Political Groups, Parties, and Organizations That Shaped America

Political Groups, Parties, and Organizations That Shaped America

An Encyclopedia and Document Collection

VOLUME 2: E–N

Scott H. Ainsworth and
Brian M. Harward, Editors

 ABC-CLIO®

An Imprint of ABC-CLIO, LLC
Santa Barbara, California • Denver, Colorado

Every reasonable effort has been made to trace the owners of copyrighted materials in this book, but in some instances this has proven impossible. The editors and publisher will be glad to receive information leading to more complete acknowledgments in subsequent printings of the book and in the meantime extend their apologies for any omissions.

Library of Congress Cataloging-in-Publication Data

Names: Ainsworth, Scott H., editor. | Harward, Brian M., editor.
Title: Political groups, parties, and organizations that shaped America : an encyclopedia and document collection / Scott H. Ainsworth and Brian M. Harward, editors.
Description: Santa Barbara, CA : ABC-CLIO, [2019] | Includes bibliographical references and index. Contents: Alphabetical list of entries—Chronological list of entries—Guide to related topics—Primary document list—Chronology.
Identifiers: LCCN 2018056083| ISBN 9781440851964 (set : alk. paper) | ISBN 9781440851988 (volume 1) | ISBN 9781440851995 (volume 2) | ISBN 9781440852008 (volume 3) | ISBN 9781440851971 (ebk.)
Subjects: LCSH: Pressure groups—United States—Encyclopedias. | Political parties—United States—Encyclopedias. | United States—Politics and government—Encyclopedias. | United States—Politics and government—Sources.
Classification: LCC JK1118 .P644 2019 | DDC 320.97303—dc23
LC record available at https://lccn.loc.gov/2018056083

ISBN: 978-1-4408-5196-4 (set)
      978-1-4408-5198-8 (vol. 1)
      978-1-4408-5199-5 (vol. 2)
      978-1-4408-5200-8 (vol. 3)
      978-1-4408-5197-1 (ebook)

23 22 21 20 19   1 2 3 4 5

This book is also available as an eBook.

ABC-CLIO
An Imprint of ABC-CLIO, LLC

ABC-CLIO, LLC
147 Castilian Drive
Santa Barbara, California 93117
www.abc-clio.com

This book is printed on acid-free paper ∞

Manufactured in the United States of America

Contents

Documents

Alphabetical List of Entries

Chronological List of Entries

Guide to Related Topics

ARTS, SCIENCES, AND MEDICINE

American Academy of Arts and Sciences (1780–)

American Medical Association (1847–)

Motion Picture Association of America (1922–)

National Academy of Sciences (1863–)

Planned Parenthood (1921–)

Union of Concerned Scientists (1969–)

BUSINESS AND INDUSTRY

American Bankers Association (1875–)

American Enterprise Institute (1938–)

American Farm Bureau Federation (1911–)

American Gaming Association (1994–)

American Medical Association (1847–)

American Petroleum Institute (1919–)

American Telephone and Telegraph Corporation (1885–1982)

American Trucking Associations (1933–)

Fannie Mae (1938–) and Freddie Mac (1970–)

Food Policy Action (2012–)

General Motors (1908–)

Grocery Manufacturers Association (1908–)

Halliburton (1919–)

Land Speculation Companies (1740–1790)

Lockheed Martin (1995–)

Mountain States Legal Foundation (1977–)

National Association of Manufacturers (1895–)

National Dairy Council (1915–)

National Rural Electric Cooperative Association (1942–)

News Corporation (1979–)

Pharmaceutical Researchers and Manufacturers of America (1958–)

Potomac Canal Company (1784–1828)

Sallie Mae (1973–)

Standard Oil Company (1870–1911)

Sunoco PAC (1975–2012)

Union Pacific Railroad (1862–)

United Fresh Produce Association (1904–)

U.S. Business and Industry Council (1933–)

U.S. Chamber of Commerce (1912–)

U.S. Steel (1901–)

CIVIL RIGHTS ORGANIZATIONS

American Anti-Slavery Society (1833–1870)

American Civil Liberties Union (1920–)

American Colonization Society (1816–1919)

American Indian Movement (1968–)

Amnesty International USA (1966–)

Anti-Defamation League (1913–)

Black Lives Matter (2013–)

Black Panther Party (1966–1982)

Center for Constitutional Rights (1966–)

Children's Defense Fund (1973–)

Congress of Racial Equality (1942–)

Disability Rights Education and Defense Fund (1979–)

Equal Justice Initiative (1989–)

Freedom Riders (1961)

GLAAD (1985–)

Human Rights Campaign (1980–)

Innocence Project (1992–)

Lambda Legal Defense and Education Fund (1973–)

Lawyers Committee for Civil Rights Under Law (1963–)

League of Women Voters (1920–)

Mexican American Legal Defense and Education Fund (1968–)

Montgomery Improvement Association and Women's Political Council (1955–1970)

NAACP Legal Defense and Education Fund (1940–)

National Abortion and Reproductive Rights Action League (1969–)

National American Woman Suffrage Association (1890–)

National Association for the Advancement of Colored People (1909–)

National Congress of American Indians (1944–)

National LGBTQ Task Force (1973–)

National Organization for Women (1966–)

National Organization on Disability (1982–)

National Urban League (1910–)

National Woman's Party (1913–1930)

Niagara Movement (1905–1910)

Organization of Afro-American Unity (1964–1965)

Rainbow-PUSH Coalition (1996–)

Southern Christian Leadership Conference (1957–)

Student Nonviolent Coordinating Committee (1960–1974)

Unidos US (Formerly, National Council of La Raza) (1968–)

United Negro College Fund (1944–)

COLONIAL AND REVOLUTIONARY GROUPS

Charter Colonies

Committees of Correspondence/ Committees of Safety (1772–1776)

Sons of Liberty (1765–1784)

Whig Society (1777–1787)

EDUCATION

American Federation of Teachers (1916–)

Disability Rights Education and Defense Fund (1979–)

Historically Black Colleges and Universities

Lambda Legal Defense and Education Fund (1973–)

Land Grant Colleges and Universities

Mexican American Legal Defense and Education Fund (1968–)

NAACP Legal Defense and Education Fund (1940–)

National Education Association (1857–)

ENVIRONMENTAL ORGANIZATIONS

Greenpeace (1971–)

National Audubon Society (1905)

Natural Resources Defense Council (1970–)

National Wildlife Federation (1936–)

Resources for the Future (1952–)

Sierra Club (1892–)

Union of Concerned Scientists (1969–)

GOVERNMENT ORGANIZATIONS

National Conference of State Legislatures (1975–)

National Governors Association (1908–)

National School Boards Association (1942–)

Parents Music Resource Center (1985–)

Political Machines

LABOR UNIONS AND LABOR ORGANIZATIONS

American Federation of Labor (1886–1955)

American Federation of Labor–Congress of Industrial Organizations (1955–)

American Federation of State, County and Municipal Employees (1936–)

American Federation of Teachers (1916–)

American Foreign Service Association (1924–)

International Brotherhood of Teamsters (1903–)

Knights of Labor (1869–1890)

Lowell Female Labor Reform Association (1844–1847)

National Association of Letter Carriers (1889–)

National Education Association (1857–)

National Farmers Union (1902–)

Professional Air Traffic Controllers Organization (1968–1981)

Service Employees International Union (1921–)

United Farm Workers (1966–)

LGBTQ RIGHTS

AIDS Coalition to Unleash Power (1987–)

GLAAD (1985–)

Human Rights Campaign (1980–)

LOBBYING AND ADVOCACY GROUPS

AARP (1958–)

American Immigration Control Foundation (1983–)

American Jewish Committee (1906–)

American–Israel Public Affairs Committee (1951–)

Americans for Democratic Action (1947–)

Americans for Prosperity (2004–)

Americans for Tax Reform (1985–)

Americans United for Separation of Church and State (1947–)

Anti-Saloon League (1893–1933)

Arab American Institute (1985–)

Association of Community Organizations for Reform Now (1970–2010)

Brady Campaign to Prevent Gun Violence (1974–)

China Lobby

Christian Coalition of America (1988–)

Citizens Against Government Waste (1984–)

Citizens for Health (1992–)

Citizens United (1988–)

Club for Growth (1999–)

CODEPINK (2002–)

Common Cause (1970–)

Democratic Socialists of America (1982–)

Eagle Forum (1972–)

Family Research Council (1983–)

Federalist Society for Law and Public Policy Studies (1982–)

Focus on the Family (1977–)

Food Policy Action (2012–)

Gray Panthers (1970–)

Greenpeace (1971–)

Home School Legal Defense Association (2000–)

Moral Majority (1979–1989)

Mothers Against Drunk Driving (1980–)

MoveOn.org (1998–)

National Association of Realtors (1908–)

National Audubon Society (1905)

National Council on Aging (1950–)

National Organization for Marriage (2007–)

National Organization for the Reform of Marijuana Laws (1970–)

Natural Resources Defense Council (1970–)

National Rifle Association (1871–)

National Right to Life Committee (1967–)

National Right to Work Legal Defense Foundation (1968–)

National Taxpayers Union (1969–)

National Women's Political Caucus (1971–)

Open Society Foundations (1993–)

Operation Rescue (1986–)

People for the American Way (1981–)

Political Machines

Public Citizen (1971–)

Rainbow-PUSH Coalition (1996–)

Republican National Coalition for Life (1992–)

Rock the Vote (1990–)

Sierra Club (1892–)

Susan B. Anthony List (1993–)

Union of Concerned Scientists (1969–)

Vote Hemp (2000–)

Women's Christian Temperance Union (1874–)

MOVEMENTS AND ACTIVIST GROUPS

Anonymous (2004–)

Antifa (2007–)

Black Lives Matter (2013–)

Fire Eaters (1850–1861) and Border Ruffians (1854–1860)

Free Staters, Jayhawkers, and New England Emigrant Aid Company (1855–1860)

Minuteman Project (2004–2016)

Non-Partisan League (1915–1956)

Occupy Movement (2011)

Sons of Liberty (1765–1784)

Students for a Democratic Society (1959–1970)

Weather Underground (1969–1975)

PHILANTHROPIC AND CHARITY ORGANIZATIONS

AIDS Coalition to Unleash Power (1987–)

American Cancer Society (1913–)

American Red Cross (1881–)

Bill & Melinda Gates Foundation (2000–)

Carnegie Corporation of New York (1911–)

Church World Service (1946–)

Ford Foundation (1936–)

Koch Family Foundations (1953–)

March of Dimes (1938–)

National Council on Aging (1950–)

Pew Charitable Trusts (1948–)

Settlement House Movement (1889)

Special Olympics (1968–)

POLICY AND RESEARCH

American Conservative Union (1964–)

American Constitution Society for Law and Policy (2001–)

American Legislative Exchange Council (1973–)

Brennan Center for Justice (1995–)

Brookings Institution (1916–)

Cato Institute (1977–)

Center for American Progress (2003–)

Center for International Policy (1975–)

Center for Security Policy (1988–)

Century Foundation (1919–)

Citizens Against Government Waste (1984–)

Competitive Enterprise Institute (1984–)

Heritage Foundation (1973–)

Open Society Foundations (1993–)

Project Vote Smart (1992–) N/A

Public Citizen (1971–)

Public Interest Research Groups (1971–)

Resources for the Future (1952–)

POLITICAL ACTION COMMITTEES

American Crossroads/Crossroads GPS (2010–)

EMILY's List (1985–)

MoveOn.org (1998–)

National Committee for an Effective Congress (1948–)

National Conservative Political Action Committee (1975–1994; 2006)

Progressive Democrats of America (2004–)

Republican National Coalition for Life (1992–)

Sunoco PAC (1975–2012)

Susan B. Anthony List (1993–)

POLITICAL FACTIONS WITHIN PARTIES

Bourbon Democrats (1876–1904)

Communist League of America (1928–1934)

Copperheads (1860–1868)

Mugwumps (1884–1888)

Tea Party Movement (2009–)

War Democrats (1860–1868)

POLITICAL PARTIES

America First Party (1944–1996)

American Independent Party (1968–)

American Labor Party (1936–1956)

American Nazi Party (1959–1967)

American Workers Party (1933–1934)

Anti-Federalists (1787–1790)

Anti-Masonic Party (1828–1840)

Anti-Monopoly Party (1884)

Citizens Party (1979–1984)

Concerned Citizens Party (1975–2013)

Constitution Party (1991–)

Democratic Party (1828–)

Democratic-Republican Party (1792–1825)

Dixiecrats (1948)

Federalist Party (1790–1820)

Free Soil Party (1848–1855)

Independence League/Party (1906–1914)

Know Nothings (1854–1858)

Libertarian Party (1971–)

Liberty Party (1840–1848)

Mississippi Freedom Democratic Party (1964–1968)

National Union Party (1864–1868)

Peace and Freedom Party (1967–)

People's Party (1887–1908)

Progressive Labor Party (1961–)

Progressive Party (1948–1955)

Progressive Party/Bull Moose (1912–1916)

Prohibition Party (1869–)

Radical Republicans (1854–1877)

Reform Party (1995–)

Republican Party (1854–)

Socialist Labor Party of America (1876–)

Socialist Party of America (1901–1972)

U.S. Pacifist Party (1983–)

Whig Party (1833–1856)

Workers World Party (1959–)

Working Families Party (1998–)

TRADE AND MEMBERSHIP ASSOCIATIONS

American Automobile Association (1902–)

American Bar Association (1878–)

America's Health Insurance Plans (2003–)

Arab American Institute (1985–)

Association of Community Organizations for Reform Now (1970–2010)

National Association of Realtors (1908–)

National Foreign Trade Council (1914–)

National Grange of the Order of Patrons of Husbandry (1867–)

VETERANS' GROUPS

American Legion (1919–)

Bonus Army (1932)

Grand Army of the Republic (1866–1956)

Swift Boat Veterans for Truth (2004–2008)

United Confederate Veterans (1889–ca. 1950)

Veterans for Peace (1985–)

Vietnam Veterans Against the War (1967–)

WOMEN'S RIGHTS ORGANIZATIONS

EMILY's List (1985–)

League of Women Voters (1920–)

National American Woman Suffrage Association (1890–)

National Organization for Women (1966–)

National Woman's Party (1913–1930)

National Women's Political Caucus (1971–)

Planned Parenthood (1921–)

Susan B. Anthony List (1993–)

E

Eagle Forum (1972–)

Founded in 1972 by conservative activist Phyllis Schlafly (1924–2016), the Eagle Forum is one of the most politically influential organizations within the social conservative movement. Eagle Forum's mission is "to enable conservative and pro-family men and women to participate in the process of self-government and public policy making so that America will continue to be a land of individual liberty, respect for family integrity, public and private virtue, and private enterprise."

Four areas of the group's mission include protecting American sovereignty, American identity, the U.S. Constitution, traditional education, and opposing radical feminists. The Eagle Forum, along with the Conservative Women of America, is one of the two most politically influential countermovement organizations opposing the women's liberation movement. The current president of the organization is Eunie Smith, who founded the Eagle Forum of Alabama and has served on the national Eagle Forum Board since 1975.

The Eagle Forum also includes an Eagle Forum Education and Legal Defense Fund and the Eagle Forum PAC, mirroring the organizational structure of women's rights organizations, such as NOW (the National Organization for Women).

Originally, Schlafly's Eagle Forum had a singular purpose and mission: to stop the ratification of the Equal Rights Amendment, which, she argued, would dismantle the family. The Eagle Forum led the STOP-ERA movement, which was an acronym for "Stop Taking Our Privileges." Specifically, the organization argued that passage of an Equal Rights Amendment to the Constitution would result in women losing various social and economic privileges, including their dependent wives' benefits under Social Security and separate bathrooms for men and women and lead to their being drafted alongside men into the military.

The Equal Rights Amendment, at the time of the STOP-ERA movement, had been overwhelmingly passed in 1972 by both the U.S. House of Representatives and the U.S. Senate and then went to the states for ratification. Thirty-eight states were needed for ratification of this proposed constitutional amendment, and within a year, 30 of the 38 states needed voted to ratify. This success of feminist groups prompted the creation of the Eagle Forum and created a sense of urgency to its countermovement mission.

To this day, the ERA is described in many American government college textbooks as the last proposed amendment to receive congressional support that failed to be ratified by the states and is one of six such proposed amendments in history. What may not always be mentioned is that this defeat in 1982 was due primarily to the campaign mobilization and lobbying work of the Eagle Forum.

The growth of the Eagle Forum and its enduring political mark on the modern conservative movement speaks to the importance not only of issues that can galvanize interest group support, but also to the important role of the individual activist who can energize others to support a cause. Phyllis Schlafly played this role masterfully when organizing Eagle Forum and in selecting the strategies it would pursue. Schlafly, who died in 2016 at the age of 92, was often credited with almost singlehandedly defeating the ERA. Jane Mansbridge argued that Schlafly's success came from making the ERA "controversial." Schlafly is credited with starting the pro-life, pro-family movement in American politics. She wrote *A Choice, Not an Echo*, arguing in support of Barry Goldwater's (1909–1998) Republican nomination for president in 1964 and opposing East Coast influence on conservatism; in essence, this work set the stage to push the Republican Party more to the right on social issues.

In Schlafly, the Eagle Forum had a leader steeped in the organizational structures and practices of politics. She was active in Republican Party organizations, heading up the Illinois Federation of Republican women, serving as a delegate to the Republican National Convention, and was herself a two-time congressional candidate. Schlafly recognized earlier than her opponents the importance of giving campaign contributions to state legislators.

In her book, *The Power of the Positive Woman*, Schlafly argued that feminism's emphasis on sexism was a "fraud" perpetrated on American women; instead, there was power in the traditional roles of women as wives and mothers. Schlafly would frequently say, "Don't call me Ms.—to me it means misery" a reference to "Ms." preferred by feminists instead of Miss or Mrs., denoting marital status (a distinction not made with "Mr." for men).

The Eagle Forum's activities led to the defeat of the ERA in 1982, with the proposed constitutional amendment falling three states short of ratification. Each year, Schlafly held Eagle Forum training conferences, where members watched tapes of Schlafly debating ERA supporters and learned how to hold a press conference, a phone bank, or a fund-raiser. Additionally members learned strategies to gain entry to women's liberation organizations to learn about their strategies as well. Communication for Eagle Forum members came in the form of *The Phyllis Schlafly Report*. The group's hierarchical structure lent consistency to trainings, communications, messaging, and strategies—all key aspects of success for Schlafly's Eagle Forum.

Equally important to its success was the diversity of members it acquired. Eagle Forum originally pulled primarily from conservatives associated with the National Federation of Republican Women, younger stay-at-home moms, and older women whose children had left home. Later the group attracted wide support from fundamentalist women's groups who were mobilized against the ERA. As Jane E. Mansbridge (1939–) notes, these women had participated in church activities that provided political skill training, such as public speaking and engaging others through evangelist practices; much of the coverage of these demonstrations missed this religious basis for many of those demonstrating for STOP-ERA in Illinois. The mobilization of these groups played a sizable role in Eagle Forum's success in defeating the ERA. Some state legislatures have recently revived the ratification process for the ERA; the Eagle Forum remains committed to stopping these current attempts as well.

The Eagle Forum endorsed Donald Trump's (1946–) presidential candidacy in 2016. Many Eagle Forum members supported the candidacy of Florida Senator Ted Cruz (1970–), yet Phyllis Schlafly and the Eagle Forum strongly endorsed Donald Trump for the Republican nomination, stating "this is the best and most conservative platform we've ever had. . . . Now we have a guy that is going to lead us to victory" (Weigel and DelReal 2016). The organization wanted Trump's campaign promise of building a border wall to deal with illegal immigration to be included as a part of the Republican Party's official platform. Schlafly died on September 5, 2016. Her last book, released one day after her death, is titled *The Conservative Case for Trump.*

Janna L. Deitz

See also: Family Research Council (1983–); Focus on the Family (1977–); National Right to Life Committee (1967–)

Further Reading

Felsenthal, Carol. 1981. *The Sweetheart of the Silent Majority: The Biography of Phyllis Schlafly.* Garden City, NY: Doubleday Press.

Mansbridge, Jane J. 1986. *Why We Lost the ERA.* Chicago: University of Chicago Press.

Marshall, Susan E. 1991. "Who Speaks for American Women? The Future of Antifeminism." *The Annals of the American Academy of Political and Social Science* 515: 50–62.

Schlafly, Phyllis. 1977. *The Power of the Positive Woman.* New Rochelle, NY: Arlington House.

Schreiber, Ronnee. 2008. *Righting Feminism: Conservative Women & American Politics.* New York: Oxford University Press.

Weigel, David, and Jose A. DelReal. 2016. "Phyllis Schlafly endorses Trump in St. Louis." *Washington Post*, March 11, 2016. https://www.washingtonpost.com/news/post-politics/wp/2016/03/11/phyllis-schlafly-endorses-trump-in-st-louis/?utm_term=.c7e8ca564563.

EMILY's List (1985–)

The most influential pro-choice political action committee (PAC) devoted to increasing the number of Democratic women in elective office is EMILY's List. Founded in 1985 by Ellen Malcolm (1947–), the name of the organization is an acronym that stands for "Early Money Is Like Yeast—it makes the dough rise" and is a reference to the strategy of this organization. Malcom and other founders of this organization noted the importance of campaign finance to winning elections—specifically the importance of candidates' abilities to raise significant sums of money early in the campaign process. Led by current president Stephanie Schriock (1973–), the organization has more than 5 million members and cites the election of over 100 pro-choice women to the House, 23 to the Senate, 12 pro-choice governors, and hundreds of state and local pro-choice women as its successes. The organization also describes itself as the "largest financial resource for minority women seeking federal office."

Prior to the founding of this group, women candidates who sought political office often were unable to get access to large donations; politics were still considered a man's pursuit, and traditional industries that gave large contributions tended to favor male candidates over women. EMILY's list was a woman-supported effort to raise the necessary campaign funds early in the election process for women so that they could be competitive.

Raising early money was the primary method by which party leaders and other donors assessed candidate viability. A viable candidate was one determined to have the ability to win elective office—proving viability increased the likelihood of winning a general election, as donors and voters tended to support those thought to have a chance to win. Viability was especially crucial for women running at the time, who were mostly challenging male incumbents. Challenging sitting officeholders required significant fund-raising for women to demonstrate that they could be competitive and win.

The EMILY's List fund-raising model relied on the practice of bundling, wherein members joined the organization and pledged to support at least two of the EMILY's List–endorsed candidates. Members wrote checks of at least $100 directly to the candidates but mailed those checks to EMILY's List. EMILY then "bundled" all contributions to a candidate and delivered them.

The advantage to this practice is that it allowed the organization to have much more of an impact than their $5,000 limit direct contribution under federal election law. So, EMILY could donate $5,000 directly, but if 1,000 of its members donated $100 each, then the organization could effectively raise $100,000 for a candidate. This model was quite effective and helped Senator Barbara Mikulski (1936–) become the first women elected in her own right to the U.S. Senate in 1986. Because of its success, the EMILY's List bundling model was quickly employed by other pro-choice and partisan women's groups like WISH List (supporting pro-choice Republican women in the Senate and House) and Susan B. Anthony List (supporting pro-life Republican women candidates).

In 1982, Harriet Woods (1927–2007) ran to be the first woman elected to the U.S. Senate but was narrowly defeated. Postelection analysis attributed the close vote margin in part to the inability to amass enough monetary support. Following this close defeat, Malcolm convened a group of friends and activists to discuss the barriers to getting women elected to office. Access to campaign funds was a resounding theme, and as Malcolm cites in her book, although other women's rights organizations had PACs, they did not have large enough sums of money to affect elections.

The women who met that day did not originally create the PAC that exists today, but they decided to write letters to women they knew and tell them about Democratic women running for office who they thought had a good chance of winning. The letters also suggested that recipients donate to these women's campaigns. Malcolm described this activity as creating a "political chain letter."

The group was then named EMILY's List, and in 1986 it became an official PAC. The campaign world of pro-choice Democratic women candidates was forever changed with this female donor network that encouraged women to write checks for women. EMILY's List is another example of an interest group formed to address a concern from the women's movement and one that led to the increased political participation of women as donors and candidates in addition to voters.

Today an EMILY's List endorsement carries with it the promise of competitive fund-raising and resources for pro-choice Democratic women running for office. Yet not all pro-choice Democratic women will get the support of EMILY's List. Eligibility criteria for an EMILY's List endorsement include expectations that the candidate is a pro-choice Democratic woman who has a good chance of winning her election. EMILY's List has been criticized by those who felt they could not get a primary endorsement when challenging a sitting Democratic male incumbent and by those who don't agree with the group's focus on the pro-choice position over other progressive policy stances.

An EMILY's List endorsement carries great weight, and its success rate is shown in both the large sums its members have raised for Democratic candidates since its beginning 32 years ago (over $500 million) and also the number of women candidates they have helped elect. EMILY's List is a sought-after endorsement with tremendous cache for pro-choice Democratic women. Many Democratic women cite the importance of EMILY's List support to their electoral success.

EMILY's List influence, however, is not confined to fund-raising activities only, although that is the core of the group's mission. In 1995, EMILY's List created Women Vote! to encourage women to participate in elections and to vote for pro-choice Democratic women. In 2000 the organization started its Political Opportunity Program, focused on candidate recruitment and training. Currently called Run to Win, EMILY's List claims to have trained over 10,000 women to run for office to date.

As soon as Hillary Clinton declared her candidacy for president in 2016, EMILY's List announced their endorsement of her and their commitment to break their fund-raising levels in support of breaking the highest glass ceiling in American politics. EMILY's List raised more than $90 million for the 2016 election cycle in support of Hillary Clinton (1947–) and other pro-choice Democratic women running around the country. Following Clinton's loss, EMILY's List created a FOCUS 2020 program, designed to get Democratic women elected to governorships and to state legislative seats across the country, to influence the redistricting process following the 2020 census. The organization also reported around 19,000 women had contacted their headquarters expressing interest in running for office following 2016.

EMILY's List is a lesson in interest group organizing that maximizes campaign finance law to create policy change by influencing elections. For many Democratic women, EMILY's List has provided the crucial early fund-raising that helped propel them past primaries and into the general election as viable nominees of their party, and ultimately as elected officeholders. The influence of this organization cannot be overstated in regards to increasing women's political representation. Following the presidential election of 2016, EMILY's List reported that they had been contacted by over 16,000 women seeking advice on running for elective office.

Janna L. Deitz

See also: Americans for Democratic Action (1947–); National Organization for Women (1966–); National Women's Political Caucus (1971–)

Further Reading

Crespin, Michael, and Janna Deitz. 2010. "If You Can't Join 'Em, Beat 'Em: The Gender Gap in Individual Donations to Congressional Candidates." *Political Research Quarterly* 63 (3): 581–593.

Malcolm, Ellen R., and Craig Unger. 2016. *When Women Win: EMILY's List and the Rise of Women in American Politics*. Boston: Houghton Mifflin Harcourt.

Pilmott, Jamie Pamelia. 2010. *Women and the Democratic Party: The Evolution of EMILY's List*. Amherst, NY: Cambria Press.

Witt, Linda, Karen M. Paget, and Glenna Matthews. 1994. *Running as a Woman: Gender and Power in American Politics*. New York: Free Press.

Equal Justice Initiative (1989–)

Bryan Stevenson (1959–) founded the Equal Justice Initiative (EJI) in 1989 and currently serves as executive director and public interest lawyer. Based in Montgomery, Alabama, the 501(c)(3) nonprofit was initially created for the sole purpose of providing legal assistance to individuals on death row, a necessity in a state that has no state-funded statewide public defender system and supplies insufficient compensation to state appointed aid, capping out-of-court compensation at $1,000. Since its founding, the organization's focus has expanded while retaining its initial purpose, with its website touting that "the Equal Justice Initiative is committed to ending mass incarceration and excessive punishment in the United States, to challenging racial and economic injustice, and to protecting basic human rights for the most vulnerable people in American society." EJI plays a prominent role within the American political system by attempting to educate the American electorate and policy makers about the nation's racial history and criminal justice and human rights–related issues as well as providing needed services like legal assistance and re-entry programs to citizens.

EJI educates people about the United States' history of racial inequality and how unfair and unequal treatment has led to racial economic injustices and inequalities within the criminal justice system. Tracing the roots of the problem back to notions of racial inferiority, EJI is involved in numerous projects that encourage people to acknowledge our nation's past and understand the long-lasting ramifications of enslavement and lynching of African Americans. One of their most prominent projects is The Legacy Museum: From Enslavement to Mass Incarceration, which is located on the site of a former slave warehouse in Montgomery, Alabama and opened in 2018 along with EJI's The National Memorial for Peace and Justice.

The museum offers an interactive look into the African American experience in the U.S. by utilizing virtual reality technology, images, artwork, and data to educate its audiences. As a part of EJI's Community Remembrance project, soil collected from lynching sites and placed in jars dedicated to each victim is on display as a memorial at the museum. EJI is also working to erect historical markers at these sites. EJI began creating an annual History of Racial Injustice calendar in 2013; this educational tool is similar to other racial justice projects coordinated by the organization in that it encourages its audiences to confront the harsh realities of our nation's past and present.

EJI is also interested in protecting the rights of children in the criminal justice system, specifically youths tried as adults. EJI's stance, according to the organization's website, that "confinement of children with adults in jails and prisons is indefensible, cruel, and unusual, and it should be banned" informs the direction of its research and outreach. EJI-produced reports such as "All Children Are Children" and "Cruel and Unusual: Sentencing 13- and 14-Year-Old Children to Die in Prison" aim to educate the public about delinquent children and their treatment within the criminal justice system.

This stance also guides the casework of EJI attorneys. In *Sullivan v. Florida* (2009), Bryan Stevenson represented Joe Sullivan, a youth sentenced to life without parole at the age of thirteen. The U.S. Supreme Court dismissed *Sullivan v. Florida* and ruled in *Graham v. Florida* (2009) that life without parole sentences for children convicted of nonhomicidal crimes were unconstitutional, ultimately entitling Sullivan to a new sentence. In 2012 the U.S. Supreme Court ruled in favor of the petitioner, represented by Stevenson, in *Miller v. Alabama* and its companion case *Jackson v. Hobbs*, that mandatory life without parole sentences were unconstitutional for juveniles convicted of homicide.

EJI has also worked to educate people about the realities and history of the death penalty. Their legal record reflects their educational goals, "hav[ing] won reversals, relief or release for over 125 wrongly condemned prisoners on death row" (EJI website). In 2015, Stevenson and his staff celebrated the exoneration of Anthony Ray Hinton, who spent 30 years insisting his innocence while on death row. Continuing their work surrounding the death penalty, EJI released the fifth version of their *Alabama Capital Defense Trial Manual* in the fall of 2017, a document created to assist attorneys in providing representation for individuals facing capital punishment charges.

EJI is also heavily involved in addressing issues related to mass incarceration in the United States. EJI conducted an investigation into abuse at Tutwiler prison, following which the organization filed a complaint which prompted a U.S. Department of Justice investigation in 2013. Because of high rates of violence and dangerous conditions created by poor prison management and overcrowding, EJI also filed a federal lawsuit on behalf of inmates at St. Clair Correctional Facility. This ultimately led to an agreement with Alabama's Department of Corrections, which required the introduction of new systems at the facility, such as an internal classification system and an incident management system as well as additional structural reforms. EJI has also done critical work to address the necessity for reentry assistance for formerly incarcerated individuals by creating the "Post-Release Education & Preparation (PREP) re-entry program [which] provides employment, daily supervision, counseling from licensed mental health professionals, and educational programming for offenders who entered state prison as children."

The organization's wide reach, addressing a multitude of issues within the American criminal justice system, and accomplishments would not be possible without the vision of Bryan Stevenson. The receiver of numerous awards, Stevenson has been awarded 29 honorary doctoral degrees and is the author of *Just Mercy*, a nonfiction book about "the story of EJI, the people [they] represent, and the importance of confronting injustice" (EJI website). EJI has been a major contributor to the existing body of work that guides criminal justice policy and reform, producing numerous studies and reports and compiling important comprehensive data sets, such as that on lynching, which was recently on exhibit at the Brooklyn Museum. Their free legal aid has made them a strong force within the judicial branch, advocating for their clients and arguing cases to the U.S. Supreme Court. Furthermore, for well over 20 years, EJI has maintained its position as a resilient influence within the American political system, clearly continuing its fight for justice and human rights by actively working to combat the actors and systems which seek to undermine them.

Heather Marie Rice and Nicole Loncaric

See also: Congress of Racial Equality (1942–); Innocence Project (1992–); NAACP Legal Defense and Education Fund (1940–); National Association for the Advancement of Colored People (1909–)

Further Reading

"EJI Annual Report 2017." 2017. *Equal Justice Initiative*. https://eji.org/files/EJI-Annual -Reort-2017.pdf.

Equal Justice Initiative. 2018. https://eji.org/.

Robertson, Campbell. 2018. "A Lynching Memorial Is Opening. The Country Has Never Seen Anything Like It." *New York Times*, April 25, 2018. https://www.nytimes .com/2018/04/25/us/lynching-memorial-alabama.html.

Stevenson, Bryan. 2015. *Just Mercy*. New York: Spiegel & Grau.

F

Family Research Council (1983–)

The Family Research Council (FRC) is a 501(c)(3) lobbying organization located in Washington, D.C., that is designed to influence policy makers to support a social and political agenda consistent with traditional Christianity. According to its vision statement, FRC seeks "a culture in which all human life is valued, families flourish, and religious liberty thrives."

FRC existed initially as an outgrowth of Focus on the Family and its founder and then-CEO Dr. James Dobson (1936–). Through his work with Focus on the Family in the 1980s, Dobson's connections to Washington, D.C., were growing. While Focus was not political per se, Dobson's parenting advice and his conception of how the family should be organized and maintained had strong political overtones.

Wary of becoming overly politicized himself (at that point), and always protective of Focus on the Family's reputation and legal status, Dobson, along with Gerald Regier (1945–) and other Christian leaders, formed the Family Research Council in 1983. Regier became FRC's first president. The initial goal was to promote friendly policy experts and connect them to sympathetic ears on Capitol Hill.

The early going was either rocky or inconsequential. Limited to a budget of $200,000 and three staffers, FRC occasionally published papers on social issues, but its efforts paled in comparison to those of the Christian Coalition and had not yet made a significant dent in D.C. Due to financial stresses, FRC was subsumed under the Focus on the Family umbrella in 1988. With Gary Bauer's (1946–) arrival as president in 1989, FRC charted a different course. A former advisor in the Ronald Reagan (1911–2004) administration, and with a reputation as a hard-edged political insider, Bauer convinced Dobson to grant him significant airtime on Focus on the Family's flagship radio program. The increased visibility was a boon to the FRC.

In 1992, FRC regained its legal independence from Focus on the Family and soon established itself as one of the most important Christian Right voices in Washington, D.C. During the Bill Clinton (1946–) presidency, FRC helped thwart Clinton's effort to rescind the ban on homosexuals in the military and, in 1996, shepherded the Defense of Marriage Act, a law that defined marriage as only between one man and one woman for the purposes of the federal code and also allowed states to refuse to recognize gay marriages licensed in other states.

During this period, two prominent Michigan families, the Princes and DeVoses (Betsy Devos would later be selected by President Trump to be the Secretary of

Education), funded the construction of a six-floor, permanent facility in downtown Washington, D.C. At that point, FRC was among the most preeminent lobbying institutions within the Christian Right. By the time of Bauer's departure in 1999, FRC boasted an annual budget of more than $14 million, a staff of 120, and a mailing list of at least 500,000 people (Gilgoff 2007, 116–118).

Also in 1992, FRC decided to spin off a sister organization, FRC Action, a 501(c)(4), to exercise more direct political activity. FRC Action is able to mobilize voters, lobby without limitation (501(c)(3) entities may lobby as a minor portion of their overall activity), and engage in issue and electoral advocacy. FRC Action, though, has not generated a significant, durable, or independent presence. According to Internal Revenue Service records, FRC Action, in the 2015–2016 fiscal year, generated less than $860,129 in contributions, grants, and revenue, while charting expenses of $763,529. FRC Action declared net assets of $590,263. These numbers show a decline from the previous year.

Beyond institutional independence, Bauer also sought to create a grassroots movement that operated outside of Washington, D.C. Building on, and sometimes imitating, the Christian Coalition's model of state chapters, Bauer forged relationships with entities across the nation with the hope of replicating FRC's model at the state legislative level. As of 2017, FRC counts 40 state affiliates, varying in terms of professionalism, staffing, and budget.

By the mid-2000s, FRC could reasonably be credited with being the most effective Christian Right organization in Washington, D.C. According to a survey of the movement's activists, FRC was rated more favorably than any other explicitly political entity attached to the Christian Right (Green et al. 2006). In fact, religion and politics scholars have used FRC-generated congressional scorecards, which measure how frequently members of the U.S. Congress support the FRC's preferred policy positions, as a proxy for support for the Christian Right.

Gary Bauer's tenure as FRC president ended in 1999, and he was replaced in 2000 by Ken Connor, a prominent Florida attorney. Connor's reign at FRC was marked by a public dispute with James Dobson, who was still exercising significant influence over the organization. Early in the George W. Bush presidency, the Christian Right mounted its most significant effort to amend the U.S. Constitution via the Federal Marriage Amendment. Authored by Matt Daniels (1989–) of Alliance for Marriage, the amendment defined marriage in the United States as between one man and one woman. It would also proscribe federal and state courts from conferring marital status or the "legal incidents" of marriage upon unmarried couples.

James Dobson threw the weight of Focus on the Family behind the amendment and expected FRC to do the same. Connor determined the amendment had two fatal flaws. One, it would not prevent state courts or legislatures from providing civil unions or domestic partnerships to same-sex couples. So for Connor, the amendment did not go far enough. Two, the probability of enacting the amendment was low. Although hundreds of constitutional amendments of all kinds have been proposed throughout the nation's history, only 27 have succeeded. Pouring millions of dollars into what would most likely be a losing effort was, for Connor, a waste of resources that would be better spent lobbying for conservative federal court appointments. Connor directed FRC lobbyists to avoid the marriage amendment and, if asked about it, supply FRC's analysis.

The rift between Dobson and FRC was unprecedented. While Connor may have miscalculated how reliant FRC had been on Focus on the Family historically, he also understood that FRC would be stronger if it maintained some distance from Dobson. Connor "saw Christian Coalition's implosion after Ralph Reed's (1961–) departure as a lesson in the perils of the evangelical world's tendency to build organizations around charismatic leaders" (Gilgoff 2007, 141–149).

In 2003, Tony Perkins (1963–), a Christian Right politician from Louisiana, was named president of Family Research Council. FRC has maintained a strong position in Washington, D.C., and adapted to a shifting issue environment. FRC, like much of the Christian Right, responded to the Supreme Court's decision to legalize same-sex marriage by trying to limit the implications of the ruling. Religious liberty, FRC argues, "is more than the right to attend a private worship service. Religious observance has a distinctly positive effect on community and national life. The fostering of religious liberty is a hallmark of our culture as intended by our Founding Fathers and practiced by tens of millions of Americans" ("Liberty Issues" 2018). By couching the conflict as between recent, judicial innovation and historic standards rooted in the American founding, FRC still succinctly reveals the Christian Right's essential approach to evolving social conflict in the United States.

According to the Evangelical Council for Financial Accountability, in 2016, the last year data were available, FRC was financially profitable. Compared to its one time competitor, Concerned Women for America (CWA), or a similar organization, like Bread for the World (Bread), FRC is still strong. At the same, FRC cannot claim to rival conservative stalwarts like the Heritage Foundation, at least in this snapshot of resources.

Mark Caleb Smith

See also: Christian Coalition of America (1988–); Focus on the Family (1977–); Moral Majority (1979–1989)

Further Reading

Gilgoff, Dan. 2007. *The Jesus Machine: How James Dobson, Focus on the Family, and Evangelical America are Winning the Culture War*. New York: St. Martin's Press.

Green, John C., Kimberly H. Conger, and James L. Guth. 2006. Agents of Value: Christian Right Activists in 2004." In *The Values Campaign? The Christian Right and the 2004 Elections*, edited by J. C. Green, M. J. Rozell, and C. Wilcox, 22–55. Washington, D.C.: Georgetown University Press.

"Liberty Issues." 2018. FRCAction. https://www.frcaction.org/liberty-issues.

Smith, Lauren Edwards, Laura R. Olson, and Jeffrey A. Fine. 2010. "Substantive Religious Representation in the U.S. Senate: Voting Alignment with the Family Research Council." *Political Research Quarterly* 63 (1): 68–82.

Fannie Mae (1938–) and Freddie Mac (1970–)

The Federal National Mortgage Association and the Federal Home Loan Mortgage Corporation, most commonly known by their humanized nicknames of "Fannie Mae" and "Freddie Mac," are two government-sponsored enterprises (GSEs) in the mortgage market. Per the Federal Housing Finance Agency, the regulator of both organizations: "They perform an important role in the nation's housing finance system—to provide liquidity, stability and affordability to the mortgage market" ("About Fannie Mae & Freddie Mac" 2018). One of the ways Fannie Mae and Freddie Mac provide that stability and liquidity is by transforming traditional mortgages into an investment product called a "mortgage backed security," allowing lenders (usually banks, but also smaller financial institutions like credit unions) to reinvest their assets into more lending. By increasing the total lending happening through banks, more consumers are able to access loaned money—allowing more consumers to access mortgages and, ultimately, own their own homes.

In 1938, the federal government founded Fannie Mae as part of President Franklin Delano Roosevelt's "New Deal." In the throes of the Great Depression, millions of Americans were out of work, and affordable housing became a national crisis. Before the creation of Fannie Mae, more than 20 percent of all American mortgages were in default—homeowners were unable to pay their outstanding debts on their homes. In President Roosevelt's view, this crisis required government action, both to ensure that American families could afford housing and to stimulate the economy out of the depression. Giving families access to mortgage funding would house them, and it would also increase the demand for construction, which could help put many unemployed Americans back to work.

Fannie Mae originally aimed to put federal funding in the hands of local banks, expanding the secondary mortgage market. It seemed like a win-win situation: banks could increase their profits through stable investment, and families could more readily buy their own homes. In 1970, Congress chartered Freddie Mac, expanding the secondary market even further so that mortgage investments could be purchased by ordinary investors on the open market. This would continue to help ensure mortgage funds throughout the country. In 1981, Fannie Mae invented a new banking product: the "mortgage-backed security." Investors could purchase the bundled debt associated with many mortgages at once, assured by the fact that their money was safe. For decades, the Fannie Mae model was relatively effective. More Americans could acquire mortgages, and the investments in mortgages generated revenue for the American economy.

Similar to a stock market, the secondary mortgage market allows mortgage lenders to sell mortgage debt holdings as a "security"—an investment that is more stable than a traditional stock. Because mortgages are typically reliably repaid over 20- or 30-year periods, buying these debts was perceived to be a very stable investment. They were sold to investors who needed stable revenue, like pension funds and insurance companies. Feeling secure in the knowledge that their assets would grow through the secondary market, local banks could expand their lending programs, allowing more families to buy mortgages.

In the 1990s, the Bill Clinton administration put Fannie Mae under increased pressure to do more to finance housing for low-income Americans. While its earlier programs had helped many middle-class Americans get access to homeownership, the poorest still lagged behind. The Federal Agency of Housing and Urban Development (HUD) used regulations to force Fannie Mae to reorient its financing away from ordinary banks and toward banks that did business in low-income areas, so that poorer Americans with less stable credit could also become home-owners. Unfortunately, this also meant Fannie Mae and its secondary markets were taking on much more risk. The low-income areas had a much higher rate of "default"—nonpayment—on their mortgages. They were less-than-ideal mort-gages: "subprime."

In 2004 HUD regulations were altered to accept high-risk, high-cost loans within the affordable housing goals mandated to Fannie Mae. These "predatory" loans charged high fees and allowed people to take on much more debt than they could afford. One of the most famous cases was Alberto Ramirez, who earned $14,000 a year as a strawberry picker and was approved by a lender to purchase a $720,000 home—more than 50 times his annual income. Typical mortgages were sold in a cautious way to families who could demonstrate through their incomes that they would reliably pay the bank back over the years. These new predatory mortgages were never designed to be paid back. They drew in borrowers with temptingly low introductory interest rates, which were structured to be variable and "kick in" to a much higher rate later on. The lender would accumulate money through high-interest payments, not unlike a payday loan, and when the family failed to pay the mortgage, the lender foreclosed on the house.

Fannie Mae's mission to generate public good—affordable housing, stable investment—had been subverted amid a push to sell high-interest, high-risk mort-gage products to people who did not really understand them. At the same time, those high-risk mortgages were being sold to prospective investors as though they were safe, "sure-thing" assets, hidden in "bundles" of mortgages. Something was clearly amiss.

In the late 2000s, it all came crashing down. The variable rate mortgages began to adjust to the much higher rates that were going to make predatory lenders huge profits. Families formerly capable of paying the mortgages on their oversized homes were suddenly unable to cover the costs. Foreclosures became frighten-ingly commonplace across the United States, and with them, the assets built on the backs of mortgage-backed securities began to collapse, too. The financial fall-out impacted not only the United States but also the whole world, rippling into what became known as the 2008 Financial Crisis, and the beginnings of the "Great Recession"—a great irony, given Fannie Mae's Depression-era roots. In Septem-ber 2008, Fannie Mae and Freddie Mac were both put into conservatorship—a type of temporary financial control for corporations—by the U.S. Treasury. The government designed the conservatorship to be a temporary measure, but as of October 2017, the U.S. federal government retains control.

For many everyday Americans, the story of Fannie Mae and Freddie Mac was perceived as an example of the misplaced focus of government institutions. The organizations that sold mortgages were financially protected, but the families who lived in the mortgaged homes those organizations had sold them were foreclosed on. When Occupy Wall Street, a social movement against the influence of the financial sector on the government, began in 2011, Fannie Mae offices were among its main sites of protest.

From FDR's New Deal, to mass investment and deceptively easy credit, to bailout, the presence of Fannie Mae and Freddie Mac looms large. Their future—whether in or out of conservatorship—remains to be seen, but their influence on U.S. society is indelible.

Lisa Jane de Gara

See also: Association of Community Organizations for Reform Now (1970–2010); National Association of Realtors (1908–); Sallie Mae (1973–)

Further Reading

"About Fannie Mae & Freddie Mac." 2018. Federal Housing Finance Agency. https://www .fhfa.gov/SupervisionRegulation/FannieMaeandFreddieMac/Pages/About-Fannie -Mae---Freddie-Mac.aspx.

Avramenko, Richard, and Richard Boyd. 2013. "Subprime Virtues: The Moral Dimensions of American Housing and Mortgage Policy." *Perspectives on Politics* 11, no. 1 (March): 111–132.

Fannie Mae. 2018. http://www.fanniemae.com/portal/index.html.

Freddie Mac. 2018. http://www.freddiemac.com/.

Lewis, Michael. 2010. *The Big Short: Inside the Doomsday Machine.* New York: W. W. Norton & Company.

Nielsen, Barry. 2018. "Fannie Mae, Freddie Mac and the Credit Crisis of 2008." *Investopedia*, March 19, 2018. https://www.investopedia.com/articles/economics/08 /fannie-mae-freddie-mac-credit-crisis.asp.

Farmers Alliance

See **People's Party (1887–1908)**

Federalist Party (1790–1820)

The Federalist Party was the first of the two major political parties to emerge in the American political system. The Federalist Party was an extension of the federalists who defended the ratification of the U.S. Constitution following the Constitutional Convention in Philadelphia in 1789.

Alexander Hamilton (1755–1804) is widely considered the founding father of the Federalist Party, although many would include John Adams (1735–1826) as an early founder as well. Despite the fact that political parties were not conceived as a part of American government, and George Washington (1732–1799) did not consider himself to be a member of any political party, two major political parties arose during Washington's presidency. These opposing factions developed as a result of disagreements in President Washington's Cabinet: Alexander Hamilton, as secretary of the treasury, vehemently opposed the political stances and philosophies of Thomas Jefferson (1743–1826), Washington's secretary of state (who is widely considered the founding father of the Democratic-Republicans, along with James Madison [1751–1836]).

The Federalist Party developed during Washington's second presidential term. A key emphasis of the party was a belief in a strong national government and extensive economic policies. Members of the Federalist Party included merchants, businessmen, bankers, and large landowners mainly in the Northeast and in the cities of early America. The party typically distrusted the general populace and felt intellectual elites were most suited to lead the new government. The Federalists sought to establish fiscal responsibility in the new government by maintaining a tariff system; favoring business, banking, and shipping interests; and creating a national bank. The Federalists also allied themselves with Great Britain, a relationship that stimulated trade in the new nation.

Hamilton's proposals to establish a national bank, assume states' debts accumulated during the Revolutionary War, and centralize power in the national government and in the executive were strongly opposed by Democratic-Republicans, who had the support of the South and other agrarian interests. President Washington, who insisted he belonged to no political party, generally agreed with Hamilton's proposals and tended to support the Federalist agenda.

The Jay Treaty that Washington negotiated with Great Britain in 1794–1795 resolved several issues between the countries, including national borders, debt owed, and trade. When Hamilton convinced Washington to issue a Proclamation of Neutrality in the war between Great Britain and France over Jefferson's insistence the United States support the French, Jefferson resigned from Washington's cabinet in protest and organized his party to challenge the Federalist agenda. Democratic-Republicans believed the centralization of power in the national government would result in a loss of individual and states' rights and that the Federalists' fiscal policy favored the upper class.

The presidential election of 1796 was the first contested by the new two-party system. John Adams ran as the Federalist Party candidate; and Thomas Jefferson ran as the Democratic-Republican Party candidate. Adams' victory continued the Federalist agenda. Many members of Congress at this time had yet to declare a political party affiliation, and many considered themselves independents. However, the growing divisiveness between the parties led Adams to convince Congress to pass the Alien and Sedition Acts, which allowed the president to deport aliens he deemed dangerous and made criticizing the national government in print an illegal act. Jefferson and Madison encouraged Virginia and Kentucky to pass their own state laws that declared the national Alien and Sedition Acts unconstitutional, insisting that states had the right to nullify national laws (despite the Supremacy Clause of the Constitution, which states when national and state laws conflict, the national government laws are "supreme").

In addition to rising public opinion against the Alien and Sedition Acts, which the population regarded as suppressing free speech, the Federalist Party split between those loyal to John Adams and those loyal to Alexander Hamilton. The Hamiltonians opposed Adams' decision to begin diplomatic relations with France and his military priorities, which led Adams to reorganize his cabinet to rid it of those who deferred to Hamilton's leadership over the president's.

This dissention in the Federalist Party resulted in Adams losing the presidential election of 1800 to his Democratic-Republican rival, Thomas Jefferson. Were it not for the three-fifths compromise, Adams likely would likely have been reelected. But due to the added political clout of Southern states due to the compromise and the heavy support the Democratic-Republicans enjoyed in the South, Jefferson became the third president in 1800. The Democratic-Republicans supplanted the Federalist majorities in Congress as well.

When the Democratic-Republican electors all voted for Jefferson and Aaron Burr (1756–1836), Jefferson's vice-presidential candidate, the election resulted in a tie, throwing the presidential election into the lame duck, Federalist-majority House of Representatives, many of whom had just lost their seats to a Democratic-Republican. After much intrigue and Federalist scheming to choose Burr as president rather than the more objectionable Jefferson, Hamilton finally intervened to direct his fellow party members to choose Jefferson as president. Hamilton and Jefferson were fierce political rivals, but Hamilton deemed Burr unfit for the executive office. The Federalist Party, virtually decimated after the election of 1800, further declined after its opposition of the Louisiana Purchase and to the War of 1812 met with public disapproval.

The Federalist Party eventually lost favor with the people and were not as adept at political organizing after the death of Hamilton in 1804. Despite electing only one president and facing declining representation in Congress after 1808, the Federalist Party continued to have a champion in John Marshall (1755–1835), who was appointed Chief Justice of the Supreme Court by John Adams and served until 1832. Marshall's leadership of the federal judiciary maintained the strong national government ideals of the Federalist Party beyond the party's influence in executive and legislative politics.

The Federalist presidential candidates following Adams' loss to Jefferson in 1800 fared no better. Charles Pinckney, the Federalist presidential nominee in both 1804 and 1808, DeWitt Clinton, the party's nominee in 1812, and Rufus King, the nominee in 1816 all lost to their Democratic-Republican opponents. In the election of 1820, the Federalist Party only nominated a vice-presidential nominee, Richard Stockton.

The membership of the Federalist Party by 1820 was absorbed into the Democratic Party and the Whig Party. However, the lasting and enduring legacy of the early domination of American government by the Federalist Party established the precedents by which the national government continues to function and guaranteed the young United States would survive. The Democratic-Republican presidents who succeeded Adams in many ways embraced Federalist ideals by increasing tariffs to protect factories, purchasing the Louisiana Territory, chartering the Second National Bank, and strengthening the army and navy. These measures were adopted by the Democratic-Republicans despite their ideological opposition to a strong national government.

Heather Frederick

See also: Democratic Party (1828–); Democratic-Republican Party (1792–1825); Republican Party (1854–); Whig Party (1833–1856)

Further Reading

Borden, Morton. 1967. *Parties and Politics in the Early Republic: 1789–1815*. Hoboken, NJ: Wiley-Blackwell Publishing.

Chernow, Ron. 2005. *Alexander Hamilton*. New York: Penguin Books.

Ferling, John. 2014. *Jefferson and Hamilton: The Rivalry That Forged a Nation.* New York: Bloomsbury Press.

Hamilton, Alexander, James Madison, and John Jay. 2008. *The Federalist Papers.* Oxford: Oxford University Press.

Knott, Stephen F. 2016. *Washington and Hamilton: The Alliance That Forged America.* Napierville, IL: Sourcebooks.

Payan, Gregory. 2004. *The Federalist and Anti-Federalist: How and Why Political Parties Were Formed in Young America.* New York: Rosen Publishing Group.

Federalist Society for Law and Public Policy Studies (1982–)

The Federalist Society for Law and Public Policy Studies, commonly known as the Federalist Society, is an organization composed of conservatives and libertarians committed to "reforming" the current American approach to law to reflect originalist and textualist points of view. The Federalist Society was founded as a student organization in 1982 at the University of Chicago, one of the most prominent law schools in the United States. Chapters soon followed at the Harvard and Yale law schools. The Federalist Society strived to challenge the perceived liberal biases that the group's founders thought were prevalent throughout many American law schools.

The Federalist Society features the founding Student Division, and it has since added a Lawyer's Division and a Faculty Division. Today, the Student Division includes more than 10,000 law students at 196 ABA-accredited law schools as well as 24 additional chapters. The Lawyers Division is composed of more than 60,000 legal professionals and others interested in the intellectual and practical application and shaping of American jurisprudence in active chapters across 80 cities. As an illustration of the clout of the Federalist Society, the first two faculty advisors to the Federalist Society were Antonin Scalia (1936–2016) and Robert Bork (1927–2012). Both Scalia and Bork were professors and leading federal judges. Antonin Scalia, of course, was an associate justice on the U.S. Supreme Court.

There are many different approaches to constitutional interpretation. Originalism is the idea that the Constitution should be interpreted via the original intent that the framers had at the time that the document was written. Another version of originalism refers to how the specific constitutional provision was originally understood at the time of ratification, which could be rather different from how it was intended. Nonetheless, originalists insist that any amendments to the Constitution should be interpreted in the same manner—via the meaning that the writers had in mind at the time the amendment was written. Originalism's companion, textualism, is the idea that the Constitution should be interpreted explicitly via the words or text that are in the document. Textualists argue that the plain meaning approach is preferable to alternatives because the language that was chosen by the framers of the text was the language that was ratified—not the inferences judges or others might make from that text. And where the meaning is not so "plain," the framers' original intent or original understanding should be used to interpret the text.

Neither of these manners of constitutional interpretation subscribe to the idea of a "living" Constitution (see *Trop v. Dulles*, 356 U.S. 86 (1958)). In originalist or textualist theory, the ideals on which the Constitution was drafted remain true to the framers' view of governance, and so too ought the manner in which the Constitution is interpreted. The meaning of the document can only be changed pursuant to the amendment procedures prescribed by Article V.

Although historically it has been the tendency of the judiciary, and occasionally the legislature, to attempt to compensate for the ambiguities and conflicting provisions in the Constitution, the document grants enumerated powers and suggests that Congress has broad implied powers to act, sometimes in areas that might otherwise be reserved to states' authority. For example, Congress has the expressed authority to regulate interstate commerce and to tax and to spend. In addition, Article I includes the "elastic clause," which grants Congress the power to pass all laws which might be "necessary and proper" for executing its enumerated powers. In addition, the supremacy clause states that the federal Constitution, and laws and treaties made pursuant to it, are the supreme law of the land. However, these broad grants of federal authority may, in the view of states' rights advocates (also known as dual federalists), run afoul of the reserved powers of states, secured by the Tenth Amendment. Adherence to dual federalism and what they see as the proper distribution of power between the federal government and the states are at the foundation of the Federalist Society's beliefs. Originalism and textualism, they argue, help to secure that proper balance of power and restrain what they see as encroaching federal authority over states.

Subsequently, the Federalist Society is committed to preserving three specific principles it deems to be at the bedrock of our nation's history: that the state exists to preserve individual freedom; that the separation of government powers is central to the constitutional order; and that it is the province and duty of the judiciary to say what the law is.

First, the Federalist Society believes that the state exists to preserve individual freedom. In their view, the nation has its origins in the unwillingness of the people to be oppressed by a foreign monarch. Colonists were oppressed both socially and economically and had little, if any, freedom to make decisions that would govern themselves and their society. As a result, the Federalist Society, along with most of its conservative and libertarian membership, asserts that the federal government exists chiefly and only to ensure that the people can govern themselves without the infringement of a foreign power into their domestic agenda.

Second, the Federalist Society is adamant that the separation of governmental powers is central to the constitutional order. Federalist Society leadership has previously noted that the freedoms the Federalist Society is trying to preserve are best protected by maintaining the separation of powers and enforcing limitation on the exercise of state authority. In particular, the Federalist Society places great importance in the even distribution of power within the federal government to ensure that ambition counters ambition and no individual or small cohort retain all the power. The Constitution, they believe, specifically enumerates the powers vested in each branch and leaves little room for ambiguity. It is solely the responsibility of the bicameral legislature to make the laws; it is the responsibility of the executive branch to enforce the law. Thus, when Congress delegates legislative power to the executive branch, for example, Congress violates the separation of powers.

Finally, and perhaps most importantly, the Federalist Society believes that, as Chief Justice John Marshall (1755–1835) reasoned in *Marbury v. Madison* (1803), it is emphatically the province and duty of the judiciary to say what the law is. It is not proper, they argue, for judges to say what the law "ought to be" by imputing their preferences for that of the legislature. In originalist or textualist approaches to constitutional interpretation, there is therefore no room for judicial discretion; they simply apply the law as written or as originally understood.

The widespread impact of the Federalist Society can be seen in several key contexts, including the federal judiciary, in bureaucratic agencies, and in law schools across the nation. First, the Federalist Society has had a considerable impact on the makeup of the federal judiciary. Every federal judge appointed during the Republican administrations of George H. W. Bush and George W. Bush was either a member of the Federalist Society or was approved by its members. Supreme Court Chief Justice John Roberts and Justices Clarence Thomas, Samuel Alito, and Neil Gorsuch, for instance, are each current or former members of the Federalist Society. As of 2018, President Donald Trump's appellate nominations also tend to come from the ranks of the Federalist Society, and, despite numerous nominees deemed "unqualified" by the American Bar Association (ABA), the Republican Senate has had sufficient votes to seat these overwhelmingly young and conservative jurists.

The Federalist Society also continues to demonstrate its incredible influence beyond the federal judiciary, with members in many cabinet and other notable positions throughout the government. Philip Perry, former general counsel of the Office of Management and Budget (OMB) and Federalist Society member, was tasked with drafting the legislation that would later create the Department of Homeland Security (DHS) in the wake of the September 11, 2001, terrorist attacks. DHS, charged with protecting the United States within, at, and outside its borders, maintains a mission that works to prevent terrorism, enforce immigration laws, safeguard cyberspace, ensure national resilience to disasters, and maintain the greater Homeland Security Enterprise. In 2005, President Bush nominated Perry to be the general counsel of the very organization for which he drafted the legislation, and Perry was unanimously confirmed by the Senate that year. In addition to his new departmental tasks, Perry was also chief counsel to then DHS Secretary Michael Chertoff. Chertoff, former Secretary of the Department of Homeland Security and Federalist Society member, was the co-author of the 2001 USA PATRIOT Act. The PATRIOT Act, hastily passed in the wake of the September 11 attacks, was a piece of legislation set to increase national security controls that was met with significant liberal opposition. The goal of the PATRIOT Act was to prevent another terrorist attack through the increased use of government interrogation and intelligence collection. Gale Norton, former U.S. secretary of the interior; C. Boyden Gray, former U.S. ambassador to the European Union; and Charles

Grassley (1933–), chair of the Senate Judiciary Committee and president pro tempore of the U.S. Senate as of this writing, are each active or former members of the Federalist Society.

The Federalist Society has also had, as its origins would suggest, an important impact on legal scholarship. Federalist Society scholarship has influenced many areas of law, including—importantly—the Second Amendment. Though long pilloried, the view that the Second Amendment guaranteed the right to keep and bear arms as an individual right was upheld by the Supreme Court in *District of Columbia v. Heller* (2008), with Justice Antonin Scalia writing for the majority. In *Heller*, Scalia articulated an originalist (as opposed to textualist) view of the Second Amendment that was a dramatic departure from the Court's previous treatments of the amendment. Scalia's understanding of the language of the Second Amendment— which has a prefatory clause which would seem (to a textualist) to limit the second, so-called operative clause—was based on legal (as opposed to peer-reviewed historical) scholarship that characterized the "original intent" of the framers of the Second Amendment. It is important to note in this context that—not surprisingly— historians and legal historians do not agree on whether securing the individual right to bear arms was the original understanding, much less the intent, of the framers of the Second Amendment.

The Federalist Society has become among the most influential organization in the United States today. It has been extremely successful in filling consequential positions in each of the three branches of government at the federal and state levels. It has influenced law professors and students for decades, and its efforts to influence scholarship have successfully affected public policy outcomes.

Sydney Franklin and Tobias T. Gibson

See also: Competitive Enterprise Institute (1984–); Libertarian Party (1971–)

Further Reading

Avery, Michael, and Danielle McLaughlin. 2012. *The Federalist Society: How Conservatives Took the Law Back from Liberals.* Nashville, TN: Vanderbilt University Press.

Breyer, Stephen. 2010. *Making Our Democracy Work: A Judge's View.* New York: Vintage Books.

Clegg, Roger, Michael E. DeBow, and John McGinnis. 1996. "Conservative and Libertarian Legal Scholarship: An Annotated Bibliography." The Federalist Society for Law and Public Policy Studies. https://fedsoc-cms-public.s3.amazonaws.com /update/pdf/urFFkbJ6p75qQKfGEoNvG84wzfbwqsaijgGRPtBJ.pdf.

Scalia, Antonin, and Bryan A. Garner. 2012. *Reading Law: The Interpretation of Legal Texts.* St. Paul, MN: West Law.

Toobin, Jeffery. 2017. "The Conservative Pipeline to the Supreme Court." *The New Yorker*, April 17, 2017. https://www.newyorker.com/magazine/2017/04/17/the -conservative-pipeline-to-the-supreme-court.

Fire Eaters (1850–1861) and Border Ruffians (1854–1860)

Politics in the United States and its territories in the 1850s involved Southern sympathizers who included both the Fire Eaters (those who wrote and politicized the continuation of slavery) and a group known as the Border Ruffians (those who defended the pro-slavery position through violence). With the impending crisis hurtling toward disaster, these proponents also wanted to see the right to extend slavery into the territories. The seeming prosperity in the wake of the Mexican-American War (1846–1848) and the Compromise of 1850 quieted the radicals on either side of the debate, but fire eaters became incensed with the debates over the Kansas-Nebraska Act of 1854. They crafted the words that fueled secessionists to remove their states from the Union. Likewise, border ruffians—or pukes, as they came to be known—flooded the lines of demarcation, in order to vote, harass, and even burn, if necessary, in the name of slavery.

Some of the Fire Eaters' most celebrated representatives included William Lowndes Yancey (1814–1863), Edmund Ruffin (1794–1865), and the most famous fire eater, Robert Barnwell Rhett (1800–1876). All of these individuals coalesced around the idea that the United States should be dissolved if slavery was not to be protected under the Constitution. They employed the legacy of Thomas Jefferson (1743–1826) and James Madison's (1751–1836) Virginia and Kentucky Resolutions, which established the states' rights theory, and were protected by the Ninth and Tenth Amendments in the Bill of Rights. Sectionalism and the right to secede had deep roots in the American past, and throughout the Revolutionary Era and the formation of the country, it was debated in some form or fashion, whether by the threats of South Carolinians to walk out of the Convention in Philadelphia or the New Englanders who disliked the direction of the nation as a result of the War of 1812, thus forming the swansong of the Federalist Party at the Hartford Convention. Sectional conflicts did not abate, though. The power of nationalism led to events such as the Missouri Controversy, the writings of John C. Calhoun (1782–1850) concerning the impact of the tariff in the early 1830s known as the Nullification Crisis, and of course, Texas's entry into the Union and the Mexican-American War. All fueled debates that lasted for over four decades during the Jacksonian Period.

Fire Eaters primarily faced attacks on their credibility during the antebellum period. For Northerners—and a good number of Southerners, too—the radical arguments for secession seemed out of place because the result, a civil war, seemed too terrible. Thus, Fire Eaters in the press were perceived as self-serving egotists who did not have the best interests of the republic at heart. Even though they claimed the mantle of antifederalism and Jefferson's ire for out-of-control, large, centralized government, people for the most part believed they were pretenders. Up until 1854, keeping the Fire Eaters in check became the goal of moderates who understood that cooler heads should prevail in order to preserve the Union.

For the most part, every state in the South had its own collection of Fire Eaters. Some were more educated or more creative in crafting their messages, but rarely did they collaborate effectively on a mass scale. They did not overtake a particular political party (but tried in 1848), and they did not ever form their own. Rhett, a hardcore secessionist through and through, best exemplified the ability to incense and ridicule anyone who stood in his path. South Carolina was a hotbed for debate about how to react to Northern abolitionism and aggression, but Rhett was as radical as they came because of his inflexibility and personality. Unlike him, Yancey, a Yankee transplant from New York, who moved to Alabama as a moderate, turned Fire Eater not because of the cause per se but, some historians argue, due to his personal hatred for his abolitionist and abusive stepfather.

Yancey, much more than Rhett, believed that the only means to politically expose the weakness of compromise was to destroy the Democratic Party. In 1848, working with his Alabama delegation, he attempted to sever the ties between the moderate Southerners and the Northerners who did not want to join the slowly fragmenting Whig Party. Though the plan fell apart, Yancey got his foot in the proverbial door by exposing threats and creating discord. All he needed was a means to prove that political tactics like "popular sovereignty," at least initially, were dangerous to slavery's future. If he could somehow show that Congress had no authority to legislate whether or not slavery could be extended into the territories, he would have his victory.

By 1854, Yancey and many of his Fire Eater brethren would have met their match. In Kansas and Nebraska, debate ensued over what kinds of places these states would become: slave or free. With the *Dred Scott* Supreme Court decision, which nullified the Missouri Compromise just three years away, the territories became engulfed in a mini-civil war. Kansas became the focal point for debate and destruction as both proslavery advocates and Free Staters struggled over the political future of the state. In an attempt to influence territorial elections, borders, especially that of Missouri, were overrun by proslavery advocates seeking to protect their own interests. Some moved there legally, and others did so illegally. Dubbed "Border Ruffians," these pukes were seen as a direct threat to democracy and the sovereignty of the people.

Beginning in late 1854 into 1855, Border Ruffians overwhelmed the Kansas plain by harassing and intimidating Free Staters. They used any means necessary to promote their cause, from hanging around polling places shouting insults to visiting local farmsteads to deliver threats. They voted early and often; sometimes tallies were far higher than the number of residents present in the regions. Territorial census data bears out these election manipulations, and the Northern press attempted to portray the Border Ruffians in juicy, thick descriptions that were wholly negative. Border Ruffians did not shy away from this persona; one of their leaders, Benjamin Stringfellow (1816–1891) from Missouri, encouraged it in order to win elections. And elections they won. In overwhelming majorities proslavery advocates swept the territorial votes, only inciting more armed violence to come.

Once the lines were drawn, Yankee influence arrived in the form of rifles, known as Beecher's bibles, after the New England minister who sent them. And of course, in Congress Charles Sumner (1811–1874) and other leading politicians of the age created a strong message of contempt for the ills of what became known in the North as "Bleeding Kansas." Armed groups became commonplace on both sides, and Jayhawkers, as they were known on the free state side, clashed throughout the period with border ruffians. The latter's name, which at first was viewed as an extreme insult, became synonymous with the cause of turning back the manipulative Yankees. Thus, a proxy war began that led to untold violence and destruction well before 1861.

The Border Ruffians, such as James Henry Lane (1814–1866) and Charles Jennison (1834–1884), led the physical fight for the expansion of slavery into the territories. Likewise, the Fire Eaters charged that the only means to keep slavery alive was secession. The ensuing Kansas-Nebraska Act spelled not only the destruction of the Whig Party but also the death knell of the Union, because for too long, the question of slavery's existence continued to be tabled for successive generations to decide. The rise of the Know-Nothing Party also destroyed the roots of the Democratic Party, which were vilified in the political cartoons of the time period for aligning themselves with the dastardly border ruffians. These political realignments led to the rise of both the Fire Eaters, exemplified by Louis Wigfall (1816–1874), and the Republican Party, best represented by Abraham Lincoln (1809–1865).

The turmoil in Kansas allowed the Fire Eaters the chance to promote Yancey's League of United Southerners, an organization that worked to not elect representatives but rather to foment revolution. The Fire Eaters, like the Border Ruffians, were out of control, feeding on any opportunity and seeking to quell any challenge by moderates. Like a tiger backed into a corner, when slavery's future became universally threatened by the result of the election of 1860, the previous events in Kansas, or even the Southern planters' repudiation of the work of Hinton Helper's (1829–1909) book, *The Impending Crisis*, which predicted the end of the system of oppression because it was wasteful, it was time for even the moderates to side with the Fire Eaters. In the end, radicals with pens and Bowie knives did not cause secession; rather, it was the inability of cooler heads to prevail.

J. N. Campbell

See also: Free Staters, Jayhawkers, and New England Emigrant Aid Company (1855–1860)

Further Reading

Davis, William C. 2001. *Rhett: The Turbulent Life and Times of a Fire-Eater*. Columbia: University of South Carolina Press.

Etcheson, Nicole. 2004. *Bleeding Kansas: Contested Liberty in the Civil War Era*. Lawrence: University Press of Kansas.

Faust, Drew Gilpin. 1977. *A Sacred Circle: The Dilemma of the Intellectual in the Old South, 1840–1860*. Baltimore, MD: Johns Hopkins University Press.

Fellman, Michael. 1989. *Inside War: The Guerilla Conflict in Missouri during the Civil War*. New York: Oxford University Press.

Freehling, William W. 2007. *The Road to Disunion: Vol. 2: Secessionists Triumphant, 1854–1861*. New York: Oxford University Press.

Heidler, David S. 1994. *Pulling the Temple Down: The Fire Eaters and the Destruction of the Union*. Mechanicsburg, PA: Stackpole Books.

Neely, Jeremy. 2007. *The Border between Them: Violence and Reconciliation on the Kansas-Missouri Line*. Columbia: University of Missouri Press.

Potter, David M. 2011. *The Impending Crisis: America before the Civil War, 1848–1861*. New York: Harper Perennial.

Focus on the Family (1977–)

Focus on the Family is a nonprofit, 501 (c)(3) organization headquartered in Colorado Springs, Colorado. The group is among the most influential elements of the

Christian Right, though its impact reaches far beyond politics. Focus on the Family, as its name implies, seeks to shape the family, primarily using a biblically-based, conservative framework. God's work springs from the family, according to Focus on the Family's mission statement:

> To cooperate with the Holy Spirit in sharing the Gospel of Jesus Christ with as many people as possible by nurturing and defending the God-ordained institution of the family and promoting biblical truths worldwide. ("Foundational Values" 2018)

In 1970, while still a clinical professor of pediatrics at the University of Southern California School of Medicine, and as part of the attending staff at Children's Hospital in Los Angeles, Dr. James Dobson (1936–) published *Dare to Discipline*. Intended as a counterpoint to Dr. Benjamin Spock's (1903–1998) *The Common Sense Book of Baby and Child Care*, *Dare to Discipline* was a call toward traditional, discipline-based parenting and away from what Dobson perceived as Spock's damaging permissiveness. The book became a sensation.

In September, 1976, Dobson asked for a one-year leave of absence, during which he formed Focus on the Family. The context was critical. Candidate, and soon president, Jimmy Carter (1924–), promoted himself as a "born again" Christian, signifying the ascendance of evangelicalism and its sociopolitical offshoot, the Christian Right. The movement, which eventually found a political home in the Republican Party, developed, to a degree, from a sense of cultural alienation.

The Christian Right was, and is, a complex, somewhat defensive response to the shifting norms of the 1960s and 1970s. Supreme Court decisions against school prayer and in favor of abortion rights both reflected and created a world at odds with elements of the Christian ethos that, for the Christian Right, defined America. Sex, marriage, childbirth, and child-rearing began to take on different meanings. James Dobson and Focus on the Family became the conservative Christian response to the sexual revolution.

Focus on the Family began humbly but grew into a colossus. Dobson started with a 25-minute weekly radio broadcast, called "Let's Get Acquainted," on 40 stations. By 1980, he had a daily, 15-minute program that aired on 200 outlets. By the 2000s, Dobson commanded a daily audience of 7.3 million people on hundreds of affiliates around the world, including the Armed Forces Radio network. These broadcasts were translated into over 35 languages.

Beyond the flagship radio program, Focus built a media empire as it launched magazines (*Focus on the Family, Focus on the Family Citizen, Clubhouse, Clubhouse, Jr., Brio*, and *Breakaway*), films (*Turn Your Heart toward Home*; *A Man Called Norman*; *Sex, Lies, and Truth*), and books by Dobson (*Bringing Up Boys, Bringing Up Girls, The Strong-Willed Child*, and *Temper Your Child's Tantrums*) and others. Focus also produced radio and video programs for children (*Adventures in Odyssey, Last Chance Detective Series, McGee and Me!*).

In 1993, the organization moved to a 45-acre campus with its own zip code. The organization has a mailing list of more than 250 million people across 155 countries. During the mid-2000s, Focus on the Family received over 10,000 letters, 7,000 phone calls, and 10,000 emails on any given day (Klemp 2007, 522).

In principle, little of this content is overtly political. At the same time, there are significant themes that feed into political issues. Focus's approach to "family values" argued against abortion; undermined most notions of homosexual rights; and defined marriage and the family as one man, one woman, and many children. By extension, in advocating for these positions, Focus exercised a significant political influence, much of it indirect, over the still unfolding "culture wars" that divide progressive and traditional Americans.

Focus on the Family's reach was lengthened by its decision to be nonsectarian and theologically inclusive. The organization's language and the biblical interpretations it relies upon are generally broad and stay above fine divisions more likely to plague other religious groups. Within its framework, Focus appeals to a varied audience, including Protestants, Roman Catholics, Jews, and Mormons. This relative inclusiveness, combined with the superficially less politicized emphasis on the family, extended its influence beyond groups more closely associated with fundamentalist (the Moral Majority) or charismatic (the Christian Coalition) religious roots. Focus on the Family shares more with the National Association of Evangelicals than with other religious organizations appealing to a splintered evangelicalism.

Though Dobson largely operated within the evangelical subculture, and did so successfully, he also built relationships with political entities tied to the Republican Party. In 1981, *Focus on the Family Magazine* highlighted one of the organization's new board members, Susan Baker, wife of President Ronald Reagan's (1911–2004) Secretary of State James Baker (1930–). In 1983, Dobson, along with others, helped form the Family Research Council (FRC), a conservative lobbying organization in Washington, D.C. The FRC was able to more fully manifest some of the politics only implied by Focus on the Family itself.

Three instances demonstrated Focus's direct political power. First, in 1980, early in the organization's history, President Carter convened the White House Conference on the American Family. Dobson was not an invited participant, so he asked his radio audience to send letters to the White House with requests he be included. Soon, Jim Guy Tucker (1943–), the conference organizer, was flooded with 80,000 letters, which led to Dobson's invitation. Second, not long after opening its new headquarters in Colorado, in 1992, Focus became embroiled in the controversy over amending the state constitution to limit gay rights laws. Dobson and Focus joined the effort, produced advertising to promote the amendment, and encouraged listeners and readers to volunteer on behalf of Amendment 2. The measure passed with 53.4 percent of the vote, though it was later overturned by the U.S. Supreme Court. Third, in 1994, the U.S. House of Representatives considered legislation that would require homeschool parents to be certified by the state in every subject they taught their children. Michael Farris (1951–), founder of the Homeschool Legal Defense Association, appeared on Focus on the Family's radio broadcast and appealed to Dobson's listeners to call Congress to voice their displeasure. Approximately one million calls jammed congressional phone banks over the next week. The measure was defeated, and alternative language, more conducive to homeschool families, was used instead (Gilgoff 2007, 33–35).

While the organization continued to propound family-centric material, through *Citizen* magazine, Focus on the Family took positions on a range of issues, some of which transcended the seemingly narrow confines of family values. Supreme Court appointments, tax exemption for religious organizations, and family friendly tax policies that might benefit single-income households were all featured prominently. Readers were also often encouraged to contact their members of Congress when important matters made their way to the legislative calendar.

Throughout the 1990s and early 2000s, Dobson sharpened his attacks on abortion rights in general and Planned Parenthood in particular, and he began to advocate against homosexual rights and the potential redefinition of marriage. By then, much of Focus on the Family's content was shifting away from advice on parenting and challenges in the household and toward social commentary. "What had been only a small, behind-the-scenes aspect of Focus in the 1980s was now becoming its primary mission" In 2004, every member of the Focus mailing list received voter registration forms (Ridgely 2017, 188–189).

In 2003, Dobson stepped down as CEO of Focus on the Family, and the next year, Focus on the Family Action (later renamed CitizenLink and Family Policy Alliance) was formed. This overtly political entity was legally separated to allow Dobson to take a more political role, especially to combat the growth of same-sex marriage, while protecting Focus on the Family's tax-exempt status. In 2009, Dobson severed himself fully from Focus on the Family.

Though there has been some decline in the number of listeners and stations, Focus's radio broadcast (now anchored by others) is still heard on over 1,000 stations. According to the Evangelical Council for Financial Accountability, Focus on the Family still took in more than $93 million in revenue in 2016, which more than covered its $90 million in expenses. Focus declared more than $54 million in existing assets.

While Focus on the Family's influence has diminished in recent years, the group was nonetheless influential in getting Donald Trump (1946–) elected president in 2016.

Mark Caleb Smith

See also: Christian Coalition of America (1988–); Eagle Forum (1972–); Family Research Council (1983–); Home School Legal Defense Association (2000–); Republican National Coalition for Life (1992–)

Further Reading

"Foundational Values." 2018. Focus on the Family. https://www.focusonthefamily.com /about/foundational-values.

Gilgoff, Dan. 2007. *The Jesus Machine: How James Dobson, Focus on the Family, and Evangelical America are Winning the Culture War.* New York: St. Martin's Press.

Klemp, Nathan J. 2007. "Beyond God-Talk: Understanding the Christian Right from the Ground Up." *Polity* 39 (4): 522–544.

Ridgely, Susan B. 2017. *Practicing What the Doctor Preached: At Home with Focus on the Family.* New York: Oxford University Press.

Food Policy Action (2012–)

Food Policy Action (FPA) is a policy-focused, nonprofit organization created in 2012 to address environmental and food justice issues. Its mission involves promoting environmentally sustainable farming practices, protecting the rights of farm workers, eliminating food waste, and creating access to nutrition for low-income people. Since its founding, FPA has primarily focused its efforts on informational campaigns designed to "hold legislators accountable on votes that have an effect on food and farming" (Food Policy Action 2014). Best known for its National Food Policy Score Card, which rates members of the U.S. Congress on food policy issues, FPA has emerged as a vocal critic of policies advocated by the Republican Party.

FPA's mission reflects the vision of two of its most prominent founding members, Tim Cook of the Environmental Working Group (EWG) and Tom Colicchio, an acclaimed chef and star of "Top Chef" on the Bravo television network. Under Cook's leadership, the EWG has provided research and organized advocacy efforts against pesticide use. The EWG has also advocated for increased funding for nutrition programs, conservation, and organic agriculture. Upon gaining a national following through his television program, Colicchio has called attention to hunger issues in the United States and has also highlighted the amount of food that goes to waste at restaurants and grocery stores. Cook and Colicchio met in 2010 when they testified before a congressional committee in support of government funding for school lunch programs. Both agreed that a lack of public information had become a major obstacle to addressing their concerns with food production and distribution in the United States. They began collaborating to create FPA soon after, leveraging Cook's decades of lobbying experience and Colicchio's celebrity status.

FPA made its debut in national politics when Congress debated the Farm Bill of 2012. Like other farm bills, the 2012 bill included subsidies to farmers, regulations pertaining to farming practices, and budget provisions for government programs for the poor, such as the Supplemental Nutrition Assistance Program (SNAP). Although Congress generally reassesses and reauthorizes farm bills every five years, and although reauthorization invariably involves conflict, the process of reauthorizing the Farm Bill in 2012 proved unusually contentious. Congressional Democrats and Republicans were starkly divided in their preferences about the scope of government, leading to conflict over a variety of governmental regulations and social programs. This partisan conflict extended to the Farm Bill of 2012.

In July 2012, the Agricultural Committee in the Republican-controlled House of Representatives put forward a bill that included several controversial provisions. This bill would have cut $16 billion dollars from SNAP over a period of 10 years—an unprecedented reduction in funds for the program. The Republican plan also called for a reduction to programs that promote conservation in farming and a reduction of the Environmental Protection Agency's authority to enforce regulations on farming practices. Republican leadership in the House of Representatives also refused to schedule time to debate the bill, ultimately allowing the previously authorized farm bill of 2008 to expire. Although Congress did pass resolutions to continue the provision of farm subsidies and SNAP benefits, funding for ecological conservation programs and research on sustainable farming stopped when the farm bill of 2008 expired. A new farm bill—the Agricultural Act of 2014—eventually passed after two years of partisan conflict. During this time, House Democrats resisted the curtailing of regulations and the cuts to SNAP and found allies in the food justice movement. FPA—formed earlier that year—stood among them.

The controversy over the farm bill in 2012 provided FPA with its first test as an advocacy organization and it responded with a large-scale public information campaign. FPA initiated its National Food Policy Score Card in October 2012 and began to promote it on television, via the Internet, and through social media. This score card rates members of Congress based on their votes on several major areas of food-related policy, ranging from hunger relief to support for farmers' markets. Scores range from zero to 100, with higher scores signifying voting records that are most consistent with FPA's position.

Scores on the National Food Policy Score Card in 2012 reflected that congressional Republicans were consistently at odds with the FPA. Congressional Democrats, meanwhile, generally supported positions endorsed by the FPA. Of the 11 senators who received a perfect score on the National Food Policy Score Card, 10 were Democrats. Joseph Lieberman—an independent who formerly belonged to the Democratic Party—also earned a perfect score. Similarly, the 10 lowest scorers in Senate—who all received scores lower than 20—belonged to the Republican Party. Likewise, in the House of Representatives, Democrats received the highest scores while Republicans received the lowest. Score card results showed a similar pattern for 2013 as the battle over the farm bill dragged on. During this time, FPA primarily focused its criticism on House Republicans who advocated for cuts to SNAP.

When Congress passed the farm bill into law in January 2014, FPA expressed disappointment over its contents, particularly cuts to SNAP funding. Although cuts to SNAP were ultimately smaller than those proposed by House Republicans, FPA criticized the reduction in funds for hurting poor families while increasing subsidies for already profitable farm businesses. The 2014 National Food Policy Score Card reflected this sentiment. In 2014, 10 Republican senators and 28 Republican House members received a zero. All 54 perfect scores went to Democrats, as did an additional 126 scores above 70 (http://foodpolicyaction.org/scorecard/).

In the aftermath of the battle over the farm bill, FPA quickly pivoted to other food-related issues. It also began to raise its political profile in the nation's capital. FPA began a nearly two-year lobbying effort to require the labeling of genetically modified food, which ultimately helped spur the passage of a new food labeling law in July 2016. The organization also supported changes to school nutrition guidelines that require lunch programs to serve more whole grains, fruits, and vegetables while also serving less fat and sodium. This once again put the FPA in conflict with Congressional Republicans, who announced plans for allowing schools to opt out of this mandate. After another multiyear conflict over legislation, Congress authorized a school nutrition policy that is largely consistent with the FPA's preferences in January 2016.

During its efforts to require labeling of genetically modified foods and preserve nutrition standards for school lunches, FPA also began to expand its lobbying efforts. Colicchio began to organize fund-raising dinners with prominent Democratic members of Congress in attempt to get food policy reforms on the political agenda. Additionally, during the 2014 election cycle, FPA made its first attempt to influence electoral politics when it actively sought the defeat of Republican Steve Southerland of Florida's second congressional district. FPA criticized Southerland for blocking the 2013 version of the farm bill in an effort to cut funding for SNAP. In the weeks leading up to Election Day, FPA targeted voters with digital advertisements. Tom Colicchio and VoteVets Chairman Jon Soltz collaborated on an op-ed that appeared in the *Tallahassee Democrat*, the major newspaper in Southerland's district. The op-ed criticized Southerland for his votes to cut nutrition assistance programs for vulnerable populations such as veterans, women, and children. On Election Day, Southerland was defeated. FPA received credit for its role in Southerland's defeat from political journalists and commentators, most notably from the online political magazine *Politico* and from MSNBC's progressive cable show, *All In with Chris Hayes*.

Along with its political achievements, FPA has also received criticism. Some congressional Republicans have publicly criticized celebrity chefs for becoming politically involved on food issues, arguing that they lack sufficient policy expertise. Others have argued that Colicchio and other food justice activists have demonstrated elitism in their approach. Some of these critics have come from the culinary community. Julie Kelly, a Chicago-based culinary instructor, criticized Colicchio for misusing his celebrity status in a 2014 *Wall Street Journal* op-ed. In the op-ed Kelly stated, "Culinary elites—like political elites—profess to want to help ordinary Americans, but their efforts often miss the mark as they aim to be the smartest guy at the food and wine festival. . . . Tom, with all due respect, please stick to your pots and pans" (Kelly 2014).

Colicchio's response to Kelly's remarks, published on FPA's website, signaled the organization's future priorities. After arguing that celebrity chefs and others have an obligation to highlight problems with food distribution and production, Colicchio reiterated the FPA's concerns about cuts to SNAP. Colicchio also put forward a critique about how the government provides subsidies to agricultural producers: "Federal subsidies, paid for with American tax dollars, are lavished on the ingredients that make unhealthy food cheap, produced by corporate mega-farms, while healthy fruits and vegetables are labeled 'specialty crops' and receive far less support." Colicchio and FPA reaffirmed these policy concerns in 2016 when they began promoting the "Plate of the Union" initiative, which called upon the next president of the United States to support policies that would promote sustainable farming practices, cut subsidies to large corporate farms, and strengthen programs that make food more affordable for low-income people.

SNAP funding and federal subsidies for agricultural producers are recurring sources of conflict when Congress debates farm bills. The periodic reauthorizations of the farm bill present the FPA with significant opportunities to influence these areas of food policy.

Andrew J. Bloeser

Related Primary Document: **Food Policy Action: Steve Southerland Campaign Target Article (2014)**

Food Policy Action: Steve Southerland Campaign Target Article (2014)

Food Policy Action (FPA) is a nonpartisan organization founded in 2012 that tracks legislators' voting records concerning the food industry and its workers in the United States. The Farm Bill is the nation's largest bill concerning food in the United States. The bill goes up for renewal every four years and governs the implementation of the Supplemental Nutrition Assistance Program (SNAP)—formerly known as food stamps. SNAP subsidizes food aid for low-income families and individuals by providing them with a monthly payment to be used for this purpose. In this article written by Food Policy Action in 2014, the organization used its resources to target Steve Southerland, representative from Florida. His food record, the FPA argues, poses a threat to public health. The FPA cites that Congressman Southerland failed to protect crops from pesticides and voted to cut SNAP benefits, among other perceived transgressions.

FOOD POLICY ACTION MAKES CONGRESSMAN STEVE SOUTHERLAND ITS #1 CAMPAIGN TARGET

October 1, 2014

Claire Benjamin

GROUP SAYS SOUTHERLAND'S RECORD ON SENSIBLE FOOD POLICIES IS ROTTEN

Washington, D.C.—Today, Food Policy Action announced that Congressman Steve Southerland of Florida's Second Congressional District will be the group's top target for defeat in the upcoming midterm elections. The organization, which is dedicated to educating the public about the votes their elected leaders take on critically important food issues, will devote significant resources in the race as part of a larger, one million dollar effort to hold elected officials accountable for the votes they make related to food quality, accessibility, and sustainability.

"Congressman Southerland has a clear history of voting against sensible food policy and has repeatedly made policy choices that are harmful to families and small farmers," said Claire Benjamin, Managing Director of Food Policy Action. "His record on food is rotten. We're letting voters in his district know that Steve Southerland is way past his sell-by date."

Over the last two years, Southerland has voted multiple times to roll back funding and regulation on food safety, pesticides, nutrition assistance, and healthy food initiatives:

*   Voted against an additional $1 million in funding to protect against E-coli contaminations for the Center for Food Safety and Applied Nutrition [Amendment 420, H.R. 2112, 6/15/2011].

- Voted to make it easier to discharge pesticides that pollute rivers and other waterways, and to eliminate the need for a permit for such activities [Voted yes on H.R. 935, 07/31/2014].
- Voted to cut Supplemental Nutrition Assistance Program (SNAP) by more than $39 billion, preventing 4 million individuals, including children, seniors, military families, and veterans from receiving critical nutrition assistance [H.R. 3102, 9/19/2013].
- Voted to eliminate the Healthy Food Financing Initiative (HFFI) and to end support for projects that increase access to healthy and affordable food in low-income communities [Amendment 30, H.R. 1947, 6/20/2013].

Southerland was also credited for being singularly responsible for blocking the 2013 Farm Bill from passage. Southerland's SNAP work requirement amendment would have given cash incentives to states for kicking SNAP recipients off the program who have not been able to find work. This was not only bad policy, it also caused the whole process to grind to a halt.

- According to the Southeast Farm Press, Southerland's amendment "was key to the bill's failure Thursday." [Southeast Farm Press, 6/25/13].
- Politico reported "the farm bill has been a beacon of bipartisanship in an increasingly rough-and-tumble chamber. The defeat of Thursday's version was propelled by the adoption of Florida GOP Rep. Steve Southerland's amendment to institute work requirements for recipients of food stamps." [Politico, 6/20/13].
- The Sunshine State News also reported that "Some disappointed House Republicans are blaming Florida colleague Steve Southerland for losing 195-234, a five-year farm bill leadership badly wanted." [Sunshine State News, 6/20/13].

In order to hold Congressman Southerland accountable for his terrible record, Food Policy Action will conduct a targeted voter turnout program, including telephone calls and digital ads, focused on educating drop-off voters about Southerland's abysmal voting record on food policy.

"Congressman Southerland is out of step with voters on the importance of common sense food policy. Parents and young voters will not stand for his continued disregard for the health and safety of the food that feeds our families," said Benjamin.

Source: Food Policy Action, 2014. All Rights Reserved.

See also: Citizens for Health (1992–); United Farm Workers (1966–)

Further Reading
Bottemiller Evich, Helena. 2014. "Celebrity Chefs Cooking Up Lobbying Agenda." *Politico*, November 27, 2014.
Colicchio, Tom. 2014. "Food Is Worth Fighting For." *Food Policy Action*, November 6, 2014. http://foodpolicyaction.org/food-is-worth-fighting-for/.
Feur, Allen. 2014. "Tom Colicchio, Citizen Chef." *New York Times*, May 16, 2014.

Food Policy Action. 2014. "Who We Are." http://foodpolicyaction.org/who-we-are/

Kelly, Julie. 2014. "Tom Colicchio's Overcooked Politics." *Wall Street Journal*, October 29, 2014. https://www.wsj.com/articles/julie-kelly-tom-colicchios-overcooked -politics-1414621705.

Severson, Kim. 2016. "When Will Food Issues Be on Politicians' Plates?" *New York Times*, July 26, 2016.

Zizza, Claire A. 2015. "Policies and Politics of US Food Supply." *Journal of the Academy of Nutrition and Dietetics* 111: 27–30.

Ford Foundation (1936–)

The family of automaker Henry Ford (1863–1947) established the Ford Foundation in 1936. Based in New York City, it is a private foundation whose stated mission is to improve the welfare of people internationally. According to its website, the Ford Foundation prides itself on investing in "innovative ideas, visionary individuals, and frontline institutions advancing human dignity around the world" (Ford Foundation 2017). Since the time of its creation, the Ford Foundation has traditionally been one the largest and most influential charitable institutions, with the greatest assets and highest annual giving.

On January 15, 1936, Edsel Bryant Ford (1893–1943), then-president of the Ford Motor Company, established the Ford Foundation with the purpose of administering funds for charitable, educational, and scientific purposes that would benefit the public. Edsel Ford was the only recognized child of pioneering automaker Henry Ford. As the founder and owner of the Ford Motor Company, Henry Ford had popularized the development of the assembly line to support mass production. He made a fortune by manufacturing the first automobile that many middle-class Americans could afford, revolutionizing the nation's transportation as well as industry in the United States. In his time, Henry Ford was one of the wealthiest and best-known people in the world, serving as president of the Ford Motor Company from 1906 to 1919.

As the sole heir to the family business, Edsel Ford served as company president from 1919 until he died of stomach cancer in 1943 at 49 years old. His elderly father, Henry Ford, returned to run the company at age 80 until Edsel's son, Henry Ford II (1917–1987), took over two years later. Henry Ford II went on to serve as company president from 1945 to 1960. The deaths of both Edsel Ford and Henry Ford took place within two years of each other. They left considerable assets to the Ford Foundation when their estates were settled in 1947. Upon their passing, in addition to serving as president of the Ford Motor Company, Henry Ford II also assumed the presidency of the Ford Foundation.

In 1947, the involvement of the United States in World War II (1939–1945) remained fresh in people's minds. Henry Ford II served in the U.S. Navy during the war. After the Allied victory, as head of the then-largest charitable foundation in the world, he felt that the Ford Foundation had a responsibility to respond to global issues. In 1948, Ford II and his board of trustees commissioned attorney H. Rowan Gaither to conduct a study in order to prioritize problems that the Foundation might address.

The Gaither Study Committee recommended that the foundation become an international philanthropy, focusing on solving the most pressing problems of humankind rather than working in any specific field. The board of the Ford Foundation adopted that recommendation in 1949. Since that time, it has concentrated its considerable resources in several major areas, including arts and culture, civil rights, education, human rights, poverty reduction, and urban planning.

The Ford Foundation's involvement in arts and culture includes support of organizations like the Dance Theatre of Harlem, Detroit Symphony, New York's Lincoln Center, the School of American Ballet, and the Museum of Modern Art in New York City as well the Kennedy Center for the Performing Arts in Washington, D.C. It has also awarded grants in the creative arts to individuals working in music, poetry, theater, visual arts, and writing. In 2017, the annual Pulitzer Prizes included honors for several Ford Foundation grantees, including author Matthew Desmond for his book *Evicted: Poverty and Profit in the American City*; playwright Lynn Nottage for her play *Sweat* about the struggles of working-class people in Pennsylvania; and Heather Thompson for her book *Blood in the Water* about the 1971 Attica Prison uprising. Thompson was instrumental in helping to develop the Ford Foundation's college-in-prison program. The Foundation was also a major underwriter for *Eyes on the Prize*, a 14-hour documentary television series covering the American civil rights movement from the 1950s to 1980s. It has also involved itself in providing funds for civil rights litigation.

The Ford Foundation has traditionally been a strong supporter of education. In 1952, the Foundation provided a grant to help found the National Educational Television Center. That organization evolved into the Public Broadcasting Service (PBS) which has brought iconic programs like *Mister Rogers' Neighborhood* and *Sesame Street* to American television. The Foundation also provided seed funding for the Head Start program to offer early childhood education, health, nutrition, and parental involvement services to low-income children and their families. Launched in 1965, Head Start is one of the longest-running programs addressing the effects of poverty by intervening to aid children. Also, from the earliest days of the Foundation, it has been a major supporter of the United Negro College Fund (UNCF), providing scholarships for African American students and general scholarship funds for 37 historically black colleges and universities.

The Ford Foundation has helped to support human rights law groups around the world, including groups focused on women's rights and the rights of indigenous people. It granted resources to establish the United Nation's International Criminal Court, which oversees cases regarding crimes against humanity, such as genocide and war crimes. It has supported the Children's Defense Fund to address the rights of children, with special attention to the needs of poor children, children of color, and those with disabilities so that all children have equal opportunities for healthy, successful lives.

The Ford Foundation has addressed poverty through programs around the world such as agricultural research, microfinance, PLANNING PROJECTS, AND technical assistance. The Foundation's initiatives in urban issues have leaned toward community engagement and economic opportunity through such efforts as funding the Bedford-Stuyvesant Restoration Corporation to revitalize a disadvantaged neighborhood in Brooklyn, New York.

In 1967, the Ford Foundation invested in a headquarters building on 43rd Street in New York City. It was innovative for being the first large-scale architectural building in the United States to devote a large portion of its square footage to an urban greenspace. The building became well known for its large garden atrium area, which was designed with a vision of being accessible to the public. Recognized as a new concept in urban construction, the design was utilized for many skyscrapers and indoor shopping malls that were built in the following decades. The New York City Landmarks Preservation Commission designated the Ford Foundation building as a landmark in 1997.

Starting in 2016, the iconic Ford Foundation building began undergoing a renovation project to update it. The Foundation's headquarters moved temporarily to an interim office at 1440 Broadway. According to the Foundation, when the building reopens, "it will be a contemporary, collaborative workspace that is open and green, and will be known as the Ford Foundation Center for Social Justice. It will feature a welcome center, an art gallery, and two full floors for events and programs—as well as space for like-minded organizations" (Ford Foundation n.d.).

Nancy Hendricks

See also: Bill & Melinda Gates Foundation (2000–); Carnegie Corporation of New York (1911–); Koch Family Foundations (1953–); Pew Charitable Trusts (1948–)

Further Reading

Bak, Richard. 2003. *Henry and Edsel: The Creation of the Ford Empire.* Hoboken, NJ: Wiley.

Berman, Edward. 1983. *The Influence of the Carnegie, Ford, and Rockefeller Foundations on American Foreign Policy: The Ideology of Philanthropy.* Albany: State University of New York Press.

Ford Foundation. 2017. https://www.fordfoundation.org/.

Ford Foundation. n.d. "Transforming Our Building." https://ff-dev.durabledigital.com/about/about-ford/transforming-our-building/.

Parmar, Inderjeet. 2012. *Foundations of the American Century: The Ford, Carnegie, and Rockefeller Foundations in the Rise of American Power.* New York: Columbia University Press.

Free Soil Party (1848–1855)

The Free Soil Party was a political party that developed in the mid-1840s in the midst of the nation's growing divide over slavery. Although the party had only the most limited electoral success, its effort to move the nation toward an end to slavery provided something of a bridge and helped pave the way for the emergence in 1856 of the Republican Party.

With the major parties, the Democrats and the Whigs, essentially ignoring the slavery question, the 1844 presidential election had seen that banner carried by the Liberty Party, a group that sought the end of slavery. While it garnered only a little more than 2 percent of the popular vote, many believe that the votes siphoned off by Liberty Party candidate James Birney in New York prevented Whig candidate Henry Clay from winning the state and, in turn, the election. The resulting victory of Democrat James K. Polk was soon followed by the Mexican-American War (1846–1848), which served to quickly exacerbate the debates over the slavery question.

The introduction in the House of Representatives by Pennsylvania Congressman David Wilmot of what became known as the Wilmot Proviso, a provision that would have prevented slavery in any land acquired by the United States from Mexico, only further highlighted the issues of both slavery itself as well as its expansion, while also raising questions about the very purpose of the war. Things were further muddied when, as the 1848 presidential election approached, and with neither the Democrats nor the Whigs wanting to address the slavery issue, remnants of the Liberty Party and some antislavery Whigs and Democrats joined with the Barnburners, a faction of New York's Democratic Party that had supported the Wilmot Proviso; and, meeting in Buffalo, New York, in August 1848, they formed the Free Soil Party. Adopting the slogan "Free soil, free speech, free labor, freemen," the new party chose former president Martin Van Buren as its presidential nominee and Charles Francis Adams, the son of John Quincy Adams, the nation's sixth president and a man who had capped his long public career as a crusading antislavery member of the House of Representatives, as its candidate for vice president and prepared to force the nation to confront the issue.

Amid the political turmoil and instability that followed the Mexican-American War, and boasting a high-profile ticket, the Free Soilers entered the campaign with high hopes. In fact, however, the campaign was not what the Free Soilers had hoped. Some saw the choice of the well-known Van Buren as little more than a cynical ploy aimed at capitalizing on his name and doubted the commitment to the antislavery cause of the onetime Democratic Party leader. Meanwhile, others saw the choice of the two well-known partisans to lead the ticket as an act of revenge, intended to take votes from the major parties and not as part of a sincere effort, or reflecting a true desire, to abolish slavery. Massachusetts senator and Whig leader Daniel Webster typified this attitude, calling the party the "Free Spoilers." At the same time, the party did gain substantive support from elements of the abolitionist movement, with Fredrick Douglass being one of the most prominent of their number to support the cause.

Despite the ongoing tensions over slavery, the Free Soilers were unable to make their message resonate with a broad national audience. In the end, rather than forcing the major parties to confront the looming problem of slavery and its expansion in the aftermath of the war, in winning only 10 percent of vote, in the view of many, all the Free Soil Party did, however unintentionally, was play the role of spoiler that had been predicted. To those analysts, the Free Soilers guaranteed a victory for Whig nominee and war hero Zachary Taylor over Democratic Senator Lewis Cass, who had tried to skirt the slavery issue by asserting that it should be determined by popular sovereignty, thus putting the onus back on the states.

The Free Soilers did achieve some local success, electing one senator, Salmon Chase of Ohio, as well as a number of members of the House of Representatives.

Estimates of their success range from as high as 15 percent to as low as 9 percent, depending on differing sources as well as which point in the party's short life one cites. The fact that historians have struggled to arrive at an exact figure reflects the political volatility of the times. Historians have argued that the movement's actual strength and influence in Congress exceeded whatever figures are reported. A number of office holders, including, most prominently, Senators John Hale of New Hampshire and Charles Sumner of Massachusetts and William Seward of New York, although clinging to their established party labels, supported political positions and pursued policies on slavery that were much like the Free Soil Party platform. In addition, regardless of the actual labels, in the deeply but closely divided Congress of the time, those who supported the Free Soil ideas represented a bloc that could tip the balance of power and were thus were able to impact policy beyond their numbers. This reality was most evident in the debates over the Compromise of 1850. All of this, coupled with the political evolution of avowed Free Soilers like Salmon Chase who became a Republican leader, offers substantive evidence of the party's influence in the subsequent development and success of the Republican Party.

Indeed, ideologically, like the later Republicans, the Free Soil Party was not an abolitionist party, and the party's agenda did not call for black equality. Rather, while the Party did, for its time, offer the only real political alternative for abolitionists willing to engage with the political process, most Free Soilers based their views on slavery in economics, not morality. They believed that slave owners, possessing a built-in labor force, had an unfair advantage over the farmer who was working their own land or hiring others to help. This economic focus was apparent in the part of the Free Soil platform that called for a tariff, but only as a method of raising revenue to pay off the national debt and not as a barrier to free trade. The party also supported a homestead act designed to encourage landownership and western migration.

But these economic views notwithstanding, the centerpiece of the Free Soil platform was its position on slavery, one that proclaimed: "We inscribe on our banner, 'Free Soil, Free Speech, Free Labor and Free Men,' and under it we will fight on and fight ever, until a triumphant victory shall reward our exertions." The Party did include some members—and leaders—whose views of blacks were advanced for the times and were not rooted in the white supremacy that characterized the period. Indeed, the Party's 1852 platform called slavery a "sin," and while acknowledging that the federal government could not, under the constitution, interfere with slavery, it did include a call for abolition. Also, reflective of an increasingly enlightened or at least humane view of the nation's blacks, those free blacks, including Frederick Douglass, who attended the Party's 1852 convention in Pittsburgh, reported being treated with a respect not seen four years before in Buffalo.

In the end, the Party's direct political impact was limited. While its success in the 1848 election was small, its impact, if only indirectly, was large. That election also represented the party's high watermark. In 1852, John Hale of New Hampshire, who, although elected to the Senate in 1846 as an independent Democrat, had in fact been an early Free Soil supporter, won the presidential nomination but received only 5 percent of the vote. In the turbulent political scene that was the 1850s, the Free Soilers quickly disappeared from the scene; and after a brief appearance by the Know Nothings, whose support cut across slavery lines, the Republican Party, aided by a major infusion of Free Soil blood, emerged first as the alternative to the Democrats in 1856 and then as the victors against a deeply divided Democratic Party in 1860.

Ultimately, the Free Soil Party proved to be a short-lived experiment whose message resonated with only a limited audience. The bulk of its electoral support came from parts of Ohio, upstate New York, and western Massachusetts, although there were pockets of support in other northern states. While its political opponents tried to stamp it as an abolitionist group, in fact, despite such allegations, the party did not advocate an absolute end to slavery. It opposed it—on many levels— and ultimately saw it as a violation of fundamental democratic ideals. But the Free Soilers also believed that given its economic inefficiency, the practice would eventually become obsolete. In the meantime, rather than engaging in an unwinnable battle to end the practice, they instead sought to focus their efforts and energies on preventing its expansion. While the free soil they sought was ultimately achieved, it was through a ghastly civil war and not their political efforts.

William H. Pruden III

Related Primary Document: **Free Soil Party Platform (1848)**

Free Soil Party Platform (1848)

Adopted at Buffalo, New York, on August 9, 1848, the platform of the newly formed Free Soil Party sought to present a clear choice for the antislavery proponents. The party was assembled from several antislavery groups from the Democratic, Whig and former Liberty parties. The Free Soil Party nominated Martin Van Buren of New York for president and Charles Francis Adams of Massachusetts for vice president as its candidates for the election of 1848, but they lost to Zachary Taylor of the Whig Party, obtaining only 10 percent of the popular vote and no electoral votes. Within six years, the Free Soil Party joined with other antislavery groups to form the Republican Party.

Whereas, We have assembled in Convention, as a union of *Freemen*, for the sake of Freedom, forgetting all past political differences in a common resolve to maintain the rights of Free Labor against the aggressions of the Slave Power, and to secure Free Soil for a Free People:

And whereas, The political Conventions recently assembled at Baltimore and Philadelphia, the one stifling the voice of a great constituency entitled to be heard in its deliberations, and the other abandoning its distinctive principles for mere availability, have dissolved the national party organizations heretofore existing, by nominating for the Chief Magistracy of the United States, under Slaveholding dictation, candidates, *neither of whom* can be supported by the opponents of Slavery-extension, without a *sacrifice of consistency, duty*, and *self-respect*.

And whereas, These nominations, so made, furnish the occasion and demonstrate the necessity of the union of the People under the banners of Free. Democracy, in a solemn and formal *declaration* of their *independence* of the *Slave Power*, and of their fixed determination to rescue the Federal Government from its control:

Resolved, therefore, that we, the people here assembled, remembering the example of our *fathers* in the days of the first Declaration of Independence, putting our trust in God for the triumph of our cause, and invoking his guidance in our endeavors to advance it, do now plant ourselves upon the NATIONAL PLATFORM OF FREEDOM, in opposition to the Sectional Platform of Slavery.

Resolved, That Slavery in the several States of this Union which recognize its existence, depends upon the State laws alone, which cannot be repealed or modified by the Federal Government, and for which laws that Government is not responsible. We therefore propose no interference by Congress with Slavery within the limits of any State.

Resolved, That the PROVISO of Jefferson, to prohibit the existence of Slavery, after 1800 in all the Territories of the United States, Southern and Northern; the votes of six States, and sixteen delegates, in the Congress of 1784, for the Proviso, to three States and seven delegates against it; the actual exclusion of Slavery from the Northwestern Territory by the ORDINANCE OF 1787, *unanimously* adopted by the States in Congress, and the entire history of that period, clearly show that it was the settled policy of the nation, *not* to *extend, nationalize*, or *encourage*, but to limit, localize, and discourage, Slavery; and to *this policy* which should never have been departed from, the Government ought to *return*.

Resolved, That our fathers ordained the Constitution of the United States, in order, among other great national objects, to establish justice, promote the general welfare, and secure the blessings of Liberty; but expressly *denied* to the Federal Government, which they created, all constitutional power to *deprive any person* of life, *liberty*, or property, without due legal process.

Resolved, That in the judgment of this Convention, Congress has no more power to make a SLAVE than to make a KING; no more power to institute or establish SLAVERY, than to institute or establish a MONARCHY. NO such power can be found among those specifically conferred by the Constitution, or derived by just implication from them,

Resolved, THAT IT IS THE DUTY OF THE FEDERAL GOVERNMENT TO RELIEVE ITSELF FROM ALL RESPONSIBILITY FOR THE EXISTENCE OR CONTINUANCE OF SLAVERY WHEREVER THAT GOVERNMENT POSSESS CONSTITUTIONAL POWER TO LEGISLATE ON THAT SUBJECT, AND IS THUS RESPONSIBLE FOR ITS EXISTENCE.

Resolved, That the true, and, in the judgment of this Convention, the *only* safe means of preventing the extension of Slavery into territory now free, is to prohibit its existence in all such territory by *an act of Congress.*

Resolved, That we accept the issue which the Slave Power has forced upon us, and to their demand for more Slave States and more Slave Territory, our calm but final answer is: No more Slave States and no more Slave Territory. Let the soil of our extensive domains be kept free, for the hardy pioneers of our own land, and the oppressed and banished of other lands seeking homes of comfort and fields of enterprise in the New World.

Resolved, That the bill lately reported by the Committee of Eight in the Senate of the United States, was no compromise, but an absolute surrender of the rights of the non-slaveholders of the States; and while we rejoice to know that a measure which, while opening the door for the introduction of Slavery into Territories now free, would also have opened the door to litigation and strife among the future inhabitants thereof, to the ruin of their peace and prosperity, was defeated in the House of Representatives, its passage, in hot haste, by a majority, embracing several Senators who voted in open violation of the known will of their constituents, should warn the People to see to it, that their representatives be not suffered to betray them. There must be no more compromises with Slavery: if made, they must be repealed.

Resolved, That we demand Freedom and established institutions for our brethren in Oregon, now exposed to hardships, peril, and massacre, by the reckless hostility of the Slave Power to the establishment of Free Government for Free Territories and not only for them, but for our new brethren in California and New Mexico.

And whereas, It is due not only to this occasion, but to the whole people of the United States, that we should also declare ourselves on certain other questions of national policy, therefore,

Resolved, That we demand CHEAP POSTAGE for the people; a retrenchment of the expenses and patronage of the Federal Government; the *abolition* of all *unnecessary* offices and salaries; and the election by the People of all civil officers in the service of the Government, so far as the same may be practicable.

Resolved, That *river* and *harbor improvements*, when demanded by the safety and convenience of commerce with foreign nations, or among the several States, are objects of *national concern*; and that it is the duty of Congress, in the exercise of its constitutional powers, to provide therefor.

Resolved, That the FREE GRANT TO ACTUAL SETTLERS, in consideration of the expenses they incur in making settlements in the wilderness, which are usually fully equal to their actual cost, and of the public benefits resulting therefrom, of reasonable portions of the public lands, under suitable limitations, is a wise and just measure of public policy, which will promote, in various ways, the interest of all the States of this Union; and we therefore recommend it to the favorable consideration of the American People.

Resolved, That the obligations of honor and patriotism require the earliest practical payment of the national debt, and we are therefore in favor of such a tariff of duties as will raise revenue adequate to defray the necessary expenses of the Federal Government, and to pay annual installments of our debt and the interest thereon.

Resolved, That we inscribe on our banner, "FREE SOIL, FREE SPEECH, FREE LABOR, and FREE MEN," and under it we will fight on, and fight ever, until a triumphant victory shall reward our exertions.

Source: Stanhope, Edward. *A History of Presidential Elections*. Boston: Houghton, Mifflin, 1896, 172–175.

See also: American Anti-Slavery Society (1833–1870); Liberty Party (1840–1848); Republican Party (1854–); Whig Party (1833–1856)

Further Reading

Blue, Fredrick J. 1974. *Free Soilers: Third Party Politics, 1848–54*. Champaign: University of Illinois Press.

Earle, Jonathan H. 2004. *Jacksonian Antislavery and the Politics of Free Soil, 1824–1854*. Chapel Hill: The University of North Carolina Press.

Foner, Eric. 1995. *Free Soil, Free Labor, Free Men: The Ideology of the Republican Party before the Civil War*. New York: Oxford University Press.

Smith, Theodore Clarke. 2009. *The Free Soil Party in Wisconsin*. Ann Arbor: University of Michigan Library.

Free Staters, Jayhawkers, and New England Emigrant Aid Company (1855–1860)

Like their counterparts, the Fire Eaters and the Border Ruffians, before the Civil War (1861–1865) the Free Staters, Jayhawkers, and members of the New England Emigrant Aid Company (NEEAC) occupied politically important positions in and around the Kansas border conflict. In essence, they were extreme actors in a war that only escalated with time as the Union moved toward dissolution. Their adversaries were proponents of secession and the continued expansion of slavery. The Free Staters, Jayhawkers, and NEEAC were aggressive, and sometimes violent, abolition and antislavery movements that pressed for the emancipation of slaves and the outlawing of slavery, especially opposing the advancement of slavery into the territories.

When Free Soilers migrated west from northern states like Massachusetts, New York, and Ohio, they helped establish the Free State Party. With the objective of making the western territories of the United States, newly acquired land from the Mexican-American War (1846–1848), into free as opposed to slave states, this new party focused establishing political authority on a national stage. In May

1854, led by Senator Stephen A. Douglas (1813–1861), Congress passed the Kansas-Nebraska Act, which continued to implement the previous principle that was applied in the Utah and New Mexico Territories of popular sovereignty. Northern Democrats and Republicans both hoped that the newly created territories, linked by railroads, in this piece of legislation would see peaceful forms of democracy bear fruit and avoid violent confrontations. Utah and New Mexico, though, were fundamentally different regions than the Midwest because they did not support slavery due to a lack of large-scale agriculture. Thus, political violence in the Midwest was inevitable, especially as the divided state of Missouri was directly next door, and its Free Staters were at the ready to support those who immigrated to the region.

The territory of Kansas boiled over a year later as the region elected a legislature with the goal of deciding whether it would be slave or free. With a porous border, Missouri-backed slave state supporters, called Border Ruffians, overwhelmed the local polls, and most voted early and often. Threat and violence resulted in the victory of 90 percent of proslavery candidates. This rampant voter fraud, some of the worst in all of U.S. political history, led to what Free Staters called the "Bogus Legislature," even though slave state proponents argued that their mere presence allowed them to cast a ballot. Northern Democrats and Republican Party members used the opportunity to support or turn their backs on the situation in order to serve their own political ends. Likewise, newspaper coverage of these incidents in Kansas became rampant as the country turned its attention to the activities in the territories. Kansas basked in the political spotlight, but it was not to be a favorable one.

Border Ruffians and their backers in Missouri also claimed that their actions were no worse than those of organizations like the New England Emigrant Aid Company (NEEAC). At the time of the vote in Kansas, businessmen back in the East, led by a representative from Massachusetts named Eli Thayer (1819–1899), helped to found a joint-stock company that promoted the cause of antislavery in the new territories headed toward statehood. Viewed by most as a charitable organization, the NEEAC provided funds for individuals to travel to Kansas, a sponsorship if you will, but those who went did not necessarily possess the agricultural skills necessary to be farmers. The ones who did stay were seen as political rabble-rousers (such as the famed abolitionist and provocateur John Brown, 1800–1859), and they did their best to form new towns and provinces such as Lawrence, named in honor of NEEAC treasurer Amon Lawrence, and others still like Topeka and Manhattan.

These towns became the locus of all antislavery activities and also attracted the ire of the border ruffians. With violence on the horizon and the inauguration of what became known as "Bleeding Kansas," help arrived in the form of firepower when the NEEAC sent Sharp's rifles to the cause secretly packed in crates that were marked "Beecher's Bibles," in reference to the Minister Henry Ward Beecher (1813–1887). These Northern settlers were well-armed militarily and politically as Kansas sunk into a mini-civil war. Before action took place in the form of spilling blood and destroying property, the Free State Party established its own legislature in Topeka in response to the proslavery advocates relocating their capital to

Lecompton, near the Missouri border. The result of this move was the passage of the Lecompton Constitution, a slavery document that promoted their cause. However, before they could issue a call for a vote, violence broke out in Kansas.

In order to check the moves of the Border Ruffians and their proslavery benefactors across the Missouri line, the Free Staters employed their own roving bands, known to some as liberators and to others as robbers. These groups became known as "Jayhawkers," and they could be ruthless in doling out frontier justice. Named after a cross between a hawk, which was a lethal hunter, and a jay, which was loud and boisterous, the Jayhawkers battled the Border Ruffians in campaigns across Kansas. Led by abolitionists, Charles R. Jennison (1834–1884) and James Montgomery (1771–1854), they fought proslavery forces in and around polling stations, and leveled their form of violence on farmsteads that did not conform to their own political ideologies. After the start of the Civil War, they were assumed into Union regiments and continued to fight fierce, pitched battles against their now Confederate enemies, known as "bushwhackers."

Although it might seem that the Free State Party was unified in its cause politically against the proslavery advocates who flooded into the territory, the situation was not that clear. Antislavery factions, like their national parties, were deeply divided over the case of black freedom. Some wanted an abolition of slavery, while others were not so sure that ending an economic way of life to Southerners was the proper legislative choice. For the latter, it was not a moral argument but a question of labor and where that force would come from if slavery was outlawed. Gradually, though, with the region engulfed in violence from all sides, the abolitionists gained control of the different factions and were able to produce a constitutional document named after the town of Topeka, where it was drafted, that could rival the one created in Lecompton. The Topeka Constitution was held up in the U.S. Senate, and the Free Soilers and abolitionists attempted to pass a more radical document a few years later with the Leavenworth Constitution. This far-ranging radical attempt at a civil rights revolution included blacks and whites as equals and even included black suffrage in name. Though that did not pass in the Senate either, it showed how progressive and organized the Free State Party had become.

By 1858, the efforts of the NEEAC and the Jayhawkers gave the Free State Party the opportunity to officially overturn the proslavery Lecompton Constitution, replaced by the new Wyandotte Constitution. Although not as radical as the one from Leavenworth, this document did extend certain rights to African Americans. After the Election of 1860, as Abraham Lincoln (1809–1865) was set to enter office, the territory of Kansas entered the Union as a free state in 1861. Kansas became a microcosm for the political machinations to come during the Civil War, and what is certain is that the conflict drove many Northern Democrats to the Republican Party. Without that support, Lincoln might not have received enough coalition votes to win the presidency.

Though the Free State Party did not last beyond 1861, the tenets of radicalism transferred to the Lincoln-opposed faction that became known as the Radical Republicans. The NEEAC continued on in name only, and by the early 20th century, it disbanded officially. Even though they were backed by Northerners, they were deeply divided over the violence that foamed in Kansas, with some groups advocating the actions of John Brown and the Jayhawkers and others opposing them. Though the Jayhawkers fought for freedom, they seemed to be more concerned with enacting violence than protecting the liberties of freemen, whether white or black. During the Civil War, they became uncontrollable in many cases, even to the Union Army, and their tactics were viewed by General William T. Sherman (1820–1891) as the only viable option during his famous March to the Sea Campaign in Georgia. The jayhawk, although later adopted by the University of Kansas as its mascot, became synonymous with plunder and destruction. In the end, political turmoil, even for antislavery and abolitionist factions during the 1850s, could not stave off the inevitability of violence and the Civil War; in actuality, their political actions did more to spur it along as the country hurtled toward disunion.

J. N. Campbell

See also: Fire Eaters (1850–1861) and Border Ruffians (1854–1860)

Further Reading

Etcheson, Nicole. 2004. *Bleeding Kansas: Contested Liberty in the Civil War Era*. Lawrence: University Press of Kansas.

Fellman, Michael. 1989. *Inside War: The Guerilla Conflict in Missouri during the Civil War*. New York: Oxford University Press.

Neely, Jeremy. 2007. *The Border between Them: Violence and Reconciliation on the Kansas-Missouri Line*. Columbia: University of Missouri Press.

Potter, David M. 2011. *The Impending Crisis: America Before the Civil War, 1848–1861*. New York: Harper Perennial, new edition.

Rawly, James A. 1969. *Race and Politics: "Bleeding Kansas" and the Coming of the Civil War*. Lincoln: University of Nebraska Press.

SenGupta, Gunja. 1996. *For God and Mannon: Evangelicals and Entrepreneurs, Masters and Slaves in Territorial Kansas, 1854–1860*. Athens: University of Georgia Press.

Freedom Riders (1961)

The Freedom Riders were white and black nonviolent civil rights activists who rode buses throughout the segregated Deep South in 1961 to assert their right to integrated interstate bus travel. The riders tested Southern compliance with Supreme Court decisions outlawing segregation in interstate transit. Meeting violent white resistance, the riders found the Southern states and the federal government unwilling to uphold their rights. However, growing media attention to mob attacks on the riders pressured the federal government to intervene, guaranteeing integrated interstate bus transit for all passengers.

The Freedom Rides were modeled after the 1947 Journey of Reconciliation in which a biracial group of 16 men rode buses and trains across the Upper South to test enforcement of *Morgan v. Virginia* (1946), a Supreme Court decision that declared the segregation of interstate bus passengers unconstitutional. During the two-week journey, riders were arrested 12 times but only encountered violent opposition in Chapel Hill, North Carolina. The Congress on Racial Equality

(CORE), one of the leading nonviolent civil rights organizations founded in 1942, organized the Journey of Reconciliation and the Freedom Rides. CORE believed the Journey of Reconciliation showed that segregation could be challenged through nonviolent, direct action without provoking widespread violence. Unfortunately, the Journey of Reconciliation received little media attention and failed to undermine segregated bus travel in the South. Nevertheless, the struggle for racial equality continued into the 1950s as civil rights advocates won key victories in the *Brown v. Board of Education* (1954) decision outlawing segregation in public schools and the Montgomery Bus Boycott (1955–1956) challenging segregated city buses.

Under the leadership of James Farmer (1920–1999), a black Southerner who cofounded the organization, CORE conceived the 1961 Freedom Rides after the Supreme Court extended the *Morgan* decision in *Boynton v. Virginia* (1960) to outlaw segregation in transportation terminals and facilities. In addition to testing Southern compliance with the court rulings, the rides were intended to push Democratic President John F. Kennedy (1917–1963) to take action on behalf of civil rights for African Americans. Although Kennedy supported racial equality, he remained reluctant to pursue new civil rights legislation against segregation out of fear of alienating conservative Southern Democrats, whose support he might need for reelection in 1964. By asserting their right to integrated interstate bus transit through nonviolent direct action, the Freedom Riders aimed to place civil rights on Kennedy's agenda. CORE also hoped that media coverage of the riders' nonviolent actions and Southern white resistance would convince most Americans to support desegregation and racial equality. Unlike the Journey of Reconciliation, the riders planned to travel throughout the Deep South from Washington, D.C., to New Orleans in May 1961.

In selecting riders, Farmer and his staff sought a mix of black and white volunteers from the North and South who were dedicated to the principles of nonviolent protest. Farmer and James Peck (1914–1993), a staunch pacifist and white veteran of the Journey of Reconciliation, were the first volunteers selected. CORE chose 11 other riders, two of whom were women. CORE feared an equal number of men and women would attract accusations of interracial relationships in the conservative, segregated South. On May 4, 1961, the Freedom Riders—seven black and six white—departed Washington, D.C., on two buses. This group included future U.S. congressman John Lewis (1940–), a rising star in the Nashville civil rights movement who later led the famed 1965 voting rights march in Selma, Alabama. To test enforcement of the *Morgan* and *Boynton* decisions, Farmer always instructed at least one black rider to sit in a seat reserved for white passengers and another to abide by segregationist practices and remain out of trouble so he or she could arrange legal counsel for arrested riders. Throughout the journey, riders attempted to patronize segregated terminal restaurants and facilitates, noting times when they received or were refused service. They also met with local civil rights activists, associations, and church congregations, generating support for the movement.

Between May 4 and May 13, the riders traveled from D.C. to Atlanta, Georgia, and met relatively little resistance. The first arrest took place in Charlotte, North

Carolina, after a black rider sat in a shoeshine chair for whites only and demanded equal service. Three riders were also beaten in front of a white waiting room in Rock Hill, South Carolina. Otherwise, the path to Atlanta was peaceful, and the riders enjoyed dinner with Reverend Martin Luther King Jr. (1929–1968), who expressed support for their cause and admiration for their courage. Unfortunately, Farmer had to leave the journey unexpectedly after his father passed away. The other riders continued on, however, and crossed into Alabama, where they met fierce mob violence.

On May 14, one Freedom Ride bus pulled into a station in Anniston, Alabama, about halfway between Atlanta and Birmingham. A white mob, organized by the Alabama Ku Klux Klan, surrounded the bus and hurled projectiles at it, smashing some windows. After 20 minutes, the local police intervened and escorted the bus out of the city. However, the mob followed the bus down the highway until flat tires forced the bus driver to pull over. Klan members then threw a firebomb through the window, filling the bus with thick smoke. As the riders exited the burning bus, the mob beat them until highway patrolmen intervened. Miraculously, none of the riders were killed, but they suffered from severe smoke inhalation and bleeding gashes. No arrests were made in the attack.

The other bus of Freedom Riders also encountered violence at a station in Birmingham. Before the riders arrived, the local police agreed to let local Klan members assault the riders uninterrupted for 15 minutes. During that time, the Klan incited a riot that spilled into the streets surrounding the bus station. The mob beat the nonviolent activists with fists and pipes, leaving many riders in need of urgent medical attention. Peck, for example, underwent emergency surgery for his injuries but surprised the press when he announced his intention to continue the ride. After the violence in Anniston and Birmingham, the riders asked the Kennedy administration to arrange protection for them as they continued their journey to Montgomery. Despite pressure from Attorney General Robert Kennedy (1925–1968), Alabama Governor John Patterson (1921–) refused to offer the riders police escorts. Viewing the activists as outside political agitators, Patterson insisted they had to leave Alabama immediately. The president refused to send federal marshals into Alabama to protect the riders, fearing such a move would inflame the violence and precipitate a political crisis. Faced with federal and state intransigence, the riders agreed to board a flight from Birmingham to New Orleans, defusing the tense situation.

The Freedom Rider movement was not over, however. Lewis worked with Nashville student activist Diane Nash (1938–) to organize a new group of riders on short notice. Within days, they departed Nashville to continue the Freedom Ride from Birmingham to Montgomery. In an effort to avoid another violent incident, the Kennedy administration coerced Patterson to grant the riders police escorts. However, the local Montgomery police colluded with the Klan to incite another riot. Recognizing he could not trust the local or state authorities, President Kennedy finally sent federal marshals into Alabama to protect the riders. The Nashville riders then continued their journey to Jackson, Mississippi, where they were arrested for disturbing the peace. At this point, Kennedy suggested CORE and other activists channel their movement towards voter registration initiatives as opposed to the highly publicized and increasingly violent Freedom Rides. The riders, however, refused to give up, and more volunteers flocked to the movement, leading to several other rides across the South throughout the spring and summer of 1961.

Swelling support for the Freedom Riders and continued Southern resistance pressured the attorney general to file a petition requesting stronger regulations against segregated interstate bus travel with the Interstate Commerce Commission (ICC)—the government agency that regulated interstate commerce and transportation—in late May. The Freedom Rides throughout the South only ended after the ICC ruled on the petition in late September by strictly prohibiting segregation in interstate transit. With this ruling, the federal government moved to uphold and enforce the *Morgan* and *Boynton* decisions. Moreover, the Freedom Riders and the media attention their movement attracted helped transform the civil rights movement from a regional issue in the South to a national, moral issue that would dominate U.S. politics and society for years to come.

Tyler P. Esno

See also: Black Lives Matter (2013–); Black Panther Party (1966–1982); Congress of Racial Equality (1942–); National Association for the Advancement of Colored People (1909–); National Urban League (1910–); Organization of Afro-American Unity (1964–1965); Rainbow-PUSH Coalition (1996–); Student Nonviolent Coordinating Committee (1960–1974)

Further Reading

Arsenault, Raymond. 2011. *Freedom Riders: 1961 and the Struggle for Racial Justice.* Abridged edition. New York: Oxford University Press.

Catsam, Derek Charles. 2009. *Freedom's Main Line: The Journey of Reconciliation and the Freedom Rides.* Lexington: The University Press of Kentucky.

Lewis, John with Michael D'Orso. 1999. *Walking with the Wind: A Memoir of the Movement.* San Diego, CA: Harcourt Brace & Company.

Niven, David. 2003. *The Politics of Injustice: The Kennedys, the Freedom Rides, and the Electoral Consequences of a Moral Compromise.* Knoxville: The University of Tennessee Press.

G

General Motors (1908–)

The General Motors Company, generally referred to as GM, is an American multinational automobile corporation headquartered in Detroit, Michigan. Products of the company are sold under a number of labels throughout 125 countries and in 2016 they delivered 10 million vehicles worldwide. William C. Durant (1861–1947) founded the company in 1908 and grew to be the largest automobile manufacturer by 1931. GM dominated the auto industry from 1931 until 2007, when sales began to slump. As a result, the company underwent government sponsored reorganization in 2009 as a requirement to receive government funding to prevent GM from going out of business.

Due to the size of the company and the numerous other companies reliant on their existence, the company has had significant political pull throughout history. GM is a single member economic interest group—a large corporation which focuses on policy associated with the business in an effort to increase revenue. Throughout their history, General Motors has lobbied the national government and used other tactics to influence policy in an effort to benefit the corporation.

In 1935, the U.S. Congress passed, and President Franklin Delano Roosevelt (1882–1945) signed, the National Labor Relations Act, also known as the Wagner Act. The new law guaranteed basic rights to private sector employees, most specifically the right to organize a union, engage in collective bargaining, and the ability to strike if necessary, in addition to creating the National Labor Relations Board, which helped enforce the right of workers to unionize. Passage of the Act provided a significant blow to GM, as it solidified the power of the United Auto Workers (UAW) union. Unhappy with the new law, GM, under the direction of Alfred Sloan (1875–1966), openly defied the legislation and attempted to stop industrial unionism from taking root at the corporation (Hoopes 2011, 53–54). Sloan's efforts ultimately failed, and workers unionized and organized a sit-down strike at two plants in Flint, Michigan, from December 1936 to February 1937.

Toward the end of World War II (1939–1945), breaking down union power and reducing government control became the primary political objective of Sloan and other corporate leaders. In the early 1940s, a political activist named Vance Muse (1890–1950) led his organization, the Christian American Association, to get "Right to Work" legislation passed. "Right to Work" refers to the ability of individuals to seek employment at a union-organized corporation, without requiring the individual to become a member of the union. "Right to Work" legislation reduces the power of unions because new employees can opt out of union membership and dues, while still benefiting from the union's collective bargaining.

Reductions in union dues and membership numbers decrease the effectiveness of the union's collective bargaining power. Throughout Muse's campaign to get "Right to Work" legislation implemented, he received financial support from GM and other large manufacturing corporations (Kaufman 2015). In 1944, Arkansas became the country's first right-to-work state. Over the next 20 years, 18 additional states adopted right-to-work laws. By 2017, 28 states implemented right-to-work acts, with the most recent and controversial being Wisconsin in 2015.

The success of right-to-work legislation is largely the result of actions taken by GM and other manufacturers following the end of World War II. During the war, unions refrained from striking in order to prevent a decrease in the production of war materials. However, following the end of the war, UAW workers at GM attempted to secure a 30 percent pay raise to compensate for the lack of pay increases during the war and to help the American economy grow in the postwar period. GM opposed the pay raise, which resulted in workers going on strike in November 1945. The strike ended in March 1946 with union workers surrendering and accepting a raise of 15 percent.

Following the end of the strike, General Motors made a strategic move by raising the prices of its automobiles. From March to November 1946, the national inflation rate rose 14 percent (Hoopes 2011, 73). With Sloan's marketing expertise, he publicized this increase as a result of the union's demand for higher wages, guiding public opinion to believe that the unions were behind inflation (Hoopes 2011, 71). New perspectives among the public about the freedom of corporations and the free market led to growing support among voters that the Republican Party was better equipped to handle the economy in the postwar era.

As a result of the new perspectives, Republicans gained control of both chambers of Congress in the midterm election of 1946 with a renewed vigor to weaken the unions. On the first day of the 80th Congress, Republican legislators introduced 17 anti-union bills (Hoopes 2011, 73). Six months later, Republicans successfully passed the Taft-Hartley Act, also known as the Labor Management Relations Act of 1947. President Harry S. Truman (1884–1972) vetoed the bill. The House of Representatives subsequently overrode the president's veto on June 20, and the Senate did the same on June 23, 1947, making the bill law. The new law dealt a blow to the unions, reversing many of the gains they made following the passage of the Wagner Act. Amendments within the Taft-Harley Act cemented the legality of states to pass right-to-work laws. Other provisions within the Act allowed the president to appoint a board to investigate union disputes when it could endanger national health or safety, as well as allowing the creation of unions only after a majority of employees voted for them. Although the Act included many additional provisions, most have been repealed with subsequent legislation.

In 1990, the United States, Canada, and Mexico began negotiations of the North American Free Trade Agreement (NAFTA). On December 17, 1992, U.S. president George H. W. Bush (1924–2018), Canadian prime minister Brian Mulroney (1939–), and Mexican president Carlos Salinas (1948–) signed the agreement. After ratification of NAFTA, tariffs between the three countries were eliminated over the next 15-year period, which started on January 1, 1994. The successful passage of NAFTA was important to many American manufacturers, including

General Motors. In a congressional testimony on September 11, 1997, before the House Ways and Means Committee, General Motors' chief economist stated:

> GM was an early and strong supporter of NAFTA. We believe that it would promote economic growth, improve living standards and enhance cooperation and goodwill between the US, Mexico, and Canada . . . NAFTA is living up to its promise three years into its implementation. (Kengor, LaFaive, and Summers 1999, 14)

In fact, prior to the implementation of NAFTA, GM had "virtually zero" exports to Mexico (Kengor, LaFaive, and Summers 1999). By the time of the congressional testimony in 1997, GM had sold over 60,000 vehicles to the country, making them "the largest seller of vehicles in Mexico" (Kengor, LaFaive, and Summers 1999). Since the passage of NAFTA, General Motors has opened numerous plants in Mexico while closing plants in the United States, causing upset among union workers.

Since 1998, the amount of money GM spends on special interest lobbying efforts has varied from $6 million in 2001 to almost $15 million in 2007. The amount of money GM spends on lobbying efforts is largely dependent upon how much attention government institutions are giving to issues that directly affect the company. Lobbying efforts of the company peaked in 2007, when it was working to convince the government to secure the company a bridge loan in efforts to prevent them from becoming insolvent. This bridge loan became known as the "auto bailout" and was included in the 2008 Trouble Asset Relief Program (TARP) funds, to address issues associated with the Great Recession. Despite receiving the TARP funding, GM still filed for bankruptcy in 2009. As a part of the bankruptcy, President Barack Obama's (1961–) administration managed the process while providing additional bridge loans, in exchange for the government receiving 60 percent of GM stock.

In addition to lobbying the national government to keep the company solvent in 2007 and 2008, other topics that GM has recently lobbied on include: the automotive industry, taxation, telecommunications, environmental policy, trade, as well as copyright, patent, and trademarks. Most often, lobbying efforts by GM are focused on the U.S. Senate and U.S. House of Representatives, however the company also regularly lobbies the Department of Treasury, Environmental Protection Agency, Federal Communications Commission, Internal Revenue Service, Executive Office of the President, White House, the Department of Commerce, as well as foreign governments.

With the passage of NAFTA, implementation of right-to-work laws by states, adoption of automation, and the bankruptcy of GM, the UAW union has seen a decline in membership, job benefits and pay, and job security. The job and financial security that used to come with a union job at GM is no longer present. This insecurity was exacerbated and harnessed by Donald Trump (1946–) in the 2016 U.S. Presidential Election. Trump routinely criticized companies like GM for moving jobs to Mexico. In order to gain the support of blue-collar workers, Trump adopted an "America First" policy, indicating that he would punish companies that ship jobs to other countries. He made renegotiating NAFTA one of the major aspects of his policy. With the belief that union jobs were being lost to Mexico, as opposed to the real reason—automation—many blue-collar workers voted for Trump, with the belief that he could bring their manufacturing jobs back.

After taking office, President Trump continued to boast his "America First" policy and reiterated his intent to renegotiate NAFTA. These actions spurred GM, along with many other auto manufacturers, to lobby Mexico's federal government to discuss the future of NAFTA. In April 2017, GM met with Mexico's Secretary of Economy Ildefonso Guajardo (1957—) to voice its support for continued access to Mexico's marketplace.

General Motors' work to influence policy transcends lobbying efforts, as the company was also a member of the American Legislative Exchange Council, most commonly referred to as ALEC. ALEC is a nonprofit volunteer organization working to promote limited government, free markets, and federalism. The organization claims to be nonpartisan, but its membership is made up of almost all conservative state legislators. As a member of the ALEC organization, businesses such as General Motors have the ability to write legislation and pass it on to legislators who then introduce the bill under their name. Many consider the organization to be a corporate bill mill. Although the specific date that GM joined ALEC is unable to be confirmed, public records indicate that they were a member in 1992. GM's financial contribution to the organization was approximately $25,000 annually. GM continued to be part of the ALEC organization until 2012, when it was pressured to drop its membership by 10,000 Michigan citizens. Departure from ALEC coincided with that of at least 31 additional corporations, following the big push by the conservative group for "stand your ground" gun laws, although no formal reasoning was given by GM.

With the competition to bring self-driving cars to market heating up, GM has been actively working to push its self-driving vehicles. In 2016, GM started to lobby Washington, D.C. on the future of self-driving cars. Specifically, in May of that year, GM participated in a Senate Commerce Committee hearing on the future of self-driving cars. However, the company's efforts to promote the future of automobile transportation is not intended to help the entire industry. More recent lobbying efforts are aimed at removing competitors of GM, in order to increase future profits. On February 23, 2017, a news story broke that GM was actively lobbying state legislators to introduce legislation that would allow GM an unfair advantage in the deployment of self-driving cars. Specifically, the legislation would require that self-driving vehicles be owned by an automaker, therefore preventing other technology companies and ride-sharing companies, like Uber, from developing their own self-driving fleet. Although GM denies the allegations, legislators from four different states reported being contacted by GM lobbyists to introduce such legislation.

Michael J. Pomante II

See also: Standard Oil Company (1870–1911); U.S. Steel (1901–)

Further Reading

Fine, Sidney. 1969. *Sit-Down: The General Motors Strike of 1936–1937.* Ann Arbor: The University of Michigan Press.

Hoopes, James. 2011. *Corporate Dreams: Big Business in American Democracy from the Great Depression to the Great Recession.* New Brunswick, NJ: Rutgers University Press.

Kaufman, Dan. 2015. "Scott Walker and the Fate of the Union." *The New York Times Magazine*, June 12, 2015. https://www.nytimes.com/2015/06/14/magazine/scott-walker-and-the-fate-of-the-union.html.

Kengor, Paul, Michael D. LaFaive, and Grady Summers. 1999. *Trade Liberalization: The North American Free Trade Agreement's Economic Impact on Michigan.* December 20, 1999. Mackinac Center for Public Policy. http://mackinac.org/s1999-09.

Sloan, Alfred P. 1972. *My Years with General Motors.* Edited by John McDonald with Catharine Stevens. Garden City, NY: Anchor Books—Doubleday & Company, Inc.

Turner Jr., Henry Ashby. 2005. *General Motors and the Nazis: The Struggle for Control of Opel, Europe's Biggest Carmaker.* New Haven, CT: Yale University Press.

GLAAD (1985–)

GLAAD, formerly Gay & Lesbian Alliance Against Defamation and Gay and Lesbian Anti-Defamation League, was founded in 1985 as a reaction to the *New York Post*'s defamatory coverage of the HIV and AIDS crisis. The first reported meeting of GLAAD was held on November 14 of its founding year, and one of the group's first actions was to protest outside of the offices of the *New York Post* to demand change in the paper's coverage of the HIV and AIDS crisis. This protest drew nearly 1,000 people and was the first of many vigorous actions pursuing their goal of combating discrimination against LGBTQ individuals in the media, thereby encouraging fair, accurate, and inclusive representations of the LGBTQ community.

GLAAD has focused its attention on advocating for positive and accurate representations of LGBTQ individuals in media and is dedicated to honoring those media outlets that do so. GLAAD's website states, "GLAAD rewrites the script for LGBTQ acceptance. As a dynamic media force, GLAAD tackles tough issues to shape the narrative and provoke dialogue that leads to cultural change. GLAAD protects all that has been accomplished and creates a world where everyone can live the life they love" ("About GLAAD" 2018). In pursuing its goals, GLAAD utilizes both proactive and reactive advocacy strategies.

The organization's proactive strategies include recognizing and awarding allies in film, television, advertising, print, and electronic media who demonstrate fair and accurate representations of the LGBTQ community and the issues affecting them. The first GLAAD Media Awards were held in 1990 and honored 34 nominees in seven categories. The 26th annual GLAAD awards were held in 2017 and honored 156 nominees in 33 categories, both English-speaking and Spanish-language. In 2009, GLAAD held its first Media Awards in Advertising to recognize corporations whose advertising is inclusive of the LGBTQ community.

GLAAD's further proactive advocacy activities include developing rankings of media outlets and advertisement organizations. Their Advertising Media Program "monitors all forms of advertising and speaks out against anti-LGBT images. GLAAD also works to promote LGBT images in mainstream advertising campaigns through educating ad agencies and corporate advertising departments on best practices for inclusion of LGBT people in the workplace and in marketing" ("Advertising Media Program" 2018). Furthermore, the Network and Studio

Responsibility Indices evaluates the quantity, quality, and diversity of LGBTQ people and issues in the prime-time programming and films out of six studios: 20th Century Fox, Paramount Pictures, Sony Columbia, Universal Pictures, Walt Disney Studies, and Warner Brothers.

Not only does GLAAD rank the various media outlets, but it also honors those media outlets that present characters and storylines that present the LGBTQ community in a fair, accurate, and inclusive light. GLAAD's also sponsors ad campaigns, one of their most prominent and successful campaigns being 1993's "Images" campaign, designed to introduce New York City subway riders to gay and lesbian New Yorkers by featuring their photos and biographies on 30,000 posters displayed throughout the system. In the same year, GLAAD won an American Advertising Award for a billboard depicting an expectant lesbian couple displayed at various spots in California.

Furthermore, in the spring of 2004, the "I Do" campaign for marriage equality included public service announcements advocating for marriage equality. In 2011, GLAAD turned their attention to LGBTQ youth. The "Amplify Your Voice" public service announcement campaign featured stories of bullied LGBTQ youth in order to direct affected youth to resources and encourage support for the bullied from the community. Then, in 2012, the "I AM: Trans People Speak" video series, which featured prominent as well as unknown trans people, allowed individuals to share their stories in their own words. In announcing the project, GLAAD stated, "Transgender people have a wide range of interests, experiences and backgrounds that are too often ignored because of their trans identity. Together we can make a positive change in the visibility and representation of transgender people by focusing on the full individual" ("I AM" 2018).

Much of GLAAD's reactive strategies revolve around education outreach. Specifically, GLAAD's reactive strategies involve outreach to media outlets, helping them give fair and accurate coverage of news stories involving the LGBTQ community. GLAAD links media outlets with LGBTQ experts to provide commentary on major news stories and to provide counter-arguments to anti-LGBTQ rhetoric. This is an especially important function in response to prominent, visible hate crimes as well as to support national dialog on major issues. For example, following the 1998 murder of Matthew Shepard (1976–1998), who was targeted because of his sexuality, GLAAD leaders traveled to his hometown of Casper, Wyoming, to coordinate media outreach and coverage. This coordination with news outlets helped to start a national dialogue on anti-LGBT hate crimes. Additionally, GLAAD was central to helping guide the national discussion regarding *Lawrence v. Texas* (2003) and other major SCOTUS decisions.

Additionally, GLAAD has helped to coordinate several high-profile protests, including of the Boy Scouts of America's ban on gay members and pack leaders, New York's Power 105.1 radio station following an on-air personality's use of an anti-gay slur in 2003, the Miss Universe Pageant's refusal to allow trans women to participate, and the Federal Drug Administration's ban on gay men donating blood.

Above and beyond their specific advocacy strategies, some of GLAAD's biggest accomplishments include successfully petitioning the *New York Times* to use the term "gay" rather than "homosexual" in 1987, spearheading an annual Spirit Day in support of LGBTQ youth in 2010, and creating LGBT history month in October. GLAAD also successfully lobbied the Associated Press to revise its stylebook to include inclusive and positive terminology when referring to LGBT individuals and the *New York Times* to open its weddings & celebrations page to gay and lesbian couples. GLAAD therefore has been and remains a champion of LGBTQ acceptance, protecting the progress that has been made and continually promoting cultural change.

On March 24, 2003, GLAAD formally adopted their acronym as their official and legal name so as to be more inclusive, highlighting their commitment to trans and bisexual issues. Some of GLAAD's work specific to trans and bisexual communities includes founding the GLAAD Transgender Media Program, which is wholly devoted to fairly and accurately telling the stories of transgender people, utilizing many of the proactive and reactive strategies detailed about. GLAAD also cofounded Bisexual Awareness Week every September since 2014, which highlights and celebrates the history, culture, issues, and policy concerns of the bi community.

Heather Marie Rice and Nicole Loncaric

See also: AIDS Coalition to Unleash Power (1987–); Center for Constitutional Rights (1966–); Human Rights Campaign (1980–); National LGBTQ Task Force (1973–)

Further Reading

"About GLAAD." 2018. https://www.glaad.org/about.

Doyle, Vincent. 2016. *Making Out in the Mainstream: GLAAD and the Politics of Respectability*. Montreal, Quebec: McGill-Queen's University Press.

GLAAD. 2018. https://www.glaad.org/.

"I AM: Trans People Speak Video Series by MTPC and GLAAD." 2018. GLAAD. https://www.glaad.org/transpeoplespeak.

Kantor, Emma. 2018. "GLAAD and Bonnier USA Partner on Publishing Program." *Publishers Weekly*, May 17, 2018. https://www.publishersweekly.com/pw/by-topic/childrens/childrens-industry-news/article/76903-glaad-and-bonnier-usa-partner-on-publishing-program.html.

Ramos, Dino-Ray. 2018. "GLAAD Media Awards New York Winners List: 'Call My By Your Name,' Samira Wiley, Ava DuVernay Among Honorees." *Deadline Hollywood*, May 5, 2018. http://deadline.com/2018/05/glaad-media-awards-new-york-winners-list-call-me-by-your-name-samira-wiley-ava-duvernay-1202383382/.

Grand Army of the Republic (1866–1956)

The Grand Army of the Republic (GAR) was the largest membership association of Union Civil War (1861–1865) veterans in the nation, at its peak attracting membership from over 400,000 veterans. While there were other veterans' groups during the era for Union soldiers, none reached the GAR's level of prominence. To place its prominence in perspective, five of the six presidents elected from 1868 to 1900 were GAR members. Therefore, its membership ranged from the White House to the small town, and it was found in Northern, Western, and even Southern states.

In the wake of the Civil War, veterans founded the GAR in 1866 as a fraternal society as Republicans of various stripes and Democrats struggled to push their visions of a recovering United States. Initially, the GAR served as a Republican Party front organization, working to help the party win the 1868 election. In Illinois, a few Radical Republican leaders, led by Dr. Benjamin Franklin Stephenson, facilitated the creation of the GAR to help with election of two Republicans in the state: Governor Richard Oglesby and, more importantly, General John A. Logan, who went on to have a Congressional career that spanned both houses. This manner of organizing spread rapidly into the nearby states of Indiana, Michigan, and Ohio before becoming a national phenomenon.

After the election of 1868, then, the GAR leadership tried to reorient the organization away from partisan politics in an attempt to create a true veterans' membership association. But it suffered mightily after Ulysses S. Grant's election to the presidency as veterans grew content and uninterested in (or turned off by) partisan political activism. Additionally, the national headquarters did not work effectively with state organizations, which often did not communicate well with "posts," as local groups were called. As a consequence, state and local organizations were disbanding by the early 1870s, veterans were not as interested in using the organization as a tool for electoral politics, and many potential members were focused on rebuilding their lives after the war. Veterans transitioned into civilian life without the need for a military-based fraternal organization. Given this confluence of factors, the GAR struggled.

Prospects for the organization improved heading into the 1876 election, as the campaign sparked interest among Republican and Democratic Party operatives in veterans as a potential base of electoral support; appeals to this group could benefit them at the ballot box. The contested nature of that election, which placed President Rutherford B. Hayes (himself a GAR member) in the White House, thus inspired veterans to join the organization. This spirit carried over into the 1880 presidential campaign as well, and even into 1884, when John A. Logan served as the Republican Party's vice-presidential candidate.

Regardless of party machinations, though, both Republicans and Democrats began to join the GAR as it emphasized nonpartisanship and sought to benefit the lives of all Union veterans. Leadership pushed membership drives, and with the pension question at the forefront, Union veterans joined the organization in record numbers. Additionally, its conservative national leadership continued to chart a course away from direct partisan political activity, instead focusing on fraternalism, brotherhood, and charity to unite these former soldiers.

Around this same time, pension issues moved to the forefront at the national level, further stimulating interest among veterans. Initial federal legislation was a start, but it was quite restrictive in its requirements. The GAR influenced the passage of the Arrears Act of 1879, but it did not go far enough for all veterans. Many group members demanded broader pension benefits. Specifically, demands for a pension based on service and not disability animated the GAR. Publisher George Lemon's *National Tribune* helped popularize the effort for pension reform among veterans, which focused on building up the GAR to pressure politicians.

The GAR's most prominent and successful lobbying efforts, therefore, focused on expanded pensions for Union veterans. In 1887, the GAR began a campaign for a pension system that simply required military service as a prerequisite for receiving benefits, but President Grover Cleveland vetoed the legislation. He argued that existing legislation covered enough soldiers; moving beyond it created a system of dependence and charity that was not the proper function of government toward these veterans. This veto further catalyzed interest in the GAR and its message, and the organization's lobbying efforts continued in Washington.

Though Benjamin Harrison sidestepped the issue in the 1888 campaign, he and a Republican-led Congress reacted soon after taking office, culminating in the adoption of the Disability Pension Act of 1890. Under this act, an applicant had to show he had a disability, but it did not have to come from his time in the service; it also only required 90 days of service and an honorable discharge. These changes were so significant that by 1893, 42 percent of the national government's income was used on pensions. In this way, the GAR played a key role in shaping the federal budget while creating an expectation of benefits that veterans would demand in the 20th century.

These increases in veterans' claims came right at the peak of GAR membership, at 427,981 in 1890. As an organization that was "born to die," as only Civil War veterans could join, death began to take a significant toll on membership by the early 1900s, though state organizations made efforts to bring aging veterans into the organization. Nevertheless, politicians still saw group members as an important voting bloc and as citizens in need. The pension reform of 1890 was eventually expanded in 1904, when President Theodore Roosevelt issued Executive Order No. 78, which reclassified disability in the Disability Pension Act of 1890 to include old age. Eventually, the Service and Age Pension Act of 1907 reorganized veterans' benefits and further increased payments.

The GAR also pursued aid from government in other ways. One direct way was through pressuring lawmakers for legislation requiring that veterans receive preferential treatment when being considered for employment. Second, the organization worked closely with the federal and state governments to create soldiers' homes for those veterans who were destitute and required care. GAR members often played a role in the administration of these facilities, serving on boards of directors.

However, the organization was not just interested in lobbying government for pensions. The GAR instituted Decoration Day, or what is now called Memorial Day, in 1868. This was part of the GAR's goal of promoting patriotism, which became a more prominent theme for the organization as time went on. GAR leadership and members even became interested in patriotic education, hoping to ensure that their version of the Civil War would be taught in schools nationwide. Overall, the organization's efforts helped to shape the narrative of the Civil War while popularizing its own version of nationalism.

The GAR also focused on building and maintaining camaraderie among members. Given the military basis of the organization, it mixed fraternal elements with language from the armed services. Annual meetings were known as encampments, which did often feature elements of "life on the frontlines," including sleeping in tents. (However, as the membership aged, such recreations became less common.) Officers of the organization also took on military titles; a few such examples are the Department Commander, the Assistant Adjutant-General, the Assistant Quarter-Master General, the Judge-Advocate, and the Chief Mustering Officer.

Military-like routines were also supposed to be followed in the posts, though devotion to the meeting standards set out by the national and state associations varied from post to post. Finally, the local posts often helped needy veterans and their families during hard times, even if the GAR was not like other fraternal organizations that had sickness insurance (like the Odd Fellows or Knights of Pythias).

It is also important to note that the GAR allowed membership for both white and black veterans. Because soldiers of both races provided support to the Union effort, the GAR leadership made this a centerpiece of the organization. It was not without opposition, especially in Southern GAR organizations, and different state organizations and posts took different approaches to the subject. There were separate black posts but also those that were integrated. Nevertheless, it was the first major, national organization with longevity that treated men of both races equally.

Other associations were created to parallel the GAR's activities. One was the Woman's Relief Corp (WRC), which served as an auxiliary organization that aided the GAR throughout its existence. Another is the Sons of Union Veterans of the Civil War (SUV), which currently describes itself as an organization that serves to promote and preserve the efforts of Union soldiers during the Civil War. As the GAR restricted membership only to those who had served, its members viewed the SUV as being the spiritual successor to the GAR. Other affiliated organizations included the Ladies of the Grand Army of the Republic (which initially competed with the WRC for official GAR support), Daughters of Union Veterans of the Civil War, and the Auxiliary to Sons of Union Veterans of the Civil War. These affiliated organizations still exist today, though their membership and activities are much more limited than in the past.

By 1920, membership had declined significantly as old age and death increasingly limited the GAR's pool of potential members. Though its political power began to wane, it still served an important function by uniting these aging veterans and allowing them to share their experiences with one another. Encampments continued annually until 1949, when the remaining membership was too small and old to continue GAR meetings. Nevertheless, the organization formally persisted until 1956, when its last remaining member, Albert Woolson, died.

In the end, the GAR's influence was quite great in its day. From pressuring governments for increased pensions and social services, which created the first extensive federal social service program, to shaping our national understanding of the Civil War, to popularizing Memorial Day, to serving as an organization open to veterans regardless of race, the GAR was an important organization that affected the course of government and society in the late 1800s and early 1900s.

Adam Chamberlain

See also: American Legion (1919–); United Confederate Veterans (1889–ca. 1950)

Further Reading

Ainsworth, Scott. 1995. "Electoral Strength and the Emergence of Group Influence in the Late 1800s: The Grand Army of the Republic." *American Politics Quarterly* 23 (3): 319–338.

Dearing, Mary R. 1952. *Veterans in Politics: The Story of the G.A.R.* Baton Rouge: Louisiana State University Press.

McConnell, Stuart. 1992. *Glorious Contentment: The Grand Army of the Republic, 1865–1900*. Chapel Hill: The University of North Carolina Press.

Gray Panthers (1970–)

With a nod to the Black Panthers, a militant organization focusing on African American civil rights, which was founded in 1966, the Gray Panthers are a group that functions through local advocacy networks to confront issues involving senior citizens as well as other areas of social justice. The organization first reached national prominence under the leadership of one of its founders, the charismatic Margaret Eliza "Maggie" Kuhn (1905–1995).

Even before her personal experience would later lead to her founding the Gray Panthers in 1970, Kuhn was an advocate for the rights of older people and effective in her efforts to address the challenges facing them. In 1961, she participated as a church member in the White House Conference on Aging. Through her work with the Presbyterian Church, she visited retirement homes. There, she observed firsthand the conditions in nursing homes and senior citizen housing, becoming appalled in many cases at what she saw. According to her autobiography, she heard one resident describe the facility as "a glorified playpen." She stated that she realized the need to reverse the tendency in American culture to treat old people not like tribal elders but like children. The tipping point for Kuhn came in 1970, when her employer forced her to retire from the job she loved, due to a mandatory retirement law that was then in effect, on the day she turned 65, even though she was valued and productive in her work.

As a longtime resident of Philadelphia, she worked outside the home for more than 40 years, also serving as a caregiver for her disabled mother and mentally ill brother. After working as a magazine editor, Kuhn became a program administrator with the social education and action department of the United Presbyterian Church. There, she saw the lack of rights available to older people. When Kuhn found herself to be a victim of the same lack of rights, she was determined not to passively accept forced retirement. She met with five other women she knew who had also been forced to retire from national religious and social work organizations. According to her autobiography, Kuhn said that the women ultimately discovered a new freedom in their retirement, especially the freedom to speak out on what they believed in.

The group decided not to accept the status quo. They began by calling themselves the "Consultation of Older and Younger Adults for Social Change." Soon they found a more appealing term: Gray Panthers.

Under Kuhn's leadership, the group did not focus solely on the rights of older people. The group actively recruited high school and college students. The Gray Panthers' slogan, "Age and Youth in Action," reflects intergenerational inclusiveness. With a diverse membership base, the issue of forced retirement expanded to challenge other laws and stereotypes regarding aging in America. These include preservation of Medicare and Social Security, intergenerational housing, advances in health care, and improvement of treatment for people in nursing homes. During the 1970s and 1980s, the Gray Panthers fought to overcome the stereotype that older people are weak, fragile, and should be shut away from society. Another stereotype they fought to shatter was that older people are an unproductive drain on the workforce.

After considerable political activism, the Gray Panthers were ultimately successful in their efforts to overturn the mandatory retirement law. In 1986, the U.S. Congress passed a law banning forced retirement solely based on age. In an example of extreme irony, the law was signed by America's 40th president, President Ronald Reagan (1911–2004) signed the bill into law; at that time, at age 70, he was the oldest person to be elected president. Exercising the political clout of its membership, the Gray Panthers vocally lobbied in opposition to Reagan's proposed cuts to Medicare and Social Security. Ultimately, those programs were saved from deep cuts to their budgets.

Kuhn stated that she saw all issues of injustice as being linked. Therefore, the Gray Panthers have not restricted themselves solely to activism involving the rights of elders. Peace, poverty, and civil liberties are among their interests. The Gray Panthers continue to address proposals that would impact Medicare and Social Security. In addition, they pursue inspections regarding nursing home violations, confront stereotypes about aging people, and spotlight issues that affect seniors. Reflecting the demographic shift as Baby Boomers, or people born between approximately 1946 and 1964, make the transition into retirement and old age, the Gray Panthers seek to improve the nation's health care and the need for family caregivers. They have also confronted big pharmaceutical companies to find ways for consumers to have access to safe, affordable prescription drugs and to hold corporations accountable when they do not. The Gray Panthers have also sought to work within the political system by adopting the means to lobby effectively. In addition to a local chapter in the nation's capital, in 1985 the Gray Panthers opened their first public policy office in Washington, D.C.

According to writer Claudia Levy in the *Washington Post*, by 1995 the Gray Panthers grew to about 100,000 members across the United States as well as several other countries. However, although it actively sought participation by college students and addressed issues affecting all ages, membership began to decrease (Levy 1995). Two factors played a significant role in the decline in numbers for the Gray Panthers. One was the rise of the American Association for Retired Persons (AARP), which grew into a powerful lobbying organization. Another factor was that Kuhn died in April 1995 from cardiopulmonary arrest at age 89, one month before she was to be honored by the White House Conference on Aging by President Bill Clinton. In her final years, Maggie Kuhn continued to combat the stereotype of old people being weak, disabled, and dependent. She survived cancer and two street muggings in Philadelphia that resulted in breaking her arm and her shoulder.

Kuhn served as a colorful symbol of the Gray Panthers. She chided President Gerald Ford in 1974 for calling her a "young lady." In 1975, she was a guest on TV's popular *Saturday Night Live*. While appearing on *The Tonight Show with Johnny Carson*, she reprimanded Carson for poking fun at old people in his monologue and sketches, such as his portrayal of "dear, kind, loveable, sweet, *old* Aunt

Blabby." According to the *Washington Post*, in 1978 she was listed by the *World Almanac* as one of the 25 most influential women in the United States.

In its early years, the Gray Panthers fought against a then-popular theory of "disengagement" that argued for old age requiring a separation from society as elders made their way toward death. Having worked in social services, Kuhn was aware of the process for grant funding of programs. She pointed out that grant money for research tended to favor gerontologists (those who study the effects of old age) who favored disengagement.

The Gray Panthers continued without Maggie Kuhn after she passed away, but her quotes about the myths of old age lived on as rallying calls. One of her observations was that in America, old age is treated as a disease. Echoing an often quoted sentiment from her autobiography, her obituary in the *Washington Post* attributed to her the following statement: "The first myth is that old age is a disease, a terrible disease that you never admit you've got, so you lie about your age. Well, it's not a disease—it's a triumph. Because you've survived. Failure, disappointment, sickness, loss—you're still here." (Levy 1995) https://www.washingtonpost.com /archive/local/1995/04/23/gray-panthers-co-founder-maggie-kuhn-dies-at-89 /a7c55189-b388-4e95-aafe-0d7d9a9163a1/?utm_term=.7cff203c1be5

Nancy Hendricks

See also: AARP (1958–); America's Health Insurance Plans (2003–); National Council on Aging (1950–)

Further Reading

Gray Panthers. 2017. https://www.facebook.com/GrayPanthers/.

Hessel, Dieter, and Maggie Kuhn. 1977. *Maggie Kuhn on Aging: A Dialogue.* Louisville, KY: Westminster John Knox Press.

Kuhn, Maggie. 1991. *No Stone Unturned: The Life and Times of Maggie Kuhn.* New York: Ballantine Books.

Levy, Claudia. 1995. "Gray Panthers Co-founder Maggie Kuhn Dies at 89." *Washington Post*, April 23, 1995. https://www.washingtonpost.com/archive/local/1995/04/23 /gray-panthers-co-founder-maggie-kuhn-dies-at-89/a7c55189-b388-4e95-aafe -0d7d9a9163a1/?utm_term=.12cd80857083.

"Maggie Growls: Panthers on the Prowl." n.d. PBS, *Independent Lens*. http://www.pbs .org/independentlens/maggiegrowls/panthers.html.

National Council of Gray Panthers Networks. 2017. https://www.facebook.com/National CouncilofGrayPanthersNetworks/.

Greenpeace (1971–)

As one of the best-known environmental groups, Greenpeace's transformation from its historically humble beginnings to its current global presence can be attributed to activism and visibility. Launching first in 1970 as the "Don't Make a Wave Committee," Greenpeace was initially purposed to thwart a nuclear test by the U.S. government off Amchitka Island, Alaska. The committee, consisting of a loosely organized group of pacifists, scientists, journalists, and environmentalists, set sail off the coast of Vancouver in a small fishing vessel (named *Phyllis*

Cormack, after the captain's wife, and later renamed *Greenpeace*) in an attempt to dissuade the U.S. government from conducting a nuclear test in the ocean.

Though the voyage was unsuccessful in its mission, the David-and-Goliath story of a tiny ship standing up to the U.S. Navy brought much attention to the cause, as well as newfound vigor on behalf of the original activists to channel the efforts of the committee in creating a new group with broader environmental goals. Today, the name "Greenpeace" is synonymous with being one of the leading nongovernmental organizations focusing mostly on global, cross-issue environmental protection.

The maiden voyage of the *Greenpeace* began as the brainchild of founding activists John Bohlen (1926–2010), Irving (1915–1974) and Dorothy Stowe (1920–2010), Bob Hunter (1941–2005), and David McTaggart (1932–2001). Though some were already members of the Canadian-based environmental group Sierra Club, the members quickly distinguished their organization by attempting to engage in direct action and activism over more passive lobbying approaches.

In fact, the group launched an effort to create what its members labeled "media mindbombs" under the encouragement of Bob Hunter. As part of its first foray into activism, the group began to organize a benefit concert to fund the excursion out to Amchitka Island. With gratis performances by Joan Baez, Joni Mitchell, and James Taylor, among others, the group raised enough money to bring their idea to fruition. In October 1970, 12 members (with an additional 2 members coordinating onshore) attempted to sail out to the Aleutians with the goal of placing the boat in the way of the nuclear test site.

Despite the best efforts of the crew, the U.S. Navy intercepted the *Greenpeace* before it reached the test site. Though the group internally considered the excursion a failure, they began to gain notoriety on an international level. The efforts of the crew and their bold approach captured the attention of environmental protectionists worldwide, who then flooded governmental phone lines in protest. As a result of their actions and growing public pressure, the U.S. government called off additional nuclear tests.

With its heightened visibility, the initial group officially established the Greenpeace Foundation in 1971. While interrupting nuclear tests continued to be a mainstay of the organization, Greenpeace began to also include commercial whaling, the killing of harp seals, dumping of toxic waste, and, more recently, climate change and deforestation as part of its commitment to the Quaker idea of "bearing witness." This idea—of taking responsibility for preserving and maintaining the environment and all its creatures—became the basis for Greenpeace to begin branching out into broader and varying environmental concerns.

As Greenpeace expanded its scope, satellite groups independent of the organization began to sprout up in countries around the world. As a result, the better part of the 1970s was spent consolidating and eventually rebranding the organization into Greenpeace International in 1979. Today, Greenpeace International maintains offices in over 50 countries as well as thousands of volunteers, all dedicated to causes of environmental protection, including country-specific issues, regional areas of concern, and even global environmental health.

Greenpeace's direct action tactics have been a source of differentiation for the group from other environmental organizations—but not without a price. On the one hand, as Greenpeace began to expand its efforts from classic environmental protection to wildlife protection, it relied on the use of the often dangerous tactic of directing its crew and ships to position themselves between harpooners and whalers. The effect has been a moratorium on whaling signed by five of the worst offending countries since 1982, resulting in the saving of thousands of whales worldwide. However, during one such expedition intending to prevent nuclear testing by France off the coast of Auckland, New Zealand, in 1985, a pair of French secret service agents planted bombs on the Greenpeace vessel *Rainbow Warrior,* killing 35-year-old photographer Fernando Pereira (1950–1985).

Despite the setback, Greenpeace has steadily maintained a largely peaceful approach to pursuing its political interests. In fact, the organization has done much to distance itself from Paul Watson (1950–), a rogue former member who founded the sometimes violent Sea Shepherd Conservation Society. By differentiating the efforts of the Sea Shepherd Conservation Society from those of Greenpeace, the organization has been able to preserve claims that its tactics are demonstrably peaceful, though potentially dangerous.

In addition, Greenpeace, while still working in the area of ending commercial whaling, has since focused its efforts into tackling newer issues such as climate change and deforestation. During the 1990s, Greenpeace actively began to speak out against chlorofluorocarbons (CFCs) as major contributors to climate change. In their effort to not only bring attention to the problem, Greenpeace also developed a cleaner product for use in refrigerators, dubbed "Greenfreeze." By 2011, two-fifths of the world's refrigerators were produced to be compatible with Greenfreeze CFC-free technology.

Currently, Greenpeace continues to pursue efforts in the areas of deforestation, dumping of toxic waste, saving the Arctic, and combatting climate change. At times, Greenpeace has been at odds with national governments, major industries and corporations, scholars, and even other activists. In one such campaign against the proliferation of the use of genetically-modified organisms (GMOs) in food designated for aid relief, Greenpeace was met with an open letter from over 100 Nobel Laureates to cease and desist in their efforts, so that famine-stricken nations could benefit from the altered food.

Greenpeace has also felt backlash from the fashion industry over conflicts resulting from accusations of toxic-waste pollution in Chinese rivers, as well as from historic preservationists over the damage caused to the Nazca lines in Peru while members of the organization engaged in protesting.

As of 2014, Greenpeace reported a budget of roughly $400 million (U.S.) garnered mainly from individual donors and supporting foundations. Since its meager beginnings in 1970 to a multimillion dollar budget in just under 45 years, Greenpeace has become among the most visible environmental organizations worldwide, and it continues to redefine and broaden its scope in order to remain relevant and keep abreast of current environmental issues. According to the organization's mission statement, Greenpeace holds "respect for global democratic principles and a need to maintain a high level of internationalism and coordination."

Laila F. Sorurbakhsh

See also: National Audubon Society (1905); Natural Resources Defense Council (1970–); National Wildlife Federation (1936–); Resources for the Future (1952–); Sierra Club (1892–); Union of Concerned Scientists (1969–)

Further Reading

Brown, Michael, and John May. 1991. *The Greenpeace Story.* New York: Dorling Kindersley, Inc.

Doyle, J. 2007. "Picturing the Clima(c)tic: Greenpeace and the Representational Politics of Climate Change Communication." *Science as Culture* 16 (2): 129–150.

Hunter, Robert. 2005. *The Greenpeace to Amchitka.* Vancouver: Arsenal Pulp Press.

Tsoukas, H. 1999. "David and Goliath in the Risk Society: Making Sense of the Conflict between Shell and Greenpeace in the North Sea." *Organization* 6 (3): 499–528.

Weyler, R. 2004. *Greenpeace: How a Group of Ecologists, Journalists, and Visionaries Changed the World.* Emmaus, PA: Rodale.

Grocery Manufacturers Association (1908–)

The Grocery Manufacturers Association (GMA) is a trade group representing the interests of around 250 companies in the food, beverage, and consumer products industry. Its members include some of the largest producers of branded consumer packaged goods (CPG) in the world. GMA considers itself the voice of the grocery manufacturing sector, which employs 2.1 million people in 30,000 communities throughout the United States, and prides itself upon supplying safe, nutritious, and affordable food to American consumers. GMA conducts scientific research, develops food safety initiatives, supports product innovation, and promotes sustainability among its members. The organization also lobbies state and federal lawmakers to shape public policies and regulatory decisions related to food, nutrition, and health.

GMA was founded in 1908, when representatives of dozens of food manufacturers met in New York City to discuss the industry's response to the Pure Food and Drug Act of 1906 and other Progressive Era laws aimed at consumer protection and food safety. Originally known as the Grocery Manufacturers of America, the organization adopted its current name in 2008 after merging with the Food Products Association. During the first half of the 20th century, GMA worked closely with the federal government to increase food production to meet wartime needs. Food manufacturers tripled their output of meat, bread, and sugar during World War I, for instance, and donated food and consumer products as part of the Marshall Plan to aid in Europe's recovery from World War II (1939–1945).

In 1967, GMA moved its headquarters to Washington, D.C., and took a more active role in promoting technological innovation and lobbying the federal government on behalf of its members. During the 1970s, in response to supermarket demands to automate inventory tracking and speed up the checkout process, GMA participated in the development of the Universal Product Code (UPC) system and barcode scanners. In 1986, GMA led opposition to the Value Added Tax, which would have imposed an incremental tax on each step in the manufacturing process for CPG. The trade association also responded to rising consumer concerns about environmental protection by supporting member initiatives that reduced grocery packaging discards by 14 percent from 1990 to 1993. In the late 1990s, GMA advocated passage of the Food and Drug Administration (FDA) Modernization Act, which eliminated the requirement for FDA approval of manufacturer changes to packaging and other substances that came into contact with food.

In the 21st century, according to its website, GMA focuses its resources and activities on five main areas: food safety, health and nutrition, sustainability, value-chain optimization, and global commerce. The organization helps its members produce safe food and comply with government regulations by developing comprehensive food safety initiatives that emphasize prevention, providing education and training, and maintaining a scientific laboratory to perform chemical analysis and contaminant diagnosis. It also funds research and provides resources and expertise to shape food and product safety regulations enacted by Congress, the FDA, the U.S. Department of Agriculture (USDA), and state legislatures.

In the area of health and nutrition, GMA worked with food and beverage manufacturers to help combat obesity by introducing 30,000 new products with lower calorie, fat, sodium, and sugar content. Many GMA member companies participated in a campaign sponsored by the nonprofit Healthy Weight Commitment Foundation that reduced the number of calories in the U.S. marketplace by 6.7 trillion from 2007 to 2014. GMA members also voluntarily limited advertising on children's television programs to messages promoting nutritious food choices and a healthy lifestyle. To help consumers make informed grocery purchasing decisions, GMA launched a voluntary nutrition labeling program called Facts up Front in 2011 and offered more detailed ingredient information in a digital format through its SmartLabel Transparency Initiative.

GMA encourages its members to adopt sustainable business practices and reduce the environmental impact of the CPG industry. One of its main priorities involves reducing the amount of packaging material used by the CPG industry by 4 billion pounds by 2020. GMA has also worked with grocery retailers to identify opportunities to reduce food waste and to standardize expiration date labeling on product packaging. Finally, GMA helps foster industry-wide collaboration throughout the value chain to promote growth and efficiency, and it works to eliminate trade barriers and streamline technical standards to open up global commerce opportunities for its members.

In its efforts to protect and promote the interests of major manufacturers of food, beverage, and consumer products, GMA has sometimes stood in opposition to legislative or regulatory measures favored by consumer advocates. Critics have referred to GMA as "the leading trade group for the junk food industry" (Ruskin 2018) and "the attack group for large companies like Kraft and General Mills" (Evich and Boudreau 2017). GMA generated a great deal of negative press by campaigning against state consumer-protection laws that would require mandatory labeling for foods containing genetically engineered ingredients, known as genetically modified organisms (GMOs). Proponents of GMO labeling argued that consumers had a right to know how foods were produced in order to make informed purchasing decisions. Polls suggested that over 90 percent of American consumers supported GMO labeling (Ruskin 2018).

Beginning in 2012, GMA spent millions of dollars fighting to prevent the passage of GMO labeling laws and ballot initiatives in such states as Washington, California, Connecticut, and Maine. In 2013, GMA petitioned the FDA to issue a rule allowing manufacturers to apply the label "natural" to foods containing GMO ingredients. In response, groups associated with the organic and natural foods movement called for a boycott of GMA member companies. When Vermont became the first state to approve a mandatory labeling law in 2014, GMA unsuccessfully sued to prevent it from taking effect.

The trade association also lobbied the U.S. Congress to pass a federal ban on state GMO-labeling laws, arguing that the food industry was not equipped to meet separate labeling requirements for different states. Congress finally passed a compromise bill in 2016 that preempted the Vermont law and established a federal standard for labeling GMO foods. Although the law required food manufacturers to disclose their use of genetically engineered ingredients, it allowed them to provide that information digitally by using QR codes that consumers scan with a smartphone, rather than by presenting written labels on product packaging. Also in 2016, a judge in Washington ruled that GMA violated campaign finance laws by intentionally hiding the source of the $11 million it spent to defeat the state's GMO-labeling referendum. Although donations from member companies such as Coca-Cola, ConAgra, Nestlé, and PepsiCo financed the effort, GMA shielded their involvement to avoid negative publicity or product boycotts.

In addition to the GMO labeling debate, GMA came under criticism for resisting federal efforts to combat childhood obesity. First Lady Michelle Obama enlisted GMA as a partner in her "Let's Move" campaign to promote healthy eating and physical activity by giving the keynote address at its 2010 Science Forum. Although GMA leaders expressed support for the program's goals, the organization also actively worked to defeat state school nutrition guidelines that imposed restrictions on junk food and sugary beverages in schools. GMA also opposed an FDA plan to update the Nutrition Facts labels on food packaging to include a category for "added sugars."

Critics—and some GMA member companies—argued that the trade association's positions on nutrition and health issues failed to account for changing consumer tastes. Between 2011 and 2017, the 20 largest food and beverage companies in the United States lost $18 billion in market share as consumers migrated toward healthier options, such as organic foods produced without GMO ingredients, antibiotics, or artificial dyes. Disagreements about how to respond to evolving consumer preferences created an ideological split within GMA, with some members fighting to preserve the status quo and others embracing the new reality. "Some of these companies are realizing that being more progressive is a good place to be, from a marketing perspective," said nutrition policy expert Melissa Musiker. "They get kudos for it" (Evich and Boudreau 2017).

The dispute led some member companies to question whether GMA represented the best interests of their brands. In 2017, nearly a dozen large food and beverage makers ended their membership in GMA, including Campbell Soup, Cargill, Dean Foods, DowDuPont, Hershey, Kraft Heinz, Mars, Tyson Foods, and Unilever. Several of these companies formed a new trade association, the

Sustainable Food Policy Alliance. The exodus sent shock waves through the CGA industry and precipitated a change in leadership at GMA. CEO Pamela Bailey retired in 2018 and was replaced by Geoff Freeman, former head of the American Gaming Association. A short time later, GMA reversed its longtime stance against GMO labeling and released a statement emphasizing its importance in building consumer trust. "If consumers do not believe that they are getting the transparency and ingredient information they demand, the repercussions will be felt most directly by the companies that make their food and beverage products," they wrote. "Consumers will hold GMA member companies and their brands accountable for any lack of product transparency" (Fusaro 2018).

Laurie Collier Hillstrom

See also: American Farm Bureau Federation (1911–); United Fresh Produce Association (1904–)

Further Reading

Evich, Helena Bottemiller, and Catherine Boudreau. 2017. "The Big Washington Food Fight." *Politico*, November 26, 2017. https://www.politico.com/story/2017/11/26 /food-lobby-consumer-tastes-washington-190528.

Fusaro, Dave. 2018. "Two New Grocery Manufacturers Associations Emerge." *Food Processing*, August 10, 2018. https://www.foodprocessing.com/articles/2018/editors -plate-august/.

Grocery Manufacturers Association. 2018. https://www.gmaonline.org/.

Ruskin, Gary. 2018. "Grocery Manufacturers Association—Key Facts." *Right to Know*, March 1, 2018. https://usrtk.org/gmo/grocery-manufacturers-association/.

H

Halliburton (1919–)

Halliburton is an American multinational energy company with significant lobbying interests and influence within the U.S. national security and foreign policy communities. Halliburton was founded in 1919 as an oil field services corporation with an expansive number of divisions, interests, and locations. It currently operates in 70 countries and employs over 50,000 workers worldwide. The company is involved in production as well as services provision related to the energy sector. Halliburton produces products for drilling, mining, transporting, refining, by-product processing, and delivering of oil and oil-related goods.

Erie P. Halliburton (1892–1957) founded the New Method Oil Well Cementing Company in 1919 at Duncan, Oklahoma, on a technological innovation that significantly modernized and advanced oil extraction. The company utilized cement to insulate oil wells from water intrusion. Later, Halliburton expanded on this idea by developing a jet-mixer and measuring line system that sped up the process and increased the efficiency of oil well cementing. Halliburton received a patent from the U.S. Patent Office in 1921 for his invention. In another advance, he applied his cementing procedure to natural gas wells beginning in 1920.

In 1922, Halliburton renamed his company the Halliburton Oil Well Cementing Company (HOWCO). The company was benefiting from the Mexia, Texas, oil boom, which provided numerous clients for HOWCO's service. In the wake of its 500th successful oil well cementing, HOWCO incorporated in 1924 with investors from seven major oil companies. However, Halliburton and his wife, Vida Halliburton (1894–1951), maintained majority stock-control in the company. Nationalization of automobile transportation with the development of the Model T and Model A cars by the Ford Motor Company was a boon for the oil industry, and HOWCO profited accordingly throughout the 1920s.

The post–World War I (1914–1918) deregulation of the economy presided over by presidents Warren G. Harding and Calvin Coolidge (1872–1933) also served as an impetus for corporate expansion which summarily benefitted HOWCO. During this period, HOWCO became involved in lobbying national and state governmental agencies in order to promote its business interests. In particular, HOWCO and other similarly minded energy sector firms lobbied to open up public and tribal lands in Oklahoma and Texas for oil and natural gas exploration. There was some pushback by the Coolidge administration (1923–1929) regarding tribal lands as Coolidge had, as a social policy interest, the promotion of Indian rights. Nevertheless, HOWCO and other energy firms tended to have a largely successful lobbying strategy with the government during these years. The Great Depression, along with the subsequent redistributive and regulatory efforts of the New Deal, lowered corporate profits. However, the regulations brought greater rationalization to the energy sector and, in fact, benefited HOWCO in the long run because it leveled the field for interfirm competition within the oil industry.

HOWCO entered the international economy early as an oil services parts seller in 1926, with sales going to the Far Eastern claims of the British Empire. At that time, the empire was the United States' number-one foreign client in terms of trade. The United States was also the number-one recipient of nonimperial-based British foreign direct investment into the American home market, including the energy sector. A feature of the political economy that positively affected energy start-ups like HOWCO, World War II (1939–1945) and its aftermath pushed HOWCO into being one of the world's fastest expanding exporters. It also became an international company by expanding its offices into Venezuela at the same time that it became a fully national company through cementing wells across the United States. In 1938, HOWCO entered the offshore oil and natural gas industry by cementing platform drillings and developing a marine cementing vessel in 1947. By 1951, HOWCO was a multimillion-dollar company with offices and plants across North America, Europe, and Asia. It developed a strong trade economy which kept it close to national and state governments; this became particularly acute given the wartime and Cold War petroleum needs of the American military.

In 1961 HOWCO renamed itself Halliburton, both to honor the passing of its founder Erie Halliburton in 1957 and to show the expansion in scope of products and services undertaken by the company. Beginning in the 1960s, Halliburton expanded its efforts. It began operating the actual extraction portion of the energy sector by developing an oil and natural gas exploration service. In addition, the company began acquiring as well as creating subsidiaries with specializations in building refineries, chemical plants, and automated cement mixing systems. Halliburton began its own oil and natural gas extraction efforts by the late 1960s with a massive effort put into place at Prudhoe Bay, Alaska. By acquiring smaller companies and then reorganizing them as subsidiaries Halliburton has been able to move into other extraction sectors of the economy like logging. It has also become a technological and policy contributor through its own internal developments at its think tank, the Halliburton Energy Institute, a research facility established in 1976 at the corporation's home site of Duncan, Oklahoma. More recent corporate acquisitions like that of Gearhart Industries in 1989 have moved Halliburton significantly in the direction of becoming a digitized technological entity specializing in the development of computer systems for fossil fuel extraction services.

The deregulatory turn of the Jimmy Carter (1977–1981) and Ronald Reagan administrations (1981–1989) allowed Halliburton to expand into these various subsectors of the global energy economy with little governmental oversight. Also, the growing energy interdependence of international markets served as an impetus for ever-larger global expansions by Halliburton. This was done in order to maintain the company's competitive edge even as it was losing comparative advantage along with the rest of America's noncoal energy companies during the 1970s and 1980s. The cartel-driven oil politics of the Arab Petroleum Producing Countries (APEC) presented both an opportunity and a challenge to Western energy sector dominance. Halliburton's expansion then was driven by the opportunity for an expanding fossil fuels market and the challenge of the relative decline of Western energy hegemony. Such decline was showcased in the recession-inducing oil shocks of the 1970s, 1990s, and early 2000s.

The organizational expansion by Halliburton coincided with its market penetration in terms of goods and services. This continues to be true but in recent decades Halliburton's economics have become particularly politicized. The key development was the close corporate relationship developed between Halliburton and leading political figures from the Bush family. This included Senator Prescott Bush (R-CT) (1895–1972), his son President George H. W. Bush (1924–), and grandson President George W. Bush (1946–). Major figures in the Bush political family entourage, most importantly, Vice President Richard "Dick" Cheney (1941–) were also key links between the energy company and political power. The seeds of the Bush family and its relationship with Halliburton lie with the elder Bush, who was once a company director of a future subsidiary.

But, it was George H. W. Bush who elevated Halliburton to the position of becoming the main energy contractor for the U.S. military during the Persian Gulf War (1990–1991). The relationship solidified as Bush's former secretary of defense Dick Cheney took over as Halliburton's CEO in 1995; a position he held until he became the younger Bush's Vice-President in 2001. Key to Halliburton's business methodology was that the actual contracting was done through a subsidiary, Brown and Root Services. Through its joint-subsidiary Kellogg-Brown and Root (KBR), Halliburton became a provider of various laundering, sustenance, and transportation services for troops in the Balkans during the U.S. peacekeeping mission there. It also continued to expand its role as an all-around provider of goods and services through its subsidiaries to U.S. and allied operations relative to Iraq in the wake of the Gulf War.

With the onset of the Iraq War in 2003, Halliburton became fully enmeshed in the political intrigues of corporate influence in the construction of foreign policy. In the early years of the war, Halliburton had an almost unchecked influence and access on issues pertaining to energy and troop provisions within the theater of conflict. As media scrutiny increased and the public turned against the war, Halliburton suffered in the court of public opinion even as its investors were amassing tremendous profits. Fellow corporate competitors, both in and out of the energy sector joined congressional, journalistic, and Democratic Party criticism against perceived excesses by the company. As a result, Halliburton has pulled back from its previously very public role in American national security. It remains a player but has now returned to its pre-Gulf War position as a single, albeit very large, megacorporate competitor in American and international political economy.

Matthew M. Caverly

See also: General Motors (1908–); Lockheed Martin (1995–); Standard Oil Company (1870–1911)

Further Reading

Franks, K. 1980. *The Oklahoma Petroleum Industry.* Norman: University of Oklahoma Press.

Haley, James Evetts. 1959. *Erle P. Halliburton: Genius with Cement*. Duncan, OK: Privately printed.

Halliburton. 2018. http://www.halliburton.com/en-US/default.page.

Hughes, Llewelyn, and Phillip Y. Lipscy. 2013. "The Politics of Energy." *Annual Review of Political Science* 16 (1): 449–469.

Heritage Foundation (1973–)

The Heritage Foundation is a conservative think tank that analyzes, develops, and promotes public policy proposals that promote the ideals of conservatism within American politics. The foundation's mission statement claims that its policy promotion activities are based on "the principles of free enterprise, limited government, individual freedom, traditional American values, and a strong national defense" (Heritage Foundation 2018). This captures the trifecta of economic, social, and foreign policy conservatism within the Foundation's intellectual orbit and political practice. Heritage is different from other right-leaning American think tanks like the American Enterprise Institute (AEI) in that it is openly partisan. Heritage does not promote itself as a bipartisan entity but rather maintains and advances an ideologically conservative core set of values.

The Heritage Foundation actually originated in a faction of conservative elites who were opposed to Republican President Richard Nixon's embrace of what they termed the "liberal consensus." These policy activists led by Paul Weyrich (1942–2008), Edwin Feulner (1941–), and Joseph Coors (1917–2003) established the Heritage Foundation in 1973 as an intellectual and practical outcrop of the "New Right" thinking which had developed during the 1950s as a within-opposition movement in American conservatism. Weyrich originally led Heritage and recently the foundation once again returned to one of its founders for leadership in Edwin Feulner, who since 2017 is serving his second stint as president of the organization.

The New Right promoted an aggressive variety of conservatism that challenged the public policy status quo in place since the New Deal Realignment (i.e., the liberal consensus). It called for a return to and the adoption of a cross-policy coherent conservatism. The only deviation of this trend was in the movement's adoption of the neoconservative stances on interventionist foreign policy and its related efforts promoting national militarist positions.

The Foundation had its moment in the policy making sun during the Ronald Reagan presidency (1981–1989). Heritage's policy promotion work, *Mandate for Leadership*, became a secular bible of sorts for the application of Reaganomics to governmental organization and policy formulation. Most of the work's 2,000 public policy proposals were adopted with little, if any, amendment by Reagan during the first year of his presidency in 1981. During the same time frame, Heritage was instrumental in developing portions of what became the Strategic Defense Initiative, better known as the "Star Wars" program for nuclear missile defense.

In the post-Reagan years, the Foundation turned its attentions to developing programs with which to lobby Republicans in Congress while continuing to try to influence the presidency. The George H. W. Bush administration (1989–1993) was not as enthusiastic an adopter of Heritage's ideas as Reagan. However, the Foundation did influence elements of the 1990 budget deal between Bush and the Democratic-controlled Congress. Additionally, Heritage spoke out strongly in favor of the Persian Gulf War on President Bush's behalf. The "Contract with America" domestic public policy platform, architected by Speaker Newt Gingrich (R-GA) (1943–), was erected with advice from the Foundation. Heritage continued to promote its ideas outside of government by sponsoring studies on labor economics, family life, military preparedness, and religious and political ethics. These efforts brought the Foundation acclaim from conservatives and earned the ire of liberals.

Heritage had a somewhat unusual relationship with the Bill Clinton administration (1993–2001) as the Foundation wholeheartedly supported Clinton's welfare reform and anticrime efforts at the same time that it staunchly opposed his efforts at health care reform. In the 2000s the Heritage Foundation became a source of ideas for the George W. Bush administration (2001–2009), which embraced them more openly and enthusiastically than Bush's father. Heritage was something of an intellectual clearinghouse for policies that ultimately found their way on the Bush and Republican congressional agendas. These policies included tax and domestic budget cutting, national defense promotion, the war in Iraq, and proposals on entitlement reform.

Much like in the 1980s, the Foundation became something of a revolving door in terms of personalities as leading fellows and executives left to do tours with the administration. In 2005, Heritage established the "Margaret Thatcher Center for Freedom" to both honor the former British Prime Minister and serve as a gathering place for lay and scholarly avocation of conservative principles. This was especially true in matters relating to capitalism and nationalist foreign policies.

In more recent years, Heritage settled into its role as intellectual oppositionists to the policies of the Barack Obama administration (2009–2017) and related Democratic Congresses. Heritage has expanded its communications network by first establishing a blogging site called "The Foundry," which was later displaced by a wider all-media news network established by Heritage titled "The Daily Signal."

Studies on poverty in the United States and cross-national studies of economic freedom have joined the Foundation's earlier work advocating limited government as points of agreement for conservatives and places of intense opposition by liberals. Heritage has taken its conservative philosophy to the video screen by producing a film titled *33 Minutes*, which took a hawkish perspective on foreign policy challenges facing the United States in 2009. By the late 1990s, Heritage had also developed an impressive speaker's series with leading politicians and policy scholars, all of a conservative bent, promoting the ideals of the think tank.

Heritage's "Index of Economic Freedom" has been one of its hallmark achievements tracking countries' level of free enterprise, government regulation, and size as well as strength of their respective welfare states since 1997 in a joint effort with the conservative-leaning newspaper, the *Wall Street Journal*. Heritage's public policy efforts have included the establishment of an academic journal, *Policy Review* in 2001, though it eventually ceded publishing authority and ownership over it to the Hoover Institution.

As an organizational endeavor, Heritage is centrally located in Washington, D.C. It originally followed a "beltway approach" to policy advocacy, trying to directly influence the holders of power in U.S. politics. This approach allowed it to reach its zenith of influence in the Reagan administration and to a slightly lesser extent the George W. Bush administration. Beginning in the 1990s, however, the Foundation turned its attentions outward to include an indirect lobbying campaign through information, formation, interpretation, and dissemination. It was during this time that Heritage developed its academic journal, journalism blog, film production, speaker's series, and publicly promoted policy studies.

Most recently, Heritage, along with fellow philosophical traveler the American Enterprise Institute (AEI), has entered presidential politics by sponsoring Republican presidential candidate debates in both the 2012 and 2016 election cycles. Heritage is governed by a board of directors led by a president. The current occupant of that office is Edwin Feulner, who replaced the previous president, former senator James "Jim" DeMint (R-SC) in 2017.

The ideology of the think tank is conservatism; unlike other conservative organizations, Heritage makes no effort to promote outreach with the opposition party (i.e., the Democrats). This is because one of the organizing principles of Heritage was the "Powell Memorandum" by Supreme Court Associate Justice Lewis Powell (1907–1998) just prior to his nomination by President Nixon in 1971. The Powell Memorandum asserted that the New Deal and its aftermath, culminating in Ralph Nader's Consumer Rights Advocacy Movement, amounted to "creeping socialism." Hence, it delegitimized liberalism and called for conservatives to rally and turn the tide through aggressive opposition. This version of "New Right" thinking is conflictual in orientation and leaves little, if any, room for compromise. Thus, Heritage sees itself as a means to turn back the political clock and return America to a pre-New Deal minimalist state as well as a more traditionalist society.

Heritage has had its most pronounced influence during the Reagan and George W. Bush years, but it has had an ongoing relationship with the Republican Party. This has come about because as the Republican Party has become more coherently and consistently conservative in terms of its ideological public policy focus, the Heritage Foundation has also developed and expanded its influencing efforts. The two work very much in synch now, and Heritage enjoys the highest level of think tank influence among Republican circles, particularly those that are oriented around conservative orthodoxy.

As a recent example of this coordination, Heritage, through Rebekah Mercer (1973–), played a major role in the incoming Donald Trump administration's (2017–) transition team by identifying and vetting candidates for appointments, setting up timetables, prioritizing policy agendas, and translating campaign pledges into policy promotion packages. Much of the deregulatory and tax reform initiatives, as well as the shifting of budgetary priorities away from domestic social programs toward national defense and homeland security, within the Trump Presidency have their basis in ideas largely formulated by and through the Heritage Foundation.

Matthew M. Caverly

See also: American Conservative Union (1964–); American Legislative Exchange Council (1973–); Center for Security Policy (1988–)

Further Reading

Edwards, Lee. 1997. *The Power of Ideas: The Heritage Foundation at 25 Years.* Ottawa, IL: Jameson Books.

Heritage Foundation. 2005. *Mandate for Leadership.* 6th ed. Washington, D.C.: Heritage Foundation.

Heritage Foundation. 2018. http://www.heritage.org/.

Historically Black Colleges and Universities (1837–)

Historically Black Colleges and Universities (HBCUs) continue to play an important role in the political development of the United States in rural and urban environments. Due to the significant contributions of their alumni, they first began as alternatives to primarily white institutions that refused to allow admittance of African Americans during the slavery and segregation periods. Beginning in 1837 at what would become Cheyney University in Pennsylvania, today over 107 of these entities exist across the country. However, they still struggle to secure private, state, and federal funding, coupled with enrollment issues into the twentieth-first century.

Two of the earliest African American institutions of higher learning were the Ashmun Institute founded in 1854 by Quakers and later renamed Lincoln University, and Wilberforce University in Ohio. The latter was founded by the Methodist Episcopal Church and the African Methodist Episcopal Church (AME) in 1856 on the eve of the Civil War (1861–1865). In the aftermath, the AME bought it outright, and built a strong program of degreed training. They employed professors like W. E. B. Dubois (1868–1963), a graduate himself of Fisk University in Nashville and Harvard University, and Charles Young (1864–1922), the third African American to graduate from West Point, who founded the military science department. Other religious missionary organizations invested in numerous private institutions that would form the backbone, especially in the North, of HBCU communities.

Once the Confederacy was defeated, Southern states continued to fund white universities, as they had before the war, with the passage of the 1862 Morrill Act, which backed land grant colleges in each state. Some of these were open in the North and West to blacks, but all schools in the South were closed. While privately funded institutions took up the slack, it would be nearly 25 years before Congress passed the Hatch Act of 1887 (for expanded funding of agricultural and mechanical schools), and the second Morrill Act of 1890. Known as the Agricultural College Act, it required states to establish alternative colleges for African Americans, thus inaugurating the principle of "separate but equal."

Some HBCUs were built as the African American communities banded together against their former white masters in the Reconstruction and Jim Crow eras. Former abolitionists and others reasoned that black institutions could not be located in cities because rural environments were remote and away from white mobs that could torch buildings and harass students. Shaw University, the first of its kind in the South, and later Roger Williams University built near the Vanderbilt Campus and Fisk University built in 1866 also built in Nashville were politically driven sites that sought solace in the face of black codes and little funding.

Eventually city campuses did become popular after the War, particularly the renamed Atlanta Baptist Seminary, which by 1913 was christened Morehouse College. But, perhaps the most significant urban HBCU was opened in 1867 in Washington, D.C. Antislavery advocates and members of the Radical Republicans demanded that a proper college for freedman be constructed in the nation's capital. Using political purse strings the first temporary building to hold classes was a former beer saloon and dance hall. This was the location of what would become Howard University.

Besides Howard, the other major HBCU of the period built before 1914 was the seed planted in a little-known part of the Deep South. Education, reading, and writing were on the rise, but Southern ways of life still stymied learning. A young teacher with political aspirations and much pluck by the name of Booker T. Washington (1856–1915) saw a vision for the African American community that included a full slate of degreed education at the highest level. Born into slavery in Virginia, Washington attended Hampton University, which would later become Virginia Union University.

Aspiring black men now with the opportunity for education took advantage of books, lectures, and the communal opportunities for advancement that the university setting provided. By the early 1880s, Washington joined a new school in Alabama that was committed to African American business training called the Tuskegee Institute. Students helped to build the university by fashioning bricks and constructing classrooms for the purpose of turning out the next generations of educators and craftsmen. In 1895, inspired by what he had seen at Hampton and his work at Tuskegee, Washington crafted his famous Atlanta Compromise, which argued for education, rather than political agitation, in order to move toward better relations with whites.

Despite a public face that argued for submission, Washington privately helped to fund court cases to fight *Plessy v. Ferguson*, the Supreme Court decision that established "separate but equal," and, interestingly enough, sent his own children to Northern schools to attend white universities. The HBCUs were quickly moving toward a political platform, with the passage of the second Morrill Act and the founding of the NAACP, with the assistance of Washington's longtime adversary, W. E. B. Dubois, as African Americans sought new forms of expressions of rights and responsibilities. Of course, at this time few schools admitted black women, one of the exceptions being Spelman College in Atlanta, as they continued to sit on the sidelines of the advanced educational systems of the time period.

After World War I (1914–1918), African American men and women tired of the Atlanta Compromise and rebuilt HBCUs in a new image that reflected what became known as the "New Negro." These institutions of higher learning, with a sturdy alumni base and slavery behind them, now looked at the urban university campus as a place for continued struggle and agitations. The 1920s and 30s afforded some opportunities politically for this. Namely, the next generation of

Civil Rights leaders from Thurgood Marshall (1908–1993), who attended Lincoln University and later, in 1933, graduated from Howard University's law school; and Dr. Martin Luther King Jr. (1929–1968), who graduated from Morehouse after World War II (1939–1945). HBCUs produced a myriad of important degreed graduates that would take part in protests against the Vietnam War, embrace the counterculture of the 1960s, and debate the merits and foibles of the Civil Rights Movement.

After World War II, HBCUs underwent a profound political transformation as debate ensued concerning their place in the U.S. educational system. Once the color barrier of public universities began to break down, with the admittance of James Meredith (1933–)at the University of Mississippi, and the failure of Alabama Governor George Wallace (1919–1998) to block African American students from registering for classes at the University of Alabama, many wondered if HBCUs were necessary any longer. Their legacy and alumni however thought differently. Federal funding from the Lyndon B. Johnson (1908–1973) administration prolonged their existence with the passage of the 1965 Higher Education Act, which offered matching assistance to keep historically significant schools of African American education operating.

While it seemed that a new era in education arrived, much like the politics of the Civil Rights Era itself, HBCUs were still considered unequal. An example of this became clear in 1970 during events at Jackson State College. Founded originally in Natchez, Mississippi, and later moved to the capital in Jackson, 10 days after the killing of white students at Kent State University in Ohio, a similar incident took place at JSC. After two nights of demonstrations against the draft for the Vietnam War (1955–1975), a violent confrontation erupted as rumors circulated that the first black mayor of Fayette, Mississippi, Charles Evers (1922–) (the brother of Medgar Evers, 1925–1963), and his wife had been assassinated. The campus confrontation ended with police and state highway patrolmen firing their weapons into a dormitory, killing 2 students and wounding 12 others. The incident at Jackson State was blamed on a supposed sniper, but the Richard Nixon–nominated Commission on Campus Unrest found no evidence to support this claim. The lack of national attention, especially compared to what transpired in Ohio, led many to believe that black lives did not matter. News of the violence at Jackson State did, however, spread to other HBCUs as political leaders grappled with how to respond.

The political history associated with HBCUs is reflection of the complex needs of African Americans who, across many generations, struggled for access to higher education. Despite intervention at the national level, southern, and some western states after 1901, like Tennessee, Kentucky, and Oklahoma, did their utmost to block entrance to their own schools by passing strict criminal measures. In the wake of the Morrill Act, 18 black land-grant institutions opened due to the progressive nature of the Congress. However, the promise of federal funding did not lead to affordable education. Only through private means did HBCUs survive the era of Jim Crow and the tumultuous Civil Rights Era. Even to this day, the legacies of these schools and the commitment of their alumni base are the only bulwarks against the ever-increasing tide of the ease of online classrooms, the more affordable community college systems, and the integrated model at major universities that draw multiethnic cohorts of undergraduates into their fold.

J. N. Campbell

See also: Land Grant Colleges and Universities; NAACP Legal Defense and Education Fund (1940–); National Association for the Advancement of Colored People (1909–); United Negro College Fund (1944–)

Further Reading

Brooks, F. Erik, and Glenn L. Starks. 2011. *Historically Black Colleges and Universities: An Encyclopedia.* Santa Barbara, CA: Greenwood Press.

Carter, Dan T. 1995. *The Politics of Rage: George Wallace, the Origins of the New Conservatism, and the Transformation of American Politics.* Baton Rouge: Louisiana State University Press.

Diner, Steven J. 2017. *Universities and Their Cities: Urban Higher Education in America.* Baltimore, MD: Johns Hopkins University Press.

Lovett, Bobby L. 2015. *America's Historically Black Colleges and Universities: A Narrative History, 1837–2009.* Macon, GA: Mercer University Press.

Mbajekwe, Carolyn O. Wilson. 2016. *The Future of Historically Black Colleges and Universities: Ten Presidents Speak Out.* Jefferson, NC: McFarland & Co.

Norell, Robert J. 2011. *Up From History: The Life of Booker T. Washington.* Cambridge, MA: Belknap Press.

Home School Legal Defense Association (2000–)

The Home School Legal Defense Association (HSLDA) is a conservative litigation, lobbying, and policy advocacy organization pressing for laws and practices at the state and federal level that support homeschooling of children. While the HSLDA started slowly, it became the primary lobbying and litigation organization for home schooling. The HSLDA was founded by Michael Farris (1951–) and Michael Smith in March 1983. The organization came into existence as a result of a series of seemingly unrelated developments that coalesced to put home schooling on the agenda of local, state, and federal governments.

During the 20th century, state and local governments became more involved in primary and secondary education by creating a system of public education. These schools expanded because the American population grew, and laws in most states required students to attend either public or private schools.

As part of a backlash against traditional government institutions starting in the 1970s, many in American society wanted to homeschool their children and not send their children to public schools. The motivations cited for this choice ranged from a reaction against a larger, increasingly impersonal and bureaucratic public education system, a concern that public education did not reflect the wishes of local citizens, a "values gap" between what was taught in public schools and what many parents wanted their children to learn, and the rise of a child-centric viewpoint in American society (Gaither 2008).

Among those who wanted to homeschool their children during this time was Michael Farris, a lawyer who worked for the Moral Majority and became the executive director of its Washington state branch. He later became chief legal counsel for Concerned Women for America and moved to Washington, D.C. By 1982, he became more involved with litigation against public schools and was convinced to explore homeschooling as an educational alternative for his ten children.

However, homeschooling was illegal in many states, and it existed on the edges of what was legal in others. Coordinating with Michael Smith, a homeschooling advocate and lawyer, the two began the HSLDA in March 1983 to make home-schooling a legal and accepted alternative to public education

The HSLDA was successful because it became a membership-based organiza-tion, rather than one sustained on private philanthropy. The primary benefit that this organization offers its members is free legal protection against any government action related to homeschooling. These benefits attracted many members because of homeschooling's legal status and resulted in substantial membership growth.

This organization grew for two other reasons as well. First, the HSLDA utilized their organizational structure to keep their members regularly informed through their monthly, "Home School Court Report." This newsletter contains accounts of many homeschooling families and their experiences with truant officers, police departments, judges, and local school districts. In many of these cases, the HSLDA portrays itself as the organization that comes to the successful defense of families that otherwise would not have the resources to fight against the state.

Second, this organization capitalized on demographic trends in which conser-vative Protestants became politically engaged while moving their children away from public schools. Conservative Protestants became aware of homeschooling as an alternative to public education through the efforts of Focus on the Family, the Moral Majority, and other similar organizations. During radio broadcasts, those who led these organizations encouraged those who went through with home-schooling to sign up for an HSLDA membership. In addition, the HSLDA bene-fited from the endorsement of prominent conservative Christian leaders at the time, like Jerry Falwell (1933–2007), Pat Robertson (1930–), and Phyllis Schlafly (1924–2016).

As the HSLDA grew, it fought to legalize homeschooling through a combina-tion of legislative advocacy and litigation. As a result of their legislative advocacy alongside other like-minded groups, between 1981 and 1991, many states updated or created laws that allowed for homeschooling. In addition, the National Center for Education Statistics (2016) estimates that the number of children who are homeschooled increased by approximately 700,000 between 2003 and 2012.

In many cases, victories in state courts created the opening for legal changes. The tactics that the HSLDA used to represent the DeJonge family (in *People v. DeJonge*) illustrates the tactics that this organization has used elsewhere. Prior to 1993, Michigan only allowed families to homeschool their children if the person teaching their children was a certified teacher in the state. In violation of this law, Mark and Christine DeJonge homeschooled their children in 1985, with the legal support of the HSLDA. They were arrested, charged, and convicted of criminal truancy for homeschooling without being certified teachers. The Court of Appeals upheld their conviction, and the couple appealed to the Michigan Supreme Court.

In a 4–3 decision, the Michigan Supreme Court overturned the trial court and the Court of Appeals judgments and ruled in favor of the DeJonges. The Michigan Supreme Court ruled that the First Amendment's Free Exercise clause allows the DeJonges to practice their religion by homeschooling their children. Further, the court erased Mark and Christine DeJonge's convictions for criminal truancy.

In 1996, Michigan passed a new law that made the state one of the most permissive with respect to homeschooling. In part, this law eliminated the teacher certification requirement for homeschooling families and repealed the requirement that families must notify local school districts if they are homeschooling their children. With HSLDA support, this law was shepherded through the Michigan legislature.

On the national level, the HSLDA has been more successful at lobbying and seeking legislative policy change than in its pursuit of litigation. In 1993, the HSLDA worked alongside a diverse array of groups to help draft and pass the Religious Freedom Restoration Act. Among other things, this law places a substantial burden of proof—a strict scrutiny standard—on governments whenever they pass laws or rules that restrict a person's religious freedom, which is often cited by families as reasons for homeschooling their children. The application of that high standard means that the government's action restricting religious liberty would likely be struck unless it could be shown to serve a compelling governmental interest and the government could demonstrate that the challenged law was the least restrictive means of serving that compelling interest.

In 1994, the HSLDA mobilized its members to oppose an amendment to H.R. 6, a bill that reauthorized the Elementary and Secondary Education Act. If passed, the amendment would have required school districts in each state to verify that all teachers were certified in the subject areas to which they were assigned. In addition, the amendment would have expanded the legal definition of a school to include nonprofits, and by extension, could have covered homeschoolers.

As a result of their advocacy, this amendment was defeated and an alternative was offered by Representative Dick Armey (R-TX) (1940–present). Drafted by Michael Farris, this amendment excluded anything that was contained in H.R. 6 from applying to homeschoolers. For the first time, homeschooling was codified into federal law. However, some homeschooling advocates worried that this step would create a precedent for federalizing homeschooling.

Beyond lobbying, the HSLDA tried to extend its influence on the national level by litigating cases in the federal courts. As with state courts, the HSLDA has represented plaintiffs against state and federal governmental agencies in federal courts. Typically, the HSLDA has argued that homeschooling is federally protected under the First Amendment's Free Exercise clause, the Fourteenth Amendment's Equal Protection Clause, and the right to privacy under the Ninth Amendment. The Free Exercise Clause guarantees each person the right to freely exercise his or her religious beliefs. The Equal Protection Clause states that each person is entitled to equal protection under the law. These claims are generally unsuccessful in federal courts and have never been litigated before the U.S. Supreme Court.

After homeschooling became legal in all states and Washington, D.C., the HSLDA became more active in influencing American political culture. Since 1998, the HSLDA political action committee (PAC) has contributed money solely to Republican candidates in U.S. House and Senate contests. In addition, the HSLDA has attempted to advance a parental rights amendment to the U.S. Constitution. If enacted, this amendment would write the ability to homeschool children directly into the Constitution.

Moreover, the HSLDA has initiated larger projects to affect U.S. society, including Generation Joshua, an organization to recruit homeschooled teens to volunteer time to Republican political campaigns. Its most ambitious project is the founding of Patrick Henry College (PHC), an institution of higher education whose mission is to train Christian students in leadership and classical education. The ultimate goal of this institution is to strategically place its graduates in positions of influence in U.S. society and politics to influence the world in a conservative direction. Many graduates of PHC come from families in which homeschooling is the predominant mode of education.

Kenneth W. Moffett

Related Primary Document: **Religious Freedom Restoration Act of 1993**

Religious Freedom Restoration Act of 1993

The Religious Freedom Restoration Act was a federal law enacted on November 16, 1993, that attempted to establish a higher level of protection for religious freedom. The act placed the burden of proof on the state and federal government, requiring them to establish a compelling interest in cases where laws substantially burdened the free exercise of religion. However, in City of Boerne, Texas v. Flores *(1997), the U.S. Supreme Court struck down the RFRA, ruling that it exceeded congressional powers under Section 5 of the Fourteenth Amendment, or the enforcement provision. The Home School Legal Defense Association supported the act, reproduced below, seeing the legislation as favorable to its cause.*

An Act to protect the free exercise of religion.

Be it enacted by the Senate and House of Representatives of the United States of America in Congress assembled,

SECTION 1. SHORT TITLE.

This Act may be cited as the "Religious Freedom Restoration Act of 1993."

SEC. 2. CONGRESSIONAL FINDINGS AND DECLARATION OF PURPOSES.

(a) Findings.—The Congress finds that—

(1) the framers of the Constitution, recognizing free exercise of religion as an unalienable right, secured its protection in the First Amendment to the Constitution;

(2) laws "neutral" toward religion may burden religious exercise as surely as laws intended to interfere with religious exercise;

(3) governments should not substantially burden religious exercise without compelling justification;

(4) in Employment Division v. Smith, 494 U.S. 872 (1990) the Supreme Court virtually eliminated the requirement that the government justify burdens on religious exercise imposed by laws neutral toward religion; and

(5) the compelling interest test as set forth in prior Federal court rulings is a workable test for striking sensible balances between religious liberty and competing prior governmental interests.

(b) Purposes.—The purposes of this Act are—

(1) to restore the compelling interest test as set forth in *Sherbert v. Verner*, 374 U.S. 398 (1963) and *Wisconsin v. Yoder*, 406 U.S. 205 (1972) and to guarantee its application in all cases where free exercise of religion is substantially burdened; and (2) to provide a claim or defense to persons whose religious exercise is substantially burdened by government.

SEC. 3. FREE EXERCISE OF RELIGION PROTECTED.

(a) In General.—Government shall not substantially burden a person's exercise of religion even if the burden results from a rule of general applicability, except as provided in subsection (b).

(b) Exception.—Government may substantially burden a person's exercise of religion only if it demonstrates that application of the burden to the person—

(1) is in furtherance of a compelling governmental interest; and

(2) is the least restrictive means of furthering that compelling governmental interest.

(c) Judicial Relief.—A person whose religious exercise has been burdened in violation of this section may assert that violation as a claim or defense in a judicial proceeding and obtain appropriate relief against a government. Standing to assert a claim or defense under this section shall be governed by the general rules of standing under article III of the Constitution.

SEC. 4. ATTORNEYS FEES.

(a) Judicial Proceedings.—Section 722 of the Revised Statutes (42 U.S.C. 1988) is amended by inserting "the Religious Freedom Restoration Act of 1993," before "or title VI of the Civil Rights Act of 1964."

(b) Administrative Proceedings.—Section 504(b)(1)(C) of title 5, United States Code, is amended—

(1) by striking "and" at the end of clause (ii);

(2) by striking the semicolon at the end of clause (iii) and inserting ", and"; and

(3) by inserting "(iv) the Religious Freedom Restoration Act of 1993;" after clause (iii).

SEC. 5. DEFINITIONS.

As used in this Act—

(1) the term "government" includes a branch, department, agency, instrumentality, and official (or other person acting under color of law) of the United States, a State, or a subdivision of a State;

(2) the term "State" includes the District of Columbia, the Commonwealth of Puerto Rico, and each territory and possession of the United States;

(3) the term "demonstrates" means meets the burdens of going forward with the evidence and of persuasion; and

(4) the term "exercise of religion" means the exercise of religion under the First Amendment to the Constitution.

SEC. 6. APPLICABILITY.

(a) In General.—This Act applies to all Federal and State law, and the implementation of that law, whether statutory or otherwise, and whether adopted before or after the enactment of this Act.

(b) Rule of Construction.—Federal statutory law adopted after the date of the enactment of this Act is subject to this Act unless such law explicitly excludes such application by reference to this Act.

(c) Religious Belief Unaffected.—Nothing in this Act shall be construed to authorize any government to burden any religious belief.

SEC. 7. ESTABLISHMENT CLAUSE UNAFFECTED.

Nothing in this Act shall be construed to affect, interpret, or in any way address that portion of the First Amendment prohibiting laws respecting the establishment of religion (referred to in this section as the "Establishment Clause"). Granting government funding, benefits, or exemptions, to the extent permissible under the Establishment Clause, shall not constitute a violation of this Act. As used in this section, the term "granting," used with respect to government funding, benefits, or exemptions, does not include the denial of government funding, benefits, or exemptions.

Speaker of the House of Representatives.

Vice President of the United States and President of the Senate.

Source: Religious Freedom Restoration Act of 1993, Pub. L. No. 103-141, 107 Stat. 1488 (November 16, 1993).

Related Primary Document: ***People v. DeJonge* (1993)**

People v. DeJonge (1993)

In 1985, parents Mark and Chris DeJonge were accused of criminal truancy for homeschooling their children without teaching certifications. The pair were arrested, and although the DeJonges lost their 1989 appeal, the Home School Legal Defense Association appealed the case twice to the Michigan Supreme Court and were finally permitted to argue the case in November 1992. On May 25, 1993, the Supreme Court decided to reverse the DeJonges' convictions with a 4–3 vote, holding that the teacher certification requirement was a violation of the Free Exercise clause. The Supreme Court held that the state failed to show that teacher certification requirement for homeschooling was the least restrictive means of achieving the state's claimed interest, and thus, the teacher certification requirement violated the Free Exercise clause. People v. DeJonge, *excerpted below, stands as a prime example of the legal actions pursued by the HSLDA.*

Supreme Court of Michigan.

Argued November 10, 1992.

Decided May 25, 1993.

AFTER REMAND

RILEY, J.

At issue is the constitutionality of MCL 388.553; MSA 15.1923, which requires parents who conduct home schooling for their children to provide instructors certified by the state. We hold that the teacher certification requirement is an unconstitutional violation of the Free Exercise Clause of the First Amendment as applied to families whose religious convictions prohibit the use of certified instructors. Such families, therefore, are exempt from the dictates of the teacher certification requirement.

I

Defendants Mark and Chris DeJonge taught their two school-age children at home in accordance with their religious faith. The DeJonges utilized a program administered by the Church of Christian Liberty and Academy of Arlington Heights, Illinois.

Because the DeJonges taught their children at home without the aid of certified teachers, the Ottawa Area Intermediate School District charged them with violating the compulsory education law, as codified in the School Code, MCL 380.1561(1), (3); MSA 15.41561(1), (3). This act requires parents of children from the age of six to sixteen to send their children to public schools or to state-approved nonpublic schools. To qualify as a state-approved nonpublic school, students must be instructed by certified teachers. MCL 388.553; MSA 15.1923.

At time of trial, the prosecution never questioned the adequacy of the DeJonges' instruction or the education the children received. Michael

McHugh, an employee of the Church of Christian Liberty and Academy, testified that his organization provided the DeJonges with "testing, individualized curriculum, and monitoring of the home school." Unpublished opinion of the Court of Appeals, decided August 8, 1989 (Docket No. 106149), p 2.

McHugh testified further that this educational program, in use since 1968, had been employed by "many of thousands of youngsters who have attended and successfully graduated from major colleges and universities throughout the United States. . . ." Indeed, with respect to the DeJonge children, the trial judge noted that he was "very impressed with the support that they have, the credentials of the witnesses that have testified and the reports that apparently are very, very favorable report on the education of the children."

The DeJonges testified that they began teaching their children at home in August of 1984 because they wished to provide them a "Christ centered education." The DeJonges believe that "the major purpose of education is to show a student how to face God, not just show him how to face the world."

That the DeJonges' opposition to the certification requirement was religiously motivated was beyond question. At the close of the proceedings, the trial judge concluded that he had no "question about the conviction or the sincerity of the DeJonges on this position," and that the teacher certification requirement conflicted with a "very, very honest and sincere religious conviction."

Nevertheless, the DeJonges were convicted and sentenced to two years probation for instructing their children without state certified teachers. They were each fined $200, required to test their children for academic achievement, and ordered to arrange for certified instruction.

The Ottawa Circuit Court affirmed their convictions, and the DeJonges appealed in the Court of Appeals, where their case was consolidated with People v Bennett. The Court affirmed both trial *272 court decisions, and reaffirmed their convictions on rehearing. 179 Mich App 225; 449 NW2d 899 (1989) (DeJonge II).

In so ruling, the Court recognized that with respect to the DeJonges the "burden of the state certification law on the belief is high, and there appears to be no room for compromise," DeJonge II, supra at 235. Nevertheless, the Court ruled that the certification requirement was constitutional as the least restrictive means to meet the state's interest.

On October 17, 1990, this Court, in lieu of granting leave to appeal, remanded the case to the Court of Appeals for reconsideration in light of recent case precedent. 436 Mich 875 (1990).

Following remand, the Court of Appeals again affirmed the defendants' convictions. 188 Mich App 447; 470 NW2d 433 (1991) (DeJonge III). The Court reiterated its prior findings, and added that "since Mr. DeJonge opposes all state involvement in the education of his children, this alternative [individual examinations] would impose just as great a burden on his religious beliefs. Accordingly, we reaffirm the DeJonges' convictions." Id. at 452.

On appeal before this Court, the DeJonges contend that the certification requirement violates their First Amendment right of free exercise of religion, and submit that the Court of Appeals misapplied the compelling interest test by not requiring the state to establish that the certification requirement is essential to and the least restrictive means of achieving a compelling state interest.

II

At issue then is whether Michigan's teacher certification requirement for home schools violates the Free Exercise Clause of the First Amendment of the United States Constitution as applied to the State of Michigan by the Fourteenth Amendment of the United States Constitution. The Free Exercise Clause proclaims: "Congress shall make no law respecting an establishment of religion, or prohibiting the free exercise thereof. . . ."

Thus, we begin our analysis by considering the historical underpinnings of the First Amendment. This Court has long held that the constitution must be interpreted in light of the original intent and understanding of its drafters. The framers' intent must be understood in conjunction with the intentions and understanding of the constitution held by its ratifiers:

The intent of the framers, however, must be used as part of the primary rule of "common understanding" described by Justice COOLEY: "'A constitution is made for the people and by the people. The interpretation that should be given it is that which reasonable minds, the great mass of the people themselves, would give it.'"

A necessary corollary of these principles is that the constitution can only properly be understood by studying its common meaning as well as "'the circumstances surrounding the adoption of a constitutional provision and the purpose sought to be accomplished. . . .'"

These rules of constitutional construction are indispensable because "[t]he literal construction of the words, without regard to their obvious purpose of protection, is to make the constitutional safeguard no more than a shabby hoax, a barrier of words, easily destroyed by other words. . . . A constitutional limitation must be construed to effectuate, not to abolish, the protection sought by it to be afforded." Lockwood v Comm'r of Revenue, 357 Mich 517, 556–557; 98 NW2d 753 (1959). Hence, a thorough examination of the historical origins of the Free Exercise Clause is essential to the proper disposition of the case at issue, and more important, to the preservation of religious freedom.

This American experiment includes an unprecedented protection of religious liberty from tyrannical government action. Springing forth from this nation's founding principle that government is "instituted for [the] protection of the rights of mankind," the Free Exercise of Religion Clause ensured protection from government interference as the first freedom in the Bill of Rights.

The prominence of religious liberty's protection in the Bill of Rights is no historical anomaly, but the consequence of America's vigorous clashes regarding religious freedom. The First Amendment's protection of religious liberty was born from the fires of persecution, forged by the minds of the Founding Fathers, and tempered in the struggle for freedom in America.

As our history forcefully attests, the Founding Fathers envisioned the protection of the free exercise of religion as an affirmative duty of the government mandated by the inherent nature of religious liberty, not one of mere "toleration" by government. Most significant in this history was the dramatic confrontation regarding the proposed renewal of Virginia's tax levy for the support of the established church. This embroilment bore James Madison's Memorial and Remonstrance Against Religious Assessments, delivered in the Virginia House of Burgess in opposition to the levy, as well as Thomas Jefferson's Virginia Bill of Religious Liberty, enacted in the levy's stead. Madison's Memorial and Remonstrance Against Religious Assessments explained as "a fundamental and undeniable truth" that religious liberty is a deeply private, fundamental, and inalienable right by which a citizen's religious beliefs and practices are shielded from the hostile intolerance of society, while Jefferson's Virginia Bill for Religious Liberty protected the right of the free exercise of religion, as well as barred state established churches. The Founders understood that this zealous protection of religious liberty was essential to the "preservation of a free government."

The Founding Fathers then reserved special protection for religious liberty as a fundamental freedom in the First Amendment of the constitution. This fortification of the right to the free exercise of religion was heralded as one of the Bill of Rights' most important achievements. Indeed, Jefferson proclaimed that "[n]o provision in our constitution ought to be dearer to man than that which protects the rights of conscience against the enterprises of the civil authority."

III

In Employment Div, Dep't of Human Resources v Smith, 494 US 872, 881; 110 S Ct 1595; 108 L Ed 2d 876 (1990), the Court ruled that the "Free Exercise Clause in conjunction with other constitutional protections, such as . . . the right of parents, acknowledged in Pierce [v Society of Sisters, 268 US 510; 45 S Ct 571; 69 L Ed 1070 (1925)], to direct the education of their children, see Wisconsin v Yoder, 406 US 205 [92 S Ct 1526; 32 L Ed 2d 15] (1972)," demands the application of strict scrutiny. Hence, Michigan's teacher certification requirement must undergo strict scrutiny to survive a free exercise challenge.

This strict scrutiny is manifested in the "compelling interest" test, which is composed of five elements:

(1) whether a defendant's belief, or conduct motivated by belief, is sincerely held; (2) whether a defendant's belief, or conduct motivated by belief, is

religious in nature; (3) whether a state regulation imposes a burden on the exercise of such belief or conduct; (4) whether a compelling state interest justifies the burden imposed upon a defendant's belief or conduct; (5) whether there is a less obtrusive form of regulation available to the state. Yoder, supra at 214–230; Dep't of Social Services v Emmanuel Baptist Preschool, 434 Mich 380, 391–396; 455 NW2d 1 (1990) (CAVANAGH, J., concurring), 430 (GRIFFIN, J., concurring).

A

The first element of the compelling interest test is met by the DeJonges because their belief is sincerely held. "[W]hile the 'truth' of a belief is not open to question, there remains the significant question whether it is 'truly held.' This is the threshold question of sincerity which must be resolved in every case. It is, of course, a question of fact. . . ." United States v Seeger, 380 US 163, 185; 85 S Ct 850; 13 L Ed 2d 733 (1965). As noted, after extensive trial testimony, the trial judge concluded that "[t]he Court does not have any question about the conviction or the sincerity of the DeJonges on this position." Furthermore, the state does not contest the sincerity of the DeJonges' beliefs.

B

Similarly, because the DeJonges' belief is religiously based, the second element of the compelling interest test is met. To be afforded the protection of the Free Exercise Clause, an individual's behavior must be religiously motivated, as the Court in Yoder, supra at 215–216, explained:

A way of life, however virtuous and admirable, may not be interposed as a barrier to reasonable state regulation of education if it is based on purely secular considerations; to have the protection of the Religion Clauses, the claims must be rooted in religious belief. . . . Thus, if the Amish asserted their claims because of their subjective evaluation and rejection of the contemporary secular values accepted by the majority, much as Thoreau rejected the social values of his time and isolated himself at Walden Pond, their claims would not rest on a religious basis. Thoreau's choice was philosophical and personal rather than religious, and such belief does not rise to the demands of the Religion Clauses.

Thus, this Court must determine whether a religious belief is sincerely held, not whether such beliefs are true or reasonable. United States v Ballard, 322 US 78, 86; 64 S Ct 882; 88 L Ed 1148 (1944). This Court must accept a worshiper's good-faith characterization that its activity is grounded in religious belief because "[i]t is not within the judicial ken to question the centrality of particular beliefs or practices to a faith, or the validity of particular litigants' interpretations of those creeds." Hernandez v Comm'r of Internal Revenue, 490 US 680, 699; 109 S Ct 2136; 104 L Ed 2d 766 (1989). This must be so because "[m]en may believe what they cannot prove. They may not be put to the proof of their religious doctrines or beliefs. Religious experiences which are as real as life to some may be incomprehensible to others." Ballard, supra at 86.

Nor is religious orthodoxy necessary to obtain the protection of the Free Exercise Clause. Religious belief and conduct need not be endorsed or mandated by a religious organization to be protected. Emmanuel Baptist Preschool, supra at 392 (CAVANAGH, J., concurring). Indeed, because popular religious beliefs are rarely threatened by elected legislators, the Free Exercise Clause's major benefactors are religious minorities or dissidents whose beliefs and worship are suppressed or shunned by the majority. To hold otherwise would be to deny that "Religion . . . must be left to the conviction and conscience of every man. . . ."

The DeJonges testified that they taught their children at home without complying with the certification requirement because they wished to provide for their children a "Christ-centered education." Because the DeJonges' faith professes "that parents are the ones that are responsible to God for the education of their children," they passionately believe that utilizing a state-certified teacher is sinful. Their faith, although unusual, may not be challenged or ignored.

C

The third element of the test is also met because the certification requirement clearly imposes a burden on the exercise of the DeJonges' religious freedom. A burden may be shown if the "affected individuals [would] be coerced by the Government's action into violating their religious beliefs [or whether] governmental action [would] penalize religious activity by denying any person an equal share of the rights, benefits, and privileges enjoyed by other citizens." Lyng v Northwest Indian Cemetery Protective Ass'n, 485 US 439, 449; 108 S Ct 1319; 99 L Ed 2d 534 (1988). Hence, "[a] claimed burden on religious beliefs may be deemed constitutionally insignificant, but only (1) if the claimant's beliefs do not create an irreconcilable conflict between the mandates of law and religious duty, or (2) if the legal requirement does not directly coerce the claimant to act contrary to religious belief. . . ." Emmanuel Baptist Preschool, supra at 393 (CAVANAGH, J., concurring). Put simply, the petitioner must prove that he has been "enforced, restrained, molested, or burdened . . . [or] otherwise suffer[ed], on account of his religious opinions or beliefs. . . ." The burden on religious liberty, however, need not be overwhelming, because "[e]ven subtle pressure diminishes the right of each individual to choose voluntarily what to believe." Lee v Weisman, 505 US ___; 112 S Ct 2649, 2665; 120 L Ed 2d 467 (1992) (Blackmun, J., concurring).

In the instant case, the findings of the trial court, to which this Court grants due deference, amply reveal that the teacher certification requirement directly and heavily burdens the DeJonges' exercise of their religion. As noted, the DeJonges believe that the word of God commands them to educate their children without state certification. Any regulation interfering with that commandment is state regulation of religion. The certification requirement imposes upon the DeJonges a loathsome dilemma: they must either violate the law of God to abide by the law of man, or commit a crime under the law of man to remain faithful to God. The requirement presents an "irreconcilable conflict between the mandates of law and religious duty. . . ." Emmanuel Baptist Preschool, supra at 393 (CAVANAGH, J., concurring).

Moreover, this is not a case in which the DeJonges must forgo a government benefit or privilege in lieu of their religious beliefs, because the state compels through criminal sanction both mandatory education and the certification requirement. In Yoder, the Court found that compulsory education for Amish children past the eighth grade violated the Free Exercise Clause because the criminal sanctions imposed compelled the Amish to violate their religious faith: "The impact of the compulsory-attendance law on respondents' practice of the Amish religion is not only severe, but inescapable, for the Wisconsin law affirmatively compels them, under threat of criminal sanction, to perform acts undeniably at odds with fundamental tenets of their religious beliefs." Id. at 218. Similarly, the state's enforcement of the teacher certification requirement compels the DeJonges to sin, as they have been coerced by the state to educate their children in direct violation of their religious faith. In other words, as applied to the DeJonges, the certification requirement "inescapably compels conduct that [plaintiffs] find objectionable for religious reasons." Bowen v Roy, 476 US 693, 706; 106 S Ct 2147; 90 L Ed 2d 735 (1986).[38] Indeed, perhaps the most striking state burden upon religious liberty imaginable, criminal prosecution, was imposed upon the DeJonges for following their interpretation of the word of God.

D

Finally, the certification requirement is unconstitutional because it fails to meet the remaining two prongs of the compelling interest test, which presume that a state's burden of the free exercise of religion is invalid unless the burden is essential to the fulfillment of a compelling state interest. Hence, strict scrutiny demands that (1) a state regulation be justified by a compelling state interest, and (2) the means chosen be essential to further that interest.

Furthermore, a compelling state interest must be truly compelling, threatening the safety or welfare of the state in a clear and present manner.

The state asserts that it has a compelling state interest in ensuring the adequate education of all children. Indeed, "[t]here is no doubt as to the power of a State, having a high responsibility for education of its citizens, to impose reasonable regulations for the control and duration of basic education. Providing public schools ranks at the very apex of the function of a State." Yoder, supra at 213 (citations omitted). The importance of compulsory education has been recognized because "some degree of education is necessary to prepare citizens to participate effectively and intelligently in our open political system if we are to preserve freedom and independence. Further, education prepares individuals to be self-reliant and self-sufficient participants in society." Id. at 221. Our commitment to education is deeply rooted in our history: "[t]he American people have always regarded education and acquisition of knowledge as matters of supreme importance which should be diligently promoted." Meyer v Nebraska, 262 US 390, 400; 43 S Ct 625; 67 L Ed 1042 (1923).

Michigan has an equally deeply rooted commitment to education. Article 8, § 1 of our constitution, paralleling the language of the Northwest Ordinance of 1787, proclaims the vital nature of education in Michigan:

Religion, morality and knowledge being necessary to good government and the happiness of mankind, schools and the means of education shall forever be encouraged.

*289 Nevertheless, our rights are meaningless if they do not permit an individual to challenge and be free from those abridgments of liberty that are otherwise vital to society:

[F]reedom of worship . . . is not limited to things that do not matter much. That would be a mere shadow of freedom. The test of its substance is the right to differ as to things that touch the heart of the existing order. [West Virginia Bd of Ed v Barnette, 319 US 624, 638, 642; 63 S Ct 1178; 87 L Ed 2d 1628 (1943).]

Hence, Michigan's interest in compulsory education is not absolute and must yield to the constitutional liberties protected by the First Amendment. The United States Supreme Court explained:

Thus, a State's interest in universal education, however highly we rank it, is not totally free from a balancing process when it impinges on fundamental rights and interests, such as those specifically protected by the Free Exercise Clause of the First Amendment, and the traditional interest of parents with respect to the religious upbringing of their children so long as they, in the words of Pierce [supra at 535], "prepare [them] for additional obligations." [Yoder, supra at 214.]

Although the state asserts that "its interest in its system of compulsory education is so compelling that" the DeJonges' religious practices must give way, "[w]here fundamental claims of religious freedom are at stake, . . . we cannot accept such a sweeping claim . . . we must searchingly examine the interests that the State seeks to promote . . . and the impediment of those objectives that would flow from recognizing the claimed [religious] exemption." Yoder, supra at 221.

Indeed, such a searching examination in the instant case is enlightening because it reveals that the state has focused upon the incorrect governmental interest. The state's interest is not ensuring that the goals of compulsory education are met, because the state does not contest that the DeJonges are succeeding at fulfilling such aims. Rather, the state's interest is simply the certification requirement of the private school act, not the general objectives of compulsory education. The interest the state pursues is the manner of education, not its goals.

Hence, the state's narrow interest in maintaining the certification requirement must be weighed against the DeJonges' fundamental right of the free exercise of religion. Because exemptions are the remedy provided in cases in which a general law abridges religious liberty, this Court must focus on the effect granting such religious exemptions would have on the purported state interest. If this Court does not find a substantial effect on the asserted interest, an exemption is warranted because no compelling interest is affected. Yoder, supra at 237; Sherbert, supra at 407. In the case at issue, if the state fails to prove that exemptions from the teacher certification requirement impair the state's asserted interest, then no balancing is necessary. The state, therefore, must establish that enforcing the certification requirement, without exception, is essential to ensure the education required by the compulsory education law. United States v Lee, 455 US 252, 257–258; 102 S Ct 1051; 71 L Ed 2d 127 (1982). If less intrusive means fulfill the government's purported interest, then an exemption must be granted and the alternative implemented.

Nevertheless, the state in the instant case has failed to provide evidence or testimony that supports the argument that the certification requirement is essential to the preservation of its asserted interest. Conversely, while the record is barren of evidence supporting the state's claim, it clearly indicates that the DeJonge children are receiving more than an adequate education: they are fulfilling the academic and socialization goals of compulsory education without certified teachers or the state's interference. Nor has the state suggested that the DeJonges have jeopardized the health or safety of their children, or have a potential for significant social burdens. In sum, the state has failed to provide one scintilla of evidence that the DeJonge children have suffered for the want of certified teachers; it has failed to prove a "clear and present" or "grave and immediate" danger to the welfare of the children that justifies the onerous burden placed upon the DeJonges' exercise of their religious beliefs.

Furthermore, the experience of our sister states provides irrefutable evidence that the certification requirement is not an interest worthy of being deemed "compelling." The nearly universal consensus of our sister states is to permit home schooling without demanding teacher certified instruction. Indeed, many states have recently rejected the archaic notion that certified instruction is necessary for home schools. Within the last decade, over twenty states have repealed teacher certification requirements for home schools. Devins, Fundamentalist Christian Educators v State: An inevitable compromise, 60 Geo Wash L R 818, 819 (1992).

The relevance of the practice of our sister states becomes clear when empirical studies disprove a positive correlation between teacher certification and quality education. A study by Dr. Brian Ray of the National Home Education Research Institute found that "there was no [statistically significant] difference in students' total reading, total math, or total language scores based on the teacher certification status (i.e., neither parent had been certified, one had been, or both had been) of their parents." National Home Education Research Institute, A Nationwide Study of Home Education: Family Characteristics, Legal Matters, and Student Achievement (Salem, Oregon: National Home Education Research Institute, 1990), p 12. The compelling nature of the teacher certification requirement is not extant.

E

In any event, even if the state possessed a compelling state interest, it has failed to prove that the certification requirement is essential to that interest. The Court of Appeals asserted that "[t]he teacher certification requirement is a backbone in the protection of" state education, and that the DeJonges did not "propose[] an alternative" to teacher certification. DeJonge II, supra at 236; DeJonge III, supra. But, the record fails to support this assertion. In Sherbert, supra at 407, the Court held that because the plaintiff had "no proof whatever to warrant" fears that its compelling interest would be endangered by alternative means, the state had failed to meet its burden. Similarly, in the instant case, the state's sweeping assertion must be turned aside when it is not supported by evidence. The state's contention is particularly suspect when no other state has such "a backbone." To find that of all the states in the Union only Michigan meets the aims of compulsory education is untenable and flies in the face of the aforementioned studies.

Moreover, in Yoder, supra at 222–223, the Supreme Court held that the success of Amish teaching methods proved that the state's compulsory *296 education system did "little to serve" the state's interest. The Court ruled that because "[t]his case, of course, is not one in which any harm to the physical or mental health of the child or to the public safety, peace, order, or welfare has been demonstrated or may be properly inferred," the state's argument that its power as parens patriae permitted it to extend secondary education to children regardless of the religious wishes of their parents, must fail. Yoder, supra at 230. Similarly, in the instant case, the success of the Church of Christian Liberty and Academy and the DeJonges repudiates the state's argument that the certification requirement is essential to the goals of compulsory education.

Indeed, the State of Michigan itself now permits noncertified teachers possessing a bachelor's degree to teach in nonpublic schools; nor is the certification requirement enforced with regard to substitute teachers in public schools. Even Michigan, then, does not command a certification requirement for the great majority of its students, but only for those taught by their parents at home.

The state, however, argues that the proposed alternative means are more intrusive upon the religious beliefs of the DeJonges than the current certification requirement. We, however, do not presume to make that judgment. We believe that the DeJonges are the best judges of which regulations are the most burdensome or least intrusive upon their religion. To entertain the notion that either this Court or the state has the insight to interpret the DeJonges' religion more correctly than they is simply "an arrogant pretension."

Similarly, the Court of Appeals assertion that because Mark DeJonge's beliefs would bar all state interference, the certification requirement is therefore constitutional, is incredulous. First, the assertion that the DeJonges' beliefs prohibit any and all types of state monitoring or guidance is erroneous; the DeJonges have administered standardized tests and emphasized at oral argument that they do not object to such testing. More important, the constitution forbids the state to impose any regulation that burdens religion and is not essential to the fulfillment of a compelling state interest. Because teacher certification does not meet that constitutional burden, the DeJonges must be exempt from it regardless of their other religious views if a less burdensome regulation may be enacted. To hold otherwise would be to sanction the most intrusive and egregious infringement of religious beliefs because another intrusion, although much less burdensome, also burdens a religious belief.

Furthermore, the Court of Appeals erroneously placed the burden of proof upon the DeJonges. The Court of Appeals, by requiring that the individual burdened by governmental regulation prove that alternatives exist, while at the same time accepting at face value unsubstantiated assertions by the state, has turned constitutional jurisprudence on its head. Our citizens need not "propose an alternative" to be afforded their constitutional liberties. Lee, supra at 257–258; Yoder, supra at 233–234. We are persuaded that the burden of proof correctly placed in the instant case is fatal to the state's certification requirement.

IV

In sum we conclude that the historical underpinnings of the First Amendment of the United States Constitution and the case law in support of it compels the conclusion that the imposition of the certification requirement upon the DeJonges violates the Free Exercise Clause. We so conclude because we find that the certification requirement is not essential to nor is it the least restrictive means of achieving the state's claimed interest. Thus, we reaffirm "that sphere of inviolable conscience and belief which is the mark of a free people." Weisman, 112 S Ct 2658. We hold that the teacher certification requirement is an unconstitutional violation of the Free Exercise Clause of the First Amendment as applied to families whose religious convictions prohibit the use of certified instructors. Such families, therefore, are exempt from the dictates of the teacher certification requirement.

Accordingly, we reverse the DeJonge convictions.

CAVANAGH, C. J., and GRIFFIN, J., concurred with RILEY, J.

LEVIN, J. (concurring).

I join in the reversal of the convictions because I agree with the majority that the state failed to discharge its burden of showing that the teacher certification requirement is the least intrusive means of discharging its interest in the education of the DeJonge children.

MALLETT, J.

Source: *People v. DeJonge*, 501 NW 2d 127 (1993).

See also: Children's Defense Fund (1973–); Christian Coalition of America (1988–)

Further Reading

"About HSLDA." 2016. Home School Legal Defense Association. http://www.hslda.org/about/.

Center for Responsive Politics. 2016. "Home School Legal Defense Association Campaign Contribution Patterns." Opensecrets.org. https://www.opensecrets.org/pacs/lookup2.php?strID=C00390526.

Gaither, Milton. 2008. *Homeschool: An American History.* New York: Palgrave MacMillan.

"Home Schooling: Fast Facts." 2016. National Center for Education Statistics. https://nces.ed.gov/fastfacts/display.asp?id=91.

"The Parental Rights Amendment." 2016. Parentalrights.org. http://www.parentalrights.org/amendment.

People v. DeJonge. 1993. Justia. http://law.justia.com/cases/michigan/supreme-court/1993/91479-5.html.

Human Rights Campaign (1980–)

Founded originally as a PAC in 1980 by Steve Endean (1948–1993), the Human Rights Campaign Fund (HRCF) has grown to become the largest advocacy group in the United States for lesbian, gay, bisexual (this is the largest group within the LGBTQ community), transgender, and queer (LGBTQ) rights. In the beginning, the organization's method of operating was to raise money and then use that money to support political candidates sympathetic to gay and lesbian rights. This strategy proved to be highly effective, with many of the supported candidates winning elections. While not always successful, HRCF quickly gained prominence, even hosting a fund-raiser in 1982 with former vice president Walter Mondale (1928–) who was running for president. In 1995, the PAC transitioned to a member-based advocacy group, changing its name to the Human Rights Campaign (HRC). Today, the organization has over 1.5 million members.

The executive director at the time of the change to a member organization, attorney Elizabeth Birch (1956–), played a key role in this reorganization that greatly expanded the outreach of the HRC. Their mission statement reads:

The Human Rights Campaign and the Human Rights Campaign Foundation together serve as America's largest civil rights organization working to achieve LGBTQ equality. By inspiring and engaging individuals and communities, HRC strives to end discrimination against LGBTQ people and realize a world that achieves fundamental fairness and equality for all. The Human Rights Campaign envisions a world where lesbian, gay, bisexual, transgender and queer people are ensured equality and embraced as full members of society at home, at work and in every community. (Human Rights Campaign 2017)

The broad focus of the HRC is political, social, economic, and legislative equality for the LGBTQ community. Specific fields of interest for the HRC include adoption (working to ensure that qualified LGBTQ people are allowed to adopt children); allies (non-LGTBQ individuals who are nonetheless supportive of the community); campus communities (helping to create safe, welcoming environments for college students); educating young people and bully prevention; providing resources for those who are "coming out"; communities of color, which often face additional discrimination; hate crimes; HIV and AIDS; marriage equality; parenting; and the workplace (ensuring a nonhostile working environment).

The Human Rights Campaign Foundation (HRCF) is the 501(c)(3) tax-exempt charitable wing of the HRC that works to benefit the LGBTQ community in a variety of ways. Outreach, educational, and advocacy programs include the All Children—All Families Project, which seeks to assist LBTQ adoptive and foster groups through working with child welfare agencies. The Welcoming Schools Project works to encourage schools to provide a positive environment for LBTQ students, with a focus on antibullying efforts and avoiding stereotyping. The Youth Well-Being Project also seeks to benefit LGBTQ youth by educating young people on the importance of inclusion and diversity. The Health & Aging Program focuses on elder care and enhancing the quality of life for senior LGBTQ people, ensuring respect and proper treatment for people in long-term care as well as health-centric advocacy for LGBTQ people of all ages. Part of this program is the Healthcare Equality Index, which reports on how well various health care providers perform when it comes to caring for the LGBTQ community. Outreach targets are not only medical providers but also include those conducting research as well as policy makers. The Religion and Faith Program concerns the inclusion of LGBTQ population in communities of faith. Parts of this program include Triumph through Faith, which is a project that advocates for policies and laws pertaining to marriage equality and other LGBTQ issues in the specific contexts of religious sensitivity. Also within the Religion and Faith Program is A La Familia, where the objective is on working toward greater inclusion of LGBTQ people in Latino communities. Another project is the Summer Institute for Religious and Theological Study, which seeks to educate and influence seminary students in LBTQ matters with the intent of making more inclusive religious spaces.

HRC also runs the Workplace Equality Program, which has two main projects designed to enhance workplace inclusion and better the professional lives of LGBTQ people. One is the Corporate Equality Index, which is an annual survey involving some of the largest businesses in America. The survey measures variables pertaining to LGBTQ community members and the workplace. This program is supported by two projects, one of which is the Buyer's Guide that shows consumers what companies are the most equitable vis-à-vis LGBTQ employment policies, and the other is the Best Places to Work annual list, which provides potential employees with information relevant to which companies provide the best workplaces for LGBTQ people. The Degrees of Equality Project is the other main project within the Workplace Equality Program; it also seeks to enhance workplace inclusion by providing resources to educate both employers and employees on LGBTQ-related employment policies.

Another important HRC sponsored is the Youth & Campus Engagement Program, which focuses on working with LGBTQ youth transitioning to college or employment, and is supported by three primary projects. One is the U Internship Project, another is the Historically Black College and University (HBCU) Project, and another is the Coming Out Project; as the names suggest, these projects focus on providing internships, assisting LGBTQ communities at HBCUs, and supporting those sharing their identities for the first time, respectively. Finally, there is HRC Global, which focuses on LGBTQ rights worldwide. Its key areas of focus include building partnerships with organizations globally; advocating for LBGTQ rights with various intergovernmental organizations, such as the United Nations; the convening of the Global Innovative Advocacy Summit, which brings in thinkers from around the world to discuss their work; Global Fellows, which identifies key LBGTQ leaders and brings them to Washington, D.C., for advanced training in advocacy; and Thought Leadership, which educates people globally.

The HRC has had many successes, both in the realm of legislative outcomes and in cultural attitude shifts. Here, perhaps the most salient dynamic is the remarkable shift in the public's attitude toward same-sex marriage in tandem with the legalization of the same. The American public went from vastly opposing such legalization to the majority supporting it, and in 2015 the Supreme Court ruled in the case of *Obergefell v. Hodges* that marriage equality was a constitutionally guaranteed right that must be recognized by all states and the District of Columbia.

Other successful lobbying outcomes include the 2009 passage of the Hate Crimes Prevention Act (also known as the Matthew Shepard Act), which expanded previous legislation that protected people based on race, color, religion and national origin, by including protections specific to the LGBTQ community, as well as for those with disabilities. Additionally, the 2009 legislation broadened the parameters of protection by negating the previous requirement that a victim needed to be engaged in a federally protected activity (for example, voting). Another example is the 2010 repeal of the "Don't Ask, Don't Tell" (DADT) policy involving LGBTQ personnel in the military. Prior to DADT (1994), it was illegal for LGBTQ people to serve in the military. DADT attempted a compromise, making it illegal for LGBTQ people to openly serve in the military. Its repeal 17 years later marked another political, legislative, and cultural milestone for civil rights. In 2009, the HRC also successfully lobbied for overturning the United States' travel restrictions for those with HIV wishing to visit or become citizens. In August 2017, President Donald Trump (1946–) signed an executive order prohibiting transgender persons from serving in the military. However, in 2018, several lower federal courts blocked its implementation.

Like most political groups, parties, and organizations that have shaped America, the HRC is not without controversy. Perhaps most notably, the HRC was against the inclusion of transgender issues throughout the 1990s and 2000s. Indeed, as executive director, Birch fought to prevent the inclusion of transgender rights in pending employment nondiscrimination legislation. Historically, gay rights advocacy has been disinclined to embrace transgender advocacy for fear of alienating the dominant culture by association with those whose lifestyle may be seen as more transgressive in nature. However, this cultural proclivity has changed overtime, and HRC's current executive director, Chad Griffin (1973–), has both apologized for the exclusionary rhetoric and conduct and taken steps to be more inclusionary toward the transgender community, including supporting legislation that would protect the LGBTQ community from workplace discrimination, which was passed by the Senate in 2013 but remains stalled in the House. Crimes against the transgender community, especially people of color, have recently increased. Furthermore, the HRC has been criticized as being elitist, or too establishment oriented, and was chided by some for endorsing Secretary Hillary Clinton over Senator Bernie Sanders in the 2016 Democratic Primary.

Evan O. Renfro

See also: AIDS Coalition to Unleash Power (1987–); GLAAD (1985–); National LGBTQ Task Force (1973–)

Further Reading

Astor, Maggie. 2017. "Violence Against Transgender People Is on the Rise, Advocates Say." *New York Times*, November 9, 2017. https://www.nytimes.com/2017/11/09/us/transgender-women-killed.html.

Cornell University Library. 2006. "25 Years of Political Influence: The Records of the Human Rights Campaign." http://rmc.library.cornell.edu/HRC/index.html.

Human Rights Campaign. 2017. http://www.hrc.org/.

I

Independence League/Party (1906–1914)

Largely the political vehicle of newspaper publisher and tycoon William Randolph Hearst (1863–1951), the Independence League was formed in 1906 as an outgrowth of the Municipal Ownership League (MOL), one of the many Progressive Era nonpartisan, antimonopoly organizations that advocated for public ownership of utilities, among other restrictions against business consolidation and the accumulation of wealth into the hands of the few.

In 1904 Hearst, who had been serving in the House of Representatives as a Democrat, unsuccessfully sought his party's nomination for president. The lack of enthusiasm at the St. Louis convention for his candidacy convinced Hearst that he could not win on his fame alone, and he began laying plans to run for the governorship of New York in 1906 as a platform to gaining the White House.

Hearst was a polarizing figure. Although wealthy himself, he touted a form of populism that decried the concentration of wealth in the form of monopolies and trusts. His supporters considered him a man of the people who exposed the corruption of the plutocrats; his enemies saw a self-serving demagogue who cynically attacked others in order to increase his newspaper circulation and, hence, his own wealth and power. The Democratic establishment did not trust him, and his partisan colleagues in the House openly ridiculed him whenever they had the opportunity.

In 1905 Judge Samuel Seabury's Municipal Ownership League (MOL) nominated Hearst as its candidate for mayor of New York City. The MOL was dedicated to clean government and the public ownership of urban utilities, long-standing Hearst positions. Despite a spirited campaign against incumbent mayor George B. McClellan Jr., a Tammany Hall machine Democrat, Hearst lost in a surprisingly close election.

As Hearst prepared to run for the governorship of New York in 1906, he saw a need to expand his appeal and name recognition to upstate voters. To appear less radical and narrowly urban, the MOL was renamed the Independence League. Hearst financed and encouraged the formation of affiliated clubs in cities, counties, and towns throughout the state. Never bashful about using his business empire to serve his political ends, Hearst formed a new publication, *Farm and Home*, to reach the rural electorate.

The Republicans nominated Charles Evan Hughes for governor, a formidable candidate who made his mark prosecuting business corruption. With no clear frontrunner of their own, the Democrats nominated Hearst at their convention in Buffalo. Having secured a major party nomination, Hearst and his small group of loyalists quickly began to the push the organization that they had created into the background as part of an effort to maximize the candidate's draw with Democrats.

Although Hearst's antimonopoly, antirailroad, pro-good government, and pro-corporate tax campaign adhered to the principles of the League, a series of conflicts erupted between Gilsey House, a name for Hearst's clique of loyalists, and local clubs over the question of fusion and nominations. In the closing days of September, for example, Hearst booted the League candidates for attorney general, controller, and engineer off the statewide ballot to give those to Democrats. The Buffalo League defied Gilsey's order to fuse with Democrats by nominating its own candidates for local offices. The local league in another district was so upset by the fusion nominee that it repudiated him and backed the Republican instead.

These sorts of battles were waged throughout the state as the local leagues sought to remain loyal to the concept of nonpartisanship while Hearst sought to solidify his standing with regular Democrats. Such high-handed disregard for the local organizations led to legal battles and courtroom drama. Max Ihmsen, Hearst's campaign manager, admitted under oath that Gilsey House made decisions without any consideration of, input from, or consultation with the local leagues.

All of Hearst's maneuverings and scheming came to naught when the voters handed a clear victory to Hughes. After this defeat, the League challenged the New York secretary of state to grant the organization party status. Under New York election laws, a party designation could be awarded only to organizations that had won 45,000 votes. According to the Canvassing Board, only 17,837 votes of the 673,268 cast for Hearst were on the Independence League line. The vast majority of ballots marked for Hearst were counted as Democrat votes. The League alleged that this was inaccurate and that the number of votes on their line was much closer to 110,000, well in excess of the number required to win party designation. Local clubs saw an advantage to gaining party status. Parties had to follow certain rules, and it opened up a possibility to challenge Hearst's monopolistic control over the League.

As the presidential election year approached, Hearst decided to take the Independence League onto the national political stage, despite a concerted effort by Democrats and others to dissuade him from doing so. Hearst harbored no illusions that the Independence League could win in 1908, but he hoped that as the public grew dissatisfied with the two major parties, his party could emerge as a genuine contender by 1912.

On February 22, 1908, the Independence League's provisional national committee met in Chicago with Hearst as chairman. The 125 delegates authorized a national convention and approved a declaration of principles that broadly included preservation of American liberty, clean elections and government, opportunity in business, and equality of all before the law. In addition to their long-standing support of public ownership of utilities, the League platform called for the direct election of U.S. senators, an income tax, campaign finance regulations, currency reform, naval construction, and the adoption of a referendum.

The Independence Party held its convention at the Orchestra Hall in Chicago in late July. Not seeking the nomination for himself, Hearst advocated for Thomas L.

Hisgen of Massachusetts, a former Democrat who had been the unsuccessful League candidate for governor of Massachusetts in a close election the year before. Hisgen was an axle grease and kerosene manufacturer who successfully fought off Standard Oil's efforts to buy him out and destroy his business, which made him something of a hero among the antimonopolists. The vice-presidential nomination went to John Temple Graves of Georgia, a newspaper editor who might appeal to populists.

Thomas Hisgen stumped the country, proclaiming the economic, political, and social evils that business consolidation was causing in the United States; however, he was frequently overshadowed by Hearst at their joint campaign appearances. In an effort to gain greater attention from the electorate, Hearst resorted to a publicity ploy that he was all too familiar with. In September, he began releasing embarrassing private correspondence that he had obtained several years before from a disaffected employee of John Archbold, a Standard Oil executive. Though the letters were damning of Archbold and Senator Joseph Foraker, a Republican from Ohio, they failed to benefit the Independence Party.

Hisgen and Graves received just 82,580 votes, or one-half of 1 percent of the total cast. The Independence Party ran far behind not only the two major parties but also the Prohibition and Socialist parties.

Such a dismal showing and the damage the Archbold letters stunt had done to Hearst's reputation ended the Independence Party's influence as a national political force. However, the party remained active in New York City and statewide, to a lesser extent, until 1914. In the 1909 primaries, the Tammany Hall regulars captured control of the Independence Party's ballot line and symbols by exploiting the naivete and inexperience of their opponents. It took a ruling by the New York Supreme Court to force their return. Hearst followed this embarrassing incident by running for mayor of New York for a second time in 1909. Unlike the first race, Hearst finished third behind William Gaynor, the Democratic candidate and winner, and the Republican. The Independence Party ran a slate of candidates in 1910, with John J. Hopper as governor and Hearst as lieutenant governor, but, again, they finished in the back of the pack.

In 1911 Hearst abandoned the Independence League and returned to the Democrats, telling members that this was the only effective way to break the hold Tammany Hall boss Charles Murphy had over New York City. The rank and file rejected this course, further dividing the already fractious Independence Party. While the party continued to exist over the next couple of elections and fused with the Progressive Party in 1912, it faded into obscurity without Hearst's financial support and notoriety. Hearst's prediction that the public would reject the two major parties in favor of his Independence Party failed to materialize, as did the illusion of emerging as the strongest third-party alternative.

Gregory J. Dehler

See also: Progressive Party/Bull Moose (1912–1916)

Further Reading

Coletta, Paola A. 1971. "Election of 1908." In *History of American Presidential Elections, 1789–1968*, vol. 3, edited by Arthur M. Schlesinger Jr. New York: Chelsea House.

Mulrine, Barbara M. 2011. *The Price of Honor: The Life and Times of George Brinton McClellan Jr.* Madison, NJ: Farleigh Dickinson University Press.

Procter, Ben. 1998. *William Randolph Hearst: The Early Years, 1863–1910.* New York: Oxford University Press.

Proctor, Ben. 2007. *William Randolph Hearst: The Later Years, 1911–1951.* New York: Oxford University Press.

Richardson, Darcy G. 2007. *Others: Third Parties During the Populist Period.* Lincoln, NE: iUniverse.

Swanberg, S. A. 1961. *Citizen Hearst: A Biography of William Randolph Hearst.* New York: Charles Scribner's Sons.

Innocence Project (1992–)

The Innocence Project, founded by Barry Scheck and Peter Neufeld, is a nonprofit legal organization focusing on litigation strategies directed toward exonerating wrongfully convicted individuals through DNA testing. Through public policy advocacy, the Innocence Project is also dedicated to redressing the causes of wrongful convictions and reforming the criminal justice system to prevent future injustices. The Innocence Project works to hold the criminal justice system accountable for unjust convictions and the imprisonment of innocent people and provides legal representation to review claims of innocence of individuals convicted in an effort to promote accuracy, integrity, and truth in the criminal justice system. The Innocence Project primarily focuses on cases where DNA is available to exonerate the wrongfully convicted, as DNA can definitively establish a defendant's innocence.

A wrongful conviction is when a person is accused and convicted of a crime he or she did not commit. The error rate of wrongful convictions is estimated to range from half of 1 percent to 10 percent of all convictions. The exact error rate cannot be calculated, but it is clear that errors are made, people are wrongfully convicted, and it is a matter of concern for the criminal justice system.

Scholars argue that there are many factors that can contribute to an innocent defendant being erroneously convicted. The factors include the race of the victim and the perpetrator; the age and previous criminal history of the defendant; the punitive nature of the state (i.e., how "tough on crime" the state is); constitutional violations, such as when the defendant is not provided an attorney; forensic science errors; eyewitness misidentification; false testimony of witnesses; faulty law enforcement practices; false confessions coerced by the police; and inadequate defense, as court-appointed attorneys are often under-resourced and thereby limited in their ability to conduct an investigation on behalf of their clients. In its work to overcome these factors that contribute to increasing the likelihood of wrongful convictions, the Innocence Project has four main areas of focus.

First, the organization aims to exonerate the innocent by providing direct legal representation, research and critical assistance through extensive investigations and new technologies to prove innocence in a court of law, but to also bring substantive changes to the system to end unjust convictions and imprisonment. To date, the Innocence Project has assisted in the exoneration of 344 people by DNA testing. The use of DNA to free innocent people is irrefutable proof that innocent people are wrongfully convicted and that these wrongful convictions are not isolated events. Indeed, the ability to demonstrate that innocent people are frequently convicted and imprisoned means that systemic shortcomings exist in the system.

Second, the Innocence Project seeks to improve the criminal justice system by reforming the laws governing the system through policy advocacy, using DNA testing to prove innocence, and securing compensation for innocent people who have been harmed by wrongful convictions. The Innocence Project's policy department prioritizes overturning wrongful convictions and reforming the use of unjust practices in the criminal justice system, such as the use of eyewitness identification, because eyewitness misidentification is the greatest contributor to wrongful convictions. In case after case, DNA has proven that eyewitness identification can be exceedingly inaccurate due to limits of vision and memory, law enforcement procedures, visual perception of the victim, conditions of the actual crime, the race of the perpetrator, and elevated emotion and duress due to distracting elements like a gun or knife (National Academy of Sciences 2014). The Innocence Project works to implement eyewitness identification reforms to reduce reliance on eyewitness identification.

The Innocence Project is also working on eliminating the use of improper forensic techniques, which is the second-greatest contributor to wrongful convictions. Many forensic techniques developed to solve crimes lack scientific standards of quality, which leads to improper forensic testimony. There is also a lack of training and insufficient resources for scientists, which can reduce the reliability of test results. The unfolding scandal in the Massachusetts state laboratory is a dramatic example demonstrating how one person in the state drug lab analysis unit can lead to wrongful convictions. Reports indicate that an analyst falsified thousands of drug tests over nine years involving 34,000 criminal cases. At the time of this writing, Massachusetts is still trying to figure out how to repair the damage wrought on the system and individuals wrongfully convicted. The defendants in these cases are represented by the ACLU of Massachusetts and are seeking new trials (or to have their convictions vacated) based on this massive fraud.

Third, the Innocence Project seeks to reform criminal justice policies by working through the legal system to change the leading causes of wrongful convictions in order to prevent future injustices. The Innocence Project's Strategic Litigation Department uses strategies to educate and inform judges, attorneys, and policy makers about the use of inaccurate and faulty evidence. The Strategic Litigation Department files *amicus curiae* briefs, supports defense attorneys, provides legal counsel to individuals, and works to pass legislation to limit the use of unreliable evidence in court.

Finally, the Innocence Project provides support for the exonerated who face the formidable task of reinventing their lives, clearing their names, reclaiming their identity, reunifying with family, and transitioning back into society. When individuals are wrongfully convicted and their conviction is overturned, they return to society, and the Innocent Project provides support for the formidable task of reentering society. Many men and women who have spent decades in prison struggle with the transition. The Innocence Project aims to meet the individual needs of clients, including helping them to secure jobs and other support to restore their lives.

Keesha M. Middlemass

See also: Equal Justice Initiative (1989–)

Further Reading

Borchard, Edwin. 1932. *Convicting the Innocent: Sixty-Five Actual Errors of Criminal Justice.* New York: Garden City Publishing.

Middlemass, Keesha. 2017. *Convicted & Condemned: The Politics and Policies of Prisoner Reentry.* New York: New York University Press.

National Academy of Sciences. 2014. *Identifying the Culprit: Assessing Eyewitness Identification.* Washington, D.C.: The National Academies Press. http://www.innocenceproject.org/wp-content/uploads/2016/02/NAS-Report-ID.pdf.

International Brotherhood of Teamsters (1903–)

The International Brotherhood of Teamsters ("teamster" was originally a term for a person who drove a team of draft animals; it has since been used in reference to truck drivers) is one of the oldest and largest labor unions in the United States. It was founded in 1903 and is the product of a merger between the Team Drivers International Union (TDIU), a group that had begun in 1901 and had a membership of 1,700, and the Teamsters National Union, a group made up of drivers who had broken off from the TDIU. At the urging of American Federation of Labor (AFL) head Samuel Gompers (1850–1924), the two unions worked out their differences, merged, and created the International Brotherhood of Teamsters (IBT) in August 1903. Cornelius Shea (1872–1929) was elected the new union's General President. Today, the union represents both blue-collar and professional workers in a variety of professions, in both the public and private sectors.

The Teamsters struggled in the beginning. Lacking supportive labor laws and victimized by judicial rulings that allowed antitrust laws to be used as anti-union weapons, the early twentieth century was a difficult time for all unions. A major setback in a strike at the Chicago-based Montgomery Ward Company in 1905 forced the union to regroup. That process began at the 1907 convention when Dan Tobin (1875–1955), a young leader from Local 25 in Boston, was elected general president. Tobin led the Teamsters for the next 45 years, setting them on the road to increased influence and prosperity.

Under Tobin the union engaged in an aggressive organizing effort, seeking to expand and broaden its membership base, and in turn its revenue and public profile. The type of driver who came under the Teamsters umbrella was broadened to include gravel haulers, beer and milk wagon drivers, as well as bakery deliverymen. In short order, the teamsters began representing drivers of the new "motor trucks," a move that put them in the forefront of the developing modern transportation industry.

Success begat success, and as the union grew, it was able to secure ever better contracts for its workers. With increased wages, the Teamsters' status in the U.S. work force was enhanced. In addition, the Teamsters cultivated a reputation for openness and inclusion, being one of the first unions to begin organizing women while also showing an early openness to racial equality declaring that the "Teamsters know no color line."

The 1920s were a challenging decade for the nation's unions as businesses continued to grow and expand unhindered by federal and state regulation, until the sudden downturn that signaled the start of the Great Depression. The Great Depression was a challenging time for labor, but the Teamsters continued their efforts until 1934, when a strike in Minnesota proved to be a watershed event.

With Minneapolis being one of the nation's major hauling centers as well as a major Midwestern distribution center, Local 574 sought to organize the area's drivers. Emboldened by victory in a local coal yard, Local 574 had a rush of new members and determined to expand its role as the union representative of the city's major workers. However, when many of the Minneapolis companies refused to recognized the newly revitalized union, Local 574 opted to strike. A full-scale, citywide strike on May 16 brought the city to a commercial standstill.

The strike benefited from widespread support, though violence soon broke out. Within 10 days most of the city's employers had agreed to a large number of the union's demands. The state's governor, Floyd Olson (1891–1936), appointed mediators, which resolved other issues associated with the strike. However, once the strikers returned to work, many companies reneged on their agreement. As a result, another strike, which began on July 17, erupted into even greater violence, much of which came at the hands of the police. While Olson declared martial law, clashes between the National Guard and the union not only added to the tension but also increased public sympathy for the strikers. The strikes led to the acceptance of the union's major demands while also serving to lay the groundwork for a strong union tradition in Minneapolis and the Midwest.

The Teamsters played an active role in World War II (1939–1945). President Franklin D. Roosevelt (1882–1945) sent Teamsters president Dan Tobin to Britain to observe and then report on how the unions there helped with the war effort. After Tobin urged organized labor to refrain from any work stoppages, the Teamsters led an effort to secure signed pledges to that effect. In addition, the union played an active role buying millions of dollars in war bonds. The union and its many locals were also tremendously active in local activities like rubber and scrap metal drives that were so important to the war effort. While Teamsters served in all branches of the service, female members helped keep the domestic part of the nation's war machine operating.

The postwar period brought prosperity and controversy to the Teamsters. The union's membership continued to climb, reaching one million in 1949. However, in 1952, following a series of fierce internal battles, Dan Tobin resigned as president, and executive vice president Dave Beck (1894–1993), allied with former rival James (Jimmy) Hoffa (1913–1975), emerged victorious. However, soon after Beck's ascension to the presidency, rumors of organized crime influence within the union began to circulate. Responding to these rumors, as well as broader concerns, in 1957, the U.S. Senate established the Select Committee on Improper Activities in Labor and Management, also known as the McClellan Committee for its chairman, Arkansas Senator John McClellan (1896–1977). The hearings cast a poor light on Beck and the Teamsters. The resulting criminal investigations led to criminal charges and a 1959 conviction of Beck for crimes relating to his work as president.

At the Teamster's subsequent annual convention, executive vice president Jimmy Hoffa was elected to succeed him. As president, Hoffa continued to enhance his reputation as a hard, effective bargainer and an advocate for his membership. He also proved a successful recruiter, increasing the Union's membership to over two million workers. Probably his greatest accomplishment was the National Master Freight Agreement, a 1964 effort that united over 400,000 drivers under a single contract. It proved to be a high-water mark for the union.

Hoffa believed that the union's efforts on behalf of its workers extended beyond the bargaining table and worked hard to enhance the union's political voice. He created a voter education campaign aimed at encouraging political activism across party lines. In addition, he recognized that with membership being the core of the union's strength, it needed to be as inclusive as possible. Consequently, under Hoffa, the Teamsters were in the forefront of organized labor's support of the Civil Rights Movement, with black and white teamsters participating in the 1963 March on Washington, and the Teamsters contributed significant funds to Dr. Martin Luther King Jr.'s (1929–1968) Southern Christian Leadership Conference.

Federal investigations of the Teamsters did not end with the downfall of Dave Beck. In fact, after Robert Kennedy (1925–1968) became attorney general in 1961, the government conducted a lengthy investigation of Hoffa and the union, as it suspected him of a wide range of criminal activity. Finally, in 1964, in two separate trials, the union leader was convicted of jury tampering, attempted bribery, and fraud. Hoffa was sentenced to 13 years and entered prison in 1967. In late 1971, though, President Richard Nixon (1913–1994) pardoned Hoffa, and he was released. Hoffa vanished at the end of July in 1975, with the whereabouts of his body remaining a mystery more than four decades after his disappearance.

Frank Fitzsimmons (1908–1981) succeeded Hoffa, but the transition represented the start of a downward slide. Over the next four decades, the Teamsters were plagued by significant infighting, changes in the national economic scene to which the union did not effectively respond, and a general diminution of labor power and influence from which the Teamsters were not immune. The Teamsters were deeply hurt by the deregulation efforts of President Jimmy Carter (1924–) and Congress in the late 1970s. The union actively opposed the deregulatory efforts. In fact, there was an attempt to bribe influential Senator Howard Cannon (1912–2002), which resulted in the conviction of Teamsters President Roy Williams (1915–1989), Fitzsimmons's successor. In addition, deregulation led to almost 200 unionized carriers going out of business, which in turn left almost one-third of the union's freight division employees out of work. Moreover, the remaining carriers demanded major concessions in other contractual areas. These challenges were exacerbated by a series of internal political battles and an increasingly anti-union economic climate that resulted in 20 years of leadership instability as well as declining membership, despite the union's efforts to merge with smaller unions to bolster its declining numbers.

Jimmy Hoffa Jr. was elected union president in 1998, a post he has held ever since. The Teamsters left the AFL-CIO in 2005, but the union appears to have fared no better on its own. Indeed, as the United States moves deeper into the 21st century, the number of union members—especially in the private sector—has declined, as has its political influence. No union has been hit any harder than the Teamsters, whose membership is barely larger than it was in 1950. Hoffa has sought to return the union to the heights they had achieved under his father, but the challenges have been daunting and only continue.

William H. Pruden III

See also: American Federation of Labor (1886–1955); American Federation of Labor and Congress of Industrial Organizations (1955–)

Further Reading

Hoffa, James. 1975. *Hoffa: The Real Story.* New York: Stein & Day, Inc.

International Brotherhood of Teamsters. 2018. https://teamster.org/.

Korth, Philip A. 1995. *The Minneapolis Teamsters Strike of 1934.* East Lansing: Michigan State University Press.

Sheridan, Walter. 1972. *The Fall and Rise of Jimmy Hoffa.* New York: Saturday Review Press.

Witwer, David. 2008. *Corruption and Reform in the Teamsters Union.* Champaign: University of Illinois Press.

K

Knights of Labor (1869–1890)

During the last third of the 19th-century American society transitioned from agricultural production to the industrial factory system in an urban setting. During this "Gilded Age," corporations grew into giant monopolies through horizontal and vertical integration, combining all production processes from extraction of raw material to manufacturing and sale of the final product into one giant company. To lower production costs, companies subdivided tasks, replaced human labor with steam and machine power, and cut wages. Wealth concentrated in ever fewer hands. This was a period of economic uncertainty owing to several up-and-down swings in the business cycle. White American workers competed for jobs with an ever-increasing and diverse immigrant population. These dramatic changes contributed to the emergence of several sectional, ethnic, and social interest groups that jostled with each other for political influence. One organization that aimed to address the needs of workers was the Knights of Labor.

The Noble and Holy Order of the Knights of Labor began as a secret society of tailors in Philadelphia in 1869 but soon grew into the first national labor organization by adding to its base of skilled workers, miners, semiskilled and unskilled industrial laborers, women, and African American wage earners. Egalitarian and republican ideals shaped the purpose of the organization, including the preservation of the dignity of work, maintenance of self-worth, and protection of the family-centered household. Knights believed that all workers, regardless of skill, ethnicity, race, or gender, experienced the same degradation of work and a wage system that contributed to poverty, not a life of independence. Knights did not advocate the overthrow of government or capitalism but insisted that government had the responsibility to establish equality between employers and laborers, because business owners (capital) had gained too much power. Government could rein in the power of capital by establishing an eight-hour workday; ending child labor; demanding that employers pay men and women equal wages for equal work; giving workers the right to organize; instituting public ownership of communication, transportation, and banking; and passing laws that improved the health and safety of workers. The Knights also believed in self-help through boycotts, lecture circuits, cooperative enterprises, political action, and strikes, although initially the latter were seen only as a last resort. Community ties and cultural practices served as the basis for solidarity between skilled and less skilled workers, furthered working-class identity, contributed to the establishment of district assemblies, and promoted rapid growth for the organization.

Political activism took the form of lobbying state and federal legislatures to draft laws friendly to labor, including the Alien Contract Labor Law in 1885, which prohibited employers from importing immigrants only to fill jobs. Knights also conducted successful election campaigns during the 1880s to fill hundreds of municipal office and state assembly positions with pro-labor candidates. Once elected, these representatives influenced passage of legislation that established nine or eight hour days for city employees and increased funding for education. Despite such successes, the Knights insisted on acting outside of organized politics because they associated established parties with corruption and privilege.

Although the Knights favored boycotts, arbitration, and political activism over violence, members took part in several strikes. Highly publicized and successful strikes in 1884 and 1885, especially against railroad magnate and financier Jay Gould's (1836–1892) Southwest railway system, contributed to an exponential increase in membership across industries and inspired establishment of Knights of Labor assemblies in cities and towns throughout the nation. A new wave of strikes began in early 1886, climaxing in a general strike in May, referred to by historians as "the great upheaval." Membership in the Knights had reached 700,000 by that time. A tragic event in Chicago on the evening of May 4, 1886, however, reversed its history. As police attempted to round up a pro-labor rally in Haymarket Square, a bomb exploded, causing a riot that resulted in the death and injury of several policemen and civilians. City officials blamed anarchist labor leaders for the bombing, and after a contentious trial, four labor leaders received the death penalty. Although there was no evidence that the Knights were involved in the bombing, this event marked the organization's decline, because as business owners and state officials reacted by using police and military force to squash demonstrations and strikes, disillusioned members began to question strategy and tactics to achieve their goals.

There are several reasons for the decline of the Knights of Labor. The very factor that contributed to its rise—various labor interests looking for solutions to their problems—also played a part in its demise after 1886. Conflict grew between the diverse groups, especially when craft oriented labor organizations, such as the Cigar Makers' International Union, excluded unskilled workers from their ranks. Laborers, consequently, joined or created special interest groups or labor parties, like the Socialist Labor Party, that addressed their own specific concerns. Structure was another reason. Although a national organization with an executive board and general assembly at its head, the Knights gave autonomous local assemblies the ability to define membership criteria, decide when and where to strike, develop tactics during walkouts, and select candidates for elected office. Such decentralization discouraged unity and contributed to disputes between national leaders, who wanted more centralized control, and local leaders, who supported establishment of separate language assemblies and independent labor parties. These disagreements only furthered ethnic and political tensions within the organization. Workers, especially unskilled laborers employed in different industrial sectors, also could not overcome the resources, government influence, and tactics such as lockouts that business owners used after 1886 to fight the labor movement. Diminished in numbers and influence, the Knights nevertheless continued to agitate for the eight-hour day and worker rights by actively participating in the Populist movement of the 1890s.

As the first national union for workers, the Knights of Labor are significant in U.S. labor history because their successes and failures influenced the organization and tactics of their successors, including the AFL and the Congress of Industrial Organizations (CIO). The Knights are also significant in the development of the American political system because they contributed to, if not heightened, the national debate over the social consequences of industrial capitalism. Their political activism at the community level inspired the creation of new labor-oriented parties and influenced the two established parties to address labor issues in their party platforms.

Petra DeWitt

See also: American Federation of Labor (1886–1955); American Federation of Labor and Congress of Industrial Organizations (1955–); American Federation of State, County, and Municipal Employees (1936–)

Further Reading

Fink, Leon. 1983. *Workingmen's Democracy: The Knights of Labor and American Politics.* Urbana: University of Illinois Press.

Voss, Kim. 1993. *The Making of American Exceptionalism: The Knights of Labor and Class Formation in the Nineteenth Century.* Ithaca, NY: Cornell University Press.

Weir, Robert E. 1996. *Beyond Labor's Veil: The Culture of the Knights of Labor.* University Park: Pennsylvania State University Press.

Weir, Robert E. 2000. *Knights Unhorsed: Internal Conflict in a Gilded Age Social Movement.* Detroit: Wayne State University Press.

Know Nothings (1854–1858)

The Know Nothings or, formally, the American Party (sometimes referenced as the Native or Nativist American Party prior to 1855) after 1855, was a political party and social movement that existed in some capacity and form from the mid-1840s until the eve of the 1860 elections. At its peak, the party elected 52 members (out of 234) to the House of Representatives in 1854 and 5 Senators to the United States Senate in 1856. The origin of the moniker "Know Nothing" stems from the secretive procedures of the Order of United Americans and the Order of the Star-Spangled Banner, two of the prominent nativist clubs of the era. When questioned over the activities of the organizations, members were instructed to reply that they "knew nothing" of said groups' activities. The result was that as members sought political office under the nativist banner, they were frequently dubbed "Know Nothings" due to their association with the nativist organizations (Desmond 1905).

There is no agreed upon origin of the Know Nothings, in part because the party emerged from various nativist social movements initially founded in the northeast and because the secretive nature of the anti-immigrant organizations lends poorly to historical documentation. What most would agree upon is the roots date back to around 1843 and the mid-Atlantic region (New York) (Leonard 1966). Initially, the party was christened the American Republican Party (1843–1845), and it won municipal elections in New York City and Philadelphia. Anti-immigrant sentiments dominated the early party and the party platform prominently called for a twenty-one-year naturalization period and severe restrictions on Catholic immigration. While the American Republican Party was short-lived, it captured rising popular sentiment at a time when public opinion was turning against immigrant populations and Catholics, more generally.

While the American Republican Party marked the beginning of the Know Nothing movement, the success of the future party depended on broader appeal, coordination, and electoral victories. Such events were quick to come. Perhaps the best-known of the early Know Nothings was Philadelphia Congressman Lewis Charles Levin (who was born in Charleston, South Carolina). Levin was a fiery orator known for his intense hatred of Pennsylvania's Catholic population. After riots broke out surrounding one of his orations, Lavin was arrested for "incitement to riot" and treason. One year later, he was elected to the U.S. House of Representatives on the 21-year naturalization platform and the pledge to elect only native-born Americans to public office (Forman 1960). Along with Lavin, in 1844, New York and Pennsylvania elected five other Know Nothings to the House of Representatives. Throughout the rest of the 1840s, the party, now called the Native American Party, continually won a handful of seats in the House until the retirement of Levin, rise of the Free Soil Party, and greater skepticism toward immigration by the Whigs completely eliminated the Know Nothings from Congress; the party still held only a handful of seats in the northeastern and mid-Atlantic state legislatures by 1850.

Following the collapse, two factors returned the Know Nothings to the national political scene. First, in the late 1840s a series of well-to-do nativist organizations sprung to action across the United States. The largest being the Order of the Star Spangled Banner, but in almost every state—North, South, and West—the newly formed organizations proliferated at a staggering rate (Anbinder 1992, 20–23). The national posturing of the organizations gave the Know Nothing cause a national base of support, something the earlier American Republican Party lacked. From California to Texas to New York the nativist clubs elevated the Know Nothing movement to various degrees of the success. While the party organizations varied from state to state, in general, they rallied to the banner of opposition to immigration and intense anti-Catholic paranoia.

The second factor, by the early 1850s, the Whig party was mired in a state of perpetual decline and increased fragmentation. As the issue of slavery ripped the party apart, existing Whig politicians faced few viable alternatives. Many Know Nothing converts were partisan refugees looking to join an opposition as opposed to true nativist believers. Perhaps the most prominent of the national Know Nothing figures, future Speaker of the House, Nathaniel Banks, emerged as a Know Nothing when it was no longer practical to remain in elected office as a Whig and ideologically imprudent to attempt to survive as a Democrat. At the state level, California's Governor J. Neely Johnson and Maryland's Governor Thomas Hicks both fell into the category of former Whig politicians who turned to the Know Nothing ballot line out of necessity. Thus, at its peak, the electoral base of the Know Nothings consisted of disaffected Whigs and true believers in American nativism.

The years 1854–1856 marked the pinnacle of the Know Nothing Party. Americans' increasing frustration with the Pierce administration and, by that point, the complete collapse of the Whigs and the second-party system made the Know Nothings the de facto political opposition for a short period of time in both the North and the South. At the state level, Know Nothings captured state legislatures in their traditional northern strongholds and remarkably seized control of virtually the entire Massachusetts governing apparatus.

At the national level, while the Know Nothings played some role in delivering the 1852 election to Franklin Pierce, in 1856 they nominated former President Millard Fillmore as their presidential candidate. While history has long debated whether or not Fillmore was a true Know Nothing, he did receive 21.5 percent of the national vote, carried the state of Maryland, and clearly harmed the nominee of the newly created Republican party, John C. Fremont in many of the mid-Atlantic states.

The Know Nothings also surged in Congress. In 1854, the party elected 52 members to the House of Representatives, and Know Nothing Nathaniel Banks was elected speaker of the house following a prolonged deadlock over candidates. While less successful in the Senate, the Know Nothings nevertheless elected a few senators, including the influential John Crittenden of Missouri and Sam Houston of Texas.

As the party enjoyed success and expansion, one element that contributed to its success also led to its downfall. Quite simply, the party was united only when it came to the broad advocacy of "Americanism" and even that was tenuous. Once other issues were placed on the table, Know Nothing consensus broke down quickly. In Massachusetts, for example, the Know Nothings were viewed as pragmatic modernizers who championed reform and an odd mix of populist policies. In New York and Pennsylvania, Know Nothings had no discernable political positions beyond violently opposing immigration and showing some hostility to slavery as an institution. And finally, in the South, Know Nothings championed the continuation of slavery and viewed immigration and Catholics, in particular, as threats to their peculiar institution, either through advocacy of abolition or by supporting immigration that would create an alternative source of cheap labor and thus devalue their slaves (Overdyke 1968). In the end, no matter the cause, a party based on secrecy and finding unity only in a couple of vague positions was not well suited to face a polarizing national crisis or settle internal divisions.

After their successes in 1854 and 1856, the *Dred Scott v. Sanford* Supreme Court decision was the crisis that facilitated the decline of the Know Nothings both as a party and as a prominent political movement. In the *Dred Scott* case, the U.S. Supreme Court ruled that slaves were not "citizens" within the meaning of the Constitution and therefore had no claim to the rights protected under the Constitution. It remains perhaps the most infamous of all Supreme Court decisions. As the nation turned its attention towards slavery, the Know Nothing party, similar to what the Whigs experienced earlier, split between northern Anti-Slavery Know Nothings and southern Pro-Slavery Know Nothings. As the Republican

Party emerged as a force, most antislavery Northern Know Nothings were simply absorbed by the Republican Party, by whom their anti-immigrant positions were tolerated but not whole heartedly embraced or prominently advertised (Anbinder 1992, 187–188). In the South, fearing an encroachment on slavery, most pro-slavery Southern Know Nothings united with other pro-slavery forces, typically in the Democratic Party but in some cases with "unity" or pro-union parties.

By the 1860 elections, the party had for all practical purposes disbanded. The Know Nothings failed to nominate a candidate for president, won no seats in the Congress, and only a handful of state officials (all in the North) carried on under the Know Nothing banner. What little political activity was generated by the movement tended to support the newly formed and short-lived Unionist Party headed by the Bell-Everett ticket. By 1861, the party officially ceased to exist; the issue of slavery had forced the demise of yet another political party.

The rise and fall of the Know Nothing Party and movement is unique within U.S. history. Many at the time, and even historians today, perceived that by the mid-1850s, the Know Nothings were a national force and even had a chance at securing the presidency in 1856 or 1860. Yet less than a decade later, the party no longer existed and many that held association with the party were tarnished by that association. The party passed no significant legislation and by most measures of evaluation had little long-term impact on the American political system. While the party, movement, and era is generally associated with anti-immigrant and anti-Catholic sentiment, it was neither the first nor the last time that those issues would briefly dominate and reorganize American politics.

Justin Moeller

See also: Free Soil Party (1848–1855); Whig Party (1833–1856)

Further Reading

Anbinder, Tyler. 1992. *Nativism and Slavery: The Northern Know Nothings and the Politics of the 1850s.* New York: Oxford University Press.

Desmond, Humphrey Joseph. 1905. *The Know-Nothing Party: A Sketch.* Washington, D.C.: New Century Press.

Holt, Michael F. 1973. "The Politics of Impatience: The Origins of Know Nothingism." *The Journal of American History* 60 (2): 309–331.

Leonard, Ira M. 1966. "The Rise and Fall of the American Republican Party in New York City, 1843–1845." *New-York Historical Society Quarterly* 50: 151.

Levine, Bruce. 2001. "Conservatism, Nativism, and Slavery: Thomas R. Whitney and the Origins of the Know-Nothing Party." *The Journal of American History* 88 (2): 455–488.

Overdyke, William Darrell. 1968. *The Know-Nothing Party in the South.* Shreveport: Louisiana University Press.

Koch Family Foundations (1953–)

The Koch Family Foundations are a group of separate, private charitable foundations controlled by the billionaire brothers Charles Koch (1935–) and David Koch (1940–). The Koch brothers made their fortune as majority owners of Koch

Industries, a Kansas-based, multinational conglomerate with interests in the oil, gas, chemical, and paper industries. The company was founded by their father, Fred C. Koch (1900–1967), and grew to become the second-largest privately held company in the United States (after Cargill) under their guidance. In addition to operating oil refineries and pipelines, Koch Industries produces such wide-ranging consumer products as Lycra fabrics, Stainmaster carpets, Brawny paper towels, and Dixie cups. Its success placed the Koch brothers among the top ten richest Americans in 2018, with net worth estimated at more than $50 billion each.

The Koch Family Foundations—which include the Charles Koch Foundation, the Charles Koch Institute, the David H. Koch Charitable Foundation, and the Fred C. and Mary R. Koch Foundation—provide financial support to many different organizations and causes, including educational institutions, cancer and medical research facilities, and arts and cultural institutions. The main focus of the Koch brothers' philanthropic endeavors, however, involves promoting libertarian and conservative political ideologies and policies, such as lower taxes, less regulation, fewer social services, smaller government, and greater reliance on free-market economic principles. The Koch brothers have funded academic research, think tanks, political action committees, and grassroots advocacy groups with the goal of advancing their vision of the United States as a free society, including such conservative organizations as the American Legislative Exchange Council, Americans for Prosperity, the Cato Institute, the Competitive Enterprise Institute, Donors Trust, and the Heritage Foundation.

The Koch brothers are widely considered to be among the biggest and most influential donors to libertarian and conservative candidates and causes. They present their goals as reshaping the American political landscape, creating a society that maximizes personal and corporate freedom and generating social progress and economic prosperity for all citizens. After operating behind the scenes for many years, the Koch brothers made headlines in the 2000s for financing opposition to many policies advanced by the Obama administration and its Democratic allies in Congress. "The central belief and fatal conceit of the current administration is that you are incapable of running your own life, but those in power are capable of running it for you," Charles Koch wrote in 2014. "This is the essence of big government and collectivism." The Koch brothers came under criticism for some of their political activities. Environmentalists expressed outrage over their promotion of climate-change denial and skepticism, for instance, while student-led groups like UnKoch My Campus claimed that their extensive funding for higher education undermined academic freedom and independence.

The patriarch of the Koch family, Fred C. Koch, earned a degree in chemical engineering from the Massachusetts Institute of Technology (MIT) and developed a cost-effective method for turning crude oil into gasoline. Facing patent litigation from powerful competitors in the U.S. oil industry, Koch took his innovation overseas and shared it with companies in the Soviet Union, Germany, and the Middle East. With the approach of World War II, he returned to the United States. Koch married Mary Robinson in 1932, and they had four sons: Frederick, Charles, David, and William. In 1940, Koch opened an oil refinery in Wichita, Kansas, that eventually expanded to become Koch Industries.

The elder Koch—a founding member of the ultraconservative, anti-Communist John Birch Society—raised his boys to distrust government. "He was constantly speaking to us children about what was wrong with government," David Koch recalls. "It's something I grew up with—a fundamental point of view that big government was bad, and imposition of government controls on our lives and economic fortunes was not good" (Mayer 2010). After earning degrees in engineering from MIT, Charles and David Koch became interested in the work of Friedrich von Hayek, an economist who advocated free-market capitalism and portrayed government regulation as a threat to individual freedom.

Charles Koch assumed control of the family business in 1966, with David as his second in command. Under their leadership, Koch Industries showed phenomenal growth over the next five decades, from $250 million in annual sales to $115 billion, and from 650 employees to 120,000 worldwide. The two brothers continued to promote their political and economic ideas by financing the creation of the Cato Institute, a libertarian think tank and public policy organization, in 1977. Two years later, David Koch became the vice-presidential running mate of Libertarian Party candidate Ed Clark. Their political ideas failed to appeal to American voters, however, and the ticket garnered less than 1 percent of the vote. In 1983, Charles and David Koch paid over $1 billion to buy out the business interests of their two brothers, and from that time forward, they each owned 42 percent of Koch Industries (the remaining 16 percent was held by the descendants of J. Howard Marshall, an early investor).

Beginning in the 1980s, the Koch brothers withdrew from the public sphere and began advancing their political ideas behind the scenes by contributing hundreds of millions of dollars to academic institutions, think tanks, and other organizations. The Koch brothers coordinate their political donations and charitable giving through several private foundations. The Fred C. and Mary R. Koch Foundation, established in 1953, focuses on improving the quality of life for the people of Kansas by providing financial support for the arts and education. It funds development programs for at-risk youth, entrepreneurial business programs for Kansas high schools, and scholarships for children of Koch Industries employees. It also supports the Bill of Rights Institute, which offers workshops for teachers that promote a conservative perspective on the nation's founding documents and principles.

The David H. Koch Charitable Foundation was founded in the early 1990s, after David was diagnosed with prostate cancer. Medical research aimed at finding a cure for cancer became a central focus of its charitable giving. The foundation also provides financial support for many institutions in the arts and sciences, such as the American Ballet Theatre, the Lincoln Center for the Performing Arts, the Metropolitan Museum of Art, the Smithsonian Museum of Natural History, and the WGBH Educational Foundation, which produces public television programming. In the early 2000s, it also provided a major source of funding for Americans for Prosperity, a libertarian/conservative political advocacy group that played an influential role in the rise of the Tea Party movement.

The Charles Koch Foundation and the Charles Koch Institute were formed in 2011, when Charles divided an earlier charitable foundation into two separate parts. The Charles Koch Foundation provides grants to nearly 300 colleges and universities to support academic research and educational programs that promote the benefits of a free society. It funds scholarship focusing on such issues as tolerance and free speech, economic freedom, technological innovation, and foreign policy. In partnership with such liberal organizations as the ACLU and the Center for American Progress, it proposed a bipartisan approach to criminal justice reform that sought to end the overincarceration of people from poor and minority communities and increase employment rates for rehabilitated offenders. The Charles Koch Institute, meanwhile, offers professional education, research, and training programs aimed at the advancement of free-market economic principles.

Critics contend that the Koch brothers funnel their charitable giving through a maze of nonprofit organizations with bland-sounding names in order to disguise the fact that they are spending hundreds of millions of dollars to promote their own libertarian philosophies and corporate interests. To qualify for tax-exempt status under federal law, charities are required to promote the public welfare. According to the National Committee for Responsive Philanthropy, however, the Koch Family Foundations "give money to nonprofit organizations that do research and advocacy on issues that impact the profit margin of Koch Industries" (Mayer 2010). Moreover, critics describe the Koch brothers' donations as "dark money" because it is often difficult to trace the funding to its source. "You take corporate money and give it to a neutral-sounding think tank," one attorney explains, which "hires people with pedigrees and academic degrees who put out credible-seeming studies. But they all coincide perfectly with the economic interests of their funders" (Mayer 2010).

Many of the conservative interest groups and think tanks that receive financial support from the Koch Family Foundations oppose environmental regulations and legislation intended to promote clean energy and combat climate change. Koch funding has supported many individuals and organizations who have attempted to create doubt about whether human activity contributes to global climate change. For instance, the Kochs granted $230,000 to Dr. Willie Soon, a climate researcher who claimed that global warming was caused primarily by the sun, and they also provided funding to the Independent Women's Forum, an organization that opposes programs presenting climate change as a scientific fact in public schools. In 2008, the Koch-funded Cato Institute took out a full-page ad in the *New York Times* contradicting President Barack Obama's assertion that climate science was "beyond dispute." Cato criticized plans to limit carbon dioxide emissions as a means of addressing global warming as expensive, ineffective, and a ploy for the government to gain greater control over industry.

Environmentalists have pointed out that Koch Industries derives much of its revenues from oil and gas and regularly ranks among the top producers of air pollution in the United States, which creates strong business incentives for it to deny climate science. "If the answer is to phase out fossil fuels, a different group of people are going to be making money," said Professor Naomi Oreskes of the University of California, San Diego, "so we shouldn't be surprised that they're fighting tooth and nail" (Mayer 2010). The campaign proved effective in creating skepticism among the American people about climate science. A 2016 Pew

Research Center survey found that 48 percent of respondents viewed human activity as the primary cause of climate change, while a majority said it either resulted from natural processes or there was no evidence that climate change was occurring (Funk and Kennedy 2016).

Some critics argue that the Koch brothers' efforts to promote their libertarian views have contributed to the growing divisiveness in American politics. During the eight years of Obama's presidency, the Kochs funded political campaigns, advocacy groups, policy organizations, and lobbyists that vocally opposed the administration's goals, such as health-care reform. Americans for Prosperity and other groups financed by the Kochs also supported the rise of the antigovernment Tea Party movement. Critics claim that the Koch political network generated antipathy toward Obama and deepened partisan divisions in the electorate. Lee Fang of the liberal blog ThinkProgress described the Koch brothers as "the billionaires behind the hate" (Mayer 2010).

By 2018, however, the Koch brothers had distanced themselves from President Donald Trump and threatened to withhold financial backing from Republican candidates who supported his agenda. Although the Trump administration's corporate tax cuts and proindustry environmental policies favored Koch Industries, Charles Koch expressed dissatisfaction with the president's divisive rhetoric and protectionist trade policies. Trump countered by calling the Koch political network "overrated" and "a total joke in real Republican circles" and saying that "I never sought their support because I don't need their money or bad ideas" (Peters 2018).

The Koch brothers also faced increasing resistance in the world of academia, which has long been considered a bastion of progressive values and liberal thought. Student-led groups such as UnKoch My Campus raised concerns that the Kochs donated millions of dollars to colleges and universities in order to gain influence over the selection of professors, the direction of academic research, and the focus of curriculum materials. They claimed that excessive donor interference stifled intellectual diversity and threatened research integrity. In response, Charles Koch issued an open letter in which he described his goals as supporting "courageous, far-sighted scholars who are grappling with our country's toughest challenges," as well as "programs and opportunities that expand open inquiry and a rigorous exchange of ideas that are essential for universities to be engines of learning, science, and the resulting discovery" (Flaherty 2018). One beneficiary of a Koch-funded research grant asserted that "Academics should rejoice that there are public-spirited citizens like Charles Koch, who in the tradition of such great wealthy philanthropists as Leland Stanford, Johns Hopkins, John D. Rockefeller and others want to expand the dissemination and creation of knowledge" (Vedder 2018).

Laurie Collier Hillstrom

See also: American Enterprise Institute (1938–); Bill & Melinda Gates Foundation (2000–); Carnegie Corporation of New York (1911–)

Further Reading

Flaherty, Colleen. 2018. "A Shift for Koch, but How Much of a Shift?" *Inside Higher Education*, July 25, 2018. https://www.insidehighered.com/news/2018/07/25/koch

-foundation-pledges-make-future-grant-terms-public-critics-want-know-more
-about.

Funk, Cary, and Brian Kennedy. 2016. "Public Views on Climate Change and Climate Scientists." Pew Research Center, October 4, 2016. http://www.pewinternet.org /2016/10/04/public-views-on-climate-change-and-climate-scientists/.

Koch, Charles G. 2014. "I'm Fighting to Restore a Free Society." *Wall Street Journal*, April 2, 2014. https://www.wsj.com/articles/charles-koch-im-fighting-to-restore-a -free-society-1396471508?tesla=y.

Koch Family Foundations. 2018. http://kochfamilyfoundations.org/.

Levinthal, Dave. 2015. "Koch Brothers' Higher-Ed Investments Advance Political Goals." Center for Public Integrity, October 30, 2015. https://www.publicintegrity.org /2015/10/30/18684/koch-brothers-higher-ed-investments-advance-political-goals.

Mayer, Jane. 2010. "Covert Operations." *New Yorker*, August 30, 2010. https://www .newyorker.com/magazine/2010/08/30/covert-operations#ixzz0yDnax8KY.

Peters, Jeremy W. 2018. "Charles Koch Takes on Trump. Trump Takes on Charles Koch." *New York Times*, July 31, 2018. https://www.nytimes.com/2018/07/31/us/politics /trump-koch-brothers.html.

Schulman, Daniel. 2014. *Sons of Wichita: How the Koch Brothers Became America's Most Powerful and Private Dynasty*. New York: Hachette Book Group.

Vedder, Richard. 2018. "Academic Freedom, Intellectual Diversity, and the Charles Koch Foundation." *Forbes*, May 7, 2018. https://www.forbes.com/sites/richardvedder /2018/05/07/academic-freedom-intellectual-diversity-and-the-charles-koch -foundation/#38582ba22719.

L

Lambda Legal Defense and Education Fund (1973–)

Lambda Legal Defense and Education Fund was founded in 1973 as the nation's first legal organization dedicated to achieving full equality for lesbians and gay people. The organization was founded by lawyer Bill Thom, who had been volunteering for the Gay Activists Alliance. He believed that an organization dedicated to legal issues would be a helpful addition to the gay rights movement. He based the framework for the organization on that of the Puerto Rican Legal Defense and Education Fund. A panel of New York judges initially turned down Lambda Legal's application for nonprofit status because the judges believed that the organization's mission was "neither benevolent nor charitable." In essence, Lambda Legal became their own first client, appealing the decision. Initially, Lambda Legal had virtually no budget and volunteer attorneys and staff ran the organization, but by 1993, the organization's budget was $2 million.

The organization works for the civil rights of lesbians, gay men, bisexuals, transgender people, and everyone living with HIV. Lambda Legal uses the legal system to achieve equality. It has been compared to the American Civil Liberties Union (ACLU) and the National Association for the Advancement of Colored People (NAACP), which use a similar legal strategy. Lambda Legal focuses on cases "which, if successful, can provide a breakthrough ruling that can benefit the greatest number of gays and people with AIDS" (Rimmerman 2000). The organization often acts as legal counsel or co-counsel for its clients. This legal strategy has worked quite well—legal avenues have often proven more successful than political ones.

The organization's strategy involves bringing test cases in the hope that court rulings will change the law. Timing is vital in this strategy. It is important that a case is not brought before judges are likely to rule favorably. If this happens, it could create a negative precedent that might prevent future change. Therefore, the organization cautions against suits brought by individuals.

Lambda Legal helped to win many early cases about gay and lesbian rights. In one of the first cases that the organization worked on, they helped a gay student group fight a ban on their activities. In the 1980s, they won the first HIV/AIDS discrimination case, which established that it is illegal to discriminate against people who have HIV. They also helped to establish privacy rights for people with HIV. The organization faced defeat with the U.S. Supreme Court decision in *Bowers v. Hardwick* in 1986, which upheld state sodomy laws. This decision was a setback as sodomy laws not only stigmatized lesbian and gay individuals but also laid the foundation for continuing to legally discriminate against the LGBTQ community.

In the 1990s, the organization won a case establishing that schools are responsible for harassment and violence against LGBTQ students. They were also successful in defending the right of gay-straight alliances to exist in schools. In 1992, Lambda Legal was able to keep a Colorado law from taking effect which would have invalidated existing anti-discrimination bans and prevented the passage of new ones. The case eventually made its way to the Supreme Court, which declared the measure unconstitutional.

Lambda Legal persuaded the Supreme Court to overturn state sodomy laws in *Lawrence v. Texas* in 2003, thus invalidating the *Bowers* ruling. The case began in 1998 when Tyron Garner (1967–2006) and John G. Lawrence were arrested for having consensual sex in Lawrence's apartment, which was illegal under Texas's Homosexual Conduct Law. This case is a good illustration of the work that Lambda Legal does. The goal of most lawyers would have been to get the charges against Garner and Lawrence dropped, but that was not the goal for Lambda Legal's attorneys. If the charges were dropped, then that would have eliminated the possibility of using it as a test case. The Supreme Court will generally not hear cases that are moot or those that have been resolved either through settlement or the dropping of charges. If the charges had been dropped, they also would have lacked standing, the legal right to bring a case to court. So with the permission of Garner and Lawrence, the Lambda Legal team kept the criminal process going. If the case were lost, Garner and Lawrence would have had criminal records, but they wanted to make a political point and so were willing to take that risk. Prior to the ruling, Lambda Legal hosted town halls in the 13 states that still had sodomy laws to provide information to the LGBTQ community and the public on the importance of the case.

The effect of the *Lawrence* decision was immediate for those who lived in the 13 states that still had sodomy laws in place. But more importantly, the decision removed the legal rationale that allowed the law to treat lesbians and gay people differently than heterosexuals. It also opened the door for equal consideration of the LGBTQ community in other legal matters, such as employment, adoption, child custody, and marriage. As former Justice Antonin Scalia (1936–2016) argued in his dissent, the ruling left state laws prohibiting same-sex marriage on "pretty shaky grounds" as the decision "dismantles the structure of constitutional law that has permitted a distinction to be made between heterosexual and homosexual unions" (*Lawrence v. Texas* 2003 Scalia Dissent, 20–21). It was also an important sign of the times that it took the Court only 17 years to overturn the *Bowers* decision, whereas it took the Court nearly 60 years to overturn its decision in *Plessy v. Ferguson* that racial segregation was constitutional.

Lambda Legal scored a major victory in 2009 after the Iowa Supreme Court legalized same-sex marriage in the state in the *Varnum v. Brien* decision. But the work on the case began in 2002. The organization had received many calls and letters from same-sex couples all over the country who had been denied the benefits of marriage. The organization made a calculated decision to file the suit in Iowa. As the lead attorney on the case said, "We try to bring lawsuits where we can do the work necessary to win" (Zahorsky 2009). Lambda Legal attorneys were hopeful that Iowa would rule favorably due to its history of applying broad equal rights and due process protection under its constitution.

In order to prevent potential backlash against the LGBTQ community, Lambda Legal laid groundwork for the case by working with local LGBTQ organizations to educate Iowans about marriage equality by speaking in places like church basements, senior centers, and high schools. The organization compiled scientific research demonstrating that there is no evidence that children do best in heterosexual homes. The team also gathered 15 amicus briefs representing forty faith denominations. The decision was not just a victory for same-sex couples in Iowa; it also signaled that the issue of marriage equality was not limited to the liberal confines of the East and West Coasts.

The organization was cocounsel in *Obergefell v. Hodges*, which declared in 2015 that denying same-sex couples the right to marry is unconstitutional. Even after the victory in that case, their work was not finished. A federal judge in Puerto Rico ruled that the *Obergefell* decision did not apply to Puerto Rico, as it is a territory and not a state. Lambda Legal appealed that decision to the U.S. Court of Appeals, which issued an opinion reaffirming that Puerto Rico's ban on same-sex marriage is unconstitutional and reassigned the case to a new judge, who promptly struck down the ban.

Lambda Legal worked with the ACLU to file suit against the controversial House Bill 2 in North Carolina, which barred transgender people from using restrooms and other single-sex facilities that match their gender identity when in government buildings, including public universities. This law was replaced by another law, which the ACLU and Lambda Legal still believe puts the state's LGBTQ residents at risk as it is unclear about the access that transgender individuals will have to public restrooms.

The organization is involved in an employment discrimination case on behalf of Jameka Evans, a lesbian who says she suffered harassment and discrimination at her job as a security guard because she's lesbian and gender-nonconforming. The U.S. Court of Appeals for the Eleventh Circuit dismissed the lawsuit because Title VII of the Civil Rights Act of 1964 prohibits sex discrimination, but not discrimination based on sexual orientation. The case was appealed to the U.S. Supreme Court, which declined review in December of 2017.

Lambda Legal now has more than 100 staff members in six offices in New York, Atlanta, Dallas, Chicago, Los Angeles, and Washington, D.C. It is currently involved in 40 open cases. In addition to its litigation work, the organization provides information campaigns to help people exercise the rights they have and to build public support for equality. These information campaigns can help to strengthen their lawsuits. In addition, they advocate for public policy to improve the lives of LGBTQ people and people affected by HIV.

Jessica Loyet Gracey

See also: AIDS Coalition to Unleash Power (1987–); American Civil Liberties Union (1920–); GLAAD (1985–); Human Rights Campaign (1980–); NAACP Legal Defense and Education Fund (1940–); National LGBTQ Task Force (1973–)

Further Reading

Pierceson, Jason. 2016. *Sexual Minorities and Politics: An Introduction.* Lanham, MD: Rowman and Littlefield.

Rimmerman, Craig A. 2000. "Beyond Political Mainstreaming: Reflections on Lesbian and Gay Organizations and the Grassroots." In *The Politics of Gay Rights*, edited by Craig A. Rimmerman, Kenneth D. Wald, and Clyde Wilcox. Chicago: The University of Chicago Press.

Zahorsky, Rachel M. 2009. "Doing 'Work Necessary to Win.'" *ABA Journal* 95 (7): 36–37.

Land Grant Colleges and Universities

In 1857, Vermont Representative Justin Smith Morrill (1810–1898) introduced in the U.S. House of Representatives a bill that proposed to open up higher education, especially the study of agriculture and technology, to lower- or working-class people by setting aside federal land for the construction of public universities. Although this land-grant bill passed Congress, President James Buchanan (1791–1868) vetoed it. Morrill reintroduced his bill in 1861 with the added stipulation that students should also be able to receive military training if they so wished. The context of the Civil War made this an attractive proposal. Congress passed, and President Abraham Lincoln (1809–1865), signed into law the Morrill Act of 1862, also known as An Act donating Public Lands to the Several States and Territories which may provide Colleges for the benefit of Agriculture and the Mechanic Arts. This act established the uniquely American system of 105 public land-grant colleges and universities that have offered access to education in a variety of academic disciplines to millions of Americans.

As the son of a blacksmith, Morrill had little opportunity for a formal education, was largely self-taught, and wanted to offer better opportunities to people like himself—farmers and artisans. Therefore, the basic concept of a land-grant college or university is to provide a practical and affordable education to ordinary people who could not otherwise attend an institution of higher education.

Precedent for federally sponsored education existed since colonial days when the English monarchs King William and Queen Mary signed a charter to establish a college (William & Mary) in Virginia. During the formative days of the United States, Congress set aside through the Land Ordinance of 1785 one section of land in each township for education purposes. The idea that higher education should no longer be the privilege of the elite but that all people should have access to it developed later, during the Second Great Awakening and the reform movement of the early 19th century. The scientific and technological advancements in transportation and manufacturing during that time also contributed to an increased demand for science-based curriculum to replace traditional studies in the classics and theology at universities. By the time Morrill introduced his bill, the state of Illinois had already petitioned Congress for land to establish industrial universities, and several states, including Michigan, offered agricultural colleges.

Morrill also noticed that farming practices in the United States led to soil depletion and decreased yields. English farmers, by contrast, used science to maintain field productivity. Morrill concluded that Americans lacked contemporary agricultural skills and knowledge and should learn about soils, fertilizers, and crop diseases by attending agricultural colleges. He also believed that these universities, as a foundation for the country's economic growth, should receive the same support from the federal government through public land grants as railroads were receiving at the time.

The original Morrill Act established a federal-state partnership by setting aside federal land in each state, amounting to 30,000 acres each for a state's senators and representatives, which a state could then sell, or the equivalent of $1.25 per each acre to which a state might be entitled, to establish a permanent endowment for the creation and long-term maintenance of a public institution. While these colleges and universities were open to anyone, the act preferred that the "sons of toil," or the sons of farmers, artisans, and industrial workers, attend. Though the Department of Agriculture would oversee the administration of land-grant funds, states could determine what subjects and degrees to offer at their institutions as long as they provided studies in agriculture, engineering, and military science.

Once the Morrill Act of 1862 went into effect, states had two years to agree to the law's provisions and five years to establish a college or university. Progress, however, was slow because few states had resources or educators available during or shortly after the Civil War, and land prices remained low owing to the Homestead Act and Transcontinental Railroad Act. Despite these problems, states established 48 colleges, such as the University of Missouri and the Massachusetts Institute of Technology. They also included the first black land-grant universities, Alcorn State University in Mississippi and Hampton University in Virginia.

To encourage agricultural research, the Hatch Act of 1887 established federal funding for an agricultural experiment station for each land-grant university. Since then, each state has received federal funding for research through the Department of Agriculture, as long as each state matches these funds, usually in the form of competitive or noncompetitive grants based on a complex formula calculating farm population versus total state population versus the nation's population.

Realizing that states could not maintain long-term financing and that racial discrimination was widespread in the institutions despite stipulations in the original law that anyone, including African Americans, could attend land-grant colleges, Morrill introduced, Congress passed, and President Benjamin Harrison (1833–1901) signed the Second Land-Grant Act in 1890. This legislation increased funding for existing colleges, but more importantly, it threatened to deny funding to states that used race as a condition for admission unless they established a separate but equally funded land-grant university for African Americans. Consequently, several southern states established segregated land-grant colleges and universities, the so-called 1890 institutions, including the Colored Normal, Agricultural and Mechanical College of South Carolina (the future South Carolina State University), and State Normal School for Colored Persons (the future Kentucky State University). The act also provided for existing black colleges, including Tuskegee Institute, to become part of the land-grant system. These historically black colleges and universities have provided education to countless first-generation college students who had limited opportunities elsewhere, and they have established programs for individuals and communities that further social and economic upward mobility.

In order to provide useful education to the public beyond the colleges, Congress passed the Smith-Lever Act in 1914, establishing the federally supported Cooperative or Agricultural Extension Service. This public service outreach program for land-grant universities shares information about home economics and developments in agricultural practices and technologies with the general population as well as teaches the practical implementation of that knowledge through hands-on workshops or instructions. The Smith-Lever Act completed the three functions of today's land-grant institution: instruction, research, and extension.

Inequalities in federal funding between 1862 and 1890 institutions, however, remained a problem for several decades because the traditionally black institutions were not eligible to receive support through the Hatch and Smith-Lever Acts. Congress did not change that until the second half of the twentieth century when the Evans-Allen Act of 1977 extended research funds for food and agricultural sciences and the National Agricultural Research, Extension, and Teaching Policy Act of 1997 provided federal funding for agricultural extension programs and activities to 1890 land-grant universities.

Since the 1960s Congress has expanded the land-grant system by creating colleges or universities in several jurisdictions, including the District of Columbia in 1967 and territories such as American Samoa and the Virgin Islands in 1972, not by providing free land but by offering cash endowments for their establishment. In 1994 Congress also authorized the inclusion of 29 tribal colleges into the land-grant system and provided additional funding for the Extension Service to set up facilities and programs focused on the needs of Native Americans.

By offering soil science, food science, veterinary, and engineering degrees, as well as hands-on research opportunities at its experiment stations, land-grant universities have had an important impact on agriculture in the United States, turning farming into an industry based on science and technology and dramatically increasing productivity of farm labor. Although family farms still exist, they have often become client-focused businesses ranging from organic products to specialized crops, in order to compete with large-scale, commercial organizations. In turn, consumers' concerns about their food have contributed to the development of new biotechnology curricula at land-grant colleges.

As research institutions, land-grant universities have undertaken important interdisciplinary research addressing subjects like food, energy, and water security. Several of the universities have recently established Research or Discovery Parks to carry out research in cooperation with private individuals or businesses, resulting in a number of discoveries, patents, and start-up companies. For example, scientists and students at Alabama A&M University have created a biodiesel initiative that uses cooking oil from cafeterias at the nearby Toyota Motor Manufacturing Company to fuel A&M's transit system buses. North Carolina A&T State University in conjunction with an industry partner has developed traditional food processing technology without chemicals or irradiation to eliminate allergens in peanuts. And the University of Maryland is addressing the declining number of honey bees by working with beekeepers across the nation to develop management strategies to assure the health of bees.

Land-grant extension services have also had an important impact in American society through their hands-on education programs. During World War I, extension programs helped the nation meet its needs by teaching farmers how to increase crop yields per acre and by demonstrating canning lessons to women to conserve foods. During the Great Depression, extension agents managed the Farm Seed and Loan Program, taught farmers management skills, and demonstrated canning and gardening practices that helped families survive the depression and drought. Since 1902, 4-H programs have been teaching children leadership, citizenship, and life skills. More recently, extension services have adjusted to fewer people living on farms or in rural areas. They, for example, offer master gardener classes to train people in the science and art of gardening, instead of farming, including water management and minimizing use of fertilizers and pesticides. Most extension services, including at the University of Wisconsin and University of Missouri, also offer Master Naturalist courses that train volunteers for work in state parks and nature preserves as leaders in educational experiences for visitors, observers of animal and plant activity, and stewards of trails or grasslands. Others have adjusted to the diversity of animals or plants the modern farmer raises. The extension service at Tennessee State University, for example, established a master meat goat producer program that provides management skills to goat farmers hoping to improve profitability, resulting in Tennessee becoming the nation's second largest goat-producing state.

Since the financial crisis of the early 2000s, land-grant colleges and universities have faced new challenges. As the federal government and states tightened their financial support, land-grant universities had to rely more on tuition increases and student fees to operate and fulfill the mandates of the Morrill Act. In order to survive, less-financially stable universities have created partnerships with other institutions or have relied increasingly on modern telecommunication technologies shared across campuses to maintain curricular offerings for students. Increased competition for fewer federal research grants has encouraged more collaboration with private business.

Despite these challenges, academicians have heralded the Morrill Act for democratizing education and bringing diversification to the student body. Over the past 150 years, millions of students have attended publicly funded land-grant colleges or universities and received undergraduate, master's, and doctoral degrees in a number of academic subjects, including but not limited to agriculture, engineering, and military tactics. Graduates include famous scientists, military leaders, and presidents of the United States. What had been the prerogative of white wealthy men became the opportunity for working-class men and women, African Americans, Native Americans, immigrants, and other minorities. The Land-Grant Act not only adjusted education to fit the needs of an ever-changing nation and its people but also set important precedent for future federal legislation, such as the Servicemen's Readjustment Act (GI Bill) in 1944, expanding higher education to all World War II veterans; the National Defense Education

Act in 1958, establishing a federal student loan program; and the Higher Education Act in 1965, which introduced work-study and federal grants into the pool of government-backed financial aid resources available to students.

Petra DeWitt

See also: Historically Black Colleges and Universities (1837–); Mexican American Legal Defense and Education Fund (1968–); NAACP Legal Defense and Education Fund (1940–); National Education Association (1857–); United Negro College Fund (1944–)

Further Reading

Christy, Ralph D., and Lionel Williamson. 1992. *A Century of Service: Land-Grant Colleges and Universities, 1890–1990.* New Brunswick, NJ: Transaction Publishers.

Cross, Coy F. 1999. *Justin Smith Morrill: Father of the Land-Grant Colleges.* East Lansing: Michigan State University Press.

Edmond, J. B. 1978. *The Magnificent Charter: The Origin and Role of the Morrill Land-Grant Colleges and Universities.* Hicksville, NY: Exposition Press.

Land Speculation Companies (1740–1790)

Land speculation companies were originally formed as joint-stock companies, whose investors would be granted thousands of acres of land by the British (and later U.S.) government to then market and sell to settlers. During the colonial and early Republic periods, land speculation company officers were generally members of the elite who possessed capital and political connections. The actions of these companies were later adopted by the federal government to organize and encourage settlement of the west.

Land speculation companies were first formed in Virginia during the 1740s to profit from the speculation of land in and around the Ohio Valley. The actions of these early companies encouraged hostilities to develop between England, France, and Native Americans and can be seen as part of the cause of the French and Indian War (1754–1763). Two of the earliest land speculation companies in Virginia were the Loyal Company and the Ohio Company. The Loyal Company was led by Dr. Thomas Walker (1715–1794), and its shareholders were from the Piedmont counties of Virginia. The Ohio Company drew its shareholders from the Tidewater counties of Virginia and included George Washington (1732–1799). The Ohio Company campaigned the Board of Trade for a grant of 500,000 acres in 1749. The Board of Trade approved, with the stipulation that a fort should be built on this land after 200 families settled on 200 acres. The Board of Trade agreed to give the Ohio Company an additional 300,000 acres on similar terms. The Board of Trade saw the value of increased trade with the Ohio Valley region as well as encouraging British settlers to occupy the Ohio Valley. The French who possessed legal claim to the Ohio Valley viewed the Ohio Company and its land grant as an attempt to drive a wedge in its Northern American empire—to create a division between French Canada and Louisiana to weaken French holdings. As a result, the French seized all English traders within the Ohio Valley and built forts throughout what is now western Pennsylvania. Native American groups viewed land speculators as threats to their community stability and became allies with the French to drive British settlers away from the Ohio Valley. These motivations served to justify many participants' actions during the French and Indian War.

Great Britain was victorious at the close of the French and Indian War, but it hindered the activities of land speculation companies through the Proclamation of 1763. After the French and Indian War, the English were deeply in debt and did not wish to increase this debt by protecting British settlers on western lands and participating in Indian wars. As a result, King George III (1738–1820) issued the Proclamation of 1763, which prohibited English settlement and hunting activities west of the Appalachian mountains. British settlement on land west of the Appalachians still occurred, however. Between 1765 and 1768 approximately 30,000 British settlers ignored the 1763 Proclamation. Despite the inability of the British to guard all land west of the Appalachian mountains, land speculation companies suffered. Land speculation companies were not able to obtain legal title to land west of the Appalachian mountains as long as the Proclamation of 1763 was in effect and therefore could not market and sell this land with confidence that the land was entirely the property of the land speculation company. Individual freeholders, however, freely moved into this area and took up residence.

Native Americans served as an additional obstacle to settlement and thwarted the plans of land speculation companies. Pontiac's Rebellion of 1763 was a largely united resistance among Native American groups against British settlers who were determined to settle on Indian land. Apart from the Iroquois, most Indian groups joined with the Ottawa leader Pontiac and waged war against British invaders. This violence served to dissuade many British settlers from making the move westward and bolstered the provisions of the Proclamation of 1763.

Land speculation companies used various Indian groups to attempt to get around the legal strictures of the Proclamation of 1763. Several leaders of land speculation companies met with Indian groups individually to purchase western land, with the idea that these transactions would not be prohibited by the Proclamation of 1763. With the Treaty of Fort Stanwix in 1768 and other treaty meetings, the Ohio Company and other companies obtained land from Indian groups under coercion. Many of the land purchase agreements emerging from these treaty meetings included land that Indian representatives had no control over and was occupied by other Indian groups. The Board of Trade ruled that many of these arrangements were not valid.

With the American Revolution (1775–1783), land speculation companies ceased to operate fully due to the exigencies of war. However, land speculation companies reemerged after the war. In addition to the motivations for profit, population and increased economic activity that came from westward expansion, postwar companies also included war veterans' land bounties as a further justification for their activities. The Ohio Company of Associates was founded in 1786 by veteran officers of the Continental Army who desired economic and social recognition for their wartime service. At the end of the Revolutionary War, the U.S. government did not make good on pay and benefits promised to soldiers and officers for their service. As a result, veterans filed hundreds of petitions with the federal government, and some used violence to attempt to persuade government leaders to pay veterans what they believed they were owed. In an attempt to placate veterans, the American confederation government issued land bounties to disgruntled veterans. The Ohio Company of Associates was formed by veterans to use these land bounties as a profitable resource to provide for those who had served in the Continental Army. Unlike other previous land speculation companies, each shareholder was limited to five shares' ownership to prevent the Company from being overrun with elite land speculators.

By 1796, the Ohio Company of Associates dissolved due to internal disagreements and post-revolutionary economic downturn. Shareholders from the west focused on clearing and settling land, while shareholders in the east were concerned with the overall profits the Company was producing. Soon, shareholders violated the five-share-limit policy and the Ohio Company of Associates became dominated by elite land speculators. Concurrently, the new nation faced severe economic downturns and inflation which increased debts the Ohio Company of Associates had taken on when it was first formed and threatened to bring the organization to financial ruin. The Ohio Company of Associates was unable to successfully organize a vehicle to support western expansion while also making a profit for its shareholders.

While the land speculation companies largely met with failure, their strategies for marketing land and encouraging settlement were taken up by the federal government with the Northwest Ordinance of 1787. This legislation was critical for establishing a process of western settlement by delineating requirements for land ownership and legal recognition of an area as a territory, and later, a state.

Angela Miller Keysor

See also: Settlement House Movement (1889)

Further Reading

Friedenberg, Daniel M. 1992. *Life, Liberty, and the Pursuit of Land: The Plunder of Early America*. Buffalo, NY: Prometheus Books.

Holton, Woody. 1994. "The Ohio Indians and the Coming of the American Revolution in Virginia." *Journal of Southern History* 60 (3): 453–478.

James, Alfred P. 1959. *The Ohio Company: Its Inner History*. Pittsburgh: University of Pittsburgh Press.

Ray, Kristofer. 2002. "Land Speculation, Popular Democracy, and Political Transformation on the Tennessee Frontier, 1789–1800." *Tennessee Historical Quarterly* 61 (3): 161–181.

Shannon, Timothy J. 1991. "The Ohio Company and the Meaning of Opportunity in the American West, 1786–1795." *New England Quarterly* 64 (3): 393–413.

Lawyers Committee for Civil Rights under Law (1963–)

The Lawyers Committee for Civil Rights under Law is a civil rights organization formed during the John F. Kennedy administration in order to identify ways attorneys could help resolve civil rights–related issues and assist other civil rights organizations and leaders with legal matters involving desegregation and other issues that arose as a result of nonviolent civil rights demonstrations. The committee formed in June 1963 at the request of President Kennedy, just a few months prior to his assassination.

Although his short administration is often referred to as Camelot, President John F. Kennedy (1917–1963) faced increasing violence associated with the Civil Rights Movement. Fueling this violence was the frustration of the black community with the repeated and systemic violation of their civil rights as well as the continuing denial of their access to voting, public facilities, and jobs. Their frustration increased after the *Brown v. Board of Education* decisions as the states' idea of "all deliberate speed" was anything but speedy.

President Kennedy wanted to find a way to encourage localities to obey court orders and voluntarily integrate. More importantly, he wanted to resolve the injustices faced by the black communities in courts and legislatures rather than through violent protests. Both President Kennedy and his brother, Attorney General Robert Kennedy, saw the potential for lawyers to help resolve these issues.

On June 21, 1963, President Kennedy invited a diverse and representative group of lawyers to the White House for a conference. President Kennedy, Vice President Lyndon B. Johnson, and Attorney General Kennedy all spoke to the group about the current state of civil unrest and the need to solve the problems within the rule of law. Lawyers, they argued, possess the training and skills to negotiate through the various issues while ensuring that the rights of all citizens were protected. As a result of their training, lawyers understand the rights involved in issues and can find agreement across different views. As a result, the president of the American Bar Association formed the Committee on Civil Rights and Racial Unrest.

The president asked Bernard Segal and Harrison Tweed, the cochairs of an independent committee, to identify ways that lawyers could help resolve the issues underlying civil unrest. Thus began the Lawyers Committee for Civil Rights under Law (LCCR). The LCCR went to work quickly asking for voluntary desegregation of public facilities and compliance with court orders. More importantly, the LCCR asked for the involvement of the private sector in civil rights issues.

Its first legal efforts were in Mississippi at the request of the National Council of Churches to help ministers who had been arrested and charged with crimes when they participated in nonviolent civil rights demonstrations. The LCCR arranged for volunteer lawyers to travel to Mississippi to find local lawyers to represent the ministers. However, any local lawyers willing to take these cases faced extreme backlash. To provide the legal representation needed by the Mississippi ministers, the LCCR opened an office in Mississippi.

The Mississippi office worked with local officials to secure appropriate permits for demonstrations and provided legal representation when permits were denied or participants arrested. Staffing for the office was provided by lawyers who went to Mississippi for two-week periods. The LCCR also worked with the Mississippi Bar, efforts that eventually resulted in the Bar passing a resolution to provide counsel without discrimination and establishing a process for court appointment of counsel when necessary.

Realizing the problems faced by the black community, the LCCR expanded its efforts from defending civil rights advocates to affirmative litigation against problems such as police harassment, suppression of civil rights activities, and discrimination in jobs and by public officials. They also worked in the community to improve relations with the police and began a program to assist black lawyers in building a black Bar. By the end of the 1960s, the LCCR added offices in Atlanta, Los Angeles, Boston, Chicago, Cleveland, Indianapolis, Kansas City, Philadelphia, San Francisco, and Washington. The LCCR also established the South African Project to provide legal assistance and support to those fighting apartheid.

Although the LCCR continued working to improve community-police relations and defend the rights of civil rights activists, expanded their efforts to protect and defend voting rights and challenge discriminatory employment practices. During the early 1970s, the LCCR began the Urban Areas Project to ensure adequate school financing, housing, and federal services. They also worked with local law offices to secure commitments from them to devote 1 percent to civil rights and poverty law cases referred to them by the LCCR.

The LCCR also started several specific projects during the 1970s. Laws and customs that denied minorities full voting rights were examined and challenged by the Election Law Project. With the help of the Rockefeller Fund, the LCCR established the Government Employment Project to combat federal discrimination against minority employees. The Ford Foundation supported the School Finance Project, which fought for adequate funding of schools in minority and disadvantaged areas. Meanwhile, efforts by the South African Project forced the South African Parliament to repeal discriminatory laws.

Over time, the LCCR expanded its efforts to assist other minorities. They fought to protect voting rights of Hispanics, address increasing violence against Southeast Asians, and protect the rights of refugees. The South Africa Project also expanded its efforts by working through the Namibian courts to protect South African refugees and fight for Namibian independence.

The LCCR has also responded to pervasive social problems with innovative legal programs. Realizing that jailing drug addicts was not effective, they began working to substitute rehabilitation for incarceration. Volunteer lawyers in the Narcotic Addict Legal Services Program represented clients on the original charges, advocated for their referral to treatment rather than prison, and assisted them with any other matters necessary, including helping them identify treatment facilities, find housing, and receive appropriate social services. Participants in this program were more likely to receive probation and remained in treatment longer. Although approximately 50 percent were rearrested within a year, this program demonstrated that the best results were achieved when legal aid was supplemented with social services.

The LCCR also began the Narcotic Addict Parole Project, in which attorneys helped clients plan before their parole and then assisted them for six months after parole. Those participating in the program had an increased likelihood of being granted parole both because of advocacy by the lawyers and the expectations of the parole board. However, they had a slightly higher occurrence of being rearrested within the year than nonparticipants.

Another innovative effort by the LCCR is its response to hate crimes, which began in 1982. This effort involves working closely with communities across the

United States to educate potential victims on their rights, educate police on the laws, promote enforcement of the laws, and build tolerance within the community to counter active recruitment by hate groups. Volunteer lawyers work with victims to prepare them for court appearances and victim impact statements, represent them when they are wrongfully charged, and represent them in claims for damages, restitution, and injunctive relief. With the help of Ford Foundation grants, the LCCR is working with the Department of Justice to improve hate crime reporting and provide education on the harm hate crimes cause for the victims and the community. Finally, the LCCR advocates for policy changes and passage of laws that broaden the groups covered and underlying crimes.

Currently, the LCCR is focusing its efforts on five projects. Election issues are seen by the LCCR as an important challenge to civil rights. The Election Protection Initiative is designed to ensure that all voters can participate in every election. This program works with local law firms to establish hotlines that voters can use to report and resolve issues such as changes in polling locations, ballot shortages, and verification of voter registration. The LCCR continues to challenge discrimination in housing and employment and advocates for equal public school and higher education opportunities for the poor and minorities. Because the poor and minorities disproportionately suffer from problems associated with poor air and water quality, the LCCR provides assistance to groups to fight these problems. In the near future, the LCCR expects to address the disproportionate incarceration of African Americans and the barriers they face to reintegration.

Kathleen Barrett

See also: American Civil Liberties Union (1920–); Center for Constitutional Rights (1966–); Equal Justice Initiative (1989–); NAACP Legal Defense and Education Fund (1940–)

Further Reading

Davis, Jenny B. 2016. "10 Questions: Kristen Clarke Is a Leader in the 21st Century Fight for Civil Rights." *ABA Journal*, August 2016, 2016. http://www.abajournal.com /magazine/article/10_questions_kristen_clarke_civil_rights_lawyer/.

Hutt, Peter Barton. 1984. "Civil Rights Papers: Washington Lawyers' Committee for Civil Rights Under Law: The Role of the Washington Lawyers' Committee for Civil Rights under the Law in the Handling of Drug Abuse." *Howard Law Journal* 27: 1243–1250.

Murphy, Clyde E. 1999. "Civil Rights Lawyers Organize A National Response to Hate Crime." *Corrections Today* (August): 88.

Tatel, Edith S. B. 1988. *The Lawyers' Committee: The First Twenty-Five Years*. Washington, D.C.: Lawyers' Committee for Civil Rights under Law.

League of Women Voters (1920–)

The League of Women Voters (LWV) is a nonpartisan civic organization that promotes political participation and awareness. With state and local chapters throughout the country, it plays a significant role in hosting voter registration drives, sponsoring state and local candidate forums, and promoting issue awareness, as well as engaging in issue advocacy focused on redistricting and restrictive voting laws, for example. The organization emphasizes the importance of the voter in democracy and pursues the mission set forth by its motto: "Making Democracy Work."

The LWV was first founded in 1920 by Carrie Chapman Catt (1859–1947). Catt was a well-known suffragette who was among those who fought for women's right to vote, which ultimately resulted in the passage of the Nineteenth Amendment in 1920. After women were granted the right to vote, Catt and others sought to make the newly enfranchised group more aware of the issues facing their nation and also to make them more directly engaged in the political process. Foreseeing the need to educate and mobilize women voters, the LWV was actually founded at the National American Women Suffrage Association's annual meeting, months before the Nineteenth Amendment was formally ratified.

The founding leaders of the LWV considered it to be a "mighty political experiment" for its endeavors in getting women to engage directly in politics. Before the Nineteenth Amendment, women in most states were unable to vote (some states allowed women to participate in presidential elections only, and a few states granted women full suffrage before the passage of the Nineteenth Amendment). As women account for roughly half of the population in any given community, the legal change that enabled them to vote essentially doubled the electorate. Leaders of the suffrage and women's movements wanted to be sure that women were civically engaged, using their new freedom to cast a ballot at the polls. They also worked to help women become politically knowledgeable, making informed decisions that best fit their views.

Officially, the LWV is nonpartisan and created that way intentionally. Its founding leadership was concerned not only that making it partisan would exclude women of an opposing political party from participating but also that the party politics would override the principles of political engagement upon which the organization was founded. In the interest of inclusivity, the LWV avoids ties with political parties.

The LWV originally only accepted women as members based on its focus in educating and encouraging female political participation. In 1973, however, the organization voted to change its policy and began admitting men. Many local chapters now have both men and women as active members, though the leadership at the national level remains predominantly female. The state and local chapters elect their own leadership separate from the national organization.

Despite its formal stance as being nonpartisan, the LWV does promote a variety of policies that tend to be progressive and encourage an expansion of enfranchisement and responsible citizenship. The national chapter of the organization sets its platform during its annual convention where members from local and state chapters across the country gather. Additional policy planks are debated and adopted during the national meeting, but local chapters can incorporate other stances that relate to the specific circumstances and interests of their own communities.

There are several major themes in the national LWV policy stances, all concentrating on different facets of supporting civic participation and maintaining the health of American democracy. Four major tenets are voter protection, voter education and engagement, campaign finance reform, and environmental protection. In addition to these primary issues, the LWV also takes a formal stance on the topics of immigration reform, health care improvements (including universal health care and abortion rights), gun safety legislation, fiscal policy improvements, responsive government reform, and global democracy initiatives.

First, protecting voters is central to the LWV's slogan of "Making Democracy Work" because of the critical role that voters play in the democratic process of elections and transparent governance. Though the organization was initially focused more on female voters, its interest has since expanded to include all eligible voters. In particular, the LWV works to ensure that voters from underrepresented groups are not disenfranchised or discouraged from participating in the political process. Citizens who have never registered before; come from lower socioeconomic status communities; or are elderly, new citizens, or minorities are all less likely to vote, though they have the same constitutional rights as other Americans.

Under the theme of voter protection, the LWV works to secure and expand voting rights, improve the election process, and support the expansion of voting rights to citizens residing in Washington, D.C. To make voting rights more accessible, the organization has advocated for increasing registration and voting opportunities, including allowing online voter registration, providing early voting, and making the process to both register and vote as easy as possible. It also works to confirm that states comply with the policies set forth by the Voting Rights Act of 1965 (which barred discriminatory practices that disenfranchised voters) and the National Voter Registration Act of 1993 (which made voter registration easier by offering it through other government agencies beyond the elections divisions).

With the recent proliferation of voter ID laws that have been established by state legislatures across the nation, the LWV has fought against these policies because of their limitations on voters' rights and the barriers to participation that may arise. By requiring an ID (in some states, one that has a picture that "substantially conforms" to the voter, an expiration date, a name matching—exactly—the one on the voter registration log, and is issued by a state agency), proponents argue that this practice maintains the integrity of the elections process by eliminating in-person voter fraud. However, the LWV counters that the kind of in-person voter fraud these measures are designed to prevent simply does not happen. Moreover, they argue, these requirements place an undue burden on individuals who do not already possess such documentation—thereby depressing turnout and increasing the likelihood that otherwise legal ballots would be thrown out.

Second, to educate and engage voters, the organization participates in a variety of programs aimed at encouraging civic involvement. Through publications, forums, open meetings, and online resources, the LWV aims to provide voters with unbiased, nonpartisan summaries of the important issues, the different candidates, and the various offices that are at stake in the elections. They also regularly sponsor voter registration drives and work to ensure that all eligible citizens are able to exercise their right to vote.

Third, the LWV also takes an active stance on the topic of campaign finance reform with the concern that the overwhelming emphasis on money in politics prioritizes the voices of wealthy interests over others in the political process. In particular, the organization opposes the *Citizens United* decision rendered by the Supreme Court in 2010 (*Citizens United v. Federal Election Commission*). The court found that previous regulations prohibiting corporations from spending money in campaigns was a violation of those corporations' First Amendment freedom of speech. This led to the creation of Super-PACs and the exponential growth in uncoordinated financial contributions supporting candidates' campaigns. The LWV challenges that this decision dilutes the influence of voters and disadvantages candidates with less funding.

Beyond the role money plays in elections, the organization is also invested in changing the way money influences interest groups and lobbying. It advocates for more transparency and accountability in government and believes that restricting the influence interest groups and PACs can have in interacting with elected officials would make the legislative process more fair and free from special interests.

Finally, the LWV has adopted a policy platform focused on protecting the environment and works to encourage legislation that furthers this endeavor. It seeks to raise public awareness of the likely causes of climate change and advocate for potential solutions that can be implemented to counteract its impact. By focusing on global climate change, clean air, and clean energy, the organization embodies a progressive attitude that citizens and their government must take an active role in environmental preservation for the current and future health of their communities.

The LWV works at the local, state, federal, and even international levels to support initiatives that ensure long-term health and stability. Specifically, it argues for the protection of natural resources and the advancement of clean energy as an alternative to fossil fuels, maintaining economic prosperity without the risk of environmental harms. The organization supported the Kyoto protocol and other national legislation involving clean air and drinking water; most recently, it opposed the proposed Keystone Pipeline for its potential environmental hazards.

In order to spread its message and pursue its initiatives, the LWV operates as a grassroots organization. Its state and local chapters provide town hall–style forums and debates during the election cycle in which candidates running for office can share their views and stances with the voters. They also regularly publish and distribute materials about the races, offices, candidates, and voting process. Because of its nonpartisan position, the LWV provides moderators and materials to other organizations hosting debates and forums as well.

Though the LWV is a self-described nonpartisan organization, the progressive stances it has taken prevent it from being purely nonpartisan. The group came under fire in 2010 by some Colorado Republicans who claimed the LWV was biased toward the liberal perspective. The argument was incited when a state senator tried to pass a resolution honoring the organization's 90th anniversary.

The League's status as nonpartisan again came into question in Minnesota concerning a new voter ID law, which was supported by Republicans. The LWV's commitment to open access in voting led to a conflict. The state legislature discussed the adoption of an amendment to the state constitution that would require voters to supply a photo ID in order to vote. The LWV argued that such a requirement would unfairly disenfranchise some voters and further suppress voter turnout.

Prior to the 2012 election cycle, the organization sponsored television advertisements to influence Senate races based on incumbents' votes on the reauthorization of the Clean Air Act. An amendment sponsored by West Virginia Senator Jay Rockefeller (1937–) proposed to curb the Environmental Protection Agency's authority to regulate. Two senators facing competitive elections, Scott Brown (1959–) from Massachusetts and Claire McCaskill (1953–) from Missouri, were among those who voted in favor of Rockefeller's proposition. The two incumbents were both targets of television spots sponsored by the LWV that challenged their commitment to their constituents based on their vote. Unlike the earlier issues from Colorado and Minnesota, the LWV's involvement was perceived to be nonpartisan, as Brown was a Republican and McCaskill a Democrat.

Since its inception nearly a century ago, the LWV has played an integral role in American politics. By educating voters and encouraging civic participation, the organization has grown into a powerful national political institution. Despite various changes in the political landscape and in the organization itself, the LWV remains steadfast in its aim of empowering voters and "making democracy work."

Laura Merrifield (Albright) Wilson

Related Primary Document: **League of Women Voters: Interest of Amici Curiae in** *Husted v. A. Philip Randolph Institute* **(2017)**

League of Women Voters: Interest of Amici Curiae in *Husted v. A. Philip Randolph Institute* (2017)

The League of Women Voters (LWV), a civic organization founded in 1920 with the purpose of encouraging women to pursue political roles after they gained the right to vote, has long advocated for both women's rights and voting rights. On September 22, 2017, the LWV created the following amicus curiae brief to fight restrictions on the voting rights of the homeless population of Ohio. The LWV filed this brief with several other organizations to fight for citizens removed from the voter registry due to their failure to vote, as detailed in Husted v. A. Philip Randolph Institute, *a Supreme Court case argued in January 2018.*

INTEREST OF AMICI CURIAE

The League of Women Voters of the United States ("League") is a nonpartisan, community-based organization that encourages Americans to participate actively in government and the electoral process. Founded in 1920 as an outgrowth of the struggle to win voting rights for women, the League now has more than 140,000 members and supporters, and is organized in approximately 750 communities and in every state. For over ninety years, the League has led efforts to remove barriers that Americans face in registering to vote and casting a ballot.

The League was deeply involved in crafting the National Voter Registration Act of 1993 ("NVRA"), having provided substantial testimony and input over the course of the NVRA's legislative history, specifically on the topic of purges for failure to vote. See, e.g., Voter Registration: Hearing Before the Subcomm. on Elections of the Comm. on H. Admin., 101st Cong. 149 (1989) (testimony of Nancy M. Neuman, President, League of Women Voters); Voter Registration: Hearing Before the Subcomm. on Elections of the Comm. on H. Admin., 103d Cong. 140 (1993) (testimony of Becky Cain, President, League of Women Voters).

The League of Women Voters of Ohio ("LWVO") is the state affiliate of the League. It is a nonpartisan political organization, which encourages informed and active participation in government. There are thirty-three local Leagues around the state. The LWVO has fought unlawful voter restrictions and believes that voting is a fundamental citizen right that must be guaranteed. The LWVO's local Leagues register voters, perform public education, conduct research, and engage with public officials on issues related to registration and voting.

The Brennan Center for Justice at N.Y.U. School of Law is a not-for-profit, nonpartisan think tank and public interest law institute that seeks to improve systems of democracy and justice. It was founded in 1995 to honor the extraordinary contributions of Justice William J. Brennan, Jr. to American law and society. Through its Democracy Program, the Brennan Center seeks to bring the idea of representative self-government closer to reality, including through work to protect the right to vote and to prevent manipulation of electoral rules. The Brennan Center conducts empirical, qualitative, historic, and legal research on electoral practices, including on voter list maintenance practices. In 2008, the Center published a comprehensive report examining the voter roll purge practices in the United States based on in-depth interviews of state and local election administrators. Moreover, the Center has litigated numerous cases involving purges of the voter rolls, and submitted numerous amicus briefs in this Court on voting rights matters.

SUMMARY OF ARGUMENT The purge provisions contained in Section 8 of the NVRA are designed to prevent states from instituting practices to remove registered voters from the rolls based on unreasonable inferences that the voter has become ineligible. The NVRA requires states to make "a reasonable effort to remove the names of ineligible voters," and bars states from taking unreasonable steps to remove voters from the rolls, such as removing individuals for non-voting or removing voters based on an unsubstantiated belief that the voter has moved. The legislative history and the NVRA's text confirms Congress sought to protect voters against having to needlessly re-register because of purges based on unreasonable inferences.

Ohio's Supplemental Process of commencing a purge based on the failure to vote in a single federal election cycle is not reasonable. It is wildly overbroad and does not target individuals who may no longer be eligible. In this case,

Ohio began the first step in purging over half its registered voters—by sending notices to some four million people—after they failed to vote in a single federal election cycle in 2010. Ohio compounded the unreasonableness of its action by not clearly informing these voters that they would be removed from the voter rolls if they did not act in response to the notice. And Ohio stands alone: it is one of only six states that expressly commences deregistration based on the failure to vote. Yet Ohio is the only state that commences such a process based on the failure to vote in a single federal election cycle. Section 8 of the NVRA was designed to prevent such practices.

ARGUMENT

I. Section 8 of the NVRA was Intended to Prevent Purges Based on Unreasonable Inferences. 1. When Congress enacted the NVRA, it did so against a historical backdrop in which states routinely imposed obstacles to voter registration to limit the franchise. Such "[r]estrictive registration laws and administrative procedures were introduced in the United States . . . to keep certain groups of citizens from voting; in the North, the wave of immigrants pouring into the industrial cities; in the South, blacks and the rural poor." H.R. Rep. No. 103-9, at 2 (1993). Indeed, "[t]hroughout the history of this country there have been attempts to keep certain groups of citizens from registering to vote—which groups specifically depending on the decade and the locale." S. Rep. No. 103-6, at 3 (1993). Congress rightly condemned "discriminatory and unfair registration laws and procedures" that had "a direct and damaging effect on voter participation in elections for Federal office and disproportionately harm voter participation by various groups, including racial minorities." 52 U.S.C. § 20501(a)(3).

Among the obstacles Congress addressed in the NVRA were efforts to deregister or "purge" voters who remained eligible to vote. Congress's reforms of purge practices are found in Section 8 of the NVRA. An animating goal of Section 8 was to prevent deregistration procedures premised on unreasonable inferences that a registered voter was no longer eligible to vote. The Senate Committee on Rules and Administration explained that Section 8 was intended to "ensure that once a citizen is registered to vote, he or she should remain on the voting list so long as he or she remains eligible to vote in that jurisdiction." S. Rep. No. 103-6, at 17 (1993). The committee further noted: "The maintenance of accurate and up-to-date voter registration lists is the hallmark of a national system seeking to prevent voter fraud. These processes, however, must be scrutinized to prevent poor and illiterate voters from being caught in a purge system which will require them to needlessly reregister." Id. at 18.

Congress heard about these problems over the course of successive legislative sessions.2 In fact, the congressional record is replete with complaints about abusive practices where persons still eligible to vote were removed from the rolls. The record established both that certain purges had been conducted in a discriminatory manner, and that other purges arbitrarily purged individuals based on an unreasonable inference that the individual was no longer eligible to vote. Among the injustices documented for Congress were "selective" purges, insufficient or no notice to registrants about their removal, purges too close to an election for citizens to refresh or renew their registrations in time to vote, and other disenfranchisement measures. See generally S. Rep. No. 103-6, at 3 (1993) (identifying specific practices that inhibited or excluded potential voters); Voter Registration: Hearing Before the Subcomm. on Elections of the Comm. On H. Admin., 101st Cong. 149 (1989) (testimony on purged voters having insufficient time to reregister to vote); id. at 134 (same); id. at 202–03 (testimony regarding absence of notice to purged voters).

Prominent among the practices condemned during the congressional testimony was the practice of purging registered voters who had not voted in the most recent election. As the Committee on Rules and Administration report summarizes:

> If there was a single point of agreement among all participants in the hearings on voter registration, it was the fact that not only is voting a right, but also, in this country, everyone has an equal right to choose not to vote. However, many States continue to penalize such non-voters by removing their names from the voter registration rolls merely because they have failed to cast a ballot in a recent election. S. Rep. No. 101-140, at 12 (1989).

During congressional hearings, witnesses not only condemned the arbitrary and discriminatory effects of purging non-voters, they also challenged the basic premise behind conducting such purges—that is, the inference that a person's failure to vote signifies that he or she has moved or is otherwise ineligible to vote. As the Senate Rules Committee observed: "[W]hile voting is a right, people have an equal right not to vote, for whatever reason." S. Rep. No. 103-6, at 17 (1993). Removals of non-voters, the Committee concluded, are overinclusive. "Such citizens may not have moved or died or committed a felony." Id.

Throughout the Congressional hearings and debate, witnesses and members of Congress explained why the failure to vote does not a support an inference that a voter is ineligible. For example, in 1989, League President Nancy M. Neuman testified at some length about the many reasons why voters do not vote in particular elections—none of which support the conclusion that voter is ineligible:

> Whatever may be a voter's reasons for choosing not to vote—lack of interest in or confusion about a particular election, disbelief that the issues presented will adequately express one's concerns or that the candidates are worthy of one's support, inaccessibility of the polling place, absence, emergency, health, even general lack of interest—one should not have the right to vote stripped away.

Voter Registration: Hearing Before the Subcomm. on Elections of the Comm. on H. Admin., 101st Cong. 149 (1989) (statement of Nancy M. Neuman, President, League of Women Voters).

Senator Wendell Ford, the Senate sponsor of the NVRA, argued that "[w]e can put an end to unnecessary reregistration by voters who choose to be heard by not voting. . . . Some, even Senators, abstain from voting. . . . And that speaks as loud as a yea or a nay. So they want to be heard by choosing not to vote. And then we penalize them under our present system for not voting." 139 Cong. Rec. S2,390 (1993) (statement of Sen. Ford). Similarly, Senator Kennedy, a co-sponsor of the legislation, observed that "[m]any people who are registered don't vote as a matter of civil protest." Equal Access to Voting Act of 1989: Hearing Before the Subcomm. on the Constitution of the S. Comm. on the Judiciary, 101st Cong. 89 (1989).

Deborah Karpatkin, Legal Director of Human SERVE, likewise pointed out that voters may abstain from voting in one or more elections

> because they don't wish to vote for any of the candidates available to them. The only way these voters can express their displeasure with the candidates is to vote with their feet—that is, to not show up. I don't know of any ballots in the country where you can check "None of the above."

Voter Registration: Hearing Before the Subcomm. on Elections of the Comm. on H. Admin., 101st Cong. 201 (1989) (testimony of Deborah Karpatkin, Legal Dir., Human Serve); see also S. Rep. No. 103-6, at 17 (1993) ("No other rights guaranteed to citizens are bound by the constant exercise of that right. We do not lose our right to free speech because we do not speak out on every issue").

These observations and the resulting legislative judgment make good sense. In every election, there are tens of millions of registered voters who do not vote. For example, in 2016, the U.S. Election Assistance Commission counted almost 74 million registered voters across the country (37.02%) who did not cast a ballot in the general election. Voter participation is even lower in non-Presidential elections: in 2014, almost 110 million registered voters across the country (57.45%) did not cast a ballot in the general election. While different data from the U.S. Census Bureau show a smaller number of registered non-voters in 2014—roughly 50 million—that number is still vast.

These numbers far exceed the number of registered voters who move outside their county each election cycle, and thus become ineligible to vote in that district. See 52 U.S.C. § 20507(e)(1)-(2). According to the U.S. Census Bureau, about ten million residents age 18 or older moved outside their county between 2015 and 2016. That means that even if one assumes that every single adult mover failed to take any steps to update their registration information, moving still would account for less than one seventh of the non-voting activity in 2016, based on figures from the U.S. Election Assistance Commission.

Survey data of registered voters who do not vote confirms that there are many reasons why an eligible voter might abstain from voting—none of which implicates ineligibility. For example, a U.S. Census Bureau survey of 18,933 registered voters who did not vote in the 2016 election found that most of these individuals did not vote because they:

- "did not like candidates or campaign issues" (24.8%);
- were "not interested" (15.4%);
- were "too busy" or had "conflicting schedule" (14.3%);
- had "illness or disability" (11.7%);
- were "out of town" (7.9%);
- "forgot to vote" (3.0%);
- had "transportation problems" (2.6%); or
- had an "inconvenient polling place" (2.1%).

Only 4.4 percent of respondents claimed that they did not vote because of "registration problems." Even if, in the unlikely event, every single one of these respondents experienced such problems because they moved, that accounts for at most 4.4 percent of those who do not vote. These data demonstrate that it is unreasonable to infer that a person did not vote because he or she has moved or is otherwise no longer eligible to vote. 2. Congress addressed this issue in Section 8 of the NVRA, which provides the basic rules for conducting purges. Section 8 directs states to make "reasonable efforts" to maintain accurate rolls of voters. Preventing eligible registrants from being purged arbitrarily is an essential aspect of reasonableness.

The NVRA specifies only five reasons for which voters may be removed from the rolls: (i) the voter requests to be removed, 52 U.S.C. § 20507(a)(3)(A), (ii) the voter is ineligible under state law due to criminal conviction, id. § 20507(a)(3)(B), (iii) the voter is ineligible under state law due to mental incapacity, id., (iv) the voter has died, id. § 20507(a)(4)(A), or (v) the voter has moved out of the jurisdiction, id. § 20507(a)(4)(B).

The first four factors—voter request, criminal conviction, adjudication of mental incapacity, and death—are derived from ascertainable, recorded facts. Accordingly, purges on those bases are relatively straightforward. In contrast, assessing whether a voter has moved but has not so informed election officials is often very difficult. Because of this, the NVRA contains additional restrictions specifically aimed at purges based on an assumed change in residence. The statute expressly recognizes only three permissible processes for purging voters on the ground that they have moved.

First, the NVRA allows states to begin the deregistration process when the Postal Service provides information that the voter has moved. Id. § 20507(c)(1). If the Postal Service has information that an individual has moved, it is reasonable for a state to infer that the individual may have, in fact, moved. Yet, Congress still insisted that the state verify the move through the Section 8(d)(2) procedure. Id. § 20507(c)(1)(B)(ii).

Second, the NVRA allows a state to remove a voter from the rolls if the voter confirms in writing that the voter has moved. Id. § 20507(d)(1)(A). If an individual confirms that she or he has moved, it is of course reasonable for the state to act on that information.

Third, after receiving or obtaining credible information that a voter has moved,10 the NVRA allows a state to send a forwardable notice to the voter with a prepaid return card requiring the voter to confirm her residence, i.e., the Section 8(d)(2) notice. If the voter does not return the card and does not vote in the next two federal elections, it is not unreasonable for the state to infer that the voter has moved. Id. § 20507(d)(2).

But even when states follow these steps, the NVRA still limits states' discretion on how to implement a removal program in a number of ways:

First and foremost is the limitation at issue in this case: the statute explicitly prohibits states from purging registered voters "by reason of the person's failure to vote. . . ." Id. § 20507(b)(2). This provision is not an isolated limitation; it is part of a series of limitations on how states can remove from the rolls individuals suspected of moving.

The statute further requires that purges based on moving (among other grounds) occur only pursuant to a "general program" involving "reasonable effort[s]." Id. § 20507(a)(3)(C), (4).

And, more generally, the statute bars any purges that are not "uniform" and "nondiscriminatory." Id. U.S.C. § 20507(b)(1).

Congress did not stop there. The NVRA also provides additional, more specific limits on state programs to purge registered voters:

- If a voter has moved to a different address in the same jurisdiction but did not update her address, the voter is nonetheless entitled to vote. Id. § 20507(c)(1)(B)(i).
- If a voter is mailed a forwardable notice with the prepaid return card and the voter does not return the card but appears to vote at any time before the next two elections, the voter may not be purged. Id. § 20507(d)(2).

These prohibitions are directed at the accuracy of inferences about ineligibility, including in particular whether a failure to vote in a single federal election cycle signifies that the voter has become ineligible. For the present case, this is significant for two reasons.

First, the "failure to vote" prohibition is part of a related series of protections against purging individuals based on unreasonable inferences that they may have moved. That provision should be interpreted in a manner consistent with that objective, and not in a way that defeats it. Cf. King v. Burwell, 135 S. Ct. 2480, 2493 (2015) ("We cannot interpret federal statutes to negate their own stated purposes.") (internal quotation marks omitted); FDA v.

Brown & Williamson Tobacco Corp., 529 U.S. 120 (2000); Reves v. Ernst & Young, 494 U.S. 56, 60–61 (1990).

Second, Congress was so deeply concerned about inaccurate purging, especially when seeking to remove a voter because she has moved, that it erected multiple safeguards to curb that practice. The prohibition on purging by reason of non-voting is a critical safeguard against inaccurate purges of individuals suspected of moving; indeed, it lies at the center of Congress's intended protections for the right to vote or not vote.

While the NVRA does not expressly address every practice a state might use to determine whether a voter becomes ineligible, and allows states some flexibility, the NVRA directs states to "conduct a general program that makes a reasonable effort to remove the names of ineligible voters." 52 U.S.C. § 20507(a)(4) (emphasis added). And it bars states from removing voters from the rolls based on change in residence unless removal is part of that general, reasonable program. Id. § 20507(a)(3)(C) (barring change-in-residence removals except pursuant to 52 U.S.C. § 20507(a)(4)). For the reasons described below in Part II, a program like Ohio's Supplemental Process, which is initiated when a voter fails to vote in just one election, does not pass Congress's test.

II. Ohio's Supplemental Process Is an Entirely Unreasonable Method of Determining Ineligibility.

Ohio's Supplemental Process is not a reasonable measure to maintain accurate voting rolls by identifying and removing ineligible voters. As Congress recognized in the NVRA, failure to vote in a single election is a lousy proxy for assessing whether a registered voter has moved or otherwise become ineligible to vote. That is why the overwhelming majority of states expressly do not rely on failure to vote at all. There are four outlier states, but none is as aggressive as Ohio.

Only Ohio deregisters voters based on their failure to vote in a single federal election cycle. As a result, the purges that are at issue in this litigation were commenced following a non-Presidential election (in 2010) in which half of Ohio registered voters—some four million people—did not vote. Such a process cannot be considered reasonable within the meaning of the NVRA.

A. Failure to Vote in One Federal Election Cycle Is Not a Reasonable Proxy for Voter Ineligibility.

1. Ohio's Supplemental Process starts from an unjustified premise. It is unreasonable to infer that a person may have moved (or died or been disenfranchised) simply because the registrant failed to vote in a single federal election cycle.

The number of affected voters is startling. For example, during the Presidential election in 2016, 28.67% of Ohio registered voters did not vote, and in 2012, 29.46% did not vote. As with the national trends, non-voting is even higher in non-Presidential elections: in 2014, 59.35% of Ohio registered voters did not cast a ballot, and in 2010, 50.78% did not vote. Those percentages translate into millions of eligible voters that choose to stay home on election day in Ohio: over 2.2 million in 2016, and over 2.3 million in 2012.13 In non-presidential election years, the numbers double. In 2014, 4.6 million registered Ohioans did not vote, and 4.1 million did not vote in 2010.14 While Ohio speculates that those numbers might be inflated by including non-eligible voters, it offers no data to substantiate that assumption. In any event, commencing a purge of all such individuals—as Ohio did here—is not reasonable.

2. Ohio compounded the unreasonableness of its program by sending ineffectual notices under Section 8(d)(2) that failed to warn voters to take a specific action or face removal from the rolls. Petitioner's argument that its notice prevents any violation of the NVRA because its purges are based on a "failure to respond to a notice," and not the failure to vote, see Pet. Br. 23–29, ignores that its own practice failed to make clear that voters needed to respond. The court below found that Ohio's 8(d)(2) notices "did not adequately inform voters of the consequences of failing to respond to the notice; rather, the form indicated that the recipient's registration 'may' be canceled if he or she did not respond, re-register, or vote in the next four years." Pet. App. 6a. Notably, Petitioner does not dispute this finding. Id. at 8a-9a. Ohio's inadequate 8(d)(2) notices cannot transform its unreasonable practice of initiating purges based on the failure to vote in a single federal election cycle into a reasonable one.

3. The Supplemental Process has had harmful consequences for Ohio's conduct of federal elections and for voters. First, thousands of voters were deregistered even though they had not moved and remained eligible to vote. The Secretary concedes that at least 7,515 citizens were struck from the rolls despite not moving; these voters had to cast provisional ballots in the 2016 election. Yet, the real toll is likely much greater. Records from just two of Ohio's 88 counties show that 66,570 registrants were removed from the rolls due to the Supplemental Process. And there is no way to know how many still-eligible voters who had been deregistered did not cast a provisional ballot because they did not know they were entitled to do so or were improperly denied a provisional ballot by confused poll workers. As the Presidential Commission on Election Administration has observed, "poll workers unaware of various legal requirements, such as those governing provisional ballots, may unintentionally turn away eligible voters." See Presidential Comm'n on Election Admin., The American Voting Experience 48 (2014). And even if Petitioner's number is correct, depriving 7,515 eligible citizens of their fundamental right to vote based on their lawful choice not to vote in a prior election is exactly what the NVRA was intended to prevent.

Second, Ohio's practice promotes confusion on election day. The Secretary concedes that thousands of people showed up to vote who were not aware they had been deregistered through the Supplemental Process. Pet. Br. 14. Poll workers had to take time to confirm that those people were not on the rolls, to figure out why not, to explain the situation to them, and to offer them a provisional ballot. See Pet. App. 94a–100a. Because people who turn out to vote but are not on the rolls require more time and attention from poll workers, they lengthen the lines and wait times for all voters. Presidential Comm'n on Election Admin., The American Voting Experience 25 (2014). Longer lines and wait times can lead would-be voters to give up, and discourage others from turning out at all. See, e.g., U.S. Gov't Accountability Off., GAO-14-850, Elections: Observations on Wait Times for Voters on Election Day 2012 26 & n.52 (2014).

This result flies in the face of "the duty of the Federal, State, and local governments to promote the exercise of th[e] right [to vote]" and the NVRA's purpose of "enhanc[ing] the participation of eligible citizens as voters in elections for Federal office." 52 U.S.C. § 20501(a)(2), (b)(2).

4. Several of Petitioner's amici (but not Petitioner himself) assert that deregistering a voter for failure to vote is somehow justified on the theory that it prevents voter fraud. See, e.g., Judicial Watch Br. 19–20; American Civil Rights Union Br. 13; Landmark Legal Found. Br. 13. No evidence bears out that argument. A broad sweep that starts with all individuals who did not vote (based on the unreasonable inference that people who do not vote must be ineligible to vote) is not a reasonable way to target individuals who may attempt to vote fraudulently. That petitioners' amici repeatedly invoke an overstated and theoretical risk does not make it true. And those unsubstantiated concerns certainly do not make Ohio's program reasonable.

B. No Other State Uses Practices as Unreasonable as Ohio's to Deregister Voters.

States have adopted a wide array of practices to remove the names of ineligible voters from the rolls. Petitioner and several of his amici suggest that Ohio's Supplemental Process is not unreasonable because it is similar to other states' practices.16 No other state, however, has a practice as hamhanded and draconian as Ohio's Supplemental Process.

A survey of other state practices reveals that no other state expressly uses the failure to vote in a single federal election cycle as the trigger to send a Section 8(d)(2) notice.

Thirty-eight other states (and the District of Columbia) have established practices that, unlike Ohio's Supplemental Process, use independent information that an individual has moved—not an individual's failure to vote—as a trigger to send a Section 8(d)(2) notice. These states are identified in the Appendix.

Their processes include:

- Consultations with other agencies in the state. State election officials often have information-sharing agreements with other state agencies to

identify individuals who may have moved or died. See, e.g., Ind. Code §
3-7-38.2-2 (election officials informed of returned jury notices); N.Y.
Elec. Law § 5-712 (election officials receive information from federal,
state or local government agencies); Wash. Rev. Code § 29A.08.620
(election officials receive information from Department of Licensing or
other agency).

- Information-sharing agreements with other states. Many states (including
  Ohio) collaborate to pool information from their various agencies to com-
  pare voter records across states for evidence that an individual has moved
  from one jurisdiction to another. See, e.g., Electronic Registration Information Center (ERIC), http://www.ericstates.org/faq (a non-profit organization (consisting of 20 states and the District of Columbia) that aggregates
  data from its members and submits a report to each state showing "voters
  who have moved within their state, voters who have moved out of state,
  voters who have died, duplicate registrations in the same state and individuals who are potentially eligible to vote but are not yet registered");
  Del. Code tit. 15, § 1704(a) ("The Department may use a list of persons
  registered to vote in Delaware and who are registered to vote in another
  state or who have obtained a Driver's License or state ID card from
  another state as a source to send an address verification request to those
  voters."); Va. Code § 24.2-404.4 ("Department of Elections shall request
  voter registration information . . . from the states bordering the Commonwealth" and "utilize data regarding voter registration . . . received through
  list comparisons with other states").
- Other election-related mailings. Certain states send mailings to all registered voters or use information about non-delivered or returned mail to
  identify individuals who may have moved. See, e.g., Ala. Code 1975 §
  17-4- 30(a) (nonforwardable mailing to all registered voters every four
  years); Ariz. Rev. Stat. § 16-166(A) (any returned election related mail);
  Cal. Elec. Code § 2225 (returned voter notification card); Colo. Rev. Stat.
  § 1-2- 605 (1) (returned election-related mail); Ind. Code § 3-7-38.2-2
  (returned election-related mail); Kan. Stat. § 25-2316c(e) (returned election-related mail); Neb. Rev. Stat. § 32-329 (biennial mailing of a nonforwardable notice to each registered voter); N.M. Stat. 1-4-28 (returned
  election-related mail).
- Canvass of all registered voters. Certain states canvass all of their voters
  to determine if they have moved. See Conn. Gen. Stat. § 9-32; Mass.
  Gen. Laws Ch. 51, § 37.
- Postal Service Information. Virtually every state, including Ohio, see
  Ohio Rev. Code § 3503.21(B)(1), uses information from the Postal Service's National Change of Address Program to identify individuals who
  have indicated they have moved. See, e.g., Ariz. Rev. Stat. § 16-166(E);
  Cal. Elec. Code § 2225; Del. Code tit. 15, § 1704; Ind. Code § 3-7-38.2-2;
  Kan. Stat. § 25-2316c(e); Mich. Comp. Laws § 168.509aa; Md. Code

Elec. Law § 3-502(b); Neb. Rev. Stat. § 32-329; N.J. Stat. § 19:31-15; Va. Code § 24.2-428.18

- Two-step process. Several states use a twostep mailing process for sending a Section 8(d)(2) notice. If an individual has not voted in a specified number of elections, election officials send a non-forwardable notice to that voter; if that notice is returned as undeliverable, only then do these states send a Section 8(d)(2) notice.19 See Alaska Stat. § 15.07.130(a); Fla. Stat. § 98.065(2); 29-250- 505 Me. Code R. § 1; Mont. Code § 13-2-220(1); 17 R.I. Gen. Laws § 17-9.1-27(b); S.D. Codified Laws § 12-4-19.

These other state practices demonstrate states can undertake efforts to clean their rolls without adopting a policy like Ohio's Supplemental Process. Only five other states (Georgia, Oklahoma, Oregon, Pennsylvania, and West Virginia) expressly use failure to vote as a trigger for deregistration at all. All provide for more protection than Ohio to prevent deregistration of eligible voters. Unlike Ohio, none of these states sends a Section 8(d)(2) notice after an individual fails to vote in a single federal election cycle. See Ga. Code § 21-2-234(a) (three years); Okla. Stat. tit. 26, § 4-120.2 (two general elections); Or. Rev. Stat. § 247.296 (five years); 25 Pa. Cons. Stat. § 1901(b)(3) (five years); W.V. Code § 3-2-25(j) (four years).20 This is especially significant in light of the fact that Ohio is the only state to have sent notices that a court found insufficient to inform voters that if they do not respond to the notice and continue not to vote, they will be deregistered.

The above survey of other state practices reveals what amici in support of Petitioner attempt to obscure: that no other state has implemented a process as aggressive or unreasonable as Ohio's Supplemental Process. Ohio's Supplemental Process is the opposite of a "best" practice. American Civil Rights Union Br. 12. Other states have not and will not be "hamstrung" if Ohio's Supplemental Process is confirmed to violate the NVRA. Landmark Legal Found. Br. 10. Nor is it "practically infeasible" for Ohio to use a different practice. The Buckeye Inst. Br. 8. Literally every other state uses a different, and more voter-protective, practice.

CONCLUSION

Ohio's Supplemental Process not only violates the NVRA prohibition against removing a lawful voter "by reason of the person's failure to vote," it is based on unreasonable and inaccurate inferences that deprive a significant number of voters of their right to vote, or not vote. This Court should affirm the judgment below.

Respectfully submitted,

WENDY R. WEISER

MYRNA PÉREZ

JONATHAN BRATER BRENNAN

CTR. FOR JUSTICE AT NYU SCHOOL OF LAW

161 Avenue of the Americas, 12th Floor New York, NY 10013 Phone: 646-292-8318 wendy.weiser@nyu.edu

JOHN A. FREEDMAN Counsel of Record

PETER J. SCHILDKRAUT

ELISABETH S. THEODORE

JEREMY KARPATKIN

ANDREW W. BEYER

ARNOLD & PORTER KAYE SCHOLER LLP

601 Massachusetts Ave., NW Washington, DC 20001 (202) 942-5000 john.freedman@apks.com Counsel for Amici Curiae

Source: *Husted v. A. Philip Randolph Institute*, No. 16-980, Argued January 10, 2018, pending.

See also: EMILY's List (1985–); National Organization for Women (1966–); National Women's Political Caucus (1971–)

Further Reading

Chappell, Marisa. 2002. "Rethinking Women's Politics in the 1970s: The League of Women Voters and the National Organization for Women Confront Poverty." *Journal of Women's History* 13 (4): 155–179.

DuBois, Ellen Carol. 1998. *Women Suffrage and Women's Rights.* New York: New York University Press.

Van Voris, Jacqueline. 1996. *Carrie Chapman Catt: A Public Life.* New York: Feminist Press at CUNY.

Young, Louise Merwin. 1989. *In the Public Interest: The League of Women Voters, 1920–1970.* Santa Barbara, CA: Praeger.

Libertarian Party (1971–)

The Libertarian Party, founded in 1971, has been the most consistently successful third party in the United States over the last third of the 20th century and into the 21st. While its electoral success at the national level has been limited, its vibrant state party organizations have helped the party achieve increasing success at the state and local levels. In addition, the party's ideological commitment has, by all accounts, impacted the national debate over issues ranging from drug use to school choice, with the major parties increasingly adopting libertarian influenced positions.

The Libertarian Party was founded in 1971 in the shadow of the ongoing war in Vietnam and the imposition by President Richard Nixon of wage and price controls. Although the formal founding of the party is generally dated to an eight-member gathering in a private home in Colorado Springs, Colorado, on December 11, 1971, the roots of that meeting can found in a smaller gathering in August at the home of party founder David Nolan, who, while watching with dismay as President Nixon announced both the imposition of wage and price controls as well as the decision to take the United States off the gold standard, determined to do something.

Indeed, Nixon's actions, coupled with ongoing questions about the legitimacy of the Vietnam War (1955–1975), were the source of continuing discussions among Nolan and his friends, and they finally led to the December Colorado Springs gathering, from which a plan and a party emerged. The following summer a small convention was held in Denver, and a ticket—John Hospers for president and Theodora Nathan for vice president—was nominated. The ticket itself won less than 4,000 popular votes, but when one elector, Roger MacBride, who would in fact be the Libertarian nominee in 1976, expressed his opposition to Richard Nixon's continuing war policies by casting his vote for the Libertarian ticket, he made Nathan the first woman ever to receive an electoral vote in a United States presidential election.

The Libertarian Party began an ongoing effort to build a grassroots movement, and every four years it has emerged from its seeming media-imposed isolation to nominate a presidential candidate while seeking to spread its message before a national audience In 1976, the Libertarian standard bearer was Roger MacBride, who garnered barely 0.2 percent of the vote. The following cycle offered more hope for those dreaming of a Libertarian overthrow of the entrenched Democratic- and Republican-based system. While ultimately little more than a footnote in the face-off between Jimmy Carter and Ronald Reagan, the performance of 1980 Libertarian nominee Ed Clark represented its then-high-water mark for the party, one that endured for over three decades until established political figure and former Republican governor of New Mexico Gary Johnson joined the party and led the ticket in 2012.

Clark, a lawyer and businessman who had won over 5 percent of the vote running as an independent in the 1978 California gubernatorial election, ran with businessman David Koch, who had recently founded the Cato Institute, a libertarian think tank, and who with his brother would become a controversial and major funder of libertarian and conservative causes in the late 20th and early 21st centuries. Together they won just over 920,000 votes, a figure that accounted for just over 1 percent of the vote. Subsequent presidential cycles have always included a Libertarian candidate, with its best presidential showing coming in 2016 when Gary Johnson, also the 2012 nominee, paired with former Massachusetts governor William Weld to win just under 4.5 million votes, good for 3.28 percent of the popular vote.

Not only did this performance represent its best electoral showing ever, but it also represented the fourth time in the party's history—the previous ones were 1980, 1992, and 1996—that the party has had its presidential nominee on the ballot in all 50 states. In 2000, the formal nominee Harry Browne was listed on all state ballots except in Arizona, where the Libertarian candidate was instead listed as L. Neil Smith. Indeed, the back-to-back 50-state ballot access of 1992 and 1996 was the first time in U.S. political history that a third party had achieved that across-the-board ballot placement in consecutive elections.

The party has not limited itself to presidential campaigns. In fact, the party has had substantive success at the local and municipal levels. Less than a decade after the party's founding, in 1978, Dick Randolph was elected to the Alaska House of Representatives, a victory that made him the first Libertarian to hold an elected office at the state level. Once in office, true to the party's agenda, Randolph led the successful effort to repeal the state's income tax. At the same time, as of 2017, no Libertarian candidate has ever been elected to Congress, although Randolph is not the lone state-level electoral victor. In fact, according to the party's website, as of July 2016, the Libertarians held elected offices in 34 states, with three being state legislators.

In addition, in recent years a number of elected Republicans have switched to the Libertarian Party, with mixed results in their next electoral efforts. Three of its presidential nominees, Ron Paul in 1988, Bob Barr in 2008, and Gary Johnson, were all former office holders originally elected as Republicans. As of November 2016, the party had about 500,000 registered voters nationwide, with state affiliates in all 50 states.

Many libertarians have rejoiced at the party's improved electoral fortunes, seeing Johnson's performance as evidence that the party is beginning to crack open the door. In contrast, others express concern about whether the nomination of onetime Republican office holders like Johnson and running mate William Weld might be a surrender of the party's principles, a trading in of their longtime beliefs for the well-known candidates against whom they have long fought. Others argue that it simply reflects the way the Libertarian message has been adopted by much of the Republican Party. These may be debates with no answer, and the question of mission has dogged the party from its beginning.

The Libertarian Party's political philosophy is fairly straightforward. It believes in individual freedom and limited government, but it pairs those beliefs with an equally strong advocacy of both personal responsibility and personal and economic liberty. It is those central beliefs that the party has sought to spread using the electoral process, and it has worked very hard to field as many candidates as possible.

And yet, from the beginning, those candidates have been hampered by the philosophical division and strategic divide based in the question of whether or not the Libertarian Party is committed to winning office and putting its philosophy into action or is satisfied with merely being a part—admittedly, an increasingly large part—of the public debate and eventually getting its ideas accepted. As recently as the party's 2016 presidential convention, debates flared, reflecting the ongoing divisions over ideological purity and practicality. Issues like abolition of the Federal Reserve and state sponsored education were all hotly debated and had strong adherents. At the same time, at that same convention, some aspirants for the presidential nomination were declaring that the goal was not to reach the White House but rather to reach the hearts and minds of Americans.

Indeed, the party's lack of electoral success has not been for a lack of effort. Reflective of its never-ending effort to establish itself as a true source of electoral competition for the long-established Democrats and Republicans, the Libertarian Party's website is a mix of history and philosophical exposition that culminates with an invitation to run for office—any office—as a Libertarian. That invitation is then accompanied by step-by-step instructions on how to take the political plunge. It is a very different approach for a party with a very different mission.

The party has a national organization based in greater Washington, D.C., in Alexandria, Virginia, as well as an active network of state affiliates. The national leadership consists of a chair, a vice chair, a treasurer, a secretary, and five at-large board members. There are also regional representatives who are members of the Libertarian National Committee. Each of them is elected according to rules established by the individual regions. There were eight such regions as of July 2016.

Though the party's electoral success has been limited, there can be no denying that many of its views have increasingly become part of the political mainstream: both conservatives and liberals, Democrats and Republicans have adopted more Libertarian-espoused positions on issues ranging from marijuana use, to abortion, to LGBT rights. This reality is arguably exactly what founder David Nolan had in mind in 1971, for Nolan had long decried the way the emphasis on winning caused parties and candidates to compromise and abandon their principles. In establishing a party that he was proud to see called the "Party of Principle," he sought to establish an organization that would take the long view, where the injection of ideas into the national political discourse would be a greater measurement of success than winning elections—certainly in the beginning.

In looking at the Libertarian Party and its place in the political landscape, it is as important to look at the way it has influenced the major parties' political positions as it is to look at its own political successes. Evidence of success in influencing the national discourse is everywhere, beginning with the increasing talk about the libertarian wing of the Republican Party, a label that, while highlighting Libertarian ideology and its increasing impact on the national political dialogue, has also served to undermine the party's effort to become the sole representative of that political worldview.

In the end, anyone who seeks to understand the Libertarians and assess their impact must recognize the party's split personality. Yet they are becoming increasingly problematic. While the Libertarian Party is definitely having a greater impact on the development of the nation's political agenda, its electoral fortunes are increasingly confused. Indeed, as they have been a more active factor on the electoral landscape, Libertarians have had to weather the criticism that comes from being a spoiler. In 2006, many saw Libertarian candidate Stan Jones's 3 percent in the Montana Senate race tipping the scales in favor of Democrat Jon Tester—a victory that helped Democrats regain the majority in that body.

Further complicating the political equation is the presence of political leaders and candidates who proclaim themselves Libertarians but are running under other standard party labels, a reality that has only hurt the party's identification efforts. Examples abound. Although elected as a Republican, Ron Paul's successful 1976 House candidacy featured a ringing call for the elimination of most federal government programs and offices, an indication of his strong Libertarian leanings as well as a harbinger of his 1988 candidacy as the Libertarian nominee for President. Another prominent example is one time Minnesota governor Jesse Ventura. Elected in 1998 running as the nominee of the Reform Party, the next year he said he was a Libertarian, having earned a perfect score on what he called the Libertarian exam, a survey of Libertarian issues. After serving his term, Ventura left office but stayed in the public eye as a political commentator and discussed seeking the Libertarian Party nomination in 2012 and 2016 but did not follow through, instead twice endorsing Libertarian Party nominee Gary Johnson, whose tenure as New Mexico governor overlapped with Ventura's years in the Minnesota statehouse.

In the end, the Libertarians must determine whether their goal is to run for office in order to make a point or run to win elective office en route to governing, however limited those efforts might be, given their philosophy. For all its recent electoral progress, not until the Libertarian Party determines what it really wants can it make an all-out effort to achieve it.

William H. Pruden III

See also: Democratic Party (1828–); Republican Party (1854–)

Further Reading

Benedict, Wes Benedict. 2013. *Introduction to the Libertarian Party: For Democrats, Republicans, Libertarians, Independents, and Everyone Else*. Scotts Valley, CA: CreateSpace, LLC.

Doherty, Brian, and Matt Welch. 2017. "Did the Libertarian Party Blow It in 2016?" *Reason*, February 2017. http://reason.com/archives/2017/01/07/did-the-libertarian -party-blow.

Johnson, Gary. 2012. *Seven Principles of Good Government: Gov. Gary Johnson on Liberty, People & Politics*. Aberdeen, WA: Silver Lake Publishing.

Libertarian Party. 2018. https://www.lp.org/the-libertarian-party/.

Liberty Party (1840–1848)

The Liberty Party arose in 1839 out of discussions within the American Anti-Slavery Society on the need for a political party that supported the abolition of slavery. At the time, neither the Whigs nor the Democrats were willing to expressly call for the abolition of slavery in a party platform. Neither party wished to alienate Southern or Northern voters needed to win majorities in Congress and the Electoral College by taking a firm position on slavery. The Gag rule in Congress in operation from 1836 to 1844 demonstrated the efforts of much of the political mainstream to sideline the issue. The larger antislavery movement had long debated the approach to be used, and many of its early leaders like William Lloyd Garrison (1805–1879) were proponents of moral persuasion rather than direct political action. For most of the 1830s, abolitionists avoided direct political involvement given the moral compromises that retail politicking entailed. After the absence of progress on the issue nationally, however, many believed they would need their own political party that could enact a political program in law rather than relying on persuasion. Antislavery advocates like Arthur Tappan (1786–1865), Theodore Weld (1803–1895), Gerrit Smith (1797–1874), Salmon P. Chase (1808–1873), Henry Stanton (1805–1887), and Joshua Leavitt (1794–1873), the editor of *The Emancipator*, argued for the need for a political party to bring about substantive change on the issue of slavery. As the Liberty Party formed, many antislavery leaders broke from Garrison's American Anti-Slavery Society to form the American and Foreign Anti-Slavery Society. That group attempted to push gradual practical political solutions to the end of slavery while also avoiding the issue of women's rights that Garrison's group had come to focus upon. Garrison's faction also saw the U.S. Constitution as a fundamentally flawed proslavery document while the Liberty Party believed the Constitution could be used to empower the federal government to limit slavery in those states where it existed such that it would ultimately be eliminated.

Tensions between the idealistic moral program of the party that grew out of the abolitionist movement and the practical compromises required to win at the state level proved difficult for the party. The ultimate goal of the movement was the abolition of slavery. Even so, while the party platform sought to bar the federal government from the protection and expansion of slavery, it did not call for the end of slavery in states where it was legally allowed. Rather, the Liberty Party sought to bar slavery from D.C. and the territories as well as barring the interstate slave trade under the interstate commerce clause. In 1840 and again in 1844, the Liberty Party nominated James G. Birney (1792–1857) as its presidential candidate. Birney, originally from Kentucky, was an Alabama planter and slaveowner whose religious convictions and interactions with Theodore Weld (1803–1895) brought him to the abolitionist movement in 1833, whereupon he freed his slaves. Birney's conversion to abolitionism, along with his support for Henry Clay (1777–1852) and John Quincy Adams (1767–1848) over Andrew Jackson (1767–1845), damaged his reputation and political prospects in Alabama. Ultimately, he chose to move back to Kentucky and then further north.

In 1840, Birney garnered less than 1 percent of the popular vote. Given its positions on slavery, the Liberty Party could not compete in the South, but in the North, it cut into some Whig constituencies. The party appealed to Quakers as well as evangelical and Protestant denominations most influenced by the Second Great Awakening. It also appealed to middle-class and lower–middle-class working men sometimes out of economic fears over slavery, but also by playing on their religious convictions. The Liberty Party had prominent African American members like Henry Highland Garnet (1815–1882), but its openness to African American voters likely hurt it with some white voters. In general terms, the party likely drew more voters from the Whigs than from the Democrats. The Liberty Party alienated the most radical abolitionists for moderating its positions in order to gain votes.

On the other hand, it also suffered, like all third-party movements, from critics who pointed to its failures to win votes given the dominance of the major parties of the second-party system. The Whigs often attacked it as a movement that only benefited Democrats by peeling off their voters, while Democrats often portrayed it as pro-black, thereby playing on the racial fears of Northern voters. Geographically, the party proved popular among New Englanders and in areas of the Midwest settled by New Englanders. Even so, as a third party, it was not in a position to actually win statewide elections in most cases. Rather, it was in closely contested states like Connecticut, Indiana, Michigan, New York, Pennsylvania, and

Ohio that the Liberty Party could play a pivotal role in taking enough votes away from the Whigs to conceivably shift an election. It also could secure victories in state legislatures when it cooperated with other groups as it did in New Hampshire in 1846. In that case, the Liberty Party combined with Conscience Whigs and a Democratic faction led by John P. Hale (1806–1873) (who had lost his Congressional seat over voting against Texas annexation), to win control of the New Hampshire state legislature and send Hale to the U.S. Senate.

In the 1844 election, Birney once again secured the Liberty Party nomination. In 1844 neither political party took a clear position on Texas annexation initially, but the Whig parties in Ohio and in New York rejected it, at least in part to win back Liberty Party voters. When James K. Polk (1795–1849) embraced Texas annexation, his Whig opponent, Henry Clay, altered his own position to support it as well, which left the Liberty Party as the only force opposed to it. The Liberty Party did significantly better in the 1844 election than its last outing, winning approximately 62,000 votes, or 2.3 percent of the popular vote, but with no electoral votes. In New York, Birney likely pulled enough votes from Clay (largely from Whigs alienated by Clay's failure to oppose Texas annexation) that Polk was able to win the state. Similarly, Birney may have cost Clay Michigan. This assumes that the vast majority of the Liberty Party voters would have cast their votes for Clay had Birney not been on the ballot—a likelihood, but not a certainty. The Whigs managed to secure Ohio's electoral votes in the contest even with a strong Liberty Party presence, so it remains unclear if the Liberty Party played a spoiler role.

Similarly, in the 1846 congressional elections, the Liberty Party may have hurt Whig congressional nominees in Vermont and Ohio. Unlike many modern third parties, the Liberty Party fielded congressional candidates, further deteriorating Whig strength in the north as some of their voters shifted to the Liberty Party. Though many of its voters and leaders came from the Whig party, they also drew from Democrats who had criticized slavery, including John P. Hale who initially received the Liberty Party nomination in 1848 with Leicester King (1789–1856) as his running mate. The creation of the Free Soil coalition, however, led to their withdrawal as the nominees.

In the 1848 election, the Liberty Party fused with two other groups: the Conscience Whigs and the Barnburners. The Conscience Whigs had been firmly antiwar and antislavery during the Polk administration but could not stomach voting for Mexican War general and slaveowner Zachary Taylor (1784–1850). The Barnburners were a Democratic faction in New York politics led by former president Martin Van Buren (1837–1841). Van Buren's recent conversion to the cause alienated some antislavery voters, however, and they turned to the National Liberty Party, which then nominated Gerrit Smith as its presidential nominee. The Free Soil Party's platform was decidedly reminiscent of the Liberty Party's in the last two presidential election cycles on the issues of slavery. Unlike in 1844, the Free Soil Coalition did not play a spoiler role in that it likely tilted New York to the Whigs (Taylor) because Van Buren's Barnburners took enough votes away from the Democratic nominee, Lewis Cass (1782–1866). In Ohio, where the Liberty Party and Conscience Whigs had more appeal, it likely took enough votes away from Taylor to allow Cass to win. Though unsuccessful in sustaining itself as a third party, the Liberty Party demonstrated the weaknesses of the Whig Party when it came to the issue of slavery. In its voter coalition, ideas, and the composition of some of its leadership, it was a forerunner to the Republican Party that emerged in 1854.

M. K. Beauchamp

See also: Democratic Party (1828–); Republican Party (1854–); Whig Party (1833–1856)

Further Reading

Brooks, Corey M. 2016. *Liberty Power: Antislavery Third Parties and the Transformation of American Politics*. Chicago: University of Chicago Press.

Holt, Michael F. 1992. *Political Parties and American Political Development from the Age of Jackson to the Age of Lincoln*. Baton Rouge: Louisiana State University Press.

Johnson, Reinhard O. 2009. *The Liberty Party, 1840–1848: Antislavery Third-Party Politics in the United States*. Baton Rouge: Louisiana State University Press.

Volpe, Vernon L. 1990. *Forlorn Hope of Freedom: The Liberty Party in the Old Northwest*. Kent, OH: Kent State University Press.

Lockheed Martin (1995–)

Lockheed Martin is a security and aerospace company created through the merger of Lockheed Corporation and Martin Marietta on March 15, 1995. The company is headquartered in Bethesda, Maryland, and employs approximately 97,000 people in more than 70 countries around the world in areas of research, design, development, and manufacturing of advanced technology products and services. Lockheed Martin currently operates in four business segments: aeronautics, missiles and fire control, rotary and mission systems, and space systems. Due to its diverse areas of expertise and considerable scale of operations, Lockheed Martin serves several private- and public-sector organizations, most notably the U.S. Department of Defense (DOD), National Aeronautics and Space Administration (NASA), and the U.S. Department of Energy.

At its inception, Lockheed Martin accounted for annual sales of more than $23 billion, which made it the largest military contractor in the United States. Since then, Lockheed Martian has continued to grow financially, with more than $47 billion in net sales and net earnings of approximately $5.3 billion in 2016. While these figures are encouraging to stockholders and board members alike, they are somewhat unsettling to others because approximately 92 percent of the company's revenue comes from contracts with the DOD. Because Lockheed Martin has generated (and continues to generate) such a sizeable proportion of revenue through government contracts, some scholars and policy makers are concerned that it may use its substantial political clout to influence future security-related expenditures and the nature of U.S. foreign policy.

Lockheed Martin has been awarded several notable government contracts in its relatively brief history. One of its more notable projects began in 2001 when it earned a contract to design and manufacture the Joint Strike Fighter (also known as the F-35 Lightning II). This highly advanced aircraft has been created to function in diverse environments, which will allow it to replace most fighter jets among all branches of the United States military in coming decades.

This program has faced harsh criticism, not only because it is considered one of the most expensive and ambitious acquisition programs by the DOD but also because Lockheed Martin and its partners have fallen behind considerably on the initial production schedule and have consistently gone over budget on the project. According to the U.S. Government Accountability Office, even if the F-35 program proceeds according to estimates, acquisition costs will exceed $400 billion, and, beginning in 2022, the DOD expects to spend more than $14 billion annually for 10 years to fulfill the terms of the contract.

Recognizing the sheer volume of government contracts granted to Lockheed Martin, there are concerns that such a close relationship between the private and public sectors increases the possibility for corruption. Some of these apprehensions have been justified in recent years, noting that Lockheed Martin or its subsidiaries have been linked to falsifying information regarding government contracts. In 2012, the U.S. government brought civil claims against Lockheed Martin under the False Claims Act, alleging that Lockheed Martin mischarged perishable tools used on numerous government contracts between 1998 and 2005. Likewise, in 2014, the Department of Justice announced that Lockheed Martin Integrated Systems overbilled the Pentagon for work performed by employees who "lacked required job qualifications" but whose work was billed at the rate for qualified ones. Both cases alleged that Lockheed Martin had willfully sought to defraud the U.S. government in an attempt to inflate profits. Rather than fight these charges, Lockheed Martin agreed to pay nearly $16 million and $27.5 million, respectively, to settle these allegations.

In addition to earning lucrative government contracts, Lockheed Martin has also had considerable involvement in lobbying efforts. According to the Center for Responsive Politics, in 2016, Lockheed Martin spent more than $13.5 million on lobbying efforts in the United States, which ranked 15th among 3,742 organizations. These expenses were spread among 26 lobbying firms operating in the Washington, D.C., area, which underscores Lockheed Martin's commitment to provide a meaningful influence on legislation that may directly influence its business practices.

Among the 95 lobbyists representing the political interests of Lockheed Martin, 71 have previously held positions in the federal government. Although prior experience in government undoubtedly allows these employees to better navigate the complicated political processes surrounding the creation and passage of legislation, it also creates concerns that members of the defense industry have too many ties with political operatives in Washington.

Critics of Lockheed Martin point to the 2016 controversy surrounding Robert Rangel, who served as the senior vice president for government affairs beginning in 2015. Although this position entails interactions with government officials, Rangel did not register as a lobbyist, which, while not technically illegal, does deviate from industry norms followed by counterparts at rival firms like Boeing and General Dynamics. This is troubling to some because Rangel previously served as chief of staff to Defense Secretaries Donald Rumsfeld and Robert Gates, and these extensive ties with the Pentagon arguably provide Lockheed Martin with a competitive edge.

Considering that Lockheed Martin is highly dependent on government contracts for revenue, it is not surprising that campaign contributions by both individuals and related PACs are distributed in a strategic manner to members of both major parties. For instance, in 2016, more than $125,000 was given in support of Republican Kay Granger, who represents the congressional district where the F-35 is assembled. Likewise, members of Lockheed Martin also contributed funds to seven of the eight House members representing Maryland, six of whom are affiliated with the Democratic Party. Both the amount and destination of campaign contributions illustrate that those associated with Lockheed Martin prioritize cultivating political relationships over partisanship.

Michael A. Morgan

See also: Halliburton (1919–)

Further Reading

Center for Responsive Politics. 2017. "Lockheed Martin." https://www.opensecrets.org /orgs/summary.php?id=D000000104.

Hartung, William D. 2012. *Prophets of War: Lockheed Martin and the Making of the Military-Industrial Complex.* New York: Nation Books.

Mizokami, Kyle. 2016. "The F-35 is Getting Cheaper—But the F-35 Program Is Not." *Popular Mechanics,* December 21, 2016. http://www.popularmechanics.com /military/aviation/a24431/the-f-35-is-getting-cheaper-but-the-f-35-program-is -growing-more-expensive.

"Who We Are." 2017. Lockheed Martin. http://www.lockheedmartin.com/us/who-we-are .html.

Wright, Austin, and Jeremy Herb. 2016. "Lockheed's Top Government Affairs Official Not Registered as Lobbyist." Politico, July 3, 2016. http://www.politico.com/story /2016/07/lockheed-lobbyist-no-registered-225044.

Lowell Female Labor Reform Association (1844–1847)

During the industrial revolution of the first half of the 19th century, rapid changes occurred in the workplace, including adoption of factory-based mass production, transformation of skilled work to unskilled labor, creation of corporations with networks of managers, long working hours, and declining wages. Workers reacted to these changed by resisting and forming labor organizations such as the New England Workingmen's Association (NEWA). Although initially a phenomenon for male workers, these changes and reactions also shaped the lives of female workers and influenced the creation of a labor movement at New England textile mills. To reduce the hours of labor per day, 15 female operatives established the Lowell Female Labor Reform Association (LFLRA) in December 1844.

A growing number of young women, mostly the daughters of respectable New England farmers, who hoped to accumulate savings for a future household of their own, but also destitute women who needed to support their families, became workers at textile mills during the early 19th century. Despite strict enforcement of traditional moral values in company sponsored housing and working regulations in the mills, these women had not challenged the authority of management because work was temporary, behavioral codes protected their status in society, and the mills offered an active social and intellectual life. During the 1830s, however, female workers in several New England textile mills, especially in Lowell, Massachusetts, expressed their opposition to what they thought were unwarranted changes that threatened their dignity, perceived social equality, and economic independence. In 1834, operatives in the Lowell mills "turned out," or went on strike, against reduction in wages. Most of the mill workers returned within a week to work at lower incomes while other left permanently. In 1836 a monthlong strike to protest increase in room and board at company-sponsored housing resulted in the temporary establishment of the Factory Girls' Association and partial—but not permanent—reduction of proposed rates.

Later, in the 1840s, the 10-hour movement emerged because working conditions continued to deteriorate rapidly at the textile mills. Managers required female workers to sign 12-month contracts under threat of blacklisting those who walked off the job without permission. Supervisors also increased productivity by speeding up machines, stretching-out work by assigning more machines to individual operatives, and paying overseers bonuses if workers increased output. Women workers, rather than focus on reversing this increased hardship, organized to reduce the hours of labor per day because efforts to lower the number of working hours had been successful for men in other trades and government occupations.

Under the leadership of their first president, Sarah G. Bagley (1806–1889), members of the LFLRA drafted a constitution that outlined the organization's purpose as a reform society for the protection of each worker's independence from oppression at the work place. It did not advocate strikes or violence but encouraged members to use any means necessary to affect reduction in working hours so that workers could continue to dedicate time to intellectual as well as spiritual matters and maintain a self-respecting status in society. These were the very aspects of life that mill owners had promised to protect when they recruited women to the textile mills in the 1820s.

The LFLRA used a three-pronged approach to achieve its goals. Organizational work through social gatherings and fund-raisers resulted in establishment of Association chapters throughout New England. Propaganda in the form of public speeches and publication of articles in the organization's official organ, *Factory Tract*, and the Workingmen's Association's *Voice of Industry*, informed the public about changes in working conditions, urged workers to organize, explained the necessity for a 10-hour day, and called for reforms in society. Political agitation, or petitions informing the Massachusetts legislature about degrading working conditions and calling for a 10-hour day, resulted in an investigation and hearings before two special state House committees in 1845 and 1846. Six female workers testified during the hearing, attesting to how air pollution and long hours had negatively affected their health. Although the committees acknowledged the authority of the legislature to regulate corporations, they did not recognize the need to interfere with the length of a working day, arguing instead that operatives could negotiate hours and wages through contracts with employers.

The lack of legislative support in Massachusetts contributed to the LFLRA's declining influence in the labor reform movement after 1847. The LFLRA lasted for just over two years, and female textile operatives in New England textile mills garnered few concessions from managers. One important factor in the organization's demise was that of the over 7,000 women who had worked in the Lowell mills between 1845 and 1847, only 500 had joined the LFLRA, and fewer than 36 percent signed the 10-hour workday petitions. An ever increasing number of native New England women left the mills during the 1840s in reaction to declining working conditions, leaving behind poor American and immigrant women who accepted long hours without resistance owing to their economic conditions. In January 1847, the Association transformed itself into the Lowell Female Industrial Reform and Mutual Aid Society and changed its focus from reform to self-help, aid to the sick, and relief for the poor.

The organization and its members, nevertheless, represent an important aspect of the labor movement in U.S. history. Although based initially on female experience, the LFLRA worked with male labor organizations, such as the Mechanics and Laborers' Association, to achieve recognition for all workers. Members of the LFLRA also served as officers in NEWA and sat on the editorial board of the *Voice*. Additional successes included the 1846 transformation of the New England Workingmen's Association into the Labor Reform League of New England (LRL), which incorporated female labor organizations into its structure, and passage of a 10-hour bill in the New Hampshire legislature in 1847.

The LFLRA also is significant in the development of the U.S. political system because women testifying before a state legislature expressed political thought even though they could not yet vote. Some members became active in the growing cooperative movement that, by the 1870s, gave rise to the Grange. Other women, including Harriet Hanson Robinson (1825–1911), joined the emerging women's rights movement. Male and female workers also continued to build on the successes and failures of the 10-hour movement of the 1840 to successfully petition the Massachusetts legislature to establish the 10-hour day in 1874 and to create politically active labor organizations such as the Knights of Labor.

Petra DeWitt

See also: American Federation of Labor (1886–1955); Knights of Labor (1869–1890); Women's Christian Temperance Union (1874–)

Further Reading

Blewett, Mary H. 1991. *We Will Rise in Our Might: Workingwomen's Voices from Nineteenth Century New England.* Ithaca, NY: Cornell University Press.

Dublin, Thomas. 1993. *Women at Work: The Transformation of Work and Community in Lowell, Massachusetts, 1826–1860.* 2nd ed. New York: Columbia University Press.

Dublin, Thomas. 1994. *Transforming Women's Work: New England Lives in the Industrial Revolution.* Ithaca, NY: Cornell University.

Early, Frances H. 1980. "A Reappraisal of the New England Labour Movement of the 1840s: The Lowell Female Labor Reform Association and the New England Workingmen's Association." *Histoire Sociale—Social History* 13 (25): 33–54.

March of Dimes (1938–)

The March of Dimes is the nation's primary nonprofit organization dedicated to protecting the health of mothers and babies by preventing birth defects, premature birth, and infant mortality. Originally dedicated to the fight against polio, the March of Dimes' mission has evolved over the past 80 years to focus more broadly on health disparities, health access, and public policies that promote healthy pregnancies. Partnering with a wide array of local, state, national, and global health partners, March of Dimes initiatives include education, advocacy, research, and family support designed to ensure positive birth outcomes for all women, especially those in traditionally underserved communities.

In the decades following the end of World War I (1914–1918), no disease inspired more fear and panic in the American public than poliomyelitis. Polio, or infantile paralysis, as it was also known, seemed a particularly cruel disease. It struck primarily children, often without warning or clear cause, with cases peaking during the hot summer months. Many afflicted were left with permanent paralysis, unable to walk or stand without aid, and in some cases, unable even to breathe on their own, destined to live the rest of their lives in massive breathing machines known as "iron lungs."

Though the infectious agent that caused polio was isolated in 1908 by Karl Landsteiner and Erwin Popper, it would take almost five decades and the work of hundreds of scientists and politicians before an effective vaccine would be developed. By far the most famous American polio survivor, President Franklin Delano Roosevelt played a major role in the fight against the disease. Believing that swimming in warm mineral springs at a resort in Georgia had greatly aided his rehabilitation and recovery, in 1927 Roosevelt purchased that resort and created the Georgia Warm Springs Foundation (GWSF). Roosevelt and his foundation expanded and revitalized the resort with the goal of offering rehabilitative services to polio victims from across the country.

Once Roosevelt was elected president of the United States in 1933, the board of the GWSF launched a new fund-raising initiative to support the facility and raise money for polio treatment and research. On January 30, in celebration of Roosevelt's birthday, local communities were encouraged to hold fund-raising "Birthday Balls," with local participants invited to dance and donate whatever small amount they could. These balls were a huge success, with hundreds of participating local communities raising over a million dollars in the first year to support the GWSF's treatment services and the work of polio researchers around the country.

Capitalizing on this success, Roosevelt and his longtime associate Basil O'Connor established the National Foundation for Infantile Paralysis (NFIP) on

January 3, 1938. With O'Connor as its president, the NFIP became the most important private foundation funding polio research in the United States. It assumed oversight of the Birthday Ball fund-raisers in addition to launching a new fund-raising campaign that would become known as the March of Dimes to promote donations in the weeks leading up to the Birthday Ball events.

The name "March of Dimes" was a play on the popular "March of Time" newsreels that ran in movie theaters at the time. It was coined by stage and screen performer Eddie Cantor as a succinct way of embodying the fund-raising model first embodied in the Balls and subsequently adopted by the NFIP. Cantor used radio to reach out to everyday Americans, particularly children, encouraging them to mail their spare change to Roosevelt to show their support for polio research by creating "a march of dimes to reach all the way to the White House." The campaign was a massive success, with tens of thousands of letters and small donations flooding the White House mail room. In a radio address on January 29, 1938, President Roosevelt described this influx:

> During the past few days bags of mail have been coming, literally by the truck load, to the White House. Yesterday between forty and fifty thousand letters came to the mail room of the White House. Today an even greater number—how many I cannot tell you, for we can only estimate the actual count by counting the mail bags. In all the envelopes are dimes and quarters and even dollar bills—gifts from grown-ups and children—mostly from children who want to help other children to get well. (Roosevelt 1938)

Roosevelt became so publicly linked with these March of Dimes campaigns that the U.S. Treasury changed the design of the dime to feature his profile in 1946.

With the money raised by the March of Dimes campaigns and the Birthday Balls, the NFIP funded both research into the prevention of polio and treatment and rehabilitation for those affected. Though polio was an indiscriminate disease, affecting white communities and communities of color equally, African American families faced additional hurdles to finding care for affected children. Recognizing this racial inequity, the foundation pledged from its beginning to support all Americans impacted by polio regardless of "race, creed, or color," but that pledge was often undermined by the strict policies of racial segregation that were enforced in most hospitals and rehabilitation facilities. Even the resort at Georgia Warm Springs admitted only white patients. Additionally, local chapters of the NFIP, which were responsible for administering the funds raised by annual March of Dimes campaigns to families in need of treatment services, were nearly all exclusively white. The March of Dimes fund-raising campaigns themselves were pitched only to white Americans, without the broad appeal to more diverse audiences. Though the NFIP helped to found a new polio treatment and rehabilitation facility for black Americans at the Tuskegee Institute's John A. Andrew Memorial Hospital in 1939, the racial divide in the NFIP's membership and fund-raising campaigns remained firmly in place.

In 1944 the foundation appointed Charles H. Bynum, a prominent educator and civil rights advocate, to oversee the NFIP's newly created department of "Negro Activities" as a way to help overcome these problems. Bynum was one of the first black men ever appointed to an executive position within a national health advocacy organization. From that position he successfully argued that the March of Dimes campaigns were limiting themselves by not appealing to African American donors. As the costs for polio treatment and research continued to climb, the NFIP needed to broaden its appeal beyond white Americans. Under Bynum's leadership the first black March of Dimes poster child appeared in NFIP fund-raising materials in 1947. In subsequent years, the March of Dimes regularly produced posters featuring black polio survivors in addition to those with white children. Bynum's work was vital to increasing the revenue from March of Dimes fund-raising, as Roosevelt's death in 1945 ended the Birthday Balls aspect of the fund-raising structure. Perhaps even more importantly, the new March of Dimes posters helped to combat public perceptions that polio was exclusively a disease affecting white people and brought greater awareness to the treatment and rehabilitation needs of black families, particularly in the American South.

The money raised by the March of Dimes campaigns in the 1940s and 1950s funded much of the crucial research into polio, including the work of Jonas Salk to create a safe and effective vaccine against the virus. In 1955, Salk's vaccine became publicly available, and reported cases of paralytic polio declined rapidly from more than 20,000 in 1952 to fewer than 100 cases by the mid-1960s. The last case of wild poliovirus in the United States was in 1979.

With the virtual elimination of polio as a significant health threat, O'Connor and the NFIP faced a dilemma. The March of Dimes campaigns had proven themselves as a model of grassroots fund-raising that could promote real improvements in public health. The NFIP had a well-established leadership structure, respected and effective committees of experts trained in evaluating scientific research proposals, and thousands of local chapters with tens of thousands of committed volunteers dedicated to helping promote children's health. What was missing now was the cause. O'Connor had been anticipating this moment for years and had begun laying the groundwork for the NFIP's transition into a more broadly focused organization even before Salk's vaccine reached the public. In 1958, O'Connor announced that the NFIP was shortening its name to the National Foundation (NF) and changing its mission to birth defects prevention. The new NF defined itself as a "flexible force" for good in the field of infant and maternal health.

The "New March of Dimes" found a powerful spokesperson in Dr. Virginia Apgar, the physician who created the "Apgar Score" for evaluating newborn health. Apgar joined the NF in 1959 and became perhaps its most important and influential advocate for its new mission, traveling, lecturing, and fund-raising to bring international attention to the previously stigmatized issue of birth defects. By the 1960s, the March of Dimes had a new slogan—"Be good to your baby before it's born"—that highlighted the growing understanding that preventing birth defects meant, in many cases, promoting healthy pregnancies. A major rubella outbreak in the mid-1960s showed just how devastating this disease could be to fetal development if a woman contracted it in her first trimester. Apgar dedicated March of Dimes campaigns to promote rubella vaccination, even testifying before the Senate in 1969 on the need for federal funding to support rubella immunization programs.

In 1970, the NF started WalkAmerica, the first-ever charity walking event, as
its new March of Dimes signature fund-raiser. Rebranded as the Walk for Babies
in 2008, the event was another major innovation in grassroots fund-raising, and it
became the model for many similar events held by other advocacy and fund-
raising organizations. Matching the popularity and success of those initial Birthday Balls, the walk-a-thons captured the public's interest once more and cemented
the association of the name March of Dimes with the cause of infant health. In
1976, the NF officially renamed itself the March of Dimes Birth Defects Foundation, eventually shortening its name to simply the March of Dimes Foundation.

Over the years the March of Dimes foundation has supported research, legislation, and public awareness campaigns targeting a host of serious threats to fetal
and child health, including major efforts to educate the public on the importance
of folic acid during pregnancy, the dangers of fetal alcohol syndrome, and the
need for universal screening of newborns for serious heritable disorders. Today
the March of Dimes continues to promote maternal and child health issues with
special emphasis on reducing the rates of premature birth in the United States.

Vesta T. Silva

Related Primary Document: **Franklin D. Roosevelt's Birthday Message (1938)**

Franklin D. Roosevelt's Birthday Message (1938)

*This document is a transcript of the radio broadcast of President Franklin D.
Roosevelt's birthday party, which also served as a fund-raiser for the "March of
Dimes Foundation." Known at this time as the National Foundation for Infantile
Paralysis, it raised research money for the children afflicted with infantile paraly-
sis, also known as polio. Adults and children were asked to send a dime to the
White House to help this cause, resulting in the donation of over 7 billion dimes.*

At 11:30 in the Waldorf-Astoria the part of the Birthday Celebration, which
was broadcast over every radio network and radio station—via short wave to
South America, Europe and the Far East—the largest network of stations
ever joined together, began with Miss Lucy Monroe singing The Star-
Spangled Banner. Then the master of ceremonies said:

"Last Tuesday afternoon in New York City the first meeting of the Board of
Trustees of the new National Foundation for Infantile Paralysis was held. At
this meeting the Trustees unanimously elected as President of this new
Foundation a very old and very dear friend of the President of the United
States, a man who has devoted many years to the fight against infantile
paralysis. Mr. Basil O'Connor of New York."

Mr. O'Connor's address:

"Ladies and gentlemen, in a few minutes you will hear the message from the
President of the United States, and we all know it is in him that you are interested. Before that takes place, however, as president of the new National

Foundation for Infantile Paralysis, I want to tell you that I am very grateful to those of you who are here at the Waldorf. I am equally grateful to the millions of people throughout the country who tonight are helping to launch this new National Foundation by their participating in some Birthday Celebration. I know that your presence at these celebrations is, in part at least, a personal tribute to the President of the United States, but I am certain that he would want me to say to you that while he appreciates the great honor which you pay him, he wants to feel and believes that he can feel that you are here because you have a real interest, as he has, in the fight against infantile paralysis. I know that your being here tonight gives him and the rest of us strength and courage to go on with the great fight until this dread disease and its maiming after-effects are eliminated.

"You are at these celebrations to enjoy yourself and I hope that you do. I am certain that there is no group in the country tonight that will be happier in your enjoyment than that group handicapped by infantile paralysis. None of these celebrations would be possible, were it not for the untiring industry and organizing ability of Keith Morgan, from whom you will now hear."

Mr. Morgan, chairman of the Committee for the Celebration of the President's Birthday, spoke next:

"Mrs. James Roosevelt, Mr. Basil O'Connor, my mother and father who are here tonight, I salute you; as well as all of my guests and friends throughout the United States.

"There are listening in tonight throughout the United States, and the rest of the world, some 15,000 chairmen with their committees who have worked hard, laboriously, for the past three months to bring this occasion to a grand and glorious climax. I salute them and I thank them again and again. We could not have done this job without the unanimous support of the country—without the great cooperation of the railroads, the hotels, the business firms, stores, the merchants, citizens, the clubs, the fraternal and labor organizations—in fact, everyone. We simply could not have done this job without their wonderful cooperation, whole-hearted enthusiasm and support to embark on this great crusade to lick this devastating disease.

"Many years ago it was my great privilege to meet Mr. Basil O'Connor. As the chairman of the Executive Committee and the Treasurer of Georgia Warm Springs Foundation, his clear-headedness, his wisdom, his guidance and his courage and leadership have been a great tonic to us all. I know of no man in the United States whom the Trustees of the new National Foundation could have chosen with more unanimous approval and enthusiastic endorsement than my old friend Mr. Basil O'Connor. I can assure all the chairmen and the committees and everyone here tonight and those listening in that under his direction the new Foundation will go forward to greater and greater accomplishments as time goes on.

A number of years ago, as a young man it was my great privilege and a rare opportunity to meet a man who had been, we might say, hit by a traffic light which never seemed to change. I watched him work, I watched him struggle, I watched him study his subject, and I watched him resolve firmly that the thing that had afflicted him would not defeat him . . . and, furthermore, I watched him right through to the end. I watched him grow until he reached the most exalted position that could possibly be bestowed by the American people, the highest gift of our land, it not of the whole world.

"Tonight to all who are listening-in in the United States and throughout the world, and to all my friends and guests here, I give you my beloved chief, the President of the United States."

Then the President himself:

"My friends, my heart goes out in gratitude to the whole American people tonight—for we have found common cause in presenting a solid front against an insidious but deadly enemy, the scourge of infantile paralysis.

"It is a very glorious thing for us to think of what has been accomplished in our own lifetime to cure epidemic diseases, to relieve human suffering and to save lives. It was by united effort on a national scale that tuberculosis has been brought under control; it was by united effort on a national scale that smallpox and diphtheria have been almost eliminated as dread diseases.

"Today the major fight of medicine and science is being directed against two other scourges, the toll of which is unthinkably great—cancer and infantile paralysis. In both fields the fight is again being conducted with national unity—and we believe with growing success.

"Tonight, because of your splendid help, we are making it possible to unite all the forces against one of these plagues by starting the work of the new National Foundation for Infantile Paralysis. The dollars and dimes contributed tonight and in the continuing campaign will be turned over to this foundation, which will marshal its forces for the amelioration of suffering and crippling among infantile paralysis victims wherever they are found. The whole country remains the field of work. We expect through scientific research, through epidemic first aid, through dissemination of knowledge of care and treatment, through the provision of funds to centers where the disease may be combated through the most enlightened method and practice to help men and women and especially children in every part of the land.

"Since the first birthday celebrations in 1931, many splendid results have been accomplished so that in literally hundreds of localities facilities for combating the disease have been created where none existed before.

"We have learned much during these years and when, therefore, I was told by the doctors and scientists that much could be gained by the establishment of this new National Foundation for Infantile Paralysis, I was happy, indeed, to lend my birthday to this united effort.

"During the past few days bags of mail have been coming, literally by the truck load, to the White House. Yesterday between forty and fifty thousand letters came to the mail room of the White House. Today an even greater number—how many I cannot tell you—for we can only estimate the actual count by counting the mail bags. In all the envelopes are dimes and quarters and even dollar bills—gifts from grown-ups and children—mostly from children who want to help other children get well.

"Literally, by the countless thousands, they are pouring in, and I have figured that if the White House staff and I were to work on nothing else for two or three months to come we could not possibly thank the donors. Therefore, because it is a physical impossibility to do it, I must take this opportunity of thanking all of those who have given, to thank them for the messages that have come with their gifts, and to thank all who have aided and cooperated in the splendid work we are doing. Especially am I grateful to those good people who have spread the news of these birthday parties throughout the land in every part of all the big cities and the smaller cities and towns and villages and farms.

"It is glorious to have one's birthday associated with a work like this. One touch of nature makes the whole world kin. And that kinship, which human suffering evokes, is perhaps the closest of all, for we know that those who work to help the suffering find true spiritual fellowship in that labor of love.

"So, although no word of mine can add to the happiness we share in this great service in which we are all engaged, I do want to tell you all how deeply I appreciate everything you have done. Thank you all and God bless you."

Immediately following and under the direction of Mr. James Sauter, the audience at the Waldorf Astoria Grand Ballroom, led by Miss Lucy Monroe, sang "Happy Birthday to You" for the President.

Source: Franklin D. Roosevelt Library.

Related Primary Document: **Virginia Apgar: March of Dimes Proposals to Senate for the Control of Communicable Disease (1969)**

Virginia Apgar: March of Dimes Proposals to Senate for the Control of Communicable Disease (1969)

The March of Dimes, an organization founded at the onset of World War II with the purpose of responding to the polio epidemic, has long committed itself to the research and education necessary to control and eradicate communicable diseases. On June 30, 1969, Dr. Virginia Apgar, a pivotal figure in the early identification of newborn birth defects and illnesses, spoke to the Senate Committee on Labor and Public Welfare on behalf of the March of Dimes regarding new proposals for the control of communicable disease. Her statement, reproduced below, focuses on the necessity of vaccination, a topic that continues to spark controversy today.

Statement by Virginia Apgar, M.D. Vice President for Medical Affairs

The National Foundation–March of Dimes, Subcommittee on Health, Senate Committee on Labor and Public Welfare June 30, 1969

The National Foundation-March of Dimes is pleased to have been invited to present its views on proposals to the Senate for the control of communicable disease. Our interest in immunization is well known and extends back to 1938, the year in which The National Foundation was organized by Franklin D. Roosevelt to lead the fight against poliomyelitis.

During an era in which government support of health research and development was minimal, The National Foundation was the principal source for the funding of major advances in virology and immunology which culminated in the licensure of the Salk vaccine in 1955 and the elimination of epidemic poliomyelitis as a public health problem in the United States. Underlying all the developments leading to subsequent virus vaccines were the laboratory techniques perfected in poliomyelitis vaccine research.

I. Since 1958 The National Foundation-March of Dimes has been dedicated to the prevention and amelioration of birth defects which are this nation's primary problem of child health. An estimated seven per cent of the liveborn—some 250,000 each year—have defects which are evident during infancy. Through programs of laboratory and clinical research, medical care, professional and public education, and community service, this organization strives to advance the fight against birth defects.

S.1662 addresses itself to the problem of the control through vaccination of certain communicable diseases of childhood, namely, poliomyelitis, diphtheria, whooping cough, tetanus, measles and rubella. S.2264 adds to this list tuberculosis, venereal disease and other 'communicable diseases determined to be of national significance.

With the exception of rubella, existing prophylactic measures have brought each of the specified diseases under control to varying degrees—from virtually complete control in the case of poliomyelitis to less-than-adequate control for tuberculosis, measles and the venereal diseases. Our particular interest, however, is directed to the prospects for prevention of rubella, since the recent approval of a vaccine for this disease represents a significant step forward in the fight against birth defects.

Rubella is usually a mild childhood disease but may cause serious defects in the unborn baby when the mother is infected in the early months of pregnancy. Young children are the principal source of the infection of pregnant women. Epidemics of rubella occur in the United States at irregular intervals of 6 to 9 years. The last major epidemic, in 1964, caused an estimated 50,000 abnormal pregnancies, resulting in some 20,000 live-born babies with birth defects and about 30,000 fetal deaths.

The consequences of rubella in pregnancy are varied and unpredictable. Spontaneous abortion, stillbirth, live birth with one or more anomalies, and normal infants are represented in the spectrum. Virtually every organ may be involved, either temporarily or permanently. Cooper and Krugman, in a review of 271 abnormal infants followed to age 18 months, found congenital heart disease in 142 (52%), confirmed or suspected hearing loss in 140 (52%), cataract or glaucoma in 107 (40%), severe or moderate psychomotor retardation in 65 (24%), and neonatal thrombocytopenic purpura in 85 (31%). The mortality rate was 13% (35 infants).

Thousands of victims of congenital rubella from the 1964 epidemic and from subsequent outbreaks of the disease have been cared for at the 107 Birth Defects Centers supported by the March of Dimes. Many of these children continue to require intensive medical and educational services if they are to realize their full potential.

With widespread immunization of children with the new rubella vaccine, this tragedy may not be repeated.

In our view, however, there are formidable obstacles to the rapid and widespread use of the rubella vaccine in time to prevent another wave of rubella babies which may occur as early as 1970 or 1971.

Some of these obstacles are educational in nature; others are fiscal. On the educational side, the idea of vaccinating children against rubella to protect unborn babies from birth defects will not be easy to get across. But public understanding is crucial if the vaccine is to prevent another epidemic. Accordingly, The National Foundation has pledged vaccine, as supplies become available. A review article on rubella has been mailed to 145,000 physicians and other health professionals throughout the nation, and millions of educational flyers are being readied for widespread public use.

We are confident that educational measures such as these, undertaken in cooperation with other voluntary health agencies, organized medicine and public health departments, can and will overcome the barriers to public understanding and acceptance.

As for the fiscal obstacles, however, we are less optimistic. There are approximately 56 million children aged 1 to 14 in the United States. This is the target group for rubella immunization. If 75% of these boys and girls are to be vaccinated—and I believe that we can achieve this level of participation—some 42 million doses would be required initially. If as much as half this amount were to be administered on a private, fee-for-service basis—and I personally view this as a probable upper limit—then governmental sources will need to furnish at least 20 million doses to achieve primary protection against another epidemic. At current prices, this is equivalent to $30 million, exclusive of necessary laboratory, surveillance and administrative costs.

In view of the cyclical nature of rubella epidemics and the consequent need to achieve rapid vaccine coverage, neither of the legislative proposals under consideration appears to be entirely adequate to meet this challenge.

The appropriations authorized in S. 2264, however, more nearly approach the requirements.

S. 2264, moreover, would permit expeditious use of rubella vaccine through the well-established mechanisms of the National Communicable Disease Center which has proven its competence in earlier programs authorized under the Vaccination Assistance Act. The coming rubella epidemic, whether it strikes next year or the year after, constitutes a real emergency for the more than 4 million American babies who will be conceived that year. Under the circumstances, it would seem ill-advised for the federal government to approach the problem of rubella prevention along a circuitous route which involves untried and necessarily slower administrative mechanisms.

In urging your favorable decision on S. 2264, we should like to call your attention to the need for amendment of the measure to comprehend the prevention of another disease which constitutes a more serious threat to children than most of the others included, and for which there is an effective vaccine. This is hemolytic disease of the newborn due to Rh incompatibility, otherwise known as erythroblastosis fetalis, or more simply, Rh disease.

Unlike the vaccines for the other diseases, this vaccine prevents, instead of fostering, immunization, in this case the immunization of Rh negative mothers against the Rh positive blood of their unborn babies. Each year an estimated 250,000 women and their families in the United States face the possibility of having an affected child.

Prevention of Rh disease now is possible with the use of a specially prepared blood fraction known as Rh immune globulin. This product has been available to hospitals since June 1968. Injected into an unsensitized Rh negative mother soon after the birth of an Rh positive baby, the Rh immune globulin effectively prevents her sensitization and the possible development of the disease in a subsequent Rh positive baby. About 8% of white maternity patients and 4.1% of Negro maternity patients are candidates for this vaccine.

With optimal use of this vaccine, the incidence of disease can be expected to decline continuously from year to year, so that in 20 to 25 years the present pool of sensitized women of childbearing age will be exhausted, thus eliminating the disease as a public health problem.

Our surveys of hospitals and our consultations with state public health departments, however, indicate that in many parts of the country substantially fewer doses of the Rh vaccine are being administered than are needed to eliminate the disease. While the situation differs from one community to another, we estimate that nationally about one out of every 4 women who need the vaccine is not receiving it. The reasons for underutilization of this preventive ore varied, but since the vaccine is relatively expensive, cost may be a serious obstacle for many low and moderate income families, especially in areas where public programs of medical assistance are absent or inadequate to meet this need. For this reason, we ask you to consider the inclusion of Rh disease in any vaccination assistance measure you approve.

Source: Apgar, Virginia. Statement to the Subcommittee on Health, Senate Committee on Labor and Public Welfare, June 30, 1969. National Institute of Health.

See also: American Cancer Society (1913–); National Academy of Sciences (1863–)

Further Reading

Cohn, Victor. 1955. "Four Billion Dimes." *Minneapolis Star and Tribune*, Minneapolis, MN.

Mawdsley, Stephen E. 2010. "'Dancing on Eggs': Charles H. Bynum, racial politics, and the National Foundation for Infantile Paralysis." *Bulletin of the History of Medicine* 84 (2): 217–247.

Roosevelt, Franklin D. 1938. "Radio Address for the Fifth Birthday Ball for Crippled Children" (speech). January 29, 1938. Online by Gerhard Peters and John T. Woolley, *The American Presidency Project*. http://www.presidency.ucsb.edu/ws/?pid =15584.

Wilson, Daniel J. 2015. "Basil O'Connor, the National Foundation for Infantile Paralysis, and the Reorganization of Polio Research in the United States, 1935–41." *Journal of the History of Medicine and Allied Sciences* 70 (3): 394–424.

Mexican American Legal Defense and Education Fund (1968–)

The Mexican American Legal Defense and Education Fund, usually known by its acronym, MALDEF, was founded in 1968 by San Antonio, Texas, attorney Pedro "Pete" Tijerina (1922–2003). MALDEF is a nonprofit civil rights advocacy organization that concentrates on defending Latino civil rights through legal actions and education. Its original headquarters was in San Antonio, but it is now headquartered in Los Angeles, California, with regional offices in San Antonio, Washington, D.C., Chicago, and Atlanta; a satellite office in Sacramento; and a program office in Houston. Pete Tijerina grew up in Laredo, Texas, and was, in the later 1960s, a state civil rights chairman for the League of United Latin American Citizens (LULAC) and a member of American G. I. Forum (AGIF), a group that specialized in Latino veteran's rights. LULAC's legal efforts were restricted due to limited funding, and the group tended to be cautious and conservative in its approach to civil rights. Many of LULAC's supporters were businessmen who did not want to annoy possible Anglo customers (Anglo is the term that is often used to identify non-Spanish-speaking, white Americans). Pete Tijerina was oriented toward being more active and aggressive than LULAC could tolerate, although the two organizations still usually cooperated. The limitations that Mr. Tijerina felt at LULAC and AGIF are among the reasons he created a new third civil rights organization that concentrated on legal action.

In a 1966 civil lawsuit, Tijerina represented a Mexican American woman who had suffered an amputated leg in a car accident in Jourdantown, Texas, a rural community 38 miles south of San Antonio. There were no Mexican Americans at all in the jury pool, and although he won the case, Tijerina thought the settlement was far too small. Tijerina was convinced that the racially skewed jury selection caused the low payout. Pete Tijerina believed this case symbolized one of the key difficulties Latinos face in the legal system—that they are not being judged by a panel of their peers but rather by (possibly bigoted) Anglos. Hence, he began to learn from the legal successes of the Legal Defense Fund of the National Association for the Advancement of Colored People (NAACP). The Legal Defense Fund (LDF) had been very successful in litigating on behalf of African American civil rights–winning cases such as *Brown v. the Board of Education of Topeka* (1954). Initially, Tijerina had wanted to work with the LDF, but University of Texas education professor and Mexican American civil rights activist George I. Sanchez (1906–1972) advised him that he thought they should found their own Mexican American Legal Defense Fund as a parallel and similar organization, because discrimination faced by Mexican Americans was, in many respects, quite different. Pete Tijerina would model MALDEF after the LDF. MALDEF won a $2.2 million five-year grant from the Ford Foundation as seed (start-up) money and would serve as head of MALDEF for its first two years.

MALDEF was established in October 1968 with six attorneys and five Volunteers in Service to America (VISTA) law student interns. Among the organization's first activities was to hold two conferences on discrimination in education, initiating the education mission of the organization. MALDEF also created scholarships for 118 Latino law school students. On the legal side, MALDEF soon had 83 cases and complaints, but many of the cases were not taken up because they were not discrimination cases. MALDEF filed class-action lawsuits that challenged school segregation, job discrimination, and voting rights. Initially MALDEF's successes were few. In *San Antonio ISD v. Rodriguez* (1973), a case concerning Texas' unequal school property tax financing system, MALDEF failed to convince the Supreme Court that education was a fundamental right protected by the Fourteenth Amendment. MALDEF was also unsuccessful in *Logue v. U.S.* (1973), but they were successful in *White v. Regester* (1973) striking down large multimember Texas state legislature districts because they diluted the voting strength of minorities. MALDEF's early troubles were caused, in part, because it was unable to fill its attorney positions with highly skilled Latino attorneys who would be sensitive to the pervasive discrimination heaped upon Latinos. At that point, there were few experienced Latino civil rights attorneys.

MALDEF lawyers successfully argued the case of *Serna v. Portales Municipal School District* (1974). In that case, the court ordered this New Mexico school district to establish bilingual education programs for English language learners. Other notable victories include *Plyler v. Doe* (1982) which struck down a Texas law requiring the parents of undocumented children to pay tuition to the local school district. This was the victory that established MALDEF as a successful civil rights advocate for Latinos. Another important early victory was *Edgewood Independent School District v. Kirby* (1984). This case revisited Texas's unequal school finance system based upon property taxes. As a result of the Texas Supreme Court's decision in the case, the state was obliged to implement a more equal school finance system, later nicknamed "Robin Hood," whereby wealthy Texas school districts were required to send some their funds to the state to be redistributed to the poor school districts. In 1999, MALDEF took the lead in overturning California's Proposition 187. Proposition 187 denied undocumented immigrants access to public education from elementary through postsecondary education, and limited their access to public social and health services. In 2013, MALDEF's argument won the day against Arizona's Proposition 200, which required proof of citizenship in order to register to vote. In April 2017, a MALDEF suit against the state of Texas struck down Texas's 2011 redistricting plan for the Texas State House districts on the grounds that it is racially discriminatory and unlawfully diluted the voting strength of Latinos.

Not all of MALDEF's achievements are marked by court victories; some are settled out of court or through lobbying. MALDEF was among several civil rights organizations that argued against the confirmation of the conservative jurist and constitutional originalist, Judge Robert Bork (1927–2012) to the Supreme Court in 1987. One out-of-court success was the South Texas Border Initiative (1989), where MALDEF argued that while 20 percent of Texans live in the border region, only 10 percent of higher education spending was spent in that region. In an out-of-court settlement, the Texas Legislature agreed to provide additional funding for nine four-year public universities in the border region. As a result, in 1990 these 9 universities awarded 5,707 bachelors, 1,675 masters, and 5 doctorate degrees. Just 20 year later, in 2010, there were a total of 13,840 bachelors, 3,994 masters, and 168 doctorates awarded in the nine border universities. The number of degrees awarded in the nine border region schools almost tripled. The increase in doctoral degrees awarded was over 30 times the 1990 figure. Another example is MALDEF's victory in a 2008 case, *Dominguez v. State of Texas,* which was settled out of court when the Texas Higher Education Coordinating Board changed its rules to have the Hazelwood Act apply to all qualified veterans regardless of their immigration status at the time they entered the military. The Hazelwood Act provides a tuition and fees waiver for Texas veterans, spouses, and dependent children at Texas public universities and colleges. An additional example of the group's legal success was MALDEF prevailing in a voting rights dispute over the city of Pasadena, Texas, in October of 2017. The city dropped its appeal of an earlier U.S. District Court decision that the city's at-large city council seats violated the Voting Rights Act and discriminated against the city's Latino voters.

After a shaky start, MALDEF has been very successful in advancing Latino civil rights and other related areas of law, and developing broad and deep professional expertise in constitutional litigation before state courts and the U.S. Supreme Court. It is recognized as a powerful voice for civil rights and a policy entrepreneur in constitutional litigation just as its founder, Pete Tijerina, intended. It fights for Latinos in the areas of immigration, desegregation, discrimination, voting rights, educational finance, bilingual education, and other educational policy areas. MALDEF also conducts policy analysis to monitor and lobby for policies that will help Latinos. Furthermore, the organization is committed to education, awarding over fifteen scholarships a year to Latino law students. MALDEF also sponsors leadership classes to over one thousand mid-career Latino professionals, in addition to a parent leadership program.

James A. Norris

See also: Amnesty International USA (1966–); Lambda Legal Defense and Education Fund (1973–); NAACP Legal Defense and Education Fund (1940–); United Farm Workers (1966–)

Further Reading

Badillo, David A. 2005. "MALDEF and the Evolution of Latino Civil Rights." *The Research Reports.* Institute for Latino Studies at the University of Notre Dame. Vol. 2005.2. https://latinostudies.nd.edu/assets/95252/original/2005.2badillofinal .pdf.

Kaplowitz, Craig A. 2005. *LULAC, Mexican Americans and National Policy.* College Station: Texas A&M University Press.

MALDEF. 2018. www.maldef.org.

Navarro, Armando. 2005. *Mexican Political Experience in Occupied Aztlán: Struggles and Change.* Walnut Creek, CA: AltaMira Press.

O'Conner, Karen and Lee Epstein. 1985. "A Legal Voice for the Chicano Community: The Activities of the Mexican American Legal Defense and Education Fund, 1968–82." In *The Mexican American Experience: An Interdisciplinary Anthology,* edited by Rodolfo O. de la Garza, Frank D. Bean, Charles M. Bonjean, Ricardo Romo, and Rodolfo Alvarez. Austin: University of Texas Press.

Rivas-Rodriguez, Maggie. 2015. *Texas Mexican Americans & Postwar Civil Rights.* Austin: University of Texas Press.

Minuteman Project (2004–2016)

The Minuteman Project was a far right–wing citizens' group that was organized to combat unauthorized migration from Mexico into the United States. Created in 2004, the Minuteman Project was organized under the notion that the U.S. federal government was not fulfilling its obligations to minimize the number of undocumented immigrants who were crossing the border between Mexico and the United States. The name "Minuteman" comes from the Minutemen who fought during the American Revolution as a militia army. The Minuteman Project was very short-lived, however, and generally ceased to be recognized as an influential voice in mainstream American politics by the late 2000s. The primary activities of the project were to raise awareness of undocumented immigration, informally patrol the Arizona-Mexico border area, and endorse politicians whom they found to be sympathetic to their cause. The Minutemen provoked strong condemnation from human rights groups who likened their detaining of suspected undocumented migrants to a form of kidnapping.

The Minuteman Project was created by Jim Gilchrist (1949–) and Chris Simcox (1961–) in 2004, and Arizona was chosen as the location for the group. Both Gilchrist and Simcox adhered to an extreme right-wing political ideology, and Arizona was selected as the locality due to its position along the U.S.-Mexico border and the large number of undocumented immigrants living in and passing through the state. After the downfall of the Minuteman Project, Simcox would be found guilty of child molestation and sentenced to nearly 20 years in prison. Gilchrist has remained active in right-wing politics, albeit at a much lower public level than during his time with the Minutemen.

The Minuteman Project arose within a far-right political camp where there was general dissatisfaction with the U.S. government's actions and responses to undocumented immigration flows. Particularly in the American Southwest, large numbers of unauthorized migrants were entering the U.S. from Mexico. While many Minuteman members were from California, they found the political environment in Arizona to be more hospitable to their ideological causes. At its peak, the Minuteman Project had several hundred loosely affiliated citizens' groups performing informal "neighborhood watches" along the U.S. border with Mexico, and membership within the group numbered in the thousands. Moreover, during this time Gilchrist and Simcox were able to exude political influence by endorsing anti-immigration politicians throughout the United States.

Minuteman patrols along the U.S.-Mexico border were relatively unorganized groups that would drive along the desolated roadways near the border. The intended goal would be to locate groups of unauthorized migrants walking on foot into the United States. When these groups were spotted, the Minuteman patrol would radio to the nearest U.S. Customs and Border Protection to request that agents be sent out to their location to retrieve the migrants. Minuteman patrols were almost always armed with handguns and semiautomatic assault rifles, which they would openly brandish in order to keep suspected migrants from fleeing while waiting for U.S. border officials to arrive. While there were many accusations of Minuteman patrols using violence against migrants, a notorious episode was depicted in a video made by Minuteman sympathizers in which a migrant was shot. In fact, the video turned out to be a hoax. Shortly after the video had gone viral on the Internet, the creators admitted that it was a fabrication they had concocted because they were "old and bored." Still, the implied threat of violence against migrants was apparent in how Minutemen dressed, spoke, and armed themselves. Even though Minutemen usually prefaced any potential violence as self-defense, their general demeanor was that of a paramilitary group.

The Minuteman Project came to fruition at the same time that social media began to play a central role in American politics. It was also a time in which legal immigration and unauthorized immigration were salient issues in American political debate. During this period, various social media outlets were becoming mainstream, enabling the leaders of the Minutemen to gain a national audience for their politics and Minuteman patrolling activities. Without social media, it is debatable whether this movement could have gained enough traction to make the political impact that it did.

While the Minuteman Project was always a controversial actor in American politics, there were notable examples of ideologically sympathetic politicians who lent credibility to the group. Particularly in Arizona and California, the Minutemen received words of encouragement from then-California governor Arnold Schwarzenegger, and it was not until a member of the Minuteman militia pointed his rifle at a Maricopa County sheriff's deputy he mistook as a drug dealer that noted anti-immigrant sheriff Joe Arpaio publicly reprimanded the paramilitary behavior of the Minutemen. Furthermore, the group received praise from right-wing media for its patrolling activities along the U.S.-Mexico border.

After achieving name recognition due to their leadership within the Minuteman Project, both Gilchrist and Simcox attempted to enter electoral politics. In 2005, only a year after founding the Minuteman Project, Gilchrist ran for an open seat in the House of Representatives from California's 48th District under the American Independent Party label (a far-right niche political party). He came in third place with a 25 percent vote share in the special election to replace Republican Christopher Cox, who had vacated his seat in order to accept a position within the U.S. Securities and Exchange Commission. In 2010, Simcox launched an exploratory bid to challenge Republican Senator John McCain for his Arizona Senate seat. Soon afterward, however, he dropped his challenge in order to support another challenger to McCain. Apart from these two attempts at elected office, Gilchrist and Simcox were largely relegated to giving political endorsements and speaking on behalf of the Minutemen during interviews and social media. Due to Simcox's incarceration, only Gilchrist remains a voice for the movement among the founders.

Following their quick rise to national attention, Gilchrist, Simcox, and the Minuteman Project began a rapid decline in political influence and the number of border patrols. Today, Gilchrist's voice is largely confined to the extreme fringes of far-right politics. Though he saw a relative reemergence during the 2016 presidential primaries, his influence no longer carries much public weight. In fact, even within Arizona politics, Gilchrist's voice is more likely to be detrimental to Republicans in general elections than it is beneficial due to his controversial statements. More broadly, though, the Minuteman Project served as a starting point in creating like-minded civilian groups across the United States. From this perspective, Gilchrist has had a sustained influence on U.S. politics by creating a template for other anti-immigration groups to follow.

Nathan Henceroth

See also: American Immigration Control Foundation (1983–)

Further Reading

Boland, Michael R. Jr. 2006. "No Trespassing: The States, the Supremacy Clause, and the Use of Criminal Trespass Laws to Fight Illegal Immigration." *Penn State Law Review* 111: 481.

Doty, Roxanne Lynn. 2007. "States of Exception on the Mexico-U.S. Border: Security, 'Decisions,' and Civilian Border Patrols." *International Political Sociology* 1 (2): 113–137.

Kil, Sang H., Cecilia Menjívar, and Roxanne L. Doty. 2009. "Securing Borders: Patriotism, Vigilantism and the Brutalization of the U.S. American Public." In *Immigration, Crime and Justice*, 297–312. Bingley, UK: Emerald Group Publishing Limited.

Walsh, James. 2008. "Community, Surveillance and Border Control: The Case of the Minuteman Project." In *Surveillance and Governance: Crime Control and Beyond*, 11–34. Bingley, UK: Emerald Group Publishing Limited.

Yoxall, Peter. 2006. "The Minuteman Project, Gone in a Minute or Here to Stay? The Origin, History and Future of Citizen Activism on the United States-Mexico Border." *University of Miami Inter-American Law Review* 37 (3): 517–566.

Mississippi Freedom Democratic Party (1964–1968)

The Mississippi Freedom Democratic Party (MFDP) was a political organization composed of African Americans and whites in the state of Mississippi. Its core purpose was to challenge the establishment and state power structures by gaining political representation for the black community, cultivating African American citizens' participation in the decisions that governed their lives, and obtaining political power and influence in the interest of black constituents. Its leadership included civil rights leaders Ella Baker (1903–1986), Fannie Lou Hamer (1917–1977), and Bob Moses (1935–).

In order to reach its goals, the Mississippi Freedom Democratic Party and its leadership had to face the racial, social, economic, and political conditions of Mississippi. In 1890, the state of Mississippi reestablished white supremacy following the Civil War and put an end to Reconstruction. The all-white Mississippi state legislature set in place a "massive resistance" agenda that was designed to disregard and exclude the black community. To ensure that the color line was maintained and enforced, Jim Crow laws, such as literacy tests and poll taxes; intimidation from white Citizens Councils; and random violence, including lynching and firebombing, kept black Mississippians away from politics and the ballot box. Although the main tool of black exclusion was disenfranchisement, the state's efforts reached into the area of education, employment, medical facilities, housing, food, transportation, criminal justice policies, and racial violence. After more than a century of systematic racism, organized racial terror and violence, and exploitation, most black residents in Mississippi could not vote, and had not voted in great numbers since Reconstruction (1865–1877). By the 1960s, the policy decisions of white Mississippians shaped the customs and laws of the state and created a political system of racial exclusion, subjugation, and violence.

In Mississippi in the early 1960s, the first modern black political organizing began around voter registration drives. The political activities were met with violence by the white Citizens Councils, who were particularly active in the Delta region, which had the highest concentration of African Americans. The official and unofficial hurdles to cross in order to register were numerous, and as a result, black voter registration was around 5 percent. Black Mississippians knew they could not rely on the federal government to intervene on their behalf; the John F. Kennedy administration had done little to guarantee racial justice and to secure the constitutional rights of black Mississippians, and the Lyndon B. Johnson administration did not want to upset the fragile relationship with Southern Democrats and the national Democratic Party. Without federal protection, civil rights organizations and workers were vulnerable to attacks carried out by the Ku Klux Klan (KKK) and local authorities, including the police.

In this environment, Mississippi civil rights leaders considered a new proposal to attack the entrenched white political power structures and the war subjugating the Black population. The "Freedom Vote" campaign emerged to provide disenfranchised black citizens a racially integrated alternative to the segregationist Democratic Party of Mississippi. The goals of Freedom Vote in the summer of 1963 were to demonstrate the political power of the black community, unify the civil rights organizations in the state, educate potential voters, have black candidates stand for election, and to encourage and support political activism. Despite the efforts of white officials to disrupt and harass, jail, beat, and threaten volunteers, Freedom Vote accomplished many of its goals. It provided the impetus for African Americans to assert their individual and collective rights and began to change the state's political landscape forever by setting the foundation for further political activities and the establishment of the MFDP.

While the gains made by the Freedom Vote were important, all of the limitations on African American participation remained in place in Mississippi. White primaries, poll taxes, literacy tests, interpretation tests, and voter intimidation all combined to depress black registration, which hovered in the single digits. In 1964, the year MDFP was founded, the rate of African American voter registration in Mississippi was 6.4 percent while white registration was at about 65 percent.

In 1964, the Council of Federated Organizations (COFO) launched the Mississippi Freedom Summer Project, which, under the leadership of Bob Moses (1935–), brought hundreds of white college students to the state to educate and register African Americans to vote. The threat of violence was ever present; the Freedom Summer workers faced constant threats of violence and intimidation. Three civil rights volunteers—James Chaney, Andrew Goodman and Michael Schwerner—disappeared on June 21 after being detained and released by local law enforcement. The disappearance captured the nation's attention and drew the involvement of the FBI. After an extensive search, their bodies were discovered in an earthen dam 44 days after they were abducted and murdered.

One of the principal goals for Freedom Summer was to further develop the capacity of the MFDP as a party structure. To do so, the MFDP expanded its focus to include electing delegates to represent Mississippi at the national Democratic Party convention, to be recognized as the official Mississippi delegation at the national convention to replace the all-White Democratic Party "regulars," and to nominate candidates for U.S. Senate and House seats. The MFDP ran candidates in the Democratic primaries and filed federal lawsuits targeting the state's policies that disenfranchised black voters.

On August 6, 1964, the MFDP held its first state convention with nearly 2,500 delegates from across the state attending; 68 MFDP delegates and 22 alternates were elected at the precinct, county, and district level meetings before being selected to attend the national Democratic convention in Atlantic City, New Jersey. The selected delegation reflected a cross-section of black Mississippians, including tenant farmers, laborers, domestics, preachers, teachers, small landowners, and entrepreneurs. The diversity reflected urban and rural Mississippi, as well as the civil rights movement more broadly. The MFDP group also included four white representatives and ten black Student Non-violent Coordinating Committee (SNCC) organizers. The most famous of the MFDP delegates was Mrs. Fannie Lou Hamer, a 46-year-old black woman who had lived her entire life in Mississippi as a sharecropper and domestic. Hamer was the vice chair of the delegation and was known for her leadership and the courage she displayed in the face of discrimination in the Mississippi Delta.

When the MFDP group arrived in Atlantic City, their goal was to be seated in place of the "Regulars" and to be recognized as the official Mississippi delegation. In order to be seated as the official Democratic delegation, the MFDP needed approval from the credentials committee, and it sought support from other states' delegations, staged a vigil on the boardwalk, lobbied the Democratic Party's credentials committee members, and gave speeches about the appalling conditions they experienced in Mississippi. However, the MFDP met resistance from President Lyndon Johnson. Earlier that year, on July 2, Johnson had signed the 1964 Civil Rights Act with the full expectation that it would cost the Democratic party votes among white southerners. To limit those losses, Johnson hoped to avoid a public fight within the party. The 1964 Civil Right Act, however, primarily focused on desegregating public accommodations and did not address poll taxes, literacy tests, and other racially discriminatory local and state laws that disenfranchised black voters. MFDP was interested in a comprehensive plan to protect African American political participation and voting rights, something that Johnson largely supported and would later sign into law with the Voting Right Act of 1965.

President Johnson was determined to avoid a public fight because he believed that seating the MFDP delegation would cost him the South in the November 1964 presidential election, and he needed Southern support for his legislative agenda. Further, President Johnson wanted a smooth path to his nomination and used government tools to serve his political agenda. Specifically, Johnson requested that the FBI survey the MFDP delegation and its key supporters, wiretap their phones, and solicit information by posing as reporters. As a result, President Johnson was aware of what was being planned before the plan was executed, including getting a key MFDP member to divulge the names of credential committee members who had pledged their support to the MFDP challenge. Those credential committee members then received phone calls threatening political and economic reprisals if they supported the MFDP.

Unaware of what the president was doing, the MFDP gave testimony at the credentials committee meeting. As Vice Chair of the Delegation, Mrs. Hamer testified about her life as a sharecropper, how she had lost her job and been evicted for attempting to register to vote, that she was shot at because of attempting to register others, and how she was arrested and beaten for trying to vote. Mrs. Hamer's potent testimony was carried live on national television. President Johnson, worried that MFDP would gain public support, announced an emergency press conference—to preempt Hamer's speech—during which he announced rather mundane items, none of which amounted to much of an emergency. In addition, LBJ sent his soon to be running mate, Hubert Humphrey, to neutralize the conflict and find a resolution that was acceptable to everyone. MFDP was offered two at-large seats (but not as representatives of Mississippi), and the racialized selection of delegates from Mississippi would be eliminated in 1968. But MFDP viewed the offer as a symbolic gesture and voted to reject the deal. Fannie Lou Hamer announced, "We didn't come all this way for no two seats" (Branch 1998, 474).

The MFDP delegation returned to Mississippi disappointed and disillusioned; the experience at the convention demonstrated that the Democratic Party was unwilling to take on the cause of the MFDP. The demarcation lines of racism were firmly in place in 1964. Despite the setback in Atlantic City, MFDP garnered national support for its cause, and shined a spotlight on the plight of African Americans in Mississippi and throughout the South. Although their efforts did not immediately change the national Democratic Party's politics, the sustained efforts of MFDP kept the national spotlight on voting rights and racially discriminatory policies, motivated more African Americans to participate in electoral politics, and influenced the passage of the Voting Rights Act in 1965.

The MFDP continued to be active at the local level by registering voters across Mississippi, supporting candidates for local and state office, and electing one of their own candidates to the state legislature in 1967. At the 1968 national convention in Chicago, the MFDP, now allied with other civil rights groups, formed the Loyalist Democratic Party, to challenge the legitimacy of the Mississippi "Regulars." Through careful documentation, MFDP demonstrated that the "Regulars" were selected illegally. The MFDP's challenge succeeded, and in 1968 the MFDP's delegation was seated as Mississippi's officially recognized delegates. The MFDP had a profound influence on Democratic Party politics, and its influence extends well beyond Democratic politics in Mississippi—reaching across the country as a result of MFDP's efforts to achieve voting rights for all.

Keesha M. Middlemass

See also: Congress of Racial Equality (1942–); Montgomery Improvement Association and Women's Political Council (1955–1970); National Urban League (1910–); Rainbow-PUSH Coalition (1996–); Southern Christian Leadership Conference (1957–); Student Nonviolent Coordinating Committee (1960–1974)

Further Reading

Branch, Taylor. 1998. *Pillar of Fire: America in the King Years, 1963–65.* New York: Simon & Schuster.

Burner, Eric. 1994. *And Gently He Shall Lead Them: Robert Parris Moses and Civil Rights in Mississippi.* New York: New York University Press.

Davis, T. 1998. *Weary Feet, Rested Souls.* New York: Norton.

Dittmer, John. 1995. *Local People: The Struggle for Civil Rights in Mississippi.* Urbana: University of Illinois Press.

McAdam, Doug. 1988. *Freedom Summer.* New York: Oxford University Press.

Montgomery Improvement Association and Women's Political Council (1955–1970)

Within 24 hours of the December 1, 1955, arrest of Rosa Parks (1913–2005) for violating Montgomery, Alabama's, segregated bus seating policy, representatives from over 50 groups from the city's African American community met at Dexter Avenue Baptist Church to plan a response. That response included a boycott of city buses, the elevation of a young Baptist minister to national and ultimately global prominence, drawing national press attention to the segregation issue, and, ultimately, federal involvement in the form of legal action abolishing segregation on city buses. The Montgomery Improvement Association (MIA) kept the boycott from falling apart or dissolving in the face of legal action and violent intimidation.

The confrontation had been brewing for years. Under the Jim Crow laws in Montgomery and throughout the South, African Americans had been relegated to a second-class existence. That included riding on city buses, which identified seats for white and black riders. But the African Americans were forced to yield their seats to white customers if all the seats dedicated for white riders were taken. In order to head off that confrontation, the Women's Political Council (WPC) of Montgomery, a group of middle-class African American educators, tried to negotiate with the city's leaders. In May of 1954, the WPC proposed a plan in which black passengers would be seated from back to front, and white passengers seated from front to back, until all the seats were full. Other cities already used such a plan, but Montgomery's commissioners consistently dismissed the idea, even though the WPC warned of plans in the African American community to stop riding public transportation.

On the day Rosa Parks was arrested, she sat in the first row of the black section of the bus and refused to move when ordered by the driver. Within hours, E. D. Nixon (1899–1987), president of the Alabama National Association for the Advancement of Colored People (NAACP), and Jo Ann Robinson (1912–1992), the leader of the WPC, set about organizing the Dexter Avenue meeting and the Montgomery Improvement Association.

Initially, community organizers called for a one-day boycott of Montgomery's buses on Monday, December 5. When virtually no black person in Montgomery rode the bus that day, Nixon, Reverend Ralph Abernathy (1926–1990), and other black religious leaders established the MIA to continue the action. But the MIA needed a leader, someone to be the face of the movement. That face had to belong to someone who could mediate between the competing factions within Montgomery's African American community as well as avoid being tagged as a radical or an activist by Montgomery's white establishment. Local leaders selected Dr. Martin Luther King Jr. (1929–1968) to lead the MIA. He was young (26), a powerful orator, and, perhaps most importantly, new to Montgomery, having arrived just six months earlier. That made him less susceptible to whatever pressures opponents might try to apply in order to end the boycott.

In the beginning, the MIA put forward modest proposals. It asked for three things: greater courtesy to black passengers, more black drivers for routes going through the African American community, and the creation of a flexible line separating black and white sections of the bus, so that when blacks made up the majority of passengers, they would not be forced to move when additional whites boarded the bus. It was the total rejection of these demands that prompted the MIA to continue the boycott and press for the complete integration of the city's public transportation system.

Over the next 381 days, the MIA kept the boycott from collapsing in the face of legal, economic, and psychological efforts to destroy it. When city leaders threatened to punish taxi drivers for helping African-Americans get around town, the MIA established carpools. When whites tried to undermine the movement to create dissension, it held weekly meetings with prayer sessions and music to keep protesters united. And when efforts to break the boycott turned violent, it helped keep a lid on emotions and focused on the bigger picture of ending segregation. It also extended its reach beyond Montgomery, synchronizing legal challenges to the city's bus segregation ordinance. Chief among those efforts was *Browder* v. *Gayle*, which challenged the Alabama state statutes and Montgomery's city ordinances legalizing bus segregation. The suit was filed in February, 1956, by Aurelia Gray and three other African American women. Montgomery mayor William Gayle, the chief of police and a host of other city officials, were named as defendants. The women charged that the state and local restrictions deprived people of equal protection under the Fourteenth Amendment. In June, a three-judge panel ruled in their favor and ordered the state of Alabama and the city of Montgomery to stop operating segregated buses. Despite the ruling, the MIA continued the boycott, while state officials pleaded their case to the U.S. Supreme Court. The MIA kept 90 percent of Montgomery's black residents off public transportation, nearly driving the bus company out of business. The boycott would end on December 21, 1956, four days after the U.S. Supreme Court rejected city and state appeals and one day after the city of Montgomery announced it would obey. Martin Luther King Jr. and other MIA leaders boarded buses that morning to commemorate the achievement.

The Montgomery Improvement Association would gradually fade in prominence, but not before it provided the foundation in 1957 for an even larger organization, the Southern Christian Leadership Conference (SCLC). The SCLC, led by Dr. King, continued the MIA's work in the struggle for civil rights.

John A. Morello

See also: Congress of Racial Equality (1942–); Mississippi Freedom Democratic Party (1964–1968); National Association for the Advancement of Colored People (1909–); National Urban League (1910–); Rainbow-PUSH Coalition (1996–); Southern Christian Leadership Conference (1957–); Student Nonviolent Coordinating Committee (1960–1974)

Further Reading

Chafe, William H. 1999. *The Unfinished Journey: America Since World War II.* New York: Oxford University Press.

Tindall, George B. 1988. *America: A Narrative History.* New York: W. W. Norton.

Moral Majority (1979–1989)

In May 1979, Reverend Jerry Falwell (1933–2007) founded the Moral Majority. This organization was formed as a reaction against the previous 17 years of liberal Supreme Court decisions and other actions by federal and state government. The goals of this organization were to mobilize the public to undo the Supreme Court decisions, inform the organization's members about what was happening politically, and to change selected public policies in a direction preferred by religious political conservatives.

From 1962 through the 1970s, the Supreme Court ruled on cases in a direction that religious conservatives consistently opposed. Beginning with *Engel v. Vitale* (1962), the Supreme Court ruled that a voluntary, nondenominational school prayer read by public school officials at the beginning of each school day in the State of New York was unconstitutional. The Supreme Court ruled this prayer unconstitutional because it was tantamount to the state establishing a religion, in violation of the First Amendment's Establishment Clause. In 1973, the Supreme Court ruled that abortion was constitutional and legally protected in *Roe v. Wade*.

Moreover, varying government agencies at the national and state levels enacted policies that religious conservatives opposed. For instance, many religious conservatives wanted to homeschool their children but were banned from doing so in many states. Further, some jurisdictions proposed laws and ordinances that would ban employment discrimination against gays and lesbians, while some in California (through Proposition 6) unsuccessfully proposed banning gays and lesbians from teaching in public schools. Finally, the Internal Revenue Service (IRS) proposed a regulation in 1978 that, if enacted, would have required Christian schools to prove that the absence of African American students in their institutions was not the result of conscious efforts.

This sequence of government actions galvanized opposition from a disparate collection of Christian conservatives. Immediately after *Roe v. Wade* (1973) was decided, the Catholic Church immediately and vehemently opposed the decision. In addition, conservative evangelicals opposed eliminating state-sponsored school prayer in public schools, state laws that prohibited homeschooling, and the IRS's proposed regulation. Finally, many political conservatives at the time opposed laws and ordinances that expanded the rights of gays and lesbians.

Despite vocal opposition to these actions from differing quarters, nobody immediately emerged to organize the opposition into a cohesive political whole. This changed in 1979 as a result of a series of behind the scenes conversations between Falwell, Paul Weyrich (1942–2008), Howard Phillips (1941–2013), Edward McAteer (1926–2004), and Robert Billings (1927–1995). These men discussed what should be done to unify theologically disparate groups into an organization that could reverse policies they saw as negative.

Paul Weyrich began their last conversation by stating, "Out there is what one might call a moral majority—people who would agree on principles based on the Decalogue [the Ten Commandments], for example—but they have been separated by geographical and denominational differences and that has caused them to vote differently" (Martin 1996, 200). Shortly thereafter, Jerry Falwell responded, "That's it! That's the name of the organization" (Martin 1996, 200).

After this conversation, Falwell traveled hundreds of thousands of miles annually to organize this collection of groups under a common banner: the Moral Majority. Initially, he held a series of "I Love America" rallies at state capitols and in Washington, D.C. During these rallies, he would call for national repentance, discuss his policy proposals, and encourage attendees to become politically active. As part of these rallies, Falwell invited all of the clergy in attendance to a free lunch afterward in which he explained the purpose and strategy of the Moral

Majority. In addition, he encouraged this diverse set of clergy members to work together despite their theological differences because they held common positions on issues like abortion, school prayer, and the rights of gays and lesbians. Many of these clergy went on to help head state and local Moral Majority chapters.

The funding to get this organization started came from a series of direct appeals to the churches of those who attended Falwell's rallies, listeners of his weekly radio program (the "Old Time Gospel Hour"), members of Falwell's church (Thomas Road Baptist Church), and broader direct mailings to those devoted to conservative causes. Quite frequently, these fund-raising letters drew upon themes ranging from patriotism to government overreach. These appeals raised several million dollars annually between 1979 and 1985.

The Moral Majority opposed abortion, socialism, the proliferation of illegal drugs, expanded rights for gays and lesbians, and pornography. The organization supported reintroducing school prayer in public schools, the Israel-United States alliance, significant increases in defense spending, homeschooling, and broader limitations on the powers of the federal government (Snowball 1991). The Moral Majority used several tactics to advance these policy objectives.

First, the organization mobilized millions of previously politically inactive conservative Christians of different denominations to vote Republican and be civically active. To do so, Falwell traveled as a guest preacher at various churches while encouraging listeners to become politically involved. In addition, the Moral Majority produced the "Moral Majority Report" that circulated to 750,000 people and 250,000 churches. This document discussed current events from a conservative Christian perspective and encouraged readers to be politically active. These mobilization efforts resulted in the successful election of Ronald Reagan as president in 1980.

Second, Ronald Reagan's election gave the Moral Majority a sufficient level of clout to become an influential presence within the Republican Party. Once Reagan became president, The Moral Majority lobbied the Executive Branch to gain support for its policies being passed by Congress and to ensure that political appointees were Moral Majority supporters. The Moral Majority had a limited degree of success in this respect. On the one hand, the Moral Majority was successful in getting Dr. C. Everett Koop (1916–2013), a staunch opponent of abortion, nominated by the president and confirmed by the Senate to be the Surgeon General. However, the Moral Majority was unsuccessful in preventing several other, less-preferred nominees from being selected and confirmed to appointed positions in the federal government.

Third, the Moral Majority also lobbied Congress to achieve its policy goals, but it had comparatively little success. Between 1981 and 1986, the Moral Majority lobbied Congress to pass a school prayer amendment to the Constitution, laws that would ban or limit abortion, and for significant increases in national defense spending. While then-President Reagan spearheaded the School Prayer Amendment, it did not get the required two-thirds support from both houses of Congress for it to be sent to the states for ratification. In addition, few laws were passed at the national level that restricted abortion. The most notable of these laws, the Hyde Amendment (which prohibits the use of federal funds to pay for abortions except in very limited circumstances), was reauthorized each year throughout this period.

Although there were significant increases in national defense spending during this time span, it is unclear how much of the increase is due to the influence of the Moral Majority.

Fourth, the Moral Majority advanced its campaigns against pornography predominantly through two unsuccessful lawsuits against *Penthouse* and *Hustler* magazines. Federal courts ruled that pornography and speech of the type found in those magazines was protected under the First Amendment. Finally, the Moral Majority formed a political action committee (PAC) whose purpose was to give money to candidates for elective office who supported this organization's goals. At its peak, this PAC gave $11,500 to nine Senate and House candidates in 1980.

The Moral Majority was at its most successful between 1979 and 1985, but it declined thereafter due to a combination of controversial statements by its founder, Jerry Falwell, and the rise of other groups that competed with it for influence and membership. For example, Falwell opposed economic sanctions against South Africa for its practice of apartheid. Apartheid was a set of South African government policies that separated whites from other races in many areas of public life. As a result of this position, fund-raising decreased, and membership declined. Also, other organizations, like People for the American Way, emerged explicitly to oppose the Moral Majority's agenda.

The organization attempted to recover by renaming itself the Liberty Federation in 1985. Just a few years later, and with little fanfare, the Liberty Foundation was disbanded by Falwell so that he could focus on his other ventures, including being the pastor of Thomas Road Baptist Church and growing the college that he founded, Liberty University. By the time the Liberty Foundation disbanded, other organizations took up the causes that Falwell championed, including Concerned Women for America, the Christian Coalition, and Focus on the Family.

Kenneth W. Moffett

Related Primary Document: **Barry Goldwater: Response to Moral Majority during Sandra Day O'Connor Confirmation Hearings (1981)**

Barry Goldwater: Response to Moral Majority during Sandra Day O'Connor Confirmation Hearings (1981)

Sandra Day O'Connor was nominated to the Supreme Court by President Ronald Reagan in 1981. During her confirmation hearings, members of the Moral Majority harshly criticized O'Connor for two votes cast while she was a member of the Arizona Senate, labeling her a supporter of abortion. In the midst of the controversy, Senator Barry Goldwater, a major supporter of Judge O'Connor, gave a speech to the Senate denouncing the Moral Majority critiques as "a lot of foolish claptrap." His statement from the hearings on July 8, 1981, follows below.

THE NOMINATION OF SANDRA O'CONNOR TO BE A JUSTICE OF THE SUPREME COURT

Mr. GOLDWATER. Mr. President, a lot of foolish clap trap has been written and spoken about President Reagan's Supreme Court nominee, Sandra O'Connor, by people who do not know what they are talking about.

I am very disturbed that the source of this uninformed criticism stems from people who have been my friends and with whom I have long shared common political positions.

Strangely enough, these people question Judge O'Connor's commitment to traditional conservative values.

Well, I ask these critics, who are associated with moral causes, to show the same Christian decency and fairness toward Judge O'Connor that they expect of others. Instead of jumping to conclusions about her views, on the basis of years-old positions that were taken in a different context and setting, why cannot these people wait until the nomination hearings and let Mrs. O'Connor discuss her views personally?

For example, she is being attacked for a vote cast in the Arizona State Legislature 7 years ago involving a bond issue. She appears to have voted against adding a rider, proposing a ban on free abortions, to a football stadium bond issue. But as I understand her interpretation of that vote, her decision had nothing to do with the merits of abortion, pro or con. As a lawyer, she read the Arizona State Constitution as forbidding unrelated legislative riders. She was merely carrying out her duty under the State constitution.

So when people ask me if she has changed or will change her position on abortion, I must reply by asking how they know what her position was. The way they interpret her stand may not at all be her own view of the matter.

And I would point out that Mrs. O'Connor was in the State legislature only for 6 years, from 1969 to 1974. She came to the bench as a State supreme court judge in January of 1975. The big Supreme Court case of Roe against Wade was just handed down in 1973, a year before she left the Senate in 1974.

In other words, she has not been in a legislator's position for 7 years. She was not called upon to take a position on the very controversial and complex and emotional issue of abortion in all these years when the issue was steadily gaining national attention.

Why, the very subject of Right of Life meant something very different even among antiabortion groups in 1974. The first Right of Life constitutional amendment was not introduced until 1973, with only nine sponsors in the Senate. There were different versions in the House. One version simply called for restoring primary jurisdiction to the State governments in this area.

It was not until later that antiabortion organizations settled on a clear-cut, national prohibition of abortion as the single acceptable approach. It was even later that prolifers generally agreed not to make any exceptions, even in case of rape or incest. It is impossible and unfair for anyone to test another person's current views by a position they took 7 years ago, especially when the subject is one in which the views of the strongest believers themselves gradually evolved.

Mr. President, the Deputy White House Press Secretary reports that Sandra O'Connor told President Reagan what her present thinking is on the matter of abortion. She reportedly announced that she is personally opposed to abortion and that it was especially abhorrent to her. She added her feeling that the subject of regulation of abortion is a legitimate subject for the legislative area.

Now, this should satisfy anyone. It is a balanced statement that is sympathetic to the right of the unborn to exist and to the power of Congress to address the subject. The Right to Life groups are totally off-base and mistaken in opposing Judge O'Connor's nomination. They can only do harm to their own credibility and should back off.

Mr. President, I have personally known Sandra O'Connor for over 20 years. I know for a fact of her strong devotion to family life. Mrs. O'Connor epitomizes the American ideal of a mother and wife and community-spirited person. She is happily married and has three sons.

Sandra O'Connor served on the Governor's Committee on Marriage and Family in 1965 and was the recipient of the prestigious National Conference of Christians and Jews Humanitarian Award in 1974.

She personally stands as the living embodiment of the decent religious woman that Moral Majority and Right to Life groups are always proclaiming, and it is shocking to me that these groups would turn against such a fine person, who deserves and has earned their respect and support.

I have heard Mrs. O'Connor's strong profamily views. I was present at the wedding of my nephew last year when she made a beautiful speech about "marriage being the foundation of the family, the basic unit of society, the hope of the world and the strength of our country." Now, what quarrel can Moral Majority take with this creed?

Mr. President, I will have more, much more, to say on Sandra O'Connor's nomination in coming days. I can easily prove to my colleagues that she is a brilliant, fair minded judge, who will make a great contribution to the Supreme Court, particularly, I think, in the area of judicial restraint.

Mr. President, I yield the floor.

Source: *Congressional Record.* Washington, D.C.: Government Printing Office, 1981, 15091–15092.

See also: Christian Coalition of America (1988–); Eagle Forum (1972–); Family Research Council (1983–); Home School Legal Defense Association (2000–); National Organization for Marriage (2007–); Republican National Coalition for Life (1992–)

Further Reading

Harding, Susan Friend. 2001. *The Book of Jerry Falwell: Fundamentalist Language and Politics.* Princeton, NJ: Princeton University Press.

Martin, William. 1996. *With God on Our Side: The Rise of the Religious Right in America.* New York: Broadway Books.

Snowball, David. 1991. *Continuity and Change in the Rhetoric of the Moral Majority.* New York: Praeger Publishers.

Wilcox, Clyde. 1992. *God's Warriors: The Christian Right in Twentieth-Century America.* Baltimore, MD: The Johns Hopkins University Press.

Winters, Michael Sean. 2012. *God's Right Hand: How Jerry Falwell Made God a Republican and Baptized the American Right.* New York: HarperCollins Publishers.

Mothers against Drunk Driving (1980–)

Mothers against Drunk Driving (MADD) is an advocacy group born out of human tragedy that has worked for over three and a half decades to raise awareness about drunk and drugged driving and to prevent the injuries and deaths that can result. The organization was founded in May 1980 by Candy Lightner (1946–), just days after her daughter Cari was killed by a drunk driver who had multiple drunk driving arrests prior to the accident but who, nevertheless, had been allowed to continue driving. Angered by the situation and wanting to channel both her anger and her grief in a positive direction, Lightner started MADD in an effort to change the way drunk driving was addressed in the United States as well as to reduce the number of drunk driving fatalities across the nation.

From the beginning, MADD has served as an example of what one dedicated person can do, not to mention how one person can make a difference. The operation started as "a one-woman show"; by the end of its third year—arguably its peak time, in terms of activity and influence—it had grown into an international organization, one that could lay claim to almost 400 chapters spread around the globe, as well as a staff of about 50 employees, 2 million members, and an annual budget in excess of $12 million. MADD hit a psychic chord with the American population, spurring unprecedented collaborative efforts to begin to rein in the devastation that had characterized drunk driving. Indeed, while it may have begun as a one-woman show, its subsequent growth showed it struck a chord and began amid a torrent of publicity and activity, all of which Lightner struggled to keep control of while seeking to channel it in the right direction.

It was a little like riding a bull. In 1982 President Ronald Reagan (1911–2004) established the Presidential Commission on Drunk Driving (PCDD) and appointed Lightner a member. Then in 1983 Lightner's efforts were portrayed in a 1983 NBC television movie, *Mothers against Drunk Drivers: The Candy Lightner Story*, in which actress Mariette Hartley (1940–) portrayed the energetic crusader. The event, coming on top of Lightner's own nonstop appearance on news and talk shows, gave widespread positive attention to MADD's efforts. The attention and publicity was almost overwhelming, but it also translated into action as the first five years of MADD's existence saw almost every state creating a governor's task force on drunk driving. In addition, during the period from 1980 to 1985, countless state laws relating to drunk driving were enacted. In addition, the Presidential Commission Group came back with a number of recommendations, one of which was a proposal for a national legal minimum drinking age, an idea adopted in July 1984 after extensive lobbying. Ironically, the enactment of the minimum age served to shift focus from drunk driving to teenage driving, but that would come later.

In its first five years, MADD spearheaded the effort to establish December as Drunk and Drugged Driving Awareness Month while also helping make the use of sobriety checkpoints a common practice. Reflective of Lightner's initial frustration over the lack of legal accountability for drunk drivers, MADD pushed hard for greater legal consequences, and by 1985, over 700 new laws relating to drunk driving had been enacted at the state level. The organization's list of accomplishments in its early years was extensive and impressive. And yet, in some ways, it left the organization wondering where to go next. When Lightner left MADD in 1985 amid controversy about finances and the organization's direction, MADD lost a big part of its identity.

Over the years MADD has continued to fight against the perils of drunk driving, but it has also expanded its message. In particular, it has continued to fight against society's mixed message about underage drinking. Given the uniform 50-state-established national drinking age of 21, the organization believes that there should be no mixed messages and nothing that runs counter to this. They disavow the teenage "don't drink and drive" campaign, for example, which, although it discourages unsafe behavior, expresses tacit acceptance of underage drinking. In addition, MADD has urged the adoption of standardized IDs given the use of fake IDs as a means of facilitating underage use and possession of alcohol. The organization has also been active in campaigns to reduce and limit college and on-campus drinking.

As it looks back on its years of fighting the impact of drunk driving, MADD proudly points to a reduction in deaths attributable to drunk driving from almost 25,000 in 1980, the year MADD was founded, to approximately 10,000 in 2014. At the same time, with many of its goals achieved, MADD has struggled to stay relevant and involved. That reality, one often faced by reform groups focused on a particular issue, may be why the organization has moved away from its drunk driving focus and has instead focused more on a broader, more prohibitionlike direction. Indeed, MADD continues to advocate not only for strict adherence to state laws but also for increased accountability for those who break the laws. MADD has encouraged alcohol-free zones, as well as social events that are alcohol free, all in an effort to show that alcohol is not a necessity for a good time. In addition, MADD is very active in the effort to increase the liability of the adults who provide alcohol to underage individuals, and it seeks to strengthen laws and standards for civil suits concerning social host liability. The group has also sought make a person's record of underage possession and use of alcohol as a condition for the ability to possess a driver's license. It has also clashed with other organizations—even the modern iteration of SADD, which was originally founded by Lightner's other daughter, Serena—which does not adhere to the zero-tolerance policy that has increasingly become a hallmark of MADD's current efforts.

All of this has led many observers, including Lightner, to believe that the modern MADD has strayed from its roots and has morphed into a different kind of organization. More and more, MADD appears to be increasingly moving in the direction of a neoprohibitionist approach to alcohol, moving beyond putting limitations on drunk or excessive driving and painting all drinking with a negative brush. It has been engaging in basic alcohol prevention efforts, and even in the area of drunk driving, the long-time centerpiece of its efforts, MAAD has increasingly been involved in pursuing ever-lower standards at the state level for what constitutes drunk driving. In addition, the group is sponsoring more advertisements aimed at drinking without making any distinctions between drinking and drunkenness or between the results that can occur. In fact, while it has pursued efforts aimed at affecting the national culture and the legal and political landscape, MADD seems to have increasingly established itself as a national scold. As one analyst observed, while MADD's initial goal was to reduce fatalities from drunk driving—and in fact they have dropped off significantly—the organization has proven to be very effective in changing the nation's views on drinking in general with public disapproval of alcohol use having risen significantly since MADD began its efforts. One newspaper editorial observed that given its current direction the group would need to change its name from "Mothers against Drunk Driving" to "Mothers against Any Drinking Whatsoever" unless it wanted to be accused of false advertising. Candy Lightner claims that although her original intention was to raise public awareness about the issue of drunk driving as well as increase accountability for those guilty of such behavior, from all appearances, the group has moved away from that focus.

MADD's current leaders dispute this claim, arguing that they remain committed to honoring the organization's long-standing goal of preventing the kinds of tragedies that are all too often the result of drunk driving. While acknowledging that the 2016 revision of its mission could be seen as a change in direction, MADD's board of directors asserted that it was an effort to more effectively align with its ongoing Campaign to Eliminate Drunk Driving, as well as its desire to more clearly define its role in the increasingly broad-based effort to combat drugged driving, a modern reality, but not something of great concern when MADD was launched in 1980. Critics perceived the changes in MADD's tactics and goals as more reflective of the antialcohol, hatchet-wielding saloon-wrecker and Temperance movement icon Carrie Nation (1846–1911) than the legacy of Candy Lightner.

Another issue that has long dogged MADD's efforts, while hurting its public image, is the matter of fund-raising. Like many nonprofits, MADD has always faced funding challenges. Indeed, Lightner left MADD in 1985 amid questions about financial mismanagement; since then, the organization often has come under fire for its financing and fund-raising. Critics have paid particular attention to the fact that its income was redirected to additional fund-raising. Indeed, so much of the money that MADD takes in is used for fund-raising that the American Institute of Philanthropy lowered its rating for MADD, believing that in spending almost twice the percentage that AIP considers appropriate, MADD's ability to pursue its service agenda is undermined. In addition, as part of its fund-raising efforts, MADD has been zealous in its pursuit of corporate sponsors and partnerships, but some of those, especially its partnership with General Motors, have raised questions about whether a large gift to MADD is buying its silence. MADD has explained its use of corporate partners by noting that they play a valuable role in the group's efforts to offer educational programs that help raise youth awareness, while also providing assistance for crime victims. As they proudly claim to have helped save over 340,000 lives, MADD makes clear its belief that the corporate partnerships have played an important role in that effort.

In the end, no one can make an accurate claim about how many lives MADD's efforts have really saved. But no objective observer can look back on the group's efforts dating to 1980 and credibly claim that the organization has had no impact. At the same time, the organization has experienced collateral issues that have distracted it from pursuing its core goals. In an effort to stay relevant and operating, it may have strayed from its original mission. Born out of tragedy, MADD is an organization that has not only affected American society on many levels but has also offered more than a few lessons along the way.

William H. Pruden III

See also: Brady Campaign to Prevent Gun Violence (1974–)

Further Reading

Hanson, David J. n.d. "Mothers against Drunk Driving: A Crash Course in MADD." *Alcohol Abuse Prevention.* http://www.alcoholfacts.org/CrashCourseOnMADD .html.

Lerner, Barron H. 2011. *One for the Road: Drunk Driving Since 1900.* Baltimore, MD: Johns Hopkins University Press.

MADD: No More Victims. 2017. https://www.madd.org/.

Reinarman, Craig. 1985. *Social Movements and Social Problems: "Mothers against Drunk Drivers," Restrictive Alcohol Laws and Social Control in the 1980s.* Berkley: School of Public Health, University of California, Berkeley.

Sadoff, Micky. 1990. *America Gets MADD!* San Diego, CA: Mothers against Drunk Driving.

Motion Picture Association of America (1922–)

The Motion Picture Association of America (MPAA), originally known as the Motion Picture Producers and Distributors Association (MPPDA), successfully avoided most attempts at government regulation of the burgeoning film industry through a combination of self-regulation and concerted efforts at public outreach and education. Key to its success was the hiring of Will Hays, a former postmaster general and chairman of the Republican National Committee, as its president. His political experience, combined with his skill as a spokesman and strategist, helped him marshal producers and distributors around a common cause of improving the film industry while protecting its profit margin, reputation, and ability to govern itself.

The MPAA was not the first attempt within the motion picture industry to work together to advance shared goals. In 1908, the Motion Picture Patents Company brought together developers of motion picture equipment with a distributor and several producers in a failed attempt at limiting the showing of motion pictures to theaters purchasing films from licensed exchanges and showing them on licensed projectors. In 1916, the short-lived National Association of the Motion Picture Industry was formed, uniting producers, distributors, and some exhibitors in a fight against censorship at the state level, but it was brought down by the mutual distrust of its members. Then, in 1922, film producers and distributors joined together to form the Motion Picture Producers and Distributors Association, which, in 1945, became the Motion Picture Association of America. The founding of this organization also coincided with a more favorable regulatory environment and governmental promotion of trade associations. Under the leadership of Hays, the organization began to simultaneously seek to avoid government censorship of films, boost the reputation of the motion picture industry among the public, and establish a favorable business climate for it, both in the United States and abroad.

The themes, images, and eventually words of early motion pictures challenged traditional morals. As the Jazz Age unfolded, the movies glorified activities that were previously seen as immoral, and newspapers told sensational stories of movie stars engaging in even more scandalous behavior offscreen. This drew the ire of concerned individuals and community groups, who pushed for government censorship of movies. They had early success in states like Pennsylvania, Ohio, and Kansas. New York adopted state censorship in 1921, and by the end of that year, dozens of state legislatures were considering censorship bills. The U.S. Supreme Court offered the movie industry little hope of protection during this time, stating motion pictures were a business and not entitled to First Amendment protections.

The MPPDA formed amid this widespread threat of government censorship of the movies at the state level. Hays and the MPPDA initially focused their efforts on fighting a censorship bill in Massachusetts, fearing that if it passed there, political censorship of movies would sweep throughout the country. Instead, they hoped a defeat of a bill would lead other states to abandon their efforts at censorship. Hays recognized that if they were to win, they needed public opinion on their side. He sent a representative of the MPPDA to talk to every small-town newspaper in the state, and he succeeded in getting a number of newspapers to oppose government censorship. He hired speakers to give public speeches and recruited citizens' committees to crusade against government censorship. As the vote grew closer, Hays also gave public speeches in Massachusetts, and he persuaded both political parties to issue written statements on government censorship of movies. A key part of all of these persuasive efforts was that the best way to protect the public interest was for the motion picture industry to regulate itself. The argument worked, and the vote for censorship failed handily. While the battle against government censorship was far from over, this practice of winning over the support of key citizens and community groups with a pitch for self-regulation remained a central part of MPPDA strategy.

Early attempts at self-regulation of movie content by the MPPDA lacked teeth, and movies with morally objectionable content continued to make it to the screen. In response to public pressure, members of Congress considered bans of objectionable content in films used in interstate or foreign commerce. Once Hays convinced movie producers that effective self-regulation was the only way to both save themselves from onerous government regulation and protect their profits, the MPPDA set out to develop a stronger (and enforceable) code of conduct for the movies. Two prominent Catholics with ties to the movie industry, Martin Quigley and Father Daniel Lord, were enlisted to write what became known as the Hays Code. Though their code focused mainly on sexual mores, Hays added a number of provisions to it, including the depiction of certain crimes, the consideration of national feelings, and the avoidance of repellant subjects. MPPDA members offi-cially voted to accept the Hays Code and made it the industry standard on March 31, 1930.

At first, the Hays Code, too, lacked teeth, and calls for censorship by religious and community groups continued. The MPPDA responded with a number of mea-sures to strengthen the enforcement of the code. In 1931, they voted to require prior review of scripts, but the MPPDA's advice about content was often ignored. In 1934, the Catholic Legion of Decency was formed, and it threatened a boycott of the movies unless the Hays Code was enforced. Other prominent religious groups joined in. In response, the MPPDA created the Production Code Adminis-tration to review all films. Films that failed to secure the Production Code Admin-istration's seal of approval would not be distributed or exhibited by MPPDA members, and violators of this rule would be faced with a $25,000 fine (equivalent to $450,000 in 2017 dollars). With these sanctions in place, movie producers began working with Production Code Administration staff throughout the filmmaking process to ensure they produced films that would secure this seal of approval and to avoid making extensive changes to a finished film. This new system of self-regulation worked. Complaints by the League of Decency and other groups disap-peared, and a papal encyclical suggested the Hays Code as a model for other countries. For the next two decades, the Hollywood films shown in the nation's movie theater's all had seals of approval.

The avoidance of government censorship was not the only battle the MPPDA waged against government regulation. The exorbitant salaries and profits of the movie industry drew government's attention during the Great Depression. So, too, did monopolistic practices in a number of industries, including motion pictures. Hays recognized that in order to effectively stop governmental interference, the motion picture industry needed to win public support for it efforts. The MPPDA routinely enlisted the public as an ally and partnered with civic groups to advance their aims. However, efforts to avoid governmental interference in these areas also required the cultivation of good relations with government officials. The MPPDA's General Coun-sel kept close watch on potential legislation that could affect the motion picture industry. Meanwhile, Hays cultivated friendships with members of both political parties. Hays limited the amount of money spent by the MPPDA in influencing legis-lation. When additional lobbying was required, he and his staff enlisted volunteer lobbyists whose interests were directly at stake as Hays believed these volunteer lob-byists would make the most compelling case. They also enlisted help from the public and engaged in community service to boost the reputation of the motion picture industry. The community service department actively worked with groups like the National Council of Teachers and the National Education Association to develop and provide films for educational use. Efforts such as these made it easy for them to recruit members of civic and community groups to testify in favor of the MPPDA and its goals, and they lessened the focus on the motion picture industry.

The success of the MPPDA in these efforts can be seen in its treatment under the National Industrial Recovery Act (NIRA), signed into law on June 16, 1933. It called for each industry to be governed by a code, but this code could be written by the industry's dominant trade association or, if the association refused, by the government. Although the monopolistic practices of the MPPDA were being challenged by the Allied States Association of Motion Picture Exhibitors, the MPPDA managed to get a sympathetic individual appointed to draw up the code. This code favored MPPDA members' practices in almost all respects. However, Hays and the MPPDA were worried their victory might not last, because President Franklin D. Roosevelt signed an executive order accompanying the code, allowing the head of the National Recovery Administration, Hugh Johnson, to modify it if there were difficulties within the industry. To ward off potential governmental interference, Hays and representatives of two of the major motion picture studios in the MPPDA met personally with Roosevelt and convinced him to order Johnson not to interfere. Meanwhile, Hays and the MPPDA agreed to a government study of exorbitant salaries in the motion picture industry. They helped the study's authors document the pay cuts movie stars, directors, and producers had taken. No action was taken against the industry as a result of the report.

However, a few years after the Supreme Court struck down the NIRA, the Roosevelt administration's Justice Department began antitrust action against the film industry. The suit named a number of MPPDA members but not the MPPDA itself. The Justice Department said the suit came in response to a number of complaints, not just from independent producers, distributors, and exhibitors but also from the theater going public. However, the MPPDA's public relations efforts over the years had won much of public opinion to their side. The trial recessed after two days. Over the next few months, Hays helped negotiate a consent decree from the Justice Department that was so favorable to the film industry that it returned to many of the practices allowed under the NIRA code.

The long-standing links between Hollywood and politics that began with the appointment of Hays as head of the MPPDA continues to this day. Jack Valenti, former assistant to President Lyndon Johnson, became head in 1966. When the Hays Code became no longer workable thanks to the rise of television, foreign films, and unfavorable court cases, Valenti and the National Association of Theater Owners developed a ratings system to replace it that was approved by the MPAA. This ratings system helps provide guidance to parents while restricting children from X-rated content, thus helping to placate those concerned about protecting children from objectionable content. These ratings remain in place in modified form today. In 2011 former United States Senator Christopher Dodd took the helm of the MPAA. Under Dodd, the MPAA continues to use a combination of public and legislative relations (aided today by campaign contributions) to advance its current goals of protecting creative freedom, stopping piracy of films, opening new global markets, and engaging in technological innovation.

Laurie L. Rice

Related Primary Document: **Hays Code (1934)**

Hays Code (1934)

The Motion Picture Production Code, known as the Hays Code, was a set of strict conduct rules that were applied to many major films released in the United States for almost three decades. The code was adopted in 1930 but not officially enforced until 1934. Films created before this era are often referred to as "pre-code." The Hays Code could be seen as a reaction to the effects of a booming film industry. Silent films fell off the radar and were replaced with more progressive content that some audiences may have been shocked to see in theaters. The Hays Code was also a means to bypass government regulation of production companies, as the companies handed the responsibility of policing film content to filmmakers themselves. The provisions of the code are listed below, and they forbid almost all suggestive behavior, as well as the perceived slander of "God" and any notion of an interracial relationship, among others.

A Code to Govern the Making of Talking, Synchronized and Silent Motion Pictures Formulated and formally adopted by The Association of Motion Picture Producers, Inc. and The Motion Picture Producers and Distributors of America, Inc. in March 1930. [Promulgated in 1934.]

Motion picture producers recognize the high trust and confidence which have been placed in them by the people of the world and which have made motion pictures a universal form of entertainment.

They recognize their responsibility to the public because of this trust and because entertainment and art are important influences in the life of a nation.

Hence, though regarding motion pictures primarily as entertainment without any explicit purpose of teaching or propaganda, they know that the motion picture within its own field of entertainment may be directly responsible for spiritual or moral progress, for higher types of social life, and for much correct thinking.

During the rapid transition from silent to talking pictures they have realized the necessity and the opportunity of subscribing to a Code to govern the production of talking pictures and of re-acknowledging this responsibility.

On their part, they ask from the public and from public leaders a sympathetic understanding of their purposes and problems and a spirit of cooperation that will allow them the freedom and opportunity necessary to bring the motion picture to a still higher level of wholesome entertainment for all the people.

General Principles
1. No picture shall be produced that will lower the moral standards of those who see it. Hence the sympathy of the audience should never be thrown to the side of crime, wrongdoing, evil or sin.

2. Correct standards of life, subject only to the requirements of drama and entertainment, shall be presented.

3. Law, natural or human, shall not be ridiculed, nor shall sympathy be created for its violation.

Particular Applications

I. Crimes against the Law
These shall never be presented in such a way as to throw sympathy with the crime as against law and justice or to inspire others with a desire for imitation.

1. Murder
   a. The technique of murder must be presented in a way that will not inspire imitation.
   b. Brutal killings are not to be presented in detail.
   c. Revenge in modern times shall not be justified.
2. Methods of Crime should not be explicitly presented.
   a. Theft, robbery, safe-cracking, and dynamiting of trains, mines, buildings, etc., should not be detailed in method.
   b. Arson must subject to the same safeguards.
   c. The use of firearms should be restricted to the essentials.
   d. Methods of smuggling should not be presented.
3. Illegal drug traffic must never be presented.
4. The use of liquor in American life, when not required by the plot or for proper characterization, will not be shown.

II. Sex

The sanctity of the institution of marriage and the home shall be upheld. Pictures shall not infer that low forms of sex relationship are the accepted or common thing.

1. Adultery, sometimes necessary plot material, must not be explicitly treated, or justified, or presented attractively.
2. Scenes of Passion
   a. They should not be introduced when not essential to the plot.
   b. Excessive and lustful kissing, lustful embraces, suggestive postures and gestures, are not to be shown.
   c. In general passion should so be treated that these scenes do not stimulate the lower and baser element.
3. Seduction or Rape
   a. They should never be more than suggested, and only when essential for the plot, and even then never shown by explicit method.
   b. They are never the proper subject for comedy.
4. Sex perversion or any inference to it is forbidden.
5. White slavery shall not be treated.
6. Miscegenation (sex relationships between the white and black races) is forbidden.
7. Sex hygiene and venereal diseases are not subjects for motion pictures.
8. Scenes of actual child birth, in fact or in silhouette, are never to be presented.
9. Children's sex organs are never to be exposed.

III. Vulgarity

The treatment of low, disgusting, unpleasant, though not necessarily evil, subjects should always be subject to the dictates of good taste and a regard for the sensibilities of the audience.

IV. Obscenity

Obscenity in word, gesture, reference, song, joke, or by suggestion (even when likely to be understood only by part of the audience) is forbidden.

V. Profanity

Pointed profanity (this includes the words, God, Lord, Jesus, Christ—unless used reverently—Hell, S.O.B., damn, Gawd), or every other profane or vulgar expression however used, is forbidden.

VI. Costume

1. Complete nudity is never permitted. This includes nudity in fact or in silhouette, or any lecherous or licentious notice thereof by other characters in the picture.

2. Undressing scenes should be avoided, and never used save where essential to the plot.

3. Indecent or undue exposure is forbidden.

4. Dancing or costumes intended to permit undue exposure or indecent movements in the dance are forbidden.

VII. Dances

1. Dances suggesting or representing sexual actions or indecent passions are forbidden.

2. Dances which emphasize indecent movements are to be regarded as obscene.

VIII. Religion

1. No film or episode may throw ridicule on any religious faith.

2. Ministers of religion in their character as ministers of religion should not be used as comic characters or as villains.

3. Ceremonies of any definite religion should be carefully and respectfully handled.

IX. Locations

The treatment of bedrooms must be governed by good taste and delicacy.

X. National Feelings

1. The use of the Flag shall be consistently respectful.

2. The history, institutions, prominent people and citizenry of other nations shall be represented fairly.

XI. Titles

Salacious, indecent, or obscene titles shall not be used.

XII. Repellent Subjects

The following subjects must be treated within the careful limits of good taste:

1. Actual hangings or electrocutions as legal punishments for crime.

2. Third degree methods.

3. Brutality and possible gruesomeness.

4. Branding of people or animals.

5. Apparent cruelty to children or animals.

6. The sale of women, or a woman selling her virtue.

7. Surgical operations.

Reasons Supporting the Preamble of the Code

I. Theatrical motion pictures, that is, pictures intended for the theatre as distinct from pictures intended for churches, schools, lecture halls, educational movements, social reform movements, etc., are primarily to be regarded as ENTERTAINMENT.

Mankind has always recognized the importance of entertainment and its value in rebuilding the bodies and souls of human beings.

But it has always recognized that entertainment can be a character either HELPFUL or HARMFUL to the human race, and in consequence has clearly distinguished between:

a. Entertainment which tends to improve the race, or at least to re-create and rebuild human beings exhausted with the realities of life; and

b. Entertainment which tends to degrade human beings, or to lower their standards of life and living.

Hence the MORAL IMPORTANCE of entertainment is something which has been universally recognized. It enters intimately into the lives of men and women and affects them closely; it occupies their minds and affections during leisure hours; and ultimately touches the whole of their lives. A man may be judged by his standard of entertainment as easily as by the standard of his work.

So correct entertainment raises the whole standard of a nation.

Wrong entertainment lowers the whole living conditions and moral ideals of a race.

Note, for example, the healthy reactions to healthful sports, like baseball, golf; the unhealthy reactions to sports like cockfighting, bullfighting, bear baiting, etc.

Note, too, the effect on ancient nations of gladiatorial combats, the obscene plays of Roman times, etc.

II. Motion pictures are very important as ART.

Though a new art, possibly a combination art, it has the same object as the other arts, the presentation of human thought, emotion, and experience, in terms of an appeal to the soul through the senses.

Here, as in entertainment,

Art enters intimately into the lives of human beings.

Art can be morally good, lifting men to higher levels. This has been done through good music, great painting, authentic fiction, poetry, drama.

Art can be morally evil in its effects. This is the case clearly enough with unclean art, indecent books, suggestive drama. The effect on the lives of men and women are obvious.

Note: It has often been argued that art itself is unmoral, neither good nor bad. This is true of the THING which is music, painting, poetry, etc. But the THING is the PRODUCT of some person's mind, and the intention of that mind was either good or bad morally when it produced the thing. Besides, the thing has its EFFECT upon those who come into contact with it. In both these ways, that is, as a product of a mind and as the cause of definite effects, it has a deep moral significance and unmistakable moral quality.

Hence: The motion pictures, which are the most popular of modern arts for the masses, have their moral quality from the intention of the minds which produce them and from their effects on the moral lives and reactions of their audiences. This gives them a most important morality.

1. They reproduce the morality of the men who use the pictures as a medium for the expression of their ideas and ideals.

2. They affect the moral standards of those who, through the screen, take in these ideas and ideals. In the case of motion pictures, the effect may be particularly emphasized because no art has so quick and so widespread an appeal to the masses. It has become in an incredibly short period the art of the multitudes.

III. The motion picture, because of its importance as entertainment and because of the trust placed in it by the peoples of the world, has special MORAL OBLIGATIONS:

A. Most arts appeal to the mature. This art appeals at once to every class, mature, immature, developed, undeveloped, law abiding, criminal. Music has its grades for different classes; so has literature and drama. This art of the motion picture, combining as it does the two fundamental appeals of looking at a picture and listening to a story, at once reaches every class of society.

B. By reason of the mobility of film and the ease of picture distribution, and because the possibility of duplicating positives in large quantities, this art reaches places unpenetrated by other forms of art.

C. Because of these two facts, it is difficult to produce films intended for only certain classes of people. The exhibitors' theatres are built for the masses, for the cultivated and the rude, the mature and the immature, the self-respecting and the criminal. Films, unlike books and music, can with difficulty be confined to certain selected groups.

D. The latitude given to film material cannot, in consequence, be as wide as the latitude given to book material. In addition:

a. A book describes; a film vividly presents. One presents on a cold page; the other by apparently living people.

b. A book reaches the mind through words merely; a film reaches the eyes and ears through the reproduction of actual events.

c. The reaction of a reader to a book depends largely on the keenness of the reader's imagination; the reaction to a film depends on the vividness of presentation.

Hence many things which might be described or suggested in a book could not possibly be presented in a film.

E. This is also true when comparing the film with the newspaper.

a. Newspapers present by description, films by actual presentation.

b. Newspapers are after the fact and present things as having taken place; the film gives the events in the process of enactment and with apparent reality of life.

F. Everything possible in a play is not possible in a film:

a. Because of the larger audience of the film, and its consequential mixed character. Psychologically, the larger the audience, the lower the moral mass resistance to suggestion.

b. Because through light, enlargement of character, presentation, scenic emphasis, etc., the screen story is brought closer to the audience than the play.

c. The enthusiasm for and interest in the film actors and actresses, developed beyond anything of the sort in history, makes the audience largely sympathetic toward the characters they portray and the stories in which they figure. Hence the audience is more ready to confuse actor and actress and the characters they portray, and it is most receptive of the emotions and ideals presented by the favorite stars.

G. Small communities, remote from sophistication and from the hardening process which often takes place in the ethical and moral standards of larger cities, are easily and readily reached by any sort of film.

H. The grandeur of mass settings, large action, spectacular features, etc., affects and arouses more intensely the emotional side of the audience.

In general, the mobility, popularity, accessibility, emotional appeal, vividness, straightforward presentation of fact in the film make for more intimate contact with a larger audience and for greater emotional appeal.

Hence the larger moral responsibilities of the motion pictures.

Reasons Underlying the General Principles

I. No picture shall be produced which will lower the moral standards of those who see it. Hence the sympathy of the audience should never be thrown to the side of crime, wrong-doing, evil or sin.

This is done:

1. When evil is made to appear attractive and alluring, and good is made to appear unattractive.

2. When the sympathy of the audience is thrown on the side of crime, wrongdoing, evil, sin. The same is true of a film that would throw sympathy against goodness, honor, innocence, purity or honesty.

Note: Sympathy with a person who sins is not the same as sympathy with the sin or crime of which he is guilty. We may feel sorry for the plight of the murderer or even understand the circumstances which led him to his crime: we may not feel sympathy with the wrong which he has done. The presentation of evil is often essential for art or fiction or drama. This in itself is not wrong provided:

a. That evil is not presented alluringly. Even if later in the film the evil is condemned or punished, it must not be allowed to appear so attractive that the audience's emotions are drawn to desire or approve so strongly that later the condemnation is forgotten and only the apparent joy of sin is remembered.

b. That throughout, the audience feels sure that evil is wrong and good is right.

II. Correct standards of life shall, as far as possible, be presented.

A wide knowledge of life and of living is made possible through the film. When right standards are consistently presented, the motion picture exercises the most powerful influences. It builds character, develops right ideals, inculcates correct principles, and all this in attractive story form.

If motion pictures consistently hold up for admiration high types of characters and present stories that will affect lives for the better, they can become the most powerful force for the improvement of mankind.

III. Law, natural or human, shall not be ridiculed, nor shall sympathy be created for its violation.

By natural law is understood the law which is written in the hearts of all mankind, the greater underlying principles of right and justice dictated by conscience.

By human law is understood the law written by civilized nations.

1. The presentation of crimes against the law is often necessary for the carrying out of the plot. But the presentation must not throw sympathy with the crime as against the law nor with the criminal as against those who punish him.

2. The courts of the land should not be presented as unjust. This does not mean that a single court may not be presented as unjust, much less that a single court official must not be presented this way. But the court system of the country must not suffer as a result of this presentation.

Reasons Underlying the Particular Applications

I. Sin and evil enter into the story of human beings and hence in themselves are valid dramatic material.

II. In the use of this material, it must be distinguished between sin which repels by its very nature, and sins which often attract.

a. In the first class come murder, most theft, many legal crimes, lying, hypocrisy, cruelty, etc.

b. In the second class come sex sins, sins and crimes of apparent heroism, such as banditry, daring thefts, leadership in evil, organized crime, revenge, etc.

The first class needs less care in treatment, as sins and crimes of this class are naturally unattractive. The audience instinctively condemns all such and is repelled.

Hence the important objective must be to avoid the hardening of the audience, especially of those who are young and impressionable, to the thought and fact of crime. People can become accustomed even to murder, cruelty, brutality, and repellent crimes, if these are too frequently repeated.

The second class needs great care in handling, as the response of human nature to their appeal is obvious. This is treated more fully below.

III. A careful distinction can be made between films intended for general distribution, and films intended for use in theatres restricted to a limited audience. Themes and plots quite appropriate for the latter would be altogether out of place and dangerous in the former.

Note: The practice of using a general theatre and limiting its patronage to "Adults Only" is not completely satisfactory and is only partially effective.

However, maturer minds may easily understand and accept without harm subject matter in plots which do younger people positive harm.

Hence: If there should be created a special type of theatre, catering exclusively to an adult audience, for plays of this character (plays with problem themes, difficult discussions and maturer treatment) it would seem to afford an outlet, which does not now exist, for pictures unsuitable for general distribution but permissible for exhibitions to a restricted audience.

I. Crimes Against the Law
The treatment of crimes against the law must not:
    1. Teach methods of crime.
    2. Inspire potential criminals with a desire for imitation.
    3. Make criminals seem heroic and justified.
Revenge in modern times shall not be justified. In lands and ages of less developed civilization and moral principles, revenge may sometimes be presented. This would be the case especially in places where no law exists to cover the crime because of which revenge is committed.

Because of its evil consequences, the drug traffic should not be presented in any form. The existence of the trade should not be brought to the attention of audiences.

The use of liquor should never be excessively presented. In scenes from American life, the necessities of plot and proper characterization alone justify its use. And in this case, it should be shown with moderation.

II. Sex
Out of a regard for the sanctity of marriage and the home, the triangle, that is, the love of a third party for one already married, needs careful handling. The treatment should not throw sympathy against marriage as an institution.

Scenes of passion must be treated with an honest acknowledgement of human nature and its normal reactions. Many scenes cannot be presented without arousing dangerous emotions on the part of the immature, the young or the criminal classes.

Even within the limits of pure love, certain facts have been universally regarded by lawmakers as outside the limits of safe presentation.

In the case of impure love, the love which society has always regarded as wrong and which has been banned by divine law, the following are important:

1. Impure love must not be presented as attractive and beautiful.
2. It must not be the subject of comedy or farce, or treated as material for laughter.
3. It must not be presented in such a way to arouse passion or morbid curiosity on the part of the audience.
4. It must not be made to seem right and permissible.
5. In general, it must not be detailed in method and manner.

III. Vulgarity; IV. Obscenity; V. Profanity; hardly need further explanation than is contained in the Code.

VI. Costume
General Principles:

1. The effect of nudity or semi-nudity upon the normal man or woman, and much more upon the young and upon immature persons, has been honestly recognized by all lawmakers and moralists.
2. Hence the fact that the nude or semi-nude body may be beautiful does not make its use in the films moral. For, in addition to its beauty, the effect of the nude or semi-nude body on the normal individual must be taken into consideration.
3. Nudity or semi-nudity used simply to put a "punch" into a picture comes under the head of immoral actions. It is immoral in its effect on the average audience.
4. Nudity can never be permitted as being necessary for the plot. Semi-nudity must not result in undue or indecent exposures.
5. Transparent or translucent materials and silhouette are frequently more suggestive than actual exposure.

VII. Dances
Dancing in general is recognized as an art and as a beautiful form of expressing human emotions.

But dances which suggest or represent sexual actions, whether performed solo or with two or more; dances intended to excite the emotional reaction of an audience; dances with movement of the breasts, excessive body movements while the feet are stationary, violate decency and are wrong.

VIII. Religion
The reason why ministers of religion may not be comic characters or villains is simply because the attitude taken toward them may easily become the attitude taken toward religion in general. Religion is lowered in the minds of the audience because of the lowering of the audience's respect for a minister.

IX. Locations
Certain places are so closely and thoroughly associated with sexual life or with sexual sin that their use must be carefully limited.

X. National Feelings
The just rights, history, and feelings of any nation are entitled to most careful consideration and respectful treatment.

XI. Titles
As the title of a picture is the brand on that particular type of goods, it must conform to the ethical practices of all such honest business.

XII. Repellent Subjects
Such subjects are occasionally necessary for the plot. Their treatment must never offend good taste nor injure the sensibilities of an audience.

Related Primary Document: **Motion Picture Association of America: Statement before House Judiciary Committee (2014)**

Motion Picture Association of America: Statement before House Judiciary Committee (2014)

The Motion Picture Association of America (MPAA) provided this statement to the House Judiciary Subcommittee's hearing on Copyright Office Oversight on November 14, 2014. In this statement, the MPAA points out the need for reform of the Copyright Office and offers its suggestions to how this may be accomplished. This document shows areas where the MPAA is active outside of movie ratings.

MOTION PICTURE ASSOCIATION OF AMERICA, INC. SUBMISSION FOR THE RECORD BEFORE THE HOUSE JUDICIARY COMMITTEE SUBCOMMITTEE ON COURTS, INTELLECTUAL PROPERTY, AND THE INTERNET

HEARING ON COPYRIGHT OFFICE OVERSIGHT

NOVEMBER 14, 2014

The Motion Picture Association of America, Inc. ("MPAA") is pleased to provide this statement as part of the record of the Subcommittee's hearing on Copyright Office Oversight, held September 18, 2014. The MPAA is a not-for-profit trade association founded in 1922 to address issues of concern to the motion picture industry. The MPAA's member companies are: Paramount Pictures Corp., Sony Pictures Entertainment Inc., Twentieth Century Fox Film Corp., Universal City Studios LLC, Walt Disney Studios Motion Pictures, and Warner Bros. Entertainment Inc. These companies and their affiliates are the leading producers and distributors of filmed entertainment in the theatrical, television, and home-entertainment markets.

The motion picture and television industries support 1.9 million jobs across all 50 states and contributed $111 billion in total wages in 2012, the most recent year for which data is available. The protections afforded by copyright law enable the MPAA's member studios to tell the stories that audiences enjoy both in the United States and around the world. The U.S. Copyright Office plays a vital role in administering that law and in ensuring that both the legislative and other branches of the federal government receive the best possible advice on copyright matters.

The MPAA greatly appreciates the hard work and dedication of the Copyright Office, from Register Pallante down through its staff. It has become increasingly clear in recent years, 2 however, that the Office is not optimally funded and positioned to address its increased workload and the challenges it faces in this era of rapid change, both in technology and in the business practices in the industries it serves.1 Below we briefly set forth two broad areas that we urge the Subcommittee to further examine as it seeks to maintain the Copyright Office's ability to meet the challenges of the twenty-first century.

REGISTRATION AND RECORDATION

The MPAA's members are large-volume users of the Copyright Office registration and recordation systems, which secure copyright protection for their content, and provide constructive notice of their rights, as well as priority between conflicting transfers of rights. Such protections are vital to the MPAA members' ability to, among other things, conduct transactions, secure financing, and to fight piracy. The MPAA member companies also rely heavily on the Office's hard-copy public records and online database in searching for and conducting business involving the copyrights of third parties. As such, we appreciate the Copyright Office's attention to improvements in the current registration and recordation systems for our members, and also for the general public who use or rely on them and their associated database.

However, it has become apparent that the Office does not currently have adequate resources to administer these systems in a timely and effective manner. As Register Pallante noted in her testimony before the Subcommittee, it currently takes the Office on average 8.2 months to process paper registration applications, and 3.3 months for electronic applications. Moreover, the Copyright Office's registration records are not fully digitized, and those electronic databases that it does maintain are relatively rudimentary, lacking the robust functionality that is typical of today's commercial database systems, and covering registrations only from 1978 forward. 2 The problem is more acute in the recordation system, where the current average processing time is around 17 months, and (with one minor, recent exception) documents must be submitted entirely on paper—more or less the same way as when the recordation system first launched in the late nineteenth century—and those documents are not searchable or accessible online.

Much could potentially be done to improve the registration and recordation systems and their associated databases. Basic web site functionality could be improved. Additional staff could be hired to reduce processing delays. The Office could implement application program interfaces ("APIs") to facilitate direct, computer-to-computer communication between copyright owners and the Office, which would eliminate the need for data re-entry, thereby increasing efficiency and reducing the potential for error. APIs would also allow for the development of third-party applications that could interface seamlessly with the Copyright Office in much the same way that various tax preparation software tools enable communication with the Internal Revenue Service's e-file system. Such APIs could also potentially facilitate appropriate connections between the Copyright Office database and databases maintained by private registries, such as the performance rights organizations' databases of musical works. Among the many benefits that would flow from improved databases is a reduction in the population of orphan works, improved connectivity between potential licensees and copyright owners, greater accuracy of search results, faster and more efficient data recovery, and valuable digital preservation of older and historical data that might be lost as time passes.

The solution to the problems noted above is clear: The Copyright Office needs additional resources, both IT and examiner staff. As Register Pallante noted in her testimony, the Office's staff has shrunk significantly in recent years; the registration program alone currently has 48 vacancies out of a staff of 180, and a full one-quarter of the remaining staff is approaching retirement. On the IT side, the Office relies on the Library of Congress for its resources, and it must compete with other departments within the Library, many of which have widely differing interests. While we recognize that this Subcommittee does not itself appropriate funds, it does have an oversight role over the Office, and our hope is that highlighting these issues will give them additional prominence and lead all involved to advocate that the Copyright Office obtain the resources necessary to fulfill its many important duties.

STRUCTURAL ISSUES

Some of the Office's challenges stem from a simple lack of resources. But others are the result of its unique position as an entity that administers the law—traditionally an executive branch function, see Intercollegiate Broad. Sys., Inc. v. Copyright Royalty Board, 684 F.3d 1332, 1341–42 (D.C. Cir. 2012)—yet is located within the legislative branch, as a division of the Library of Congress, operating under the supervision of the Librarian of Congress. See 17 U.S.C. §§ 701–02. The time is now ripe for a serious discussion about whether the Copyright Office should remain housed within the Library, or whether it would be more appropriately placed within executive branch, or made an independent agency. MPAA takes no position at this early stage whether such a move is warranted, or, if so, where within the government the Copyright Office should land. But we do believe that Congress would benefit from taking a close look at these issues, and, with input from the Copyright Office and other stakeholders as to the pros and cons of various potential scenarios, arrive at a conclusion that best serves the Office's various 5 mandates, which include: administering the copyright law; creating and maintaining public records of copyright ownership through registration of claims and recordation of documents pertaining to those claims; providing technical assistance to the Congress and to executive branch agencies; and serving as a resource to the domestic and international copyright communities.

There are various potential benefits to relocating the Copyright Office within the government's administrative structure, including increasing its prominence and stature; providing it with an independent budget adequate to meet its staffing and IT requirements; and eliminating some of the inherent tension between an agency that administers a copyright system and yet is overseen by a library, which has a very different mission that includes making copyrighted works available to the public.

CONCLUSION

We thank the Subcommittee for the opportunity to provide this statement, and welcome the opportunity to examine issues related to modernization of the Copyright Office in the next Congress.

Source: U.S. Copyright Office n.d.

See also: American Academy of Arts and Sciences (1780–); National Education Association (1857–)

Further Reading

Afra, Kia. 2016. *The Hollywood Trust: Trade Associations and the Rise of the Studio System.* Lanham, MD: Rowman & Littlefield Publishers.

Kindem, Gorham, ed. 1982. *The American Movie Industry: The Business of Motion Pictures.* Carbondale: Southern Illinois University Press.

Moley, Raymond. 1945. *The Hays Office.* Cornwall, NY: The Cornwall Press.

U.S. Copyright Office. n.d. Pages 123–124. https://archive.org/stream/gov.gpo.fdsys.CHRG -113hhrg89810/CHRG-113hhrg89810_djvu.txt.

Mountain States Legal Foundation (1977–)

The Mountain States Legal Foundation (MSLF) is a conservative nonprofit law firm that describes itself as "dedicated to individual liberty, the right to own and use property, limited and ethical government, and the free enterprise system." It is governed by a volunteer board of directors that approves legal actions taken by MSLF, and it is assisted in the selection of its lawsuits by a volunteer board of litigation. The organization employs a full-time staff, which includes attorneys who conduct the lawsuits in which MSLF engages. In its litigation, MSLF seeks to establish binding legal precedents. Among its activities, MSLF also files *amicus curiae* (friend of the court) briefs.

In defense of its interpretation of constitutional liberties and the rule of law, MSLF defends its clients, who include businesses, corporate bodies, individuals, local governmental entities, and trade associations. To provide litigation on behalf of those who cannot afford private counsel or whose goals do not justify the expense of private counsel, MSLF offers pro bono (work undertaken without charge) litigation against governmental entities, primarily the federal government.

In pursuit of its goals, MSLF says that it seeks victory for its clients at the highest level possible, including the Supreme Court of the United States; establishment of binding legal precedents; and education of the American public on what it terms is the "threat to their liberties that unrestrained government presents." MSLF states that it is supported by tens of thousands of donors from all across the country who are committed to preserving the liberties guaranteed by the Constitution. Through that funding, MSLF is able to provide its legal services.

MSLF claims that the support it receives from major corporations and foundations is small compared to national environmental groups. According to its website, MSLF's annual budget is a "tiny $2.1 million." The group states that it depends heavily on the support of private individuals who share what it calls MSLF's commitment to the Constitution.

The organization states that it reflects broad-based support. MSLF's directors are said to represent more than a dozen states and numerous industries, including agriculture, trucking, construction, forestry, mining, oil and gas, and ranching.

According to its mission statement, MSLF strives to provide effective legal representation for those who share its commitment to fight for individual liberty and the free enterprise system. Its vision is to build the Mountain States Legal Foundation into "the preeminent foundation for litigation aimed at securing and protecting constitutional freedoms and the rule of law" (Mountain States Legal Foundation n.d.).

Citing "life, liberty and property" as the "cornerstones of American democracy" and the factors that account for America's prosperity, the purpose of the Mountain States Legal Foundation is to "defend and secure these precious rights, thus preserving and advancing the American dream."

MSLF states that its core values represent the moral compass that governs U.S. culture, including accountability, commitment to purpose, integrity, and persistence. Its core competencies are the ability to utilize life experiences and commitment to the Constitution as well as the ability to litigate zealously and effectively to advance its purpose and goals. Its stated ideal client base includes individuals, small businesses, and/or local governments that lack financial resources for and expertise in litigation and who have "a winnable and relevant case."

MSLF was incorporated in Colorado in 1977 by business leaders who were concerned that advocates for constitutional liberties, property rights, and economic activity were not present during important legal battles. It was initially created with funding by the National Legal Center and Joseph Coors (1917–2003), grandson of brewer Adolph Coors and then-president of the Coors Brewing Company of Golden, Colorado, which is among the largest single brewery facilities in the world.

The organization's first president was James G. Watt (1938–), who served as secretary of the interior from 1981 to 1983. One of President Ronald Reagan's most controversial cabinet appointments, Watt was opposed to much of the nation's environmental laws and regulations.

Author Russ Bellant states that on behalf of MSLF, Watt filed lawsuits that argued for the repeal of Idaho's ratification of the Equal Rights Amendment, opposed an affirmative action program at the University of Colorado Law School, sought to limit health and safety inspections of businesses, and block reduced utility rates for the elderly (85).

MSLF has argued cases before the Supreme Court of the United States and in federal appeals courts, often in the areas of affirmative action, which it terms "reverse discrimination." It has also litigated regarding property rights and in cases involving the federal Antiquities Act, Clean Water Act (especially regarding wetlands), the Endangered Species Act, the National Environmental Policy Act, and the National Forest Management Act. It opposes restrictions on the ability to develop natural resources such as energy sources, forest utilization, and mineral rights. Although the case was dismissed in 2002, MSLF sued President George W. Bush for failing to overturn a designation of national monuments by former president Bill Clinton.

The president and chief legal officer of Mountain States Legal Foundation is William Perry Pendley, who is described as a former Capitol Hill lawyer and Reagan administration official. In that capacity, he served as deputy assistant secretary for energy and minerals of the Department of Interior, authoring President Reagan's National Minerals Policy and Exclusive Economic Zone proclamation.

The MSLF office is in Lakewood, Colorado. The organization publishes a quarterly newsletter, *The Litigator,* and a quarterly *Action Update* that addresses legal issues of interest to its constituents.

Nancy Hendricks

See also: American Conservative Union (1964–)

Further Reading

Bellant, Russ. 1991. *The Coors Connection: How Coors Family Philanthropy Undermines Democratic Pluralism.* Cambridge, MA: South End Press.

Lindstrom, Matthew J. 2010. *Encyclopedia of the U.S. Government and the Environment: History, Policy, and Politics.* Santa Barbara, CA: ABC-CLIO.

"Mountain States Legal Foundation." *Charity Navigator.* https://www.charitynavigator.org/index.cfm?bay=search.summary&orgid=7353.

Mountain States Legal Foundation. n.d. "Mission Statement." https://www.mountain stateslegal.org/about/mission-statement#.XGmm7M9KjjA.

Pendley, William Perry. 1995. *War on the West: Government Tyranny on America's Great Frontier.* Washington, D.C.: Regnery Publishing.

MoveOn.org (1998–)

MoveOn.org is among the largest and most influential of the new liberal "netroots" organizations. MoveOn, and other organizations like it, have sought to combine online communications with community-focused offline social events. The development of the Internet enabled many politicians and political organizations to raise large sums of money from small donors and to create a movement-style means of political communication and activism that has been credited with pulling the Democratic Party further to the left since the early 2000s.

There is little evidence that the creators of MoveOn.org had any intention of making the group an enduring vehicle for progressive activism. The organization was founded in 1998 by Joan Blades (1956–) and her husband Wesley Boyd (1960–), the founders of Berkeley Systems, a Silicon Valley software company.

The group was originally merely a website where visitors could sign a petition encouraging Congress to censure President Clinton and move on to other matters, rather than following through on impeachment proceedings. The group's success in gathering the email addresses of visitors who signed the petition, however, led it to prospect among the signatories for funds to be used in support of campaigns against members of Congress who had supported the president's impeachment. The group reported raising over $1.85 million in the 2000 election cycle from over 40,000 different contributors, and in 2002 its total was $4.1 million.

Over the subsequent four years, MoveOn expanded its staff and increased its communication with members. Because membership is free, the group managed to grow very quickly, to over two million members in 2004. In 2003 Eli Parisier (1980–), a college student, created an online petition opposing the Iraq War; the number of signers of the petition grew into the millions very quickly. Parisier and MoveOn ultimately merged their lists, and Parisier became the executive director of the group in 2004. Tom Matzzie (a veteran of the AFL-CIO's online outreach efforts) also joined the group. MoveOn has deliberately kept its number of employees small—it is, essentially, a list of names, and individual members have substantial latitude to use this list to generate support for causes. Since 2004, it has maintained two separate organizations – MoveOn Civic Action, a 501(c)(4) nonprofit wing, which circulates petitions and engages in communication with members about progressive issues, and MoveOn Political Action, a political action committee that engaged in independent expenditures and at times donates money to candidates.

Although the group has emphasized raising donations in small amounts, in 2002 and 2004, it benefited from very large donations from Peter Lewis (1933–2013) and George Soros (1930–); these donations enabled the group to become the second-largest advertiser in the 2004 election among Democratic-leaning groups, with a total of over $30 million in expenditures. In addition to its advertisements and on line communication, MoveOn coordinated get-out-the-vote activities with other large liberal groups. MoveOn also held the "MoveOn Primary" in 2004, which led to its endorsement of Howard Dean's (1948–) campaign.

Following the model of the Dean campaign's Meetups, MoveOn made its list available for members across the country to organize community events, circulate petitions, and champion state and local candidates and causes. The large membership of the organization has, according to the group, enabled it to organize community events in places with little or no history of progressive activism. One story circulated by the organization, for instance, was that members of the group in Sugarland, Texas, home of former House Majority Whip Tom DeLay (1947–), had several very successful events. As the story goes, progressives in Sugarland felt alone and isolated until they discovered through MoveOn that there were others in the community who shared their political views.

MoveOn continued to grow after the 2004 election, reaching an estimated four million members by 2010. It also forged closer ties with other Democratic "Netroots" organizations, such as Democracy for America (an offshoot of the Dean campaign) and followers of blogs such as DailyKos or Talking Points Memo. These groups frequently participated in the same events, including the Yearly Kos and Netroots Nation annual gatherings. Its coalitional work with these groups has been credited with providing financial and volunteer support for a variety of progressive candidates in the 2006 and 2008 elections. MoveOn spent over $40 million in support of Democratic candidates in 2008.

Like the conservative group Club for Growth, MoveOn has also sought to support challenges to a select number of primary challengers to what it considers to be insufficiently partisan members of the House and Senate. MoveOn raised money for Ned Lamont's (1954–) 2006 primary challenge to incumbent Connecticut Democrat Joseph Lieberman (1942–) and Bill Halter's (1960–) 2010 challenge to Arkansas Senator Blanche Lambert Lincoln (1960–). Although neither challenge was successful, these efforts were designed in part to promote MoveOn's agenda and to put pressure on centrist Democrats. MoveOn was more successful in its 2006 and 2008 efforts on behalf of Donna Edwards (1958–), who succeeded in 2008 in ousting incumbent Maryland Democrat Al Wynn (1951–).

Because it is a decentralized organization with a very small leadership staff, many of MoveOn's ideas are generated by members. Many of these ideas have ultimately benefited liberal candidates, but some have also led to controversy. In 2004, the group sponsored a "Bush in 30 Seconds" contest, where members were encouraged to make short videos describing the consequences of the Bush presidency. The videos that won were creative commentaries on the economy and the Iraq War, but some entries caused controversy because of the links they drew between Bush and various totalitarian leaders. A similar advertising campaign promoting the Obama campaign, however, was more successful. In 2007, the group took out a full-page ad describing General David Petraeus (1952–) as "General Betray Us" that also drew widespread condemnation from Democrats and Republicans.

In recent election cycles, MoveOn has continued to promote a variety of liberal causes, although its overall spending has declined. In 2014, the group pledged over $1 million in support of an Elizabeth Warren (1949–) presidential campaign, and began a petition drive encouraging her to run. When that was unsuccessful, the group, using the same sort of informal member primary it had used in the past chose in January 2016 to endorse Bernie Sanders (1941–) for president. MoveOn endorsed Hillary Clinton (1947–) in June, once it became apparent that Sanders could not win the nomination. MoveOn has to an extent been eclipsed by the new Democratic Super PACs as a source of funding for independent expenditure campaigns, and its function as a small dollar-bundling organization has declined following the development of ActBlue, an on line contribution portal for Democratic candidates. The group remains, however, one of the largest and most-influential multi-issue progressive groups in American politics.

Robert G. Boatright

See also: Americans for Democratic Action (1947–); EMILY's List (1985–); National Committee for an Effective Congress (1948–)

Further Reading
Boatright, Robert G. 2011. *Interest Groups and Campaign Finance Reform in the United States and Canada.* Ann Arbor: University of Michigan Press.

Karpf, David. 2012. *The MoveOn Effect.* New York: Oxford University Press.

Kerbel, Matthew R. 2009. *Netroots: Online Progressives and the Transformation of American Politics.* Boulder, CO: Paradigm Press.

McKenna, Elizabeth, and Hahrie Han. 2014. *Groundbreakers: How Obama's 2.2 Million Volunteers Transformed Campaigning in America.* New York: Oxford University Press.

Mugwumps (1884–1888)

In the election of 1884, Republican political activists supported Grover Cleveland, Democratic candidate for president of the United States. These defectors left the Republican Party due to dissatisfaction with Republican candidate James G. Blaine's financial corruption. These Republicans became known as "Mugwumps" by their critics, who labeled them as being aloof or "holier than thou" for leaving the party and supporting Cleveland. Support from the Mugwumps helped Cleveland win the election and become the 22nd president of the United States.

Toward the end of 19th century, Democrat Grover Cleveland and Republican James G. Blaine were in fierce competition for the presidency of the United States. During the election of 1884, American voters faced a choice between Blaine, a statesman originally from Pennsylvania who went on to become a senator representing Maine, and Cleveland, who served as governor of New York in the late 1800s. Both Blaine and Cleveland shared extensive political backgrounds, though both represented very different political perspectives. While candidate Grover Cleveland insisted on working against political corruption and creating a government that would uphold the moral standards expected by constituents it represented, Blaine's platform painted him as more of a serious politician who frequently dabbled with business deals in the railroad industry.

As citizens on both sides of the political spectrum struggled with whom to vote for, a particular group of Republican voters, known as Mugwumps, deserted their own party during the election to vote for the candidate they believed more suitable for the job, Democrat Grover Cleveland. The term "Mugwumps" was used to describe those party-switching Republicans in 1884 who, at the last minute, left their Republican Party loyalties to cross party lines.

For a majority of Mugwumps, the road to defection was rooted in the Republican Party itself. In the years leading up to the 1884 election between Blaine and Cleveland, the party was controlled by a spoils system. A spoils system is a political system in which government officials allocate bureaucratic positions to advocates of their own party, personal friends, and family and so forth, regardless of the experience or expertise in the policy area. Many Republican members witnessed political positions being handed to people who were not always deserving of the political jobs they were given and sought to end a system that favored the "friends" of their party.

Moreover, Republican supporters grew worried that the spoils system had become so entrenched that it would become a permanent staple in the party, which would lead to a decline in ethics and morality among its members. A number of Republicans were concerned that if the party became less concerned with ethics and morality, there would be increased corruption among party members and inaction on issues that voters cared about. This concern was only heightened with the nomination of Blaine.

Blaine, who was loyal to his party, was not viewed as very loyal when it came to making promises to the people he claimed to represent. Many of those who would become Mugwumps looked at Blaine as a part of the problem with politics, rather than the solution. This distrust for Blaine by many Republican voters stemmed from a number of questionable choices he made earlier in his political career. His public failures in business and politics, along with the increasing influence of the spoils system within the party, had voters troubled and anxious about how Blaine would act as president.

As some voters contemplated the possibility of Blaine becoming president, the rest of the country was trying to picture Grover Cleveland in the White House. Unlike Blaine, Cleveland pushed for a political system guided by moral and ethical actors and choices, but he too had been plagued by political and personal problems. However, by advocating for a more moral and ethical government, Cleveland was able to attract the attention of those Republican voters who were still on the fence about the moral credibility of Blaine.

Ultimately, it was not the fact that Cleveland had not made mistakes as a politician but rather his respect and passion for ethical politics that first interested those who would become Mugwumps. Those Republicans who finally left their party and were dubbed Mugwumps believed that they had good reason for fracturing their party loyalties lines. From their point of view, Blaine was not to be trusted with executive power, but Cleveland gave them hope for a better future—one without the spoils system.

Though the Mugwumps jumped to vote for Cleveland over Blaine in 1884, it did not necessarily mean that they fully pledged their alliance to the Democratic Party. For a majority of the Mugwumps, their vote for Cleveland served two purposes: they wanted to make Republican spoils leaders change the way the party operated (a number of the Mugwumps hoped to return to their party only after some essential changes were put into place), and they wanted new members to join them in their fight for change within their own party. The Mugwumps believed that if they were able to secure enough support, they could change the future outcome of the election as well as the structure of the Republican Party.

However, the Mugwumps were typically not supported by Republicans who decided to stay true to their party. Republican Party loyalists believed that the Mugwumps were traitors, distrustful, and irrational when it came to political matters. They warned all voters that the Mugwumps were not to be trusted because they could not even remain devoted to their own party. Furthermore, loyal Republicans wished for Mugwump members to never try to return to the Republican Party after they had so quickly betrayed it during the election.

Naturally, Democrats greeted the Mugwumps' defections in a friendly fashion. The Democrats understood the Mugwumps more as a group of independent voters who were not as worried about which party they belonged to, as long as they were voting the "right" candidate into the White House. For the most part, the Democrats were pleased to see voters who sided with them during such an important election. Yet, regardless of the two parties' opinions of their actions, the Mugwumps were only concerned with doing what they perceived to be the best thing for the country.

While statistically the Mugwumps did not have a huge overall impact on the election, they did manage to sway enough people in some key states, particularly New York. Grover Cleveland's election deflated members of the Republican Party, but for the winning Democrats, it helped boost party morale towards a more hopeful moral and ethical government. As Cleveland took the election, the Mugwumps' efforts amounted to more than simply a win for the Democrats. The Mugwumps' struggle represented a group of voters who were able to change the political environment, even though they would likely not be able to return to the Republican Party. Mugwump members demonstrated to many frustrated voters who did not support their party's candidate that they could, indeed, vote for a different nominee.

The Mugwumps' devotion to voting for the candidate they believed would be the better choice for America, instead of the nominee their party heavily favored, in some ways changed the way voters thought about political parties and their political choices. Though members of the Mugwumps were not the first to defect from their party, they were certainly among the first to form a decent-sized group of citizens to make a difference in a presidential election. Although the impact of their defection was small in terms of numbers during the election, the Mugwumps were ultimately able to change the course of American political history.

In addition, the election of 1884 demonstrated that American voters were not going to stand by and allow their party to direct their vote whichever way they wanted. At a time when the spoils system dominated the Republican Party, the Mugwumps encouraged those citizens who felt stuck in their party to vote for who they wanted to vote for, rather than their party's candidate. This movement toward more independent voting was immensely important in helping citizens feel like they were not at the mercy of their political party and could vote freely without party restrictions.

The Mugwumps began as a small group of Republican Party members who were tired of political scandals and the spoils system that had taken over their party. Though other groups have attempted to repeat the actions of the Mugwumps, most have failed. However, the Mugwumps' decision to leave the Republican Party in 1884 to vote for Democrat Grover Cleveland began as a small movement. However, after Cleveland's defeat of Blaine in the election, it proved to be one of the biggest moves in American political history.

Brittany Page Brake

See also: Copperheads (1860–1868)

Further Reading

Hofstadter, Richard. 1955. *The Age of Reform: From Bryan to F.D.R.* New York: Alfred A. Knopf.

Hoogenboom, Ari. 1961. *Outlawing the Spoils: A History of the Civil Service Reform Movement, 1865–1883.* Urbana: University of Illinois Press.

McFarland, Gerald W. 1975. *Mugwumps, Morals, & Politics, 1884–1920.* Amherst: University of Massachusetts Press.

Murphy, Kevin P. 2008. *Political Manhood: Red Bloods, Mollycoddles, & the Politics of Progressive Era Reform.* New York: Columbia University Press.

Schneider, Robert W. 1965. *Five Novelists of the Progressive Era.* New York: Columbia University Press.

N

NAACP Legal Defense and Education Fund (1940–)

The NAACP Legal Defense and Education Fund is the nation's preeminent civil rights legal organization. An offshoot of the National Association for the Advancement of Colored People (NAACP), the Legal Defense Fund was formally launched in 1940 in part to take advantage of new laws that granted tax exempt status to nonprofit organizations for which lobbying was not their primary purpose. The Fund, as it is known in civil rights circles, engineered a long-term legal campaign that chips away, case by case, year by year, at the long-entrenched system of legal segregation.

Headed by Thurgood Marshall (1908–1993) from its beginnings in 1940 until his appointment to the Federal Court of Appeals in 1961, the Fund had its roots in the NAACP's legal department, an operation established and run by Charles Hamilton Houston (1895–1950). Houston, who also served as Dean of the Howard University School of Law, meshed his interests, turning the Howard Law School into a training ground for a generation of civil rights pioneers. After Marshall graduated at the top of his class from Howard in 1933, he opened a private practice in his hometown of Baltimore, Maryland, but having come under Houston's influence while in school, the young lawyer became increasingly involved working with Houston and the NAACP on a range of civil right cases. In 1935, Marshall represented the local chapter of the NAACP in a suit challenging the segregation policy of the University of Maryland, a policy that had prevented Marshall from pursuing his legal education there. After winning the landmark victory in *Murray v. Pearson*, in 1936 Marshall joined the national staff of the NAACP, beginning a professional association that would continue until his appointment to the federal bench.

Roaming the South, looking for and pursuing civil rights actions, Marshall developed a network, a feel for the legal landscape, and a courtroom expertise, all of which proved central to the organization's subsequent effort to mount a full-scale, but methodical, attack on the legal basis of segregation in America. That effort began in earnest when he assumed the leadership of the organization's efforts. That opportunity came in 1938 when Marshall moved to New York, succeeding an ailing Houston as head of the NAACP's legal department. Two years later, the Fund was born, with Marshall as its helm.

Over the course of the next almost quarter century, Marshall was the driving force, chief strategist, and dominant courtroom presence for a campaign that chipped away—one step and one case at a time—at the legal barriers to racial equality in the United States. Beginning with the 1944 victory in *Smith v.*

Allwright, which ended the restrictive white primaries that had prevented the South's blacks from any meaningful participation in the political process, to their 1948 victory in *Shelly v. Kraemer*, a case that struck down racially restrictive home ownership covenants, Marshall and his NAACP colleagues mounted an attack on the many legally supported aspects of American life that had long served to deny equal opportunity to the nation's minority population. Recognizing the critical importance of education to achieving success in America, Marshall and company turned their attention to the inequalities of the public school systems in the late 1940s. Initially demanding that separate facilities be, in fact, equal as required by the Supreme Court's decision in *Plessy v. Ferguson* (1896), Marshall won victories that determined that allegedly equal factors were in fact not. Courts began to recognize that in education, tangible items like desks and books are necessary—but not sufficient—to ensure equal educational experiences. Intangibles, like the human dimensions of education, the availability of mentors and former students, and especially the interactions among students, were in fact central to quality education. This approach led in 1950 to victories in the Supreme Court cases of *Sweatt v. Painter* and *McLaurin v. Oklahoma State Regents*, rulings in which the Court ended segregation in graduate and professional schools. Then in 1954, in *Brown v. Board of Education*, a multischool district challenge to the "separate but equal" doctrine established under *Plessy*, the Supreme Court, in a 9–0 decision, ruled that in education "separate was inherently unequal" and not only ordered an end to segregated public education, but also gave new meaning to the equal protection clause of the Fourteenth Amendment. It was the culmination of a decade and a half campaign by the Marshall-led NAACP Legal Defense Fund, but it was by no means the end of their efforts.

While the campaign to end segregation that culminated in the *Brown* decision tends to dominate the story of the Fund, that was actually only a part of the story. During the same period that Marshall led the effort to win the big precedent-setting cases that would ultimately greatly contributed to breaking down the legal basis for segregation that had long prevented the nation's African Americans from achieving equal rights, NAACP lawyers, especially Marshall, and local lawyers affiliated with the Fund, also handled countless local cases. Their efforts often times were the only things that stood between an accused individual and the implementation of "Southern justice," a process often administered at the end of a rope. Indeed, though the NAACP worked tirelessly, if unsuccessfully, to achieve the enactment of a federal anti-lynching law, the Fund was no less engaged in the efforts to prevent the imposition of the death penalty in instances where the saving of the accused's life, while perhaps not truly justice, nevertheless represented a major triumph. Indeed, in the 1940s and 1950s, to an accused Southern black, the news that "Mr. Marshall is coming" was a godsend, whereas the white population did everything it could to prevent him from getting involved.

Marshall constantly received threats, and each foray into the Deep South was a dangerous venture. It was not unusual for him to sleep in a different place every night during a trial, and he was also known to use multiple cars to get out of a town, especially when he had been victorious in court. Central to Marshall's effort, as well as the man himself, was a courage that was not a part of any law school curriculum, but which was at the heart of his efforts and those of the NAACP Legal Defense Fund.

All of these efforts took a toll on Marshall's health, as did the 1955 death of his wife, Buster; but despite the victory in *Brown*, the battle continued, with the NAACP forced into action on behalf of those who sought to integrate the schools in the face of major Southern—and later Northern—resistance. The organization was in the forefront of the legal efforts that resulted in the integration of Little Rock's Central High School as well as cases like *Swann* v. *Charlotte-Mecklenburg*, that extended into the 1970s, but finally established guidelines and means—including busing—to achieve Brown's promised desegregation of the nation's public schools. As the Civil Rights Movement, especially the effort led by Dr. Martin Luther King Jr. (1929–1968), began to utilize mass marches and non-violent protests, Marshall and the Legal Defense Fund were kept busy defending the thousands who were arrested after engaging in the large-scale protests and acts of civil disobedience that became the hallmark of that next wave of civil rights activism.

While Marshall and the NAACP Legal Defense Fund were almost inseparable in the public mind, the activist attorney, whose Court colleague Sandra Day O'Connor (1920–) was reported to have once said that he was the only one among the Court's members who would be in the history books had he not sat on the High Court, had, in fact, built a powerful organization, which, public perceptions, notwithstanding, was never a one-man band. In fact, the Fund had long been a training ground for young lawyers who cut their teeth on movement cases only to later emerge as some of the nation's best litigators and legal strategists. Consequently, when Marshall left the Fund in 1961 following his appointment to the Federal Court of Appeals, the appointment of Jack Greenberg (1924–2016), a long-time Fund staff attorney, who had been intimately involved with the *Brown* litigation, as director counsel made for a seamless transition and a continuation of the kinds of efforts the Fund had represented for over two decades. Indeed, Greenberg held the post until 1984, when he was succeeded by Julius Chambers (1936–2013), who had also had experience in civil rights law working for the Fund and who would serve until 1993 when he returned to his native North Carolina to assume the role of Chancellor at North Carolina Central University.

While school, jobs, and voting rights took center stage in the Fund's ongoing efforts to end segregation and achieve equality, it did not happen in one fell swoop, but rather, in case after case, big and small, Fund lawyers were winning less heralded victories that toppled long-standing barriers to integration. In 1962, the Fund secured James Meredith's (1933–) right to attend the University of Mississippi, and the next year, it won a case in Memphis that ended segregation in the city's parks. Another 1963 victory ended segregation in hospitals that received federal funding. Meanwhile, in 1969 the Fund won the seminal *Loving v. Virginia* case, which ended Virginia's ban on interracial marriage; and two years later, it played a central role in the Supreme Court's decision to overturn the conviction of heavyweight boxing champion Muhammad Ali (1942–2016), whose effort to achieve conscientious objector status in response to the Vietnam War was initially denied.

In the 1960s and beyond, the Legal Defense Fund began to pursue cases involving employment discrimination, as well as voting rights and redistricting and legislative representation cases where districts and election processes had been drawn and set up in ways intended to dilute the influence of African Americans. In addition, in the later part of the 20th century into the 21st, the organization was a leader in efforts to defend affirmative action in both college admissions and the workplace.

As noted, another important legacy of the Legal Defense Fund has been its role as a training ground for attorneys, public officials, and legal scholars. Prominent Fund alumni include William Coleman (1920–2017), secretary of transportation under President Gerald Ford; Marian Wright Edelman (1939–), the founder of the Children's Defense Fund; Eric Holder (1951–), the nation's first black attorney general who served under president Barack Obama (1961–); Drew Days, who served as solicitor general under Bill Clinton (1946–); and Elaine Jones (1944–), who successfully argued the death penalty case of *Furman v. Georgia* and succeeded Chambers as the Fund's director counsel, the first woman to hold the position. The Fund's roster also featured at different times Deval Patrick (1956–), who served as governor of Massachusetts; Constance Baker Motley (1921–2005), the first African American woman appointed to the federal bench; widely renowned Constitutional scholar Pamela Karlan (1959–); and voting rights advocate and the first women to be granted tenure at Harvard Law School, Lani Guinier (1950–).

Though the organization's agenda has changed in response to changing times, the organization's stature as the preeminent legal advocate for civil rights remains unchallenged. Indeed, the list of cases, large and small, in which the Fund has had a hand over the course of the last few decades is lengthy and wide-ranging, with the only common denominator being an unwavering commitment to individual's right to equal protection of the law and equal opportunity. Whether it is defending affirmative action in the workplace or in college admissions, attacking the death penalty, defending voting rights, or, more recently, getting involved with police reform while also speaking out against the increased racial violence inspired by white supremacy groups, the Fund continues to build upon its long legacy. The efforts of the Legal Defense Fund have done much to level the playing field in the United States.

William H. Pruden III

See also: Historically Black Colleges and Universities (1837–); Lambda Legal Defense and Education Fund (1973–); Mexican American Legal Defense and Education Fund (1968–); National Association for the Advancement of Colored People (1909–); United Negro College Fund (1944–)

Further Reading

"History." *The NAACP Legal Defense and Educational Fund (LDF)*. http://www.naacpldf.org/history.

James, Rawn Jr. 2010. *Root and Branch: Charles Hamilton Houston, Thurgood Marshall, and the Struggle to End Segregation*. New York: Bloomsbury Press.

Kluger, Richard. 2004. *Simple Justice: The History of Brown v. Board of Education and Black America's Struggle for Equality* (Rev. Exp. Edition). New York: Knopf.

Williams, Juan. 1998. *Thurgood Marshall: American Revolutionary*. New York: Crown.

National Abortion and Reproductive Rights Action League (1969–)

Like many other groups in the United States, the National Abortion and Reproductive Rights Action League (NARAL) emerged from a rich history of interactions between religious, professional, and identity organizations. NARAL was originally known as the National Association for the Repeal of Abortion Laws. It has also been known as the National Abortion Rights Action League and NARAL Pro-Choice America. Regardless of its official name, NARAL has worked to ensure ready access to abortion and abortion-related services for women. NARAL is often considered the oldest abortion rights group, but it was not the first entity to push for legal reforms that would ensure access to contraception, abortion, and abortion-related services. Professional organizations focused on abortion rights included entities from both the medical and legal fields. Religious organizations from various faith traditions struggled to find an appropriate stand for themselves on abortion and women's rights. The Catholic Church and the more conservative evangelical churches were always strongly opposed to abortion, but other faith traditions sought a more nuanced approach.

Through the 1800 and early 1900s, abortion received little or no attention from the federal government, but several state laws did address access to abortion procedures. In the early 1900s, many of the state-level abortion laws had the support of the nascent medical profession as physicians were seeking ways to limit the influence and market encroachments of midwifery services. Nonphysicians acting as abortionists typically failed to follow carefully established medical procedures and limited the overall viability of the small but growing professional medical community. In the first half of the 20th century, abortion under most circumstances was illegal in many states. Nonetheless, abortions were still provided by so-called "back alley" providers as well as physicians working surreptitiously. Although few people ever spoke of abortion or abortion services, and although abortions were illegal in many states, they did still regularly occur.

The legal context in the 1950s and 1960s leading up to NARAL's founding varied by state. Most states limited access to abortion procedures, but enforcement was erratic at best. Viewed from the national level, the overall affect was a hodgepodge of contradictory state laws that were erratically enforced. Planned Parenthood, the earliest national organization in the United States to promote birth control measures as a way to bolster women's autonomy, asked the American Law Institute (ALI) to consider ways to coordinate the various state laws and to recommend ways to update the varied abortion laws. ALI was neither pro-choice nor pro-life, but it was concerned about laws that were unenforced as written, somehow archaic, or applied differently across individuals or circumstances. The centerpiece of the ALI plan was to require the assent of two doctors before allowing abortion to save the life or ensure the health of the woman and in cases of rape, incest, or severe abnormalities. The American Baptist Convention in 1967 supported ALI-type reforms at the state level. Indeed, a wide range of groups was supportive of what those groups deemed "common-sense" ALI reforms.

States adopting the ALI-type reforms included California, the nation's most populous state at the time. Indeed, California's law easing access to abortion services was signed in 1967 by then-governor Ronald Reagan (1911–2004). Reagan would go on to serve two terms as president of the United States and become known for his subsequent opposition to abortion. Other states with ALI-type laws were from the South (Georgia), the Midwest (Kansas), the northwest (Oregon), and the mid-Atlantic (Delaware and Maryland).

Although abortion access was opening up by the 1960s in a variety of states, inconsistencies in abortion access still existed across the states. A confluence of circumstances in the late 1960s led to the development of NARAL in 1969. The women's movement of the 1960s moved beyond concerns of enfranchisement and *de jure* (or "by law") discrimination. In the 1960s, the women's movement embraced reassessments of family life, sexuality, workplace tensions, reproductive rights, and *de facto* (or "in fact") discrimination. The National Organization of Women (NOW) founded in 1966 was developing considerable prominence as the leader of the women's movement in the late 1960s. At its second national convention, NOW dramatically shifted its focus. Previously, NOW had targeted its efforts narrowly on economic issues and gender discrimination in schools, colleges, universities, and workplaces. Equal access to education and economic opportunities motivated NOW membership in its first year. At the second annual convention in 1967, NOW included abortion reform efforts to its set of main goals. NOW created an informal network of people involved with NOW, including public health groups and population control advocates. At a 1969 meeting in Chicago, that informal group, along with representatives from over 20 other organizations, established a planning committee to coordinate all futures efforts. That planning committee was charged with creating the National Association for the Repeal of Abortion Laws (NARAL). The immediate focus of NARAL was the repeal of restrictive abortion laws in the states. From NARAL's perspective, those restrictive laws were a legal quagmire: sometimes enforced, sometimes ignored, and leaving everyone in legal limbo. NARAL viewed back-alley procedures and dangerous pregnancies as clear public health hazards. Notably, NARAL rejected the widely advocated ALI reforms, preferring *ad libitum* (or "on demand") abortion rights for women. Only *ad libitum* access, NARAL argued, would ensure women had discretion over abortion procedures and hence dominion over their own bodies and control of their own fates.

NARAL, like many groups active in the United States, emerged from an already existing group. As a spin-off from NOW, NARAL did not have to bear the full burden of coordinating its collective efforts. From NOW, NARAL secured membership lists and connections to professional, identity, and religious groups with concerns about abortion access and reproductive rights. Even with such crucial support from NOW, NARAL's first years were challenging. NARAL started with just over 100 individual members, about 18 organizational members, and a mailing list with about 1,000 names. NARAL today is organized as a nonprofit with affiliates is many states. NARAL lobbies state and federal legislators to seek more open access to abortion procedures, provides electoral support to pro-choice candidates, and, from time to time, sponsors lawsuits. In 2004, NARAL coordinated the March for Women's Lives, which attracted between 500,000 and one million participants. NARAL's membership in 2018 numbers over one million individuals.

Scott H. Ainsworth

See also: EMILY's List (1985–); Planned Parenthood (1921–)

Further Reading

Ainsworth, Scott H., and Thad E. Hall. 2011. *Abortion Politics in Congress: Strategic Incrementalism and Policy Change*. New York: Cambridge University Press.

Barakso, Maryann. 2004. *Governing NOW: Grassroots Activism in the National Organization for Women*. Ithaca, NY: Cornell University Press.

Risen, James, and Judy L. Thomas. 1998. *Wrath of Angels: The American Abortion War*. New York: Basic Books.

Staggenborg, Suzanne. 1994. *The Pro-Choice Movement: Organization and Activism in the Abortion Conflict*. New York: Oxford University Press.

National Academy of Sciences (1863–)

Founded during the Civil War in 1863, the National Academy of Sciences (NAS) continues to serve as an important emissary between the scientific community and the federal government. Although inaugurated during Abraham Lincoln's presidency, its roots stretch back into the antebellum period as the Academy was influenced by the politics of nationalism, the bequest that became the Smithsonian Institution, and the visionary work of Alexander Dallas Bache (1806–1867). Today the NAS serves as a nonprofit NGO, as it did over 150 years ago, and is part of a consortium of organizations that include the National Academy of Engineering and the National Academy of Medicine. Although committed to serving the international scientific community, the NAS and its partners still grapple with how best to serve politics and government as they attempt to publish, promote, and increase understanding of the most important, complex, and pressing scientific issues of the day.

Regional scientific societies, a byproduct from Europe, were, up until 1840, the province of gentlemen and amateurs. By the 1840s and 1850s, territorial expansion under the auspices of Manifest Destiny and an expanding empire dictated that the United States think broadly about its borders and how best to keep them. The largest scientific entities of the time were the Smithsonian Institution, founded at the bequest of an Englishman named James Smithson (1765–1829), and the United States Coast Survey. The latter was the most celebrated organization within the government at the time and Alexander Bache was its chief superintendent and provocateur.

Bache began his career, after growing up in Philadelphia and being associated with his prominent relatives that included Benjamin Franklin (1706–1790), by conducting surveys. With the training he received as a cadet at the United States Military Academy at West Point, Bache was well-connected politically as he was a classmate of Jefferson Davis (1808–1889), the first president of the Confederate States of America, and later became quite close with Joseph Henry (1797–1878), the first president of the Smithsonian Institution. After resigning from the military, Bache became a professor of chemistry and natural philosophy at the University of Pennsylvania, and conducted a study of the European educational systems in order to ascertain the direction that American should take in this regard. He was later appointed the head the U.S. Coastal Survey, a post he led with vigor and with a strategic political point of view. Bache lobbied everyone from President John Tyler (1790–1862) to members of Congress for funding that would benefit science and the goals of an expanding nation.

As one of the leaders of science in America, Bache knew that a strong nation needed maps, defined borders, and protection against enemies. He was driven by his belief that the means by a nation's future could be shaped by scientific inquiry and discovery. Employing what at the time was considered a massive staff of mathematicians, surveyors, and a bevy of assistants, he orchestrated the federal government's defining of the coastline, essential for the building of safe and efficient shipping lanes.

Research coupled with education became a lifelong mission for Bache as he settled into apprising himself of the state of science in the 1850s. Politicians liked his bravado and understood that funding for science could be used to advance their own ideas and interests. America needed a national scientific-led organization which could represent the needs of the ever-growing community. If America was to compete with the other nations of the world in ideas, as well as land acquisitions in the form of colonies, the country would have to move as one. With the building of a blue water navy in the Pacific and the opening of Japan in 1851 by Matthew C. Perry's (1794–1858) expedition, the Union was well on its way to expanding a broad vision of freedom and opportunity.

By the 1850s, though, tumult and revolution were on the horizon. Little did Bache know that his world of science would play an integral role in the what would become known as the first modern war. He took the tack that serious research was not a part of American scientific discovery. Something had to change based on the European model that had set the pace across the disciplines over the past 40 years. The way to garner support for his cause for important scientific inquiry was to align himself with peers that would support his initiatives. These professional chemists, biologists, and other investigative minds, calling themselves the Lazzaroni (sardonically named after the beggars that could be found in Naples, Italy), would become the first lobbyists for their fields. Speaking at public events, engaging in funding debates with members of the government, and publishing in university publications, they probed and prodded for more exposure and money. Bache reasoned that both the North, South, and Western states could all benefit from the building of a national science-focused university system.

As opinionated and political as Bache was, he of course developed enemies. One was a Harvard botanist named Asa Gray (1810–1888). A correspondent with Charles Darwin (1809–1882) and a leading antislavery activist, Gray believed Bache and the Lazzaroni went too far in shutting out those who wanted access to science. By limiting thought, Gray believed, you would only be crushing new opportunity for discovery. The debate over national science though had to wait, as the Civil War broke out in 1861.

The Lazzaroni at this point were unable to get a national academy off the ground. But by 1863, as the war ground to an agonizing set of movements and sieges, Bache saw an opportunity. Wars he knew were fought by men and their generals, but they were won by science and superior technology. The Civil War became the moment when new developments in science could create more efficient ways to kill people. The more killed, the faster the conflict would come to an end. Bache had his angle.

In the Congress, with no Southern opposition to federal expansion, the Moderate and Radical Republicans had a free hand to legislate. Led by Charles Sumner (1811–1874) in the Senate and Thaddeus Stevens (1792–1868) in the House, they imposed their federal will on a myriad of topics. With the passage in 1862 of the Morrill Land Grant Act, which established funding for public universities, Bache was able to realize two visions at once—research and a science academy. On March 3, 1863, President Lincoln signed legislation officially establishing the National Academy of Sciences. Bache's dream became a reality.

NAS moved into an era in which appreciation for science was ascendant. With Bache's death after the war, a new phase ensued as the Academy began to build a strong following. Technology and the first modern conflict had accelerated developments in medicine and war-making ability. Though later thoroughly repudiated, theories of the social and economic implications of Darwin's *Origin of the Species* were fueling a new era in the social sciences. Science-based education opened fresh opportunities for research and the philanthropic activities of the Rockefellers and Carnegies of the era spawned developments by institutions like Johns Hopkins University and later a host of other non-profit associations devoted to specific scientific disciplines. By the First World War (1914–1918), the NAS reaped the benefits of connectivity with the federal government when it began to officially advise on official matters of science. The Progressive Era promoted a better and more just society, and professionalized public agencies and their scientific staffs.

By the Second World War (1939–1945), American science had finally kept pace and began to outdistance its European brethren. Now more than ever, the United States was poised to triumph over fascism and its insidious use of science. Unlike in previous periods, World War II proved that if the federal government invested in science, wars could be won, diseases could be vanquished, and new frontiers (including even space) could be glimpsed. Today, the NAS is an active and important resource for science policy and inquiry. Topics of recent reports from the NAS include climate change, planetary exploration, coastal community resilience, opioids, and understanding atomic nuclei are.

J. N. Campbell

See also: American Academy of Arts and Sciences (1780–); American Medical Association (1847–); Pharmaceutical Researchers and Manufacturers of America (1958–)

Further Reading

Bruce, Robert V. 1987. *The Launching of Modern American Science, 1846–1876*. New York: Alfred Knopf.

Geiger, Roger L. 1986. *To Advance Knowledge: The Growth of American Research Universities, 1900–1940*. Oxford: Oxford University Press.

Jansen, Axel. 2011. *Building the American Nation through Science and Education in the Nineteenth Century*. Chicago: University of Chicago Press.

Jansen, Axel, ed. 2016. *Legitimizing Science: National and Global Public, 1800–2010.* Chicago: University of Chicago Press.

National American Woman Suffrage Association (1890–)

The National American Woman Suffrage Association (NAWSA) was a group formed by two suffrage organizations, the National Woman Suffrage Association, founded by Elizabeth Cady Stanton and Susan B. Anthony in 1869, and the American Suffrage Association, formed by Julia Ward Howe and Lucy Stone during the same year. The National Woman Suffrage Association attempted to obtain voting rights for women through a national constitutional amendment. In addition, the group fought for women's rights in areas such as divorce disparities and pay and employment discrimination. The American Suffrage Association's sole objective was to obtain female voting rights through state legislatures. Another major difference between the two groups was that the American Suffrage Association was led by both men and women. Alternatively, the National Suffrage Association allowed men to participate, but only women were allowed formal membership and leadership in the organization.

The origins of both groups stemmed from the American Equal Rights Association, formed in 1866 to fight for equal rights—especially voting rights—for African Americans and women. The proposed Fifteenth Amendment to the United States Constitution, which extended voting rights to African Americans but not to women, led to the collapse of the American Equal Rights Association. The two women's suffrage groups were formed after its demise over a disagreement over whether to support the proposed Fifteenth Amendment. Susan B. Anthony and Elizabeth Cady Stanton opposed the amendment's ratification because it enfranchised African American voters but not women. Lucy Stone, Henry Blackwell, and Julia Ward Howe supported the ratification of the amendment on the belief that the extension of suffrage rights to African Americans was a positive step toward the enfranchisement of women. The creation of the two competing women's suffrage organizations led those citizens in favor of women's suffrage to have to choose between the two groups, which resulted in a bitter rivalry between the National Suffrage Association and the American Suffrage Association.

Eventually, the differences between the two groups diminished, and the coexistence of two separate woman suffrage organizations frustrated younger women, who believed the separation had more to do with the individuals involved than with the overall goal of obtaining voting rights for women. In 1890, the two organizations merged to form the National American Suffrage Association, with Elizabeth Cady Stanton elected its first president and Susan B. Anthony elected vice president. Lucy Stone was elected chair of the executive committee of the new organization.

Although Stanton tended to have more radical views about women attaining equality with men in all areas of society, most of the younger women believed

Stanton's strategies would harm the overall goal of obtaining suffrage rights for women. Stanton traveled to Great Britain for a long visit with her daughter, essentially leaving Anthony in charge, who was formally elected to the presidency of NAWSA in 1892. The membership of NAWSA grew from 7,000 to over two million members in 1920, making it the largest interest group in the country at that time.

When the United States Senate rejected a national constitutional amendment to enfranchise women in 1887, NAWSA decided to focus its efforts on state legislatures. Upon Susan B. Anthony's retirement from the presidency of NAWSA in 1900, Carrie Chapman Catt assumed the role. Catt decided to pivot from the national campaign to focus on women gaining voting rights in individual states. By 1893, NAWSA was spending all of its resources at the state level.

Henry Blackwell believed he could convince Southern state legislatures to enfranchise educated women, who were predominately white and against African American suffrage. Blackwell's activities appealed not only to the Southern state legislators, who wanted to ensure white dominance throughout the South, but also to those who wanted to maintain suffrage decisions at the state level to prevent national determinations of suffrage rights. Catt agreed with this strategy and campaigned with Blackwell throughout the South. As part of this appeal to segregationists in the early Jim Crow era, African American members of NAWSA were not allowed to participate at the NAWSA national convention held in New Orleans in 1903.

Catt focused on recruiting well-off women from women's clubs to bring their money, experience, and connections to the suffrage movement. In 1914, the General Federation of Women's Clubs endorsed the cause of women's suffrage. Catt strategically downplayed the more radical beliefs of Stanton and Anthony, which did not appeal to the middle- and upper-class women in the women's clubs. These women were willing to support voting rights for women but not necessarily the ideas of changing divorce laws, fighting for pay equity and employment rights for working women, and other issues originally part of NAWSA's efforts. Catt focused the group on advocating solely for women's suffrage.

When Catt resigned from the presidency of NAWSA in 1904 to care for her ailing husband, Anna Howard Shaw was elected president. Although Shaw did not possess Catt's skills of organization and strategy, Shaw did increase the membership of NAWSA and ended the racist tactics of the group's Southern strategy, saying NAWSA would not endorse policies that "advocated the exclusion of any race or class from the right of suffrage."

In 1912, Alice Paul and Lucy Burns were chosen to lead NAWSA's national campaign for a federal suffrage amendment and led NAWSA's Congressional Committee. The two women, however, employed more radical tactics than those with which the more conservative national leadership of NAWSA were comfortable, so Paul and Burns left NAWSA to begin the more radical National Woman's Party in 1916.

In 1915, Carrie Chapman Catt resumed the presidency of NAWSA and realized that while it had some successes, the state-based suffrage campaigns were limited because some states would never vote for women's suffrage. Catt decided NAWSA's best strategy was to continue to fight for women's suffrage in states where the goal was realistic, but to also concentrate considerable effort on advocating for an amendment to the United States Constitution permitting women's suffrage. Around this time, NAWSA transformed from an educational organization into a full-fledged interest group dedicated to pressuring government for women's suffrage.

When the United States entered World War I in 1917, NAWSA supported the war movement and even shifted its focus to supporting the war effort. In November the same year, the state of New York voted to give women the right to vote. These events provided much-needed momentum for the suffrage movement nationally.

The United States House of Representatives passed the suffrage amendment in 1918, and President Wilson spoke in support of the amendment as well. NAWSA began campaigning against senators up for reelection that year who opposed women's suffrage, successfully contributing to two of the opposing senators' defeats. On June 4, 1919, President Wilson convened a special session of Congress to consider the suffrage amendment as a positive war measure. The amendment passed through both houses of Congress and was sent to the states for ratification. NAWSA organized ratification committees throughout the states to lobby state legislators to ratify the amendment. On August 26, 1920, Tennessee became the last state needed to ratify the Nineteenth Amendment guaranteeing women's suffrage throughout the nation. Following the ratification of the Nineteenth Amendment, NAWSA became the League of Women Voters, an organization which still exists today as a nonpartisan political organization dedicated to informing and engaging all voters.

Heather Frederick

See also: League of Women Voters (1920–)

Further Reading

Buhle, Mari Jo, and Paul Buhle. 2005. *The Concise History of Woman Suffrage: Selections from History of Woman Suffrage, by Elizabeth Cady Stanton, Susan B. Anthony, Matilda Joslyn Gage, and the National American Woman Suffrage Association.* Urbana: University of Illinois Press, Revised edition.

Flexner, Eleanor, and Ellen Fitzpatrick. 1996. *Century of Struggle: The Woman's Rights Movement in the United States, Enlarged Edition 3rd Revised Edition.* Cambridge, MA: Belknap Press.

Kraditor, Aileen S. 1981. *The Ideas of the Woman Suffrage Movement: 1890–1920.* New York: W. W. Norton & Company.

McConnaughy, Corrine M. 2015. *The Woman Suffrage Movement in America: A Reassessment.* Cambridge: Cambridge University Press.

Spruill Wheeler, Marjorie. 1995. *One Woman, One Vote: Rediscovering the Women's Suffrage Movement.* Troutdale, OR: NewSage Press.

National Association for the Advancement of Colored People (1909–)

The National Association for the Advancement of Colored People (NAACP) was founded between 1909 and 1911 and broadly acted as a successor to the smaller, black-run Niagara Movement set up by W. E. B. Du Bois (1868–1963) in 1905. It rose to far greater prominence than its predecessor, incorporating both black and white activists, and became the leading civil rights pressure group of the early 20th century—and the largest such group in U.S. history. The driving force behind most of the civil rights challenges through the U.S. court system—most famously *Brown v. Board of Education* (1954)—the NAACP was gradually eclipsed by more high-profile activists in the 1960s, at least from a public perspective. However, the NAACP exists to this day, with aims that are largely in line with what they always have been: to achieve political, educational, social, and economic equality without discrimination based on race.

During the gradual dissolution of the earlier Niagara Movement in 1909, Oswald Garrison Villard (1872–1949), editor of the *New York Evening Post* and *The Nation* (and grandson of prominent abolitionist William Lloyd Garrison), issued "The Call," which effectively led to the foundation of the NAACP. On the centenary of Abraham Lincoln's birth, in February 1909, Villard's summons suggested that if Lincoln were alive in 1909, 'he would be disheartened and discouraged' by the numerous ways in which white Americans still discriminated against African Americans, most clearly shown the previous year in the Springfield race riots in Lincoln's electoral home of Illinois. This call was signed by a number of prominent black leaders who were in sympathy with the need for a greater voice for African-American rights, such as Du Bois and anti-lynching campaigner Ida B. Wells-Barnett (1862–1931), as well as white sympathizers such as Villard himself and Mary White Ovington (1865–1951).

"The Call" led to a series of meetings in New York City that resulted in the organization of the first National Negro Conference in June of 1909. The leading African American spokesperson in the nation prior to this point had been Booker T. Washington (1856–1915), who stood in opposition to figures like Du Bois and William Monroe Trotter (1872–1934), and what Washington saw as their overly radical approach to black civil rights activism. Washington felt that calls for equality were damaging and advocated a more gradual approach to the improvement of conditions in the U.S. for African Americans, focused on matters such as vocational education and self-help. Washington opted not to join the conference in 1909, and thus the emphases of the new movement, and the National Negro Committee that headed it, turned more towards the vision of Du Bois and the earlier Niagara Movement. However, the new group's prominence – like that of the Niagara Movement before it – was overshadowed in its earliest years by Washington's pre-existing powerbase. The existence of an established alternative starved the NAACP of many early potential black supporters, just as it had the Niagara Movement.

It was only in 1910, at the second National Negro Conference, that the organization chose to adopt the name which it still bears; it was Du Bois who was integral to the choice of the word "colored" being used as a more inclusive term than alternatives. Members of the Du Bois-led Niagara Movement generally heeded its leader's advice to join the new movement in 1909–1910, though technically the NAACP was only formally incorporated the following year in 1911 (nevertheless most histories still date its foundation as 1909). From its founding until the civil rights era of the 1950s and 1960s, the NAACP was the foremost pressure group campaigning for African Americans to receive constitutional rights enshrined in the post-Civil War Fourteenth and Fifteenth Amendments. Like the Niagara Movement before it, the NAACP sought to make its challenge primarily through the courts, and at first suffered the same lack of funds as its predecessor movement to take on such an expensive course of action. Du Bois, as director of publicity and research, founded the NAACP's magazine, *The Crisis*, in 1910 to further spread the movement's message. On occasion the organization also got behind protests, such as that witnessed during the release in 1915 of the film *The Birth of a Nation,* a film that lionized the Ku Klux Klan.

The key concern for the early NAACP was the crime of lynching, which was most prevalent in the South during the early-twentieth century and was perpetrated mainly by white Americans against African Americans. Early member of the NAACP, Ida B. Wells-Barnett, had devoted much of her life to campaigning against lynching, and the organization supported efforts to make lynching a federal crime due to the dearth of successful convictions of offenders in southern state courts. The group sponsored anti-lynching measures such as the Dyer Bill of the 1920s and the Costigan-Wagner Bill of 1930s, though neither was ultimately successful. As the 1930s drew to a close, and the prevalence of lynching in the South declined, the focus of the NAACP moved away from lynching to wider issues of injustice, such as segregated education and black disenfranchisement.

By the 1920s, the NAACP had become a much larger organization, with a growing number of African Americans joining. Black activists such as James Weldon Johnson (1871–1938) and Walter White (1893–1955) took on key positions in the movement and ushered in an era when the NAACP would gradually become a predominantly black organization. However, though Booker T. Washington had died in 1915, opposition from within the black community did not end. Marcus Garvey (1887–1940), leader of a black nationalist movement that attracted mass support in the 1920s, saw the NAACP as a sellout in much the same way Du Bois had critiqued Washington's approach in the preceding decade. Importantly, unlike the Niagara Movement or Garveyism in the 1920s, the NAACP adhered to a policy of working with white Americans toward greater racial integration in the United States and opposed working separately toward those ends.

Other potential rivals for black support in the early 20th century were labor unions and socialist movements, both of which offered to help secure black prosperity and spoke more directly to those African Americans who were no longer affected by Southern disenfranchisement, such as the thousands who had moved north to urban centers as part of the "Great Migration" that began around the time of the First World War. However, the NAACP frequently chose to quietly support rather than fight such potential competition. Steering clear of wholehearted alliances with socialist movements or radical trade unions proved tactically farsighted, especially during the Cold War, when suspicion of such leftist movements was at its height.

The most notable successes of the NAACP came though their increasingly successful court challenges. In 1930, the organization successfully mobilized its resources to block President Hoover's attempt to appoint John Parker (1885–1958) to the U.S. Supreme Court because of his previous record on black rights. The following year, Walter White began his two decades of leadership of the NAACP by stepping up its efforts to frustrate the appointment or election of white supremacists. In the early years, these efforts were largely spearheaded by white lawyers such as Moorfield Storey, but in later years, black lawyers began to play an integral role. The NAACP recorded notable successes in the 1940s in cases concerning black participation in primary elections, housing discrimination, and segregation in graduate education. However, clearly the landmark success of the NAACP was the Supreme Court decision of *Brown v Board of Education, Topeka* (1954). NAACP lawyers Thurgood Marshall (1908–1993) (later an associate justice of the United States Supreme Court) and Robert L. Carter (1917–2012) were instrumental in the success of this famous case, which overturned the "separate but equal" doctrine that had sustained segregated education in the United States, an issue that the NAACP had pursued for decades. The *Brown* decision is perhaps the best example of the way the NAACP, unlike the more direct action-oriented groups of the 1950s and 1960s, fought for civil rights throughout its history, and it was a strategy that they largely adhered to despite criticism from other groups in the decades that followed. Nonetheless, the year after *Brown*, the Montgomery bus boycott began after Rosa Parks refused to give up her seat on a segregated Alabama bus. What is often overlooked is that Parks was an active member of the NAACP—a fact that not only provides a different perspective on her actions for some but also stands in contrast to the general aversion to direct action taken by the NAACP and its members during the period.

Although founded as a movement that was headed by both black and white Americans, by the 1960s, at the height of the civil rights movement, the NAACP board was made up entirely of African Americans (Meier and Bracey 1993, 29). By the late 1960s, headed by figures such as Roy Wilkins (1901–1981), the NAACP could boast more than 450,000 members nationwide, in spite of competition from Martin Luther King's Southern Christian Leadership Conference (SCLC), the Congress of Racial Equality (CORE) and the Student Nonviolent Coordinating Committee (SNCC) (Jonas 2005, 4). The legislative breakthroughs of the mid-1960s—the Civil Rights Act of 1964 and Voting Rights Act of 1965—came, at least partially, as a result of the NAACP's decades of pressure as well as the more high-profile direct action of the SCLC, CORE, and SNCC. The NAACP maintained its traditional line on fighting for integration and avoiding the use of direct action under the leadership of Roy Wilkins between 1955 and 1977 and, as a sign of their success, the NAACP was the only civil rights organization to maintain a mass membership in the South after 1965 (Minchin 2008, 670).

In the years that have followed the civil rights movement, the NAACP has remained an active organization. Indeed, President Barack Obama, the first African American president, addressed the group in 2009 on its centenary, noting the progress the organization had helped bring about over the course of the 20th century. In 2011, the group issued a list of six "game-changing" areas where they would focus their efforts for the 21st century: economic sustainability; education; health; public safety and criminal justice; voting rights and political representation; and expanding youth and young adult engagement.

Adam D. Burns

See also: Black Panther Party (1966–1982); Congress of Racial Equality (1942–); Montgomery Improvement Association and Women's Political Council (1955–1970); NAACP Legal Defense and Education Fund (1940–); National Urban League (1910–); Organization of Afro-American Unity (1964–1965); Rainbow-PUSH Coalition (1996–); Southern Christian Leadership Conference (1957–); Student Nonviolent Coordinating Committee (1960–1974)

Further Reading
Jonas, Gilbert. 2005. *Freedom's Sword: The NAACP and the Struggle Against Racism in America, 1909–1969.* New York and London: Routledge.

Meier, August, and John H. Bracey Jr. 1993. "The NAACP as a Reform Movement, 1909–1965: 'To Reach the Conscience of America.'" *Journal of Southern History* 59 (1): 3–30.

Minchin, Timothy J. 2008. "Making Best Use of the New Laws: The NAACP and the Fight for Civil Rights in the South, 1965–1975." *Journal of Southern History* 74 (3): 669–702.

Rudwick, Elliott. 1982. "W. E. B. Du Bois: Protagonist of the Afro-American Protest." In *Black Leaders of the Twentieth Century*, edited by John Hope Franklin and August Meier, 63–84. Urbana: University of Illinois Press.

Sullivan, Patricia. 2009. *Lift Every Voice: The NAACP and the Making of the Civil Rights Movement.* New York: The New Press.

National Association of Letter Carriers (1889–)

The National Association of Letter Carriers (NALC) is a labor union representing 278,000 active and retired city letter carriers who work for the U.S. Postal Service (USPS), which operates as an independent agency within the federal government. NALC comprises 2,500 local branches and 15 regional offices covering every U.S. state and territory. Although union membership is not mandatory, and employees cannot be compelled to join under federal law, NALC represents more than 90 percent of letter carriers (NALC 2015). Several additional labor unions represent other categories of USPS employees, including the National Rural Letter Carriers' Association, the National Postal Mail Handlers Union, and the American Postal Workers Union.

NALC engages in collective bargaining with the USPS on behalf of its members. It negotiates labor contracts that define wages, benefits, and working conditions, including such elements as uniforms, route changes, delivery methods, and the amount of weight letter carriers lift and transport. NALC also conducts legislative outreach and lobbying activities to defend its members' interests among federal lawmakers. Finally, NALC operates a political action committee (PAC) that solicits voluntary donations from members to finance the election campaigns of candidates who support the organization's priorities. Formerly called the Committee on Letter Carrier Political Education (COLCPE), it became known as the Letter Carrier Political Fund in 2016.

NALC was founded in 1889, when 60 letter carriers from 13 states gathered in Milwaukee, Wisconsin, to discuss long work hours and other employment complaints. The organization grew quickly, from 52 local branches in 1890 to 335 two years later. NALC waged a legal battle to force the Postmaster General to honor an 1888 law mandating an eight-hour workday for federal employees. Its efforts paid off in 1893, when the U.S. Supreme Court awarded letter carriers $3.5 million in retroactive overtime pay. In 1917, NALC joined the American Federation of Labor (AFL).

As a labor union representing public employees, the Taft-Hartley Act of 1947 prohibited the NALC from organizing strikes that would disrupt essential government services. Nevertheless, letter carriers walked out for eight days in 1970 to protest low wages that failed to keep up with inflation. Although NALC President James Rademacher reached an agreement with President Richard Nixon to keep mail delivery going during the 1969 Christmas rush, letter carriers from Branch 36 in New York City remained dissatisfied. In March 1970, they launched a strike that was soon joined by 150,000 other USPS employees nationwide. Nixon mobilized the U.S. Army to deliver mail until the two sides reached an agreement. The dispute led to passage of the Postal Reorganization Act of 1970, which established the USPS as an independent agency, recognized NALC's collective bargaining rights, and awarded letter carriers an 8 percent pay increase.

In the 21st century, NALC offers many benefits to its members, including access to a private retirement community called Nalcrest in central Florida, a health benefit plan, and a life insurance program. NALC also sponsors several charitable initiatives and community service programs. During the 2014 Stamp Out Hunger food drive, which has been held nationwide on the second Saturday in May since 1992, letter carriers collected 72.5 million pounds of nonperishable food items to restock food pantries across the country. NALC became the first national sponsor of the Muscular Dystrophy Association (MDA) in 1952, and its annual Deliver the Cure fund-raising campaign raised $1.2 million in 2017. NALC also sponsors a National Heroes program to recognize letter carriers who perform acts of extraordinary service on the job, such as assisting victims of car accidents, preventing crimes, or alerting authorities when elderly or homebound residents fail to collect their mail.

Through its Letter Carrier Political Fund, NALC supports political candidates and campaigns that promote the interests of its members. It also encourages its members to become involved in political activities within the limitations imposed on all federal employees by the Hatch Act. Under amendments adopted in 1993, federal employees are not allowed to engage in partisan political activity while in the workplace (including government vehicles), in uniform, or serving in a work capacity. They are also prohibited from using federal resources for political purposes, including such online communication channels as email or social media. Even on their own time, active letter carriers are not allowed to run for office in a partisan election or raise money for partisan political groups or campaigns. Retired letter carriers are not bound by the provisions of the Hatch Act.

Prior to the 2016 presidential election, NALC asked USPS officials to grant several weeks of "union official leave without pay" to 97 union members. The USPS granted the time-off requests in the interest of preserving harmonious labor relations, even though some local post offices complained that releasing those employees would leave them understaffed. The active letter carriers used the leave time to participate in campaign work for Labor 2016, a project intended to generate support for pro-worker candidates in swing states, such as Florida, Ohio, Pennsylvania, and Wisconsin. The union members stuffed envelopes, made phone calls, and did door-to-door canvassing to encourage voters to elect candidates endorsed by NALC and the AFL-CIO, including Democratic presidential nominee Hillary Clinton. The Letter Carrier Political Fund compensated the employees during their unpaid leave. Meanwhile, the USPS spent an estimated $90,000 on overtime pay to cover their absence.

A USPS employee from Wisconsin filed a complaint with the United States Office of Special Counsel (OSC), an investigative agency for personnel practices relating to federal employees. In July 2017, the OSC released a report claiming that the USPS decision to grant employees unpaid leave to participate in partisan political activities constituted a "systematic violation of the Hatch Act." OSC said the arrangement conveyed an "institutional bias" and "gave the appearance that USPS favored or supported the union's endorsed candidates" (Watson 2017). Postmaster General Megan Brennan challenged the findings, asserting that USPS officials only granted employees' requests for time off and "did not in any way guide union leadership in selecting the candidates for whom NALC employees could campaign" or "ask the union to advocate for political candidates on behalf of the Postal Service" (Singman 2017). NALC leaders claimed that the complaint was politically motivated, pointing out that union members had used unpaid leave to volunteer for political campaigns since the 1990s without any objections.

OSC ordered USPS to change its practices to comply with the Hatch Act. In October 2017, Brennan announced a new policy prohibiting USPS employees from using unpaid time off to campaign for political candidates. NALC and other postal employee unions immediately filed a grievance, arguing that the new policy violated their collective bargaining agreements as well as their First Amendment rights. In August 2017, an arbitrator ruled in favor of the unions and directed the USPS to rescind the ban. The arbitrator found that the USPS could not make unilateral policy changes affecting wages, hours, or working conditions without negotiating those changes with union leaders. "The award protects employees' right to request [leave without pay] to volunteer through their union to participate in important political activities, like the upcoming November elections," a union representative stated. "Postal employees have the legal right to campaign and participate in politics, subject to limits under the federal Hatch Act" (Katz 2018).

As part of a larger effort to streamline the federal government, the administration of President Donald Trump considered reform measures that included converting the Postal Service from a government agency to a privately held corporation. Along with other postal employee unions, NALC voiced strong opposition to this proposal. "The White House is making very clear that privatization of the Postal Service is its goal," said NALC President Fredric V. Rolando. "No one has floated the idea of privatization except private shippers, who would love nothing more than to see the Postal Service dismantled. . . . NALC will work tirelessly with other stakeholders and Congress to oppose this faulty privatization plan every step of the way to preserve this public institution, which is based in the Constitution" (Rolando 2018).

Laurie Collier Hillstrom

See also: American Federation of Labor (1886–1955); American Federation of State, County, and Municipal Employees (1936–)

Further Reading

Katz, Eric. 2018. "USPS Must Rescind Its Ban on Employees Taking Leave to Campaign for Union-Backed Candidates." *Government Executive*, August 16, 2018. https://www.govexec.com/pay-benefits/2018/08/usps-must-rescind-its-ban-employees-taking-leave-campaign-union-backed-candidates/150609/.

National Association of Letter Carriers. 2015. *The Letter Carrier's Guide.* https://www.nalc.org/about/nalc-and-the-u-s-postal-service/body/Letter-Carriers-Guide-2015.pdf.

National Association of Letter Carriers. 2018. https://www.nalc.org.

Rolando, Fredric V. 2018. "NALC's Statement on OMB's Proposal to Privatize the Postal Service." NALC, June 21, 2018. https://www.nalc.org/news/nalc-updates/nalcs-statement-on-ombs-proposal-to-privatize-the-postal-service.

Singman, Brooke. 2017. "USPS Broke Law in Allowing Workers to Boost Clinton Campaign, Watchdog Says." Fox News, July 19, 2017. http://www.foxnews.com/politics/2017/07/19/watchdog-postal-service-broke-law-by-letting-employees-do-clinton-campaign-work.html.

Watson, Michael. 2017. "Union Official Leave Leads to 'Systematic' Violations at Postal Service." Capital Research Center, July 20, 2017. https://capitalresearch.org/article/union-official-leave-leads-to-systematic-hatch-act-violations-at-postal-service/.

National Association of Manufacturers (1895–)

The National Association of Manufacturers (NAM) was established in 1895 as an advocacy group to promote the export of U.S. manufactured goods to overseas markets. At the time, the United States was in the midst of a major economic downturn. A financial panic in 1893 led to increased unemployment throughout the nation. Consumption declined and resulted in the overproduction of manufactured products and agricultural goods.

Cincinnati businessman Thomas P. Egan (1847–1922), whose company built woodworking machinery, sought to bring together the nation's leading industrialists in a broad organization that would help coordinate economic strategies among firms and encourage export-friendly trade policies. More than 500 industrialists attended a meeting on January 25, 1895, hosted by Egan. The group launched NAM, which subsequently began lobbying to maintain high tariffs on imported goods and open foreign markets.

NAM collected and published information on trade opportunities and assisted firms seeking new opportunities overseas. The organization's legal staff provided advice and aid to corporations as they negotiated contracts with foreign buyers. NAM was an important resource, especially for smaller companies that did not otherwise have the staff or capabilities to interact with potential consumers overseas. NAM even provided some translation help. The organization grew quickly to represent more than 5,000 companies, responsible for as much as 75 percent of the nation's manufactured goods.

In the 1896 presidential elections, the Republican Party platform endorsed existing protectionist measures, while high tariffs were opposed by Democrats.

NAM-backed Republican candidate and former Ohio governor William McKinley (1843–1901), who had sponsored the highly restrictive Tariff Act of 1890 (also known as the McKinley Tariff), won the election, defeating Democratic candidate William Jennings Bryan (1860–1925). Republicans controlled the White House from McKinley's election until 1913. To better promote industry and coordinate trade policy, NAM backed the creation of a cabinet-level department within the federal government. In 1903, the Department of Commerce and Labor was established (oversight of labor issues was transferred to the newly-created Department of Labor in 1913). The new department was one of the organization's most significant early victories. Over the next decade the Department of Commerce and Labor dramatically expanded its size and role as a promoter of U.S. firms, both at home and abroad.

In order to better harmonize trade policy between manufactures and other economic sectors, NAM supported the foundation of a nationwide business group. The resulting National Council of Commerce (NCC) worked closely with the Department of Commerce and Labor in a partnership to promote U.S. business until the NCC was superseded by the U.S. Chamber of Commerce in 1912. The Chamber forged even closer ties with government over the next decade.

Through its early history, NAM staunchly opposed organized labor. Like other leading industrial and business groups, NAM and its membership generally sought to suppress efforts to unionize. Into the 1920s and 1930s, NAM funded various public relations campaigns that were highly critical of unions. The organization also developed advice and tactics for companies seeking to block unionization. To counter organized labor, NAM's legal counsels helped companies file suits and seek injunctions. NAM also worked with other organizations to draft and support anti-union legislation at the state and national level. The organization also worked to defeat or weaken pro-union bills. For instance, NAM and other business groups were successful in eroding many of the union protections in the original version of the 1914 Clayton Anti-Trust Act.

From the early 1900s into the 1930s, NAM was a major backer of the anti-organized labor Citizens Alliance. The Citizens Alliance was a loose collection of state-level groups that were formed with employer support to combat unionization efforts. Along with a variety of employer associations, these local entities used their superior financial backing to oppose collective bargaining efforts and various priorities of the labor movement that ranged from the eight-hour workday to a minimum wage.

NAM developed a considerable public relations capability in its first decade, including the trade publication, *American Industry*, founded in 1902. NAM used the journal and other in-house publications in campaigns to sway public opinion against organized labor and to promote the economic benefits of manufacturing in the country. Extolling the virtues of manufacturing became an even higher priority of NAM during the 1930s. The onset of the Great Depression and the election of Franklin D. Roosevelt (1882–1945) reduced NAM's influence in the nation's capital. Instead, many of Roosevelt's New Deal programs endeavored to better balance the needs and rights of workers against the economic interests of the business community. NAM initiated a decade-long, $15 million public-relations effort to stress the importance of manufacturing to the U.S. economy. The campaign included print and broadcast media. Typical of the initiative was the 1940 film *Your Town*, which emphasized rugged individualism by personifying industry as a hero, responsible both for bringing economic benefits and for defending the nation against dangers.

Following the entry of the United States into World War II in 1941, NAM's relations with the Roosevelt administration improved significantly. The administration recognized the potential assistance that the organization could provide, while NAM accepted the need to work closely with the president and cabinet to meet the nation's military and industrial needs. The group shifted its public relations efforts to support the war effort. Propaganda flyers, leaflets, radio broadcasts, and films were produced for the general public and for industrial workers. These highlighted the contributions of manufacturing sectors and the importance of the home front in the conflict. NAM concurrently launched a range of programs to assist companies in navigating the increasingly complex wartime economy. The organization provided firms with information on government contracts and new rules and regulations. NAM further offered aid in identifying increasingly scarce resources and altering manufacturing processes to account for wartime scarcities.

In late 1944 and 1945, NAM coordinated strategies among corporations on how to deal with the transition from wartime manufacturing back to civilian production. However, the financial rewards accrued by companies during World War II led an increasingly influential group within the organization to endorse a robust national defense. The economic benefits of the growing industrial-defense complex included ever-larger government contracts, more research and development funding, and an interventionist foreign policy that opened new markets to U.S. manufactured goods. Throughout the Cold War (1947–1991), NAM was staunchly anticommunist and supportive of larger defense budgets. NAM became an aggressive backer of U.S. involvement in Vietnam (1964–1974), mainly as a result of the deep anticommunism of many of its senior leaders. It also continued its deep ties with the Republican Party.

Meanwhile, the organization continued to battle organized labor. NAM and other business groups launched a broad campaign in 1946 to limit collective bargaining at the federal, state, and local levels. The culmination of their efforts was the Taft-Hartley Act of 1947, which limited some practices used by unions and permitted states to enact right-to-work legislation, limiting the ability of labor organizations to require employees to join a union as a condition of employment. It also ended support for most protectionist measures, instead embracing free trade as a means to expand access to overseas markets. For example, NAM endorsed the 1962 Trade Expansion Act, which reduced tariffs by up to 50 percent on certain imports in exchange for reciprocal reductions in barriers to U.S. exports by European nations.

NAM was one of a number of business groups that worked with the administration of President Ronald Reagan (1911–2004) on economic and tax reforms in the 1980s. The organization endorsed Reagan's economic program in 1982. Over the next four decades, NAM generally backed Republican candidates at the state and federal level. NAM opposed a succession of Democratic economic initiatives in the 1990s and 2000s, including the failed effort to reform the health care system in 1993. The ties between the group and the Republican Party were further affirmed with the appointment of former three-term Republican governor of Michigan, John Engler (1948–), as president of the NAM in 2004.

In the early 2000s, NAM remained the largest manufacturing group in the United States. The political action committee of the mainly conservative group focused its resources on Republican candidates in the 2016 elections. However, in that year's balloting, differences emerged between the organization and Republican presidential candidate Donald J. Trump (1946–) over free trade. The organization supported the Trans-Pacific Partnership (TPP) free trade accord, while Trump opposed U.S. participation in the agreement. NAM did endorse Trump's 2017 tax reform initiative because of the proposal's reduction in corporate taxes from 35 percent to 20 percent.

Tom Lansford

See also: American Bankers Association (1875–); American Trucking Associations (1933–); Grocery Manufacturers Association (1908–); National Association of Manufacturers (1895–); Pharmaceutical Researchers and Manufacturers of America (1958–); U.S. Business and Industry Council (1933–); U.S. Chamber of Commerce (1912–)

Further Reading

Becker, William H. 1982. *The Dynamics of Business-Government Relations: Industry and Exports, 1893–1921.* Chicago: University of Chicago Press.

McQuaid, Kim. 1994. *Uneasy Partners: Big Business in American Politics, 1945–1990.* Baltimore, MD: Johns Hopkins University Press.

Millikan, William. 2001. *A Union against Unions: The Minneapolis Citizens Alliance and Its Fight against Organized Labor, 1903–1947.* St. Paul: Minnesota Historical Society Press.

Soffer, Jonathan. 2001. "The National Association of Manufacturers and the Militarization of American Conservatism." *The Business History Review* 75: 775–805.

St. John, Burton, and Robert Arnett. "The National Association of Manufacturers' Community Relations Short Film, *Your Town*: Parable, Propaganda, and Big Individualism." *Journal of Public Relations Research* 26: 103–116.

National Association of Realtors (1908–)

The National Association of Realtors (NAR) is an American trade association focused on people who work in and/or support the real estate industry. More than a million professionals who work in all aspects of residential and commercial real estate comprise NAR's membership. In addition to serving as a self-regulatory professional organization for the field of real estate, NAR's large membership and its lobbying efforts make it one of the strongest political action groups in the United States. Since 1969, the Realtors Political Action Committee (RPAC) has involved itself in the political process across the nation, mobilizing its members for or against candidates and issues that involve their interests.

The National Association of Realtors is headquartered in Chicago, Illinois, and maintains a presence in Washington, D.C. NAR's 1.2 million members include residential and commercial real estate brokers and real estate salespeople along with appraisers, counselors, property managers, and others in areas of the real estate profession where a state license is required in order to practice. NAR members must also belong to at least one of the nation's 1,600 local real estate boards or associations.

In 1908, over 100 realtors gathered in Chicago to found the organization as the National Association of Real Estate Exchanges. The organization adopted a code of ethics and standards of practice for its members in 1913. In 1916, the group changed its name to the National Association of Real Estate Boards, becoming the National Association of Realtors in 1972.

Members of NAR are known as Realtors. Charles Chadbourn proposed the term in 1916 in an article in the *National Real Estate Journal*. At that time, practitioners of the profession were called real estate agents, but Chadbourn suggested that a professional title be adopted by the national association to be conferred on members of good standing, to differentiate their level of professionalism from others in the field.

Chadbourn further suggested copyrighting the term so it could be defended in order to avoid misuse. In 1949, what was then the National Association of Real Estate Boards sought and received a trademark registration for the term "Realtor." Therefore, "Realtor" is considered a trademark, setting it apart from "real estate agent," which is a generic term.

Apart from providing services to its members, the National Association of Realtors is one of the country's largest political action groups. NAR routinely lobbies federal and state officials on issues affecting NAR members. Some of NAR's interests parallel the business sector, including bankruptcy legislation, healthcare issues, housing, lending, insurance, small business legislation, and tax rates.

NAR has traditionally been known for its strength as a lobbying organization. It is consistently ranked among the largest trade associations in terms of funding for its lobbying efforts as well as spending on state and local campaign activities. In an article called "The Meaning of Political Power" for the International Real Property Association, Richard Mendenhall, the 2001 president of NAR, stated that the organization has been recognized in *Fortune* magazine's listing of America's 25 most powerful lobbying organizations for several years. He said that in addition to the monetary resources needed for lobbying efforts, there are three elements that the most powerful political action committees such as NAR have in common: (1) a highly competent and knowledgeable staff; (2) funding for political contributions and issue advocacy campaigns on the state and local levels; and (3) a large, politically active membership that is dispersed in all areas of the country (Mendenhall 2001).

With advancing technology and the diversification of financial institutions in the 21st century, NAR has been active in some areas its founders could scarcely have imagined when the organization was created in 1908. For example, in the early 2000s, some large banks pursued the possibility of entering the real estate brokerage business. The NAR opposed legislation that would have enabled such a move, with NAR's lobbying efforts halting the proposal. According to Mendenhall "NAR generated more than 100,000 letters, faxes and emails to the Federal Reserve Board, U.S. Treasury, and Congress in opposition to a regulatory proposal that would allow the nation's largest banks to add real estate to their growing list of business activities. The Fed alone got 44,000 letters and emails commenting on the proposal it put forth with the Treasury Department, virtually all of them from Realtors. There is no other U.S. trade association or lobbying group that can garner that kind of widespread participation in any campaign" (Mendenhall 2001).

An ongoing issue for NAR is protection of the traditional brokers' commissions on most home sales which runs around 6 percent. This often involves strategic opposition to Internet-based real estate companies and discount brokerage firms that might offer individual services in which customers can choose only the services they desire, a system those companies state can sometimes reduce costs for consumers.

Some opponents to NAR's lobbying efforts to protect its Realtors cite the fact that NAR limits access to property listings through the Multiple Listing Service (MLS) to its members and NAR's state and local affiliates. MLS listings were once kept in large books, but with the rise of the digital age, the lists are now maintained electronically. Information on MLS is often used to market properties on the Internet. Some opponents of this system argue that the MLS data should be open to the public. They voice concerns that large, traditional brokers gain an unfair advantage over smaller firms because bigger brokers supply a larger number of listings.

Other areas of NAR's political advocacy include developments in flood insurance, home ownership, real estate investment tax policies, credit and lending policies, residential real estate finance, refinancing of commercial properties, and topics involving business operations for its members, such as independent contractor status and worker classification of Realtors.

Among its many activities, the National Association of Realtors provides informational materials for its membership as well as material for the general public such as the pamphlet "What is a REALTOR®?" which discusses the advantages of working with a NAR member.

Apart from permitting its members to use the trademarked term "Realtors" to describe themselves professionally, NAR also provides certifications and designations that can be earned by meeting NAR's educational requirements. These include Certified Residential Specialist, Certified International Property Specialist, Real Estate Professional Assistant, and Seniors Real Estate Specialist, which addresses the needs of homebuyers over age 50, one of the nation's largest and most affluent demographics. Recent policy advocacy by the NAR has included involvement with state and federal legislators on tax policy and the mortgage interest deduction, Americans with Disabilities Act (ADA) compliance issues, and more. NAR is an important trade association that has members across every congressional district, making them a key constituency for most members of Congress.

Nancy Hendricks

See also: American Bankers Association (1875–); Fannie Mae (1938–) and Freddie Mac (1970–); U.S. Business and Industry Council (1933–)

Further Reading

Hester, Hathaway. 2016. "Trademark in the Archives, Part I: The Invention of REAL-TOR®." *National Association of Realtors Information Services*, March 23, 2016. http://infoservices.blogs.realtor.org/2016/03/23/trademark-in-the-archives-part-i -the-invention-of-realtor/.

Justice, Glen. 2006. "Lobbying to Sell Your House." *New York Times*, January 12, 2006. http://www.nytimes.com/2006/01/12/business/lobbying-to-sell-your-house.html ?mcubz=3.

Mendenhall, Richard. 2001. "The Meaning of Political Power." *International Real Property Association.* https://www.nar.realtor/AMR.nsf/pages/Lobbying.

National Association of Realtors Political Advocacy. 2017. https://www.nar.realtor/poli tical-advocacy.

National Audubon Society (1905–)

The National Association of Audubon Societies for the Protection of Wild Birds and Animals was officially incorporated in New York on January 30, 1905. In 1940 its name was shortened to the National Audubon Society. At the time of its founding, two North American bird species, the Great Auk and the Labrador Duck, had been pushed to extinction and others seemed likely to soon follow. A small group of committed ornithologists, made up of both academics and citizen scientists, grew alarmed over the rapid declines in a number of species and became convinced that birds must be protected. They began a multipronged approach aimed at winning over public support for the protection of birds, lobbying legislatures for effective bird protection laws, securing adequate enforcement for existing laws, and developing bird sanctuaries.

As the 20th century approached, millions of birds were killed each year in support of fashion. The most fashionable women's hats of that era featured birds' feathers and sometimes even entire birds. The mating plumes of snowy egrets were so popular that a number of breeding colonies were wiped out—the adults killed so their plumes could be removed and the young in the nest left to starve.

Birds faced threats on other fronts as well, though. Large flocks of migrating birds, viewed as pests, lost thousands at a time to small groups of hunters. Both eating and collecting a wide variety of bird species' eggs was so popular that some of them went several seasons with few successful breeding pairs. Even small songbirds were sold in markets for food. Meanwhile, colorful varieties like painted buntings and northern cardinals were trapped and shipped across state lines for sale as pets.

The efforts to protect wild birds and form an Audubon society began two decades before its official incorporation. The American Ornithologist Union formed the Bird Protection Committee in 1884 and soon drafted the "model law" for bird protection, a piece of legislation it hoped states would enact. Some of its members would also become leaders of the Audubon movement. Among these was George Bird Grinnell (1849–1938), who launched the first effort to form the Audubon Society in the pages of *Forest and Stream* in 1886. The society's purpose was to protect wild birds and their eggs through furthering the efforts of the

Bird Protection Committee. The price of admission was a pledge from men and boys that they would not kill birds or rob nests and a pledge from women and girls that they would not wear birds or their feathers or use them for household decoration. Over 18,000 signed the pledge by year's end, and its membership ranks swelled to nearly 50,000 by the following year. However, without membership dues, the Audubon Society lacked the finances to carry on its efforts. The few bird protection laws on the books went unenforced, and birds continued to be killed for use in women's fashion. Grinnell abandoned efforts for the Audubon Society, and it lay dormant until 1896 when it was revived by a small group of Boston society women who joined with ornithologists and naturalists to form the Massachusetts Audubon Society. The group drafted and distributed pamphlets, engaged in outreach to school children, and pushed for strengthened bird protection laws in Massachusetts. Over the next two years, more than a dozen Audubon Societies sprang up in other states, where they engaged in similar actions. Soon, ornithologist Frank Chapman (1864–1945) launched the magazine *Bird-Lore*; its pages featured reports from the state Audubon Societies and helped link them together.

William Dutcher (1846–1920) chaired the AOU Bird Protection Committee. In this role, he worked closely with the state Audubon societies and soon became the unofficial head of the national Audubon movement. He worked with several state societies to get versions of the AOU model law passed, but they soon discovered that securing enforcement was a separate issue. Three early developments helped their cause. First, in 1900, Congress passed the Lacey Act—under its Article I authority to regulate interstate commerce—to prohibit shipping birds and other animals killed in violation of state laws to other states. This gave the Audubon movement increased encouragement to secure the passage of additional state laws. Second, Theodore Roosevelt, a dedicated conservationist with ties to the Audubon Society of the District of Columbia, became president of the United States in 1901. Many of the nation's top political leaders were now sympathetic to the plight of birds. Finally, artist and AOU Bird Protection Committee member Abbott H. Thayer (1849–1921) agreed to raise funds for Dutcher to hire wardens to protect sea bird colonies. Roosevelt began creating federal bird and wildlife refuges through executive orders, and when Congress failed to allocate funds, the AOU and Audubon societies hired and paid for wardens to protect them.

By 1901 there were 36 Audubon societies across the United States. Near the end of 1904, Albert Wilcox (1847–1906), a wealthy businessman with a fondness for birds, approached Dutcher with a promise to bequeath $100,000 to the Audubon societies and provide funds in the meantime to support their work. His gifts came with conditions, however. He required that the state societies incorporate into a national organization and that they use his annual contributions to hire a secretary to recruit more members and fund-raise. Dutcher immediately embarked on both tasks. The National Association of Audubon Societies was founded in January 1905, Dutcher became its president, and he recruited Thomas Gilbert Pearson (1873–1943) to be its secretary. Pearson was a talented public speaker, educator, and fund-raiser who had worked to build public support for bird protection in North Carolina, founded the Audubon Society of North Carolina in 1902, and successfully lobbied the North Carolina legislature to pass a version of the

Model Law on March 6, 1903, that would fund wardens to enforce it through requiring hunters from out of state to pay a hunting license fee. Together, Dutcher and Pearson built the newly incorporated National Association of Audubon Societies and advanced its multipronged approach to bird protection. When Dutcher was incapacitated by a stroke in 1911, Pearson assumed most of these responsibilities and officially became president of the National Association of Audubon Societies after Dutcher's death in 1920.

While the National Audubon Society continued to advance public knowledge and concern for birds through pamphlets, public lectures, and wildlife photography and paintings, much of its public education efforts were aimed at children. Pearson had long promoted education about birds in the public schools of North Carolina—he found that children were a naturally sympathetic audience for bird protection pleas—and under his leadership, these efforts became part of a national campaign. Pearson solicited support from Margaret Olivia Slocum Sage (1828–1918), the widow of financier Russell Sage, for an education campaign to get laws passed prohibiting the killing of American robins. The campaign was immensely popular, and they eventually distributed more than five million pamphlets. Afterward, she pledged three years of support to efforts to form junior Audubon societies in the south. These societies housed in school classrooms eventually spread nationwide. Many of the next generations of Audubon leadership began as members of these Junior Audubon societies.

Public education alone was not enough to sway women's fashion away from the use of birds and feathers. The AOU had struck a deal with the Millinery Merchants Protective Association of New York (where the millinery industry and most of the traffic in birds and their feathers was based) in 1903. Milliners agreed not to traffic in or use birds protected under current bird protection laws as long as the Audubon Society did not lobby to make additional birds protected under law. This ended after three years, and the use of feathers and birds in women's hats seemed as popular as ever. Dutcher and Pearson successfully lobbied the New York legislature to pass the Audubon Plumage Act in 1910. Although they faced intense opposition from the millinery industry, they successfully debunked claims that feathers used in hat making were collected from the ground and provided graphic testimony and evidence that birds were being slaughtered for their plumes. The law banned the sale or possession of the feathers of birds in the same family as others protected in the state. This blocked the importation of a number of birds' feathers. Similar protections reached the national level in 1913 when William T. Hornaday (1854–1937) joined with Audubon leaders to get a clause banning importation of bird plumes inserted into the Federal Tariff Act.

In 1918 the Senate ratified the Migratory Bird Treaty between the United States and Great Britain (on behalf of Canada) which placed migratory birds under national government protection and overruled a number of state laws and practices. When the constitutionality of the federal government's enforcement of the treaty was challenged in *Missouri v. Holland* (1920) as a violation of the Tenth Amendment, the U.S. Supreme Court ruled that the Supremacy Clause grants Congress the authority to regulate pursuant to the treaty independent of states' objections. The National Audubon Society no longer had to worry about passing and monitoring state laws and could instead focus on protection and enforcement.

Throughout this period, the National Audubon Society continued the practice began by the AOU of hiring wardens to enforce bird protection laws and, later, to guard sanctuaries as well. This was dangerous work at times. One of their wardens was murdered by a poacher in Florida in 1905, and two more were murdered in 1908—one in Florida and one in South Carolina. No one was convicted of these crimes.

The National Audubon Society lobbied for more national wildlife sanctuaries and also began to open bird sanctuaries of its own. In 1924, it opened its first sanctuaries: the Rainey Sanctuary in the marshes of Louisiana and the Theodore Roosevelt Sanctuary on Long Island, New York. That same year Congress also approved the Upper Mississippi Wildlife and Fish Refuge. Then, in 1929, Congress passed the Norbeck-Andersen Act which allocated funds for the buying of additional wetlands as refuges.

In 1931, Rosalie Edge (1877–1962) challenged Audubon leadership when she learned the society was profiting from muskrat trapping at the Rainey Sanctuary in Louisiana. Her very public attacks against leadership and its practices continued for several years and weakened the Audubon Association's public prestige. Pearson was criticized for a proposed partnership with a gun manufacturer who wanted to work to preserve wild game and for declining memberships (caused both by Edge's attacks and the Great Depression) and was forced out of the presidency in 1934. He was replaced by John Baker, an investment banker and avid birdwatcher, who became the executive director and Kermit Roosevelt, son of Theodore Roosevelt, became president. The following year it purchased *Bird-Lore* from Chapman, known today as *Audubon* magazine.

During Baker's tenure as leader of the association, it opened the Audubon Nature Camp on Hog Island off Maine's coast and began hosting conservation education for adults in 1936. It soon also began to provide research fellowships for scientific studies of endangered birds and publish their findings in *Audubon Research Reports*. In 1937, Congress passed the Pittman-Robertson Act that placed an excise tax on guns and ammunition used for hunting that would be used to fund wildlife restoration projects, including those that helped restore birds' habitats. In 1945, Carl Buchheister joined Audubon leadership as vice president and persuaded local bird clubs to become branches of the Audubon Society, establishing the basis for the branch and chapter system it still uses today.

While the National Audubon Society's efforts came too late to save the passenger pigeon (extinct in 1914) and the Carolina parakeet (extinct by 1939), it helped protect a number of once threatened birds from similar fates. For example, the California condor, the brown pelican, and the Northern spotted owl are all species that benefited from its efforts in the 20th century. The Christmas Bird Count, first proposed by Chapman in *Bird-Lore* in 1900, has spread throughout the world and serves an important tool for measuring bird populations. Meanwhile, the National Audubon Society's number of sanctuaries and centers has grown to 41, and it has designated 2,500 important bird areas where it works to protect bird habitats. It continues to support scientific research, lobby legislators to protect birds, and engage in conservation. By 2015, its work was supported by almost 500 local chapters and a budget of roughly $100 million. Its membership remains a committed partnership of ornithologists, citizen scientists, and avid birdwatchers.

Laurie L. Rice

Related Primary Document: **The Lacey Act (1900)**

The Lacey Act (1900)

The Lacey Act of 1900 was the first federal environmental conservation law ever passed in the United States, and it had resounding implications that stand today. The Act prohibited the transfer of any animals (including birds and fish) that were obtained through illegal practices. Though the Lacey Act was primarily related to hunting, the federal government was concerned that certain species could be exploited for sale across state borders or abroad. It penalized those who failed to correctly document any cargo containing wildlife. The act set the stage for the Migratory Bird Treaty Act of 1918, which later transformed into a debate over the balance of state and federal powers. The Lacey Act of 1900 has been expanded multiple times since its enactment to protect plants (both native and nonnative) and plant products, as well more obscure classes of animals. The following document is an excerpt of the act.

An Act to enlarge the Powers of the Department of Agriculture, prohibit the transportation by Interstate Commerce of Game killed in Violation of Local Laws, and for other Purposes.

Be it enacted by the Senate and House of Representatives in the United States of America in Congress assembled,

That the duties and powers of the Department of Agriculture are hereby enlarged so as to include the preservation, distribution, introduction, and restoration of game-birds and other wild birds. The Secretary of Agriculture is hereby authorized to adopt such measures as may be necessary to carry out the purposes of this act and to purchase such game-birds and other wild birds as may be required therefor, subject, however, to the laws of the various States and Territories. The object and purpose of this act is to aid in the restoration of such birds in those parts of the United States adapted thereto where the same have become scarce or extinct, and also to regulate the introduction of American or foreign birds or animals in localities where they have not heretofore existed.

The Secretary of Agriculture shall from time to time collect and publish useful information as to the propagation, uses, and preservation of such birds. And the Secretary of Agriculture shall make and publish all needful rules and regulations for carrying out the purposes of this act, and shall expend for said purposes such sums as Congress may appropriate therefor.

SEC. 2.—That it shall be unlawful for any person or persons to import into the United States any foreign wild animal or bird except under special permit from the United States Department of Agriculture: Provided, That

nothing in this section shall restrict the importation of natural history speci-
mens for museums or scientific collections or the importation of certain cage
birds, such as domesticated canaries, parrots, or such other species as the
Secretary of Agriculture may designate.

The importation of the mongoose, the so-called "flying-foxes" or fruit bats,
the English sparrow, the starling, or such other birds or animals as the Secretary of Agriculture may from time to time declare injurious to the interest of
agriculture or horticulture is hereby prohibited, and such species upon arrival
at any of the ports of the United States shall be destroyed or returned at the
expense of the owner. The Secretary of the Treasury is hereby authorized to
make regulations for carrying into effect the provisions of this section.

SEC. 3.—That it shall be unlawful for any person or persons to deliver to any
common carrier or for any common carrier to transport from one State or
Territory to another State or Territory, or from the District of Columbia or
Alaska to any State or Territory, or from any State or Territory to the District
of Columbia or Alaska, any foreign animals or birds the importation of
which is prohibited, or the dead bodies or parts thereof of any wild animals
or birds where such animals or birds have been killed in violation of the laws
of the State, Territory, or District in which the same were killed: Provided,
That nothing herein shall prevent the transportation of any dead birds or
animals killed during the season when the same may be lawfully captured
and the export of which is not prohibited by law in the State, Territory, or
District in which the same are killed.

SEC. 4.—That all packages containing such dead animals, birds, or parts
thereof, when shipped by interstate commerce, as provided in Section 1 of
this act, shall be plainly and clearly marked, so that the name and address of
the shipper and the nature of the contents may be readily ascertained on
inspection of the outside of such packages. For each evasion or violation of
this act the shipper shall, upon conviction, pay a fine of not exceeding two
hundred dollars; and the consignee knowingly receiving such articles so
shipped and transported in violation of this act shall, upon conviction, pay a
fine of not exceeding two hundred dollars; and the carrier knowingly carrying or transporting the same shall, upon conviction, pay a fine of not exceeding two hundred dollars.

SEC. 5.—That all dead bodies, or parts thereof, of any foreign game-animals
or game- or song-birds, the importation of which is prohibited, or the dead
bodies or parts thereof of any wild game-animals or game- or song-birds
transported into any State or Territory, or remaining therein for use, consumption, sale, or storage therein, shall, upon arrival in such State or Territory, be subject to the operation and effect of the laws of such State or
Territory enacted in the exercise of its police powers, to the same extent and
in the same manner as though such animals and birds had been produced in
such State or Territory, and shall not be exempt therefrom by reason of being
introduced therein in original packages or otherwise. This act shall not

prevent the importation, transportation, or sale of birds or bird plumage manufactured from the feathers of barn-yard fowl.

Source: "The Lacey Bird Law." In *Birds in Their Relations to Man: A Manual of Economic Ornithology for the United States and Canada*, edited by Clarence M. Weed and Ned Dearborn. Philadelphia, PA: J.B. Lippincott, 1903, 320–322.

Related Primary Document: **Migratory Bird Treaty Act (1918, Amended 2004)**

Migratory Bird Treaty Act (1918, Amended 2004)

The Migratory Bird Treaty Act of 1918, which was one of the first pieces of federal legislature concerning the environment in the United States, forbids the transfer of migratory birds and game mammals through all means in an effort to preserve the species and their environments. The treaty did not differentiate between living or deceased animals, though it did allow migratory birds to be bred under proper protocol for sale as food. Perhaps benevolent on the surface, this treaty garners more significance than meets the eye. The categorization of "migratory" birds is crucial, as the United States claimed that such birds crossed international borders and were therefore subject to federal regulation. Yet some states argued that this was not always the case, sued for jurisdiction, and often won. Thus, federal and state governments were at odds. The treaty was then disputed in the Supreme Court in 1920 over whether the government could constitutionally regulate the land as a federal entity, especially as the land pertained to hunting practices in different states. In the case, called State of Missouri v. Holland, 252 U.S. 416 (1920), the Supreme Court ruled that treaties are protected in the Constitution under the treaty enforcing authority of Congress and are therefore above state affairs. The case became precedent for other international and environmental treaties that followed. The following document is the treaty upheld by the court.

MIGRATORY BIRD TREATY ACT

[Chapter 128, Approved July 3, 1918, 40 Stat. 703]

[As Amended Through P.L. 108–447, Enacted December 8, 2004]

CHAP. 128.—An Act to give effect to the conventions between the United States and other nations for the protection of migratory birds, birds in danger of extinction, game mammals, and their environment.

Be it enacted by the Senate and House of Representatives of the United States of America in Congress assembled, That this Act shall be known by the short title of the "Migratory Bird Treaty Act."

SEC. 2. 16 U.S.C. 703 (a) IN GENERAL.—Unless and except as permitted by regulations made as hereinafter provided, it shall be unlawful at any time, by any means or in any manner, to pursue, hunt, take, capture, kill, attempt to take, capture, or kill, possess, offer for sale, sell, offer to barter, barter, offer to purchase, purchase, deliver for shipment, ship, export, import, cause to be shipped, exported, or imported, deliver for transportation, transport or cause to be transported, carry or cause to be carried, or receive for shipment, transportation, carriage, or export, any migratory bird, any part, nest, or egg of any such bird, or any product, whether or not manufactured, which consists, or is composed in whole or part, of any such bird or any part, nest, or egg thereof, included in the terms of the conventions between the United States and Great Britain for the protection of migratory birds concluded August 16, 1916, the United States and the United Mexican States for the protection of migratory birds and game mammals concluded February 7, 1936, the United States and the Government of Japan for the protection of migratory birds and birds in danger of extinction, and their environment concluded March 4, 1972 and the convention between the United States and the Union of Soviet Socialist Republics for the conservation of migratory birds and their environments concluded November 19, 1976.

(b) LIMITATION ON APPLICATION TO INTRODUCED SPECIES.—

(1) IN GENERAL.—This Act applies only to migratory bird species that are native to the United States or its territories.

(2) NATIVE TO THE UNITED STATES DEFINED.—

(A) IN GENERAL.—Subject to subparagraph (B), in this subsection the term "native to the United States or its territories" means occurring in the United States or its territories as the result of natural biological or ecological processes.

(B) TREATMENT OF INTRODUCED SPECIES.—For purposes of paragraph (1), a migratory bird species that occurs in the United States or its territories solely as a result of intentional or unintentional human-assisted introduction shall not be considered native to the United States or its territories unless—

(i) it was native to the United States or its territories and extant in 1918;

(ii) it was extirpated after 1918 throughout its range in the United States and its territories; and

(iii) after such extirpation, it was reintroduced in the United States or its territories as a part of a program carried out by a Federal agency.

SEC. 3. 16 U.S.C. 704 (a) That subject to the provisions and in order to carry out the purposes of the conventions, the Secretary of Agriculture is authorized and directed, from time to time, having due regard to the zones of temperature and to the distribution, abundance, economic value, breeding habits, and times and lines of migratory flight of such birds, to determine when, to what extent, if at all, and by what means, it is compatible with the terms of the conventions to allow hunting, taking, capture, killing, possession, sale, purchase, shipment, transportation, carriage, or export of any such bird, or any part, nest, or egg thereof, and to adopt suitable regulations permitting and governing the same, in accordance with such determinations, which regulations shall become effective when approved by the President.

(b) It shall be unlawful for any person to—

(1) take any migratory game bird by the aid of baiting, or on or over any baited area, if the person knows or reasonably should know that the area is a baited area; or

(2) place or direct the placement of bait on or adjacent to an area for the purpose of causing, inducing, or allowing any person to take or attempt to take any migratory game bird by the aid of baiting on or over the baited area.

SEC. 4. 16 U.S.C. 705 That it shall be unlawful to ship, transport, or carry, by any means whatever, from one State, Territory, or District to or through another State, Territory, or District, or to or through a foreign country, any bird, or any part, nest, or egg thereof, captured, killed, taken, shipped, transported, or carried at any time contrary to the laws of the State, Territory, or District in which it was captured, killed, or taken, or from which it was shipped, transported, or carried. It shall be unlawful to import any bird, or any part, nest, or egg thereof, captured, killed, taken, shipped, transported, or carried contrary to the laws of any Province of the Dominion of Canada in which the same was captured, killed, or taken, or from which it was shipped, transported, or carried.

SEC. 5. 16 U.S.C. 706 That any employee of the Department of Agriculture authorized by the Secretary of Agriculture to enforce the provisions of this Act shall have power, without warrant, to arrest any person committing a violation of this Act in his presence or view and to take such person immediately for examination or trial before an officer or court of competent jurisdiction; shall have power to execute any warrant or other process issued by an officer or court of competent jurisdiction for the enforcement of the provisions of this Act; and shall have authority, with a search warrant, to search any place. The several judges of the courts established under the laws of the United States, and United States commissioners may, within their respective jurisdictions, upon proper oath or affirmation showing probable cause, issue warrants in all such cases. All birds, or parts, nests, or eggs thereof, captured, killed, taken, sold or offered for sale, bartered or offered for barter, purchased, shipped, transported, carried, imported, exported, or possessed contrary to the provisions of this Act or of any regulation prescribed thereunder shall, when found, be seized and, upon conviction of the offender or upon judgment of a court of the United States that the same were captured, killed, taken, sold or offered for sale, bartered or offered for barter, purchased, shipped, transported, carried, imported, exported, or possessed contrary to the provisions of this Act or of any regulation prescribed thereunder, shall be forfeited to the United States and disposed of by the Secretary of the Interior in such manner as he deems appropriate.

SEC. 6. 16 U.S.C. 707 (a) Except as otherwise provided in this section, any person, association, partnership, or corporation who shall violate any provisions of said conventions or of this Act, or who shall violate or fail to comply with any regulation made pursuant to this Act shall be deemed guilty of a misdemeanor and upon conviction thereof shall be fined not more than $15,000 or be imprisoned not more than six months, or both.

(b) Whoever, in violation of this Act, shall knowingly—

(1) take by any manner whatsoever any migratory bird with intent to sell, offer to sell, barter or offer to barter such bird, or

(2) sell, offer for sale, barter or offer to barter, any migratory bird shall be guilty of a felony and shall be fined not more than $2,000 or imprisoned not more than two years, or both.

(c) Whoever violates section 3(b)(2) shall be fined under title 18, United States Code, imprisoned not more than 1 year, or both.

(d) All guns, traps, nets and other equipment, vessels, vehicles, and other means of transportation used by any person when engaged in pursuing, hunting, taking, trapping, ensnaring, capturing, killing, or attempting to take, capture, or kill any migratory bird in violation of this Act with the intent to offer for sale, or sell, or offer for barter, or barter such bird in violation of this Act shall be forfeited to the United States and may be seized and held pending the prosecution of any person arrested for violating this Act and upon conviction for such violation, such forfeiture shall be adjudicated as a penalty in addition to any other provided for violation of this Act. Such forfeited property shall be disposed of and counted for by, and under the authority of, the Secretary of the Interior.

SEC. 7. 16 U.S.C. 708 That nothing in this Act shall be construed to prevent the several States and Territories from making or enforcing laws or regulations not inconsistent with the provisions of said conventions or of this Act, or from making or enforcing laws or regulations which shall give further protection to migratory birds, their nests, and eggs, if such laws or regulations do not extend the open seasons for such birds beyond the dates approved by the President in accordance with section three of this Act.

SEC. 8. 16 U.S.C. 709 That until the adoption and approval, pursuant to section three of this Act, of regulations dealing with migratory birds and their nests and eggs, such migratory birds and their nests and eggs as are intended and used exclusively for scientific or propagating purposes may be taken, captured, killed, possessed, sold, purchased, shipped, and transported for such scientific or propagating purposes if and to the extent not in conflict with the laws of the State, Territory, or District in which they are taken, captured, killed, possessed, sold, or purchased, or in or from which they are shipped or transported if the packages containing the dead bodies or the nests or eggs of such birds when shipped and transported shall be marked on the outside thereof so as accurately and clearly to show the name and address of the shipper and the contents of the package.

SEC. 9. 16 U.S.C. 709a That there is authorized to be appropriated, from time to time, out of any money in the Treasury not otherwise appropriated, such amounts as may be necessary to carry out the provisions and to accomplish the purposes of said conventions and this Act and regulations made pursuant thereto, and the Secretary of Agriculture is authorized out of such moneys to employ in the city of Washington and elsewhere such persons and means as he may deem necessary for such purpose and may cooperate with local authorities in the protection of migratory birds and make the necessary investigations connected therewith.

SEC. 10. 16 U.S.C. 710 That if any clause, sentence, paragraph, or part of this Act shall, for any reason, be adjudged by any court of competent jurisdiction to be invalid, such judgment shall not affect, impair, or invalidate the remainder thereof, but shall be confined in its operation to the clause, sentence, paragraph, or part thereof directly involved in the controversy in which such judgment shall have been rendered.

SEC. 11. That all Acts or parts of Acts inconsistent with the provisions of this Act are hereby repealed.

SEC. 12. 16 U.S.C. 711 Nothing in this Act shall be construed to prevent the breeding of migratory game birds on farms and preserves and the sale of birds so bred under proper regulation for the purpose of increasing the food supply.

SEC. 13. That this Act shall become effective immediately upon its passage and approval.

Source: Migratory Bird Treaty Act of 1918 (16 U.S.C. 703-712; Ch. 128; July 3, 1918; 40 Stat. 755) as amended by: Chapter 634; June 20, 1936; 49 Stat. 1556; P.L. 86-732; September 8, 1960; 74 Stat. 866; P.L. 90-578; October 17, 1968; 82 Stat. 1118; P.L. 91-135; December 5, 1969; 83 Stat. 282; P.L. 93-300; June 1, 1974; 88 Stat. 190; P.L. 95-616; November 8, 1978; 92 Stat. 3111; P.L. 99-645; November 10, 1986; 100 Stat. 3590 and P.L. 105-312; October 30, 1998; 112 Stat. 2956.

See also: Natural Resources Defense Council (1970–); National Wildlife Federation (1936–); Resources for the Future (1952–)

Further Reading

Graham, Frank Jr., with Carl W. Buchheister. 1990. *The Audubon Ark: A History of the National Audubon Society.* New York: Alfred A. Knopf.

Line, Les, ed. 1999. *The National Audubon Society: Speaking for Nature: A Century of Conservation.* New York: Hugh Lauter Levin Associates, Inc.

Orr, Oliver H. Jr. 1992. *Saving American Birds: T. Gilbert Pearson and the Founding of the Audubon Movement.* Gainesville, FL: University Press of Florida.

Pearson, Thomas Gilbert. 1937. *Adventures in Bird Protection.* New York: D. Appleton Century Company.

National Committee for an Effective Congress (1948–)

The National Committee for an Effective Congress (NCEC) is an influential PAC organized to improve the quality of the national government by supporting progressive, liberal-minded candidates for the U.S. Senate and the U.S. House of Representatives. Eleanor Roosevelt (1884–1962), Maurice Rosenblatt (1915–2005), Harry Louis Selden (1908–2004), and other leading liberals founded NCEC in 1948 to help elect progressive candidates to the U.S. Senate and to defend the domestic and foreign policy of the New Deal from conservative attacks. Its primary means for accomplishing this mission involved distributing campaign contributions and endorsements to liberal and moderate Democratic and Republican congressional candidates. NCEC's mission and electoral activities have changed drastically from this independent, nonpartisan PAC to a staunchly pro-Democratic organization that works closely with Democratic candidates and party committees for Senate and House elections. The committee has evolved from its traditional work and capacity of supporting candidates financially and now has become an important provider of in-kind campaign technical assistance.

The NCEC emerged in American politics to support and ensure the victory of "forward-looking," "constructive," and "progressive" candidates who would work in Congress to give the American people "responsive, humane" government. The committee did not speak for any section of the United States, any interest or any special group, but rather supported congressional candidates who would work "to preserve and advance the liberties and rights of all Americans" (Poole 1978). In addition, the NCEC sought to influence the formation and implementation of national public policy along liberal lines. NCEC distinguished its activities from other prominent political groups at the time by limiting its role to fund-raising and to giving campaign contributions directly to general election candidates. The NCEC did not focus on candidate recruitment, voter mobilization or strategic planning with the main Democratic Party machine. The NCEC emphasized its pragmatic, centralized role as an independent, congressional elections organization.

During its early history, the NCEC attempted to provide bipartisan electoral assistance for people already politically astute and knowledgeable. The influential PAC concerned its resources foremost on campaigns, but also engaged in related educational activities, including the publication of newsletters and the formation of research organizations, such as the Fair Campaign Practices Committee and the McCarthy Clearinghouse. Beginning with the 1948 election and then continuing through the elections of the 1950s, the NCEC identified and supported Senate candidates who were self-starting, independent liberals, in need of campaign funds, and likely to win. The committee focused on senatorial contests because of the relatively small number of candidates, allowing for a manageable practice and exercise in electoral politics. Moreover, the potential successes would mean NCEC had more influence on those leaders shaping national policies. In the 1952 election, the NCEC first collected almost 400 individual contributions and distributed these funds to liberal candidates. It also experimented with direct-mail fund-raising to raise $13,000, accounting for roughly half its total candidate disbursements.

NCEC became one of the pioneers, not only in direct-mail fund-raising but also in initiating personal meetings between candidates and potential financial backers and campaign supporters. These successful "meet and greets" for candidates and supporters resulted in NCEC becoming a significant broker in the campaign finance community. The NCEC contributed to the victories of progressive candidates and enabled the Democratic Party to maintain control of Congress throughout most of the first three decades post-World War II.

By the late 1970s, the NCEC reported contributions and income approaching half a million dollars. Over the next two decades, it increased its fund-raising capabilities, amassing contributions in excess of $2 million. NCEC campaign contribution receipts increased significantly, with over $2.5 million collected in 2000. Since 2004, NCEC contributions have declined, and over the last three electoral cycles (2012, 2014 and 2016), the committee has expensed less than $400,000 on candidate campaigns (Center for Responsive Politics 2017).

Holding to its mission and philosophy to elect liberal officeholders, the NCEC continued its distinctive position to elicit monetary support and to contribute funds to candidates in marginal Senate and House district races. However, technological and legal developments in the political environment led NCEC to innovate and rethink its role in congressional elections. Instead of only giving cash to its candidates of choice, NCEC began to provide campaign services to candidates. The committee supplied candidates and campaigns with electoral data, including polling and precinct voter demographics, media services, and campaign strategic analysis.

Nevertheless, Ronald Reagan's (1911–2004) election to the presidency in 1980 along with the Republican Party's landslide victories had a decisive effect on the NCEC. The committee recognized that Democratic control of Congress secured its liberal agenda, and without a Democratic majority, that agenda could not be guaranteed. Therefore, the NCEC rejected its previous bipartisan orientation to become a fully pro-Democratic partisan political action committee. By 1986, NCEC would no longer identify Republicans with proper moderate, liberal credentials. The committee instead turned its full attention to assisting and electing Democrats.

The NCEC has evolved in the 21st century as an influential, partisan Democratic PAC that disseminates campaign information, strategic campaign assistance, and small candidate contributions. The NCEC's key political concern is on maintaining and enlarging the Democratic congressional majorities; therefore, the committee does not focus on lobbying or advancing specific policy agendas. It continues to choose liberal, progressive candidates and campaigns to assist in order to advance the Democratic Party in Congress. NCEC selects first those candidates who are Democrats, and then it evaluates the competitiveness of electoral contests. It provides electoral assistance to those candidates with well-organized campaigns and the means to utilize the PAC's in-kind services and small contributions. Most NCEC monies and campaign data assistance are targeted to Democratic incumbents who are in electoral jeopardy or Democratic contestants in marginal, close partisan districts. NCEC's political strength lies in its formulation of campaign strategies for Democrats, its ability to connect individuals and groups to candidates, its precinct-level elections data, and the campaign assistance offered in data analysis and media-targeted services.

Members of the NCEC are diverse individuals, representing all regions of the United States. Historically, members of the committee were chosen on the basis of their liberal credentials, prominence in elite political and social circles, and the impact their names could have on the PAC's ability to fund-raise. The NCEC had four officers—chairman, vice chairman, secretary, and treasurer—along with an executive board composed of 7 to 15 members. Over time, its influential members and supporters of NCEC have included James Roosevelt (1907–1991), California Democratic representative; Robert E. Sherwood (1896–1955), the playwright; Frederick Lewis Allen (1890–1954), former editor of *Harper's* magazine; Evans Clark (1888–1970), director of the 20th Century Fund; Sumner Wells (1892–1961), former secretary of state; General Telford Taylor (1908–1998), U.S. prosecutor at the Nuremburg Trials; Oscar Hammerstein II (1895–1960), songwriter; Walter Mondale (1928–), vice president of the United States; and Andrew Young (1932–), former representative from Georgia and UN ambassador. Today, any individual may contribute and donate to the NCEC and its mission to support Democratic candidates and campaigns. Small-dollar donors as well as wealthy individuals, estates, and foundations' gifts provide necessary resources in order for Democratic candidates and campaigns to garner NCEC data, analysis, and financial support at no cost to them.

The National Committee for an Effective Congress has significantly changed in its 70-year existence. Founded as an organization for contributing campaign funds to liberal candidates for the U.S. Senate, NCEC has become a resolute Democratic political organization working to elect Democratic candidates to both the U.S. Senate and House. The NCEC leads Democratic political action committees in America as one that disseminates key electoral and campaign information to the Democratic Party, its candidates, other PAC and interest group organizations, and contributors.

Karen L. Owen

See also: Americans for Democratic Action (1947–); Democratic Party (1828–); MoveOn.org (1998–); Progressive Democrats of America (2004–)

Further Reading

Biersack, Robert, Paul S. Herrnson, and Clyde Wilcox, eds. 1994. *Risky Business? PAC Decisionmaking in Congressional Elections.* Armonk, NY: M. E. Sharpe.

Center for Responsive Politics. 2017. "The National Committee for an Effective Congress." Open Secrets. https://www.opensecrets.org/orgs/totals.php?id=D000000 0146&cycle=2016.

National Committee for an Effective Congress. www.ncec.org.

Poole, William. 1978. "Political Process Report. The National Committee for an Effective Congress." The Heritage Foundation. http://www.heritage.org/political-process /report/the-national-committee-effective-congress.

Scoble, Harry M. 1967. *Ideology and Electoral Action: A Comparative Case Study of the National Committee for an Effective Congress.* San Francisco: Chandler Publishing.

National Conference of State Legislatures (1975–)

The National Conference of State Legislatures (NCSL) is a bipartisan organization whose mission is to serve and support state legislatures and their members and staffs and to enhance the role of the states in the federal system of government. In order to do this, the NCSL provides a variety of services, including researching and monitoring legislation that may affect state politics. NCSL also maintains a 501(c)(3) foundation, the NCSL Foundation for State Legislatures, that engages corporations and other organizations with state legislatures. NCSL's offices are located in Denver, Colorado, and Washington, D.C.

Up until the 1970s, there were three separate national organizations for state legislators: the National Legislative Conference, the National Conference of State Legislative Leaders, and the National Society of State Legislators. The groups began negotiating a merger in 1971, and though these particular discussions broke down, the three began cooperating on a broad, common set of issues, most notably in the area of federal representation.

In 1973, legislators William Ratchford (1934–2011) (D-CT), Charles Kurfess (1930–) (R-OH), Herbert Fineman (1920–2016) (D-PA), George Firestone (1931–2012) (D-FL), Tom Jensen (1935–2018) (R-TN), and staffers William Snodgrass (1922–2008) (TN) and George McManus (PA) revived the merger talks, commissioning Alan Rosenthal (1932–2013) and the Eagleton Institute of Politics to create and implement a survey of state legislators and their staffs about the need for a consolidated national organization. In August 1974 the three existing organizations met in Albuquerque, New Mexico, and voted to dissolve their respective organizations in favor of the National Conference of State Legislatures as of January 1, 1975.

As the first order of business, the newly formed NCSL executive committee was tasked with choosing an executive director. There were several candidates nominated, two of whom had been directors at the predecessor organizations. The executive committee ultimately selected Earl S. Mackey (1938–), a former member of the Missouri House of Representatives and a staffer in the U.S. Senate as the first NCSL director. Mackey served as the director for 12 years and was succeeded in 1987 by William T. Pound, then Joshua Franzel who remains in the position as of 2019.

The merger of the three organizations into the one National Conference of State Legislatures has had a direct impact on how NCSL is organized and managed. Each of the original groups had some key issues that it wanted addressed within this new organization, and each left a legacy that can still be seen in the structure of NCSL. The National Conference of Legislative Leaders, for example, wanted to make sure that legislative leadership continued to play an important role in the new organization, so the bylaws require that the president of NCSL and at least 10 members of the executive committee be made up of legislative leadership. Similarly, the National Legislative Conference argued for the continuing support for legislative staff; thus the bylaws state that three of the officers shall be staff and that staff shall be represented on the executive committee in a 1:2 ratio with legislators.

Day-to-day operations of the organization are in the hands of the executive director; however, NCSL is actually governed by a 63-member executive committee. This committee consists of 7 officers (including a legislator serving as president and a staffer serving as staff chair), 30 at-large members, 4 regional legislators drawn from the Council of State Government, 6 ex-officio members, and 16 legislative staff members. In the spirit of the bipartisan nature of the organization, each year the NCSL presidency alternates between legislators of the Democratic and Republican parties. In 1994, 20 years after its inception, NCSL got its first female president, Karen McCarthy (1947–2010) (D- MO), followed four years later by its first black president, Daniel Blue (1949–) (D-NC).

The executive committee is charged with managing NCSL's funds and implementing its policies; however, the decision-making power of the organization resides largely in the membership. Annual meeting participants elect officers and executive committee members, adopt policy positions, approve the budget, and review audit reports.

NCSL has nine standing committees that are composed of legislators and legislative staff appointed by organizational leadership. These committees are as follows: Budgets and Revenue; Communications, Financial Services and Interstate Commerce; Education; Elections and Redistricting; Health and Human Services; Labor and Economic Development; Law, Criminal Justice, and Public Safety; Legislative Effectiveness; and Natural Resources and Infrastructure.

NCSL also adopts policies that inform the lobbying efforts made by their staff in Washington, D.C. For example, NCSL took the position recently that states should have the right to regulate gaming and sports betting without federal interference. They, along with other national organizations, filed an amicus brief in support of the states' position on the issue, and in May 2018, the Supreme Court agreed, striking down the 25-year-old Professional and Amateur Sports Protection Act.

When issues arise that span multiple committee jurisdictions or that have a temporal aspect, NCSL creates task forces. Unlike the permanent standing committees, task forces are temporary, created for a specific time period and for a particular topic or problem. These task forces are generally made up of 20–30 legislators and legislative staff appointed by the NCSL president or staff chair. There are 7 task forces: Agriculture; Energy Supply; Immigration and the States; International Relations; Military and Veterans Affairs; and State and local Taxation.

The mission statement of NCSL is as follows: "NCSL is committed to the success of all legislators and staff. Our mission is to improve the quality and effectiveness of state legislatures; promote policy innovation and communication among state legislatures; and ensure state legislatures a strong, cohesive voice in the federal system."

In order to fulfill its mission, NCSL hosts two annual live events, the Capitol Forum and the Legislative Summit. The Capitol Forum is a meeting of the NCSL standing committees, the main organizational unit of NCSL. The Forum gives committees an opportunity to come together and address important state and federal issues and to develop the policies and agendas that drive the organization. This meeting's location rotates between Washington, D.C., and other locations within the sates.

Each summer NCSL holds its Legislative Summit, which is the largest meeting of its type in the country. In addition to meetings of the standing committees and task forces, the Summit regularly features over 100 sessions for more than 5,000 attendees. This meeting also features keynote speakers that are nationally or internationally known experts on salient issues. The location of the Legislative Summit moves from city to city each year.

In addition to the Capitol Forum and the Legislative Summit, NCLS supports the legislative community by hosting web seminars, leadership meetings, and access to online documents and databases throughout the year. From the organization's inception, NCSL's staff has prioritized the dissemination of information in a prompt, accurate, and bipartisan manner. In order to do this in the most efficient way, in the late 1970s, it developed an electronic information exchange system called LEGISNET. In the mid-1990s the system was made available through an electronic bulletin board system and ultimately evolved to an Internet database. Today there are over 500,000 documents available to legislators and their staffs via NCSLnet.

NCSL has also been involved in providing additional training and professional development programs for legislative staff. The development of these programs was initially facilitated by a grant called Project TRAIN from the federal government under the Intergovernmental Personnel Act, beginning in 1976. Even though this grant is no longer funded, NCSL has continued to provide these programs for legislative staffers.

The organization also has a flagship publication, the *State Legislatures* magazine, which has been in circulation since 1975. It is currently published 10 times per year as a modern four-color print magazine and is also offered online.

Today, NCSL is involved in more than 100 programs in more than three-quarters of the states in the United States each year. Further, in the 1990s NCSL expanded its reach, moving into the international arena to provide support for emerging democracies in the areas of federalism and state governance.

Jayme Renfro

See also: National Governors Association (1908–); National School Boards Association (1942–)

Further Reading

Greenblatt, A. 2018. "Why It's So Hard for Lawmakers to Win Governor's Races." *Governing.* http://www.governing.com/topics/politics/gov-lawmakers-governor-races-2018-elections.html.

Marijuana Policy Project. 2017. "National Conference of State Legislatures Urges De-Scheduling Marijuana." MPP. https://www.mpp.org/news/press/national-conference-state-legislatures-urges-de-scheduling-marijuana/.

Odom, C. 2018. "Model Act Clarifies Procedural Issues in State Partnership Audits." *Bloomberg BNA*, March 26, 2018. https://www.bna.com/model-act-clarifies-n57982090381/.

Prete, R., and K. Basu. 2018. "Backers of Federal Digital Tax Provision Come Up Empty-Handed." *Bloomberg BNA*, March 21, 2018. https://www.bna.com/backers-federal-digital-n57982090167/.

National Congress of American Indians (1944–)

The National Congress of American Indians (NCAI) is the oldest and largest intertribal interest group in the country. The NCAI advocates for broad interests of American Indian tribal governments and American Indian communities at a national level. Since its founding in 1944, the NCAI has continued to pursue its original purpose to offer a forum for policy developments among all tribal governments in the United States. The NCAI has focused on federal policy related to tribal governance and treaty rights, economic development, and health and welfare. The NCAI also has a goal of educating the general public about American Indian and Native Alaskan tribes.

Prior to the organization of the NCAI, American Indian tribes had been subject to a history of profound mistreatment by the federal government. The original inhabitants of North America, American Indian tribes (also known as First Nations), were initially approached as political sovereigns and engaged in a government-to-government relationship through treaty making in the 18th and early 19th centuries. The federal government, however, did not honor the terms of the treaties, and by the late 18th century had ended treaty making entirely. Native peoples were subject to forced removals, military aggression, and the widespread loss of land.

The needs and concerns of American Indians in the 20th century were deeply connected to disastrous national Indian policy during the 1800s. At the close of the 19th century, the toll on American Indian peoples and nations was enormous. After the forced removals and relocations of the 1800s, the scope of the United States had reached the western edge of the continent, and yet pressure for land continued. Federal policy shifted to allotment, further going against already broken promises for Native peoples to be secure in their lands. Allotment policy meant that tribal reservation lands would be broken up into parcels for individuals and families (or "allotted"), and the surplus (which was often extensive) went to the federal government or states to keep or allocate to white settlers. By the close of the Allotment period, 118 out of 234 reservations had been allotted and 90 million acres removed from reservation status.

Allotment was a disaster for Indian peoples. The land allotted to American Indians was generally too small and not well suited for agriculture; the ostensible goal to turn them into self-sustaining farmers was a dismal failure. At the same time, the push to end tribal communities meant even fewer supports for impoverished Indians. The Meriam Report of 1928, commissioned by the federal government to investigate the situation of American Indians, made it clear that federal policies, particularly Allotment, had been a failure for Indian peoples.

The organization of the NCAI began to take shape in the wake of the Great Depression and the emergence of the New Deal, during the presidency of

President Franklin Delano Roosevelt (1882–1945). Roosevelt appointed John Collier (1884–1968) as the commissioner of Indian Affairs, a position which he held from 1933–1945. Collier, a sociologist who had worked with several tribes on land rights, was a strong advocate for ending Allotment and supporting tribal culture and government. Collier proposed what would become the Indian Reorganization Act (IRA) of 1934 as a means of restoring tribal government. As part of developing the IRA, Collier organized a series of meetings with multiple tribes throughout the 1930s. These conferences helped bring together tribal leaders and supported the development of inter-tribal networks. These connections were very significant for helping to form the NCAI.

The NCAI is the oldest intertribal organization in the United States, but it was not the first. Prior to the organization of the NCAI in 1944, a few other pan-Indian organizations proved viable for only short periods of time. The Society of American Indians (SAI) was founded in 1911 in Columbus, Ohio, by Indians who had integrated into American society and promoted further assimilation for all Indians. The SAI failed to gain enough support or unify various urban and reservation communities, and it faded by the mid-1920s. Gertrude Bonnin (1876–1938), who also went by the name Zitkala-Sa, had served as the secretary of the SAI and its liaison in Washington and went on to found the National Council of American Indians in 1926. The National Council of American Indians advocated for citizenship rights, educational opportunities, and cultural preservation for American Indians. The National Council of American Indians was short-lived as it failed to gather widespread support in Indian country. The American Indian Federation (AIF) was organized in 1934 to counter the policies of reorganization under John Collier. The AIF attacked the IRA as a government-imposed plot and supported Indian assimilation. The AIF broke apart due to internal disagreements by the mid-1940s.

These early Indian organizations, while not pursuing the same goals, represented advocacy that went beyond tribal identities to create pan-tribal organizations. They were based on individual membership. The NCAI was distinct in its organization as it was initially established as both a federated body (with tribal entities as members) and as an individual membership organization.

The initial meeting of the NCAI was in Denver, Colorado. The Constitutional Convention of the NCAI in 1944 brought together almost 80 delegates from 50 tribes and associations. The founding members were focused on promoting tribal unity and cooperation, working for the security and protection of treaty rights, and improving the quality of life for American Indian people. In particular, the founders of the NCAI sought to ensure the continuation of federal governmental and tribal agreements and secure the federal government's obligations to those tribes under those agreements.

The NCAI's objectives were to work as a pan-tribal organization to influence federal policy through established government channels, such as lobbying and litigation. One the first priorities of the NCAI was to file lawsuits in Arizona and New Mexico to support Indian voting rights. All American Indians had become federal citizens in 1924, but several states continued to discriminate against American Indian prospective voters. Another early priority also represented a widespread concern: a call to create the Indian Claims Commission (ICC) to resolve Indian land claims against the government.

One of the major early victories of the NCAI was the creation of the ICC. This represented the success of a variety of very different interests whose advocates, for different reasons, felt that the federal government needed to create a mechanism to hear and resolve the outstanding claims of American Indian tribes against the federal government related to violations of treaty arrangements. The ICC was established in 1946 when President Harry S. Truman signed the ICC's enabling legislation into law. The ICC was empowered to resolve Indian claims with financial compensation. It was inundated with tribal claims and operated, with multiple extensions, from 1948–1978.

Another concern of the NCAI related to federal legislative support for policies of termination, which would end federal recognition and accompanying obligations of the federal government to tribes. To bring attention to their concerns, the NCAI called an emergency conference in 1954 that was covered by more than 4,000 newspapers and radio and television stations, including the BBC and other foreign press. Throughout the 1940s and 1950s, the NCAI was the major interest group representing Indian interests in federal politics.

The NCAI supported the American Indian Chicago Conference in 1961, which brought together Indian leaders and scholars to consider the concerns of American Indians around the country. The conference became a very significant event for supporting American Indian efforts and organization during the 1960s and beyond. The conference produced the "Declaration of Indian Purpose," a document that emphasized tribal sovereignty and the preservation of native identity and culture. This statement would become instrumental in outlining policy changes in the self-determination that began under Presidents Lyndon B. Johnson and Richard Nixon. The Chicago conference also highlighted some of the differences that were arising between the relatively conservative NCAI and others, like the American Indian Movement (AIM), who advocated for more radical approaches and goals. These dissenting voices were often younger, urban Indians.

The first of these organizations, the National Indian Youth Council (NIYC), organized as a result of the Chicago conference and the dissatisfaction of young, urban Indians with the NCAI. They argued that working within established government channels would not get enough traction or attention and that the NCAI was out of touch with grassroots, daily concerns of American Indians. The NIYC began protest actions, starting with "fish-ins" to protest the violation of treaty-protected fishing rights in the Pacific Northwest in the mid-1960s. Throughout the decade, the NIYC was active in marches, demonstrations, and other protests. The NIYC was joined by other groups such as the American Indian Movement in bringing new forms of political action behind Indian interests. The NIYC remains active today and consults with the United Nations. The NIYC and the group's actions were important for supporting the broader movement for recognizing American Indian rights, even as they often disagreed with the NCAI.

The NCAI persisted in its advocacy for tribal rights throughout the tumultuous 1960s and 1970s. Ultimately, due to various advocacy groups, media attention,

international attention, and the broader policy changes of the Civil Rights Movement and President Johnson's Great Society reforms, federal policy shifted against
termination. The advocacy of the NCAI helped support the policies of tribal self-
determination initiated with the 1975 Indian Self-Determination and Education
Assistance Act. This Act allowed for tribes to administer federal programs and
take control of many aspects of their own affairs. The NCAI has also continued
to advocate for tribal control of environmental protection and resource
management.

The NCAI's areas of attention have historically been legal aid, legislative
action, education for American Indians, and special training for Indians in the
Bureau of Indian Affairs (BIA). Today, the NCAI works on a range of issues that
affect both individual Indians and American Indian tribes, ranging from the
courts to health care to tribal tax policy. In recent years, the NCAI has expanded
its work, introducing the Tribal Sovereignty Protection Initiative, the NCAI Policy
Research Center, and the Native Vote campaign. The NCAI has also been active in
seeking to promote positive intergovernmental relationships between tribes and
states.

The NCAI continues to advocate for federal policies and programs on behalf of
pan-Indian interests as well as to support tribal governments in various ways.
Since 1944, the NCAI has had a profound impact in shaping federal policy and
supporting tribal self-determination and success as the largest American Indian
interest group. The NCAI has been an enduring interest group, able to gather
widespread support from American Indian tribes and individuals across the
United States and to facilitate significant changes in federal Indian policy.

Anne F. Boxberger Flaherty

Related Primary Document: **Indian Self-Determination and Education Assistance Act (1975)**

Indian Self-Determination and Education Assistance Act (1975)

*The Indian Self-Determination and Education Assistance Act of 1975 was signed
by president Ford on January 4, 1975. The act marked a significant step forward
in United States policy toward the Native American population living in the United
States. The U.S. government was willing to acknowledge the sovereignty of Native
American Nations, following decades of disastrous attempts to assimilate those
populations into American life. This era, between 1940 and 1960, was known as
the termination era. The era defined the U.S. government's failure to uphold its
commitment to treaties made with tribal nations and jeopardized the preservation
of Native American cultures. Facing backlash from tribal nations and seeing no
positive results from its efforts, the U.S. government decided to change its position with this legislation. Sovereign tribal nations could now run their own
schools, propose grants to fund their own programs, gain access to federal
resources such as health services, and function overall as autonomous governing
bodies. This document outlines the parameters of tribal nations' "self-determination" under the act.*

Sec. 450a. Congressional declaration of policy

(a) Recognition of obligation of United States. The Congress hereby recognizes the obligation of the United States to respond to the strong expression of the Indian people for self-determination by assuring maximum Indian participation in the direction of educational as well as other Federal services to Indian communities so as to render such services more responsive to the needs and desires of those communities.

(b) Declaration of commitment. The Congress declares its commitment to the maintenance of the Federal Government's unique and continuing relationship with, and responsibility to, individual Indian tribes and to the Indian people as a whole through the establishment of a meaningful Indian self-determination policy which will permit an orderly transition from the Federal domination of programs for, and services to, Indians to effective and meaningful participation by the Indian people in the planning, conduct, and administration of those programs and services. In accordance with this policy, the United States is committed to supporting and assisting Indian tribes in the development of strong and stable tribal governments, capable of administering quality programs and developing the economies of their respective communities.

(c) Declaration of national goal. The Congress declares that a major national goal of the United States is to provide the quantity and quality of educational services and opportunities which will permit Indian children to compete and excel in the life areas of their choice, and to achieve the measure of self-determination essential to their social and economic well-being.

...

PART A—INDIAN SELF-DETERMINATION

Sec. 450f. Self-determination contracts

(a) Request by tribe; authorized programs.

(1) The Secretary is directed, upon the request of any Indian tribe by tribal resolution, to enter into a self-determination contract or contracts with a tribal organization to plan, conduct, and administer programs or portions thereof, including construction programs—

(A) provided for in the Act of April 16, 1934 (48 Stat. 596), as amended (25 U.S.C. 452 et seq.);

(B) which the Secretary is authorized to administer for the benefit of Indians under the Act of November 2, 1921 (42 Stat. 208) (25 U.S.C. 13), and any Act subsequent thereto;

(C) provided by the Secretary of Health and Human Services under the Act of August 5, 1954 (68 Stat. 674), as amended (42 U.S.C. 2001 et seq.);

(D) administered by the Secretary for the benefit of Indians for which appropriations are made to agencies other than the Department of Health and Human Services or the Department of the Interior; and

(E) for the benefit of Indians because of their status as Indians without regard to the agency or office of the Department of Health and Human Services or the Department of the Interior within which it is performed. The programs, functions, services, or activities that are contracted under this paragraph shall include administrative functions of the Department of the Interior and the Department of Health and Human Services (whichever is applicable) that support the delivery of services to Indians, including those administrative activities supportive of, but not included as part of, the service delivery programs described in this paragraph that are otherwise contractable. The administrative functions referred to in the preceding sentence shall be contractable without regard to the organizational level within the Department that carries out such functions.

(2) If so authorized by an Indian tribe under paragraph (1) of this subsection, a tribal organization may submit a proposal for a self-determination contract, or a proposal to amend or renew a self-determination contract, to the Secretary for review. Subject to the provisions of paragraph (4), the Secretary shall, within ninety days after receipt of the proposal, approve the proposal and award the contract unless the Secretary provides written notification to the applicant that contains a specific finding that clearly demonstrates that, or that is supported by a controlling legal authority that—

(A) the service to be rendered to the Indian beneficiaries of the particular program or function to be contracted will not be satisfactory;

(B) adequate protection of trust resources is not assured;

(C) the proposed project or function to be contracted for cannot be properly completed or maintained by the proposed contract;

(D) the amount of funds proposed under the contract is in excess of the applicable funding level for the contract, as determined under section 450j-1(a) of this title; or

(E) the program, function, service, or activity (or portion thereof) that is the subject of the proposal is beyond the scope of programs, functions, services, or activities covered under paragraph (1) because the proposal includes activities that cannot lawfully be carried out by the contractor. Notwithstanding any other provision of law, the Secretary may extend or otherwise alter the 90-day period specified in the second sentence of this subsection, if before the expiration of such period, the Secretary obtains the voluntary and express written consent of the tribe or tribal organization to extend or otherwise alter such period. The contractor shall include in the proposal of the contractor the standards under which the tribal organization will operate the contracted program, service, function, or activity, including in the area of construction, provisions regarding the use of licensed and qualified architects, applicable health and safety standards, adherence to applicable Federal, State, local, or tribal building codes and engineering standards. The standards referred to in the preceding sentence shall ensure structural integrity, accountability of funds, adequate competition for sub-contracting under tribal or other applicable law, the commencement, perfor-mance, and completion of the contract, adherence to project plans and specifications (including any applicable Federal construction guidelines and manuals), the use of proper materials and workmanship, necessary inspec-tion and testing, and changes, modifications, stop work, and termination of the work when warranted.

(3) Upon the request of a tribal organization that operates two or more mature self-determination contracts, those contracts may be consolidated into one single contract.

(4) The Secretary shall approve any severable portion of a contract proposal that does not support a declination finding described in paragraph (2). If the Secretary determines under such paragraph that a contract proposal—

(A) proposes in part to plan, conduct, or administer a program, function, service, or activity that is beyond the scope of programs covered under paragraph (1), or

(B) proposes a level of funding that is in excess of the applica-ble level determined under section 450j-1(a) of this title, subject to any altera-tion in the scope of the proposal that the Secretary and the tribal organization agree to, the Secretary shall, as appropriate, approve such portion of the pro-gram, function, service, or activity as is authorized under paragraph (1) or approve a level of funding authorized under section 450j-1(a) of this title. If a tribal organization elects to carry out a severable portion of a contract pro-posal pursuant to this paragraph, subsection (b) of this section shall only apply to the portion of the contract that is declined by the Secretary pursuant to this subsection.

(b) Procedure upon refusal of request to contract. Whenever the Secretary declines to enter into a self-determination contract or contracts pursuant to subsection (a) of this section, the Secretary shall—

(1) state any objections in writing to the tribal organization,

(2) provide assistance to the tribal organization to overcome the stated objections, and

(3) provide the tribal organization with a hearing on the record with the right to engage in full discovery relevant to any issue raised in the matter and the opportunity for appeal on the objections raised, under such rules and regulations as the Secretary may promulgate, except that the tribe or tribal organization may, in lieu of filing such appeal, exercise the option to initiate an action in a Federal district court and proceed directly to such court pursu-ant to section 450m-1(a) of this title.

(c) Liability insurance; waiver of defense.

(1) Beginning in 1990, the Secretary shall be responsible for obtaining or providing liability insurance or equivalent coverage, on the most cost-effective basis, for Indian tribes, tribal organizations, and tribal contractors

carrying out contracts, grant agreements and cooperative agreements pursuant to this subchapter. In obtaining or providing such coverage, the Secretary shall take into consideration the extent to which liability under such contracts or agreements are covered by the Federal Tort Claims Act.

(2) In obtaining or providing such coverage, the Secretary shall, to the greatest extent practicable, give a preference to coverage underwritten by Indian-owned economic enterprises as defined in section 1452 of this title, except that, for the purposes of this subsection, such enterprises may include non-profit corporations.

(3)(A) Any policy of insurance obtained or provided by the Secretary pursuant to this subsection shall contain a provision that the insurance carrier shall waive any right it may have to raise as a defense the sovereign immunity of an Indian tribe from suit, but that such waiver shall extend only to claims the amount and nature of which are within the coverage and limits of the policy and shall not authorize or empower such insurance carrier to waive or otherwise limit the tribe's sovereign immunity outside or beyond the coverage or limits of the policy of insurance.

(B) No waiver of the sovereign immunity of an Indian tribe pursuant to this paragraph shall include a waiver to the extent of any potential liability for interest prior to judgment or for punitive damages or for any other limitation on liability imposed by the law of the State in which the alleged injury occurs.

(d) Tribal organizations and Indian contractors deemed part of Public Health Service. For purposes of section 233 of title 42, with respect to claims by any person, initially filed on or after December 22, 1987, whether or not such person is an Indian or Alaska Native or is served on a fee basis or under other circumstances as permitted by Federal law or regulations for personal injury, including death, resulting from the performance prior to, including, or after December 22, 1987, of medical, surgical, dental, or related functions, including the conduct of clinical studies or investigations, or for purposes of section 2679, title 28, with respect to claims by any such person, on or after November 29, 1990, for personal injury, including death, resulting from the operation of an emergency motor vehicle, an Indian tribe, a tribal organization or Indian contractor carrying out a contract, grant agreement, or cooperative agreement under sections 450f or 450h of this title is deemed to be part of the Public Health Service in the Department of Health and Human Services while carrying out any such contract or agreement and its employees (including those acting on behalf of the organization or contractor as provided in section 2671 of title 28 and including an individual who provides health care services pursuant to a personal services contract with a tribal organization for the provision of services in any facility owned, operated, or constructed under the jurisdiction of the Indian Health Service) are deemed employees of the Service while acting within the scope of their employment in carrying out the contract or agreement: Provided that such employees shall be deemed to be acting within the scope of their employment in carrying out such contract or agreement when they are required, by reason of such employment, to perform medical, surgical, dental or related functions at a facility other than the facility operated pursuant to such contract or agreement, but only if such employees are not compensated for the performance of such functions by a person or entity other than such Indian tribe, tribal organization or Indian contractor.

(e) Burden of proof at hearing or appeal declining contract; final agency action.

(1) With respect to any hearing or appeal conducted pursuant to subsection (b)(3) of this section, the Secretary shall have the burden of proof to establish by clearly demonstrating the validity of the grounds for declining the contract proposal (or portion thereof).

(2) Notwithstanding any other provision of law, a decision by an official of the Department of the Interior or the Department of Health and Human Services, as appropriate (referred to in this paragraph as the "Department") that constitutes final agency action and that relates to an appeal within the Department that is conducted under subsection (b)(3) of this section shall be made either—

(A) by an official of the Department who holds a position at a higher organizational level within the Department than the level of the departmental agency (such as the Indian Health Service or the Bureau of Indian Affairs) in which the decision that is the subject of the appeal was made; or

(B) by an administrative judge.

Sec. 450g. Repealed or Transferred. Pub. L. 100-472, title II, Sec. 201(b)(1), Oct. 5, 1988, 102 Stat. 2289.

Sec. 450h. Grants to tribal organizations or tribes

(a) Request by tribe for contract or grant by Secretary of the Interior for improving, etc., tribal governmental, contracting, and program planning activities. The Secretary of the Interior is authorized, upon the request of any Indian tribe (from funds appropriated for the benefit of Indians pursuant to section 13 of this title, and any Act subsequent thereto) to contract with or make a grant or grants to any tribal organization for—

(1) the strengthening or improvement of tribal government (including, but not limited to, the development, improvement, and administration of planning, financial management, or merit personnel systems; the improvement of tribally funded programs or activities; or the development, construction, improvement, maintenance, preservation, or operation of tribal facilities or resources);

(2) the planning, training, evaluation of other activities designed to improve the capacity of a tribal organization to enter into a contract or contracts pursuant to section 450f of this title and the additional costs associated with the initial years of operation under such a contract or contracts; or

(3) the acquisition of land in connection with items (1) and (2) above: Provided, That in the case of land within Indian country (as defined in

chapter 53 of title 18) or which adjoins on at least two sides lands held in trust by the United States for the tribe or for individual Indians, the Secretary of Interior may (upon request of the tribe) acquire such land in trust for the tribe.

(b) Grants by Secretary of Health and Human Services for development, maintenance, etc., of health facilities or services and improvement of contract capabilities implementing hospital and health facility functions. The Secretary of Health and Human Services may, in accordance with regulations adopted pursuant to section 450k of this title, make grants to any Indian tribe or tribal organization for—

(1) the development, construction, operation, provision, or maintenance of adequate health facilities or services including the training of personnel for such work, from funds appropriated to the Indian Health Service for Indian health services or Indian health facilities; or

(2) planning, training, evaluation or other activities designed to improve the capacity of a tribal organization to enter into a contract or contracts pursuant to section 450g of this title.

(c) Use as matching shares for other similar Federal grant programs. The provisions of any other Act notwithstanding, any funds made available to a tribal organization under grants pursuant to this section may be used as matching shares for any other Federal grant programs which contribute to the purposes for which grants under this section are made.

(d) Technical assistance. The Secretary is directed, upon the request of any tribal organization and subject to the availability of appropriations, to provide technical assistance on a nonreimbursable basis to such tribal organization—

(1) to develop any new self-determination contract authorized pursuant to this subchapter;

(2) to provide for the assumption by such tribal organization of any program, or portion thereof, provided for in section 450f(a)(1) of this title; or

(3) to develop modifications to any proposal for a self-determination contract which the Secretary has declined to approve pursuant to section 450f of this title.

(e) Grants for technical assistance and for planning, etc., Federal programs for tribe. The Secretary is authorized, upon the request of an Indian tribe, to make a grant to any tribal organization for—

(1) obtaining technical assistance from providers designated by the tribal organization, including tribal organizations that operate mature contracts, for the purposes of program planning and evaluation, including the development of any management systems necessary for contract management, and the development of cost allocation plans for indirect cost rates; and

(2) the planning, designing, monitoring, and evaluating of Federal programs serving the tribe, including Federal administrative functions.

Source: Indian Self-Determination and Education Assistance Act (1975). Public Law 93-638, 88 Stat. 2203.

See also: American Indian Movement (1968–); Congress of Racial Equality (1942–)

Further Reading

Cowger, Thomas. 1999. *The National Congress of American Indians: The Founding Years.* Lincoln: The University of Nebraska Press.

Hertzberg, Hazel. 1971. *The Search for an American Indian Identity: Modern Pan-Indian Movements.* Syracuse: Syracuse University Press.

Wilkins, David E. 2007. *American Indian Politics and the American Political System.* Lanham, MD: Rowman & Littlefield Publishers.

National Conservative Political Action Committee (1975–1994; 2006)

The National Conservative Political Action Committee (NCPAC) was active in electoral politics throughout the late 1970s until the 1990s. NCPAC was started in 1975 by four young conservatives actively seeking to revitalize the Republican Party in the post-Watergate era and to defeat liberal Democratic Party candidates. NCPAC was more conservative than older, more traditional Republican organizations. Watergate had hollowed out the moderate elements of the Republican Party, but NCPAC aimed to reenergize the most conservative bases left in the party. Founders included John "Terry" Dolan (1950–1986), Roger Stone (1952–), Brent Bozell (1955–), and Robert Krieble (1916–1997). Dolan was the single, major force behind NCPAC, and after he died, NCPAC withered rather quickly. The Center for Responsive Politics reports the last NCPAC financial activity as 1994, while the FEC has documentation until 2006. Stone and Bozell have remained active in politics through the Trump era.

In technical senses, PACs were neither interest groups nor business entities. PACs were organizations that were solely designed to influence elections. In the late 1970s, most PACs were *connected* to an already existing business or organization. NCPAC was one of the first large *nonconnected* PACs to gain considerable sway in electoral politics. Connected PACs held considerable advantages over nonconnected ones because connected PACs were allowed to use resources tied to their parent organizations. Indeed, a parent organization could cover all of the overhead expenses of its connected PAC. Connected PACs also had a list of members, stockholders, or employees, which made finding and contacting prospective contributors much easier. A nonconnected PAC, like NCPAC, had to start from scratch, covering its entire overhead and finding contributors. NCPAC's success is particularly noteworthy because of the organizational obstacles it had to overcome as a nonconnected PAC.

NCPAC was one of the first PACs to master direct mail techniques to raise large sums of money. In the 2000s, direct mail sounds quaint, but in the 1970s and 1980s, direct mail was a tremendously powerful tool. The language in direct appeals was typically inflammatory and meant to stoke fear. Fear was an important tactic because it has been shown to be an efficient mobilizer. NCPAC appeals were mailed to specifically targeted individuals. The value of a mail campaign depended on the quality of its targeting. As NCPAC fine-tuned its mailing lists, access to its list became valuable. At its heyday, NCPAC had one of the most valued lists of conservative contributors in the United States.

NCPAC used strong, forceful messages against Democratic candidates, primarily in the U.S. Senate. NCPAC credited its advertisements with their first success in the defeat of Senator Richard "Dick" Clark (1928–) of Iowa in 1978. NCPAC claimed that the advertisements they used against Clark were responsible for Clark losing the 30-point advantage that he held just three weeks prior to the general election. Whether those NCPAC's claims were accurate or not, candidates and election observers took note. NCPAC used these same aggressive tactics in subsequent races. NCPAC claimed credit for defeating several candidates in the 1980 elections. Aggressiveness was once again the distinguishing feature of NCPAC advertising against Birch Bayh (D-Indiana, 1928–), John Culver (D-Iowa, 1932–2018), Frank Church (D-Idaho, 1924–1984), George McGovern (D-South Dakota, 1922–2012), Alan Cranston (D-California, 1914–2000), and Thomas Eagleton (D-Missouri, 1929–2007). In the 1980 campaign cycle, only Cranston and Eagleton survived.

NCPAC activities were regulated most directly by the Federal Election Campaign Act (FECA) passed in 1971. Key amendments passed in 1974 provided greater clarity and regulatory authority to the Federal Election Commission (FEC). NCPAC, staying at the forefront of legal challenges to these campaign finance laws, was one of the first and most active PACs to push against the restrictions on campaign spending. To understand these legal challenges, it is important to consider the differences between individual contributions and the aggregation of individual contributions by PACs. Unlimited contributions from individuals to candidates might invite corruption—a concern that dated back to the 1800s. In addition, large contributors might drown out the voices of smaller contributors. PACs, it was initially thought, could balance these forces by aggregating many, smaller contributions that could then be given to a candidate without risking the same corrupting influence.

Rather than giving aggregated contributions to candidates, NCPAC, as well as some other PACs, relied heavily on independent expenditures in the 1970s and 1980s. An independent expenditure allows PACs, individuals, and ideological organizations to spend unlimited amounts of money independently on political parties or candidate campaigns. Independent expenditures cannot be coordinated in any way with parties or candidates or they risk violating campaign finance laws. However, independent expenditures can expressly advocate the election or defeat of a particular candidate. NCPAC, however, was accused of using its independent expenditures to circumvent the limits on direct contributions to candidates. Direct contributions to candidates were clearly limited by the new campaign finance laws, but it was less clear whether independent expenditures in support of a candidate were similarly limited. In 1976, the Supreme Court ruled in *Buckley v. Valeo* that limitations on independent expenditures were an abridgement of freedom of speech. The *Buckley* decision unleashed NCPAC independent expenditures and led to an explosion in the number of registered PACs.

NCPAC continued to challenge campaign finance regulations in the 1980s. In *FEC v. NCPAC* (1985), the question before the court was whether the FECA violated NCPAC's first amendment rights of free speech and association. The court ruled that the FEC violated NCPAC's rights by limiting its expenditures. The majority opinion of the court held that spending money supporting one candidate over another was the same as speech. The court continued to distinguished between contributions given directly to a candidate and contributions given to the independent organizations that support candidates, but the *Buckley* distinction between coordinated activity and uncoordinated activity was blurred. Giving unlimited monies in support of a candidate was eased.

These earlier court cases affected subsequent campaign finance cases heard by the Supreme Court. After the Supreme Court's 2010 ruling, *SpeechNow v. FEC*, Super PACs emerged. In *SpeechNow*, the Supreme Court ruled that groups making independent expenditures could accept unlimited funds from any source as long as the contributors were not coordinating with candidates or parties. Indeed, Super PACs are technically known as independent expenditure-only committees. There are no limits on how much money Super PACs can raise or spend. *Speech-Now* is an important case, even if not as well known as *Citizens United v. FEC*. In *Citizens United*, the Supreme Court ruled that corporations enjoyed all of the same freedom of speech rights as individuals. *Citizens United* is widely considered to be one of the most important freedom of speech cases in decades. Each of these campaign finance cases relied heavily on the earliest cases brought before the court by NCPAC.

Although it is relatively easy to see and evaluate campaign-related PAC activities, it is more difficult to ascertain the actual impact of PACs. PACs might have reasons to exaggerate their influence if they think that such exaggerations will prompt more contributions. PACs certainly played a role in many federal elections, but it is hard to know whether their roles were more influential than other factors, such as candidate quality, the state of the economy, and the political climate. Money has always been involved in the political process, and concerns about the possibility of corruption are ongoing. Finding a way to regulate money in elections to prevent corruption while still allowing for freedom of speech and freedom of association remains a paramount question in campaign finance and was an issue that NCPAC affected for many years.

Mary Jo Shepherd and Eric S. Heberlig

Related Primary Document: **Federal Election Commission: Summary of** ***Buckley v. Valeo*** **(1976)**

Federal Election Commission: Summary of *Buckley v. Valeo* (1976)

The Federal Election Commission (FEC) is a United States federal agency designed to regulate campaign and finance laws in the country. The commission was created in 1974 as a result of an amendment to the Federal Election Campaign Act of 1971 (FECA) which tightened campaign finance rules and regulations in United States elections. Such measures might be seen as a reaction to the Watergate scandal, which ended with former president Nixon's resignation in 1974. The Supreme Court ruled in Buckley v. Valero, *424 U.S. 1 (1976), that certain campaign expenditures would violate the Constitution, while others would not, according to the following per curium opinion. The case would later become precedent for* FEC v. NCPAC, *470 U.S. 780 (1985).*

On January 30, 1976, the Supreme Court issued a per curiam opinion in Buckley v. Valeo, the landmark case involving the constitutionality of the Federal Election Campaign Act of 1971 (FECA), as amended in 1974, and the Presidential Election Campaign Fund Act.

The Court upheld the constitutionality of certain provisions of the election law, including:

The limitations on contributions to candidates for federal office (2 U.S.C. §441a);

The disclosure and recordkeeping provisions of the FECA (2 U.S.C. §434); and

The public financing of Presidential elections (Subtitle H of the Internal Revenue Code of 1954).

The Court declared other provisions of the FECA to be unconstitutional, in particular:

The limitations on expenditures by candidates and their committees, except for Presidential candidates who accept public funding (formerly 18 U.S.C. §608(c)(1)(C-F));

The $1,000 limitation on independent expenditures (formerly 18 U.S.C. §608e);

The limitations on expenditures by candidates from their personal funds (formerly 18 U.S.C. §608a); and

The method of appointing members of the Federal Election Commission (formerly 2 U.S.C. §437c(a)(1)(A-C)).

Background

On January 2, 1975, the suit was filed in the U.S. District Court for the District of Columbia by Senator James L. Buckley of New York, Eugene McCarthy, Presidential candidate and former Senator from Minnesota, and several others.1 The defendants included Francis R. Valeo, Secretary of the Senate and Ex officio member of the newly formed Federal Election Commission, and the Commission itself.2 The plaintiffs charged that the FECA, under which the Commission was formed, and the Presidential Election Campaign Fund Act were unconstitutional on a number of grounds.

On January 24, 1975, pursuant to Section 437h(a) of the FECA, the district court certified the constitutional questions in the case to the U.S. Court of Appeals for the District of Columbia Circuit. On August 15, 1976, the appeals court rendered a decision upholding almost all of the substantive provisions of the FECA with respect to contributions, expenditures and disclosure.

The court also sustained the constitutionality of the method of appointing the Commission.

On September 19, 1975, the plaintiffs filed an appeal with the Supreme Court, which reached its decision on January 30, 1976.

Supreme Court Decision

Contribution Limitations

The appellants had argued that the FECA's limitations on the use of money for political purposes were in violation of First Amendment protections for free expression, since no significant political expression could be made without the expenditure of money. The Court concurred in part with the appellants' claim, finding that the restrictions on political contributions and expenditures "necessarily reduce[d] the quantity of expression by restricting the number of issues discussed, the depth of the exploration, and the size of the audience reached. This is because virtually every means of communicating ideas in today's mass society requires the expenditure of money." The Court then determined that such restrictions on political speech could only be justified by an overriding governmental interest.

The Court upheld the contribution limitations in the FECA,3 stating that they constituted one of the election law's "primary weapons against the reality or appearance of improper influence stemming from the dependence of candidates on large campaign contributions" (the other weapon being the disclosure requirements). Although it appeared that the contribution limitations did restrict a particular kind of political speech, the Court concluded that they "serve[d] the basic governmental interest in safeguarding the integrity of the electoral process without directly impinging upon the rights of individual citizens and candidates to engage in political debate and discussion."

The Court found no evidence to support the appellants' allegations that the contribution limitations discriminated against non incumbent candidates. With respect to the appellants' charge that the contribution limitations discriminated against minor and third parties and their candidates, the court noted that the FECA, "on its face," treated all candidates and parties equally. Furthermore, the Court said there was a legitimate argument that the limitations, in fact, appeared to benefit minor parties, since major parties and candidates received a greater proportion of their funding from large contributions.

The appellants had additionally challenged the limitations on certain expenses incurred by volunteers working on behalf of candidates or political committees. While the FECA placed no limits on most unreimbursed volunteer activities, it did limit unreimbursed travel expenses and certain costs of organizing campaign functions. Beyond these limits the costs were considered in-kind contributions (§431(8)(B)(i, ii, and iv)). The Court upheld the provisions for limited spending by volunteers, stating that they were a "constitutionally acceptable accommodation of Congress' valid interest in encouraging citizen participation in political campaigns while continuing to guard against the corrupting potential of large financial contributions to candidates."

Expenditure Limitations

In contrast to its ruling on contribution limitations, the Court found that the expenditure ceiling in the FECA imposed "direct and substantial restraints on the quantity of political speech" and invalidated three expenditure limitations as violations of the First Amendment.

The overall limitations on expenditures by federal candidates and their committees were struck down by the Court. The appellees had argued that these limitations (formerly 18 U.S.C. §608(c)) served a public interest by equalizing the financial resources of candidates, but the Court determined that the amount of money spent in particular campaigns must necessarily vary, depending on the "size and intensity" of the support for individual candidates. Furthermore, expenditure ceilings "might serve not to equalize the opportunities of all candidates but to handicap a candidate who lacked substantial name recognition or exposure of his views before the start of the campaign." The appellees had also claimed that the expenditure limitations would reduce the overall cost of campaigning, and they cited statistics demonstrating the dramatic increases in campaign spending that had occurred nationwide in preceding years. The Court decided, however, that "[t]he First Amendment denies government the power to determine that spending to promote one's political views is wasteful, excessive or unwise." The Court ruled, therefore, that the limitations on overall expenditures were unconstitutional.

The appellants had charged that the $1,000 per candidate annual limitation on independent expenditures—i.e., expenditures made by persons "relative to a clearly identified candidate...advocating the election or defeat of such candidate" (formerly 18 U.S.C. §608(e)(1))—was both unconstitutionally vague and an excessive hindrance on First Amendment rights of free expression. The Court resolved the vagueness question by reading "relative to" to mean "advocating the election or defeat of such candidate" in the same subsection, and by construing the provision to apply only to "expenditures for communications that in express terms advocate[d] the election or defeat of a clearly identified candidate for Federal office." While the Court of Appeals had accepted the appellees' argument that the provision was necessary to prevent circumvention of the contribution limitations, the Supreme Court found that the "governmental interest in preventing corruption and the appearance of corruption"—which justified the contribution limitations— was not sufficient to warrant the limitation on independent expenditures. If expenditure ceilings were to apply only to situations of express advocacy, the limitation would be easily circumvented by "expenditures that skirted the restriction on express advocacy of election or defeat but nevertheless benefited" a candidate. Moreover, the Court pointed out, abuses that might be generated by large independent expenditures did not appear to pose the same threat of corruption that large contributions posed since the "absence of prearrangement or coordination of the expenditure with the candidate or his agent alleviates the danger that expenditures will be given as a quid pro quo for improper commitments from the candidates." Thus finding that no substantial governmental interest was served by the limitation on independent expenditures, the Court concluded that such expenditures were protected as political discussion and expression under the First Amendment.

Regarding the limitations on a candidate's use of personal funds, the Court found that the provisions unconstitutionally interfered with the protected and valued right of an individual "to engage in the discussion of public issues and vigorously and tirelessly to advocate his own election." The Court continued that no governmental interest supported the limit on such personal funds. To the contrary, the Court noted that "the use of personal funds reduces a candidate's dependence on outside contributions and thereby counteracts the coercive pressures and attendant risks of abuse to which the contribution limitations are directed."

Finally, the Court added that its invalidation of the expenditure limitations was severable from Subtitle H, which provides for the public financing of Presidential elections. The limitations on expenditures by Presidential candidates who received public funds was legitimate since the acceptance of public funds was voluntary. Therefore, with regard to publicly financed elections, the consequent societal and governmental benefits weighed more heavily in favor of expenditure limitations.

Reporting and Disclosure Requirements

The appellants had sought a blanket exemption from the public disclosure provisions for all minor parties, claiming that contributors to minor parties, unlike contributors to the Republican and Democratic Parties, were more vulnerable to threats, harassment and reprisal as a result of the public disclosure of their names. The appellants claimed the provisions constituted a violation of their rights to free association under the First Amendment and to equal protection under the Fifth Amendment. Recognizing that "compelled disclosure, in itself, can seriously infringe on privacy of association and belief guaranteed by the First Amendment," the Court nevertheless ruled that the Act's reporting and disclosure provisions were justified by governmental interest in (1) helping voters to evaluate candidates by informing them about the sources and uses of campaign funds, (2) deterring corruption and the appearance of it by making public the names of major contributors, and (3) providing information necessary to detect violations of the law.

The Court acknowledged the potential disadvantage for minor parties that could result from the public disclosure provisions of the law, but it noted that none of the minor parties that were appellants in this suit had demonstrated that their contributors had been injured by the disclosure provisions. Therefore, the Court ruled a blanket exemption unnecessary. The Court left open the possibility, however, that minor and new parties might successfully claim an exemption from FECA disclosure requirements by showing proof of injury.

Presidential Election Campaign Fund

The Court upheld the constitutionality of Subtitle H of the Internal Revenue Code, which established the public financing of Presidential campaigns through a voluntary income tax checkoff. The Court determined that the appellants' claim that Congress violated the First Amendment in not allowing taxpayers to earmark their $1.00 checkoff to any candidate or party of their choice was not sufficient to invalidate the law. In the Court's opinion the checkoff constituted an appropriation by Congress, and as such it did not require outright taxpayer approval. Furthermore, "every appropriation made by Congress uses public money in a manner to which some taxpayers object."

The appellants had also argued, by analogy, that just as Congress may not subsidize or burden religion under the freedom of religion clause of the First Amendment, the freedom of speech clause prohibits it from financing particular political campaigns. The Court ruled the analogy inapplicable, however, finding that Subtitle H furthered rather than abridged political speech because its purpose was "to facilitate and enlarge public discussion and participation in the electoral process."

The appellants further claimed that the public funding provisions violated the Fifth Amendment's due process clause, arguing that the eligibility requirements for public funds were comparable to unconstitutionally burdensome ballot access laws. The Court found no merit in the argument; the denial of public funds to candidates did "not prevent any candidate from getting on the ballot or prevent any voter from casting a vote for the candidate of his choice."

"In addition," the Court said, "the limits on contributions necessarily increase the burden of fundraising, and Congress properly regarded public financing as an appropriate means of relieving major-party Presidential candidates from the rigors of soliciting private contributions."

The Court also rejected appellants' contention that the public financing provisions discriminated against minor and new party candidates, in violation of the Fifth Amendment. Specifically, the appellants had argued that Subtitle H favored major parties and their nominees by granting them full public funding for their conventions and general election campaigns, while minor and new parties and their candidates received only partial public funding according to a formula based on percentage of votes received.

Similarly, the appellants challenged the provision that restricted the payment of primary matching funds to only Presidential candidates who met certain requirements. These requirements included a provision for payments to candidates who had raised a minimum amount of contributions in at least twenty states (26 U.S.C. §9033(b)(3-4)). The Court found that such requirements for receiving public funds were reasonable; rather than preventing small parties from receiving public financing, the law only required them to demonstrate that they had a minimum level of broad-based support in order to qualify for federal subsidies. The Court concluded, "Any risk of harm to minority interests . . . cannot overcome the force of the governmental interests against the use of public money to foster frivolous candidacies, create a system of splintered parties, and encourage unrestrained factionalism." Furthermore, the Court noted that the advantage of receiving public financing was balanced by the requirement to adhere to strict expenditure limitations. As mentioned above, the Court upheld the constitutionality of expenditure limits as they applied to candidates and parties receiving public funds.

Appointment of the Commissioners

The appellants had challenged the method of appointing the six members of the Commission, as specified in the FECA, which provided that the President, the Speaker of the House of Representatives and the President pro tempore of the Senate each appoint two members. Arguing that the FEC's powers were executive rather than legislative, the appellants contended that the Congressional appointment of Commissioners violated the separation of powers principle embodied in the appointments clause of Article II of the Constitution. The Supreme Court determined that the appointments clause permitted only the President, with the advice and consent of the Senate, to appoint officers to exercise such executive authority as the Commission was granted. The Court ruled that the Commission, as it was then constituted, could not exercise its authority to enforce the law, conduct civil litigation, issue advisory opinions or determine eligibility for public funds, because these functions could not properly be regarded as legislative. The Commission's informational and auditing powers, however, were found to be legislative in nature, and therefore constitutional.

The Court accorded de facto validity to all acts of the Commission prior to the ruling and granted a 30-day stay of judgment—during which time the agency could exercise all of the authorities given to it under the FECA—so that Congress could reconstitute the Commission according to the provisions of Article II of the Constitution. The initial 30-day stay expired on February 29, 1976, but was extended to March 22. On March 23 the FEC's executive powers were suspended, and they remained suspended until May 21, when the Commissioners were reappointed by the President pursuant to the FECA Amendments of 1976, Pub. L. No. 94-283 (May 5, 1976).

Source: Federal Election Commission, fec.gov.

Related Primary Document: **Federal Election Commission: Reply to NCPAC Advisory Opinion Request (1983)**

Federal Election Commission: Reply to NCPAC Advisory Opinion Request (1983)

The following document is a response from the Federal Election Commission (FEC) to the National Conservative Political Action Committee (NCPAC), which asked the FEC for its opinion on certain anticipated expenditures to former president Regan's campaign in 1983. The FEC was created by the Federal Election Campaign Act of 1971 (FECA), which posited that no political action committee (PAC), such as the NCPAC, could make a donation in support of any campaign that exceeds a certain limit, outlined below. According to this letter, the NCPAC could not legally make the expenditures they planned to, as the expenditures would have exceeded the legal limit. At the time FECA was enacted, there was debate over whether or not imposing monetary limitations on certain groups was a violation of the First Amendment. Such concerns continued on for over a decade. Then in 1984, the NCPAC and the FEC took their opposing viewpoints to the Supreme Court in the case FEC v. NCPAC, 470 U.S. 480 (1985). The Supreme Court decided in a 5–4 decision that FECA was, in fact, in violation of the First Amendment. Any limitation of expenditures by any group or individual was deemed a violation of freedom of speech. The correspondence that follows between the FEC and the NCPAC set the stage for the case.

May 18, 1983

CERTIFIED MAIL

RETURN RECEIPT REQUESTED

ADVISORY OPINION 1983-10

J. Curtis Herge, Esq.

Sedam & Herge

8300 Greensboro Drive

McLean, Virginia 22102

Dear Mr. Herge:

This responds to your letter dated March 17, 1983, requesting an advisory opinion concerning application of 26 U.S.C. 9012(f) to your client, National Conservative Political Action Committee ("NCPAC"), a multicandidate political committee.

Your letter sets forth the following factual situation. NCPAC expects that President Reagan will be nominated in 1984 by the Republican Party for re-election to the office of President and has publicly announced its intention to make expenditures on behalf of President Reagan's reelection. For purposes of this request, NCPAC assumes that President Reagan will be certified by the Commission as eligible to receive, and will in fact receive, Federal funds in 1984 under the Presidential Election Campaign Fund Act ("the Fund Act"). NCPAC will not at any time be an authorized committee with respect to President Reagan.

According to the request, NCPAC proposes to make expenditures to further Mr. Reagan's reelection; such expenditures would be of the kind which, if made by President Reagan's authorized campaign committee, would constitute qualified campaign expenses of such committee. NCPAC proposes to make these expenditures in amounts exceeding $1,000 and throughout the United States, including the District of Columbia. In view of the foregoing factual representations, the Commission assumes that NCPAC's expenditures are proposed to be made at a date after President Reagan receives Federal funds in 1984 pursuant to the Fund Act. NCPAC also asks the Commission to assume that its expenditures on behalf of President Reagan's reelection would constitute "independent expenditures" as defined in 2 U.S.C. 431(17) and Commission regulations at 11 CFR 109.1.

The specific issue raised by your request is whether NCPAC's proposed expenditures, under the circumstances and assumptions set forth, are limited by 26 U.S.C. 9012(f)(1) to an aggregate amount not exceeding $1,000. The Commission concludes that the proposed expenditures are so limited by 26 U.S.C. 9012(f)(1). The cited 9012(f)(1) provides, in pertinent part: it shall be unlawful for any political committee which is not an authorized committee with respect to the eligible candidates of a political party for President and Vice President is a presidential election knowingly and willfully to incur expenditures to further the election of such candidates, which would constitute qualified campaign expenses if incurred by an authorized committee of such candidates, in an aggregate amount exceeding $1,000.

By its terms, the quoted provision limits NCPAC to $1,000 of expenditures that further the election of President Reagan, assuming he is an "eligible candidate" under the Fund Act when any such expenditure is incurred, and assuming further that the expenditure is of the kind that would constitute a "qualified campaign expense" if made by an authorized campaign committee of President Reagan. See, Federal Election Commission v. Americans For Change, 512 F.Supp. 489 (D.D.C. 1980), (three judge court), and the following discussion in this advisory opinion. The terms "eligible candidate" and "qualified campaign expense" delineate the applicability of 9012(f)(1) in several respects. As defined in 26 U.S.C. 9002(4), an "eligible candidate" means the candidate of a political party for president (or vice president) who has met all applicable conditions for eligibility to receive payments under the Fund Act. These conditions are specified in 26 U.S.C. 9003. With respect to a candidate nominated by a major political party, one of the significant eligibility conditions in 9003 is the occurrence of that candidate's nomination. See 26 U.S.C. 9003(b) and 9002(2)(A). The term "qualified campaign expense" is also used in 9012(f)(1) thereby indicating that to be the equivalent of a "qualified campaign expense" incurred by the authorized committee of an eligible presidential candidate, a 9012(f)(i) expenditure must be incurred within the expenditure report period.1 It may, however, be made before that period if incurred for property, services, or facilities to be used during such period. 26 U.S.C. 9002(11)(B); see generally 26 U.S.C. 9002(11) which sets forth other requirements of a qualified campaign expense. Accordingly, the question of whether NCPAC's proposed expenditures are subject to the 9012(f) limit would be determined with reference to the above cited provisions of the Fund Act.

By reference to the decision Federal Election Commission v. Americans for Change, 512 F.Supp. 489 (D.D.C. 1980), (three-judge court), aff'd by an equally divided Court, 455 U.S. 129 (1982), this advisory opinion request appears to suggest that the district court's decision vitiates the continuing "applicability and effect of 26 U.S.C. 9012(f)(1) to the factual situation presented in the request. The cited district court decision found that 9012(f) prohibited certain expenditures made by various unauthorized political committees in 1980 on behalf of the election of then presidential candidate Ronald Reagan; the court then held, however, that 9012(f) was unconstitutional. On January 19, 1982, the Supreme Court affirmed the judgment of the district court by an equally divided Court, Justice O'Connor not participating.

While the Court's decision effectively concludes the civil litigation in FEC v. AFC, supra, the equally divided nature of the Court's affirmance leaves the issue of the constitutionality of 9012(f) still unresolved. Moreover, since the Court's affirmance of the decision below was by an equally divided Court, it has no precedential effect. The operative principle is that "nothing is settled" by such a 4-4 split, Ohio ex rel. Eaton v. Price, 364 U.S. 263, 264 (1960).2 Such an affirmance does not indicate any approval of the reasoning of the court below, nor does it even stand for the proposition that the result reached below was correct. See, Trans World Airlines v. Hardison, 432 U.S. 63, 73 n.8 (1977); Neil v. Biggers, 409 U.S.188 (1972). The Court has long held that "the principle of law involved not having been agreed upon by a majority of the court sitting prevents the case from becoming an authority for the determination of other cases, either in this or in inferior courts." Hertz v. Woodman, 218 U.S. 205, 213–14 (1910).

Given the law regarding the nature of equally divided Supreme Court affirmances and the foregoing statutory analysis, the Commission concludes that NCPAC's proposed expenditures would be subject to the $1,000 limitation of 26 U.S.C. 9012(f)(1).

This response constitutes an advisory opinion concerning application of the Act, or regulations prescribed by the Commission, to the specific transaction or activity set forth in your request.

See 2 U.S.C. 437f.

Sincerely yours,

(signed)

Danny L. McDonald

Chairman for the Federal Election Commission

Note: Commissioner Aikens voted against approval of this opinion and has indicated that she will file a dissenting opinion at a later date. Commissioner Elliott voted to approve this opinion but has indicated that she will file a separate concurring opinion at a later date. Both of these individual opinions will be forwarded to you when they are submitted.

Source: Federal Election Commission, fec.gov.

See also: American Conservative Union (1964–); American Crossroads/Crossroads GPS (2010–); Sunoco PAC (1975–2012)

Further Reading

Ainsworth, Scott H. 2002. *Analyzing Interest Groups: Group Influence on People and Policies.* New York: W. W. Norton.

Ansolabehere, Stephen, John M. de Figueiredo, and James M. Snyder Jr. 2003. "Why Is There So Little Money in Politics." *Journal of Economic Perspectives* 17: 105–130.

FEC. August 2016. www.fec.gov.

FEC v. NCPAC. No. 83-1082. The Supreme Court. https://www.oyez.org/cases/1984/83 -1032:1985.

Gais, Thomas. 1996. *Improper Influence: Campaign Finance Law, Political Interest Groups, and the Problem of Equality.* Ann Arbor: University of Michigan Press.

Jacobson, Gary C. 1980. *Money in Congressional Elections.* New Haven, CT: Yale University Press.

Maisel, L. Sandy, and Mark D. Brewer. 2012. *Parties and Elections in America: The Electoral Process.* Plymouth, UK: Rowman & Littlefield Publishers.

OpenSecrets.org. August 2016. www.opensecrets.org.

O'Reilly, Jane, B. J. Phillips, and John F. Stacks. 1982. "No Thunder from the Right." *Time.*

National Council on Aging (1950–)

The National Council on Aging (NCOA) is a nonprofit organization that provides programs and services "to improve the lives of millions of older adults, especially those who are vulnerable and disadvantaged" (National Council on Aging 2018). NCOA is made up of 3,500 member organizations—including senior centers, senior housing, health centers, employment services, meal providers, agencies on aging, and faith congregations—that help people age 60 and older meet the challenges of aging. NCOA also works to raise public awareness of the challenges facing older Americans and advocates for funding and legislation to improve their health and economic security.

NCOA's programs, services, and online resources are mainly aimed at helping the estimated 23 million senior citizens affected by economic insecurity in the United States. Many individuals in this population have difficulty meeting expenses for food, housing, utilities, health care, prescriptions, and other needs.

NCOA coordinates with government agencies, businesses, voluntary organizations, and community groups to help seniors access benefits, find employment, stay healthy, manage their finances, and live independently in the community rather than going into nursing homes. NCOA reported on its website that it improved the lives of 1.47 million older Americans in fiscal year 2017.

NCOA was founded in 1950 as the National Committee on Aging by activists who opposed a trend among employers to impose a mandatory retirement age on workers. The organization quickly emerged as a national voice expressing the concerns of older Americans on many issues. In 1957, NCOA conducted a study on conditions in nursing homes that led to licensing requirements and other improvements. After adopting its current name in 1960, the organization produced a report on local meal-delivery programs serving seniors that served as the impetus for development of the federal Meals on Wheels program. In 1965, NCOA successfully advocated for passage of the Older Americans Act (OAA) as well as establishment of the federal Medicare and Medicaid health insurance programs. Other achievements from this period include launching the Intergenerational Service Learning Project, which connects seniors with students interested in careers in aging, and the Family Friends initiative, which matches older volunteers with young people with disabilities or chronic illnesses.

In the 21st century, NCOA's programs and services focus on two main areas: economic security and healthy living. Its economic security programs help seniors manage their finances, take advantage of their home equity, find employment, and access benefits. Benefits Checkup, launched in 2001, is a comprehensive online screening tool that helps older adults gain access to government or private benefits to help them pay for food, housing, utilities, taxes, legal services, health care, medications, or transportation. Savvy Saving Seniors is a financial education toolkit designed to help older people create budgets, manage money wisely, reduce debt, and avoid being victimized by scams. NCOA and its partners also provide mature workers with access to job training and placement through the Senior Community Service Employment Program (SCSEP).

NCOA's health and wellness programs address some of the common health-related challenges of aging. The Falls Free Initiative raises awareness of the danger of falling for older adults and provides programs aimed at reducing the likelihood of falls, both in the home and in the community. Restart Living provides resources to help the 80 percent of elderly Americans with chronic diseases—such as diabetes, hypertension, or arthritis—manage their health and improve their quality of life. The program covers such topics as self-management of pain, taking medications safely, and coping with depression or anxiety. NCOA also sponsors programs aimed at addressing hunger and promoting good nutrition for older Americans. The organization offers all of its programs and services free of charge.

An important facet of NCOA's mission involves advocating for public policies that benefit seniors, especially those in vulnerable situations due to health problems or economic insecurity. The organization lobbies to increase federal funding for programs and services for aging Americans, and it opposes budget cuts to programs for low-income seniors. Ensuring access to affordable health care ranks among NCOA's priorities, so it has opposed efforts to limit eligibility for federal Medicare and Medicaid benefits. NCOA also advocates for legislation to help seniors and people with disabilities remain at home, with support from caregivers and community-based services, as a cost-effective alternative to nursing homes. Another policy priority for NCOA is securing funding for the Elder Justice Act of 2010, which provides research, law enforcement training, and "silver alert" programs to combat the problem of elder abuse.

NCOA advocacy contributed to Congress reauthorizing the OAA in 2016. The act covers a variety of services intended to help older adults live healthy, productive, independent lives, including nutrition services, job training, senior centers, caregiver support, transportation, and legal services. NCOA has continued to lobby for funding and expansion of the OAA to promote strategies to help older adults attain economic security, such as credit counseling, debt management, and affordable housing. NCOA also seeks to enhance the SCSEP by making eligibility requirements more flexible and coming up with innovative ways to create jobs in various sectors for older adults. The organization also seeks funding for the OAA to modernize senior centers, increase capacity, and improve service delivery. Finally, NCOA seeks additional federal funding for research and development of innovative, evidence-based healthy aging initiatives to prevent disease and disability among older Americans.

NCOA's political advocacy assumed new urgency under the administration of President Donald Trump, which has pursued policies that threatened to reduce funding for programs and services benefiting older adults who face economic insecurity. The Republican-controlled Congress attempted to repeal the Affordable Care Act, which offered health care to millions of Americans who did not have employer-sponsored coverage, and also proposed legislation that would limit eligibility for Medicare and Medicaid, reduce Social Security and Supplemental Nutrition Assistance Program (SNAP) benefits, and cut funding for other programs important to seniors, including Meals on Wheels, SCSEP, affordable housing programs, and elder abuse prevention initiatives. James Firman, president and CEO of NCOA, released a statement opposing the Trump administration's proposed budget for 2018. "This budget proposal decimates critical programs that struggling older adults and their families have relied on for more than five decades," he wrote. "NCOA is committed to working with both parties in Congress to craft a more realistic budget that is fair to all Americans and provides older adults the means to age in the community with their friends and families" (NCOA 2018).

Laurie Collier Hillstrom

See also: AARP (1958–); Gray Panthers (1970–)

Further Reading

National Council on Aging (NCOA). 2018. https://www.ncoa.org.

Prindiville, Kevin. 2017. "High Stakes for Older Adults in 2017." Justice in Aging, January 4, 2017. http://www.justiceinaging.org/high-stakes-older-adults-2017/.

"Strengthening the Voice of Older Adults and the Aging Network." 2011. National Council on Aging (NCOA), September. https://www.ncoa.org/wp-content/uploads /Strengthen-Voice-White-Paper-web.pdf.

National Dairy Council (1915–)

The National Dairy Council (NDC) is a trade association that represents the interests of the U.S. dairy industry, including dairy farmers, food producers, suppliers, and distributors. Its main role is to help generate demand for dairy products by promoting the nutritional benefits of milk to American consumers, lawmakers, educators, health professionals, and media. Since 1983, NDC's industry promotion activities have been funded through the national dairy checkoff program. Administered in partnership with the U.S. Department of Agriculture (USDA), this program requires dairy producers to contribute 15 cents per hundredweight of milk to finance new product development, nutrition education, market expansion, and promotional campaigns to increase consumption of dairy products, such as milk, cheese, and yogurt.

A group of dairy farmers established NDC in 1915 to educate the public about the safety of the milk supply during an outbreak of foot-and-mouth disease in the nation's cattle. Based on the work of pioneering vitamin researcher E. V. McCollum, NDC provided science-based information on the nutritional and health benefits of dairy products. Its work helped double milk consumption in the United States between 1918 and 1928. NDC's strong focus on the importance of milk for children's health and growth influenced the development of the USDA's school lunch program in 1929. The American Dairy Association, founded in 1940 to promote U.S. milk products to consumers, merged with NDC in 1970.

The national dairy checkoff program was established in 1983 with the passage of the Dairy and Tobacco Adjustment Act, which authorized the USDA to create a National Dairy Promotion and Research Board to oversee it. Following several legal challenges to the checkoff system, the U.S. Supreme Court ruled in 2005 that producer-funded, government-sponsored marketing programs designed to increase demand for homogenous agricultural commodities were permitted under the First Amendment. In addition to financing the operations of NDC, the dairy checkoff program led to the development of national advertising campaigns to promote milk consumption, such as the famous "Got Milk?" series of television and print ads.

In the 21st century, NDC focuses on conducting scientific research and providing educational materials, nutrition information, and media tools emphasizing the health benefits of dairy products and the positive contributions of the dairy industry. NDC employs a staff of nutrition researchers and dietitians and funds academic studies on the benefits of milk consumption. They present milk as a fresh, natural, wholesome product that contains nine essential nutrients, including calcium that promotes bone growth. "It's hard to find any other single food that will give you the levels of nutrients you get in dairy," said Professor Robert P. Heaney of the Creighton University School of Medicine (Dairy Good 2018). NDC research and education efforts influenced the USDA's dietary guidelines recommending that Americans eat three servings of low-fat and fat-free dairy foods each day for good health.

Through its "farm to table" initiatives, NDC works to forge connections between American consumers and the dairy farmers who produce the milk, cheese, and yogurt served in homes, schools, and restaurants across the country. The trade association notes that the majority of the 41,000 dairy farms in the United States are family-owned businesses and that the dairy industry provides 1.5 million jobs to strengthen the U.S. economy. Recognizing an increasing consumer interest in food ingredients and production techniques, NDC features stories, slideshows, and videos on its website about the agricultural practices that produce dairy products. These resources focus on efforts to preserve the family farming tradition and to care for the nation's nine million milk cows.

NDC also emphasizes the dairy industry's commitment to conserve natural resources and protect the environment. In 2008, the industry set a voluntary goal of reducing its emissions of greenhouse gases by 25 percent by 2020 through investment in research, innovation, and continuous improvement toward sustainability. NDC also partnered with a dozen other industry groups to create Further with Food, an online information-sharing site aimed at reducing food waste by 50 percent by 2030.

NDC also participates in several programs intended to improve child health and reduce food insecurity. The dairy industry partnered with the National Football League and the USDA to create Fuel Up to Play 60, a school-based nutrition and exercise program that has reached 11 million students in 73,000 schools nationwide (National Dairy Council 2018). NDC also presents dairy foods as a solution to hunger because of their protein content, nutritional value, reasonable cost, and easy availability. The organization helps bring food to people in need through partnerships with Feeding America, Future of Food, the Great American Milk Drive, and other programs. It also promotes the inclusion of dairy foods in school lunch menus as a way for students to improve nutrition as well as academic performance.

Critics of NDC question the objectivity of the nutritional research conducted by its industry-funded scientists and academics. This research has served as the basis for decades of marketing campaigns and educational materials that have helped convince millions of Americans that milk products are the best possible source of the calcium needed to keep their bones strong and healthy. Critics have described NDC's messages as manipulative, claiming that they overstate milk's nutritional benefits. In 2007, the dairy industry was forced to retract claims that dairy consumption promotes weight loss. Opponents also contend that dairy industry lobbyists hide or deny the results of competing studies that link milk consumption with harmful health effects, such as an increased risk of prostate cancer.

Critics also assert that NDC exerts too much influence over federal nutrition guidelines, which the USDA revises every five years with input from scientists, nutrition experts, food industry representatives, and special interest groups. In 2004, the federal guidelines increased the daily recommended allowance of dairy products from two to three servings per day. These guidelines help shape the types of food produced, sold, and consumed in the United States. The standards factor into decisions relating to consumer purchases, government-funded nutrition programs, and school lunch menus, leading to increased sales and profits for the dairy industry. In addition, federal nutrition guidelines determine which agricultural sectors receive taxpayer money to support marketing campaigns for their products.

In the 21st century, an increasing number of health-conscious Americans have decreased their dairy consumption due to concerns about the industry's products or practices. Some critics avoid dairy because of the industry's environmental impact, pointing out that milk cows consume large amounts of water and grain that could be consumed by people while also generating large amounts of waste and carbon dioxide. Others worry about the potential human health effects of hormones, antibiotics, and genetically modified feed often used in milk production. Declining milk consumption has led to the growth of the plant-based beverage industry, which offers consumers such options as almond, cashew, coconut, rice, and soy milks. Market analyses project a drop in overall U.S. dairy milk sales of $15.9 billion between 2015 and 2020. Sales of plant-based dairy alternatives, like almond milk, are expected to grow to $3 billion during that same period (Caballero 2018).

NDC responded to the market threat posed by plant-based beverages by lobbying Congress to pass the Dairy Pride Acts of 2017. The legislation would prohibit any product that was not derived from cow's milk from bearing the label "milk." Proponents argued that the measure was needed to prevent confusion among consumers and to ensure that all beverage producers were held to the same standards. Representatives of the plant-based beverage industry argued that consumers chose their products intentionally because they sought a healthier alternative to cow's milk. They asserted that the dairy industry's declining market share occurred because consumers educated themselves about the misleading information long propagated by NDC. "We need to realize the economic and health effects of drinking that much milk," said David Levitsky, a professor of nutritional sciences at Cornell University, "and the role that the dairy industry plays in setting the agenda" (Harkinson 2015). Nonetheless, the bill failed to make it out of the Senate committee on Health, Education, Labor, and Pensions.

Laurie Collier Hillstrom

See also: American Farm Bureau Federation (1911–); Citizens for Health (1992–); Food Policy Action (2012–); Grocery Manufacturers Association (1908–); National Association of Manufacturers (1895–); United Fresh Produce Association (1904–)

Further Reading

Caballero, Martin. 2018. "Almond Milk Growth Brings Change for Suppliers." https://www.bevnet.com/news/2018/almond-milk-growth-brings-change-suppliers.

"Concerns about Dairy Industry Sponsorship." 2016. Dietitians for Professional Integrity, September 26, 2016. https://integritydietitians.org/2016/09/26/concerns-dairy-indus try-sponsorship/.

Dairy Good. 2018. "About Us." Dairy Management Inc. https://dairygood.org/about-us.

Dewey, Caitlin. 2017. "The Surprisingly Heated Political Battle Raging over the Word 'Milk.'" *Washington Post*, February 10, 2017. https://www.washingtonpost.com /news/wonk/wp/2017/02/10/the-surprisingly-heated-political-battle-raging-over -the-word-milk/?noredirect=on&utm_term=.93fcc4c0eaf3.

Harkinson, Josh. 2015. "The Scary New Science That Shows Milk Is Bad for You." *Mother Jones*, November/December, 2015. https://www.motherjones.com/enviro nment/2015/11/dairy-industry-milk-federal-dietary-guidelines/.

National Dairy Council. 2018. https://www.nationaldairycouncil.org/.

National Education Association (1857–)

The National Education Association (NEA), founded in 1857 as the National Teachers Association, is the oldest education interest group and currently the largest labor union in the United States. The development of the NEA over 160 years reflects the development of the women's labor movement, progressive professionalization and bureaucratization, and public sector unionism in the 19th and 20th centuries. It has played a major role in increasing the federal influence over education policy, developing collective bargaining rights for public sector employees, and drawing the nation's attention to racial disparities in education.

For all of the 19th century, the NEA represented the interests of school administrators and, notably, *not* average teachers. From its founding until 1900, the membership of the NEA rarely exceeded 2,000 members. For the sake of comparison, the Chicago Teachers Federation (CTF), founded in 1897 as a union of women elementary school teachers just in Chicago, had a dues-paying membership of over 2,000 by the end of its first year. Indeed, even though most teachers in the United States at the turn of the 20th century were women, women teachers were excluded from membership in the NEA until 1866, and for parts of the 19th century, women members of the NEA were only allowed to sit in the gallery and listen to discussions among male members. When women were allowed to speak, many were hesitant to do so for fear of employment retaliation from the male administrators who dominated the meetings. And until the early 1900s, women held few, if any, positions of power in the NEA.

It is useful to consider the NEA in relation to its more labor-oriented counterpart, the American Federation of Teachers (AFT), because of their complementary and often rivalrous relationship. The NEA focused on ideas of "professionalism" as a foil to the more militant and less genteel tactics of organized labor. Professionalism especially appealed to women teachers, who did not quite view themselves as manual laborers and who saw their political power as being more tenuous than that of male workers. The conflict between "professionalism" and "lady labor sluggers" would define the tensions between the NEA and the AFT (among other teachers' unions) for much of the 20th century.

The NEA meetings were a place for schoolmen (male school administrators) to share ideas about school administration. These discussions reflected a managerial perspective and Progressives' attitudes about the scientific management of organizations and the elimination of corruption. As public education proliferated at the end of the 19th century, teaching positions became a fundamental part of local party machine politics; teaching positions were given to unmarried women based less on qualifications and more on political connections. The schoolmen of the NEA, like many of the other Progressive municipal reformers, sought to limit corruption and take the "politics" out of schooling through centralization, by increasing formal qualifications for professional training, and by dismissing underperforming teachers. Just as the nation as a whole was dealing with increased immigration, the need for nationalization, and the creation and management of new public services, so were schools. For instance, some accounts claim that in 1909, half of the children in urban public schools could not speak English.

In contrast, some female elementary schoolteachers and teachers' unions saw Progressive reforms as an increase in monitoring of female teachers and a delocalization of the profession. While the NEA sought to take the politics out of education, teachers' unions sought to make teaching more political. Teachers—and especially elementary teachers, who were predominantly female—complained that the reformers spoke about teachers in factory terms, focusing on efficiency, supervision, and accountability rather than the art of pedagogy. Progressive reformers also often proposed freezes on teachers' salaries as well as on the construction of new buildings.

In the early 1900s, internal and external conflict forced the NEA to pay more attention to the views of women teachers. Margaret Haley (1861–1939), one of the trailblazers of organized teachers and a vice president of the CTF, led a demonstration at the NEA's national convention in 1903 and became the first woman to speak at the national convention in 1904. In 1910, Haley led the effort to have Flagg Young (1845–1918) elected as the first female president of the NEA. With increased pressure from competing teachers' unions (such as the CTF), the NEA created a committee to examine the condition of classroom teachers and teachers' salaries. Throughout the early 20th century, the NEA spent much of its time focusing on achieving pay equity between male and female teachers. Starting in 1915 and continuing into the 1970s, the NEA also had a policy of electing a woman as president every other year.

In the 1910s, the NEA, along with the American Federation of Labor, pushed for the expansion of trade schools, eventually leading to the Smith-Hughes Act of 1917, which provided federal funds for vocational agricultural training.

In the 1930s, with female teachers joining the NEA in larger numbers due to internal conflict in the AFT and the less militant nature of the NEA, the NEA sought to expand federal funding for public education, especially in response to fiscal crises created by the Great Depression. While the NEA certainly did not afford women great power within its organization, it was no longer run exclusively by male university presidents, and it sought to address the concerns of female elementary school teachers.

In 1933, the NEA was further legitimized by becoming a member of the Federal Advisory Committee on the Emergency in Education. Through the 1930s, the NEA lobbied for more federal funding for public education. The Harrison-Fletcher bill would have provided $100 million for education in its first year and $300 million after five years. Despite assembling a coalition of the NAACP, the AFT, the AFL, and the Catholic lobby, the NEA was ultimately unsuccessful due to opposition by President Roosevelt, who was worried that the bill would force New Deal Democrats to take an uncomfortable stance on federal funding for segregated schools.

In the 1940s and 1950s, the NEA continued to advocate for pay equity between men and women. Older systems of pay, which paid elementary school teachers less, often underpaid women, who dominated elementary schools. During the 1904–1905 school year, for instance, fewer than 20 percent of female teachers had pay equity with male teachers. By 1951, 98 percent of districts paid teachers based on scales determined by professional qualifications and experience. The NEA also focused on raising qualifications for teachers in general. As the school-age population increased following World War II, less than half of teachers in 1947 had completed college, and many teachers were teaching on emergency certification. Continuing their push for a larger federal role in education, the NEA also lobbied for the G. I. Bill, which, among other things, providing federal funding for returning veterans to receive secondary, postsecondary, or vocational education.

With a shortage of teachers in the 1940s and 1950s, and with an increasingly labor-friendly environment in the 1950s, the NEA teetered between maintaining its prior no-striking stance and competing with the more militant AFT for influence among public school teachers. While the NEA maintained its no-strike policy—reflecting fears during the McCarthy-era Red Scare and the NEA's historical position as the more "professional" organization—it did create policies for "professional sanctions," which resembled strikes, and "professional negotiations," which resembled collective bargaining. With the creation of the nation's first collective bargaining law for public employees in 1959 in Wisconsin, and with President Kennedy's Executive Order 10988 in 1962, public school teachers were invigorated to start pushing for collective bargaining, and a collective bargaining consensus between the NEA and the AFT was reached. This, in effect, led to the NEA becoming a full-fledged labor union. Whereas there were only 57 teacher strikes from 1946–1949, there were over 1,000 strikes in the 1960s. By the 1970s, 72 percent of public school teachers in the United States had some form of collective bargaining. Additionally, the NEA and AFT won important victories for teachers regarding tenure, salaries, and pensions.

The NEA's involvement in racial equality has been much more tenuous than that of the AFT. In the early-to-mid 1900s, the Southern Association of Schools and Colleges often did not accredit black schools, a barrier that made it impossible for black students in the South to attend many colleges. Starting in the 1920s, the NEA and the American Teachers Association pressured the Southern Association of Schools and Colleges to accredit black schools via their Joint Committee for Justice. Through the 1950s, however, the NEA's state organizations in the South remained more segregated than those of the AFT, and although the NEA supported the desegregation of schools, it did not go as far at the AFT, which wrote an amicus brief in *Brown v. Board of Education* (1954).

In the 1960s, the NEA seized on conflicts caused by the United Federation of Teachers (UFT), a local of the AFT, to paint itself as the more racially progressive of the two organizations. In 1962, the UFT started a citywide strike in New York City over the decentralization of the school system. Although the school system sought to give more control to communities like Ocean Hill-Brownsville, a largely black and Puerto Rican neighborhood, it resulted in the firing of white teachers in favor of black teachers. As part of its response, the NEA in 1967 elected its first Hispanic president, and in 1968, it elected its first black president.

Though the NEA had been closed to women during its early years, it became the preferred union of women by the mid-to-late 1900s, largely due to its less militaristic style. Whereas the AFT often laughed off women's concerns about disseminating birth control and gender discrimination, the NEA much more strongly embraced the feminist movement, endorsing the Equal Rights Amendment in the 1970s and supporting women in positions of power within its organization. The NEA also used divisions within the AFT over affirmative action to recruit more members. By 1969, membership in the NEA had swelled to over one million compared to the AFT's membership of 135,000.

At the end of the 20th century, the NEA opposed various school "accountability" measures begun in the 1980s. It was also influential in Jimmy Carter's administration and was fundamental to the creation of the Department of Education. Although opponents of public sector unions were invigorated by Ronald Reagan's busting of the 1981 PATCO strike, the NEA and its state chapters are still some of the most powerful lobbyists in Congress and state legislatures. In the 21st century, the NEA has remained opposed to school vouchers, in favor of increased funding for Title I schools, and ambiguous about charter schools. While the NEA has supported increased standardized testing for public schools through legislation like No Child Left Behind, it has been critical of the lack of efficacy of the tests in producing proficiency for all students and for creating schools based solely around testing.

Matthew Tyler

Related primary document: **John F. Kennedy: Executive Order 10988 (1962)**

John F. Kennedy: Executive Order 10988 (1962)

Executive Order 10988, also known as the "Task Force on Employee-Management Relations in the Federal Service," was signed into law by president Kennedy on January 17, 1962. The order stated that federal workers were allowed to strike, and that federal workers had the right to "collective bargaining" as well. Collective bargaining is an organization's right to negotiate its wages, benefits, working conditions, and more. The order could be seen as a response to the Taft-Hartley Act of 1947, which was originally vetoed by president Truman for fear that imposing limitations on a union's right to strike would compromise the First Amendment. However, the veto was overridden by Congress and enacted by a government that was under pressure from unions after barrages of strikes, and recovering from World War II. It was the Taft-Hartley Act of 1947 which made it illegal for federal workers to strike at all—and if federal workers wanted to bargain, they were required to take unpaid leave from their positions. After Executive Order

10988 was passed, many federal unions sprung up and expanded. Public school teachers who were members of the National Education Association (NEA) could now bargain their wages and conditions, for example. The document that follows is the order that gave federal workers the right to unionize, strike, and more.

January 17, 1962

WHEREAS participation of employees in the formulation and implementation of personnel policies affecting them contributes to effective conduct of public business; and

WHEREAS the efficient administration of the Government and the well-being of employees require that orderly and constructive relationships be maintained between employee organizations and management officials; and

WHEREAS subject to law and the paramount requirements of the public service, employee-management relations within the Federal service should be improved by providing employees an opportunity for greater participation in the formulation and implementation of policies and procedures affecting the conditions of their employment; and

WHEREAS effective employee-management cooperation in the public service requires a clear statement of the respective rights and obligations of employee organizations and agency management:

NOW, THEREFORE, by virtue of the authority vested in me by the Constitution of the United States, by section 1753 of the Revised Statutes (5 U.S.C. 631), and as President of the United States, I hereby direct that the following policies shall govern officers and agencies of the executive branch of the Government in all dealings with Federal employees and organizations representing such employees.

SECTION 1. (a) Employees of the Federal Government shall have, and shall be protected in the exercise of, the right, freely and without feel of penalty or reprisal, to form, join and assist any employee organization or to refrain from any such activity. Except as hereinafter expressly provided, the freedom of such employees to assist any employee organization shall be recognized as extending to participation in the management of the organization and acting for the organization in the capacity of an organization representative, including presentation of its views to officials of the executive branch, the Congress or other appropriate authority. The head of each executive department and agency (hereinafter referred to as "agency") shall take such action, consistent with law, as may be required in order to assist that employees in the agency are apprised of the rights described in this section, and that no interference, restraint, coercion or discrimination is practiced within such agency to encourage or discourage membership in any employee organization.

(b) The rights described in this section do not extend to participation in the management of an employee organization, or acting as a representative of any such organization, where such participation or activity would result in a conflict of interest or otherwise be incompatible with law or with the official duties of an employee.

SEC. 2. When used in this order, the term "employee organization" means any lawful association, labor organization, federation, council, or brotherhood having as a primary purpose the improvement of working conditions among Federal employees or any craft, trade or industrial union whose membership includes both Federal employees and employees of private organizations; but such term shall not include any organization (1) which asserts the right to strike against the Government of the United States or any agency thereof, or to assist or participate in any such strike, or which imposes a duty or obligation to conduct, assist or participate in any such strike, or (2) which advocates the overthrow of the constitutional form of Government in the United States, or (3) which discriminates with regard to the terms or conditions of membership because of race, color, creed or national origin.

SEC. 3. (a) Agencies shall accord informal, formal or exclusive recognition to employee organizations which request such recognition in conformity with the requirements specified in sections 4, 5 and 6 of this order, except that no recognition shall be accorded to any employee organization which the head of the agency considers to be so subject to corrupt influences or influences opposed to basic democratic principles that recognition would be inconsistent with the objectives of this order.

(b) Recognition of an employee organization will continue so long as such organization satisfies the criteria of this order applicable to such recognition; but nothing in this section shall require any agency to determine whether an organization should become or continue to be recognized as exclusive representative of the employees in any unit within 12 months after a prior determination of exclusive status with respect to such unit has been made pursuant to the provisions of this order.

(c) Recognition, in whatever form accorded, shall not—

(1) preclude any employee, regardless of employee organization membership, from bringing matters of personal concern to the attention of appropriate officials in accordance with applicable law rule, regulation, or established agency policy, or from choosing his own representative in a grievance or appellate action; or

(2) preclude or restrict consultations and dealings between an agency and any veterans' organization with respect to matters of particular interest to employees with veterans' preference; or

(3) preclude an agency from consulting or dealing with any religious, social, fraternal or other lawful association, not qualified as an employee organization, with respect to matters or policies which involve individual members of

the association or are of particular applicability to it or its members, when such consultations or dealings are duly limited so as not to assume the character of formal consultation on matters of general employee-management policy or to extend to areas where recognition of the interests of one employee group may result in discrimination against or injury to the interests of other employees.

SEC. 4. (a) An agency shall accord an employee organization, which does not qualify for exclusive or formal recognition, informal recognition as representative of its member employees without regard to whether any other employee organization has been accorded formal or exclusive recognition as representative of some or all employees in any unit.

(b) When an employee organization has been informally recognized, it shall, to the extent consistent with the efficient and orderly conduct of the public business, be permitted to present to appropriate officials its views on matters of concern to its members. The agency need not, however, consult with an employee organization so recognized in the formulation of personnel or other policies with respect to such matters.

SEC. 5. (a) An agency shall accord an employee organization formal recognition as the representative of its members in a unit as defined by the agency when (1) no other employee organization is qualified for exclusive recognition as representative of employees in the unit, (2) it is determined by the agency that the employee organization has a substantial and stable membership of no less than 10 per cent of the employees in the unit, and (3) the employee organization has submitted to the agency a roster of its officers and representatives, a copy of its constitution and by-laws, and a statement of objectives. When, in the opinion of the head of an agency, an employee organization has a sufficient number of local organizations or a sufficient total membership within such agency, such organization may be accorded formal recognition at the national level, but such recognition shall not preclude the agency from dealing at the national level with any other employee organization on matters affecting its members.

(b) When an employee organization has been formally recognized, the agency, through appropriate officials, shall consult with such organization from time to time in the formulation and implementation of personnel policies and practices, and matters affecting working conditions that are of concern to its members. Any such organization shall be entitled from time to time to raise such matters for discussion with appropriate officials and at all times to present its views thereon in writing. In no case, however, shall an agency be required to consult with an employee organization which has been formally recognized with respect to any matter which, if the employee organization were one entitled to exclusive recognition, would not be included within the obligation to meet and confer, as described in section 6 (b) of this order.

SEC. 6. (a) An agency shall recognize an employee organization as the exclusive representative of the employees, in an appropriate unit when such organization is eligible for formal recognition pursuant to section 5 of this order, and has been designated or selected by a majority of the employees of such unit as the representative of such employees in such unit. Units may be established on any plant or installation, craft, functional or other basis which will ensure a clear and identifiable community of interest among the employees concerned, but no unit shall be established solely on the basis of the extent to which employees in the proposed unit have organized. Except where otherwise required by established practice, prior agreement, or special circumstances, no unit shall be established for purposes of exclusive recognition which includes (1) any managerial executive, (2) any employee engaged in Federal personnel work in other than a purely clerical capacity, (3) both supervisors who officially evaluate the performance of employees and the employees whom they supervise, or (4) both professional employees and nonprofessional employees unless a majority of such professional employees vote for inclusion in such unit.

(b) When an employee organization has been recognized as the exclusive representative of employees of an appropriate unit it shall be entitled to act for and to negotiate agreements covering all employees in the unit and shall be responsible for representing the interests of all such employees without discrimination and without regard to employee organization membership. Such employee organization shall be given the opportunity to be represented at discussions between management and employees or employee representatives concerning grievances, personnel policies and practices, or other matters affecting general working conditions of employees in the unit. The agency and such employee organization, through appropriate officials and representatives, shall meet at reasonable times and confer with respect to personnel policy and practices and matters affecting working conditions, so far as may be appropriate subject to law and policy requirements. This extends to the negotiation of an agreement, or any question arising thereunder, the determination of appropriate techniques, consistent with the terms and purposes of this order, to assist in such negotiation, and the execution of a written memorandum of agreement or understanding incorporating any agreement reached by the parties. In exercising authority to make rules and regulations relating to personnel policies and practices and working conditions, agencies shall have due regard for the obligation imposed by this section, but such obligation shall not be construed to extend to such areas of discretion and policy as the mission of an agency, its budget, its organization and the assignment of its personnel, or the technology of performing its work.

SEC. 7. Any basic or initial agreement entered into with an employee organization as the exclusive representative of employees in a unit must be approved by the head of the agency or an official designated by him. All agreements with such employee or organizations shall also be subject to the following requirements, which shall be expressly stated in the initial or basic agreement and shall be applicable to all supplemental, implementing, subsidiary or informal agreements between the agency and the organization:

(1) In the administration of all matters covered by the agreement officials and employees are governed by the provisions of any existing or future laws and regulations, including policies set forth in the Federal Personnel Manual and agency regulations, which may be applicable, and the agreement shall at all times be applied subject to such laws, regulations and policies;

(2) Management officials of the agency retain the right, in accordance with applicable laws and regulations, (a) to direct employees of the agency, (b) to hire, promote, transfer, assign, and retain employees in positions within the agency, and to suspend, demote, discharge, or take other disciplinary action against employees, (c) to relieve employees from duties because of lack of work or for other legitimate reasons, (d) to maintain the efficiency of the Government operations entrusted to them, (e) to determine the methods, means and personnel by which such operations are to be conducted; and (f) to take whatever actions may be necessary to carry out the mission of the agency in situations of emergency.

SEC. 8. (a) Agreements entered into or negotiated in accordance with this order with an employee organization which is the exclusive representative of employees in an appropriate unit may contain provisions, applicable only to employees in the unit, concerning procedures for consideration of grievances. Such procedures (1) shall conform to standards issued by the Civil Service Commission, and (2) may not in any manner diminish or impair any rights which would otherwise be available to any employee in the absence of an agreement providing for such procedures.

(b) Procedures established by an agreement which are otherwise in conformity with this section may include provisions for the arbitration of grievances. Such arbitration (1) shall be advisory in nature with any decisions or recommendations subject to the approval of the agency head; (2) shall extend only to the interpretation or application of agreements or agency policy and not to changes in or proposed changes in agreements or agency policy; and (3) shall be invoked only with the approval of the individual employee or employees concerned.

SEC. 9. Solicitation of memberships, dues, or other internal employee organization business shall be conducted during the non-duty hours of the employees concerned. Officially requested or approved consultations and meetings between management officials and representatives of recognized employee organizations shall, whenever practicable, be conducted on official time, but any agency may require that negotiations with an employee organization which has been accorded exclusive recognition be conducted during the non-duty hours of the employee organization representatives involved in such negotiations.

SEC. 10. No later than July 1, 1962, the head of each agency shall issue appropriate policies, rules and regulations for the implementation of this order, including: A clear statement of the rights of its employees under the order, policies and procedures with respect to recognition of employee organizations; procedures for determining appropriate employee units; policies and practices regarding consultation with representatives of employee organizations, other organizations and individual employees; and policies with respect to the use of agency facilities by employee organizations. Insofar as may be practicable and appropriate, agencies shall consult with representatives of employee organizations in the formulation of these policies, rules and regulations.

SEC. 11. Each agency shall be responsible for determining in accordance with this order whether a unit is appropriate for purposes of exclusive recognition and, by an election or other appropriate means whether an employee organization represents a majority of the employees in such a unit so as to be entitled to such recognition. Upon the request of any agency, or of any employee organization which is seeking exclusive recognition and which qualifies for or has been accorded formal recognition, the Secretary of Labor, subject to such necessary rules as he may prescribe, shall nominate from the National Panel of Arbitrators maintained by the Federal Mediation and Conciliation Service one or more qualified arbitrators who will be available for employment by the agency concerned for either or both of the following purposes, as may be required: (1) to investigate the facts and issue an advisory decision as to the appropriateness of a unit for purposes of exclusive recognition and as to related issues submitted for consideration; (2) to conduct or supervise an election or otherwise determine by such means as may be appropriate, and on an advisory basis, whether an employee organization represents the majority of the employees in a unit. Consonant with law, the Secretary of Labor shall render such assistance as may be appropriate in connection with advisory decisions or determinations under this section, but the necessary costs of such assistance shall be paid by the agency to which it relates. In the event questions as to the appropriateness of a unit or the majority status of an employee organization shall arise in the Department of Labor, the duties described in this section which would otherwise be the responsibility of the Secretary of Labor shall be performed by the Civil Service Commission.

SEC. 12. The Civil Service Commission shall establish and maintain a program to assist in carrying out the objectives of this order. The Commission shall develop a program for the guidance of agencies in employee-management relations in the Federal service; provide technical advice to the agencies on employee-management programs; assist in the development of programs for training agency personnel in the principles and procedures of consultation, negotiation and the settlement of disputes in the Federal service, and for the training of management officials in the discharge of their employee-management relations responsibilities in the public interest; provide for continuous study and review of the Federal employee-management relations program and, from time to time, make recommendations to the President for its improvement.

SEC. 13. (a) The Civil Service Commission and the Department of Labor shall jointly prepare (1) proposed standards of conduct for employee organizations and (2) a proposed code of fair labor practices in employee-management relations in the Federal service appropriate to assist in securing the uniform and effective implementation of the policies, rights and responsibilities described in this order.

(b) There is hereby established the President's Temporary Committee on the Implementation of the Federal Employee-Management Relations Program. The Committee shall consist of the Secretary of Labor, who shall be chairman of the Committee, the Secretary of Defense, the Postmaster General, and the Chairman of the Civil Service Commission. In addition to such other matters relating to the implementation of this order as may be referred to it by the President, the Committee shall advise the President with respect to any problems arising out of completion of agreements pursuant to sections 6 and 7, and shall receive the proposed standards of conduct for employee organizations and proposed code of fair labor practices in the Federal service, as described in this section, and report thereon to the President with such recommendations or amendments as it may deem appropriate. Consonant with law, the departments and agencies represented on the Committee shall, as may be necessary for the effectuation of this section, furnish assistance to the Committee in accordance with section 214 of the Act of May 3, 1945, 59 Stat. 134 (31 U.S.C. 691). Unless otherwise directed by the President, the Committee shall cease to exist 30 days after the date on which it submits its report to the President pursuant to this section.

SEC. 14. The head of each agency, in accordance with the provisions of this order and regulations prescribed by the Civil Service Commission, shall extend to all employees in the competitive civil service rights identical in adverse action cases to those provided preference eligibles under section 14 of the Veterans' Preference Act of 1944, as amended. Each employee in the competitive service shall have the right to appeal to the Civil Service Commission from an adverse decision of the administrative officer so acting, such appeal to be processed in an identical manner to that provided for appeals under section 14 of the Veterans' Preference Act. Any recommendation by the Civil Service Commission submitted to the head of an agency on the basis of an appeal by an employee in the competitive service shall be complied with by the head of the agency. This section shall become effective as to all adverse actions commenced by issuance of a notification of proposed action on or after July 1, 1962.

SEC. 15. Nothing in this order shall be construed to annul or modify, or to preclude the renewal or continuation of, any lawful agreement heretofore entered into between any agency and any representative of its employees. Nor shall this order preclude any agency from continuing to consult or deal with any representative of its employees or other organization prior to the time that the status and representation rights of such representative or organization are determined in conformity with this order.

SEC. 16. This order (except section 14) shall not apply to the Federal Bureau of Investigation, the Central Intelligence Agency, or any other agency, or to any office, bureau or entity within an agency, primarily performing intelligence, investigative, or security functions if the head of the agency determines that the provisions of this order cannot be applied in a manner consistent with national security requirements and considerations. When he deems it necessary in the national interest, and subject to such conditions as he may prescribe, the head of any agency may suspend any provision of this order (except section 14) with respect to any agency installation or activity which is located outside of the United States.

Approved—January 17th, 1962.

JOHN F. KENNEDY

THE WHITE HOUSE,

January 17, 1962

Source: Exec. Order No. 10988, 27 Fed. Reg. 551 (January 17, 1962).

See also: American Federation of Labor (1886–1955); American Federation of Teachers (1916–); Historically Black Colleges and Universities (1837–); Land Grant Colleges and Universities

Further Reading

Murphy, Marjorie. 1990. *Blackboard Unions: The AFT and the NEA, 1900–1980.* Ithaca, NY: Cornell University Press.

Tyack, David B. 1974. *The One Best System: A History of American Urban Education.* Cambridge, MA: Harvard University Press.

Urban, Wayne. 1976. "Organized Teachers and Education Reform during the Progressive Era: 1890–1920." *History of Education Quarterly* 16 (1): 35–52.

Urban, Wayne. 2001. "Courting the Woman Teacher: The National Education Association, 1917–1970." *History of Education Quarterly* 41 (2): 139–166.

National Farmers Union (1902–)

The National Farmers Union (NFU) was—and remains—a mass organization dedicated to the economic viability of the small farmer and rancher. The second most significant farm organization in the United States, the NFU finds its organizational strength in the Upper Midwest and Great Plains. The most direct descendant of the 19th-century Grange and Populist movements, the NFU reflects those organization's radical agrarian edge. Conspicuously nonpartisan in its early years, the NFU eventually became a liberal interest group. Today, the organization remains active in 33 states and boasts 200,000 members. The NFU ranks in the second tier of politically potent farm bodies, but it remains the most powerful Democratic Party–aligned agricultural organization.

The NFU is rooted in the agrarian protest culture of the late 19th century. The rise of industrial capitalism and agricultural technological innovations pushed commodity prices downward. Coupled with high and static interest rates, agriculturalists found post–Civil War America increasingly inhospitable to small farms and ranches. As a result, farmers organized the Populist Movement of the 1880s and 1890s.

A significant political force in the South, Great Plains, and Mountain West, Populists held local, state, and national offices throughout their regional strongholds. In 1891, they organized the People's Party, which endorsed a Democrat, William Jennings Bryan (1860–1925), for the presidency in 1896; he very nearly won the White House. The Populist Movement constituted the NFU's roots and the movement's worldview remains relevant to the political philosophy of NFU's members.

The sustained prosperity of the late 1890s sapped the agrarian rebellion's momentum. In the decade after the Populist Movement's zenith in 1896, the U.S. economy averaged an aggressive 7.3 percent rate of growth. This, however, was not shared prosperity. Small farmers of the South and Great Plains continued to struggle with slumping commodity prices and tight credit. In 1902, Texas farmers organized the National Farmers' Union (NFU). The heir to the agrarian rebellion impulse, the NFU's founders were a motley collection of populists, socialists, Democrats, and political independents. Imbued with a Populist critique of farmers' issues, the NFU held "railroads, monopoly capital, speculators, and middlemen" in contempt.

Within three years of its inception, the NFU reached 200,000 members. Comprising almost wholly hardscrabble cotton farmers of Texas and the Deep South, the NFU excelled in organizing cooperative marketing techniques for its members. From warehouses to mutual purchasing and marketing, the NFU gave its members pragmatic and tangible economic benefits. Though the NFU exhibited an official disdain for modern capitalism and economies of scale, the cooperative's economic enterprises—not its political philosophy—attracted and maintained its membership base. At root, the NFU's defense of the "family farm," based upon the Jeffersonian ideal, was (and remains) its ideological core.

The predominance of sharecropping (an arrangement in which a farmer rents land from a landowner and then shares a portion of the crops with the landowner) and relative lack of small landed farmers in the South pushed the NFU's center of gravity northward. By the late 1920s, the NFU had become a vital economic and political organization in the wheat belt and dairy regions of the Great Plains and Upper Midwest. In terms of the latter, the early NFU conspicuously avoided what it termed "partisanry." With many old populists still angry over the People's Party fusion with the Democrats, the NFU pushed for its members' interests but avoided the development of an independent political movement.

The post-1917 economic slump in commodity prices prompted a revival of agricultural discontent. With the American electorate in no mood for Progressive crusades, farmers trod carefully. Working with the NFU and the staid American Farm Bureau, the Congressional Farm Bloc coalesced. Comprised of congressmen from states with significant agricultural interests, the Farm Bloc pushed for stable commodity prices and access to credit. With the farm economy lagging, the NFU moved into direct political action by supporting Robert LaFollette's (1855–1925) 1924 Progressive Party presidential bid.

The presidency of Franklin D. Roosevelt (1882–1945) marked a turning point in the NFU's history. During the Great Depression, the NFU clung to dated populist clichés. In addition to calling for "currency inflation," the organization balked at the New Deal's Agricultural Adjustment Act, which set limits on the production of key crops, like wheat, in order to stabilize prices during the Great Depression. The NFU objected to these measures, maintaining that agriculture remained the nation's economic foundation.

In 1940, James G. Patton (1902–1985) was elevated to the NFU presidency. During his tenure, Patton reconfigured the NFU's ideology from populist to agrarian liberalism. Remarkable for his black eye patch, Patton also transformed the NFU into a major player in national politics. Born in Kansas, the same year as the NFU's founding, Patton was immersed in the region's populist political culture. An ally of former vice president and secretary of agriculture Henry Wallace (1888–1965), Patton updated the NFU's populism for the New Deal order. In return, Roosevelt allowed the NFU's agrarianism into mainstream liberalism. As a result, the NFU doubled its membership between 1939 and 1945.

Under Patton, the NFU developed a thoroughgoing political philosophy that placed it largely within the liberal mainstream. First, the NFU accepted a tough reality: agriculture, and by extension rural America, was not the centerpiece of the American economy and experience. This was no small concession; for decades, populists had maintained the utter economic centrality of the farmer to American economic life. Realizing rural America had become secondary to its urban counterparts in the labor movement, Patton pushed the NFU to make common cause with it. Claiming producers and consumers shared common interests, he pushed for a political coalition of farmers and labor within the New Deal coalition.

Although Patton conceded rural America's secondary economic position, he maintained the classic Jeffersonian, and populist, belief in the family farm's centrality to the democratic experiment. To save small farmers and buttress democracy, significant federal intervention was necessary. Proffering a new-fangled agrarian liberal philosophy, Patton combined old populist shibboleths with New Deal liberalism. To Patton, small farmers faced a "monopoly squeeze" wherein they could only buy equipment from two companies that charged what they wanted. Once they harvested their crops, farmers encountered a distribution market controlled by a few firms. Forced to produce maximally to reap ever-smaller profits, the NFU pushed for federal subsidies paid directly to the farmer. Thus, the urban consumer—workers—could enjoy low food prices while small farmers could earn profit.

Boosted by postwar optimism in the efficacy of federal interventions and the bright future of American life, Patton hitched the NFU wagon to the New Deal coalition. Temporarily, the family farmer held an important political place in the New Deal coalition. Dominated by urban interests, postwar liberals directed agricultural policy toward lowering consumer costs. Thus, farmers, regardless of their landholdings, received subsidies, but the NFU's ideal of preserving the family farm never became central liberal orthodoxy.

In the early Cold War era, the NFU behaved politically akin to labor unions. Under Patton's strong leadership, the NFU pushed its members' bread-and-butter concerns. At the same time, the NFU also pressed for a broad array of liberal social issues and foreign policy goals that ran afoul of its membership. This loyalty was very nearly rewarded handsomely by the Harry Truman administration's ambitious Brannan Plan. The Plan would have paid farmers a predetermined "parity" price for commodities; the resulting overproduction of commodities would have benefited consumers with lower prices. Undone by the Korean War (1950–1953) and McCarthyism, the Brannan Plan, nevertheless, marked the NFU's high-water mark in national politics.

Marked by McCarthyism as a farm organization rife with communists, the NFU fared poorly in the 1950s. Successive Republican presidents turned to the Farm Bureau, which pushed the interests of its larger landholding members. When the Democrats regained control during the John F. Kennedy and Lyndon B. Johnson years, the NFU enjoyed elite access. Despite this, the NFU faced stiff economic headwinds.

Mechanization of agriculture simultaneously reduced commodity prices and substantially raised the costs associated with farming. Thus, postwar small family farmers, the NFU's backbone, encountered an increasingly complicated agricultural economy. With small margins between profit and loss, small farmers found themselves increasingly unable to navigate the trials of recession, inclement weather, and commodity markets. By the 1970s, millions of small farmers faced the reality of bank foreclosures. Temporarily, the NFU's populist, rabble-rousing appeal enjoyed a rebound. From the American Agriculture Movement to Wayne Cryts's (1946–) 1981 Bean Raid, the Farm Belt witnessed tumult not seen since the 1890s. The NFU, however, was unable to permanently capitalize on this turnabout.

Since the NFU's high-water mark of 1950, small farmers have lost political power. In 1950, 44 percent of Americans lived on a farm or in a small town. Both utterly dependent upon agriculture, farmers and voters in those towns backed farming concerns. By the time of the farm crisis in the 1980s, only 23 percent of Americans lived on a farm or in small towns. Thus, when family farmers faced a spate of foreclosures, the NFU lacked the political heft to rally a substantial policy response. As a result, the NFU is an organizational shadow of its former self. Reflecting the economic realities of rural America, the NFU is home to a dwindling number of farmers and ranchers who proffer a populist worldview critical of free markets and corporate agriculture and supportive of a political coalition with urban liberals.

Jeff Bloodworth

See also: American Farm Bureau Federation (1911–); Grocery Manufacturers Association (1908–); National Dairy Council (1915–); United Farm Workers (1966–); United Fresh Produce Association (1904–)

Further Reading

Crampton, John. 1965. *The National Farmers Union: Ideology of a Pressure Group.* Lincoln: University of Nebraska Press.

Feld, Bruce. 1998. *Harvest of Dissent: The National Farmers Union and the Early Cold War.* Lawrence: University Press of Kansas.

Flamm, Michael. 1994. "The National Farmers Union and the Evolution of Agrarian Liberalism, 1937–1946." *Agricultural History* 68, no. 3 (Summer): 54–80.

Matusow, Allen. 1967. *Farm Policies and Politics in the Truman Years*. Cambridge, MA: Harvard University Press.

Mooney, Patrick, and Theo Makja. 1995. *Farmers' and Farm Workers' Movements: Social Protest in American Agriculture*. New York: Twayne Publishers.

National Foreign Trade Council (1914–)

The National Foreign Trade Council (NFTC) is a trade association founded by James Ferrell (1863–1943), president of U.S. Steel between 1911 and 1932. The NFTC has long advocated for a free trade agenda though it supports its regulation by national and international governance procedures to ensure a relatively fair level of competition. Like other trade associations, NFTC is a mostly private interest–oriented political group and its notion that regulated free trade is one in which its own member corporations received the largest benefit. It is also a confederation of smaller corporations, which allows it to mobilize a high level of resources. But, at times, this is offset by the tendency for internal conflict as its constituents are actually in business competition with one another.

The NFTC was founded during the Progressive Era in the late 19th and early 20th centuries when efforts to regulate big business in the United States and around the world were on the rise. Along with the earlier Populist Movement, activists of the Progressive Era raised awareness about the ill effects of unbridled capitalism both at home and abroad. In addition, the Mugwumps, a group of political activists who called for the reform of basic political, economic, and social institutions in the United States, had leveled trenchant criticism against corporate greed and corruption. At the same time, muckraker investigative journalists like Ida Tarbell (1957–1944) and Nellie Bly (1864–1922) covered the business practices of capitalist elites and the exploitation of labor. But it was the Progressive Movement's policies of increased government regulation of large companies, including the development of bodies of law protecting labor and consumer alike, that led to industrywide pushback. Progressives promoted their ideas at the state level with the support of prominent politicians like Robert M. Lafollette (1855–1925) and Hiram Johnson (1866–1945). Such activities were expanded upon and applied nationally by President Theodore Roosevelt (1858–1920). In turn, this spurred corporations' collective efforts to protect previous gains against what they initially saw as an unwarranted and anticapitalistic intrusion by the public into the private sector.

The development of the global free trade regime was instrumental in the formation of NFTC. The free trade of goods and services across international boundaries was a key concept to the theoretical development of capitalism. Its trade regime counterpart, protectionism, had been the status quo of world economic history since ancient times. Adam Smith's (1723–1790) *Wealth of Nations* indicted the extant mercantilist system of imperially bounded trade networks as the principal cause of great power conflict. Nevertheless, despite the advance of capitalism through the global industrial revolution, countries held firmly to protectionist trade policies.

In the United States, the trade issue was only partially embedded in the two-party system as both parties had strong protectionist wings. Conservative ideology at the time was dominantly protectionist, sharing that view with the British Conservative Party. In the wake of the Civil War (1861–1865), the Republicans were the nationally dominant party. However, after Reconstruction (1866–1877), the Democrats had regained ascendancy in the South with some inroads into the West and maintained their strength in the Northern cities. The Democrats were more favorable to free trade, something they held in common with the British Liberal Party. But because they were more disparate in organizational influence across the country than the more concentrated Republicans; their views took a national backseat toward the end of the 19th century.

However, the idea of expanding the invisible hand of unrestrained capitalism beyond the water's edge in order to develop a truly international free trade economic society had been growing since the mid-nineteenth century. The British were the progenitors of, and greatest practitioners in, the application of this new definition of economic freedom. In 1845, with the ascent of Queen Victoria, the British Parliament set a goal of free trade. The might of the wealthiest and most powerful country in the history of the world up to that time was reengineering itself as a prophet for the expansion of an unrestrained international capitalist agenda. And central to that agenda was the articulation and imposition of a boundless trade ideology. Hence the twin historical paths: the Progressives trying to rein in industrial and trade capitalism domestically and the international free trade movement backed by the might of the British Empire served as the impetus for American business to respond in a big way.

When Ferrell founded NFTC, its concerns were strictly trade based. However, Ferrell recognized that he was trying to pull together interests that were not only disaggregated but often opposed one another. Maintaining a relatively simple focal point for issue orientation, then, became a steady feature of NFTC's organizational politics for many decades to come. Initially, the group was composed of large industrial trade interests like Ferrell's own U.S. Steel. It began with a lobbying strategy that was focused on the Republican Party's conservative wing of legislators and the federal judiciary. The goal was to promote its ideas about tariff reduction while trying to offset further national-level domestic regulation of the industries that comprised NFTC. The judiciary was particularly targeted because both trade disputes and labor as well as consumer policy protections were adjudicated there.

Due to the expansion of the executive branch during World War I (1914–1918), NFTC quickly adapted by including Woodrow Wilson administration (1913–1921) officials as well as civil service bureaucratic administrators in its lobbying efforts. They also, expanded to a larger "target audience" for NFTC's lobbying strategy as progressives, liberals, and Democrats became a pool of potential responders to NFTC efforts. The war and its aftermath brought about a tremendous expansion of global trade; NFTC responded accordingly with professionalized lobbyist development. Additionally, NFTC adapted progressive calls for corporate regulation. NFTC even made a larger compromise with protectionists by adding an opening within its preferred umbrella of issues and policies for trade regulation, both domestically and internationally.

The Great Depression and World War II (1939–1945) were boons to the policy goals of the NFTC because of changes within the international climate regarding the virtues of free trade. Led by the United States, Great Britain, France, and China, the victorious capitalistic powers aggressively implemented and promoted free trade as a means to quicken the post-war recovery. This was also done to deter future conflicts through trade-based economic interdependence along lines of comparative advantage. In addition, the efforts sought to apply liberalism's notions of economic freedom to a war-weary world in the face of potential fascist authoritarian resurgence. And, importantly the measures were advocated as a counterbalance to the emergent Cold War threat of communistic totalitarianism. Thus, the NFTC found itself on the front edge of the expansion of trade markets and as a defender of capitalism in the face of the Second World's Marxist-Socialism.

NFTC continues to engage in a lobbying strategy that is mostly oriented at the national level of government. It does this through showcasing business and political elites' messages, the production of working papers, issuance of news briefs, and fund-raising as well as disseminating funds to politicians deemed friendly to NFTC's interests. It lobbies Republicans mostly but not exclusively, as it has also found supporters among the centrist wing of the Democratic Party. NFTC's preference for usage of the insider strategy is because of Washington, D.C.'s prominent role in trade policy making. However, it has increasingly become involved in trade bargaining that occurs at the business-to-business level. Thus, its New York-based business lobbying has moved the organization towards a less explicitly political and more intensively economic approach. Also, the organization has moved beyond being an advocate for big business and now actively recruits smaller corporations. Much of this has appeared in the years since the 1960s when the Cold War began to decline and eventually end, opening up previously cut-off trade routes to Western interests. In addition, the expansion of labor markets into the developing world as well as the corresponding increase in consumer markets in Global North countries has been a boon for NFTC and its members. As a result of its "economic turn," NFTC has added financial lobbying in both business and political avenues to its retinue of services offered to affiliates. In particular, NFTC has become very involved in the development of corporate taxing policies as they relate to trade issues.

Finally, the pushback against the free trade agenda by protectionists in both the Democratic and Republican parties is something that NFTC has to take seriously. The neoliberal consensus that developed across both parties by the 1980s has been placed under pressure. This was due to externalities that left many domestic constituencies out of the benefits of the liberal international economic order's (LIEO) perceived wisdom. NFTC has recently renewed its efforts to reshape the political and economic landscape toward free trade.

Matthew M. Caverly

See also: American Foreign Service Association (1924–)

Further Reading

Baumgartner, F., and B. Leech. 1998. *Basic Interests: The Importance of Groups in Political Science*. Princeton, NJ: Princeton University Press.

Gourevitch, P. 1978. "The Second Image Reversed: The International Sources of Domestic Politics." *International Organizations* 32 (1): 881–911.

Gourevitch, P. 1996. "Squaring the Circle: The Domestic Sources of International Relations." *International Organizations* 50 (1): 349–373.

Levy, P. 1997. "A Political-Economic Analysis of Free Trade Agreements." *American Economic Review* 1 (1): 506–519.

National Foreign Trade Council. 2018. http://www.nftc.org/?id=1.

National Governors Association (1908–)

The National Governors Association (NGA) is an organization that serves as the collective voice of the nation's governors on issues of national policy relevant to the states. The organization helps coordinate interstate programs while also sharing best practices among the states, all the while serving as a representative for the interest of the states in the halls of Congress, and among the executive agencies. Its mission statement declares, "The National Governors Association (NGA) is the bipartisan organization of the nation's governors. Through NGA, governors share best practices, speak with a collective voice on national policy and develop innovative solutions that improve state government and support the principles of federalism." The Association's members include the chief executive from the nation's 50 states as well as the five U.S. territories—American Samoa, Guam, Northern Mariana Islands, Puerto Rico, and the U.S. Virgin Islands.

What is now known as the National Governors Association has its roots in a gathering called by President Theodore Roosevelt (1858–1919) in 1908. Then called the National Governors' Conference, the first meeting came in the aftermath of the creation in 1907 of the Inland Waterways Commission. Given that the Commission's work touched on numerous states, Roosevelt thought that a gathering of governors to consider issues of conservation, a national issue in the eyes of the president, as well as some of the issues particular to the inland waterways would be valuable. From that initial meeting came the development of an annual conference of the nation's chief executives which continues to this day under the auspices of the NGA, which itself has grown and developed into a vital organization supporting the interests of the state governors from coast to coast.

In its current form, the National Governors Association serves as a liaison between the federal government and the different and diverse state governments. Reflective of its commitment to bipartisan advocacy of states' interests, in 1977 the group formally adopted its long-standing practice of having the chairmanship of the organization alternate annually between the parties, with the vice chair usually being of the opposite party of the chair as well as the one who, in most cases, ascends to the chairmanship the following year. The chair, the vice chair, and eight additional governors comprise the organization's executive committee. Elected annually, they are responsible for the oversight of the association's operations and have responsibility for all policy issues.

One of the political perks, so to speak, of being NGA chair is the opportunity to pursue a singular initiative with the full weight of the organization behind it. Reflective of the nature of politics, those efforts have often served to highlight some of the chair's own efforts and accomplishments to his or her broader political benefit, but at the same time, they have also allowed the NGA to engage in many of the ongoing national debates. Over the years, these efforts, representing the full range of issues the governors confront, have included Bill Clinton's (1946–) "Making America Work: Productive People, Productive Policies," Howard Dean's (1948–) "Governor's Campaign for Children," Mark Warner's (1954–) "Redesigning the American High School," Mike Huckabee's (1955–) "Healthy American: Wellness Where We Live, Work and Learn," Tim Pawlenty's (1960–) "Securing a Clean Energy Future," Terry McAuliffe's (1957–) "Meet the Threat: States Confront the Cyber Challenge," and John Sununu's (1939–) "Restoring the Balance: State Leadership for America's Future." Over the years, the initiatives have also addressed issues of infrastructure, employment for disabled citizens, and health care reform.

As a body dedicated to supporting the work of the federal government and the states' governments, NGA provides a number of different services. The organization has developed the NGA Center for Best Practices, which looks at and shares the ways states seek to address issues ranging from education to technology, from economic development to the environment. These efforts have yielded numerous reports that have supported and affected efforts across the country. Typical of this approach was the 2014 report titled "The Cybersecurity Workforce: States Needs and Opportunities." Similarly, in the midst of the debates over health care, the NGA weighed in with a report entitled "The Role of the Physician Assistant in Health Care Delivery."

Meanwhile, the 2014 report "Financial Empowerment: How Delaware Improved Financial Security Through Coaching" was an example of the way that through NGA, one state's efforts can be shared with others and can then be adapted and used as appropriate. Other recent NGA sponsored publications include "The Promise of the State-Federal Partnership on Workforce and Job Training," "Advancing the Energy-Water Nexus: How Governors Can Bridge Their Conservation Goals," and "How Maryland Policymakers Are Working Together to Improve School Principal Quality." Beyond such issue-oriented initiatives and ideas, the NGA also provides management and technical assistance to governors across the country.

By virtue of their shared experiences and fundamental responsibilities, the NGA seeks to strip away some of the usual trappings of politics from their work. The NGA promotes debate on the issues facing the states, and no members campaign or fund-raise while meeting to conduct business. Similarly, as a group they seek to promote ideas, working together to find solutions to policy challenges. In that same vein, the group is committed to ensuring that their gatherings are open for policy discussions focused on solutions, accepting of various viewpoints, and committed to compromise.

In fact, notwithstanding that all members of the NGA are politicians, the organization's meetings are intended to provide a respite from the pressures of the political world and instead offer an opportunity to focus on policy with "collaboration not rhetoric" another NGA principle, being the watchword as NGA "provides a trusted, bi-partisan environment for high level exchange of ideas and viewpoints." Finally, the group is deeply committed to being inclusive; any corporation or organization wanting to partner with the NGA needs to be similarly committed.

While these connections fostered by their corporate fellowships emphasis are intended to be non-partisan, they also seek to encourage a partnership aimed collaborative effort that mesh economic development with efficient and effective delivery of state services. The NGA believe that both sides—as well as the public at large—can profit when governors and corporate leaders together look at developing trends and emerging factors as they plan their future endeavors.

A centerpiece of the modern NGA's operation is the NGA Center for Best Practices. A support organization that helps develop solutions to the problems of the day, it provides a tremendous resource from which governors can draw, adapting the ideas and findings of the center to the specific problems and challenges in their individual states. With a stable of policy experts as well as access to countless more, the Center for Best Practices is a unique operation in that it is the only research and development type organization that exclusively serves the nation's governors.

To further strengthen their voice in the governing process, the NGA and its representatives offer frequent testimony at congressional hearings. Whether it is their own expert staff members, state officials that NGA identifies as effective spokespeople, or the governors themselves, the NGA is an active contributor to this part of the legislative process, ensuring that federal elected officials are fully informed about the way proposed legislation may impact the states and their interests.

In support of the governor's efforts, the NGA has a number of committees that conduct research while developing programs to address the issues they study. These committees, which are coordinated with the divisions focused in the association's Center for Best Practices include the Health & Human Services Committee, Economic Development & Commerce Committee, Education & Workforce Committee, Homeland Security & Public Safety Committee, and Natural Resources Committee. Each of these committees may be a source of independent, evidence-based information as well as policy proposals for governors and their administrations as they seek to address problems in these areas.

Interestingly, in an organization with as a long a history as the NGA, Bill Clinton is the only former NGA chair to become president. Meanwhile, the increased role of women in politics has carried over into the NGA with Janet Napolitano (1957–) of Arizona becoming the first female chair in 2006, while Oklahoma's Mary Fallin (1954–) followed suit in 2013.

As debates about the extent of government, as well as the role of federalism, sweep and in many ways divide the nation, the NGA remains an organization dedicated to providing a forum for support of the chief executives of the nation's 50 states and 5 territories as they seek to carry out their own responsibilities as well as those that come their way in the complex and multidimensional American system.

William H. Pruden III

See also: National Conference of State Legislatures (1975–); National School Boards Association (1942–)

Further Reading

Descant, Skip. 2017. "National Governors Association Forms Tech Division." Future-Structure, October 4, 2017. http://www.govtech.com/fs/automation/National -Governors-Association-Forms-Tech-Division-.html.

Miller, Zeke J. 2015. "Governors in D.C.: Beset by Lobbyists, Riven by Partisanship." *Time*, February 23, 2015. http://time.com/3717941/national-governors-association/.

National Governors Association (NGA). 2018. https://www.nga.org/cms/home.

Shapiro, Gary. 2017. "As Head of National Governors Association, Sandoval Will Spark Innovation." *Las Vegas Sun*, July 14, 2017. https://lasvegassun.com/news/2017/jul /14/as-head-of-national-governors-association-sandoval/.

National Grange of the Order of Patrons of Husbandry (1867–)

The National Grange of the Order of Patrons of Husbandry, better known simply as the Grange, is an agricultural membership association founded in 1867 that continues to function today. A Minnesota farmer, Oliver Kelley, and seven other key founders established the organization after Kelley took a job with the United States Bureau of Agriculture in 1864, and became convinced that farmers needed organized representation to deal with the government and to promote agriculture-friendly policies with lawmakers. Also, farmers needed a social organization that could unite them when not working on the farms, and many rural communities lacked social groups. Kelley was a Mason himself, and likely used that experience as a basis for the Grange's secret, fraternal activities.

The Grange spread rapidly in the early- to mid-1870s, where receptive farmers joined the ranks in the Midwest and South; in the Northeast, support was much lower. This rapid increase in membership, termed the First Granger Movement, centered attention on the political issues related to farming. It is noted as being at the forefront of demands for government regulation of railroad pricing to lower costs for shipping agricultural products, attacks on monopolies, and efforts to cut out middlemen from the process of buying and selling products. The Panic of 1873 was a key force behind the national organization's call for direct political involvement, as farmers were suffering from economic hardship.

These attacks on the established social order did attract attention, and some of the ideas espoused found a willing audience with state lawmakers. So-called "Granger Laws" that regulated railroads and grain warehouses made it through state governments in Iowa, Illinois, Minnesota, and Wisconsin during the early 1870s. However, the importance of the role played by the Grange in pressuring governments to adopt these laws is debatable, even though the name of the organization is associated with the laws. Still, the fact that some state Grange organizations lobbied for such reforms places the overall organization in line with this legislation.

These laws were challenged in the state of Illinois in two Supreme Court cases, *Munn v. Illinois* (1876) and *Wabash, St. Louis & Pacific Railway Company v.*

Illinois (1886). In the former, the Supreme Court decided that state governments could regulate private industry, but this was reversed in the latter case, as the court's decision increased the federal government's authority to regulate interstate commerce at the expense of the states. Because of this decision, Congress reacted and passed legislation to create the Interstate Commerce Commission in 1887. Considering the constitutional importance of these cases, and the laws that led to them, the Grange's pressure for government regulation of railroads was a catalyst, ultimately recreating how the federal government interacted with the economy.

Outside of government, the Grange of this era sought to provide its members with better prices for their crops, and for purchasing seed and machinery. To do this, efforts were put forth to incentivize membership through the creation of cooperative arrangements which helped Grangers eliminate middlemen in order to buy and sell products and machinery at favorable rates. Success was minimal, and these efforts ultimately failed by the mid-1870s. (After this, sometimes Grangers went outside the organization to help found cooperative associations.)

However, this First Granger Movement was short-lived. Numerous factors have been floated for the problems faced by the Grange in the late 1870s and into the 1880s, but it is likely a combination of failed business ventures through the cooperatives, organizational leadership unprepared for such a rapid increase in membership and the number of granges, internal fights over policy, and the secret fraternal elements creating claims of fraud and deception among local, state, and even national leadership. The advent of the Farmers' Alliance, which was much more radical in its calls for agricultural reform, also played a role. Farmers in the South and Midwest were attracted by this new organization's message and flocked to it, and it would eventually serve as the rural backbone of the Populist Party. The Grange found its bases of support diminishing, and state Granges even ceased operations altogether in a few cases.

Yet not all farmers left the organization. Some devoted Grangers stood by it, and with a more conservative approach than other farming organizations, it rebounded years later. The rebirth of the Grange occurred in the late 1880s and early 1890s. This Second Granger Movement, as it is called, was located not in the South and Midwest but in New England, New York, Pennsylvania, and Ohio, where agriculture faced a downturn. Many farmers had left the Eastern states for cheaper, more readily accessible land out West, and those remaining in the East wanted to find an organization to promote their interests. Despite these regional shifts in the Grange's base of support, demands for particular policies did not change significantly; its core message remained intact. But instead of emphasizing antipathy to railroad rates and monopolies, the Grange placed greater focus on other aspects of the organization, namely the creation of regulatory bodies interested in agriculture and the promotion of education among all levels and classes of farmers.

Broadly conceived, then, the Grange's policy activities during the late 1800s and early 1900s stressed government support for agriculture. Nationally, the Grange wanted the federal government to take agriculture seriously, and lobbying was directed toward receiving a cabinet-level department. This came to fruition in 1889, when Congress, with President Grover Cleveland's approval, passed legislation making the Department of Agriculture a cabinet-level department.

A similar push for state-level agencies committed to supporting agriculture occurred, too. Ultimately, these activities aimed to institutionalize government support for agriculture, and in these efforts the Grange succeeded.

In a continuation of this goal, the Grange was also a critical component of efforts to reform and expand agricultural education and educational opportunities for those employed on farms. When it came to higher education, the Grange wanted the federal and state governments to properly execute the land-grant program, specifically through the creation and support of separate agricultural colleges. Additionally, the Grange supported agricultural experimentation as a means of improving farming methods, and the organization's influence played a role in the passage of the Hatch Act of 1887. This law provided federal government money to state land-grant colleges, with an explicit goal of establishing experimental agricultural stations.

When it came to general education for adults and children alike, the organization pushed its members to read more, through agricultural publications and materials in grange libraries. The Grange also advocated for the creation of extension programs through which those involved in farming could learn about new agricultural methods and, at times, how to improve and preserve the rural lifestyle that was in decline during this industrializing, urbanizing era. It also wanted improved rural schooling for children, who often did not receive a good education in the local schools.

But there were other major issues of the era that the Grange was interested in, and it was one organization among many that pushed for the postal service to establish free rural delivery and for regulations to ensure only "pure foods" were bought and sold. For example, the Grange adamantly opposed weakening laws that would make it easier for oleo (margarine) producers to create a product that looked like butter.

Like many so-called voluntary associations of the era, the Grange relied on the rites and rituals of fraternal organizations to keep people interested and involved, above and beyond its policy missions. Members could rise up the seven ranks, or "degrees," which corresponded to different levels of the organization. For example, the sixth-degree Flora (Charity) and Ceres (Faith) were conferred only by the national organization. To ensure that this order properly represented the interests of farmers, only those individuals who were 16 years of age or older and who were involved in agriculture could become members. In this way, the Grange relied on the social and educational opportunities to engage farmers in the organization, not on economic incentives.

The Grange was also unique in its acceptance of both men and women as voting participants and leaders, even though women could not (or did not) rise to the most senior positions in the organization. Nevertheless, men and women served important functions on an equal footing, and husband-and-wife pairings were critical to the organization's leadership. Because of its heritage of equality, the national organization stepped outside its traditional policy focus in order to support granting women the franchise. In many respects, then, the Grange represented a progressive and modernized agenda for a more educated, inclusive American society, while still attempting to preserve an agrarian outlook.

But the Grange's prominence during the Golden Age of Associations (1875–1920) left them at a disadvantage, as newer farm organizations entered with more direct political intentions and as organizations focused on particular agricultural commodities began to increase their influence in Washington, D.C., and in state capitols. These included the Farmers' Union, the Farm Bureau, and the National Farmers' Organization, to name a few. Increasingly, the Grange focused on providing an organizational social sphere for farmers as other organizations became the political arm of the agricultural lobbying community.

Today, the National Grange of the Order of Patrons of Husbandry remains active in this capacity, and it does continue to advocate at times for policy change while supporting rural farming communities through its organization. In terms of policy, the Grange wants government to improve rural infrastructure (including high-speed Internet and a well-maintained postal service); maintain aid to support rural health care services; and clearer, more stable immigration and visa standards to help farm owners and foreign-born laborers alike.

Adam Chamberlain

See also: American Farm Bureau Federation (1911–); National Farmers Union (1902–); National Rural Electric Cooperative Association (1942–); United Farm Workers (1966–)

Further Reading

Marcus, Alan I. 1986. "The Ivory Silo: Farmer-Agricultural College Tensions in the 1870s and 1880s." *Agricultural History* 60 (2): 22–36.

Miller, George H. 1971. *Railroads and the Granger Laws*. Madison: The University of Wisconsin Press.

Nordin, D. Sven. 1974. *Rich Harvest: A History of the Grange, 1867–1900*. Jackson: University Press of Mississippi.

National LGBTQ Task Force (1973–)

The National LGBTQ Task Force is the oldest national LGBTQ advocacy group in the United States. New York activists who had met in the Gay Activists Alliance founded the organization in 1973 to "fill the void where no national work was being done on behalf of gays" (Rimmerman 2000). Much of the work of the Task Force focuses on building grassroots power by training state and local activists. This was crucial during the 2000s when much of the legislation that targeted the gay and lesbian community was being passed on a state and local level, such as same-sex marriage bans.

The National LGBTQ Task Force began as the National Gay Task Force, was changed to the National Gay and Lesbian Task Force in 1985, and is now known as the National LGBTQ Task Force, or often simply the Task Force. According to historian John D'Emilio (1948–), "No account of the changes in the laws and public policies that shape gay lesbian life in the United States would be complete without attention to [the history of the National Gay and Lesbian Task Force]" (D'Emilio 2002). The initial goals of the Task Force were to bring "gay liberation into the mainstream of American civil rights" and "to focus on broad national issues" (Rimmerman 2000). The organization served as a source of information and advice to local groups.

The organization earned many early accomplishments. It persuaded the American Psychiatric Association to no longer classify homosexuality as a mental illness. The organization was able to convince Rep. Bella Abzug (1920–1998) (D-NY) to introduce the first gay civil rights bill to Congress in 1974. It initiated the first meeting in the White House between gay leaders and a top presidential adviser to President Jimmy Carter (1924–). It encouraged the National Council of Churches to adopt a resolution condemning antigay discrimination. It persuaded the American Bar Association to announce support for the repeal of sodomy laws. It successfully lobbied the Civil Service Commission to end its practice of employment discrimination on the basis of sexual orientation in 1975. The Task Force accomplished all of this at a time when it was still quite small, with an annual budget in 1980 of only $260,000—the equivalent of about $772,000 in 2018.

Women were treated equally within the organization from the beginning. Board membership was divided equally between men and women, and a female coexecutive director was hired in 1975. The Task Force worked with women's organizations to encourage them to support lesbian rights.

The Task Force moved from New York to Washington, D.C., in 1986. The organization grew following the 1987 March on Washington for Lesbian and Gay Rights. During this time the organization mostly focused on issues of violence, privacy, and AIDS, but by the end of the 1980s, this widened to include the military ban on gays and lesbians, and family issues, including relationship recognition and adoption. In 1984, the Task Force issued the first extensive report on anti-gay hate crimes. The Task Force worked with friendly members of Congress to organize congressional hearings on the AIDS epidemic.

The organization became more diverse in the late 1980s, especially in its leadership roles with the appointment of Urvashi Vaid as Executive Director in 1989. As a result, the organization began to focus more on the intersection of race with lesbian and gay politics. The organization also became much larger and better funded – by 1996 the Task Force boasted 40,000 members and an annual budget of $2.4 million.

In the 1990s, the Task Force widened its scope even further, focusing on coalition politics. The organization believed that there needed to be a more explicitly progressive voice within the LGBTQ community and began labeling itself as the "progressive voice of the queer movement" and the "queer voice of the progressive movement." The Task Force began speaking out on issues such as welfare reform, immigration, affirmative action, and the death penalty and began to explicitly include the concerns of the bisexual and transgender members of the community. In 1995, the Task Force established its own think tank, the Policy Institute, to produce research and progressive analysis that could be used by activists. The Policy Institute produces research on a range of issues that affect LGBTQ individuals, such as anti-LGBTQ ballot measures, health issues, and parenting concerns.

The Task Force established its Creating Change conference in 1988, and it was quickly recognized as the premier gathering of LGBTQ activists in the country.

The goal of the conference is to make contacts with activists at the grassroots level. However, as the Creating Change conference has grown from 300 attendees in 1988 to over 4,000 attendees in 2017, there has been an increase in conflict.

At the 2016 conference, over 200 people protested a reception planned for an LGBT Israeli group, shutting down the reception. There was so much backlash prior to the conference that the reception was canceled, but that decision faced backlash as well and so the reception was reinstated, leading to the protest. There was also conflict over a planned workshop with officials from Immigration and Customs Enforcement, prompting organizers to cancel the session. Many activists and the leadership at the Task Force believe that this tension is a reflection of divisions within the broader LGBTQ community. Following victories on the issues of marriage equality and military service, there is now less to unify the community.

Even with all the victories of the Task Force, the organization has faced difficulties in its forty-three-year history. It has often been accused of overreaching and has therefore faced major budget crises. There have been several issues that the organization began to address and then dropped without explanation. There have also been times when it has faced rapid turnover in its leadership. One former leader argues that the Task Force has failed to live up to its potential to be a mobilizing force for the LGBTQ community because "they're an organization without a vision" (Rimmerman 2000).

Jessica Loyet Gracey

See also: GLAAD (1985–); Human Rights Campaign (1980–)

Further Reading

Brydum, Sunnivie. 2016. "Creating Change Conference Reflects a Movement in Transition." *The Advocate*, February 1, 2016.

D'Emilio, John. 2002. *The World Turned: Essays on Gay History, Politics, and Culture.* Durham, NC: Duke University Press.

Rimmerman, Craig A. 2000. "Beyond Political Mainstreaming: Reflections on Lesbian and Gay Organizations and the Grassroots." In *The Politics of Gay Rights*, edited by Craig A. Rimmerman, Kenneth D. Wald, and Clyde Wilcox. Chicago: The University of Chicago Press.

National Organization for Marriage (2007–)

In an attempt to garner support for Proposition 8, a ballot initiative intended to ban same-sex marriage in California, Maggie Gallagher (1960–), Robert P. George (1955–), and current president and former executive director Brian Brown (1974–), founded the National Organization for Marriage (NOM), a nonprofit organization with 501(c)(4) status, in 2007. Though a federal court ultimately struck down the initiative, NOM stuck around, fulfilling what it felt was a necessary opposition to same-sex marriage at the state and local levels across the nation.

NOM's mission statement according to its website is "to protect marriage and the faith communities that sustain it" ("About Us" 2018). NOM seeks to achieve this goal by building its membership, swaying public opinion by educating the public about their cause, and fighting to defend the definition of marriage as a union between a man and woman within legislatures and courts nationwide.

In a recent attempt to expand and maintain its base, NOM announced a Sustaining Membership Drive in the fall of 2017, asking members to support the organization's efforts by pledging a reoccurring monthly donation to the group. NOM has an active blog linked to the organization's website, updating its members about events and activities such as the "Dump Starbucks" and "Dump General Mills" campaigns, boycotts enacted to voice the group's disapproval for political stances taken by the companies, or the "Thank Chick-fil-A" campaign, which encourages members to send thank you notes to the company for "standing up for marriage."

Additionally, NOM created a separate 501(c)(3) classified arm of its organization, the NOM Education Fund, in order to promote their vision by producing pro-traditional marriage research which is dispersed to numerous parties including policy makers, religious officials, and the general public. NOM produces resources, such as a list of talking points for interacting with same-sex marriage supporters, which includes methods for diverting conversation from topics like discrimination, benefits, homosexuality, gay rights, and federalism and redirecting it back to their main argument that the most important issue is maintaining the traditional definition of marriage. The group also creates research briefs regarding a plethora of topics on same-sex marriage, such as "Is Same Sex Marriage Good for the Economy?" or "Why Libertarians Should Oppose Same-Sex Marriage."

NOM is also responsible for organizing several events protesting same-sex marriage such as the annual March for Marriage in D.C., though attendance has reportedly been on a steady decline since the *Obergefell v. Hodges* decision in 2015, the Supreme Court decision which effectively legalized same-sex marriage in the states; and the 2010 Summer for Marriage Tour, a 17-state tour of rallies protesting the overturning of Proposition 8. In partnership with its international affiliates, the International Organization for the Family (IOF) and Spain's CitizenGO, NOM helped to organize another tour of numerous cities in 2017 utilizing its antitransgender "Free Speech Bus," which proudly displayed the following text: "It's Biology: Boys are boys . . . and always will be. Girls are girls . . . and always will be. You can't change sex. Respect all."

NOM has also been responsible for several ad campaigns, the best-known being "A Gathering Storm" and "No Offense." In this 60-second television ad campaign from 2009, the ominous ad features a diverse group of what seem to be average Americans expressing their fears and complaints regarding same-sex marriage against a backdrop of an intense storm. The ad ultimately became the source of ridicule online as numerous groups created parody videos mocking the ad and its content. The "No Offense" ad campaign utilized similar tactics, showing clips of Miss USA contestant Miss California Carrie Prejean (1987–) and detailing the backlash she faced following her anti-same-sex marriage comment during the interview portion of the 2009 pageant. The video ends with a vague warning about the legal battles and devastation caused by the legalization of same-sex marriage.

In recent years, expanding upon the organization's initial purpose, President Brian Brown has accepted several speaking engagements internationally and has been a vocal supporter of numerous anti-LGBTQ movements abroad. Continuing the momentum in this direction, Brown announced the founding of a new organization, the previously mentioned IOF, in 2016, to increase the group's influence and spread its mission worldwide.

NOM has also been heavily involved in campaigns and courtroom battles revolving around ballot measures and elections, including legislative elections, judicial elections, and presidential elections. For example, in the spring of 2009, the Iowa Supreme Court unanimously decided in *Varnum v. Brien* that a 1998 statute defining civil marriage as that between a man and a woman violated the Iowa State Constitution, effectively legalizing same-sex marriage in the state. Following NOM's classification of this court's behavior as legislating from the bench, the organization worked to retaliate by organizing and contributing to an antiretention campaign, which successfully unseated three of the Iowa Supreme Court's justices in a retention election in the fall of 2010.

The group has also been involved in campaigns surrounding several pieces of legislation at the federal level and in numerous states, such as the campaign in support of a voter referendum in 2009 to defeat a bill passed in Maine's legislature that legalized same-sex marriage in the state. NOM has poured money into campaigns and utilized its super PAC, the NOM Victory Fund, to support fellow same-sex marriage opponents and defeat same-sex marriage proponents in various elections, like its 2011 vow to unseat the four Republican "turncoats" who voted in favor of a same-sex marriage bill in the New York legislature or its defeat of U.S. House candidate Richard Tisei (1962–) of Massachusetts or U.S. Senate candidate Monica Wehby (1962–) of Oregon in 2014. The organization also urged candidates in the 2012 presidential election to sign a marriage pledge, committing candidates to actions like supporting a constitutional amendment defining marriage as a union between a man and a woman. In 2016, the organization ardently backed Ted Cruz (1970–) and opposed Donald Trump (1946–) as the Republican presidential candidate, though the organization now seems willing to work with the Trump administration.

Over the years, NOM has come under criticism from groups like the Southern Poverty Law Center, which follows the moves of far-right groups on its Hatewatch blog. The SPLC has specifically criticized NOM for its anti-LGBTQ rhetoric, which often relies on outdated or debunked research or outright falsehoods about LGBTQ individuals. Similarly, the Human Rights Campaign, in partnership with the Courage Campaign, created the website NOM Exposed, which follows the actions of the organization in a fact-checking fashion. NOM has also been surrounded by controversy regarding campaign finance laws, with legal conflicts in multiple states regarding the group's unwillingness to disclose its donors for apparent fear of retaliation by same-sex marriage proponents as well as its disapproval of states' disclosure of petition signers, which the organization feels is a violation of privacy.

While the above organizations have sought to expose what they feel are hateful speech and actions expressed by NOM, the group feels that it is actually their membership and same-sex marriage opponents who are on the receiving end of the negativity. Consequently, NOM created Marriage Anti-Defamation Alliance to protect and defend the rights of individuals who are anti-same-sex marriage and create a community of individuals who share their personal experiences and support one another. The organization seeks to gather evidence for its claims that same-sex marriage opponents are threatened, harmed, and harassed at high rates.

Although it was ultimately overturned, NOM once held a prominent and even powerful position within U.S. politics following its support of Proposition 8 in California. The organization's success in California provided it with the motivation necessary to expand its vision of marriage nationwide. The group saw several achievements as well as losses from 2007 to 2019 at the state and national level, but its loss of steam following the *Obergefell v. Hodges* decision has forced the group into serious efforts to boost its membership and funding, increasing its efforts outside of the U.S. in less progressive arenas, where the idea of same-sex marriage is still very much an issue, and further expanding its mission in the United States to include opposition to issues like transgender student accessibility to sports teams, locker rooms, and restrooms of their preferred gender, which are more central to current U.S. political debates.

Heather Marie Rice and Nicole Loncaric

See also: Americans United for Separation of Church and State (1947–); Christian Coalition of America (1988–); Family Research Council (1983–)

Further Reading

Brown, Brian S. 2018. "Kavanaugh Kills It." *National Organization for Marriage Blog*, September 10, 2018. https://www.nomblog.com/41635/.

Hatewatch Staff. 2016. "National Organization for Marriage President Announces International Anti-LGBT Group." Southern Poverty Law Center, December 19, 2016. https://www.splcenter.org/hatewatch/2016/12/19/national-organization-marriage -president-announces-international-ant.

Karger, Fred. 2017. "The National Organization for Marriage May Be Collapsing before Our Eyes." *Advocate*, February 24, 2017. https://www.advocate.com/commentary /2017/2/24/national-organization-marriage-may-be-collapsing-our-eyes.

National Organization for Marriage. 2018. https://www.nationformarriage.org/.

Reilly, Peter J. 2015. "National Organization for Marriage Denied Attorney Fees in IRS Lawsuit." *Forbes*, December 9, 2015. https://www.forbes.com/sites/peterjreilly /2015/12/09/national-organization-for-marriage-denied-attorney-fees-in-irs -lawsuit/#4a8a806823f6.

National Organization for the Reform of Marijuana Laws (1970–)

The National Organization for the Reform of Marijuana Laws, better known as NORML, is a nonprofit, national organization that seeks to legalize nonmedical marijuana use for adults in the United States. It was founded in 1970 in Washington, D.C., by lawyer Keith Stroup (1944–), and its headquarters continue to be located in the capital. Several state and local chapters have also formed, and international branches have been founded in New Zealand, France, and the United Kingdom.

NORML is one of the most visible promarijuana lobbying groups in the country, in part due to its long history in Washington. Stroup (whose name rhymes with "cop") is also one of the most visible promarijuana activists in the United States. Stroup feels that the current era of legalization, in which laws against marijuana possession and use have been repealed in nine states and Washington, D.C., is, in part, a product of NORML's nearly 50 years of activism, and he feels that NORML's greatest accomplishment has been legitimizing the role of the responsible adult cannabis user, whose positive image has, in turn, shaped America's drug laws.

Prior to NORML's foundation, marijuana had a long history of use in the United States, but it was made federally illegal in 1970 with the passage of the Controlled Substances Act. Use of marijuana had been rising throughout the 1960s as the drug became popular among counterculture youth and on college campuses. In 1970, as state arrest rates for marijuana were rising, President Richard Nixon placed the drug in Schedule I of the Controlled Substances Act, meaning that the drug was federally illegal, viewed as easy to abuse, and considered to have no medical value.

Stroup founded NORML that same year. A graduate of Georgetown Law School and a former member of Ralph Nader's National Commission on Product Safety, Stroup considered himself a public-interest lawyer who sought to represent the interests of adult marijuana users on Capitol Hill. He viewed marijuana users as legitimate citizens and consumers, and he built NORML as a traditional lobbying group to promote the value of legalization to elected officials. He and his staff testified at congressional hearings, hosted national events and conferences, and produced numerous educational materials that promoted the legitimate use of marijuana and portrayed adult cannabis users as citizens deserving of equal rights and protection.

As a lobbying group, NORML had a rocky start. Considered Washington's "weakest lobby" by the *Washington Post*, Stroup ran the organization from his home, and, despite his traditional appearance and suit and tie, he was often laughed out of politicians' offices. In 1972, however, the results of the National Commission on Marijuana and Drug Abuse were released, and its conclusion that marijuana should be federally decriminalized bolstered NORML's standing and approach.

The National Commission on Marijuana and Drug Abuse was formed in 1970 by the Controlled Substances Act, in order to understand the scope and breadth of marijuana use in the United States. By studying rates and effects of marijuana use, the Commission sought to determine if marijuana should remain a Schedule I drug. In public comments, President Richard Nixon, who convened the commission, linked the drug to what he viewed as the larger problems of the time: adolescent rebellion, social turmoil, widespread social protest, and "deviant" behavior. If the commission agreed in that judgment, marijuana could stay a Schedule I drug and remain illegal nationwide.

The Commission, however, found otherwise. After two years of research, it determined that 24 million Americans had tried the drug at least once, and that marijuana users were no different than the average nonmarijuana user. It also recommended that marijuana be decriminalized nationwide, because, as commission members argued, laws against marijuana were more harmful than useful.

The commission argued that antimarijuana laws wasted local and federal resources and made young people distrust the government. Nixon was furious with the group's findings and publicly dismissed them. As a result, marijuana remained a Schedule I drug.

The Commission's report was published commercially, however, and NORML began working with state legislatures to enact the commission's recommendations on the state and local levels. Between 1973 and 1978, a dozen states, including Oregon, Minnesota, Mississippi, and South Dakota, decriminalized the drug. Jimmy Carter ran for president in 1976 in part on a platform that supported states' rights to decriminalize. And when Carter won the election and came to Washington, he brought physician Peter Bourne with him as his chief drug advisor. Bourne and Stroup became close and often collaborated on marijuana policy. Because of the results of the National Commission on Marijuana and Drug Abuse and Stroup's relationship with the White House, NORML members believed that marijuana would be decriminalized nationwide, and perhaps even legalized, by 1980.

An antimarijuana counterrevolution formed in the summer of 1976, which thwarted NORML's success. Parents in Atlanta, Georgia, were furious when they discovered their preteen children were using the drug, and they blamed what they viewed as an overly relaxed culture surrounding decriminalized marijuana for children's increased access to cannabis. A growing coalition of concerned parents formed the grassroots antimarijuana "parent movement," which soon spread nationwide. When Ronald Reagan was elected president in 1980, parent activists teamed with members of his administration, including first lady Nancy Reagan, to promote new, stricter antidrug laws that would protect a child's right to grow up drug-free. By the early 1980s, all state decriminalization laws had been overturned, and new, more punitive drug laws took their place.

NORML continued to represent the interests of marijuana smokers, however, and the organization's office in Washington continued its lobbying and education efforts. When the HIV/AIDS crisis began in the 1980s, promarijuana activists also began working with those suffering from this strange new disease and found that marijuana was helpful in battling AIDS's debilitating effects. Arguing that cannabis had clear medical benefits for those suffering from HIV/AIDS, as well as other diseases like glaucoma and cancer, NORML helped pass the first medical marijuana law in California in 1996. In response to this success, NORML published its "Principles of Responsible Use," which outlined how NORML promoted healthy cannabis use for adults, and sought to remind cannabis users to avoid abuse, dangerous driving, or violating the rights of others.

Through continued lobbying and activism, NORML continued to experience success. Medical marijuana laws were passed in 29 states and Washington, D.C., over the next two decades, and in 2012, the nation's first recreational marijuana legalization laws were passed in Colorado and Washington State. Since then, seven more states and Washington, D.C., have followed suit, legalizing recreational adult cannabis use.

Stroup was the executive director of NORML from 1970 to 1978, and again from 1994 to 2004, and remains active as the group's legal counsel. He says that NORML's greatest achievement has been legitimizing the role of the marijuana smoker. When he began his work, marijuana users were treated like deviants and misfits, living on the edges of society. Because of NORML's continued activism, Stroup argues that cannabis users are now generally seen as ordinary Americans who use marijuana as other adults drink a beer or a glass of wine. He continues to promote responsible cannabis use for adults, and NORML remains active in Washington, D.C.

Emily Dufton

See also: Pharmaceutical Researchers and Manufacturers of America (1958–); Vote Hemp (2000–)

Further Reading

Anderson, Patrick. 1981. *High in America: The True Story behind NORML and the Politics of Marijuana.* New York: The Viking Press.

Dufton, Emily. 2017. *Grass Roots: The Rise and Fall and Rise of Marijuana in America.* New York: Basic Books.

Stroup, Keith. 2013. *It's NORML to Smoke Pot: The 40-Year Fight for Marijuana Smokers' Rights.* New York: Trans High Corporation.

National Organization for Women (1966–)

The National Organization for Women (NOW), founded in 1966, advocates for gender equality and is one of the foremost interest groups associated with the modern women's movement. The group's stated purpose is "to take action through intersectional grassroots activism to promote feminist ideals, lead societal change, eliminate discrimination, and achieve and protect the equal rights of all women and girls in all aspects of social, political, and economic life." The 51-year-old organization claims over 500,000 contributing members and remains one of the largest women's rights interest groups. Terry O'Neill (1953–), a feminist civil rights attorney and law professor, serves as the current president.

Key activists and leaders of the women's movement created NOW as they advocated for gender equality in the workplace. At issue was Title VII of the 1964 Civil Rights Act—legislation designed to end discriminatory practices in employment and create more equitable economic standing for men and women in the workforce. Common practice at time of the legislation was for businesses to post "Help Wanted" ads announcing job openings for male or female employees specifically. Title VII of the Civil Rights Act was intended to end these types of gender discrimination in employment; additionally, the Equal Employment Opportunity Commission (EEOC) was created to enforce this new law. However, gender discrimination in employment practices persisted. Because the new standards under Title VII of the Civil Rights Act were not enforced as expected, women's movement leaders felt the need for an organization to push forward this policy and others related to women's rights.

By 1966, at the National Conference of Commissions on the Status of Women, women's movement leaders were unable to pass a resolution that would require active enforcement of Title VII. In response, these women met to create an organization for women's advancement similar to the National Association for the Advancement of Colored People (NAACP) in order to address these issues. Feminist activist Betty Friedan (1921–2006) reportedly jotted down "NOW" on a napkin, giving the organization its name. Friedan authored *The Feminine Mystique,* a seminal book for the women's movement published in 1963 that described the effects of social and economic gender inequality as "the problem that has no name" and had helped spark the women's movement. Twenty-eight women's rights activists present at the conference that day served as the original founders. Friedan became NOW's first president, serving from 1966 to 1970.

In its statement of purpose, NOW criticized U.S. laws and practices that contributed to gender inequality. At its first national convention in 1967, the organization adopted a Bill of Rights that included calls for passing the Equal Rights Amendment (ERA), advancing reproductive rights, and ending gender discrimination in the workforce. The organization also cited the need to change the demeaning and limiting images of women portrayed by the mass media as one of its goals.

NOW has made effective use of various means of applying pressure to create policy change; the group has employed marches, demonstrations, letter-writing campaigns, and lobbying. Marches in particular were used to bring visibility to the issue of gender equality and to show the strength of the organization's support. NOW's 1970 Women's Strike for Equality, held in New York City as well as other cities, was one example. Thousands in New York City demonstrated that day on behalf of the equal treatment of women, carrying signs with statements like "Don't Iron While the Strike Is Hot." Key leaders, including Gloria Steinem (1934–), Bella Abzug (1920–1998), and Shirley Chisholm (1924–2005), often spoke at these rallies and marches.

NOW continued to organize marches through its 50-plus year history. Many marches were held around the country in support of the Equal Rights Amendment and in support of lesbian and gay rights. Started in the early 1970s, Take Back the Night marches, designed to raise awareness of sexual assault and violence against women, still continue today. NOW's 2004 March for Women's Lives in Washington, D.C., drew over one million participants in support for abortion rights and reproductive health, according to the group.

NOW's activity includes both efforts to raise awareness and visibility of gender inequality and activism aimed at policy and political change across many issue areas. The organization has fought against pro-life Supreme Court nominees and in support of LGBTQI rights, transgender rights, and gay marriage, as well as the expansion of health care and child care, among many other issues connected to gender equality. In 1990, NOW formed a committee to explore creating a third party in U.S. politics and has a candidate action fund, supporting and endorsing candidates for local, state, and federal office. The organization's activity necessarily spans many policy issues, reflecting its commitment to advancing gender equality and empowerment.

Importantly, NOW incorporates legal expertise in its strategy to produce policy changes as well. In 1971, the group created and partnered with a separate organization, the NOW Legal and Education Defense Fund (known since 2004 as Legal

Momentum), to provide legal advocacy and education. Legal Momentum's resources and expertise spans the issues of violence, workplace rights, Title IX, and human trafficking, among others.

Since the 1970s, the group has influenced numerous court decisions and public policy though submitting briefs, bringing lawsuits, publishing legal education guides, and pushing for federal legislation. Its first victory came in *Sellers v. Colgate Palmolive Co.* (1973), brought under Title VII of the 1964 Civil Rights Act that prohibited employment discrimination on the basis of sex. The Court struck down a policy barring women from jobs that required lifting more than 35 pounds. Legal Momentum was also actively involved in task force work that contributed to the Violence Against Women Act that was signed into law in 2006.

Through its National Judicial Education Program, Legal Momentum trains those in the justice system, from judges to court professionals, on issues such as gender bias in the courts, child abuse and issues of custody, equal treatment in the courts for women of color, sexual assault prevention in the military, and intimate partner sexual abuse. Most recently, Legal Momentum is educating and advocating for policy changes to end online sexual extortion and sex trafficking of women and teenage girls.

NOW's influence in the area of women's rights is not without criticism; arguments about whether the group was inclusive enough can be traced to the early days of the organization. Early critiques included the lack of non–middle-class women and an absence of perspectives of women of color, as well as decisions made by the group to not explicitly advance lesbian rights. Early leaders defended their positions as trying to keep the focus on women's rights more generally. Regardless of the controversies surrounding the organization, no discussion of the successes of the women's movement would be complete without attributing many of the public policy, legal, and cultural changes to the work of keys early women's rights groups like NOW.

Janna L. Deitz

See also: League of Women Voters (1920–); National Abortion and Reproductive Rights Action League (NARAL) (1969–); National Women's Political Caucus (1971–)

Further Reading

Barakso, Maryann. 2004. *Governing NOW: Grassroots Activism in the National Organization for Women.* Ithaca, NY: Cornell University Press.

Carden, Maren Lockwood. 1974. "National Organization for Women: Emergence and Growth." In *The New Feminist Movement*, 103–118. New York: Russell Sage Foundation.

Ferree, Myra Marx, and Beth B. Hess. 2000. *Controversy and Coalition: The New Feminist Movement Across Four Decades of Change.* London: Routledge Press.

Friedan, Betty. 1963. *The Feminist Mystique.* New York: W. W. Norton & Company.

National Organization for Women. 2018. https://now.org/.

Perlman, Allison. 2016. "Feminists in the Wasteland Fight Back: The National Organization for Women and Media Reform." In *Public Interests: Media Advocacy and Struggles over U.S. Television*, 65–93. New Brunswick, New Jersey; London: Rutgers University Press.

National Organization on Disability (1982–)

The National Organization on Disability (NOD) is a nonprofit organization that works to increase employment opportunities for individuals with disabilities. "Tens of millions of working-age Americans with disabilities are able and eager to work," said NOD President Carol Glazer. "By joining forces with employers and 57 million Americans with disabilities—that's one out of every five of us—we can harness the talent of every willing worker and vastly expand the productive power of the national labor force" (National Organization on Disability 2018). Chronic unemployment affects up to 80 percent of working-age Americans with disabilities, contributing to a poverty rate more than twice as high as that of nondisabled adults (Kittaneh and Hess 2015). NOD offers programs, services, and resources to help employers break down barriers to accessibility and inclusion and promote full participation in the workforce for people with disabilities.

In 1981, American disability rights activist Alan A. Reich became the first person in a wheelchair to address the United Nations General Assembly. His speech marked the start of the International Year of Disabled Persons, a UN initiative aimed at promoting equal rights and full participation for people with disabilities worldwide. The following year, Reich and other disability activists from across the United States formed a nonprofit organization, the National Office on Disability, to advocate for legislation, programs, and services to fulfill the UN mandate. Reich served as the first president of the new organization, which became known as the National Organization on Disability in 1983. From the beginning, NOD presented itself as a cross-disability organization that represented the interests of all Americans with disabilities.

In 1986, NOD commissioned the first in a series of comprehensive public-opinion surveys by Harris Interactive measuring the level of community participation among people with disabilities. Repeated every two to six years, these surveys have guided the development of NOD programs and services and increased public understanding of disability issues. Poll data has also helped policy makers identify gaps, establish goals, and measure improvements in community participation for individuals with disabilities. In the late 1980s, NOD leaders joined with other disability rights activists and organizations in advocating for passage of the Americans with Disabilities Act (ADA) by giving speeches and interviews, lobbying in Congress, and building grassroots support. This landmark civil rights legislation, which President George H. W. Bush signed into law in 1990, extended equal protection of the law to people with disabilities.

Following passage of the ADA, NOD provided information to help businesses understand and meet their obligations under the new law. In 1992, the organization launched its Corporate Leadership Council, a group of prominent business leaders who promoted the competitive advantages available to companies that hired qualified employees with disabilities. Two years later, NOD introduced Start on Success, a paid internship program to increase the employability of high school students from low-income backgrounds. In 1995, NOD led a successful campaign to raise money and gain congressional approval to expand the Franklin D. Roosevelt Memorial in Washington, D.C., to include a statue of the president in his wheelchair. In 2001, NOD responded to the September 11, 2001, terrorist attacks by launching its Emergency Preparedness Initiative, which involved distributing thousands of educational pamphlets to help communities and businesses ensure the safety of people with disabilities in emergency situations.

In 2006, NOD shifted its focus toward increasing employment opportunities for people with disabilities. The organization touted individuals with disabilities as a largely untapped resource whose talents, energy, and unique contributions offered businesses a source of competitive advantage. It also presented expanding opportunities for Americans with disabilities as an important component in allowing the nation to succeed in a global economy. NOD established close working partnerships with more than three dozen large companies—including such industry leaders as Coca-Cola, Lowe's, Starbucks, UPS, Walmart, and Xerox—to develop, test, and share successful models and approaches.

NOD provides many innovative employment programs to help businesses recruit, hire, retain, and support talented employees with disabilities. The Wounded Warrior Careers Demonstration, launched in 2007, offers career support to U.S. military veterans who returned from Iraq and Afghanistan with severe injuries. The Bridges to Business program, established in 2010, helps connect job-seekers with disabilities to available positions with local businesses. The Disability Employment Tracker, introduced in 2013, provides a tool for companies to assess their employment practices and identify opportunities to build a more inclusive workforce. Companies that achieve high scores may be recognized with NOD's Leading Disability Employer Seal.

NOD also offers consulting services to help companies become more disability friendly, including assistance with program design and planning, etiquette and awareness training, and ADA compliance. Glazer asserted that both employers and prospective employees stand to benefit from disability-inclusion programs. "Every employer who has tried this has had enormously positive experiences with it," she stated, and "has come away almost evangelical about the experiences that they had" (Kittaneh and Ness 2015).

With three decades of expertise in disability employment issues, NOD provides input and advice to government agencies and lawmakers seeking ways to promote inclusion in the nation's workforce. NOD leaders advocated for the passage of a UN treaty protecting international disability rights. They achieved a victory in 2013, when the U.S. Department of Labor issued new regulations for federal contractors under Section 503 of the Rehabilitation Act mandating the inclusion of employees with disabilities and establishing a target of 7 percent of the workforce. Glazer called it "the most far reaching affirmative action and civil rights policy that has ever happened" for individuals with disabilities (Kittaneh and Hess 2015).

In 2018, NOD leaders expressed concern about the ADA Education and Reform Act, legislation proposed by Republican members of Congress and supported by the administration of President Donald Trump that would make it more difficult for people with disabilities to exercise their right of access to public accommodations under the ADA. Disability rights advocates argued that the bill weakened key enforcement mechanisms that were vital to ensuring that businesses complied with the accessibility provisions of the ADA. Tom Ridge, NOD chairman and former governor of Pennsylvania, issued a statement opposing the legislation. "It is unacceptable to roll back the civil rights of people with disabilities," he wrote. "We should expect businesses to know and comply with their obligations, not require our neighbors and colleagues with disabilities to shoulder the burden of informing and educating businesses about those obligations" (Ridge 2018). NOD leaders argued that the legislation would also harm businesses, because those that remained inaccessible to people with disabilities would lose out on talented employees as well as an important customer base.

Laurie Collier Hillstrom

See also: Disability Rights Education and Defense Fund (1979–)

Further Reading

Kittaneh, Nada, and Deirdre Hess. 2015. "Influencer Series: National Organization on Disability." Heron Foundation, March 12, 2015. https://www.heron.org/engage /pulse/influencer-series-national-organization-disability.

National Organization on Disability. 2018. https://www.nod.org/about/.

Ridge, Tom. 2018. "Rolling Back the Civil Rights of the Disabled Harms Us All." *The Hill*, February 13, 2018. https://www.nod.org/rolling-back-civil-rights-disabled -harms-us/.

National Rifle Association (1871–)

The National Rifle Association (NRA) is an organization that claims to speak on behalf of American gun owners. The NRA calls itself the oldest civil rights organization in the United States. The organization has grown, and its efforts to impact policy have changed over the ensuing decades. Around the time of its founding, the NRA was primarily concerned with policies that increased the shooting skills of the state militia and brought funding to the organization. Today it has become the voice against limitations on the individual ability to own and use firearms. This has led the organization to get involved in both lobbying the federal and state governments and providing resources to gun-friendly candidates.

On November 16, 1871, William Conant Church (1836–1917) and George Wood Wingate (1840–1928) chartered the National Rifle Association in the state of New York. As editors of *The United States Army and Navy Journal and Gazette of the Regular and Volunteer Forces*, they proposed that the Army faced several problems including a lack of skill in marksmanship. They argued that while it would be preferable for excursions and other events intended to promote marksmanship to be held by the state militias, practicality required that a private organization was needed to fill this void.

Before the Civil War (1861–1864), there were hundreds of rifle clubs in both the North and the South. Rifle clubs in the North provided comradery as well as the entertainment of shooting competitions. Southern rifle clubs served and continued to serve for a period after the Civil War as a means to organize repression of outside influences as well as preventing people of color from changing their position in the social structure. While Northern rifle clubs often sent teams to large competitions, this was a rare occurrence for Southern rifle clubs.

The article announcing the formation of the National Rifle Association also noted that in England there was the British National Rifle Association, which the NRA founders saw as a good model for the new U.S. organization. Ambrose Burnside (1824–1881), a former commander in the Union Army of the Potomac and inventor of the Burnside carbine, served as the first president of the NRA.

NRA founders and early members who either were serving or had served in the military hoped the organization would alleviate the inaccuracy of the contemporary infantryman. Findings after the Civil War showed that for every thousand rounds fired by the Union Army, a single Confederate soldier was hit. The purpose of the organization, as stated by William Church, was to "to promote and encourage rifle shooting on a scientific basis."

The organization, with financial assistance from the state of New York, established its Creedmoor shooting range and began holding marksmanship competitions in 1872. In the years after its founding, prominent former generals such as Winfield Hancock (1824–1886), Ulysses S. Grant (1822–1885), and Philip Sheridan (1831–1888) served as NRA presidents. The organization's leaders had achieved positions of importance in both the military and politics. Based on writings from the time period, most of the organization's efforts were focused during its first decades on appealing for aid from friendly state governments for the various shooting events held by the organization.

During the 1870s, the organization experienced growth as Civil War veterans longed for the comradery they had during the conflict, while those who grew up during the conflict saw service in the militia as a means of projecting masculinity and manliness. During the NRA's early years, it established a close relationship with the National Guard. When the National Guard experienced growth, the NRA usually did as well. This close relationship was forged by George Wood Wingate (1840–1928), an NRA founder who also helped found the National Guard Association.

The 1880s saw the organization struggle under fiscal issues related to the organization's reliance on government funding for its mission. Many of the NRA's struggles were the result of a waning memory of the Civil War and a feeling of perpetual peace perceived by politicians. The governors of New York no longer saw the NRA's goal of improving the accuracy of militiamen as a goal that was worth the added expense. This did not mean that politicians had soured on the organization itself, but they had instead seen that the era of peace had rendered its goal unnecessary.

Other funds had been raised by charging spectators a fee to watch competitors at their Creedmoor range shooting events. During the 1880s these events saw a decline in the number of shooting competitors as well as spectators, which reduced this form of revenue to the organization. There were also issues about which rifles could be used in the competitions. Different states had adopted different rifles for their militias. This was in part created by the U.S. Army changing the rifles it used, and some states (but not others) changed their militia's rifles when it did. This drop off in the number of competitors and spectators was not a trend that other rifle clubs experienced during this decade.

By 1890 the NRA was insolvent. The organization moved its national shooting competitions to its New Jersey affiliate organization. The organization called for a closer relationship with the U.S. government but did little of note for the rest of the decade. The New Jersey affiliate managed to have superb matches that greatly improved the shooting competence of its militiamen.

The Spanish-American War (1898) showed that the quality of state militias varied widely and that there was much to be done, both within the federal government and from other actors, to reform the current militia system. Before this conflict, the state militias had served under state control during peacetime and dual (national and state) control during times of emergency. After the conflict, multiple pieces of legislation passed with the result that the state and federal government jointly controlled state militias during times of peace, and the federal government controlled the militias during times of conflict. Moreover, there was a realization that marksmanship was in need of improvement following the conflict. These efforts to improve the organization of the National Guard on one hand and the accuracy of American shooters on the other hand would get additional support following the lessons learned from the punitive expedition against Pancho Villa (1916–1917).

In the early 1900s, the NRA led the way in promoting marksmanship among younger Americans by promoting the establishment of marksmanship clubs at colleges and universities.

The Legislative Affairs Division was established in 1934. This division of the NRA was intended to encourage members to make their voices heard when legislation was proposed that the organization saw as threats to the Second Amendment. The Legislative Affairs Division was transformed into the Institute for Legislative Action in the 1970s to deal with a new set of legislative actions that the organization saw as infringements on their members' Second Amendment rights. Often when citizens who are not NRA members think about the organization, they are thinking about the work of the Institute for Legislative Action.

The NRA established the *American Rifleman* magazine in 1923 to keep the organization's members abreast of firearms-related legislation as well as advances in firearms technology. With information being an important tool in lobbying, this magazine shares information that the organization wants its members to know and at times will contain calls for members to contact their members of Congress. At the time of this writing, the association also runs a television program on the Outdoor Channel called *American Rifleman TV*. While recurring segments like "I have this Old Gun" and some segments involving celebrities are intended to entice shooters to seek more information about firearms and the NRA, there are usually several NRA commercials throughout the program. Since the early 2000s, the trend of the organization's commercials has become increasingly partisan. With assets like the *American Rifleman* magazine and *American Rifleman TV*, the organization has attempted to spread its political message without neglecting news about firearms invitations and information.

The NRA has found the ability to play a major role in American politics. In September 2016, in an effort to impact the elections to eight Senate seats, the organization was only outspent by the candidates seeking office and their associated Super PACs. The NRA has also been thrust into the public spotlight during the multitude of mass shootings in the previous two decades. The NRA has become the face of the anti–gun control movement. Its political influence and lobbying efforts have succeeded in preventing many proposed gun control laws following shootings at Santa Fe and Parkland High Schools; Virginia Tech; Newtown, Connecticut; Orlando, Florida; and Las Vegas, Nevada. The NRA has found the national Republican Party largely supportive of their goals of limiting any new legislation restricting the ability to purchase firearms. In order to foster the support of the Republican allies, the National Rifle Association has increasingly gotten involved in partisan elections. The Institute for Legislative Action has spent significant amounts of money and contested Congressional and Senate elections. Less high-profile actions, such as editorials in the *American Rifleman* condemning politicians seen as pro–gun control (like Hillary Clinton), have become common around election time.

The NRA was established by important members of the post–Civil War military leadership and had strong backing from powerful political backers. Today the NRA claims that it has 4 million members. Starting out with a single shooting range to train individuals in the scientific method of shooting, the organization has expanded to numerous training programs for people of all ages as well as establishing a charitable organization, the NRA Foundation, and has become one of the most powerful lobbying efforts in Washington, D.C.

John Marshall Dickey

See also: Brady Campaign to Prevent Gun Violence (1974–); National Right to Life Committee (1967–)

Further Reading

Feldman, Richard. 2011. *Ricochet: Confessions of a Gun Lobbyist.* Hoboken, NJ: John Wiley & Sons.

Keene, David A., and Thomas L. Mason. 2016. *Shall Not be Infringed: New Assaults on Your Second Amendment.* New York: Skyhorse Publishing.

National Rifle Association. 2018. https://home.nra.org/.

Patrick, Brian Anse. 2013. *National Rifle Association and the Media: The Motivating Force of Negative Coverage.* London: Arktos.

"Rifle Shooting Association." 1871. *Army and Navy Journal and Gazette of the Regular and Volunteer Forces,* August 12, 1871.

National Right to Life Committee (1967–)

The National Conference of Catholic Bishops (NCCB) took the lead on coordinating antiabortion efforts in the 1960s. At that time, most of the NCCB efforts focused on state-level activities to affect abortion access laws. In an attempt to broaden the antiabortion movement beyond the Catholic faithful, the NCCB formed the National Right to Life Committee (NRLC) in 1967. The NCCB and the NRLC were so closely tied that early in its history, the NRLC was run out of the NCCB offices. The NRLC became the first single-issue antiabortion group to form in the United States. It emerged during the sexual revolution of the 1960s, which was marked by greater access to and use of contraceptive devices. The NRLC predates the U.S. Supreme Court's 1973 *Roe v. Wade* decision, which created a foundation for constitutional protections for women seeking abortion services during the first two trimesters of a pregnancy.

The NRLC ties to the NCCB illustrate how the emergence of the NRLC was entwined with the complex history of the Catholic church. The Second Vatican Council, better known as Vatican II (1962–1965), created the most immediate and most important backdrop for the antiabortion movement. Vatican II fundamentally reshaped the relations between Catholic clergy and parishioners as well as the relations between the Catholic faithful and non-Catholics. In many ways, Vatican II was considered a liberalization of Catholic practices. Catholic leaders were urged to be more socially and politically active. The antiabortion movement dovetailed with this new focus. Vatican II also urged the church to be more open and more involved in the events around them. In other words, the Catholic faithful were to be more active in the world, even if they were not of the world. Finally, even as Vatican II liberalized practices and traditions in their own church services by moving away from Latin and having the priests face the parishioners, Vatican II forcefully reinforced the church's long-held opposition to abortion.

Individual Catholic parishioners became active in the antiabortion movement, but none more so than Eunice Kennedy Shriver (1921–2009), the sister of John F. (1917–1963), Robert F. (1925–1968), and Theodore (Ted) Kennedy (1932–2009). In the 1960s and 1970s, the Kennedy family was one of the most powerful political forces in the United States. Shriver is perhaps best remembered for developing and leading the Special Olympics, but having a Kennedy at the head of the antiabortion movement illustrated the strength of the antiabortion ties to the Catholic tradition and to members of the Democratic Party. Shriver's concerns about abortion were clearly tied to her concerns for the well-being of mentally handicapped individuals. Shriver wrote and widely distributed *The Terrible Choice*, a collection of conference presentations that highlighted misfortunes tied to abortion. Pearl S. Buck (1892–1973), a popular public intellectual of the time and a Nobel laureate in literature, wrote an introduction for Shriver.

Protestant and Catholic divisions appeared from time to time in the NRLC, and during the 1970s disputes arose related to focus and strategy. As the leader of the NRLC from 1973–1975, Fred Mecklenburg (1935–) maintained strong support for family planning services and the Planned Parenthood organization, even as most Catholics forswore contraception and frowned on family planning. The American Citizens Concerned for Life (ACCL), another group active at the time, emphasized the importance of direct support for pregnant women and young mothers. ACCL sought to reduce the demand for abortion services rather than limit access to them. Interests in limiting access to abortion services became more prominent among antiabortion groups in the 1980s and 1990s, even though the NRLC was not initially a driving force in those efforts.

Spinoff antiabortion groups such as Pro-Life Action Network (PLAN), American Life League (ALL), and Operation Rescue sought greater militancy. NRLC focused on legislative successes, but PLAN, ALL, and Operation Rescue preferred direct action to physically limit access to abortion clinics. The so-called "rescue movement" was marked by sidewalk counseling of visitors to clinics, blocked clinic entrances, and sometimes the destruction of clinic property. The Operation Rescue of the 1980s aggressively adhered to those tactics, thereby garnering considerable media attention. In contrast to the hands-on approach of Operation Rescue, the most strident action taken by the NRLC in the 1980s was its coproduction of *The Silent Scream*, a movie that depicted stark images of abortions in process via ultrasound imagery.

The Silent Scream aside, Operation Rescue accused the NRLC of being too compliant, too willing to go along with minor measures that even some pro-choice proponents supported. For instance, when NRLC was moving to restrict abortion as a means of sex selection, Operation Rescue pushed legislation in the state of Missouri stating that life began at conception. The aggressiveness of Operation Rescue and its success in gaining media attention forced the hand of the NRLC leaders. Operation Rescue sought to supplant the NRLC as the spearhead of the antiabortion movement. In light of the Operation Rescue successes, the NRLC altered its stand and supported the Missouri legislative efforts. By the time the Supreme Court of the United States reviewed the Missouri law in *Webster v. Reproductive Health Services* in 1989, the NLRC was firmly onboard the "life begins at conception" drive.

During the 1980s, the antiabortion movement's roots in the Democratic Party gave way. Ronald Reagan's (1911–2004) successful 1980 presidential bid marked a shift from largely Democratic allegiance to largely Republican allegiance. Catholic voters tended to favor Democratic candidates up through the 1970s. Indeed, the first antiabortion candidate on a national ticket was Eunice Shriver's husband Sargent Shriver (1915–2011), George McGovern's (1922–2012) vice presidential running mate in 1972. McGovern and Shriver lost to Richard Nixon (1913–1994) in the 1972 presidential election, but Democratic President Jimmy Carter (1924–) was in the White House after winning the 1976 election, and he too was antiabortion.

By 1980, Reagan and the Republican Party had come to realize that economic and foreign policy issues alone could not attract enough voters for national races. Reagan's 1980 campaign highlighted the concerns of social conservatives, who focused their attention on traditional family values, education issues, and abortion. Reagan's 1980 election was eased by the emergence of socially conservative Republicans and "Reagan Democrats," who were often anti-abortion. The NRLC became part of what was soon called the New Right or the Christian Right. For the NRLC, the ability to offer the Republican Party and Republican candidates direct ties to socially conservative voters became a new measure of success. The election of President George W. Bush (1946–) in 2000 again exemplified the importance of the NRLC and its links to the Republican Party and its candidates. During the 2000 campaign, Bush spoke to both the NRLC and the Christian Coalition's national conventions. During his eight years in office, Bush invited the NRLC leaders to key bill-signing ceremonies, enhancing their legitimacy in the eyes of members who sought channels to those in power.

The eventual prominence of the NRLC was never guaranteed as long as Operation Rescue secured the headlines. Debates about the Hyde Amendment illustrate the ebbs and flows in the prominence of the NRLC and Operation Rescue. In the 1970s and 1980s, the NRLC secured considerable legislative success with the repeated adoption of the Hyde Amendment, but those successes were often overshadowed by the more media-savvy Operation Rescue. The Hyde Amendment was designed to take incremental steps to curtail abortion access by limiting the federal funds that could be used for abortion services. To Operation Rescue, the Hyde Amendment was indicative of a movement that was too stodgy and too prone to compromise. In fact, the Hyde Amendment was used hundreds of times in the United States Congress to limit access to abortion services, but the NRLC still struggled to secure attention and acclaim similar to that of Operation Rescue. While Operation Rescue focused on clinics and dramatic face-to-face confrontations, the NRLC focused on Congress and behind-the-scenes lobbying.

Indeed, the NRLC feared that storming abortion clinics and destroying property, which was tied to the rescue movement, would offer the federal government and pro-choice advocates another front on the abortion debate. The NRLC believed that the federal government might squelch the antiabortion movement if it appeared to be violent and bent on denying basic constitutional rights related to access to abortion clinics. Indeed, the federal government did respond in the 1990s with legislation protecting access to clinics, thereby making the Operation Rescue tactics more and more costly. FACE, the Freedom of Access to Clinic Entrances Act of 1994, was the most prominent of these protections. After the key tactics adopted by Operation Rescue were constrained by statute, the NRLC reemerged as the sole leader in the antiabortion movement.

The NRLC was always strongly antiabortion, but its members did not constantly pursue the limelight and generally avoided the most aggressive tactics of the movement. The NRLC was leery of a frontal assault on *Roe v. Wade*, fearing a tremendous backlash that might cement the policy guidance inherent in *Roe*. Pursuing bans on abortion as a means of birth control; banning sex-selection abortions; securing informed consent, spousal notification, and parental consent; and preventing the use of public resources for abortion procedures seemed to be a safer pathway for the NRLC's antiabortion efforts.

In the 2000s, the NRLC pursued court cases and legislative efforts at the federal and state levels and organized boycotts of pharmaceutical companies tied to abortifacients. It has also tied its right-to-life stand with a stand against euthanasia.

In 2018, the NRLC had more than 3,000 chapters and is organized in each of the 50 states in the United States. The organization continues to be the most prominent and influential antiabortion interest group in American politics—in Congress, with presidents, at the state level, and in the courts.

Scott H. Ainsworth

See also: American Conservative Union (1964–); Christian Coalition of America (1988–); Focus on the Family (1977–); Susan B. Anthony List (1993–)

Further Reading

Ainsworth, Scott H., and Thad E. Hall. 2011. *Abortion Politics in Congress: Strategic Incrementalism and Policy Change.* New York: Cambridge University Press.

Critchlow, Donald T. 1996. *The Politics of Abortion and Birth Control in Historical Perspective*. University Park: The Pennsylvania University Press.

Critchlow, Donald T. 1999. *Intended Consequences: Birth Control, Abortion, and the Federal Government in Modern America*. Oxford: Oxford University Press.

Halva-Neubauer, Glen. 1990. "Abortion Policy in the Post-Webster Age." *Publius* 20: 27–44.

Rennie, Indya. 2018. "Pro-Life Advocate Carol Tobias Talks About the #1 Pro-Life Goal in 2018 and How to Stop Abortion." *Life News*, February 23, 2018. https://www.lifenews.com/2018/02/23/pro-life-advocate-carol-tobias-talks-about-the-1-pro-life-goal-in-2018-and-how-to-stop-abortion/.

Risen, James, and Thomas, Judy L. 1998. *Wrath of Angels: The American Abortion War*. New York: Basic Books.

National Right to Work Legal Defense Foundation (1968–)

The National Right to Work Legal Defense Foundation (NRTWLDF) was established in 1968 as a nonprofit organization dedicated to providing legal support to oppose organized labor and unionization efforts. The NRTWLDF specifically uses legal action to promote right-to-work laws and to oppose what the organization terms "compulsory unionism"—requirements that employees join unions or provide financial support to organized labor for political or social causes that the worker opposes.

The establishment of the NRTWLDF represented a strategic change for groups opposed to organized labor. Most antiunion organizations endeavored to influence legislation or directly prevent unionization drives. The NRTWLDF narrowed its focus to the legal system to defend businesses accused of interfering with union drives and to support individual workers who asserted that their rights were violated by organized labor.

The 1935 National Labor Relations Act (NLRA) contained a variety of measures to make it easier for unions to organize and engage in collective bargaining. The 1947 Taft-Hartley Act amended the NLRA and outlawed closed-shops—contracts through which businesses agreed to hire only union members and which required union membership to remain employed. There was a major exception to this part of the statute in that the law allowed compulsory union membership if the employer and the union included such a precondition as part of any labor contract. Known as union security agreements, these clauses required employees to join the union within 30 days of their hire or pay special union dues known as agency fees. These types of arrangements were known as union shops.

Organized labor groups argued that all workers in a company would benefit from their collective bargaining efforts; therefore, nonunion members should pay some portion of the costs of union activities. Union security agreements were allowed in the case of the union shop in which organized labor groups agreed to allow any employee to join a union after he or she had been hired. Union security agreements could also be used to create an agency shop whereby employees did not have to join, or remain part of, the union but did have to pay dues to support its activities.

After its formation, the NRTWLDF sought court cases to challenge agency fees, union shops, and support right-to-work laws. In 1977, the group was part of the legal team for the claimants in the Supreme Court decision *Abood v. Detroit Board of Education*. In the case, teachers challenged the public school system's union shop, which required them to pay agency fees. In a unanimous decision, the Court found in favor of the school system, determining that teachers who were not members of the union were still required to pay fees to defray the costs of collective bargaining and activities to protect employees. Teachers were not required to contribute monies that were used for political activities by the union, including donations to candidates or political parties. Over the next four decades, the NRTWLDF was involved in a succession of cases that endeavored to limit the scope of, or overturn, the *Abood* decision.

The NRTWLDF and allied groups secured a major victory in 1988 with the Supreme Court decision *Communications Workers of America v. Beck*. The decision narrowed the range of activities that nonunion employees could be required to financially support to include only activities related to representing the workers. The case created what became known as "Beck rights"—the ability of workers to request a refund from the union of any dues collected that were used for political purposes that the employee did not support. The Court's majority based its decision on the principle that requiring workers to contribute for activities for which they did not agree violated their First Amendment rights of freedom of expression.

Many of the subsequent cases that the NRTWLDF became involved in were those related to Beck rights. In some cases, employees were unaware of their Beck rights; in other instances, the NRTWLDF contended that unions deliberately sought to deny workers the ability to recover their eligible dues. The organization followed the *Beck* decision by becoming involved in the 1991 case, *Lehnert v. Ferris Faculty Association*. Faculty at Ferris State University were required to pay a service fee to unions which represented them in contract negotiations. The plaintiffs argued that the fees were also used to conduct political activities, ranging from campaign contributions to lobbying, that were outside of the collective bargaining function. However, the unions contended that the political activities enhanced their stature and therefore made the groups more effective when bargaining with employers. The Court found for the NRTWLDF-backed plaintiffs and refined its decision from the Beck case to ensure that the costs of collective bargaining were defined narrowly. The basis for the decision was again the First Amendment and the unconstitutionality of requiring employees to contribute to political causes to which they objected. The Court also required that unions provide nonunion members a detailed breakdown of how any agency fees were spent.

In 2012, the NRTWLDF provided legal support to plaintiffs suing California when the Service Employees International Union (SEIU), which represented all of the state's public service workers, implemented a new agency fee to back its Political Fight Back Fund. The Fund was designed to provide support for causes endorsed by the union. The Supreme Court decided 7–2 in *Know v. SEIU* that the union had violated the First Amendment and the equal protection clause of the Fourteenth Amendment by not announcing the purpose and scope of the new dues in a timely enough manner to allow workers to opt out of the fees. The Court rejected arguments by the SEIU that unions could not always exactly determine in advance the costs of collective bargaining. Instead, the majority of the justices backed instructions for organized labor to err on the side of caution and undercharge, rather than overcharge, when estimating agency fees for future collective bargaining.

The NRTWLDF won a significant, but limited, victory in the 2014 Supreme Court case *Harris v. Quinn*. The NRTWLDF provided financial support for a group of home health care workers who challenged an Illinois provision that required them to pay agency fees. The workers claimed they were private contract employees who worked for the state, but not as full-time public service workers. Therefore, requiring them to contribute to the union violated their First Amendment right of free association and free speech. In a 5–4 decision, the majority found in favor of the plaintiffs. The majority opinion asserted that the Court had previously interpreted past precedent in too broad a fashion. The Court found that the *Abood* decision did not apply to the home health workers, as the union representation and collective bargaining had only a minimal impact on the contract workers. The ruling did not invalidate *Abood*, but it was seen by both its supporters and critics as weakening organized labor although it left intact agency fees for public service employees.

Throughout its history, the NRTWLDF has been heavily criticized by organized labor, progressive groups, and the Democratic Party, all of which assert that the organization serves as conduit to channel funds from conservative groups into antiunion efforts. The NRTWLDF does not make its contributors public. The organization has been accused by progressive groups of illegally coordinating with individual political campaigns.

The NRTWLDF is the legal arm of the National Right to Work Committee (NRTWC), and both organizations are led by the same president. The NRTWC supports right-to-work legislation, whereby employees are not required to join unions or contribute agency fees. The NRTWC has worked extensively at the state level to promote right-to-work laws. Between 2012 and 2017, 6 additional states enacted right-to-work laws, bringing the total with such statutes to 28.

By 2016, an estimated 14.6 million employees in the United States paid approximately $9 billion in union dues or agency fees. That year, about 10.7 percent of workers belonged to unions, the lowest level since 1983. One-third of all union members were public service employees. The NRTWLDF has a budget of approximately $9 million per year. The majority of expenditures were for legal cases. The organization also supports public initiatives to ensure that workers are aware of their rights. The long-term priority of the group was to overturn the *Abood* decision and end agency fees.

Tom Lansford

See also: American Federation of Labor (1886–1955); Service Employees International Union (1921–)

Further Reading

Hogler, Raymond, Steven Shulman, and Stephan Weiler. 2004. "Right-to-Work Laws and Business Environments: An Analysis of State Labor Policy." *Journal of Managerial Issues* 16: 289–304.

Leef, George. 2005. *Free Choice for Workers: A History of the Right to Work Movement.* Ottawa, IL: Jameson Books.

Lichtenstein, Nelson, and Elizabeth Tandy Shermer, eds. 2012. *The Right and Labor in America: Politics, Ideology, and Imagination.* Philadelphia: University of Pennsylvania Press.

Roof, Tracy. 2011. *American Labor, Congress, and the Welfare State, 1935–2010.* Baltimore, MD: Johns Hopkins University Press.

National Rural Electric Cooperative Association (1942–)

Founded in 1942, the National Rural Electric Cooperative Association (NRECA) is the national organization representing the interests of cooperative electric utilities, their member-owners, and the consumers they serve.

As late as 1935, 9 out of 10 rural homes did not have electrical service, whereas the opposite was true in most urban and near-urban areas, in which 9 out of 10 homes did have electrical service. While modern employers like factories and businesses situated themselves in cities and larger towns with electrical service, the common assumption that rural families and farms did not require electricity kept rural economies almost entirely dependent on agriculture—and often outdated modes of agriculture at that. Seemingly sound business practices kept existing electric companies from expanding into rural areas as the cost of establishing and maintaining lines in those areas would often outweigh profit potentials. Even when rural dwellers did have access to power, it was often at a far higher cost relative to more urban settings.

The Tennessee Valley Act of 1933 opened the door to rural electric service by authorizing the Tennessee Valley Authority (TVA) Board to build electrical lines to serve rural areas. However, the real catalysts were President Franklin D. Roosevelt's (1882–1945) New Deal and his 1935 executive order creating the Rural Electrification Administration (REA) and the resulting low-interest, long-term lending program designed to encourage new and existing for-profit electric companies (IOUs, investor-owned utilities) to expand into rural areas. When private companies proved reluctant to invest in the necessary required infrastructure—even with these government loans and the extensive technical and managerial assistance the REA offered—the idea of electric cooperatives was born.

In 1937 the REA crafted a model law (the Electric Cooperative Corporation Act) to govern the creation and operation of rural electric cooperatives (RECs) that would be user-owned, not-for-profit entities. RECs either purchase power and deliver it to users (often referred to as distribution cooperatives) or generate it and transmit energy themselves (generation and transmission cooperatives), depending on the area in which the cooperative is located and the amount of equity put into the cooperative by user-owners.

Within two years, over four hundred rural electric cooperatives were operating, serving over a quarter of a million rural American households. Due to an explosion in the number of rural electric cooperatives, the number of rural electric customers tripled in just over a decade. And, less than two decades after the founding of the REA, over 90 percent of American farms were connected to the electrical grid. Today that number is just shy of 100 percent, and although electric cooperatives are not the dominant suppliers of energy in the United States, they are the main providers in the rural areas of the country.

What makes the NRECA and its member cooperatives unique is the cooperative structure by which they all operate following the Rochdale Cooperative Principles. Those principles were first laid out in 1844 in Rochdale, England, by a group of 28 craftspeople who, in the face of the Industrial Revolution, found themselves and their families sliding into poverty. By each contributing a very small sum, the group opened a small food store with all products priced fairly and with profit split equitably among the user-owners. The Rochdale Cooperative Principles come from this early cooperative venture and the approximately 1,000 similar ventures that cropped up in the decade after.

Although the principles have been amended and altered over time to reflect new and changing social realities, seven core principles remain foundational: (1) voluntary and open membership without discrimination; (2) democratic control so that the cooperative is run by user-owners and such that one member has one vote; (3) member economic participation, with a limited return on investment to user-owners to be reinvested; (4) honest business practices, which assure the independence and autonomy of the cooperative; (5) education for members and the larger world about the value of cooperation and the cooperative endeavor; (6) cooperation among cooperatives; and (7) concern for community, with all decisions benefiting not just the cooperative but the larger community that it serves.

Because they were almost entirely created and funded through Roosevelt's New Deal programs, government support for rural electric cooperatives has been fairly consistent and strong. This policy of support is evident not only in the initial lending and support assistance programs dating back to the 1930s and 1940s but also through power supply preference programs, community-cooperative grants and loans designed to maintain and revitalize rural communities through economic development programs, and a variety of other policy initiatives. Direct subsidies have not generally been a key mechanism of government support, in part due to the cooperative structures of rural electric cooperatives.

This progress was not without its setbacks, especially during World War II, when leaders of cooperatives came together to defend themselves from charges of copper wire hoarding. Recognizing the need for a common, united front, not only in the face of such charges but also on Capitol Hill, the leaders formed the NRECA in 1942. NRECA grew as the number of cooperatives grew. Its mission now includes lobbying; policy monitoring; public relations initiatives; coordinating a variety of cooperative and individual member programs; management and director training and regional and national conferences; and community, youth, and owner-member services.

Changing economic times have also challenged cooperatives. The energy crisis of the 1970s signaled the end of some cooperatives, while others began to venture into nuclear energy. The latter endeavor has had only minimal success, as many user-owners expressed strong antinuclear sentiment and used the democratic structure of the cooperatives to limit or end ventures into nuclear power.

The NRECA, though serving as the umbrella service organization for hundreds of rural electric cooperatives, is not always able to dictate the actions of its members and often finds itself out of alignment with member cooperatives. For example, after being in existence for decades, many cooperatives have built large equity reserves currently valued in excess of $30 billion, returning little to user-consumers and investing little in cooperative or community development, putting some cooperatives in danger of losing tax-exempt status. Similarly, many user-owners' rates are 5 to 30 percent higher than average large cooperative rates because smaller cooperatives have resisted merging to make power generation and transmission more efficient on a per-customer basis.

This has perhaps run afoul of some of their cooperative principles, and it has raised the possibility of cooperation dissolution as they are bought out by larger for-profit electrical companies who can offer user-owners sizable buyout sums and lower monthly electrical bills. Local cooperative managers argue that unless user-owners address such issues and seek such changes through the open, democratic process of the cooperative structure, they have no obligation (or authority) to do so themselves.

The NRECA has also come under attack for its less-than-enthusiastic support for some climate protection legislation, especially bills and policies put forth in the past 15 years in Congress or by governmental agencies like the Environmental Protection Agency. Environmental groups, including those located in its service areas, see this as a violation of the cooperative principles on which the NRECA and its member cooperatives are built. The source of NRECA's opposition to such bills and policies seems to be financial. Because of their history of dependence on coal-powered electricity rather than on power generated from hydropower, renewable, or nuclear power, proposed legislation and policies limiting greenhouse emissions or requiring reductions in such emissions would disproportionately affect rural electric cooperatives and their user-owners.

The NRECA's stance on such legislation is based largely on historical grounds. The government supported the creation and growth of rural electric cooperatives during a time when coal was king, from the 1940s and 1950s and through the natural gas and oil shortages of the early 1970s. The enactment of legislation that imposes costs on the cooperatives is perceived as an unfair penalization of choices made when no other choices were available. The cooperatives also argue that such policies would create a very heavy burden on low-income families and the fixed-income senior citizens who populate many of the areas served by the cooperatives.

Critics counter that the NRECA and its many member cooperatives have been too slow in investigating and utilizing energy sources other than coal, although that seems to be changing. Perhaps as a result of a general shift in public, scientific, and regulatory attitudes toward climate issues, and perhaps owing to the sharp decrease in costs of cleaner energy sources, the NRECA and its members are allocating sufficient resources to increase solar capacity to nearly five times what it was in 2015. This is a particularly unique development, as for many years, solar power has been seen as the provenance of the wealthy and of particular solar-friendly states. This increase in solar energy production in rural areas of the United States, which are home to a massive population of lower-income families, and in states that have not until recently been seen as solar-friendly (like Georgia and Arizona) will likely be among the catalysts used by pro–solar energy groups to seek additional support for solar energy. The NRECA's role in the shifting energy market continues to unfold.

Milton W. Wendland

See also: American Telephone and Telegraph Corporation (1885–1982)

Further Reading

Cooper, Jim. 2008. "Electric Co-Operatives: From New Deal to Bad Deal?" *Harvard Journal on Legislation* 45 (2): 335–375.

Doyle, Jack, and Angela Wright. 1979. *Lines Across the Land: Rural Electric Cooperatives, the Changing Politics of Energy in Rural America.* Edited by Vic Reindeer. Washington, D.C.: The Rural Land & Energy Project of the Environmental Policy Institute.

National Rural Electric Cooperative Association [corporate author]. 1954. *NRECA Facts.* Washington, D.C.: National Rural Electric Cooperative Association.

Rathke, Wade. 2016. "Rural Electric Cooperatives Need Democracy and Diversity." *Social Policy* 46 (2): 5–38.

National School Boards Association (1942–)

The National School Boards Association (NSBA) is a nonprofit federation of 49 state school boards associations across the United States. Through these state associations, NSBA represents 90,000 individual members of local school boards who govern the operations of 13,800 public school districts serving 50 million students. School board members are elected or appointed by their local communities and given responsibility for setting goals, establishing policies, managing finances, and overseeing the administration of public primary and secondary schools within their districts.

NSBA provides information, services, and support to state school board associations and local school boards. It also represents the perspectives and interests of its members to state lawmakers and federal agencies involved in education policy making. NSBA describes itself as the "premier advocate for public education" (National School Boards Association 2018). It presents public education as a civil right and engages in legislative, legal, and public advocacy to promote excellence in education for all American children.

Although Pennsylvania organized the first state school boards association in 1895, only a few states followed its lead until 1913, when the number of associations began to increase steadily. In 1938, attendees at the National Education Association's annual convention discussed the potential benefits of creating a national federation to represent the state groups. Two years later, they formally established the National Council of State School Boards Association, which eventually became known as the National School Boards Association.

NSBA provides a wide range of services to its members, from assistance with training or policy writing to legal advice and legislative advocacy. Its National Connection program, for instance, works in partnership with state school boards associations to develop tools and resources for local school boards. The Council of School Attorneys (COSA) serves as a centralized resource for the 3,000 school attorneys representing public school districts across the country. COSA assists with legal issues involving student rights, school safety, racial and gender discrimination, religion in schools, health and nutrition policies, curriculum coverage, and other areas of education.

NSBA's Federal Policy Coordinators Network updates members with federal education policy developments, while the Federal Relations Network organizes grassroots efforts to connect local school board members with their congressional representatives. The Technology Leadership Network offers resources and assistance to help school boards evaluate and select technology. Finally, NSBA also includes special councils to help address the education challenges faced by local school boards in urban districts and districts serving high percentages of African American, Hispanic, or Native American students.

As the main organization representing local governance of public school districts, NSBA engages in extensive political lobbying and legislative advocacy with the goal of influencing the national debate over education in the United States. It works to secure laws and policies to promote educational equity for all students and close the achievement gap between students from different racial, ethnic, and socioeconomic backgrounds. It also works to increase federal funding for the nation's public school system while preserving the role of local school boards in establishing policies and programs to meet the learning needs of students in their districts.

Among its many federal legislative priorities, NSBA has voiced support for passage of the Carl D. Perkins Career and Technical Education (CTE) Act, which would enable local school boards to expand apprenticeships, dual enrollment options, and other innovative programs designed to prepare students for successful careers. NSBA has also advocated for reauthorization and reform of such federal education laws as the Every Student Succeeds Act (ESSA), the Individuals with Disabilities Education Act (IDEA), and the Higher Education Act (HEA). Other issues of concern to NSBA include adopting state-led, voluntary Common Core academic standards for schools; securing funding for child nutrition programs and early childhood education programs such as Head Start; and expanding access to educational technology and digital learning opportunities while also protecting data privacy for students and schools.

NSBA has also weighed in on the contentious issues of school choice, education vouchers, and charter schools. During the 2016 presidential campaign, Republican Donald Trump promised to adopt an education policy that significantly expanded school choice. Supporters of the school choice movement argue that public schools should not have a monopoly on primary and secondary education in the United States. They seek to shift control of education away from local school boards, state boards of education, and teachers' unions and give more power to students and parents. They want parents who are unhappy with the type or quality of education that their children receive in public schools to have the freedom to choose among other options, such as home schooling, virtual education, private schools, or charter schools. They believe that federal tax dollars for education should go to students and families—in the form of private school vouchers, education savings accounts, or tax credit scholarship programs—rather than to state governments, local school boards, and public schools.

In 2018, the Trump administration proposed an education budget that allocated $1.1 billion in federal aid to states that supported education vouchers or open enrollment plans in which "the money follows the student." NSBA vigorously opposes the administration's plans to expand school choice, describing it as an effort to privatize public education. NSBA leaders argue that diverting sorely needed funds from public schools to subsidize tuition vouchers for private and religious schools would weaken the U.S. education system and widen the achievement gap. They contend that local school boards represent the interests of students, parents, and the communities they serve, and that public schools offer many innovative options for students. Critics of school choice initiatives assert that voucher systems tend to leave behind vulnerable students—such as students with disabilities and English language learners—because private schools cannot accommodate their special needs. They also point to studies suggesting that voucher programs do not lead to improvements in student performance (Charles 2018). Although NSBA supports public charter schools that are authorized by local school boards, it also encourages Congress to make all education systems that receive federal funding subject to the same laws, regulations, and accountability standards.

Laurie Collier Hillstrom

See also: Home School Legal Defense Association (2000–); National Conference of State Legislatures (1975–); National Education Association (1857–)

Further Reading

Charles, J. Brian. 2018. "Trump Proposes Unprecedented Expansion of School Choice." *Governing*, February 12, 2018. http://www.governing.com/topics/education/gov-trump-doe-education-budget-schools-states.html.

National School Boards Association. 2018. https://www.nsba.org/.

"National School Boards Association—History and Development." 2018. *Education Encyclopedia*. http://education.stateuniversity.com/pages/2287/National-School-Boards-Association.html#ixzz5RYMyvvpP.

National Taxpayers Union (1969–)

The National Taxpayers Union (NTU) is a conservative, nonpartisan, and non-profit organization founded in 1969. It seeks to simplify and reform the U.S. tax code and reduce the federal deficit and national debt while simultaneously shrinking the size and role of the federal government. James Dale Davidson (1938–), a conservative financier and author, founded the organization. Throughout its history, the NTU has played an important role in mentoring young conservatives and being a prominent voice opposed to higher taxes and greater government intervention in the economy. For instance, Grover Norquist (1956–), a noted proponent of small government and limited taxes who founded the influential conservative group Americans for Tax Reform, served as executive director of the NTU from 1978 to 1983.

The NTU has consistently endorsed the elimination of the current progressive U.S. tax system with its graduated marginal tax brackets based on income. The organization has instead endorsed a "flat tax," a single rate for all taxpayers of approximately 15–20 percent, with a minimum threshold of $30,000–$40,000, depending on the specific flat tax proposal. The NTU has alternatively called for the replacement of the income tax with a national sales tax of 23 percent (less affluent households would receive a monthly rebate on the tax). The NTU helped draft some of the provisions of the landmark 1986 Tax Reform Act, which lowered the top income tax rate from 50 percent to 38.5 percent and consolidated the number of tax brackets from fifteen to four, while eliminating a range of tax loopholes and exemptions. The group also supported later tax reforms and reductions, including the 2001 tax cuts under President George W. Bush (1946–), and the 2018 tax cuts under President Donald J. Trump (1946–).

The NTU prepares a nonpartisan annual rating of members of Congress based on the representatives' or senators' support or opposition to tax increases, government spending, and increased regulations. The scores range from 0 to 100. The higher the number, the more resistant the member of Congress is to raising taxes or increasing regulations. Scores of 84 or higher rate an A and earn the member the title "Taxpayers' Friend," while 79–83 is a B+, 73–78 a B, and so forth. Scores of less than 32 are ranked an F and a "Big Spender." For the 114th Congress, through 2016, the average Senate Democrat score was 22, the House Democrat average was 18, the Senate Republican average was 64, and the House Republican was 77. No member of Congress has ever received a perfect score.

In addition to its opposition to tax increases, the NTU generally opposes increased government spending. The national debt rose from 56.8 percent of the country's total economic output or Gross Domestic Product (GDP) in 2001 to 105.4 percent of GDP by 2017. The NTU argued that the dramatic expansion of the debt undermined economic growth and financial stability. The organization routinely decried increases in the nation's debt ceiling, the total amount of money that the federal government may borrow. It vehemently opposed the series of suspensions of the debt limit, beginning in 2011, under President Barack Obama (1961–) which were implemented to avoid potential government shutdowns. Instead, the NTU argued that spending reductions should be used to avoid the need to borrow additional funds.

In order to constrain federal spending, the NTU has endorsed a balanced budget amendment to the Constitution. The amendment would require the federal government to balance spending with revenues in any given year. In the 1980s, the NTU backed a Republican effort to pass a balanced budget amendment through Congress, which would then be sent to the states for the necessary ratification by three-fourths of the states. However, backers of the initiative were unable to garner the necessary two-thirds majorities in both houses of Congress. Successive efforts, including a 2011 proposal, also failed to get the necessary supermajorities in the legislature. In response, the NTU endeavored unsuccessfully in the 1980s to have two-thirds of the states call for a constitutional convention, a second, and as of yet unused, method to change the Constitution. The NTU and other fiscal conservatives had more success at the state level. By 2017, 45 states had legislation or constitutional stipulations requiring balanced budgets, and 29 states had enacted resolutions calling on Congress to pass a balanced budget amendment on at the national level.

The NTU played a major role in promoting the legislation that led to the succession of military facility consolidations through the Base Realignment and Closure (BRAC) process. There were five rounds of BRAC from 1988 to 2005. BRAC resulted in the closure of approximately 350 facilities with savings of more than $57 billion.

The grassroots, antitax Tea Party movement, which began in 2009, began to coalesce with the September 12, 2009, Taxpayer March on Washington. The protest was organized by the NTU and other conservative groups. It sought to highlight public discontent with increased government spending and regulation. The NTU has continued to support the Tea Party movement, and the U.S. House Freedom Caucus, a group of conservative and Libertarian representatives with ties to the Tea Party.

The NTU's headquarters is in Washington, D.C. The organization has more than 360,000 members in 2017, and was led by Pete Sepp who began working for the NTU in 1988. The organization established the NTU Foundation in 1973 to educate taxpayers and to influence policymakers. The NTUF published research reports, policy papers, and an online publication, *The Taxpayer's Tab*. Through 2014, the NTUF also published *BillTally*, which analyzed the fiscal and spending bills of each Congress.

Tom Lansford

See also: American Enterprise Institute (1938–); Americans for Tax Reform (1985–); Competitive Enterprise Institute (1984–); Libertarian Party (1971–); Tea Party Movement (2009–)

Further Reading

Koopman, Douglas. 1996. *Hostile Takeover: The House Republican Party, 1980–1995.* Lanham, MD: Rowman & Littlefield.

Murray, Alan, and Jeffrey Birnbaum. 1988. *Showdown at Gucci Gulch: Lawmakers, Lobbyists, and the Unlikely Triumph of Tax Reform.* New York: Vintage Books.

National Taxpayers Union. 2017. "NTU Rates Congress: 114th Congress, Second Session." https://www.ntu.org/library/doclib/NTU-Rates-Congress114-2nd-Session .pdf.

National Union Party (1864–1868)

The National Union Party, formed in essence to bring together numerous factions, was created during the nomination phase of the presidential election of 1864. With the addition of Tennessee Senator Andrew Johnson (1808–1875), one of the only Congressional Southerners to remain loyal to the Union, as Lincoln's new vice-presidential nominee, the choices made by the National Union Party had a reverberating effect on not only the future of the two-party system in the United States and the fate of the Republican Party but also, more immediately, the outcome of Reconstruction following the Civil War (1861–1865).

In 1864, the Republican Party attempted to uphold the U.S. Constitution and risked losing everything they had gained politically in 1860. Unlike the Confederacy's one-party rule, the Union states held a presidential election, despite the state of the Union, because it gave them the best chance to remain in power. With the Civil War winding down, the incumbent, Abraham Lincoln (1809–1865), attempted to hold together a fragile coalition of radical and moderate Republicans, along with a host of pro-Union Democrats who did not agree with the pro-Confederate Democrats (also known as Copperheads).

Even though the battles of Gettysburg and Vicksburg were simultaneous victories for the Union against the Confederacy, the War between the States still raged throughout the South in 1864. General Robert E. Lee (1807–1870) during the Battle of the Wilderness, stymied General Ulysses S. Grant (1822–1885), while Southern General Joseph E. Johnston (1807–1891) kept General William T. Sherman (1820–1891) occupied in the South near Tennessee and Georgia. Lincoln hoped for a speedy end to the conflict as the death toll mounted. Despite his political popularity being on a severe downturn, he attempted to hold the Union together by crafting a set of political policies that could save the Union. His focus was to find a way for the Republicans to offer former Confederates peace while simultaneously bringing the South to heel. As one of the most skilled politicians in U.S. history, Lincoln understood that inclusivity would not only help the party but also keep his political enemies at bay.

Starting at the local level in St. Louis in 1862, political organizations calling themselves Union parties were trending. It was a means by which to set aside the focus on issues like slavery and bring to the forefront their most cherished issue—the preservation of the Union. As support for the Civil War in the North underwent transformations and a crisis of faith, the idea of a Union Party spread to the national level. Despite misgivings by the Radical Republicans, a faction that adhered to the ideology of abolitionism and severe punishment of the South, Lincoln understood that keeping the border states (i.e., Kentucky, Maryland, Delaware, and Missouri) in the Union was a top priority if he wanted his party to stay in power. Radicals did not perceive Lincoln as a party leader who would adhere to their principles, so during the nomination phase, they selected their own candidate, former frontiersman and the first Republican Party national candidate in 1854, General John C. Fremont (1813–1890). When it looked like the Radicals would split the Union Party vote and give the presidency to the Democrats, Fremont dropped out, but not before extinguishing the career of a political rival, U.S. Postmaster Montgomery Blair (1813–1883), whom Lincoln forced to resign as political collateral.

The incumbent president was given two gifts during the election of 1864 that would help ensure his victory. The first was his pro-Union Democratic opponent, political neophyte and former general, George B. McClellan (1826–1885), who had been relieved of command by Lincoln during the war for poor performance. Granted, he had the difficult task of bringing together Democrats who were divided by the Copperheads and wanted nothing but an end to the war through an immediate cessation of hostilities. However, despite these limitations, McClellan was aided by Lincoln's decline in popularity and gave him all he could handle. The second gift was the war itself. With Sherman's advance to Atlanta right before the Democratic National Convention and Admiral Farragut's victory at Mobile Bay thereafter, McClellan had a difficult time arguing against staying in the war. By this point the National Union Party under Lincoln was victorious.

Despite a resounding throttling of the Democrats, the Republicans, under the cloak of the National Union Party name, had more long-term difficulties than immediate ones. The outcome of choosing Andrew Johnson is a particular example of something Lincoln and his political lieutenants did not foresee. Going into the Baltimore Convention, Republican leadership in smoke-filled backrooms decided that Lincoln's previous vice president, Hannibal Hamlin (1809–1891) of Maine, had to go. Lincoln explored the option of adding General Benjamin Butler (1818–1893) to the ticket, but his political enemies were legion, and the plan was dropped.

The president had no idea who Hamlin's replacement would be, and he had no say. The most likely candidate was Andrew Johnson, a senator from Tennessee, whom Lincoln had appointed as a military governor in 1862. Johnson performed satisfactorily in that position and party leadership knew that he palatable enough for membership to back him. As an enemy of the South, Johnson's rhetoric sounded harsh when he spoke of the Confederacy, and it was thought that after he brought Democrats into the fold, he would be a valuable addition to the National Union Party.

The Congressional elections held in 1864 were also a resounding victory for the National Union Party. In both the Senate and the House of Representatives, candidates held the line under several different forms of the Union Party name. However, the spirit of the Union and Johnson's support of the party after Lincoln's assassination gradually eroded as the war came to a close. Most of this stemmed from the fight that ensued between Johnson and the Radical Republicans over the direction of Reconstruction.

Radicals wanted to see the Union Party move in a direction that would punish the South, whereas Johnson was much more conciliatory in tone and readied his pen for a slew of vetoes against Radical bills. In the end, Johnson was impeached (but not removed from office, as the Senate vote to convict him failed), and became one of the last Union Party members. As the election of 1868 neared, Republicans kept the name "National Union" during the Convention when they printed posters and broadsides, but they reverted to the previous name of Republican Party by the time Election Day rolled around.

Historians and political scientists have regarded the Union Party years as simply part of the Republican Party's past. However, a more nuanced approach speaks to the fact that this was more than just the renaming or rebranding of a party; rather, it was a struggle by party leadership to define itself ideologically during a time of tumultuous upheaval that included issues from emancipation of slaves to their incorporation into the franchise. Lincoln, as party chief, attempted to hold the Union together by finding a middle course that most factions could agree on, all the while trying to defeat the South militarily. The issue became, with his death, whether Andrew Johnson could pick up that mantle and lead the party through the gauntlet of Reconstruction. With such political divisiveness, it would have been difficult for anyone to take that position, although there were many who thought they could. What is for certain is Johnson was not up to the task, and he quickly angered party members, which only increased the power of Radical Republicans.

Ironically, the National Union Party did not have the constitutional authority to act with any guarantee of protecting the territorial integrity of the country because the Confederate States would not be fully reincorporated for some time. Therefore, the National Union Party could be construed as another of Lincoln's promises to protect and restore the United States in an uncertain time. What could be surmised from this political period is that the two-party system was never the same again. Secession and war were officially off the table for good, and thus the ballot box was the only means of settling political conflicts moving forward. Certainly, violence would spill over from the picket line, the factory complex, the college campus, or on any given street in any given town or city, but the federal government proved it had the mechanisms in place to serve justice, social or otherwise—although imperfectly. In that, the Union could endure, even if the Party of the same name did not.

J. N. Campbell

See also: Radical Republicans (1854–1877); Republican Party (1854–)

Further Reading

Donald, David H. 1995. *Lincoln*. New York: Simon and Schuster.

Goodwin, Doris Kearns. 2005. *Team of Rivals: The Political Genius of Abraham Lincoln*. New York: Simon and Schuster.

Johnson, David Alan. 2012. *Decided on the Battlefield: Grant, Sherman, Lincoln, and the Election of 1864*. New York: Prometheus Books.

Selinger, Jeffrey S. 2016. *Embracing Dissent: Political Violence and Party Development in the United States*. Philadelphia: University of Pennsylvania Press.

Waugh, John C. 1997. *Reelecting Lincoln: The Battle for the 1864 Presidency*. New York: Crown Press.

White, Jonathan W. 2014. *Emancipation, the Union Army, and the Reelection of Abraham Lincoln*. Baton Rouge: LSU Press.

National Urban League (1910–)

The National Urban League is one of the nation's oldest civil rights advocacy groups. Founded shortly before the large-scale northern migration of blacks during the World War I era, the organization was an early pioneer in the effort to both expand job opportunities and provide social services that could ease the transition to urban life.

The National Urban League was the product of a merger among three African American reform groups in New York City that was finalized in 1911. The driving force behind this merger was the Committee on Urban Conditions among Negroes, developed by Ruth Standish Baldwin (1863–1934) and Dr. George Edmund Haynes (1880–1960) in 1910. The organization was dedicated to helping African Americans who had emigrated from the South adjust to the realities of Northern urban life. However, the founders recognized the breadth of the challenges that confronted the city's black population and determined that a merger with the Committee for the Improvement of Industrial Conditions among Negroes in New York, which had been founded in 1906, and the National League for the Protection of Colored Women, whose roots went back to 1905, would better serve the city's black population. The resulting organization was named the National League on Urban Conditions among Negroes, a label that was shortened to the National Urban League in 1920.

Although the National Urban League's focus was on the challenges facing New York's black population, the organization had a biracial founding coalition. Baldwin, a member of New York's white establishment and Columbia University Professor Edwin Seligman (1861–1939), the group's chairman from 1911 to 1913, were just two of the many prominent white civic leaders who actively supported the league from the beginning.

The group's first president was George Edmund Haynes. A social worker, Haynes focused on local efforts aimed at fulfilling the League's mission "to enable African Americans to secure economic self-reliance, parity, power and civil rights" (Morial n.d.). In 1918, Eugene K. Jones (1885–1954), a civil rights activist, succeeded Haynes. Under his leadership, the League aggressively expanded its efforts to break down the barriers to black employment that characterized life during the boom times of the 1920s and the depression-ridden years that followed. Jones steered the League through the Great Depression and was succeeded by Lester Blackwell Granger (1896–1976), who served for two decades, from 1941 to 1961. Under Granger, the organization began to edge closer to the mainstream of the developing civil rights movement, and in fact, Granger is reported to have played a role in convincing President Harry Truman (1884–1972) to desegregate the nation's Armed Forces in 1948. Granger was followed by Whitney Moore Young (1921–1971), who led the organization during the tumultuous 1960s, a period during which, given the changing landscape of civil rights and race relations in the United States, the League looked to reassess its operations.

Under Young, the League undertook a number of new programs. He expanded the organization's fund-raising efforts while also moving the League into the mainstream of the civil rights movement. Indeed, Young became part of a group sometimes referred to as the "Big Six," which played a central role in the planning for the 1963 March on Washington and was often invited to the White House as Lyndon Johnson (1908–1973) pursued the passage of the Civil Rights Act of 1964 and the Voting Rights Act of 1965. In addition, the Urban League developed new programs, including the "Street Academy," an alternative school that brought high school dropouts back into the academic arena to prepare them for college, and "New Thrust," a program that sought to encourage local black leaders to identify and develop solutions to problems in their own neighborhoods. Young also was an advocate for increased financial aid to cities, something that became a major program under President Johnson, whose creation of the Department of Housing and Urban Development reflected the president's commitment to revitalization of the cities and their minority populations. After Young's death in 1971, attorney Vernon E. Jordan Jr. (1935–) assumed the presidency of the Urban League. In the course of his almost-decadelong tenure as head of the organization, Jordan tripled the budget and put a greater focus on cultural pluralism. In addition, in 1980 he launched the *State of Black America* reports. This annual publication offers scholarly statistical analysis of social and economic progress among the nation's black population. Under the politically connected Jordan, the League also began a civic education program that was designed to increase the African American vote.

When Jordan resigned in December 1981, he was succeeded by John E. Jacob (1934–), a longtime Urban League officer who had most recently been serving as executive vice president. Over the course of a tenure that extended until 1994, Jacob improved the organization's long-term financial outlook while also developing a number of programs dedicated to strengthening and improving the quality of the staff who worked in and with the League. In addition, he established a new youth development program and also put a new emphasis on programs that sought to reduce teen pregnancies, provide assistance to single female heads of household, and reduce crime. Carrying on Jordan's focus on political involvement, the League continued to work to increase black voter registration.

Given the ever-changing nature of the civil rights landscape, the Urban League, like other organizations, worked hard to stay relevant while serving the needs of its constituents. Under Hugh B. Price (1941–), who assumed the League presidency in the summer of 1994, the National Urban League focused its efforts in three broad areas: education and youth development, affirmative action, and the promotion of inclusion and individual and communitywide empowerment efforts. In the pursuit of the goals he established the Institute of Opportunity and Equality in Washington, D.C. The institute is a think tank that produces research and policy analyses on urban issues. In addition, under Price, the League created the Campaign for African American Achievement, an effort to encourage community action and advocacy to raise awareness and promote the importance of achievement for individuals and communities.

From its New York roots, the Urban League has continued to grow and expand its operations while seeking to remain relevant by addressing key emerging issues in a changing world. Currently, the National Urban League has almost 100 affiliates that serve approximately 300 communities. In providing direct services that improve the lives of over two million people across the country, the National Urban League continues to make a mark on the country's urban communities. It has been a longtime member of the Coalition to Stop Gun Violence, and in 1989, Stop the Violence Movement donated all the proceeds from its hip-hop single to the organization. In 2010, reflective of the organization's ongoing effort to undertake beneficial entrepreneurial initiatives, the Urban League of Essex County, New Jersey, announced the creation of a partnership with the National Association of Professional Women to form a national project called Open Doorways. The program offers inner-city middle school girls an opportunity to work with and learn from professional women.

Recently, Marc Morial (1958–), the former mayor of New Orleans who became the Urban League's president in 2003, has sought to reenergize the organization while raising the group's public profile. Morial has undertaken an effort to both strengthen the organization and expand and reaffirm its community operations. Under his leadership, the annual *State of Black America* report has been revamped, and he has created a legislative conference and developed a new strategic plan for the League. That plan is focused on closing the equality gaps that continue to exist between the African American community and other groups in the important areas of education, economic empowerment, health and quality of life, civic engagement, civil rights, and racial justice.

Indeed, to achieve these goals, the modern Urban League has developed a wide range of programs and initiatives in the areas of housing, jobs, education, and health. Its housing programs include efforts to help people prepare to own a home with counseling about what homeownership entails. It also offers programs aimed at helping prevent foreclosure. The League also offers programs designed to foster and support entrepreneurial efforts, both in terms of training and financial support. In the educational arena, programs including Project Ready and Youth Development are designed to help young people develop the foundations they need for their subsequent educational efforts.

The Urban League of the 1960s was right in the middle of the battles of the civil rights movement and had a seat at the table with the leaders of that effort. As the political and social landscape has changed, the Urban League's longtime focus on the nation's cities and on jobs meant that it had only to adapt to the changing nature of the country's urban needs. Unlike other organizations, the Urban League's core concerns and mission have remained rather painfully relevant. Indeed, as it moves into its second century, the National Urban League remains a vital and vitally important organization, one that does much to create and enhance opportunities for the nation's urban population—and especially its minority youth.

William H. Pruden III

See also: Center for Constitutional Rights (1966–); Congress of Racial Equality (1942–); National Association for the Advancement of Colored People (1909–); Organization of Afro-American Unity (1964–1965); Southern Christian Leadership Conference (1957–)

Further Reading

Jordan, Vernon, with Annette Gordon-Reed. 2001. *Vernon Can Read!: A Memoir.* New York: Public Affairs.

"Mission and History." National Urban League. http://nul.iamempowered.com/who-we -are/mission-and-history.

Morial, Marc H. n.d. "National Urban League." Racial Equity Resource Guide. http:// www.racialequityresourceguide.org/orgs/national-urban-league.

Weiss, Nancy J. 1974. *The National Urban League, 1910–1940.* New York: Oxford University Press.

Weiss, Nancy J. 1990. *Whitney M. Young, Jr., and the Struggle for Civil Rights.* Princeton, NJ: Princeton University Press.

National Wildlife Federation (1936–)

Americans who are concerned about declining populations of game animals, birds, fish, and wildlife habitats have been debating since the late 19th century how to protect their environment, how to manage it, and for what purpose. One group, following the ideals of John Muir (1838–1914), advocated the protection of American natural features in their pristine form, with limitations and regulations on human usage. Outdoorsmen supported by Theodore Roosevelt (1858–1919), Gifford Pinchot (1865–1946), and Aldo Leopold (1887–1948) formed an opposing group, advocating for the conservation and management of natural resources for recreational purposes, especially hunting and fishing, in a sustainable manner. Sportsmen and wildlife managers created the National Wildlife Federation in 1936 for this purpose. It has since grown into one of the largest and most influential conservation organizations in the United States.

Political cartoonist Jay Norwood "Ding" Darling (1876–1962), an avid duck hunter who witnessed the loss of marshland during the Dust Bowl in the 1930s, reproduced its impact on wildlife in several of his drawings published in the *Des Moines Register* and *New York Herald-Tribune*. Darling believed that although private organizations could help purchase and manage wildlife refuges, he opposed the establishment of game reserves. He advocated some government oversight and cooperation between private and public entities for the management of wildlife habitat to benefit the public at large, including hunters and fishermen. President Franklin Delano Roosevelt (1882–1945), impressed by Darling's message, appointed him in 1934 to the U.S. Biological Survey, the agency that in 1939 became the U.S. Fish and Wildlife Service (USFWS). In that capacity, Darling established the Federal Duck Stamp system as a fund-raiser to purchase or lease wetlands for the protection of waterfowl and to place them under the management of the USFWS. Envisioning a national organization that would unite various hunting, birding, fishing, conservation, and social clubs to work in tandem with the USFWS, Darling convinced President Roosevelt to call for a North American Wildlife Conference in Washington, D.C., in 1936. This meeting of outdoorsmen, hunters, anglers, and wildlife enthusiasts established the General Wildlife Federation, renamed the National Wildlife Federation (NWF) in 1938.

Structurally, the NWF is a federation of state chapters that are autonomous and focus on local conservation issues and related legislation. Those chapters convene every year for a national convention where state delegates select national officers. Prior to World War II (1939–1945) the NWF did not collect membership fees but received funds through the American Wildlife Institute, a consortium of gun manufacturers who hoped to protect the interests of hunters and fishermen. The NWF stopped this financial connection after the war in favor of raising revenue for the federation through the sale of conservation stamps depicting the images of different species of animals drawn by acclaimed artists. Despite this change, it remains opposed to gun control legislation and regulations limiting hunting and fishing in national parks. Since 1943, the NWF has held the status of a tax-exempt not-for-profit educational institution, thus attracting members who wish to preserve wildlife and limit restrictions on gun ownership and hunting while deducting their membership fees from their income taxes as a donation.

Darling's philosophy shaped many of the NWF's activities. It uses several means to educate the public about environmental concerns, including the publication of books like *The Foundations of Conservation Education* (1942), *National Wildlife* magazine (since 1962), testifying before congressional committees, bringing lawsuits, distributing free education kits to schools, as well as funding scientific studies. The group's effective lobbying activities resulted in the passage of several federal statutes, including the Duck Stamp Act of 1934, which imposed a one-dollar fee on a federal hunting license; the Pittman-Robertson Act of 1937, which raised fees through the sale of sporting equipment and ammunition; and the Dingell-Johnson Act in 1950, which placed a tax on fishing tackle. The Dingell-Johnson Act was particularly important in that it generated the revenue necessary to purchase over 800,000 acres of land for protection, establish over two dozen wildlife refuges, support various federal wildlife research projects, and assist state wildlife agencies.

By the 1950s, the NWF expanded beyond its traditional base of sportsmen for membership by appealing to children. Books like *Would You Like to Have Lived When—?* or the *Adventures of Rick Raccoon* (which would give birth to the Federations' popular *Ranger Rick* magazine in 1967), as well as a series of wildlife conservation stamps taught children about the environment. The publications explored an array of themes in biodiversity, encouraged children to interact with nature for scientific and aesthetic—not consumptive—reasons, and explained the need to protect all species of wildlife for future generations to appreciate.

During the 1960s, under the leadership of executive director Thomas Kimball (1918–1999), the NWF joined the growing modern environmental movement inspired by Rachel Carson's (1907–1964) *Silent Spring* (1962). Carson's book advocated heightened awareness of humans' impact on nature. As part of that larger effort, the Federation expanded its environmental agenda by opposing new dam construction in the West, supporting research related to the impact of toxic chemicals on wildlife habitats, and lobbying for several landmark federal laws. These new statutes included the Wilderness Act of 1964, which directed several government agencies to preserve wilderness on federal land in its natural state; the Clean Air Act of 1970, which was a comprehensive federal environmental statute directed at limiting air pollution; another major environmental law, the Clean Water Act of 1972, which regulated the release of pollutants into the waters of the United States; the Toxic Substances Control Act of 1976, a law that required the Environmental Protection Agency to test chemicals before they enter the environment; and the Federal Land Policy and Management Act of 1976, which tasked the Secretary of the Interior with developing and enforcing plans for the use of public lands. One of the most important pieces of legislation that NWF lobbying efforts shaped was the Endangered Species Act of 1973. That statute empowers the USFWS to list and protect species that are in danger of becoming extinct.

Despite legislative successes that benefit wildlife and society, the NWF also receives much criticism for being too cozy with big business. Offering membership in the NWF to major oil and chemicals companies like ARCO, DuPont, and Monsanto certainly benefits the NWF's funding. Those relationships may also create the opportunity to address disputes between environmental and industrial interests and promote collaboration in the private cleanup of hazardous waste sites. Critics, however, see such cooperation as a willingness to be less assertive in the push to regulate corporate behavior, especially the handling of chemicals that are harmful to the environment.

During the 1970s, the NWF broadened its membership by launching the certified backyard wildlife habitat program, which encouraged homeowners to grow native plants and protect water resources. What had begun as a narrowly focused interest group of conservationist outdoorsmen had grown by the 1970s into a national environmental organization with a broad public base that enjoyed wildlife for aesthetic purposes in their own backyards.

During the 1990s, the NWF began a long-term relationship with various Native American tribes to learn about their centuries-long natural resource management practices and to apply their knowledge to the preservation of wildlife. Partnership with the Intertribal Bison Cooperative contributed not only to the restoration of bison to the Yellowstone region but also to the establishment of the NWF's Tribal Lands Conservation Program. This alliance focuses on natural as well as cultural preservation because animals, plants, and land are essential factors in tribal medicinal, ceremonial, and conservation practices. Combining science with historical knowledge from tribes has contributed to restoration plans for the lower Colorado River. Moreover, the collaborations have resulted in tribes gaining a larger share of federal conservation funds.

The NWF remains one of the nation's premier advocates for wildlife preservation; sustainable hunting; and protecting habitat from pollution, urban expansion, and excessive resource extraction. The federation has expanded its original interest group of hunters and fishermen to now include birdwatchers, hikers, nature photographers, and backyard gardeners. While its political power has resulted in legislation that benefits all wildlife, not just game or fish, the NWF also remains closely associated with many corporate interests to maintain funding and to support collaborate preservation practices that benefit the interests of both environmentalists and industrialists.

Petra DeWitt

See also: National Audubon Society (1905–); Natural Resources Defense Council (1970–); Resources for the Future (1952–); Sierra Club (1892–)

Further Reading

Allen, Thomas B. 1987. *Guardian of the Wild: The Story of the National Wildlife Federation, 1936–1986.* Bloomington: Indiana University Press.

Gottlieb, Robert. 1993. *Forcing the Spring: The Transformation of the American Environmental Movement.* Washington, D.C.: Island Press.

Voggesser, Garrit. 2009. "When History Matters: The National Wildlife Federation's Conservation Partnership with Tribes." *Western Historical Quarterly* 40 (Autumn): 349–357.

National Woman's Party (1913–1930)

The National Woman's Party was formed in 1916, not as a political party but as a group solely dedicated to achieving women's suffrage at the national level. Alice Paul and Lucy Burns reunited in the United States after their work in the militant suffrage movement in Great Britain. The two women were appointed to lead the Congressional Committee of the National American Woman Suffrage Association (NAWSA) in 1913 and were sent to the nation's capital to lobby for women's right to vote.

Paul and Burns organized a peaceful parade in Washington, D.C., the day before Woodrow Wilson's inauguration in 1913 to demonstrate for suffrage rights.

The parade included between 5,000 and 8,000 women who wore costumes representing their heritage or educational achievements. The parade quickly turned into a riot when antisuffrage spectators began attacking the women. The D.C. police stood by, but the Massachusetts National Guard, the Pennsylvania National Guard, and boys from the Maryland Agricultural College created a barrier to protect the women from the angry crowd.

Paul used the publicity from the event to create a larger association, the Congressional Union for Woman Suffrage. The Congressional Union's strategies were viewed as too radical by NAWSA's leadership, so Paul and Burns split from the organization in 1914. The two women were frustrated by NAWSA's strategy of focusing on gaining suffrage for women through individual state referenda and viewed NAWSA's tactics and its president, Carrie Chapman Catt, as too tame to be effective.

In 1916, the members of the Congressional Union formed the National Woman's Party to focus solely on achieving the ratification of a constitutional amendment to guarantee women's suffrage. The National Woman's Party was a more radical organization than NAWSA and used public dissent to raise awareness of and attention to women's suffrage. Because the Democratic Party was the majority party in the country, the National Woman's Party attempted to pressure the Democrats and President Wilson to support the suffrage amendment. The group did not endorse any candidates for president during the election, and it only supported candidates who openly supported the group's cause.

The National Woman's Party was a single-issue interest group focused on a constitutional amendment to achieve women's voting rights. The National Woman's Party was synonymous with Alice Paul, who believed strongly in nonviolent, but aggressive, protest to achieve the group's goal. The National Woman's Party sent delegations of women to Capitol Hill to lobby members of Congress for passage of the amendment and often spoke on street corners to rally support for their cause. The group also traveled throughout the country to encourage women to join their movement, circulated mass petitions, and publicly burned Wilson's speeches in protest of the president's defense of human rights overseas while, in their estimation, he refused to address women's rights in the United States.

The National Woman's Party began a daily picket at the White House in 1916. These "Silent Sentinels" displayed colorful banners demanding equal voting rights. After the United States entered World War I, the women continued their picketing and sharpened the political rhetoric on their banners, with messages referring to "Kaiser Wilson," for instance. Unlike NAWSA, the National Woman's Party chose not to endorse the United States' entry into the war, arguing that their single-issue activism prevented them from addressing other issues but also because their membership included many pacifists and socialists. As patriotism engulfed the country during the war, the National Woman's Party's strategy of protesting a wartime president was viewed as un-American. Before the war, the Silent Sentinels were tolerated—Wilson would often "tip his hat" to the women as he passed through the White House gates—but after the war, the protesters provoked violence from onlookers and were arrested for "obstructing traffic." Members of the National Woman's Party continued to picket the White House, knowing they also would be arrested and sent to the Occoquan prison workhouse. The suffragists were treated harshly at Occoquan, where they protested their illegal imprisonment with hunger strikes. The women were force-fed and subjected to unsanitary living conditions in addition to other indignities. When public opinion about the treatment of the female prisoners turned in favor of the suffragists, many of the women were released.

Eventually, President Wilson publicly supported women's suffrage as a war measure and urged Congress to adopt the amendment. The Nineteenth Amendment passed the House and Senate on June 4, 1920, and was ratified by the states the same year. The milder and less radical NAWSA is generally credited with securing ratification of women's suffrage, but the National Woman's Party's more aggressive tactics certainly contributed to the success of the movement.

Following the ratification of the Nineteenth Amendment, the National Woman's Party, finding itself without a cause, quickly disbanded and reorganized under the same name to strive for the ratification of the Equal Rights Amendment, written by Alice Paul. The National Woman's Party remained a single-issue interest group led by Paul to end sex discrimination. Although the Equal Rights Amendment failed to gain the three-fourths of the states needed for ratification in 1982, the National Woman's Party was responsible for over 300 pieces of legislation passed for the cause of women's equality after 1920. In addition, the National Woman's Party was instrumental in adding "sex" into the protections guaranteed to citizens in the Civil Rights Act of 1964, which eventually led to policy gains for women in a range of issue areas.

Heather Frederick

See also: League of Women Voters (1920–); National Abortion and Reproductive Rights Action League (NARAL) (1969–); National American Woman Suffrage Association (1890–); National Organization for Women (1966–); National Women's Political Caucus (1971–)

Further Reading

Cahill, Bernadette. 2015. *Alice Paul, the National Woman's Party and the Vote: The First Civil Rights Struggle of the 20th Century.* Jefferson, NC: McFarland Publishing.

Ford, Linda G. 1991. *Iron-Jawed Angels: The Suffrage Militancy of the National Woman's Party, 1912–1920.* Lanham, MD: UPA Publisher.

The Library of Congress American History. 2014. *Historical Overview of the National Woman's Party.* Damascus, MD: Penny Hill Press.

Stillion Southard, Belina A. 2012. *Militant Citizenship: Rhetorical Strategies of the National Woman's Party, 1913–1920.* College Station: Texas A&M University Press.

National Women's Political Caucus (1971–)

The National Women's Political Caucus (NWPC) was founded in 1971 as a nationwide multipartisan organization in the United States to identify, recruit, train, and support women candidates for elected and appointed offices. Those include potential legislators, state and federal judges, and delegates to national conventions. With a "caucus" defined as a group of people sharing similar aims and interests that are usually political, the National Women's Political Caucus advocates more female participation in American politics.

The goal of NWPC is to provide insight, leadership, time, and resources in order to achieve a wide range of female involvement at all levels of the political process. As part of its mission, NWPC offers training for potential candidates as well as technical assistance and advice in such areas as choosing campaign managers, engaging volunteers, and raising funds.

According to the U.S. Census Bureau, women have traditionally made up about half of the nation's population. Starting in 1950, the percentage of females in the United States grew to about 51 percent, or slightly over half.

During World War II (1939–1945), many American women entered the workforce. After the war, there was increased attention to women's issues in the United States. In 1963, *The Feminine Mystique*, a groundbreaking book by author Betty Friedan (1921–2006), was published, spotlighting women's concerns.

In 1966, female activists, including author Gloria Steinem (1934–), founded the National Organization for Women (NOW). One of NOW's goals was for the U.S. government to pass an Equal Rights Amendment to the Constitution. After a proposed federal Equal Rights Amendment failed to pass in 1970, a group of NOW members and others concluded that equality would come only with women's full representation in political office. At that time, with women making up 51 percent of the population, women were only about 2 percent of the U.S. Congress.

On July 10, 1971, more than 300 women from across the country met in Washington, D.C., to create the National Women's Political Caucus. With involvement from both Democrats and Republicans, they represented economic, ethnic, political, and racial diversity. NWPC's founders included Friedan and Steinem along with feminist leaders Bella Abzug (1920–1998) and Shirley Chisholm (1924–2005), among others. The goal was to increase the number of women in all aspects of the nation's political life.

In Houston, Texas, during February 1973, the National Women's Political Caucus held its first national conference. With more than 1,500 women in attendance, the NWPC gathering in Houston was the first major women's political conference since the historic Women's Rights Convention held in Seneca Falls, New York, in 1848.

Frances "Sissy" Farenthold (1926–) was elected as NWPC's first chairperson. During her two-year tenure, five more women were elected to the U.S. Congress, with more women also being elected to state legislatures or appointed to other offices.

Currently, NWPC has state and local caucuses across the country to help identify candidates, issues, and needs specific to individual states or communities. State caucuses currently include those in Arizona, California, Florida, Georgia, Indiana, Kentucky, Massachusetts, Maryland, Missouri, New Jersey, New York, Ohio, Tennessee, Texas, and Washington.

As part of its mission, NWPC considers candidates for the group's endorsement. Candidates under consideration are required to publicly favor NWPC's concerns such as support of the following: passage of a federal Equal Rights Amendment (ERA) to the U.S. Constitution; a woman's right to choose termination of a pregnancy; and increased access to child care and other dependent care.

NWPC also sponsors recognitions such as the Good Guys Award to honor men who demonstrate a commitment to the advancement of gender equality, the Good Corporation Award for companies that encourage a more equitable workplace, and the Martin Abzug Good Spouse Award, named in honor of Bella Abzug's husband, for men who have been supportive spouses of female leaders.

NWPC's Exceptional Merit Media Awards (EMMAs) recognize journalists and mass media who provide information to the public about critical issues impacting women and girls in the United States as well as around the world.

The records of the National Women's Political Caucus are housed in Cambridge, Massachusetts, at the Schlesinger Library on the History of Women in America at Harvard University's Radcliffe Institute for Advanced Study.

Nancy Hendricks

See also: League of Women Voters (1920–); National Organization for Women (1966–); National Woman's Party (1913–1930)

Further Reading

Dolan, Julie, Melissa Deckman, and Michele Swers. 2017. *Women and Politics: Paths to Power and Political Influence*. Lanham, MD: Rowman & Littlefield.

Friedan, Betty. 1963. *The Feminine Mystique*. New York: W. W. Norton.

National Women's Political Caucus. 2018. http://www.nwpc.org.

Weatherford, Doris. 2012. *Women in American Politics: History and Milestones*. Thousand Oaks, CA: CQ Press.

Natural Resources Defense Council (1970–)

The Natural Resources Defense Council (NRDC) is an international environmental advocacy group. With its slogan proudly proclaiming that it is "The Earth's Best Defense," the New York based organization boasts well over two million members and has offices in New York City, Washington, D.C., San Francisco, Los Angeles, Chicago, Bozeman, Montana, and Beijing, China. Through litigation, advocacy, and education, the organization seeks as its website states "to ensure the rights of all people to the air, the water, and the wild."

More specifically, as new environmental challenges have arisen, the organization has developed a list of priorities such as stopping global warming, reviving the planet's oceans, protecting endangered animals and natural lands, preventing pollution so as to protect people's health, and guaranteeing a safe and adequate water supply, while also developing "sustainable communities."

The NRDC was founded in 1970 by John H. Adams (1936–) and a group of fellow lawyers with the intention of enacting environmentally oriented statutes and then using those laws as the basis for a litigation-based campaign to fight polluters and pollution. With an initial grant from the Ford Foundation, the organization quickly moved to the forefront of the emerging environmental effort, helping first to secure passage of the Clean Air Act and then using its provisions to launch its legal campaign against corporate polluters.

While the NRDC remains focused on using the law to protect the environment, it has also established the NRDC Action Fund to further the organization's agenda. The Action Fund is separate and distinct from the NRDC. As a 501(c)(4) nonprofit, it is able to engage in both advocacy and political activities that the tax-exempt status of the NRDC prevents it from undertaking. In addition, NRDC has a partnership with E2, a nonpartisan group that engages in focused advocacy on economic and environmental issues.

Drawing upon a stable of scientific experts who complement its legal resources, the NRDC has been both an active source of policy analysis as well as litigation. As the environmental challenges have grown, its efforts have as well. In response, NRDC has expanded its financial base and moved beyond its early reliance on foundations. While the organization continues to receive substantial support from foundations including environmental activist Tom Steyer's (1957–) Energy Foundation, the William and Flora Hewitt Foundation, George Soros's (1930–) Open Society Foundation, and the SeaChange Foundation, it has also actively sought financial support from donors who believed in the issues it addresses.

Among NRDC's many programs is the BioGems Initiative. Begun in 2001, it sought to mobilize concerned citizens in the effort to protect endangered ecosystems, merging NRDC's assets and expertise with the energies of local citizens. Another NRDC effort involved a study and subsequent report on the health impact of the September 11, 2001, attacks, and it has joined with local New Orleans activists to address some of the issues that arose in the aftermath of Hurricane Katrina. Similarly, in the aftermath of 2017 hurricanes Harvey and Irma, NRDC was immediately involved in both helping the victims and assessing the environmental impact on the regions. Meanwhile, in December 2006, together with Green Day, NRDC launched a website dedicated to raising awareness of U.S. oil dependence. Another NRDC program is the Center for Market Innovation, or CMI. It works with businesses to develop new and greener approaches to the economy, seeking both greater productivity and more environmentally friendly as well as more economically inclusive approaches. Working with both the public and private sectors, it aims to create more efficient, inclusive, and environmentally aware investment approaches.

Over the years, NRDC has run an array of ever evolving environmental programs aimed at addressing some of the many challenges now facing an ever-growing world population. These have included the Clean Air and Energy Program, an effort that focuses on a range of issues including global warming, renewable energy, energy efficiency and transportation. In contrast, the Save the Bees Initiative has urged presidential action to get a ban on the bee toxic neonics that are posing a major threat and leading to a substantive decline in the bee population. Meanwhile NRDC's Health Program is focused on issues relating to drinking water and chemical damage to the environment as well as other environmental dangers that threaten health, all with an eye to limiting the toxins released into the environment. The organization's international program is involved with a range of issues with worldwide ramifications. From concerns about the threat posed to the rainforests to the dangers of nuclear arms and global warming, the International Program workshop, often in concert with other organizations and programs, seeks to address issues of global importance. Similarly, the Land Program focuses on issues relating to national parks and forests as well as other public lands and private forests, all with an eye to preserving and protecting those areas while also working to reduce the manufacture of wood products. The Nuclear Program, in addition to its long-standing opposition to nuclear weapons, works to block the reprocessing of spent nuclear fuel (SNF) while supporting SNF disposal in appropriate, safe geological repositories. It also seeks improved safety standards in uranium mining and power plants.

NRDC's Urban Program and its successor, Cities and Green Living, have sought to spotlight the environmental issues of particular concern to urban and surrounding areas. These include garbage and recycling, the quality of the area's air and water, urban sprawl, and transportation. They have also worked to develop urban parks. Meanwhile, the Water and Oceans Program focuses on issues related to water quality, fish populations, wetlands, and the oceans of the world. It has undertaken a number of regional programs in places like the Everglades, San Francisco Bay, and California's Channel Islands. Recognizing that environmental concerns transcend cultural and language barriers, the NRDC has also run a Latin Outreach Program that seeks to communicate with and involve the Spanish-speaking Latino community in the environmental issues on which the NRDC is working.

In an effort to raise public awareness on environmental issues and make people aware of the group's efforts and how they can get involved, the NRDC also publishes a quarterly magazine, *OnEarth*, which focuses on environmental challenges. Launched in 1979 as the *Amicus Journal*, in 1983, under that name, it was awarded the George Polk Award for special-interest reporting.

The NRDC is well respected for its expertise and its effectiveness. Indeed, on the legal front, it has played an important role in a number of Supreme Court cases that have shaped the development and interpretation of administrative law. These efforts have not always gone the way the NRDC has wanted, but all have played an important role in shaping public policy. The major rulings stemming from NRDC initiated litigation include *Vermont Yankee Nuclear Power v. Natural Resources Defense Council, Inc.*, a 1978 decision in which the Court ruled that courts could not impose additional procedural requirements on an administrative agency beyond what was already required by either the agency's basic statute or the Administrative Procedure Act.

In 1983, in *Baltimore Gas & Electric Co. v. Natural Resources Defense Council, Inc.*, the organization suffered a setback when the Supreme Court upheld a Nuclear Regulatory Commission (NRC) rule that said the licensing process for a nuclear power plant should proceed under the assumption that the permanent storage of nuclear waste has no environmental impact. However, in 1984, in *Chevron U.S.A., Inc. v. Natural Resources Defense Council, Inc.*, the Court ruled that administrative interpretation of Congressional statutes would prevail in the absence of clear statutory meaning. The effect of this ruling was that courts would defer to an administrative agency's interpretation of a statute if the agency's interpretation was based on a "permissible construction of the statute." This gives agencies rather broad discretion to implement laws in accordance with their interpretations of the statutes. The importance of this ruling is reflected in the fact that it is one of the most cited cases in American case law, exceeding iconic rulings like *Marbury v. Madison, Brown v. Board of Education*, and *Roe v. Wade* combined.

Not surprisingly, given its status as a frequent defender of the environment against corporate and developmental interests, NRDC has earned the enmity of some major organizations. Many of its critics see it as responding in little more than a knee-jerk, "guilty until proven innocent" manner to development or chemical programs that might have environmental impacts. It has also been accused of engaging in scare campaigns in an effort to protect ongoing environmental conservation work. Indeed, the battle over the Water Rights Protection Act, wherein the NRDC and its allies think the appropriate regulatory bodies are being hamstrung in their efforts, whereas the bill's advocates seek to restore the balance to a process they believe overly limits private parties from using public land whose use they have already paid for, highlights many of the divisions and pressures at the heart of the NRDC's efforts.

In the end, with each passing day bringing increased awareness of the challenges that the world and its natural resources face, the NRDC continues to pursue its distinctive vision of an environmentally safe planet and the type of society that is needed to sustain it.

William H. Pruden III

See also: Greenpeace (1971–); National Audubon Society (1905–); National Wildlife Federation (1936–); Resources for the Future (1952–); Sierra Club (1892–)

Further Reading

Adams, John H., and Patricia Adams. 2010. *A Force for Nature*. San Francisco: Chronicle Books.

Natural Resources Defense Council. 2009. *NRDC: Simple Steps Deck: A Healthy Home. A Healthy Planet*. San Francisco: Chronicle Books.

Natural Resources Defense Council. 2018a. https://www.nrdc.org/.

"Natural Resources Defense Council." 2018b. Big Green Radicals. https://www.biggreen radicals.com/group/natural-resources-defense-council/.

News Corporation (1979–)

Since its founding in 1979, Rupert Murdoch's (1931–) News Corporation has shaped political discourse and other political development in several countries, including the United States. At its height, News Corporation, also known as News Corp, represented one of the largest media conglomerations in the world. Its holdings included 20th Century Fox, television networks, and newspapers in the United States as well as in the United Kingdom and Murdoch's native Australia. News Corp's hegemony and influence serve as testaments to the role of media in politics in the late 20th century and early 21st century. News Corp's reach has also raised questions about the partisanship of media companies and about the proper ethical boundaries in which those companies should operate.

News Corp's roots extend far beyond its formal founding in 1979 and reveal a consistent pattern found in many of the company's media properties. Although Murdoch worked briefly as an editor of a British newspaper, his true start in the media industry came when his father, Keith, died in 1952. The elder Murdoch had gained attention as a war correspondent during World War I (1914–1918), and he later purchased a newspaper based in Adelaide, Australia. Rupert Murdoch inherited those newspapers from his father, transformed them into tabloid-style publications, boosted their circulations, and then moved to purchase other newspapers in Australia.

With his successes in Australia, Murdoch moved into the newspaper business in the United Kingdom and the United States before establishing News Corp in 1979. As he did in his home country, Murdoch practiced tabloid-style, sensationalistic journalism. Murdoch's newspapers, however, marked only the beginning of the media empire he would amass as part of his News Corp. He spent the rest of the 20th century adding more companies to News Corp and bringing entertainment elements into the political world.

Under the umbrella of News Corp, Murdoch diversified his holdings by purchasing magazines, publishing houses like HarperCollins, television stations, and television networks. Those purchases came in addition to the newspapers that Murdoch owned in the United States, the United Kingdom, and Australia. In the United States, Murdoch concentrated on adding television stations and networks to his News Corp empire because he recognized the power of television over American political culture.

His first move into the U.S. television industry came in 1985 when he purchased independent television stations from Metromedia. Those stations formed the basis for the fourth broadcast network, the Fox Broadcasting Company, that originally operated in the shadows of the other three broadcast networks. In the 1990s, however, the Fox Broadcasting Company experienced significant growth thanks to several successful television shows and to a deal with the National Football League to air both regular season and playoff games. Those moves presaged Murdoch's and News Corp's move into the cable news industry, a move that gave Murdoch and News Corp a powerful platform for political influence.

Within the United States, Fox News embodies the most overt aspect of News Corp's influence over the country's political discourse and political culture. Fox News launched in 1996 under the aegis of Roger Ailes (1940–2017), a Republican political consultant who had long understood the importance and power of television. Ailes began his consultant career working for Richard Nixon in 1968 and successfully used television commercials to sell Nixon to American voters. His style easily complemented the journalistic style that Murdoch favored and that characterized other media holdings within the News Corp empire.

With Ailes at the helm, Fox News hired anchors with big personalities—anchors like Bill O'Reilly (1949–) and Sean Hannity (1961–)—and pledged to provide a "fair and balanced" approach to the news. While Ailes did not personally develop Fox News's "fair and balanced" slogan, he emphasized it in development meetings with the network's employees and used it to further distinguish the new network from its cable competitors. The "fair and balanced" slogan slyly implied that the other cable news networks, CNN and MSNBC, offered biased views and that Fox News would remain free from bias in its news coverage.

Despite its "fair and balanced" slogan, Fox News adopted an overtly partisan identity, something that it shared with other media companies within the News Corp umbrella. In the United Kingdom, for example, Murdoch used his News Corp holdings to promote Tony Blair (1953–) and the Labour Party before their victories in the 1997 Parliamentary election. Due to the influence of Ailes, Fox News's partisanship leaned toward the Republican Party, and that partisanship showed in the network's coverage. The first president the network covered, Bill Clinton (1946–), provided the network with the kind of scandals that fit the tabloid-style journalism prevalent within News Corp properties. Ailes brought Matt Drudge (1966–), whose website broke stories concerning President Clinton and Monica Lewinsky (1973–), into the network. Consistent with the market appeal of sensationalism that News Corp outlets identified, much of the coverage of that story emphasized the more salacious aspects of Clinton's scandals.

In the early 21st century, Fox News's partisanship hardened during the presidencies of George W. Bush (1946–) and Barack Obama (1961–). On the heels of the September 11, 2001, terrorist attacks, Ailes worked with George W. Bush's administration in selling its War on Terror and the invasion of Iraq in 2003. Fox News's rating success moved the other cable news networks, particularly MSNBC, to modify their tone and remove anchors critical of the Bush administration.

With Barack Obama's first inauguration in 2009, Ailes and Fox News moved to capture the wave of opposition that rose in response to policies like the stimulus and the Affordable Care Act (ACA). The network hired people like Karl Rove (1950–), a Republican strategist who had worked for President Bush, and Sarah Palin (1964–), the former governor of Alaska, Republican vice-presidential nominee, and frequent critic of the ACA, known for erroneously declaring the legislation would establish "death panels."

Palin's contract with Fox News and her contract with HarperCollins placed her firmly in the middle of the New Corp empire in the United States. In his capacity as the president of Fox News, Ailes helped to bring the News Corp empire directly into the Republican Party by adopting a leading role in the recruitment and selling of the 2012 Republican nominee for president. His attempts to recruit Chris Christie (1962–) and David Petraeus (1952–) failed, yet he succeeded in making Fox News, and by extension News Corp, an indispensable facet of the Republican Party.

The linkage of News Corp, Fox News, and the Republican Party came into focus with the election of Donald Trump (1946–) as the nation's 45th President. Fox News gave Trump space to enter the political world and to gain a reputation as a political authority among the network's viewers. In the years before he launched his successful presidential bid, Trump frequently called into *Fox & Friends*, the network's morning show, to discuss and criticize President Obama's policies. During the 2016 campaign, Trump regularly appeared on the network, and Ailes assisted him in preparing for the debates. Since his inauguration, President Trump and officials from his administration continued to appear on the network, especially on Sean Hannity's weeknight program. Hannity in particular emerged a leading voice in helping promote the administration's policies and in shaping perceptions of the new president.

With Fox News at the forefront of its influence in the United States, News Corp ranked as one of the most valuable companies in the world, but it also endured a number of controversies. Beginning in 2011, News Corp became embroiled in a phone-hacking scandal in the United Kingdom that damaged the company's reputation and led to an investigation of the company's practices in the United States. As a result of the scandal, Murdoch moved to split News Corp into two new entities in 2014. The two new entities consisted of a streamlined News Corp and 21st Century Fox, a company that housed the old News Corps' entertainment holdings.

In 2016, News Corp faced more scandal in the United States when two Fox News anchors, Gretchen Carlson (1966–) and Megyn Kelly (1970–), accused Ailes of sexual harassment. Their allegations led to revelations of a culture at Fox News that fostered harassment of women. Ailes resigned from Fox News in June 2016, less than a year before his death at the age of 77. In 2017, Fox News's troubles continued as other anchors, including Bill O'Reilly and Eric Bolling (1963–), faced harassment claims. Fox News fired both anchors, but the stories added to the list of scandals News Corp faced in the past decade.

Despite its scandal-stained reputation, News Corp ranks as one of the most powerful and valuable companies in the world. Its diversified media holdings provide the company and its officials, like Murdoch and Ailes, powerful platforms to shape politics, establish narratives about specific politicians, and help candidates win elections. The partisan slant of News Corp entities like Fox News raise questions about the role of the press in democratic societies. Additionally, the prominence of News Corp entities like Fox News has influenced the way the American electorate consumes political news and determine the fitness of candidates for office. With Fox News, a variety of newspapers, and a publishing house, News Corp has the means to shape political narratives in multiple media platforms. Even though it has faced scandals, News Corp remains positioned to continue its hegemony over American politics for the foreseeable future.

Courtney Michelle Smith

See also: American Telephone and Telegraph Corporation (1885–1982); Motion Picture Association of America (1922–); Republican Party (1854–)

Further Reading

Chozick, Amy. 2013. "News Corporation Board Approves of Split of Company." *New York Times*, May 24, 2013.

McKnight, David. 2010. "Rupert Murdoch's News Corporation: A Media Institution with a Mission." *Historical Journal of Film, Radio, and Television* September: 303–316.

Roberts, Tom D. C. 2015. *Before Rupert: Keith Murdoch and the Birth of a Dynasty.* Queensland: University of Queensland Press.

Sherman, Gabriel. 2014. *The Loudest Voice in the Room: How the Brilliant, Bombastic Roger Ailes Built Fox News—And Divided a Country.* New York: Random House.

Wolff, Michael. 2008. *The Man Who Owns the News: Inside the Secret World of Rupert Murdoch.* New York: Broadway Books.

Niagara Movement (1905–1910)

The Niagara Movement was a prominent early African American–led civil rights group formed in the United States. By the early 20th century, most states of the former Confederacy had taken steps to systematically disenfranchise and segregate African Americans. The Niagara Movement challenged the U.S. government to address key civil rights abuses against black Americans, such as segregation, disenfranchisement, and lynching. Led by the Harvard-educated intellectual W. E. B. Du Bois (1868–1963), among others, the movement broke with what its members saw as the compromising stance of the most prominent African American spokesperson of the day, Booker T. Washington (1856–1915). Instead, the Niagara Movement called for increased action to move the issue of rights for African Americans forward. Though the movement was short-lived and suffered from serious internal divisions, it did set the groundwork for the National Association for the Advancement of Colored People (NAACP), which has been in existence since 1909.

The dawn of the 20th century saw the first real split in what might be termed the early civil rights movement. Prior to this split, the primary African American pressure group in the United States was the National Afro-American League, established in 1887 by New York–based black newspaper editor T. Thomas Fortune (1856–1928). Like its successors, the Niagara Movement and NAACP, the League aimed to combat many of the race-based injustices of post-Reconstruction America. After a slow start, the League was reformed as the National Afro-American Council in 1898 with Booker T. Washington as a key figure within the organization. Washington was the best-known black leader of the decade following his 1895 "Atlanta Compromise" speech, where he had outlined an accommodationist approach to progress for African Americans that would focus on vocational education and "self-help," but not seek to broach the far more divisive and pressing issue of social equality. Some historians note that Washington worked behind the scenes for more radical changes in civil rights for African Americans. His clout with politicians like Theodore Roosevelt, they reason, came from his more public, moderating approach. It was his public stance of gradualism and the seeming dominance of Washington (who also controlled the influential National Negro Business League) that caused great tension within the Council. Critics of Washington, such as Boston newspaper editor William Monroe Trotter (1872–1934) and Du Bois, felt compelled to leave the League to establish their own rival movement in 1905.

It was on the Canadian side of the 49th Parallel at Fort Erie, Ontario (though often recorded as in Buffalo, New York), near Niagara Falls, that those opposed to an organization dominated by Booker T. Washington asserted their independence in the first meeting of what would come to be known as the Niagara Movement. The movement offered an alternative—and more radical—approach to seeking change for African Americans across the United States. Du Bois and the Niagara Movement moved clearly away from the vision articulated by Washington. Their 1905 Declaration of Principles outlined a host of relatively radical measures that emerged from their July conference. Although the Declaration began by accepting that some progress had been made on racial matters in the previous decade, it asserted that "we believe that this class of American citizens should protest emphatically and continually against the curtailment of their political rights."

The Declaration of Principles is the most significant document in the short history of the Niagara Movement, and it sets out a far more radical stance than any groups led by Washington. It called for African American male suffrage, civil rights, and equal treatment—all rights that had seemingly been assured by the Fourteenth and Fifteenth Amendments to the U.S. Constitution, but had been denied throughout the Southern states. The Declaration also called for equal opportunities in "economic life" where Southern blacks were kept in a state of "virtual slavery," as well as for compulsory, free public school education. The Declaration also listed many areas of life in which African Americans were discriminated against, including the justice system, the military, employment practices, and union membership. It challenged "Jim Crow" segregation laws in the South and made clear the position of the Niagara Movement toward discrimination in general. In all, the Declaration was directly critical of white supremacy in the United States, brushing aside the concessions Booker T. Washington had made in his Atlanta Compromise speech 10 years earlier.

Membership in the newly established organization faltered early, as those at the founding decided to establish local branches rather than a more centralized national movement. For Du Bois, however, the "quality" of its membership was perhaps far more important than its number. He envisioned a so-called "Talented Tenth" of black Americans shaping the future for all African Americans; those who attended the Niagara meeting surely would have fit that vision. However, even if it was aiming to be small and select, the size of the movement was not entirely a matter of choice. Booker T. Washington was not happy to allow any form of rival power to arise, and he used his network of affluent and influential supporters to continually challenge and critique the Niagara Movement. Thus, the Niagara Movement was starved of many of the "Talented Tenth" who, for one reason or another, were unwilling to throw in their lot with Du Bois and risk the wrath of Washington. In addition, Washington's followers proved adept at presenting the Niagara Movement as something of an elite cadre of intellectuals, adding to the problems the movement had in spreading its message.

The second meeting of the movement was held in 1906 at the heavily symbolic venue of Harper's Ferry in Virginia, the site of John Brown's famous raid in 1859, which had sought to ignite a slave rebellion in the antebellum South. The third and best-attended conference was held in Boston in 1907 at Faneuil Hall (a Revolutionary landmark), and the fourth meeting was held at in 1908 in Oberlin, Ohio (the site of the first college to admit students regardless of race); it was during this period that the movement was perhaps at its most successful and high-profile, yet it was also becoming less united. Unlike the Afro-American Council, where Washington held a powerful and charismatic sway over its members, Du Bois lacked the charisma or authority to hold the Niagara Movement together.

In addition to being an all-black organization from its founding, the Niagara Movement started off as an all-male movement. However, women played a role in the movement from the beginning, even if they were not formal members. An ancillary organization was set up for women who wished to join the movement in 1906, led by Gertrude Morgan, the wife of another key Niagara member, Clement Morgan (1959–1929). Over time, women came to make up a significant portion of the overall membership of the organization, yet there was always a sense of separateness.

Indeed, the role of women in the movement played a key role in dividing the group's leaders. Clement Morgan, a close ally of Du Bois, fell out with William Monroe Trotter over a variety of decisions regarding how the movement was organized, including the involvement of women. As the interpersonal dynamics became increasingly public and unpleasant, Du Bois struggled to maintain peace within the movement's leadership. Trotter eventually left the movement in 1908 and set up his own organization, the Negro American Political League. Trotter's departure was not just a high-profile loss that suggested the movement was unstable, it was also a heavy blow to the movement's influence in the New England press.

Despite Trotter's departure, the group's wider activities were advertised in the Niagara Movement's own newspapers—first in the *Moon* (which ran from December 1905 to the summer of 1906) and later in the *Horizon* (which began in January 1907 and ended in 1910)—as part of the group's plan to spread its messages. The group used letter-writing campaigns and petitions to put pressure on politicians and create a stir that did not rely on mass protest or direct action, for which such a small, geographically dispersed group was ill-suited. Another method of action used by the group was legal support for African Americans in U.S. courts. In fact, a legal strategy would come to be a key element of the Niagara Movement's successor, the NAACP. The Niagara Movement's small size, however, affected its fund-raising abilities and undermined any potential for large-scale legal challenges. Nevertheless, important test cases were made for subsequent, more high-profile challenges on matters such as segregation on public transportation.

The loss of Trotter and the grinding criticism from Washington and his supporters, combined with the organization's lack of funding and united leadership, saw the Niagara Movement decline after 1908. The final two years of the group's existence were low profile in contrast to what had come before. In addition to the many problems facing the Niagara Movement, there were calls from a number of black and white civil rights activists for a new movement. Although two final modest gatherings were held in 1909 and 1910, the Niagara Movement had become effectively obsolete. From 1909 on, Du Bois encouraged its members to join the newly formed organization that would become the NAACP. Although short-lived and lacking in a great number of concrete accomplishments, the Niagara Movement was an important counterweight to Booker T. Washington's domination of the African American political agenda. Many of its leaders went on to become significant black voices in the substantially more successful NAACP.

Adam D. Burns

Related primary document: **W. E. B. Du Bois: "Address of the Niagara Movement, to the Country" (1905)**

W. E. B. Du Bois: "Address of the Niagara Movement, to the Country" (1905)

In 1906, W. E. B. Du Bois helped found the short-lived Niagara Movement, with goals that included attaining voting rights for African Americans, the end of racial segregation, and enforcement of the Fourteenth Amendment. On August 16, 1905,

*at Harpers Ferry, West Virginia, he shared the aims of the Niagara Movement
with the nation.*

The men of the Niagara Movement coming from the toil of the year's hard
work and pausing a moment from the earning of their daily bread turn
toward the nation and again ask in the name of ten million the privilege of a
hearing. In the past year the work of the Negro hater has flourished in the
land. Step by step the defenders of the rights of American citizens have
retreated. The work of stealing the black man's ballot has progressed and the
fifty and more representatives of stolen votes still sit in the nation's capital.
Discrimination in travel and public accommodation has so spread that some
of our weaker brethren are actually afraid to thunder against color discrimination as such and are simply whispering for ordinary decencies.

Against this the Niagara Movement eternally protests. We will not be satisfied to take one jot or tittle less than our full manhood rights. We claim for
ourselves every single right that belongs to a freeborn American, political,
civil and social; and until we get these rights we will never cease to protest
and assail the ears of America. The battle we wage is not for ourselves alone
but for all true Americans. It is a fight for ideals, lest this, our common
fatherland, false to its founding, become in truth the land of the thief and the
home of the Slave a by-word and a hissing among the nations for its sounding
pretensions and pitiful accomplishment.

Never before in the modern age has a great and civilized folk threatened to
adopt so cowardly a creed in the treatment of its fellow-citizens born and
bred on its soil. Stripped of verbiage and subterfuge and in its naked nasti-
ness the new American creed says: Fear to let black men even try to rise lest
they become the equals of the white. And this is the land that professes to
follow Jesus Christ. The blasphemy of such a course is only matched by its
cowardice.

In detail our demands are clear and unequivocal. First, we would vote; with
the right to vote goes everything: Freedom, manhood, the honor of your
wives, the chastity of your daughters, the right to work, and the chance to
rise, and let no man listen to those who deny this.

We want full manhood suffrage, and we want it now, henceforth and forever.

Second. We want discrimination in public accommodation to cease. Separation in railway and street cars, based simply on race and color, is un-
American, un-democratic, and silly. We protest against all such discrimination.

Third. We claim the right of freemen to walk, talk, and be with them that
wish to be with us. No man has a right to choose another man's friends, and
to attempt to do so is an impudent interference with the most fundamental
human privilege.

Fourth. We want the laws enforced against rich as well as poor; against Capitalist as well as Laborer; against white as well as black. We are not more

lawless than the white race, we are more often arrested, convicted, and mobbed. We want justice even for criminals and outlaws. We want the Constitution of the country enforced. We want Congress to take charge of Congressional elections. We want the Fourteenth Amendment carried out to the letter and every State disfranchised in Congress which attempts to disfranchise its rightful voters. We want the Fifteenth amendment enforced and No State allowed to base its franchise simply on color.

The failure of the Republican Party in Congress at the session just closed to redeem its pledge of 1904 with reference to suffrage conditions at the South seems a plain, deliberate, and premeditated breach of promise, and stamps that party as guilty of obtaining votes under false pretense.

Fifth. We want our children educated. The school system in the country districts of the South is a disgrace and in few towns and cities are Negro schools what they ought to be. We want the national government to step in and wipe out illiteracy in the South. Either the United States will destroy ignorance or ignorance with destroy the United States.

And when we call for education we mean real education. We believe in work. We ourselves are workers, but work is not necessarily education. Education is the development of power and ideal. We want our children trained as intelligent human beings should be, and we will fight for all time against any proposal to educate black boys and girls simply as servants and underlings, or simply for the use of other people. They have a right to know, to think, to aspire.

These are some of the chief things which we want. How shall we get them? By voting where we may vote, by persistent, unceasing agitation; by hammering at the truth, by sacrifice and work.

We do not believe in violence, neither in the despised violence of the raid nor the lauded violence of the soldier, nor the barbarous violence of the mob, but we do believe in John Brown, in that incarnate spirit of justice, that hatred of a lie, that willingness to sacrifice money, reputation, and life itself on the altar of right. And here on the scene of John Brown's martyrdom we reconsecrate ourselves, our honor, our property to the final emancipation of the race which John Brown died to make free.

Our enemies, triumphant for the present, are fighting the stars in their courses. Justice and humanity must prevail. We live to tell these dark brothers of ours scattered in counsel, wavering and weak that no bribe of money or notoriety, no promise of wealth or fame, is worth the surrender of a people's manhood or the loss of a man's self-respect. We refuse to surrender the leadership of this race to cowards and trucklers. We are men; we will be treated as men. On this rock we have planted our banners. We will never give up, though the trump of doom finds us still fighting.

And we shall win. The past promised it, the present foretells it. Thank God for John Brown! Thank God for Garrison and Douglass! Sumner and

Phillips, Nat Turner and Robert Gould Shaw, and all the hallowed dead who died for freedom! Thank God for all those to-day, few though their voices be, who have not forgotten the divine brotherhood of all men white and black, rich and poor, fortunate and unfortunate.

We appeal to the young men and women of this nation, to those whose nostrils are not yet befouled by greed and snobbery and racial narrowness: Stand up for the right, prove yourselves worthy of your heritage and whether born north or south dare to treat men as men. Cannot the nation that has absorbed ten million foreigners into its political life without catastrophe absorb ten million Negro Americans into that same political life at less cost than their unjust and illegal exclusion will involve?

Courage brothers! The battle for humanity is not lost or losing. All across the skies sit signs of promise. The Slav is raising in his might, the yellow millions are tasting liberty, the black Africans are writhing toward the light, and everywhere the laborer, with ballot in his hand, is voting open the gates of Opportunity and Peace. The morning breaks over blood-stained hills. We must not falter, we may not shrink. Above are the everlasting stars.

Source: Du Bois, W. E. B. "Address of the Niagara Movement, to the Country." *The Public* 9, no. 418 (April 7): 1906.

See also: Center for Constitutional Rights (1966–); Congress of Racial Equality (1942–); National Association for the Advancement of Colored People (1909–)

Further Reading

Jones, Angela. 2011. *African American Civil Rights: Early Activism and the Niagara Movement.* Santa Barbara, CA: ABC-CLIO.

Lewis, David Levering. 1994. *W. E. B. Du Bois: Biography of a Race.* New York: Henry Holt & Co.

Rudwick, Elliott. 1957. "The Niagara Movement." *Journal of Negro History* 42 (3): 177–200.

Thornbrough, Emma Lou. 1961. "The National Afro-American League, 1887–1908." *Journal of Southern History* 27 (4): 494–512.

Various [Niagara Movement Special Issue]. 2008. *Afro-Americans in New York Life & History* 32 (2).

Non-Partisan League (1915–1956)

The Nonpartisan League (NPL) was an organization of North Dakota farmers founded in 1915 by flax farmer Arthur C. Townley. The NPL capitalized upon the frustration of North Dakota farmers over poor treatment by out-of-state businesses that determined pricing policies for grain. The NPL advocated for state-owned grain mills and elevators and for a variety of loan programs designed to help farmers.

Townley's goal in forming the NPL was to establish a highly regimented organization that stood outside of the party system but used the party primaries to elect candidates. A contemporary study of the NPL described it as the only political organization of the time that used commercial methods of salesmanship to develop a membership base. Townley established the NPL as a dues-based organization. NPL organizers collected annual dues from farmers in the form of post-dated checks; this ensured that the NPL could ensure a pledge of support from needy farmers, hedged against adequate crop sales. If the farmers failed to earn enough money when crops were harvested, or grew suspicious of the NPL, they could cancel their checks. Membership in the NPL entitled one to, among other things, a subscription to the *Nonpartisan Leader*, the League's newspaper. By 1916, the *Leader* had a readership of over 30,000.

As the NPL grew, Townley began to recruit candidates for state political offices. All candidates signed a pledge to advocate for state ownership of terminal elevators, mills, packing houses, and cold storage plants; state inspection of grain; state hail insurance and rural credit banks; and exemption of farm improvements from taxation. Although this agenda was not inconsistent with the policies advocated by socialist or left-wing movements elsewhere in the country, Townley initially declined to pursue alliances with labor organizations or with Democratic or Republican politicians already in office. The result of this decision was to create a focused, regimented organization that addressed the needs of North Dakota farmers while avoiding entanglement in the national issues that divided the two major parties. Townley chose not to run for office himself in order to emphasize the purity of his motives.

The NPL exploited North Dakota's newly enacted direct primary law to gain control of the state legislature. All NPL members were entitled to a vote at the League's preprimary convention, and the preprimary convention winners ran in the primary of the party with the most support in their area of the state. In 1916, NPL candidates swept all of the primaries they entered. In the general election, NPL candidates won 81 of 113 seats in the state House. NPL candidates also won 18 of 49 state Senate seats—enough, with the aid of sympathetic holdovers, to establish a working majority. The NPL also swept the governor's race and other state races. The NPL wave was substantial enough that the opposition was split—some incumbent legislators acceded to much of the NPL program even though they themselves were not NPL members, whereas others dug in against the NPL. In 1918, the NPL established majority control over the North Dakota legislature. It also successfully ran a candidate in a special election to the U.S. House of Representatives.

The NPL's activities beyond North Dakota varied, as did its level of success. In Saskatchewan, the NPL laid the groundwork for creating a viable party of its own. The legacy of this party endured decades later in the form of the Cooperative Commonwealth Federation (CCF), which governed the province during the early 1960s and mounted successful parliamentary campaigns between the 1930s and 1960s in Saskatchewan, Manitoba, and Alberta. The CCF was the direct forerunner of the New Democratic Party, which continues to play a significant role in Canadian politics as of this writing.

The NPL had its greatest recruiting success in Minnesota, at one time having as many as 40,000 members there. The NPL set up a national office in St. Paul.

Following its failure in statewide races, however, the League sought to strengthen its alliance with organized labor, resulting in the creation of the Farmer-Labor Party, which would eventually elect several governors before merging with the Democratic Party in 1944. In other Midwestern states, the NPL had somewhat less success. Several states already had elected officials who were sympathetic to the NPL's agenda and welcomed its support. In Montana, the NPL endorsed the campaign of the nation's first female House member, Jeanette Rankin, who ran as an incumbent in the Republican primary, and then, following her defeat, as a third-party candidate. In Idaho, the NPL organized itself following the North Dakota model, convening before the primaries and selecting a full slate to run in the state's Democratic primaries. Idaho NPL members were largely satisfied with the state's two incumbent senators, so it opted to endorse these two rather than field its own candidates. Such practical decisions enabled the NPL to boast that it had won all of the races it entered in Idaho—an interest group tactic not uncommon in contemporary politics. In South Dakota, Texas, and Iowa, NPL chapters deemed themselves too weak for the moment to field slates; in Iowa, the emergence of rival (and slightly less radical) farmers' organizations had diminished the appeal of the NPL.

While NPL leaders were exploring expansion, they were running into increasing trouble at home. The NPL had little ability to expand their coalition beyond farmers. By 1919 NPL members had embarked on an aggressive plan to reform the state's education system, consolidating several different school boards into one body with a state-appointed administrator. This created intense divisions across the state, as many presumed that the state administrator would wield extraordinary control over the curriculum, potentially leading to the indoctrination of schoolchildren by the NPL. By 1919, NPL officeholders had staked out positions on a wide range of issues that went well beyond matters of agricultural policy; the NPL's official program on post–World War I reconstruction, for instance, included calls for women's suffrage, support for the League of Nations, and a graduated income tax. Whatever the popularity or wisdom of such proposals, they clearly did go beyond the organization's original mission.

As the NPL's tenure in office wore on, opposition to the NPL in North Dakota coalesced. An anti-NPL paper, the *Red Flame*, was published by an organization calling itself the Citizens Economy League and featured a variety of attacks on the NPL—some of which were policy critiques, but most of which were crude innuendo. As World War I got underway, and as Americans became accustomed to anti-German propaganda, the German surnames of many NPL members were frequently invoked as part of the rhetorical attack. The occasional pacifist statement by an NPL member was often taken as a sign of covert sympathy for the Germans.

At the same time as the *Red Flame* was making its appeals, several rival "leagues" were formed. The most successful of these was the Independent Voters Association (IVA). The IVA made a point of welcoming disgruntled NPL voters and politicians, working to separate the more popular parts of its platform (such as those having to do with grain prices) from less popular instances of overreach such as the school board decision and a variety of proposed constitutional amendments to establish several state- run banks and businesses. Beyond this, the IVA's initial concerns had to do with process—the governor's appointment power, the NPL's bloc voting—rather than with the specific policy results of this. The IVA, furthermore, took aim squarely at Townley and his control of the legislators, seeking to frame the NPL as a dictatorship and link it more directly with the emerging Soviet regime.

When schisms had emerged within the NPL, the IVA presented a power base for dissidents. Following a conflict between NPL Governor Lynn Frazier and Attorney General William Langer, Langer ran as the IVA candidate against Frazier in the 1920 Republican primary, losing by merely 5,000 votes out of 100,000. The IVA also won one U.S. House seat (with a Republican) and, with a coalition of Republican and Democratic candidates, gained control of the state House. Conflict between the IVA House and the NPL Senate severely disrupted the North Dakota economy, and as the governing party, the NPL took the blame for this. Frazier was successfully recalled in 1921 and replaced by an IVA candidate, and the NPL lost control of the state senate in 1922. Frazier would, however, go on to win the 1922 Senate election and serve three terms as a NPL Republican in the Senate. The IVA, having achieved its objective, quickly disintegrated.

Elsewhere, the NPL faced a similar mixture of rhetorical attacks and calculated political maneuvering. In Minnesota, the NPL posed the greatest threat to the existing political power structure; much of the NPL's initial appeal in North Dakota had, in addition, been framed as a response to the alleged rapaciousness of Minnesota's merchants. Furthermore, there was a harsh rhetorical side to the battle with the NPL as well as legislative maneuvering by mainstream politicians in Minnesota. NPL recruiters were repeatedly harassed, beaten, and tarred and feathered, and Townley himself was banned from visiting several Minnesota towns and was jailed for defying one such ban. At the same time, Minnesota Republicans began to hold preprimary endorsing (or "eliminating") conventions, during which a standard bearer would be chosen. The Republican Party introduced this practice in 1920, with the expectation that those candidates who were not endorsed would drop out, leaving one candidate to confront the NPL candidate. Montana, Idaho, Nebraska, and Kansas all saw their primaries abolished in 1918 or 1919 by state legislatures seeking to ward off the NPL. Repeal legislation was also introduced in Minnesota and Colorado, and South Dakota passed laws restricting primary voting to party members of long standing. These laws did not remain on the books for long; in Nebraska and Montana, primaries were reinstated by referendum in the early 1920s. For the elections in which it was seeking to expand beyond North Dakota, however, the NPL was compelled to run in these states as a third party or issue endorsements of regular Democratic or Republican politicians.

Although it would not regain control of state government—at least in its original incarnation—the NPL did not disappear during the 1920s. Townley decided that the NPL would be more effective if it were to operate more like a traditional interest group; he also decided to resign from the organization and to establish another organization, the National Producers' Alliance. This change of strategy allowed individual legislators to claim allegiance to the NPL without officially joining it; it redirected attention toward policy and away from individual candidates; it reduced hostility toward the NPL on the part of many established political actors; and it prompted competing candidates to vie for NPL support. Although the NPL waned as a political force, many individual politicians who were associated with the NPL went on to long careers in the U.S. House and Senate. The NPL officially merged with the North Dakota Democratic Party in 1956.

The NPL stands as one of the most successful nonparty political organizations of the early 20th century. Although no other organization has replicated its electoral success, its member recruitment techniques and use of new electoral reforms served both as a model for other nonparty organizations and as a caution to political parties about the threat posed by the direct primary.

Robert G. Boatright

See also: Democratic Socialists of America (1982–); Socialist Labor Party of America (1876–); Socialist Party of America (1901–1972)

Further Reading

Gieske, Millar L. 1979. *Minnesota Farmer-Laborism: The Third-Party Alternative*. Minneapolis: University of Minnesota Press.

Glaab, Charles Nelson, and Thomas William Howard, eds. 1981. *The North Dakota Political Tradition*. Ames: Iowa State University Press.

Lansing, Michael J. 2015. *Insurgent Democracy: The Nonpartisan League in North American Politics*. Chicago: University of Chicago Press.

Morlan, Robert L. 1955. *Political Prairie Fire: The Nonpartisan League, 1915–1922*. Minneapolis: University of Minnesota Press.

Schwartz, Mildred. 2006. *Party Movements in the United States and Canada: Strategies of Persistence*. Lanham, MD: Rowman and Littlefield.